Alexander Graham Bell

Adolf Hitler

902
irst transatlantic
wireless message
ransmitted

1903
Berlin wireless tele-
graph conference

1912
Titanic disaster, 1,500
perish for lack of
adequate international
wireless regulation

1914
Belgium begins "grand
concerts" via wireless

1922
Benito Mussolini becomes
premier of Italy

1924
First experimental
transatlantic wire-
less transmission of
still photographs

1932
BBC inaugurates
the "Empire Ser-
vice"; International
Telecommunication
Union created

| 1885 | 1890 | 1895 | 1900 | 1905 | 1910 | 1915 | 1920 | 1925 | 1930 |

1906
Second Berlin wireless
telegraph conference;
electromagnetic spectrum
divided into bands for
different services;
"SOS" adopted as inter-
national distress signal

1907
United Press Asso-
ciations established

1911
U.S. maritime wireless
law goes into effect

1914–1918
World War I

1917
TASS created

1919
United States linked
with Japan via wire-
less; RCA created,
David Sarnoff

1927
BBC created, Sir
John Reith; AP be-
gins newsphoto
distribution

1933
Adolf Hitler
becomes chancellor
of Germany

1929
First transatlantic
facsimile trans-
mission; Radio
Moscow goes on
the air; Germany
begins broadcasting

Guglielmo Marconi

INTERNATIONAL COMMUNICATION
History, Conflict, and Control of the Global Metropolis

INTERNATIONAL COMMUNICATION

History, Conflict, and Control of the Global Metropolis

Robert S. Fortner
Calvin College

Wadsworth Publishing Company
Belmont, California
A Division of Wadsworth, Inc.

Communication Editor: Kristine M. Clerkin
Editorial Assistant: Patty Birkle
Production Editor: Jerilyn Emori
Managing Designer: Carolyn Deacy
Print Buyer: Randy Hurst
Art Editor: Kelly Murphy
Permissions Editor: Jeanne Bosschart
Interior and Cover Designer: Harry Voigt
Copy Editor: Thomas Briggs
Technical Illustrators: Tony Jonick, Carole Lawson,
    Jill Turney
Time Line Photos: Intelsat launched and
    communication satellite, NASA; all others, Bettman
Compositor: TypeLink, Inc.
Printer: R. R. Donnelley and Sons, Crawfordsville

 This book is printed on acid-free recycled paper.

1 2 3 4 5 6 7 8 9 10—97 96 95 94 93

Library of Congress Cataloging-in-Publication Data

Fortner, Robert S.
    International communication : history, conflict, and control of
the global metropolis / Robert S. Fortner.
        p.   cm.
    Includes bibliographical references and index.
    ISBN 0-534-19092-8
    1. Communication, International.   2. Communication—
International cooperation.   I. Title.
P96.I5F67   1992
    302.2—dc20   92-14549

CHRONOLOGICAL CONTENTS

2   The Global Metropolis: A Theoretical Perspective   23

8   Periphery Versus Core in the Global Metropolis: 1970–1985   177

9   Political and Economic Turmoil
      in the Global Metropolis: 1986 — Present   215

TOPICAL CONTENTS

Each chapter has an introduction and conclusion that are not otherwise indicated here. Often they extend the theoretical perspective developed in Chapter 2, provide a historical context for understanding the communication developments of the period covered by the chapter, or provide linkage to the previous or subsequent chapter.

Communication and Imperialism

Definitions, Characteristics, and Examples of International Communication

Economics, Trade and Flow of International Communication

Human Rights and International Communication

Intellectual Property and Cultural Aspects of International Communication

Law and Regulation of International Communication

Politics and Propaganda in International Communication

Technology and Its Application in International Communication

Digital Technology and Data Communication

PREFACE

International communication is part and parcel of our everyday lives, often functioning in the background of our experience, unacknowledged and largely unknown. Yet it touches us profoundly, affecting the supply of goods in our stores, the nature of our political and cultural life, the dimensions of our religion. When we do acknowledge its existence (when we sit glued to television sets or radios to hear whether the nation is again to be at war, or which hostages will be released in Beirut), we do so unreflectively. Perhaps we are disappointed with what journalists tell us, or we abhor what we see, but we give little thought to how the pictures arrived in our homes from afar, or whether the rest of the world's peoples see things the way we do. Most of them do not. We may even know more about the government in a distant country than its own people do. We live in an information-rich environment, where we can listen to the radio, watch television (even dozens of channels), read newspapers and magazines, choose to attend the cinema or rent one of hundreds of videotapes, pick up the telephone at will and call people around the globe. Perhaps a few brief stories will explain why the subject of international communication is so fascinating, and yet so difficult to explain.

When I was living in the United Kingdom, a close friend who had visited the United States on many occasions marveled that people in the United States could see more of the ongoing business occurring in the British House of Commons on C-Span than he could see at home. His access to the proceedings of Parliament was limited to the clips used on the evening news.

Once, when this friend and I were together in Chicago waiting to buy train tickets, he began laughing, and explained that he kept half-expecting to have someone stick a gun in his ribs and say, "stick 'em up." It seemed, he said, that whenever anyone lined up before a barred ticket window in U.S. films, it was always to rob them. Why should our experience be any different?

I spent 5 years living in Washington, DC. During that time I was asked to lecture on over a hundred occasions to foreign visitors who worked in either broadcasting or telecommunications organizations in their home countries. My job was to explain the situation in the United States: how our broadcasting or common carrier systems are organized, how our political system works, what our journalistic standards are, how the press decides what is news, and so on. It was not unusual that, having tried to explain the complexities of the United States, I would be challenged by one of the visitors to say what I thought our system accomplished. Our locally biased newspapers puzzled them; our notion of journalists as "watchdogs" over the government baffled them; the "waste" of having 10,000 different radio stations on the air confounded their own assumptions.

Is international communication a technical problem, a political issue, an economic question, or a cultural quandary? Is broadcasting a matter of putting a signal in a predetermined target, or of attracting audiences with a message? Is international television a trade issue or a cultural one? Are the economic priorities of countries of concern if all we are trying to do is sell audiocassettes? How quickly should new technologies be exploited to increase the capacity of the international communications system to handle telephone calls or data transfer? Should the copyright that authors obtain in one country protect their work in another? What responsibilities do rich countries have for the flow of information into, or within, poorer countries? Is the so-called right to communicate a real and enforceable right? Are the philosophies undergirding free expression in the West applicable around the world? Should they be? Who should control the technologies that make up the international communications system: private for-profit corporations, state monopolies, or international consortia?

Discussing international communication adequately is a most complex task. There are a variety of ways to limit the discussion, however. Some discussions limit themselves to the political, economic, or cultural dimensions of transnational activity. These discussions deal with such issues as propaganda, transnational corporations, and the results of control of the trade in film or television programs. Other discussions limit themselves to a particular technology or professional activity, such as the role of satellites, the practice of international journalism or broadcasting, or the activities of wire services. Still others focus on particular controversies, such as the debate about a new world information and communication order.

All such scholarship contributes its share to people's understanding of particular aspects of international communication. Most such studies also deal with these aspects in more detail than can be accomplished in an overview such as this work. What this book hopes to provide is a context within which the more specific treatments of international communication can be placed. It integrates the political, economic, technological, social and cultural, and legal and regulatory aspects of international communication into a whole. It provides a perspective that requires the reader to see specific international communication activities as part of a single system with these various dimensions, and to puzzle about how balance is achieved in a system that countries and private companies have variously attempted to dominate for their own ends. It asks how the political ideologies of countries have affected their positions about the just allocation of limited resources (economic or technical) among the world's peoples. It asks how the widely acknowledged right to communicate has been guaranteed, and how it has been circumvented. It asks how the rights of people to profit from their ideas or talents have been protected or abused in the international marketplace. To achieve these ends I chose not to limit the work to only one or two technologies, but to integrate them all. I chose, too, to include the perspectives of a variety of critics of the international system, to give voice to those who think the system ideologically or economically biased in favor of the most developed countries.

My own bias is that the international system, with all its complexity and rapid change, remains largely in the hands of the most powerful countries, particularly the United States. Despite the economic difficulties of Western nations in the late 20th century, their most potent adversary has collapsed, along with the alternative networks and perspectives that it provided. The developing countries remain saddled with debt, exploding population growth, and economic stagnation, and the alternatives they would provide thus continue to be more possibility than reality. Some alternative networks, such as Arabsat and PANA, continue to function, but often find themselves in economic straits. The Japanese, although they have purchased some important U.S.-based entertainment companies, remain on the periphery while CNN, MTV, and the BBC's World Service Television rapidly expand around the globe.

The global village also remains a myth, nurtured by the media themselves as part of their own self-legitimizing puffery, as what David Sarnoff once called agents of publicity. The media, and those who would use the international system for their own ends — whether good or evil — continue to make preposterous claims about television audiences of one billion or more for global events: world cup soccer, the Olympic Games, or various humanitarian concerts. These claims and myths should not blind us to the realities of most of the world's peoples, who continue to live their lives without access to much of the international system, and who are largely disenfranchised by the economic decisions of powerful elites, both domestic and foreign.

I hope this book provides the basic information needed to make discussion of these questions possible. While no book can be absolutely "up to date," this book tries to suggest that the basic issues and problems of international communication are recurring ones. Propaganda is a continuing issue, although its practice changes over the years. The economic viability of technologies is a continuing question even when the technologies of concern vary over time. Those of you who read this book will be able to put the most current controversies into the framework that the book addresses. The book is a foundation, not the definitive explanation of a most complex and controversial subject.

Many people have assisted me in the effort to create this foundation. They deserve my, and I hope your, gratitude for their contributions. They are Graham Mytton of the British Broadcasting Corporation, London; Stanton Burnett of the Center for Strategic and International Studies, Washington, DC; Christopher Sterling, George Washington University; James Schwoch, Northwestern University; Douglas Boyd, University of Kentucky; and Kenneth Harwood, University of Houston. A number of engineers, librarians, archivists, and policymakers also helped keep me on course as I completed the research for this book, including those at the BBC, Voice of America, the National Archives, the Public Records Office and Post Office Archives in London, the International Telecommunication Union in Geneva, the European Broadcasting Union in both Brussels and Geneva, and the European Space Agency in Paris. Finally, I owe a special debt to the 18 students in my International Communication course at Calvin College who, during the spring semester of 1991, read and critiqued the manuscript from the perspective of those for whom it is written.

ABBREVIATIONS AND ACRONYMS

ABC American Broadcasting Company

ABU Asia-Pacific Broadcasting Union

ADAPSO Association of Data Processing Service Organizations

ADX automatic data exchange

AED Academy for Educational Development

AFP Agence-France Presse

AM amplitude modulation

AMA American Medical Association

AP Associated Press

APN Novosti Press Agency

ARABSAT Arab Satellite Organization

AT&T American Telephone and Telegraph

ATV advanced television

AWR Adventist World Radio

BBC British Broadcasting Corporation

BIB Board for International Broadcasting

CAEF Conseil de l'Audiovisuel Exterior

CANA Caribbean News Agency

CBC Canadian Broadcasting Corporation

CBS Columbia Broadcasting System

CBT Commercial Benefits Tax

CCIR International Consultative Committee for Radio

CCITT International Consultative Committee for Telephone and Telegraph

CFI Canal France International

CIA Central Intelligence Agency

CNN Cable News Network

COMSAT Communications Satellite Corporation

CONECOM Eastern European Economic Community

COPUOS Committee for the Peaceful Use of Outer Space

DBS direct broadcast satellite

DPA Deutsche Press Agency

EBU European Broadcasting Union

EEC European Economic Community

ELWA Eternal Love Winning Africa

ESA European Space Agency

EUROVISION Western European television program exchange operated by the EBU

EUTELSAT European Telecommunications Satellite Organization

FBIS Foreign Broadcast Information Service

FCC Federal Communications Commission

FEBA Far East Broadcasting Association

FEBC Far East Broadcasting Company

FM frequency modulation

FRC Federal Radio Commission

FRG Federal Republic of Germany (West Germany)

GDR German Democratic Republic (East Germany)

GE General Electric

gHz gigahertz (1 billion cycles per second)

GMT Greenwich mean time

GTE General Telephone and Electronics

HCJB Heralding Christ Jesus' Blessings

HDTV high-definition television

HF high frequency (also called shortwave)

IBAR International Broadcasting and Audience Research

IBRA International Broadcasting Association

IDRC International Development Research Council

IEC International Electromechanical Commission

IFPI International Federation of the Phonographic Industry

IFRB International Frequency Registration Board

ILO International Labor Office

IMF International Monetary Fund

INMARSAT International Maritime Satellite Organization

INS International News Service

INTELSAT International Telecommunications Satellite Organization

INTERSPUTNIK International Satellite (Sputnik) Organization

INTERVISION Eastern European International Television exchange program operated by the OIRT

INTIB Industrial and Technological Bank

INTUG International Telecommunications Users Group

IPU International Postal Union

ISDN integrated services digital network

ISO International Standards Organization

ITA international telegraph alphabet

ITAA Information Technology Association of America

ITU International Telecommunication Union

Kc/s kilocycles per second

kHz kilohertz (1,000 cycles per second)

LW long wave (153–525 kHz)

MENA Middle East News Association

mHz megahertz (1,000,000 cycles per second)

MPAA Motion Picture Association of America

MW medium wave (525–1605 kHz)

NAB National Association of Broadcasters

NASA National Aeronautics and Space Administration

NAN News Agency of Nigeria

NATO North Atlantic Treaty Organization

NBC National Broadcasting Company

NHK Nippon Honsai Kyoki

NTIA National Telecommunications Information Administration

NTSC National Television Standards Committee

NWEO new world economic order

NWICO new world information and communication order

OECD Organization for Economic Cooperation and Development

OIRT Organization for International Radio and Television

OSS Office of Strategic Services

OWI Office of War Information

PAL phase alternate line

PANA Pan-African News Agency

PHOHI Philips Omroep Holland-Indie

PLO Palestine Liberation Organization

PRC People's Republic of China

PTT posts, telegraph, and telephone administration

RARC Regional Administrative Radio Conference

RIAS Radio in the American Sector

RITA Russian Information Telegraph Agency

RFE Radio Free Europe

RL Radio Liberty

RMI Radio Méditerranée Internationale (Médi 1)

RTL Radio Télé-Luxembourg

RTTY Radio Teletype

RVOG Radio Voice of the Gospel

SECAM Séquence Coleur á Mémoire

SIM Sudanese Interior Mission

SIS Secret Intelligence Service

SOFIRAD Société Financière de Radiodiffusion

SONET synchronous optical network

SSB single sideband

STL studio-to-transmitter link

SW Shortwave (also called HF)

TASS Telegraphic Agency of the Soviet Union

TAT transatlantic cable

TBDF transborder data flow

TDFL Televisione Diffusion de France

TELENET Telecommunications Network (a U.S. public data network; another similar network is TYMNET)

TNC transnational corporation

TWR Trans World Radio

UCC Universal Copyright Convention

UHF ultra high frequency

UK United Kingdom of Great Britain and Northern Ireland

UN United Nations

UNESCO United Nations Educational, Scientific, and Cultural Organization

UNIDO United Nations Industrial Development Organization

UP United Press (merged with INS to form UPI)

UPI United Press International

UPITN United Press International + Independent Television News, a jointly operated newsfilm organization

UPT universal personal telecommunications

USIA United States Information Agency

USSR Union of Soviet Socialist Republics (in Russian, CCCP)

USTTI United States Telecommunications Training Institute

UTC coordinated universal time

VHF very high frequency (used for both radio and television)

VOA Voice of America

WARC World Administrative Radio Conference

WIPO World Intellectual Property Organization

WRNO Radio New Orleans

1

INTRODUCTION TO INTERNATIONAL COMMUNICATION

1.1

Why Study International Communication?

If John Dewey (1926, p. 166) was correct in asserting that "of all affairs, communication is the most wonderful," then international communication must surely be the most wonderful of all. Studying it leads to one complex issue after another. International communication encompasses political, economic, social, cultural, and military concerns. It requires a focus on human rights, technology, and the right to own the products of the mind itself — that is, intellectual property. The following list contains some brief examples of the activities of international communication.

- In 1984 the United States, which had led the effort to form the international telecommunications satellite organization (Intelsat), decided that competition in international satellite communication

would better serve its national interests. The U.S. government assumed that competition would be a useful device to drive down the costs of international satellite communication, particularly between North America and Europe. U.S. pressure on Intelsat eventually resulted in new services, each of which had to be coordinated, under the Intelsat treaty, with the existing system. Many other countries objected to this approach, however, since they saw competition as a potential threat to their own interests, as well as to Intelsat's economic viability. The failure of Intelsat, they thought, would result in poorer service for them, since profit-making satellite companies would not want to serve low-density satellite routes.

- In late 1987 President Ronald Reagan sent a group of FB-111 fighter-bombers, based in England, to bomb Libya in retaliation for Moamar Ghadaffi's support for international terrorism. Voice of America (VOA), one of the United States' international radio services, broadcast an appeal to Libyans during that time calling for them to overthrow Ghadaffi. Such an appeal arguably violated international law prohibiting the use of propaganda to incite violence or to interfere in the internal affairs of another country.

- In May 1989, during the student protests in Tiananmen Square, Beijing, against corruption in the government of the People's Republic of China, the Chinese government began to jam the transmissions of VOA and the British Broadcasting Corporation (BBC), a practice that it had abandoned in 1978. The government acted ostensibly because the students were listening to these radio services to gauge the degree of their public support in China, and the Chinese government therefore saw them as an encouragement to further unrest (Trescott, 1989). Following the June crackdown on and massacre of students and workers in Beijing, Chinese students in the United States began to use **facsimile (fax)** machines to send news stories appearing in the U.S. press to their peers in China.

- Two Pakistanis visiting the United States for the first time in 1989 were relieved to discover how friendly Americans were. They had expected, they told me, to confront aggression and violence, based on what they had seen in U.S.-made films and television programs. They couldn't understand why U.S. film and television producers, when they created their entertainment material, didn't consider what members of their foreign audiences would think about the United States.

- In August 1991, during the short-lived Soviet coup, Russian President Boris Yeltsin was able to announce the coup and ask for help from contacts in Washington, DC, using a fax machine. Soviet President Gorbachev, detained in a vacation dacha by the military, was able to monitor events in Moscow by listening to the BBC and VOA on a shortwave radio. Other information made its way to the West via electronic mail systems employed by Soviet academics using personal computers and modems.

These examples indicate some of the activities that comprise the international communications system. Through this system journalists report news nearly instantaneously from anywhere in the world; governments communicate directly with foreign citizens via state-operated radio stations; individuals carry on telephone conversations, send faxes of documents, or retrieve information from computer databases in other countries. This system also allows people to access banking, stock transaction, and airline reservation systems, and companies to trade in film, audio, and video products.

The United States has a major stake in the development and use of this international system. U.S. citizens and businesses own over one quarter of all the telephones in the world, a third of the radios, the highest percentage of personal computers, and the greatest number of satellite earth stations. The United States has the world's most extensive network of communications satellites, and it exports more films and television programs than its next four competitors combined. Its citizens and companies also hold more patents than any other industrial democracy. In addition, it broadcasts more hours of international radio programs than any other nation and spends a billion dollars a year on public information activities directed to the peoples of other countries.

Yet most U.S. citizens are unaware of the significance of the international communications system to their country. A BBC survey done in the United States in 1983, for instance, found that many Americans thought **shortwave** radio, the medium for most international broadcasting, was used in microwave ovens (BBC International Broadcasting and Audience Research, 1983).

Many people in the United States also take the international news they see on television for granted, giving little thought to the problems of linking distant foreign sites to New York newsrooms or to the restrictions journalists encounter reporting the news — unless a reporter is evicted from a country or killed covering a story. They pay little attention to the notation of Associated Press (AP), Reuters, or United Press International (UPI) on stories they read in the newspaper, and even less to the less obvious clues given in programs such as National Public Radio's evening news show "All Things Considered."

Ignorance Is Not Bliss

Such realities are unfortunate. Consider that the U.S. telephone system was developed under the premise that the value of the system was directly related to the number of persons that people could dial up using their own telephones. Why should this logic not apply as much to telephones in other countries as to those in the United States, even if they are dialed less frequently? The more telephones that exist, the more connectivity for social, political, economic, and cultural relations is available. Such connections affect how U.S. businesses conduct their affairs abroad, and the

ease with which people learn of, and respond to, natural or political crises. In addition, the sales of U.S.-made films and television programs abroad affect the U.S. trade deficit. Increasingly the U.S. government depends on the channels of "public diplomacy" (principally government-operated broadcasting stations and the news media) to influence the opinion of distant peoples about its foreign policies and to inform them about life in the United States. Dozens of other countries, from the United Kingdom to Iraq, Nigeria, Russia (as well as the former Soviet Union), Hungary and Cuba, direct radio signals into the United States, some providing information, others propaganda, and still others information to foreign nationals living in the United States. Banks transfer U.S. and foreign currency electronically through an international communications system, and people trade stocks 24 hours a day using one national exchange after another — a factor in the October 1987 stock market "crash." U.S. computers store information necessary to construct flight schedules for foreign airlines, and computer programmers now provide foreign language versions of software programs. U.S. musicians participate in international fund-raising efforts linked with their counterparts in other countries by satellite, and sporting events such as the Olympic Games are available around the world to anyone with a satellite dish pointed in the right direction.

U.S. citizens cannot afford to ignore international communication, nor to continue in their well-documented ignorance of world geography or in the provincialism that suggests that local concerns are their highest priority. The depletion of the earth's ozone layer, the movement toward (or away from) nuclear disarmament, the extension of free trade principles — all require global cooperation. Such cooperation will depend on the international communications system and on U.S. public opinion influencing the policies of its government. The United States is too powerful a country in world affairs—politically, militarily, economically and culturally—for its citizens to remain aloof from world events. Commentators even refer to the United States as the "last remaining superpower." Exercising such power responsibly will require the active participation of an informed citizenry.

A fully functioning democracy, too, requires citizen participation; that is only feasible with an informed electorate, one that knows what its government is saying to the citizens of other countries and how it is pursuing its trade and foreign policies (see, for instance, Hutchins, 1947, p. 9; and Tuch, 1990, pp. 4, 5). This, in turn, depends on people in the United States paying attention to sources and channels of international communication, to the role of international law and regulation on these sources and channels, and to the application of human rights guarantees in other countries. To participate meaningfully in democracy, an alert public should also know what other countries think of their country, how foreign perceptions are influenced, and to what ends. International communication, conducted by or directed to U.S. citizens, influences all of these attitudes, understandings, and activities.

1.2

The Significance of International Communication

U.S. citizens probably know little either about the operation of international communications organizations in general or about the specific activities of such U.S.-based organizations. Their contact with such activities is limited; the organizations' activities thus go largely unnoticed. For example, people view television with rapt attention when fellow citizens are held hostage on airplanes or ocean liners, or in embassies abroad. They watched each night during the TWA airliner hijacking in Beirut, the *Achille Lauro* piracy, the Iranian hostage crisis, and the Iraqi "human shield" strategy. The Vietnam War was called the "television war" (at least until the Gulf War erupted) as newsfilm was used night after night to bring the carnage of the battlefield into living rooms. The Cable News Network (CNN) became nearly indispensable as a window on U.S. and allied bombing at the beginning of the Gulf War in 1991. (This was true even for Saddam Hussein; see Roberts, 1990.) CNN also became a catalyst for Europeans to argue for a similar news service on that continent (see LaFranchi, 1991). And yet people seldom consider, or even know about, the people and the technology behind these images. People also expect to pick up their daily newspapers and see headlines about the activities of U.S. military forces, diplomats, and businesspeople abroad, based on stories provided through wire services, or to see or hear "on-the-scene" coverage of summit talks, royal weddings, assassinations, coups—all brought via satellite to National Public Radio affiliates or to network television news operations. They would judge the absence of such reports to be a failure of U.S. newsgathering organizations, even while ignoring the complex technologies, negotiations, and finances that make such routine reporting possible.

In addition, people expect to be able to pick up their telephones and call virtually any place in the world, or to call home from abroad. They also expect to be able to "wire" money across international boundaries or to have credit cards honored worldwide, but don't give much thought to the international communications and financial systems that make such transactions possible.

Finally, people expect to have the actions of their country understood and appreciated abroad. They expect that a speech by the president or their concerns about the trade deficit will be communicated to other countries, although many of them would be hard-pressed to explain exactly how that might occur. In fact, however, it does occur on a daily basis, through the activities of foreign journalists working in the United States and reporting to their home countries, through the reports carried by the United States' official international radio operations, such as VOA, and increasingly through the worldwide activities of CNN.

International communication, in other words, is significant in U.S. citizens' lives and in those of other peoples around the world. This is true despite the fact that few people give it much thought or are able to explain how it occurs. If it suddenly ceased, however, many citizens in nearly every country of the world would notice it in short order: International telephony would cease; international stock and commodity trading, and financial transactions would grind to a halt; the significant actions of foreign political and military figures would suddenly be hidden; U.S. citizens living or traveling abroad would effectively "disappear" for days or weeks at a time. The world would suddenly seem more threatening, and its peoples more anonymous. The age of *glasnost* (or publicity and openness) brought to all the world by communications

would cease, and a new age of fear and darkness would again be possible.

The Origins of International Communication

International communication has no precise origins. It clearly existed as soon as communication began between modern nation-states, which themselves began to form in the 11th century.[1] It also existed prior to that, however, since the great ancient empires of Rome, Greece, Egypt, Babylon, and the like all established means to communicate across vast territories comprised of many distinct political, linguistic, and cultural entities (see Innis, 1972).

The late Canadian economic historian Harold A. Innis suggested that these empires could be understood by examining the artifacts of communication—the clay and stone tablets, papyrus scrolls, signet rings, and roads—that defined for him their methods of political control and authority. It was the "bias" of these "technologies," he said, that defined the nature of the societies themselves. Some of these early technologies were time-biased, he argued, based in media that were difficult to transport but that lasted for decades, even centuries, such as carved stone or pressed clay tablets. Others were space-biased, based in easily transported, lightweight, and disposable media, such as papyrus. The time-biased media favored tradition and continuity over the years, while space-biased media favored the expansion of political authority geographically, that is, imperialism (Innis, 1951, pp. 3–60, and 1972, pp. 12–115). These same territories today encompass dozens of nations around the Mediterranean basin.

Clearly it would be unfair to discount the "imperial" communication established by these regimes; their systems for rule and linkage via communication were indeed international.

Defining International Communication

International communication, simply defined, is communication that occurs across international borders, that is, over the borders of nation-states. It is sometimes referred to as transborder or transnational communication, particularly among economists who study transborder data flow, or TBDF.

This definition says both too much and too little. It suggests, for instance, that a Belgian and a Frenchman standing on either side of their border and conversing are practicing international communication. While they are indeed doing just that, it is more the province of "intercultural" communication, which examines the *interpersonal* contact of peoples of different cultural backgrounds. The definition also says too little, however: obviously it does not define the parameters of communication. Does it include a letter sent from Ghana to the United Kingdom? Or a telephone call from Buenos Aires to Lima? Or does it include only the activities of international broadcasters and associations such as Intelsat?

This chapter is designed to establish a clear definition of international communication. The practice of international communication includes many activities, as well as specific treaties, organizations, and events, that receive more comprehensive treatment later on.

The Characteristics of International Communication

There are six significant characteristics of international communication. While these attributes will not confine the concept so completely that all questions about whether any instance of communication is, in fact, international, they do provide important dimensions to consider when assessing particular activities. They will serve to include rather than exclude communication transactions.

These dimensions are significant as a means to avoid simplistic views of international communication. While it is easy to suggest that international communication is comprised primarily of radio and television activities directed across national frontiers, for instance, this notion is misleading. Equally misleading is the emphasis on international news flow (thereby excluding non-news content) or on the economic impact of data communication, or the exclusion of international voice, fax, or telex transmissions.

Studies in the sphere of international communication, however, typically do concentrate on only a single aspect of this global phenomenon, and perhaps inadvertently prevent complete understanding. The dimensions of international communication included here are means to avoid too narrow a focus. At the same time, however, this book cannot discuss everything. Its focus, therefore, will be on *electronic* communication, including radio, television, voice, fax, telegraph, **telex**, satellite, data, and news content. It will not address person-to-person communication or non-general-audience (i.e., diplomat-to-diplomat) diplomacy, and will have little to say about film or newspaper distribution, although these latter topics are occasionally included in the analysis.

What, then, are the characteristics of international communication?

Intentionality

International communication can be either *intentional* or *unintentional.* That is, the communication can be directed purposely across an international border, or it can spill across it. The activities of international broadcasters, such as VOA or Radio Russia, which target audiences in foreign countries, are obviously intentional international communication. The spillover of U.S. radio and television stations' signals into Canada or Mexico, or that of U.S. domestic communications satellites (DOMSATs) into the Caribbean, is also international communication. Such spillover (both terrestrial and satellite) has often generated more controversy than communication obviously directed across borders by rival political camps.[2] It can have cultural, political, and economic consequences for the country into which it spills, particularly when commercially financed, like that of the United States, or politically threatening, like that of West Germany to those in the German Democratic Republic prior to German reunification.

Channels

International communication can be either *public* or *private.* Public communication is available to all. Broadcasting is obviously public, although it can use either public or private channels. International high-frequency shortwave (SW) broadcasters use public channels; such channels are not assigned or reserved for individual services.[3]

Public communication occurring on private channels (or channels reserved for non-public use, for example, dedicated channels requiring special decoders or receivers tuneable to particular frequencies) does not currently have much application. An example of such communication domestically would be the use of radio signals to carry information that can only be heard on special receivers.[4] The proposed systems for international **direct broadcast satellites (DBS)** would qualify, as would experiments run by India using the American ATS-6 satellite.[5] Such systems use small satellite receiving dishes to tune in signals.

Private communication, however, is available to a restricted audience. Private communication occurring over public channels would include telegraph and telephone traffic carried through submarine cables or via satellites from country to country. Often such communication is **encrypted,** or coded, to prevent unintended recipients from determining its meaning. Its content may include military or trade secrets, financial information, or personal data that should not be widely shared.

Private communication can also occur on private channels, when, for instance, an American transnational corporation (TNC) leases a satellite transponder for its exclusive use in linking corporate offices with manufacturing plants or sales offices in other countries, or embassies establish satellite links with their home countries. Some private communication is also encoded to prevent "listening in" by others. It is thus doubly protected by encryption and restrictions on private channel access. In both cases, too, the content (whether encoded or not) may be identical: The difference is in the access afforded to individuals or organizations by the owners of the channel.

Distribution Technologies

Information in the international communications system is transmitted via *radio waves,* contained within *wires* or *cables,* or transported on *film stock* and *audio-* or *videocassettes.* Radio waves carry terrestrial radio and television signals and the microwave signals used for both up- and downlinks between satellites and earth transmitting and receiving stations.[6] Wires and cables, which may take the form of twisted copper pairs and coaxial or fiber optic cables, also carry communications traffic. The essential difference between these two distribution forms is the type of communication they carry. Radio waves typically carry broadcast communication, although they can be used for the point-to-point communication normally carried by wire and cable systems. Companies and governments use ships or airplanes to move recorded material for duplication and redistribution, either legally or illegally.

Content Form

International communication can take a variety of forms. It includes the entertainment, public affairs, and news programming carried by international radio services; the raw news copy carried by international wire services such as the Associated Press or Reuters, computer data and software provided by international data processing and database companies; voice and telegraph traffic carried by companies such as AT&T; encrypted messages carried on military frequencies for organizations such as the North Atlantic Treaty Organization (NATO); and diplomatic messages exchanged between embassies. It also includes faxes and telex messages requiring specialized transmitting and receiving equipment and electronic addresses.

Cultural Consequences

All communication, since it is a symbolic activity, has cultural consequences. Some scholars have argued that the international communications system allows dominant countries to impose their cultural values (including news values, social mores, and political and economic values) on weaker states (see, for instance, Schiller, 1971, 1976, 1989; or Mattelart & Schmucler, 1985). Debate rages between countries that try to protect what they define as indigenous culture (or meaning-laden) practices and forms of communication, and those that claim such practices are destructive of transcultural values, such as the free flow of information and the right to communicate (see chapter 8).

Political Nature

All international communication is political in one way or another. The communication can be overtly political or subtly political, or can merely be affected by countries' politico-economic policies. Political considerations, however, are intrinsic to the practice of international communication, even if the practices of particular organizations, such as international religious broadcasters, are not usually aimed at the exercise of political power. They are political because they cross the boundaries of nation-states, and because uncontrolled information threatens monopolies of knowledge used as the basis of political power (see Innis, 1951, pp. 35–38; and Carey, 1989, pp. 149–156).

Overt Political Communication

Overtly political communication is obvious. The programs of VOA or Radio Moscow, designed to present official points of view or to analyze world events from a U.S. or Soviet viewpoint, are obviously politically motivated. So is **propaganda,** which the United States Information Agency (USIA) defines as information "so selective and biased as to constitute propaganda . . . [information] adapted to indoctrinate, convert and influence the viewer. . . ."[7] Finally, so is **"disinformation,"** or the practice of planting false information that will be picked up and reported by domestic media in another country, and then possibly rebroadcast by international broadcasters and wire services. The United States often complained about alleged Soviet disinformation campaigns, but it used disinformation itself to mislead Iraq prior to beginning the February 1991 ground offensive into Kuwait. During the 1987 Reagan-Gorbachev summit in Washington, USIA director Charles Z. Wick sought assurances that the Soviet Union would discontinue disinformation used against the United States. On January 9, 1988, USIA claimed, the Soviets began a new campaign, however, using old accusations that the United States was "developing a biological weapon designed to kill individuals of a particular ethnic group or race." These stories were reportedly circulating in Africa, and originated in Accra, Ghana (Ottaway, 1988b).

More Subtle Political Communication

More subtle political considerations affect debates held under the auspices of the United Nations. These would include such activities as treaty discussions in the Committee on the Peaceful Uses of Outer Space (COPUOS) or meetings called by the International Telecommunication Union (ITU), or in working groups that prepare for ITU-sanctioned meetings. They also would include the activities of other specialized UN organizations, such as the United Nations Educational, Scientific, and Cultural Organization (UNESCO), or commissions, such as the temporary International Commission for the Study of Communication Problems. Although such organizations, commissions, and assemblies are ostensibly apolitical, their proceedings and recommendations cannot help but be affected by the realities of shifting international rivalries, the difficulties of coordinating the interests of wealthy and technologically advanced nations with those of poorer and less technologically sophisticated countries, and the desires of all countries to have their concerns accepted and taken into account during negotiations or discussions. It is through such debates and ongoing negotiations that international organizations assign **electromagnetic frequency** assignments for radio services, determine the rules governing assignments of **satellite orbital slots** or **spillover** of satellite signals, adopt the technical parameters for new communication services such as **high-definition** or **advanced television** (HDTV or ATV), and arrange other guarantees for protection of "national sovereignty" in an information and communication age. Political commitments, alliances, and animosities affect not only the paper outcome of these discussions, but also the activities of what might be considered nonpolitical entities, such as AT&T or international commercial broadcasters.

Political and Economic Policies

Perhaps most difficult to pinpoint are the political and economic policies that impinge on international communication. These policies can affect the practice of international communication in two principal ways. In the arena of radio and television broadcasting, many countries have adopted various measures to restrict the import of electronic equipment. These restrictions can take the form of import quotas, heavy duties or other taxes and fees, or simple refusal (or inability) to import at all. Although such practices are justified in many cases by the need to protect hard currency reserves or by the lack of such reserves, they restrict the availability of reception equipment needed to participate in international broadcasting activity. The recent difficulties of African and Latin American countries in repaying massive foreign debts have compounded the problem, since many of the radio receivers imported in the 1960s (the age of inexpensive transistor radios) are, 20 years later, becoming inoperable. New receiver designs, and the "bells and whistles" added to them, have made the receivers of choice very expensive to import (see Fortner & Durham, 1986; or Fortner, 1991c).

In telecommunications a similar difficulty exists. Many countries establish discriminatory pricing policies for telecommunications circuits that favor domestic or regional links over longer distance international ones — even when there is no cost factor that demands such practices — to generate revenue from TNCs or to discourage long-distance communication. Some countries also require equity participation to grant franchises or sign cooperation agreements allowing private networks to function in conjunction with international links.

Such policies in both broadcasting and telecommunications do generate revenue for many poorer countries and provide hard currency necessary to trade in world markets, but they also provide the means to suppress citizen contact with the outside world, particularly where people are too poor or isolated to avoid government controls. International communication can amount to only a trickle in such cases. People in remote areas, for instance, who have no telephone service or electricity have, until recently, had little access to the outside world except through battery-powered radios. Also, these radios have been operational only when batteries were available. Loans from the World Bank for telecommunications development, the advent of videocassette recorders (VCRs) and battery-powered televisions, and construction of homemade satellite dishes, among other developments, are now beginning to remove age-old barriers to communication.

International Communication and Political History

As previously stated, international communication has no precise origins. For purposes of analysis, however, this book will look back only as far as 1835, for the following reasons. Successful electric telegraph experiments began as early as 1837. By 1840 France was using an optical telegraph system; it had constructed towers across its territory, and men with flags received and transmitted messages cross-country (see International Telecommunication Union, 1965, pp. 11–16). By 1844 a working telegraph line was operational in the United States, and railroads were under construction that would require international negotiations to establish common rail gauges to facilitate traffic flow between countries (see Czitrom, 1982, p. 6; and International Telecommunication Union, 1965, p. 29). It was the train, steamship, and telegraph that quickened the pace of international news flow, financial transactions, and even interpersonal communication. These technologies also tightened the grip of imperial capitals on their developing empires (see Andrew, 1857, p. 140; Briggs & Maverick, 1858, pp. 21, 22; Burt, 1956, p. 435; and Kalb, 1990, p. x).

During these middle decades of the 19th century, too, countries began the negotiations that would establish an international communications *system,* negotiations that national leaders, cognizant of the power of communication, knew technological developments required. These technologies, and those that followed, would eventually provide power to create mass audiences for propaganda, establish news as a major consideration in international politics, and tie the world's economies into an ever more interdependent whole.

To facilitate understanding, this book is divided roughly into three periods: 1835–1932, 1933–1969, and 1970 to the present. Each of these periods is, in turn, subdivided around major historical events. None of these dates, however, are "hard and fast," since some developments also straddle them.

The Period of International Conventions: 1835–1932

This first period witnessed the development of the initial technologies of international communication: electric telegraph (1837), submarine cable (1866), telephone (1876), wireless (1897), and radio (1907).[8] And in the 1920s major developments in international point-to-point telephony using radio waves and international radio broadcasting took place. The application of electricity to the problem of communication led to the first international convention and organization concerned with communication, the International Telegraph Union, formed in 1865.[9] The newer wireless technologies of

the 20th century led to similar developments. In 1912, in the aftermath of the *Titanic* disaster, various countries signed an international convention requiring ships to have wireless equipment in working order and trained operators on board. National radio administrations began to meet as well, with the first meeting occurring in Berlin in 1903. This meeting resulted in the formation of a working group that became known as the International Radiotelegraph Union, although it never existed officially as an international organization. In 1932 the Telegraph Union and the Radiotelegraph Union merged to form the International Telecommunication Union (ITU). In 1906 the radio convention established fundamental radio regulations that led to certain frequencies being designated for particular services, such as long-distance communication and government use (see Headrick, 1991, pp. 120, 121).

Such efforts shared one major goal: to facilitate international communication. The Telegraph Convention signed in Paris in 1865, for instance, establishing the original ITU, created a body whose tasks included setting technical interconnection standards among nationally directed telegraph services, as well as mechanisms for overseeing tariffs, sharing revenue for telegrams crossing international borders, using encryption, and assuring privacy of messages. Similar problems had to be resolved when countries began to use the telephone for international communication, and again when Marconi introduced wireless services.

The 1903 and 1906 **radiotelegraph** conferences also dealt with the problem of monopolization. The Marconi companies had adopted a policy that forbade their coastal stations to communicate with ships using non-Marconi equipment. Efforts to break this policy were in vain until the *Titanic* disaster proved the necessity of non-discriminatory communications policies. The U.S. Radio Act of 1912, for instance, required shipboard wireless stations to be of sufficient power to broadcast "by day over sea a distance of one hundred miles," all receiving stations to give distress signals "absolute priority," and "each shore station open to general public service between the coast and vessels at sea . . . to exchange radiograms with any similar shore station and with any ship station without distinction of the radio system adopted by such stations . . ." (Provisions 8, 9, and 11 of the Radio Act of 1912, passed on August 13, 1912).

The Period of Politicalization and Propaganda: 1933–1969

The second period opened with development of overt international propaganda organs in several countries.[10] The Third Reich emerged in Germany in 1933 under Adolf Hitler, who appointed Joseph Goebbels, advocate of the "big lie," to be minister of propaganda.[11] The BBC, which had started broadcasting internationally in English in 1932, began to consider the possibilities of foreign-language broadcasting in 1935. By the following year an editorial in the *Indianapolis Star* was being quoted by Alan Dudley of the BBC to voice his misgivings about foreign language programming. The editorial claimed that Great Britain and the United States were perhaps the only countries in the world "not broadcasting propaganda in a foreign tongue" (quoted in Mansell, 1982, pp. 43–44). The BBC did begin German language broadcasting during the Munich crisis in 1938, but maintained the position that "all British information should be truthful and objective."[12] On May 26, 1940, however, a British-sponsored **clandestine radio** station began beaming

material into Nazi Germany, the first of many such operations throughout the war (see Soley & Nichols, 1987, pp. 25–32). The United States created VOA following U.S. entry into World War II to begin broadcasting to the people of the Third Reich.

The politicalization of radio was clearly underway with such operations. Although some services, such as the BBC and VOA, attempted to maintain a nonpropaganda posture, the fact that Great Britain and the United States began such services, and directed programming to hostile countries in foreign languages, indicated the political underpinnings of the broadcasts, irrespective of the actual content.

During the war years, too, submarine cables became military targets, and national news agencies became means to try to influence foreign public opinion.[13] The Nazis established an elaborate system to direct the output of both their domestic and international news operations, and the Allies subsidized or supported their wire services as well. Such activities continued following the war, as did the **jamming** activity the Nazis had initiated to drown out the clandestine radio broadcasts sponsored by the British. With the onset of the Cold War, the emerging adversaries adopted new strategies, with the United States establishing three separate services capable of reaching behind what was called the "Iron Curtain." These were Radio Free Europe (RFE), directed into Eastern Europe; Radio Liberty (RL), directed into the Soviet Union; and Radio in the American Sector (RIAS), located in West Berlin, a city then surrounded by East Germany.

The Soviets, in turn, directed Radio Moscow to the West, beginning its North American service in 1943, and started jamming frequencies of RFE/RL, VOA, the BBC, and eventually Radio Israel, which in turn began broadcasting to the Soviet Union in 1949.

Throughout the years that followed, tensions between East and West would flare and smolder, ignited by a variety of events.[14] In the United States the "red scare" and the McCarthy years kindled renewed anti-Communist sentiment, as did regular accusations of Soviet expansionism in the developing world.

Throughout this period international communication was always a potential threat to some societies, particularly those that closely supervised, or actually dictated the content of, domestic media operations. The extent of such threats can perhaps best be seen in the abortive 1956 Hungarian uprising against Soviet hegemony in Eastern Europe. During this period RFE falsely broadcast messages that Western assistance would be provided to Hungarian rebels fighting Soviet troops. When Soviet troops then entered Hungarian cities, their first act was to retake the radio stations that had been occupied by rebels. One station, Radio Free Rakoczi, broadcast a message as it was being attacked: "Attention, Radio Free Europe, hello, attention. This is Roka speaking. The radio of revolutionary youth . . . Help, help, help . . . Radio Free Europe . . . forward our request" (quoted in Wise & Ross, 1964, p. 327).[15]

The Period of Increasing Complexity and Proliferation: 1970–Present

The period of politicalization and propaganda never really ended. But in the third period a newly complex environment emerged, resulting from both the application of new communications technologies and the proliferation of new nations with the breakup of Europe's colonial empires. One could argue that this third period began as early as 1965, when the first Intelsat satellite was boosted into orbit. By 1975 a critical mass of new technologies had developed sufficiently to alter the dominant politicalization/propaganda bias of the second period by propelling international communication into the third period, one in which economic factors competed equally with political ones in determining international communication activity and content. By 1975 the portable radio, for instance, had waned as the dominant form of consumer electronics expenditure (see *Japan Electronics Almanac 1985*, 1985, p. 176). In both developed and developing countries automobile radios, audiocassette players (both portable and auto), high-fidelity components, televisions, and videocassette players had overtaken the portable radio as consumer technologies of choice. The capacity of satellites had increased many times over, from the 240-voice channel and single black-and-white television channel capacity of the 1965 Early Bird to 12,000 **voice circuits** and two color television channels on Intelsat V, launched in 1980 (Williamson, 1984). The number of satellite paths (providing point-to-point capability) for Intelsat grew from less than 10 paths in 1965 to over 640 by 1978. And **coaxial cable,** which was first used for transatlantic telegraphy and telephony in 1956, provided 104,000 circuits by 1978 (Dawidziuk & Preston, 1979, pp. 3.4.11.3–3.4.11.4).

These changes, in aggregate, introduced new economic and political imperatives into the practice of international communication. Both international broadcasters and telecommunications providers had to contend with new competition, provide new programming that would alter the context of international programs, and reconcile new expectations with established systems. For instance, the fidelity of both broadcasting and voice circuits became newly significant issues, rekindling the 1930s argument over the superiority of **frequency modulation (FM)** versus **amplitude modulation (AM)** in radio broadcasting. The ability of **telecommunications** systems to provide **broadband** services for television and data transmission became increasingly important. The use of the frequency spectrum itself became a contentious issue as potential users argued for new service assignments, based largely on technical and economic grounds, and developing countries, in response, tried to reserve frequencies for their own future use, asserting political prerogatives.

International meetings on communications issues were often contentious during the 1970s. Numerous declarations were adopted in meetings of developing countries. A new world information order (NWIO) debate emerged, modeled on the earlier disputes over a new world economic order (NWEO). Both UNESCO and the ITU commissioned major studies on communications problems, particularly as they existed in developing countries.[16]

1.7

The Role of International Conventions

All international communications services depend on agreements signed among sovereign states to work. In broadcasting, for instance, both international and domestic services must use the electromagnetic spectrum, a naturally occurring physical phenomenon that allows radio waves to carry information from transmitter to receiver. International agreements establish particular services, such as **medium-wave** (what "Americans" call AM) radio, **very high frequency** (VHF, or what "Americans" call

FM) radio, television, terrestrial microwave and satellite communication, marine and land mobile communication, and so forth.[17] Since the electromagnetic spectrum is a single worldwide phenomenon, and since radio waves cannot necessarily be confined within the border of a single country,[18] international conventions (or agreements) assign certain portions of the frequency spectrum to particular services. The ITU does not allow uses of the spectrum that have no specific assignments, although experimental services are often allowed, either by the ITU or by domestic agencies such as the Federal Communications Commission (FCC), within frequency bands that have been reserved for specific uses.

In telecommunications conventions establish the standards that allow communication across international circuits, both wire and wireless, to occur. The connection of wires between two domestic services, for instance, requires that a common standard exist for **bandwidth, impedance, voltage,** and so on, so as to prevent one system from damaging the other. Also, the components of satellite dishes must be designed to **down-link** voice, data, or broadcast information **up-linked** from other countries in a particular form, or only gibberish will result. Incompatible television standards also must be converted at either up- or down-link sites to allow broadcast over domestic cables or broadcast systems. Companies must record videocassettes, too, in appropriate television formats before exporting them to other countries.

International conventions, then, signed by countries that belong to the ITU or by countries in bilateral discussions establish the **frequencies** assigned to specific services — or divide up a band into frequencies to be used by countries bordering one another — determine the technical standards for particular services, and, more generally, set up what we might call the "moral expectations" of international communications practice. These general expectations, for instance, condemn the practice of jamming (or deliberately interfering with the radio signals of a broadcaster) and require countries using satellites for domestic direct broadcasts to homes to limit the spillover of such signals into adjacent countries.

The necessity of such conventions, of course, often politicizes the technical questions that come before the ITU, since countries disagree about what standards ought to be adopted for particular services, or even whether frequencies ought to be reserved for specific uses. The most effective restrictions on individual countries' activities are those signed bilaterally and those that establish engineering specifications for equipment linked to foreign systems. Manufacturers prefer worldwide standards for such equipment, since it allows them to make better use of the economies of scale in producing it, and this provides an additional incentive for agreement on such issues.[19] This preference, too, means that competing manufacturing companies press their governments to assure that standards they own through patents become worldwide standards. This can slow down technological development, frustrate the efforts of countries to decide how best to commit limited resources to provide the best connection to international communications systems, and politicize what would otherwise be economic or technical questions.

The Right to Disregard International Conventions

In broadcasting countries find it more difficult to establish universally held conven-

tions. Any country has the right, under the ITU charter, to take a "reservation" on any portion of a protocol adopted by international assemblies. That is, a country reserves the right to disregard those portions of the protocol that it specifically stipulates when signing it. This makes the role of the ITU in policing broadcasting activity difficult, a situation compounded by the lack of effective and dependable sanctions to apply to those defying international conventions.

1.8

Examples of International Communication Activity

International communication takes many forms. It can occur merely as spillover—that is, as radio or television signals crossing an international boundary, an everyday occurrence, for instance, along the border of the United States and Canada. Or it can be purposeful, using channels dedicated to carrying international messages.

International Broadcasting

More than 100 countries engage in international broadcasting. The United States, for instance, operates or funds five distinct radio services: Voice of America (VOA) and Radio Martí, which are under the direction of the United States Information Agency (USIA), and Radio Free Europe (RFE), Radio Liberty (RL), and Radio Free Afghanistan (RFA), all under the direction of the Board for International Broadcasting (BIB). In June 1991 VOA broadcast 1,187 hours per week, RFE 539, RL 499, Radio Martí 162, and RFA 14. The United States, then, broadcast a total of 2,401 hours that year, making it the largest international broadcaster in the world, a distinction held by Radio Moscow through 1984. In June 1991 Radio Moscow broadcast 1,951 hours, the People's Republic of China 1,537, the Federal Republic of Germany (West Germany) 841, and the BBC 778.

Clandestine and Pirate Broadcasting

In addition to these official broadcasts, countries and political movements use both clandestine and **pirate broadcasting** internationally. Clandestine broadcasting refers to the practice of one country funding broadcasting aimed at another, but concealing its activities. Perhaps the most famous clandestine broadcasting efforts were those of the United Kingdom during World War II, aimed at Nazi Germany, and those of the Central Intelligence Agency in funding RFE/RL from the 1950s until the creation of the BIB in 1973 (see Tyson, 1983, p. 60; see also pp. 61–65). A number of clandestine radio stations still operate in the Middle East and Latin America, aimed particularly at Iran and Iraq, Nicaragua and El Salvador.

Pirate broadcasting is similar to clandestine, but is funded not by governments but by individuals. A number of pirates operate around the world. The most famous cases historically have been in Western Europe, particularly directed into the United Kingdom and the Netherlands. Pirates have been credited with forcing change in the BBC's domestic radio services, which eventually dedicated a network to airing American and British rock 'n' roll and pop music, and with broadening television activities in the Netherlands, where one pirate operation eventually grew popular enough to qualify under the Dutch system for government money and then became an official service (see Briggs, 1985, p. 345; Browne, 1989, pp. 139–142; and Madge, 1988,

p. 106). Pirate stations have also been set up in Mexico and in the Atlantic Ocean, aimed into the United States (see Fowler and Crawford, 1987).

Telecommunications

International telecommunications takes a variety of forms. All countries of the world use international telecommunications systems of one kind or another. Services provided by these systems include (1) voice communication, (2) record services (telegraph, fax, and telex), (3) wire services, (4) data communication, and (5) international television traffic. Such services are provided by three types of distribution systems: underseas (i.e., submarine) coaxial and **fiber optic** cables, **high-frequency radio,** and satellites.

Voice Communication

In 1982, 9,200 voice circuits were available for U.S. transoceanic telephony, and U.S. citizens originated more than 150 million international telephone calls. Worldwide more than 40,000 transoceanic voice circuits existed, up from only 678 in 1964. By 1986 over 190,000 voice circuits were in worldwide use, and by the year 2000 this total is expected to increase to the equivalent of 2 million circuits (Pelton, 1986b, p. 40).

Record Services

Record services are carried on the same distribution systems as voice communication. In submarine cables both voice and telegraph traffic is carried on voice circuits, reflecting the decline of international telegraphy to the point that providers could no longer justify dedicating circuits for this service. The decline in telegraphy has been off-set to a degree, however, by the increasing use of international telex and fax services, as well as specialized data networks for scientists, academics, the military, and business enterprises. By 1991, for instance, "Americans" were spending 4 trillion minutes on the telephone each year, with 17 percent of this time (680 billion minutes) devoted to machine-to-machine communication: fax machines, automated teller machines (ATMs), credit card checks, and electronic mail (Suplee, 1991).

Telegraphy employs a "limited switched system": It is capable of directing messages to a limited number of termination points, each of which is owned by the service provider. Telex, by contrast, is an "unlimited switched system": Messages are steered directly to addressable subscriber instruments, as in telephony. Facsimile works similarly, but provides the means to reproduce not only words but also the composition (or format) of documents, images, and photographs — that is, a complete reproduction of an original, not just its word content. Facsimile was first introduced for international services on January 1, 1979.

Wire Services

Wire services operate internationally using primarily slow-speed circuit teleprinters and high-frequency radio. Each of the major international services, including the U.S. agencies Associated Press (AP) and United Press International (UPI), the British agency Reuters, the French Agence France-Presse (AFP), and the Russian International Telegraph Agency (RITA) sends news copy to subscribers worldwide.[20] Each provides approximately 80,000 words per day to developed countries, such as the United States or countries in Western Europe, and 25,000 to

30,000 words per day to countries in Africa. The Kyodo agency of Japan, for example, receives about 600,000 total words per day of foreign coverage from various services, including 69,000 from UPI, 64,000 from Reuters, 52,000 from AP, and 20,000 from its own correspondents (Fenby, 1986, p. 91). More than 50 smaller news agencies also currently operate and are increasingly important in the Middle East and some areas of Africa.

Data Communication

Data communication using computers, which provides access to airline reservation systems, financial, stock, and commodity trading, banking, and various information databases, is increasingly significant in international communication. In 1986, 35 database firms and 17 data-processing firms in the United States were active in international trade. It is difficult, however, to disaggregate the amount or value of transborder data flow (TBDF) from figures provided more generally for "services," which include exports of personal, marketing, advertising, franchising, and other business activities. Also, a large amount of such activity occurs within corporations with branch plants, distribution centers, and sales offices in several countries. This activity is thus internal and remains unreported in international statistics. Still other important information is proprietary. Divulging it would mean disclosing important marketing strategies or trade secrets. This makes discussion of TBDF as an element of international communication the most difficult of all.

In 1982 international on-line database revenues were estimated to be growing at an annual rate of 25%. In 1985 the total worldwide trade in services was over $600 billion, although it is not yet known how much of this was in TBDF. Electronically delivered services included data processing, computer programming, training and education, legal, accounting, engineering, banking, insurance, research and development, publishing, advertising, public relations, and managerial communications and information services. The European Economic Community (EEC) estimated that there were nearly 800 million data transactions in Western Europe in 1987 using approximately 1.6 million termination points. Between 1979 and 1987 the EEC saw a rise in international transactions of between 10 and 15%. In banking alone two separate international systems operate: CIDEL, linking 51 countries together to handle stock transactions, and SWIFT, linking 21 countries for the purpose of handling interbank transactions (Branscomb, 1986, p. 9).

International Television

International television traffic is carried in three distinct systems: (1) satellite links, (2) videotape networks linking producers with broadcasters, and (3) videocassette distribution and sales operations. The amount of international television broadcast material is estimated at over 328,000 hours per year, or enough to fill over thirty-seven 24-hour-per-day networks ("A $3 Billion International Program Market," 1982, p. 41). The average country imports about one third of its daily television programming, with some countries importing as much as four fifths of their total programming. The United States' second leading export (behind airplanes and other aeronautical products) is its television and cinema products. U.S. entertainment is so popular around the world that Japanese electronics firms, beginning with Sony's acquisition of Columbia Records in 1988 for $2 billion, began buying U.S. re-

cord, film, and television production companies to assure a supply of "software" for their consumer electronics products into the next century. Sony paid $3.6 billion for Columbia Pictures in 1989, and Matsushita subsequently bought MCA ("Show Business Tries to Balance Books," 1991, p. 5).

Televised news exchanges are also gaining momentum, both through regional efforts occurring on every continent in one form or another and through Intelsat. In 1991 the former Soviet Union became the 121st member of Intelsat ("News Drives Global Satellite Traffic," 1991, p. 4); Russia assumed the Soviet Union's membership in 1992. In addition, both CNN and the BBC continued to expand their daily video news programming, with CNN reaching 129 countries in February 1992 and the BBC inaugurating its television news service to 38 Asian countries ("BBC Launches Asian News Channel," 1991, p. 58).

The Videocassette Recorder

International television trade is reinforced by another increasingly important technology: the videocassette recorder (VCR). VCRs are unevenly distributed around the world, but are beginning to have a major impact on the distribution of television and cinema material, particularly in such areas as Latin America and the Middle East. In 1982, for instance, over 21 million prerecorded videocassettes were sold worldwide (Dunham & Hering, 1986, p. 97). By 1988 videocassette rentals were earning 50% more for the West German film industry than were cinema screenings ("Videocassettes Earned 50% More," 1991, p. 67). Films are also distributed to cinema houses worldwide. The popularity of U.S. films and television programs is so great, too, that in 1990 alone antipiracy operations seized over 885,000 illegally produced videocassettes in 41 different countries (Motion Picture Export Association of America, 1991).

1.9

Conclusion

International communication is both more complex and more significant than most people in the United States realize. Most take it for granted. People's daily lives, however, are influenced by the various means and content of international communication.

International communication is actually too important for people to ignore. Their governments use it to attempt to influence the citizens of other countries and to monitor or survey the activities of their adversaries, such as Saddam Hussein did with CNN during the Gulf War. Their banks, brokerage houses, and manufacturing and service companies all use it for international financial transactions. Their own perceptions of the world—its dangers and possibilities—are influenced by the activities and choices of newspapers and network and cable television services concerning what they shall come to know. Their jobs may be affected by international trade that depends on these international systems. Their ability to contact friends and relatives in other countries depends on the linkages maintained by international telecommunications carries and on the tariffs established to charge for telegraph, telephone, fax, and data transfers.

The international communications system, however, is more significant than any person's individual stake in it. Issues of national identity and culture, human rights and coercion, justice and freedom, are also involved. The remainder of this book attempts to make sense of these issues. It describes, analyzes, and explains this international communications system from both a theoretical and a historical point of view.

Notes

1. Nations themselves did not come into being, but the process by which they eventually emerged began in the 11th century. Probably crucial was the Battle of Hastings on October 14, 1066, that resulted in William I being crowned in England; the emergence of the Spanish national hero El Cid, who drove the Moors from Valencia in 1094; the rule of Frederick I in the 12th century in what eventually became Germany; the sealing of the Magna Carta at Runnymede (England) by King John in 1215; and the publication of the first imperial law in the German language in 1235 (see Grun, 1979).

2. Some "spillover" of broadcast signals may be welcomed by the broadcaster as a means to increase audience size or to propagate a particular point of view. But since radio and television stations are licensed in particular countries, it is also fair to judge their signals—which cross national frontiers—as spillover, outside the area covered by their domestic license and beyond the audience they are presumably licensed to serve.

3. International broadcasting uses frequencies in the high-frequency (HF) bands. Technically, then, it is referred to as HF broadcasting. The most common term applied to it, however, is shortwave (SW) broadcasting.

4. Muzak, or "elevator music," is carried on subcarrier frequencies of licensed radio stations, but these frequencies can only be detected by special receivers that tune in frequencies within the channel allocation of the regular signal.

5. Direct broadcast satellites (DBS) are those designed to deliver a signal powerful enough

to be received directly by individual home satellite dishes. Both Voice of America (VOA) and the British Broadcasting Corporation (BBC) External Services have studied the possibility of using such systems as supplements to or replacements for their current terrestrial HF transmitters. DBS can be used for delivery of either radio or television signals.

6. Radio waves exist at varying frequencies in the electromagnetic spectrum. The spectrum is divided up into portions dedicated for particular services, such as AM radio (using medium waves — MW), very high frequency (VHF) television or radio (VHF radio is referred to as FM in the United States), land mobile or cellular telephony, microwave communication, and so on. The term *radio waves,* then, does not refer to a particular service, but to the natural phenomenon used by such services to move their signals from one point to another.

7. This definition was adapted from a USIA action in denying a U.S.-produced film duty-free certification under a UN-sponsored treaty designed to promote educational, cultural, and scientific material exchange among countries. Tuch (1990, p. 3) defines public diplomacy as "a government's process of communicating with foreign publics in an attempt to bring about understanding for its nation's ideas and ideals, its institutions and culture, as well as its national goals and current policies."

8. These dates are not absolute, particularly in the cases of wireless and radio. Guglielmo Marconi filed for his first wireless patent in London in 1897, but the first transatlantic wireless broadcast occurred in 1901, and regular transatlantic service was established the following year. In radio Lee De Forest established the De Forest Radio Telephone Company in 1907 to demonstrate the audion, a sending and receiving tube he had patented in 1906 that made possible practical radio broadcasting.

9. The Universal Postal Union was formed in 1847, but communications historians have tended to treat the ITU as the first truly international communications-oriented organization (see, for instance, Codding & Rutkowski, 1982. p. 3).

10. Propaganda was actually used by several countries prior to 1933, but its modern manifestations are seen most clearly after this date. See chapter 5.

11. Hitler's and Goebbel's radio strategies may have owed much to Benito Mussolini, who actually preceded Hitler in achieving power in Italy a full decade earlier. The "big lie" refers to the belief that, while little or minor lies might be discovered, because people might have independent knowledge that allows them to question specific statements, lies about larger issues are more difficult to contradict. A small lie, for instance, might be that a country's army had occupied a particular city. Radio transmitters continuing to operate in that town, or a letter from a soldier to his parents saying that an attack had been repulsed, however, might give away the fact that it was still in enemy hands. By contrast, a larger lie, such as a claim that thousands of tons of enemy shipping had been sunk by U-boats, or that Germany continued to persevere, would both frame the understanding that people would have of the conduct of the war and be general enough that it would be more difficult to question or doubt.

12. Statement of Lord MacMillan at the first meeting of the Ministry of Information's Advisory Council, September 7, 1939, as recorded in notes by F. W. Ogilvie (quoted in Mansell, 1982, p. 89).

13. Knightley (1975, chapter 5) also discusses the role of war correspondents and domestic newspapers as vehicles of propaganda during World War I. Buitenhuis (1989) likewise discusses the role of literature as a vehicle of propaganda during the First World War; and Kenez (1985) addresses the role of the press in the birth of the Soviet "propaganda state" between 1917 and 1929. MacKenzie (1984, p. 35), discussing the British Empire after 1880, notes the role of both press and film, and says,

"The period 1870 to 1914 saw the appearance of several new communications techniques and the development of some old ones. All these rapidly became the servants of the dominant ideology of the age, patriotic, militaristic, and imperialistic." Likewise, Golomstock (1990, p. xi) notes, "Ghengis Khan had no telegraph system; it is only in our day that such ideologies have found themselves the necessary material and technological basis on which to establish themselves as stable political systems." Again, the dates I have used for analysis in the text are fluid, not definitive.

14. Significant events during this period included the 1948–49 Berlin blockade and airlift, the 1950–53 Korean conflict, the 1956 Hungarian and Polish uprisings and Soviet invasions, the 1960 U-2 spying incident in which Francis Gary Powers was shot down over Soviet territory, the 1961 U.S.-sponsored invasion of Cuba at the Bay of Pigs, the 1962 Cuban missile crisis, the 1968 Czechoslovakian uprising and Soviet invasion, and the Vietnam War.

15. See also Soley and Nichols (1987, pp. 64–67). RFE "promises," now damning in hindsight, should perhaps be seen as the result of naivete during a period of politically charged rhetoric when words were not necessarily grounded in facts. This does not excuse RFE, but perhaps provides a useful context for understanding its actions.

16. UNESCO sponsored the International Commission for the Study of Communication Problems, which issued what became popularly known as the MacBride Report, after its chairman, Sean MacBride, in 1980, and the ITU created the Independent Commission for World Wide Telecommunications Development—the Maitland Commission—which reported in 1985. Both of these documents will be discussed later in the text.

17. I used the term *Americans* here advisedly. In this context it refers to citizens of the United States, known throughout much of the world as "Americans," despite the fact that people from as far north as the Canadian Arctic Circle to as far south as the tip of Chile all live in "the Americas." When this term appears in the text in quotation marks, it will refer only to U.S. citizens.

18. All radio waves do not have the same propagation characteristics, so some are more easily controlled than others. Also, all countries are not the same size, nor do they have the same geographical relationships with other countries. The use of the electromagnetic spectrum for some services is less severe, for instance, for a country such as Australia, surrounded by water and with few close neighbors, than it is for the relatively small countries of Western Europe.

19. The term *economies of scale* refers to the lower per unit cost of producing a commodity or providing a service, created by an increase in the total number of units produced or volume of service provided. As the quantity of production increases, the cost per unit falls, allowing for sale at lower prices. Larger scale achieves economy.

20. The Republic of Russia inherited the Soviet wire service organization, TASS, and reconstituted it as the Russian International Telegraph Agency (RITA) in January 1992.

2

THE GLOBAL METROPOLIS: A THEORETICAL PERSPECTIVE

2.1

"Global Village" Versus "Global Metropolis"

People have become accustomed to hearing from journalists, news broadcasters, and columnists that they live in a "global village." This term, coined by McLuhan and Fiore (1968), expressed their belief that communications technologies were leading to a re-emergence of the aural communication (speaking and listening) of village life as the dominant means of communication. The difference was that global linkages through television and telecommunications would expand the confines of the village to global proportions.

The notion of a "global village," however, is an unfortunate metaphor, as it conceals more than it reveals. Village life dependent on oral-aural communication occurs in an atmosphere of intimacy. People in villages know one another; they do not merely know *about* one another. They share geography, that of their living environs as well as that of sacred and profane places, places of authority, and places of exile.[1] Their lives are entwined together: they marry, give birth, and die among those with whom they share daily experience. Their ways of life are molded by shared values, history, and lore, by common knowledge of their enemies and friends. The relationships that exist between people (men and women, elders and youth, warriors and children) are known to all. Members of the village know the penalties—including communication deprivation, even exile itself—for breaking village taboos. Refusal to abide by the norms of village (or tribal) life can lead to loss of identity in exile: a cutting away of the bonds that have defined who people are (see Benge, 1972, pp. 64–66).

Communication does not itself provide this degree of completeness, of identity and intimacy, although it is the means by which people construct and maintain individual and corporate identities. In the village, as well as in global society, communication can signal events, show portrayals of life, indicate potentially common elements in the way people conduct their lives even when separated by thousands of miles (see Lasswell's classic conception of communication, 1960, pp. 117–118, and Lerner's discussion of the shift from oral to mediated society, 1960, pp. 131–133). Communication allows people to learn about others whom they do not know, to recognize their similarities and differences as individuals and as members of culture-specific communities. Communication can provide the means to understand distant complex activities and can unite diverse people in extraordinary circumstances (for example, the Ukrainian earthquake, summit meetings, the destruction of the Berlin Wall, the unfolding events in Tiananmen Square in Beijing, the Gulf War, the attempted Soviet coup, the Madrid peace talks on the Middle East). Communication across distances, however, does not reproduce the intimacy that is the hallmark of village life. Rather it provides the basis to control aspects of daily life, favoring either self-control or elite and bureaucratic (centralized) control.[2] It does not necessarily bring them into greater intimacy or involve them democratically (see Pleydell-Bouverie, 1991).

Despite the rapid increases in the speed and complexity of communication systems, then, McLuhan's vision of a "global village" remains as distant as ever. What has actually been created, to alter the metaphor, is a "global metropolis." Unlike in the village, people living together in a metropolis may know little of one another's affairs.

Only the spectacular crime, for instance, may raise the consciousness of one group in the metropolis about the conditions of another. Some groups in the metropolis will be better known than others: their weddings will be reported on the society pages of the local newspaper and their deaths will command extensive obituaries. Other groups will toil in obscurity, meriting little attention from the media until some unusual event (usually violent or bizarre) commands media notice. In other words, the information flow among segments of the metropolitan population is unequal: the population at large knows more about elites than about other members of the community. Intimacy is thus restricted and often artificial.

Access to the Means of Communication

Metropolises are replete with inequalities such as these. A metropolis is full of "haves" and "have-nots." The implication of this in communication terms is twofold. First, people will have different levels of access to the means of communication *reception*. Some groups will own all the means to hear and see what is happening in the world. They can afford to subscribe to magazines, newspapers, and cable television services, to own multiple radio and television sets, to buy videocassette recorders and even satellite dishes. Other groups will make more sparing use of such subscriptions and devices, by choice or by necessity.

Second, people will have differing access to the means of communication *initiation*. Computers (for on-line access to data services), fax machines, telephones (including mobile or cellular telephones) are all within the financial reach of the more affluent members of a metropolis, but even basic telephone service is limited in its poorer sections. Not only does communication not solve the gross inequities in the conduct of daily life, the expense of communication may itself exacerbate them. Enhanced choices for some, at increasing cost, are offset by diminished options for other, poorer, people. Some will be "information rich," others "information poor."

The Control of Communication Systems

In a metropolis, too, control of communication systems is centralized, operated by either the state or private companies. The give-and-take of village discussion is largely absent. Whereas village communication is often hierarchical (usually flowing from the top down), in a metropolis it is both hierarchical and centrally controlled: Access to the system is granted or denied by bureaucratic arrangements. State and/or corporate bureaucracies choose where to extend systems, what price to charge for services, and what content to include within them.

Communication in a metropolis also reflects the ethnic, racial, and sexual inequalities that exist generally in the society. These differences affect more profoundly the levels and types of participation that people have in the system than is the case in the village. Social inequalities are perpetuated in the metropolis: different groups live in geographically separate enclaves; they espouse different values, and have contrasting histories and lore; they define their enemies using different criteria; they deal with threats using differing strategies. Even the degree of respect they give constituted authority differs, as does the legitimacy of authority itself. In addition, communication among those not in the elite circles of a metropolis is often haphazard and irregular,

practiced outside the boundaries of the routinized and bureaucratically controlled systems of communication. These organized systems of communication themselves are legitimized based on the efforts of privileged status groups to preserve or enhance their lifestyle. These systems must exclude those on the outside to function as the elites in the metropolis intend them to (see Duncan, 1969, p. 39). The value of the system, then, rests both in what (or whom) it includes and what (or whom) it excludes. A metropolis (to overgeneralize) is, in other words, actually a collection of villages with different degrees of socioeconomic, cultural, and political status that must interact as a function of their proximity, but that often do so in tension and sometimes with violent results.

The Role of Communication Systems

What, then, should one conclude about the often-stated contention that communications technology has eliminated time and space, that is, has collapsed the distance between peoples and brought them into temporal proximity? Given the continuing incongruities of access, representation, and flow, coupled with bureaucratically controlled centralized systems operated by elites for their own benefit, this claim is true only in a limited perceptual sense, not in actuality. Perceptions, too, are continually being modified; a sense of solidarity with one group can dissolve into a seemingly unbridgeable gulf. The United States' relations with the former Soviet Union, with Iran or Japan, even with Western European countries, have all been startlingly altered as a function of distant events. The gulf between the United States and countries in the Southern Hemisphere has remained since the post–World War II independence movement began, even while widening and narrowing over time, while perceptions in Arab countries of the United States have shifted rapidly in response to changing circumstances. The euphoria over the dissolution of the Iron Curtain in 1989–90 had to be tempered with recognition of the fears in African and Latin American countries, created by thawing relations in Europe, that their economic development, dependent on Western aid, would suffer as resources were shifted to rebuilding Eastern Europe (see Mufson, 1991). The perceptions of the possibility of constructing a "new world order" were rudely jarred by the invasion of Kuwait by Iraq, the invasion itself apparently fueled by the misperception that the United States would not intervene militarily in the region.

The role of communications systems in these changes was to signal their occurrence, survey and report on them, and assess their implications. Some elements of these systems also linked people at great distances, facilitating conversation and personal assessment of the events, but did not create intimacy, new identities, or the dissolution of inequality. The global village did not emerge; the metropolis merely became more inclusive.

2.2

A Theoretical Basis for International Communication

If one cannot expect communication actually to eliminate space and time — to create a "global village" — if the inequalities of the metropolis are likely to persist despite burgeoning channels of communication and increasing use of them, what should people expect of international communication?

How are they to explain its workings and results?

International Communication and Social Control

Chapter 1 already began to sketch out the rudiments of a theoretical approach to international communication. According to Innis the space or time bias of the means of communication defines the nature of society. Societies establish and attempt to maintain "monopolies of knowledge" based in these means, providing them with a measure of social control. This control is strongest near the political center of a society, and weakest on its fringes, where other means of communication may threaten central control (see Innis, 1972 and 1951, especially pp. 33–60).

Domestic Versus Global Frameworks

The social control exercised should be understood, too, as existing within two frameworks: a national (or domestic) framework and an international (or global) one. Within countries political and economic elites, or the state, may attempt to achieve control over populations: defining objectives for the society, establishing norms of behavior and enforcing them, determining what people will do for a living and what products they can purchase, and so on. Internationally, certain countries may attempt to exercise control over others by influencing their foreign policies, import-export practices, technical standards for their telecommunications or broadcasting systems, and so on.

Historically, the Western industrial states, particularly the former colonial powers of Western Europe and the United

States, have influenced other countries most decisively.[3] Since World War II the Soviet Union has also had significant influence, and more recently, the economic strength of Japan and Germany has increased their influence. Still other countries, such as Brazil, Nigeria, Egypt, and the People's Republic of China, have had strong regional influence on their neighbors.

International communication is often controversial. Even in the case of well-established services, such as international shortwave (SW) radio, countries find information broadcasts to be objectionable. They jam them by purposely transmitting another signal (or noise) on the same frequency as an incoming signal, restrict import of radio receivers that can detect particular objectionable frequencies, even move their own domestic broadcasting to different services either to compete more effectively with incoming signals or to decrease the necessity of importing receivers capable of detecting SW signals.

With new services, such as satellite broadcasting, VCRs, or computer communication, some countries attempt to deny access altogether or to provide it as a monopoly. The Soviet Union for many years severely restricted the import of both VCRs and personal computers (and even licensed typewriters) to prevent access to potentially threatening information, and Brazil placed import restrictions on computer hardware and software imports to protect its own developing information technology industries. Many countries justify similar activities with claims that they are protecting **hard currency** reserves or newly established industries, but such claims (even when true) may obscure the fact that the effect of such practices is to exert a measure of social control over their citizens. This control effectively denies citizens access to hardware or software of particular kinds, and perhaps

creates a monopoly of information or production that can serve as the basis of national economic and political authority. Governments around the world recognize the truth in Vladimir Artemov's (1981, p. 154) observation that "information is a powerful ideological and political weapon and can be used to subvert sovereign nations." All have taken steps to control its power in one way or another.

Free Flow of Information and Social Control

U.S. citizens may have difficulty understanding such efforts, for they are accustomed to the idea of a "free flow of information." But it is merely part of the prevailing "American" mythology to claim that the United States has such a free flow, and that countries where the government has more control over information do not. Controlling communication has always been an effective means to exercise social control. This statement is as true for the United States as it is for other countries. The United States tried to restrict the import of **digital audiotape (DAT)** players, for instance, to protect the copyrights of its recording artists. It prevents foreign ownership of U.S. radio and television stations, too, even while U.S.-based firms invest in such enterprises abroad (see "Foreign Ownership," 1991).

The essential difference between the United States and many other countries is that the former has chosen to allow private owners of communication channels to exercise primary social control; in other countries the state is primary. In satellite communication, for instance, the current U.S. commercial and military stake in the status quo may in fact lead to a conservative policy with regard to potential changes in international agreements governing satellites and satellite communication. It has thus chosen to exert social control in a particular way in this instance. In other words, social control always exists in one form or another, and to varying degrees.

Strategies for Social Control

Those who control the means of communication exercise social control using a variety of strategies. As already mentioned, the use of disinformation campaigns and propaganda can serve to confuse or direct attention in such a way that people find it difficult to separate truth from fiction. When confusion, error, or inaction results from such strategies, the organization practicing the deceit has effectively exercised social control.

Countries also deny reports made by adversaries, or refuse to confirm or deny them, thereby ostensibly allowing people to think what they will. Such strategies are also designed to introduce confusion, however; people don't know precisely what to believe. Therefore, they don't hold any resultant belief strongly, and can be convinced to alter it more easily at a later time. This, too, is a form of social control.

In addition to these efforts to confuse, there is also the more straightforward tactic of denying access to information. Attempting to control the import of technology or "software," whether in the form of audio- or videocassettes, computer programs, and data services, or through the act of jamming radio signals; attempting to establish international conventions to prevent satellite spillover without consent; controlling the activities of journalists or diplomats; denying access to available satellite up-links — all are means to deny people access to information. These tactics prevent either the collection of information or its distribution. Countries use each of them regularly, either

to exercise social control over domestic populations (as the Israelis sought to do during their 1987–90 Palestinian difficulties in the Gaza, or the South Africans during the so-called state of emergency) or to prevent foreign populations from knowing about, and possibly objecting to, domestic situations. In other words, many countries regard restrictions on the reporting of unrest by journalists as a means to exercise social control.

Some organizations oppose these efforts by providing information to people who would otherwise be denied access to it. This is the overriding rationale for the operations of the U.S. government's Radio Free Europe (RFE) (directed into Eastern and Central Europe), Radio Liberty (RL) (to the Soviet Union) and both Radio and Television Martí (to Cuba). It is also part of the rationale for the operations of the Voice of America (VOA) and the British Broadcasting Company (BBC) World Service. It was certainly the single most important impetus for the establishment of Britain's and the United States' external broadcasting activities in the 1930s and 1940s directed into Nazi Germany.

This, too, is the basis for less well known activities of the United States' external radio broadcasters. RFE/RL, for instance, for most of its history, regularly published engineering reports on technical means to counteract Soviet and Eastern European jamming activities. These reports were designed for nontechnical readers and required only materials readily available in Eastern bloc countries. RFE/RL broadcast these reports into such countries, and distributed them in printed form so people could carry them through "underground" networks to other interested parties.

Providing information to people otherwise denied access to it, however, is also an effort to exercise social control. Such information circumvents the social control attempted by communication denial, thus introducing a different form, albeit less controlled, of the same phenomenon. Both the Soviet Union's efforts to restrict information flow and RFE/RL's efforts to increase it, in other words, arose from the same desire to exert social control.

Finally, international communication may be used to attain a competitive advantage over other countries or companies by gaining quick access to market and commodity information, inventory supplies, sources of parts, energy, or transportation, and so on. Transnational corporations (TNCs) establish private networks, for instance, to gain such information for planning activities; governments do the same for commodity marketing strategies; and international brokerage houses and central banks do likewise for trends in stock and bond prices, exchange rates, and trade balances. Gaining a competitive edge provides a measure of control over competitors, and over one's own fortunes.

Examples of efforts to exercise social control can be found in both economic and political spheres. On the economic side, for instance, **electronic funds transfer (EFT)** arrangements, coupled with international brokerage activities and efforts of central banks to control **currency exchange** rates, are all interrelated. International computer linkages, and the ability of brokers to trade stocks and bonds nearly 24 hours a day in markets in New York, Tokyo, Hong Kong, Australia, and London, were blamed for the sudden decline in stock prices worldwide in October 1987.

Social control exercised in the political sphere is also significant. Historians have suggested that the Hungarian uprising of 1956 was at least partly caused by promises

of U.S. military intervention carried by RFE, and more recently, political figures have credited the relatively quick acknowledgment of the Chernobyl nuclear plant disaster by the Soviets to the fact that RFE/RL broadcast reports of the accident into the Eastern bloc, causing the normally slow-to-react Soviet media apparatus to respond with its own version of the situation. VOA, during the time of the 1987 bombing raid on Libya, even called for the Libyan people to depose their leader, Moamar Ghadaffi, although in this case the appeals apparently went unheeded.

Following the failed coup in the Soviet Union, the director of international services for the All-Russian State Television Radio and Broadcasting Company thanked VOA on the air for inspiring its Russian listeners "with faith and determination to fight dictatorship" ("VOA, RFE/RL Victorious," 1991, p. 37). Mikhail Gorbachev also acknowledged that he had been able to keep up with developments during the coup by using aging radios and a rigged shortwave antenna to listen to the BBC, RL, and VOA ("BRF—Gorbachev—Radio," 1991).

An interdependent world leads to expanding international communication linkages and enhanced efforts to exercise social control through them. Manipulating information itself, and access to information via communication systems, will become an increasingly prevalent activity over the next several decades. Political, economic, and military power will depend to a greater and greater extent on access to information, and on the ability to trust and make use of it.

Avoiding Social Control

To return briefly to Innis, new forms of social control exercised through control of communication may be the most obvious effect of the development of new communications systems. Innis argued that every society would use communication for social control, establishing what he called a "monopoly of knowledge" based in a medium of communication. He suggested, however, that the farther away from the center of power people were, the weaker would be the state's ability to exercise effective control (Innis, 1972, p. 117). The result, he said, was that people on the fringes of society would create alternative monopolies of knowledge, and eventually challenge the dominant monopoly.

This is precisely the situation with international communication. It enters countries along their borders (at the fringe), providing information that states would like to control, denying official domestic versions of events, allowing organizations within countries to be controlled from the outside, giving people greater choice than they might otherwise have. This penetration from the fringe can be seen in the use of audiocassettes by the Ayatollah Khomeini, while still in exile, to communicate with his followers in Iran. It is also prevalent in the activities of black marketers bringing audio and video technologies into African countries, pirates distributing **bootleg** American videocassettes in Southeast Asia and Indian pornographic tapes in the Middle East, and people constructing homemade **satellite dishes** in remote areas of Latin America and the South Pacific (see, for instance, Graham, 1988). In each instance, an alternative technology or content to that made available through state channels exists, and serves as a counter to the monopoly of knowledge centered in urban elites around the world (see Fortner, 1986a, 1987).

The social control exercised, either domestically or internationally, thus varies, as Innis recognized, depending on the strength of the central elites or the state, and the completeness of the monopoly of knowledge. This social control should be understood, too, as seeking comprehensive authority; it not only affects social relations, or the extent and means of political participation, but also economic and cultural relations between peoples.[4]

The Central Concern of Communication Theory

Communication theory's central concern is the nature and role of messages (or meaning) in life and society: the nature of social interaction achieved through messages (see Gerbner, 1967, p. 43). Communication content is an independent element in people's social reality; one that influences the nature of that reality, and thus society itself (McQuail, 1983, p. 219).[5] To understand international communication, then, requires an examination of the comprehensive set of relationships that have developed among those engaged in it. Communication theory seeks, too, to identify those attempting to exercise social control, the strategies and technologies they employ, and the impacts of these efforts on various communities. These impacts can affect individual states, nations, and economies.[6]

The Flow of Messages Across Frontiers

Traditionally, international communication study has been concerned with the flow of messages across frontiers. This has been the case largely because the systematic study of international communication arose following the First World War, during which countries made the first widespread use of propaganda aimed at foreign populations (see Bobrow, 1972, pp. 36–37). The study of international communication has thus concentrated on the flow of messages, and the "symbolic inducement" of action by them, either through propaganda itself or the more indirect method of **"cultural imperialism"** accomplished through media software (audio, video, and film) exports. (The term *symbolic inducement* is Gregg's, 1984; see also Mañach, 1975, for a developing country perspective on "frontiers" and culture.)

Comprehensive Theory and International Communication

International communication theory, however, must be more comprehensive than this traditional approach implies. Beyond these concerns it must also account for the role (and subtle message) of technology (hardware) exports from one country to another, the flow of messages between individuals or private companies over telecommunications links, and the effects of international treaties, **conventions, standards,** and organizations on the various flows that make up international exchange. It must recognize the shifting impacts and expectations of communication flow occasioned by new historical realities (such as the post–World War II independence movement or the development of new technologies) and by changing ideological perspectives (on such issues as "free flow of information") that are both philosophically grounded and affected by economics and politics.

International communication theory must recognize, too, that the messages to be examined are often hidden: they are not merely those of obvious efforts to appeal to foreign populations via an international radio service. Countries employ a variety of more subtle strategies: subsidies to private companies, careful selection of delegates to international conferences, selection of standards for domestic services, rhetorical defenses of their communications practices that obscure motives as much as illuminate them, implied condemnations of other states' practices, or arguments for extensions of domestic communication philosophies to international issues. Perhaps even more subtle are those messages carried by the extension of systems themselves, the technological prowess thus suggested, or the implications of a strong defense of **intellectual property** protection or free trade in such property, especially when coming from countries enjoying strong trade positions in such "software" products.

This more comprehensive effort recognizes, too, that the impact of international communication does not merely occur across national borders, but also across cultural and economic borders. Cultures often transcend national boundaries; several individual cultures or economic units may also exist within national borders. The social control exercised by one entity, be it a country, government, private company, or whatever, on another may affect only part of a population within a given country, or may impact on several countries simultaneously. While the principal concern of international communication must be flow across borders, it must also take account of flow across cultures and regions, and to subsets of national populations, such as political and economic elites.

2.3

Symbols and Meaning in International Communication

Perhaps the most difficult task for international communication theory is to suggest specific impacts that can be traced to its practice. Studies of propaganda conducted within countries have not found it particularly effective (see Lasswell & Blumenstock, 1970, pp. 247–248).[7] The discrediting of the so-called hypodermic needle model of persuasion, which assumed that messages could be injected like a powerful drug into the "body politic" or that this body could be inoculated against such messages, also had its impact on propaganda study, banishing it "to a lonely and peripheral region of mass communications theory: the study of **psychological warfare** and operations" (Robins, Webster, & Pickering, 1987, p. 4).

The "Effects" of International Communication

Such observations should not lead too quickly, however, to the conclusion that international communication does not matter. Elites do not exercise social control only through direct and effective propaganda appeals to non-elite populations; they may not even use such vehicles at all. Nevertheless, their control of the communication system through ownership of technology, domination of the international regulatory apparatus, or production of content, may often be more effective than overt use of propaganda.

When countries do choose to practice propaganda, it is often impossible to know how effective it is. Countries at war do not allow audience researchers from their adversaries' broadcast services to enter and survey reactions to their broadcasts. Anecdotal evidence collected during conflict situations has found that people listen to outside broadcasts; that, in itself, is indicative of effects that many countries, desirous of protecting their own monopoly of information, have seen as undesirable. At the beginning of the Gulf War, U.S. and allied warplanes focused on Radio Baghdad as one of their initial targets, ostensibly to deny Saddam Hussein a vehicle to reach either his own people or those of the outside world. This was as much to protect the allies' "monopoly of knowledge," a monopoly enforced by strict controls on the press covering the war from Saudi Arabia, as it was to staunch propaganda. Yet VOA also broadcast Hussein's speeches picked up from the damaged Radio Baghdad to maintain its objectivity in reporting news of the Gulf conflict (see Fortner, 1991a).

The issue of "effects" is further complicated by the role of audiences in processing the information received. People transform the information they attend to (Nevitt, 1982, p. 125); the degree of control enjoyed by information providers (or propagandists) is therefore never complete, even if ostensibly unchallenged. What matters perhaps more than the existence of information monopoly or of alternative information is the meaning to the audiences to whom they are directed of the symbols employed in the information. We should not expect that information, or symbols qua symbols, will control people, but that people will respond to the meaning of a given symbol as it relates to their own experience. The meaning of a dictator's saber-rattling changes, for instance, when he directs his troops to invade another country, even when his words remain constant (see Beninger, 1986, p. 95, for an elaboration of this argument).

This makes arguments about cultural imperialism more problematic. On the one hand, to demonstrate that Western cultural materials (films, videos, and musical recordings, particularly pop and rock, and computer programs) dominate cinemas, radio and television programming, or computer software sales in non-Western countries is not hard to do. On the other hand, it is more difficult to demonstrate, beyond the obvious economic effects, precisely what the impacts of this material are: how people think differently, for instance, as a result of exposure to such information over time. Some behaviors do change, to be sure: people watch television who had not done so before. The widespread changes expected, however, have been more difficult to demonstrate.[8] Culture has proved more resilient and absorptive than anticipated, and media messages less potent than feared. Two thirds of the world's population still awaits the arrival of the telephone; its impact has therefore also been spotty.

In the meantime, too, non-elites in many developing countries have used new technologies, such as audio- and videocassette recorders, to bypass the central control exercised by their own domestic elites and to threaten state-dominated monopolies of knowledge. This choice by non-elites of international over domestic information hegemony further complicates arguments about cultural imperialism.

The Centrality of People in Assessing Effects

Thus, one must recognize the centrality of two aspects of international communication if its effects are to be understood. First is the role of *people* — those who use the systems and who constitute the audiences for international communications materials. They live within cultures (systems of meaning) that serve as "terministic screens" for attending to, interpreting, and applying information (messages) ("terministic screens" is Burke's term, 1966, pp. 44–47). They are active in the international communications system, although many continue to be excluded from it based on economic in-

ability to participate. This problem of exclusion is exacerbated, too, by the decreasing role of the public service philosophy in communications (originally developed within the BBC), and its replacement by a U.S.-inspired private enterprise, "choice and variety"–based philosophy. This change in dominant philosophy has increasingly meant that those with economic ability to participate in the international communications system are given preference over those without such ability. In other words, the impact of the system is to favor elites over non-elites.

The Reality of History in Assessing Effects

The second key aspect of international communication is the reality of *history,* and historically embedded cultures. Cultures are dynamic: They change both in response to environmental (external) inputs and as a result of internal transformations, such as in the use of language or alterations in the means of representation of experience (for example, new techniques of artistic expression or new technologies for the communication of experience) (see Carey, 1989; Czitrom, 1982; Eisenstein, 1979; Meyrowitz, 1985; or Ong, 1982, for discussions of changes introduced by technology).

Since international communication began to occur in an organized fashion following the invention of the telegraph in the middle of the 19th century, its development has paralleled the continuing development of national consciousness, particularly in Europe where countries signed the first international agreements. Rising nationalism gave rise to increasing political and economic competition among the states of Europe, the aggregation of military power, and competitive efforts to attain legitimacy as "major powers."[9] By the middle of the century, when international electric telegraphy became a real possibility, the European powers were busily extending global empires. By the 1870s they were partitioning Africa into colonial enclaves and extending their hegemony through expansion of **submarine telegraph** cables. In 1879, for instance, the Eastern Telegraph Company laid a submarine cable from Aden to Durban, in southern Africa, via Zanzibar. "This cable," Weinthal argued (1923, p. 215), "immediately proved of such value that it was unable to cope with public demands, and whenever an interruption occurred, which was not infrequently, clamours for a coast line were heard." In 1887 the British Colonial Conference addressed cable communication as a major element in the adequate defense of the empire. As Jan Hendrick Hefmeyr, the representative of the Cape of Good Hope, put the issue: "I think that to make the defence of the empire complete, we should in reality have a cable both across the Pacific Ocean, and another [from England via southern Africa to Mauritius and western Australia]" (Colonial Conference, 1887, p. 226).

Communication became a method of exerting control over these empires, and led to struggles over control of submarine telegraph cables, the wireless, and eventually radio. Communication technologies reduced the authority of the "man on the spot," who had previously been responsible for responding to local crises, by investing greater authority in those at a distance (see Headrick, 1981, pp. 163–164, and 1988, pp. 99–101). Headrick disagrees, however (1988, p. 101), that the authority of the "man on the spot" was reduced by submarine cables. Efforts to influence to a purpose, what Beninger (1986, p. 7) defines as "control,"

were initiated, too, almost as soon as radio became a viable technology.

In addition to exerting political and economic control over imperial possessions, using new technologies to establish connections with their neighbors, and seeking international legitimacy through efforts to influence both domestic and foreign populations, some countries also sought to control their people's access to foreign information as well. The result was what Beninger (after Max Weber) called "rationalization" (1986, p. 15): attempting to increase control over people by (1) increasing the capability to process information (hence applications of new technologies) and (2) decreasing the amount of information to be processed (hence domestic propaganda).

The meaning of such efforts was at once obvious and obscure. Propaganda aimed at foreign populations to induce sympathy was obvious. Less apparent, however, were the struggles to provide a competitive edge to institutions to control news flow (such as Reuters), or the interpretations given to information or technological systems by people who used them. People understood each system they apprehended within a historical context, seeing it as abusive or benign.[10] These interpretations influenced their evaluations of it (and, therefore, its legitimacy). These evaluations affected, in turn, the role the technology and its content could play as a vehicle of social control, legitimation, bureaucratization, or public administration, or for the cultivation of public opinion.[11]

Cooperation and Competition in Systems

The meaning of technological or information systems was also influenced by the often contradictory uses to which states or private entities put them. In some instances it was essential that organizations (or bureaucracies) work in *cooperation;* often, however, they found themselves in *competition.* Competition implied that such organizations also sought economic advantages. This could rapidly become an effort to *control* (or monopolize) a technology, or the content it carried.

The role of cooperation is apparent in such activities as the successful establishment of international organizations, such as the International Telecommunication Union (ITU) or the International Telecommunications Satellite Organization (Intelsat). Treaties subdividing the frequency spectrum into designated services, standards development for technical interfaces between domestic telecommunications systems, the creation of international standards of conduct (regulating, for instance, copyright relations or declarations of human rights), even government contracts granted to foreign companies to build domestic telephone or radio systems — all are examples of cooperation. Such efforts usually result in enhanced legitimacy for the systems that emerge, increased willingness to use such systems, and greater international understanding. Their meaning thus is positive.

Countries also act, however, in what they perceive as their national interests. It is not unusual for them to see these interests as coincidental with those of private companies operating from their territory. The United States has protected U.S.-based companies' telegraph, wire service, telephone, radio, and electronic manufacturing companies. Great Britain has subsidized Reuters and protected British Marconi, and Cable and Wireless; Germany has likewise preferred Telefunken, France Thomson,

and Japan and several Southern Hemisphere countries their electronics manufacturing or telecommunications companies.

National interests often collide. The result can be confusion of international standards (and thus reduced communication capability) or rhetorical rivalries with the attendant accusations and denials, even international piracy (clandestine or surrogate radio stations, or pirate audio- or videocassette duplication facilities).

National interests can also lead to trade protectionism, refusals to sign international conventions, efforts to enlist allies to establish international legitimacy for a nationally developed technical standard, such as high-definition television (HDTV), or **"public diplomacy"** and "propaganda" activities designed to appeal directly to foreign populations. Such competition often reduces opportunities for international cooperative efforts, embroils ostensibly "nonpolitical" organizations (such as the ITU) in drawn-out debates on issues extraneous to their missions, and leads to incompatible technical standards — thus frustrating communication efforts.

When competition leads to strategies designed to control a system, communication can break down entirely. Countries have often attempted to establish domestic ideologies, such as the concept of a "free flow of information," as an international standard of conduct, even when selectively applying the concept to the activities of their own nationally based organizations. They have pursued obviously self-serving interpretations of international "moral" standards, such as those applied to propaganda or human rights, thus compromising their application entirely. They have vigorously exploited temporary technological advances to gain competitive advantages, as in the use of the

geostationary satellite orbit, or exploited production capability to establish near monopolies in the flow of communication content or the production of hardware.

Although it is possible to describe the technological realities of telecommunications systems, and those of the production and distribution of content, it is difficult to sort out the "effects" of such strategies and practices for international communication, particularly as they affect audiences and users. Since audiences actively interpret the meaning of these activities, as well as the content they receive from broadcast or artifactual (i.e., film) media, and decide for themselves the value of participation in telecommunications systems (when they are available), one can only speculate as to what meanings they attach.

If the approach to international communication emphasizes the role and perspective of the state, instances of cooperation and competition are often easy to see. Even here, however, the meaning of rhetorical strategies — often self-serving — must be interpreted, even when seemingly grounded in reality. Countries do strive in the international arena for their interpretations (meanings) of terms and concepts (e.g., freedom, democracy, freedom of expression, etc.) to be accepted (legitimized) by the world community. They each have strategies, too, to avoid the consequences of legitimated interpretations that they see as contrary to their national interests. They can ignore the interpretation, claim inability to comply, assert adherence although violating the interpretation, even declare an alternative justification for their actions. All of this is made possible by the fact that international standards of conduct are not necessarily consistent. They allow international communication to be used as an ideo-

logical weapon, while recognizing communication itself as a basic human right. On the one hand, standards demand that people have the right to receive information, while on the other, the world community recognizes the immense magnitude of inequality among the world's people in access to the means to communicate.

International communication, in short, is a complex set of issues. The investigation of social control historically sought by countries through application of communications systems requires, in turn, an examination of propaganda, technological control, rhetorical and political strategies in treaty making and the design of international organizations, the inequalities of access among the world's people and the reasons for them, and efforts to achieve social justice even while protecting economic interests. In addition, the investigation requires familiarity with the technologies of communication, the history of technology, and economic and political theory, particularly as applied to international communication issues. Communication may be the most wonderful of all affairs, as Dewey said, but its wonder is in its complexity, and in the interrelationships of its various aspects.

2.4

International Communication: A Systems Analysis

What is most significant from a systems perspective are the interrelationships among the various parts of the system constructed (purposively and accidentally) to conduct international communication. This system includes *technical* components (wires, recorded materials, radio waves), *economic* components (trade issues, tariffs, taxation, capital investment strategies), *political and regulatory* components (issues of sovereignty, treaty making, alliances, geo-political balance), *cultural* components (portrayals of nations and peoples, domination in the production of, or dependence on other nations for the production of, cultural products), and *social control* components (propaganda, information flow, the right to communicate). These components link together the various participants in international communication: governments, regulatory and representative agencies, corporations, and audiences. These components also have a history, are subject to criticism from a variety of ideological viewpoints, and have implications for the conduct of relations between nation-states, the conduct of business internationally, the formation of **international public opinion,** and the ability of peoples to construct, alter, and maintain distinctive cultural identities.

A systems analysis provides the basis for understanding international communication from several different perspectives: technological, political, economic, cultural, and social. It recognizes, for instance, that international radio communication, such as that undertaken by VOA, occurs not in a vacuum but within an international system with many other dimensions that affect interpretations of U.S. communications activity. The United States, for instance, operates the most extensive international radio network in the world. That, in itself, is significant. That significance is magnified by the dominance of other U.S. communication activity in international religious broadcasting, film and video distribution, data and voice traffic, and technological development. The United States has also led the Western democracies in the debate over the right to communicate versus the free flow of

information. Wherever we look, whatever the issue in international communication, whether technological, economic, cultural, or ideological, a consideration of the U.S. role is crucial.

While certain antisystemic forces — for instance, unexpected phenomena, such as pirates or clandestine users — can upset the routines adopted within the global system, the history of international communication is largely that of a developing complex system. It is a system, however, that people are occasionally able to use for unorthodox purposes.

Single Versus Separate Systems of Communication

The systems approach recognizes that, in some respects, all the activity that comprises international communication is part of a *single system.* International radio programming, for instance, must take account of the wire copy that has appeared in foreign newspapers, as well as economic trade relations and other cultural material, such as films and television programs. This approach also acknowledges that in other respects individual parts of the system (such as international radio activity) may function (wholly or partially) as *separate systems.* Both of these configurations must be accounted for in the analysis.

Also, the systems approach appreciates the various components of both the single system and its separate systems (which might reasonably be thought of as subsystems). These components would include the following:

- the *technologies* used for international communication
- the *philosophies* (e.g., politics or ideologies) that control the approach taken by

various countries to the creation, mainte- nance, and use of the system

- the *goals* that countries seek to attain by developing and using the system, and by attempting to interfere with the opera- tion of the system

- the *content* of the system (and the reason for its creation)

- the *consequences,* both anticipated and unanticipated, of developing and using the system

- the *relationships* between the single sys- tem and its various subsystems and components

- the *audiences* for and *users* of the var- ious system components—their attention to and sense making of both the system and its content

Also, as with any systems analysis, cer- tain characteristics of systems must be con- sidered. There include the following:

- Systems are the result of a *process*— in this case a communications process that itself has no beginning and no end; sys- tems, too, develop in response to exter- nal demands, and the process they serve evolves in such a way that it is difficult to determine precisely their genesis (e.g., although the date for the invention of the electric telegraph can be specified, its de- velopment as a system for international communication evolved from early do- mestic uses).

- Systems are *dynamic:* they are ever- changing and respond to outside influ- ences by altering these influences or by incorporating them into their structure.

- The *relationships* of the parts of an evolv- ing process-responsive system are not necessarily *linear:* the parts can be exam- ined in any order and should be under- stood as existing together in any order

(e.g., a technology used for communica- tion may be created in response to a need, or may create new needs; informa- tion may be created by using a system, or may be the basis for altering the means of using a system).

The Value of a Systems Approach

The value of the systems approach is that it focuses attention on relationships between the constituent elements of the *system of communication* itself, as well as those of the subsystems. It is easy to think of radio fre- quencies, for instance, as the means by which audiences receive radio or television programs. However, radio waves also serve as the medium for the transmission of wire copy that may appear in the next edition of a daily newspaper, or even of data and fac- simile traffic carrying weather maps, docu- ments, and financial information. It is not just the technical system that is important, but also the uses to which it has been put, for what reasons, and to what ends.

To return briefly to but one example, the Chinese students protesting in Tiananmen Square listened to the BBC and VOA to gauge the extent of their support outside Beijing. The government of China eventually responded by jamming these foreign ser- vices that were providing information not available to the students through domestic media. U.S. networks were beaming stories via satellite back to the United States and electronically altering faces to prevent them from being recognized by Chinese authori- ties. Reporters could not be sure, however, that the Chinese were not picking up the **back-feeds** from China before the images had been altered. Eventually, they discov- ered that Chinese authorities were, in fact, using these reports to identify and punish protesters. Reports from China appeared in the U.S. press, too, and these reports, along with others picked up off wire services and from correspondents, served as the basis for international radio broadcasts back into China. Likewise, Chinese students in the United States were reading reports that appeared in the U.S. press and then sending faxes back to China. All the available technologies, and the interrelationships between these technologies, were exploited by people interested in the demonstrations. Some of those involved acted from economic impulses, others from widely differing political convictions. The results of these official and unofficial activities affected the unfolding of later events, social relations between students and other possible supporters, and political (and eventually military) decisions made by the Chinese government (see chapter 9).

2.5

Social Control and Human Rights

A further advantage of the systems approach to examining international communication is that it illuminates significant aspects of the operation of this system. Because the system is one that must involve nation-states (the signatories of international conventions, ratifiers of **technical standards**, and so on), the role of these nations in facilitating, or impeding, international communication, as has already been suggested, is a significant question.

Political Sovereignty Versus the Right to Communicate

The impacts on people of nations collectively operating the system are thus an issue. As the system developed, two fundamental principles in international relations governing the flow of information and communication have often conflicted. Different countries have emphasized various aspects of the question of social control. Many have focused on the importance of political sovereignty in making decisions about communication. Others, often for their own political and economic reasons, have demanded that the international community recognize a **"right to communicate":** the right to seek out information and to practice free expression.

Political sovereignty implies that a nation has the right to run its own internal affairs as it sees fit. In other words, a principle of noninterference in the internal affairs of other states exists, even when the results of such a policy may have international implications for, to name but one example, the flow of news. However, nations have also signed a variety of guarantees suggesting that people have a right to communicate.

Human Rights

Behind the argument that people have a right to communicate is the issue of human rights. In the United States the idea of "inalienable rights" of individuals enshrined in the Declaration of Independence led to enumerated civil liberties in the Bill of Rights. Such rights, however inalienable they may have seemed to U.S. citizens, were not necessarily adopted by other countries. In the aftermath of World War II and the holocaust perpetrated against Jews, Slavs, the infirm and crippled, and Christian dissidents by the Nazis, the United Nations undertook the task of defining the relationship between individuals and the state. The Universal Declaration of Human Rights, adopted December 10, 1948, obliquely referred to this context in its preamble, claiming that "disregard and contempt for human rights have resulted in barbarous acts which have outraged the conscience of mankind," and stated that "freedom of speech and belief and freedom from fear and want [were] the highest aspiration of the common people." The Declaration that followed was to be a "common standard of achievement for all peoples and nations," and included the claim that "everyone has the right to freedom of opinion and expression; this right includes the freedom to hold opinions without interference and to seek, receive and impart information and ideas through any media and regardless of frontiers" (Article 19).

The Universal Declaration was followed by others. Article 19 of the International Covenant on Civil and Political Rights, adopted in 1966, included a similar provision for freedom of expression, as did the West European Convention for the Protection of Human Rights and Fundamental Freedoms (1950), the American Convention on Human Rights (1969), and the African Charter on Human and People's Rights (1981). Perhaps the best-known declarations designed to protect such rights were the Helsinki Accords, adopted by the Conference on Security and Co-Operation in Europe, and signed by both Western and Socialist states in 1975.

Western Governments and Human Rights

Because of the strong endorsement evidenced by these documents for the principles that free expression and freedom of information—regardless of national frontiers—are fundamental human rights, Western countries have considered themselves free to criticize activities of other na-

tions in restricting these rights. The United States, for instance, identified freedom of expression as being as significant as arms control in summit meetings held with the Soviet Union in 1987 and 1988. President Reagan celebrated the anniversary of the Helsinki Accords on his way to Moscow to meet with General Secretary Gorbachev in 1988, and met with Soviet dissidents while there (as George Bush later, and unsuccessfully, attempted to do in China) (see Fortner, forthcoming).

The difficulty of the West's position, however, is twofold. First, Western governments have defined the issue too narrowly: they have recognized a conflict between human rights and social control only in the arena of *state* action. They have not acknowledged the social control exercised in their own societies by the activities of profit-seeking communications institutions (the press, radio and television networks, satellite companies, wire services, telephone monopolies, and so on). In other words, their own philosophy of free expression has not been broad enough to encompass non-state social control.

The Problem of Interference in Countries' Internal Affairs

Second, despite the international guarantees of the right to communicate, various international bodies have adopted an equally long list of resolutions that, while affirming the principle of free expression, deny legitimacy to practices interfering in the **"internal affairs"** of other countries. The 1970 UN Declaration on Principles of International Law Concerning Friendly Relations and Co-operation Among States in Accordance with the Charter of the United Nations, for instance, stated that "no State or group of States has the right to intervene, directly or indirectly, for any reason whatever, in the internal or external affairs of any other State," and that "every State has an inalienable right to choose its political, economic, social and cultural systems, without interference in any form by another State." The UN reaffirmed these statements on December 9, 1981, in its Declaration on the Inadmissibility of Intervention and Interference in the Internal Affairs of States.

The United Nations has also adopted resolutions condemning the use of propaganda, such as Resolution 110, adopted by the General Assembly in 1947, and recalled in the Declaration of Fundamental Principles Concerning the Contribution of the Mass Media to Strengthening Peace and International Understanding, to the Promotion of Human Rights and to Countering Racialism, Apartheid and Incitement to War, adopted on November 28, 1978 (these documents are reprinted in Nordenstreng, Manet, & Kleinwächter, 1986).

Many nations have appealed to such resolutions in defending their choice of media and press systems, or in stifling dissent by those advocating the overthrow of their governments. They have also argued that the requirements of public order justify such practices as the licensing and/or accrediting of journalists, which Western countries have condemned.

The two principles, one guaranteeing the practice of free expression as a basic human right and the other denying legitimacy to interference in internal affairs of states and to the use of propaganda, have been used by both East and West in their historical rhetorical battles pitting Western-style democracy against communism. Likewise, various nations have used them as justifications for measures to control information.

To provide but one example, during the long Cold War confrontation between East and West, one Soviet spokesperson claimed that "Western radio propaganda tries to exert constant pressure on the socialist countries to achieve aims prohibited by the Final Act [of the Helsinki Accords]" (Artemov, 1981, p. 155). Leonid M. Zamyatin, chief of the International Information Department of the Soviet Communist Party, made a similar claim in *Literaturnaya Gazeta* in 1984, delivering a "blistering denunciation of American 'propaganda . . . aimed, in effect, at shaking and undermining the Soviet system'" (quoted in "Wick Proposes," 1986, p. 80). TASS carried a report in 1988, too, claiming that the CIA funded Radio Constitucion, a clandestine radio station in Panama. This station, it said, was "obviously aimed at destabilising the situation in that country" (BBC Monitoring Service, 1988e).

The United States, for its part, claimed that "under Article 19 of the Declaration of Human Rights of the United Nations, to which the Soviets are a signatory, there is a prohibition against any hindrance of a free flow of information across transnational boundaries. So, the stated policy of multilateral signatories does not inhibit the free flow of information. And unless that changes, that would be a very drastic change, I think you're going to find the free world resisting that very much [sic]" (statement of Charles Z. Wick, quoted in "Wick, Worldnet, and the War of Ideas" 1986). The Presidential Study Commission on International Radio Broadcasting, too, claimed in 1973 (United States, p. 8) that "limitations on freedom of information existing in the Soviet Union and its area of political and military hegemony . . . merit extraordinary concern. The Soviet sphere constitutes one of the two great power centers of the world." The United States also objected strenuously to the jamming of "American" broadcasting signals into the Soviet Union and Socialist Europe, although these countries ended jamming beginning in 1987.

The conflict of these two principles, then, has complicated the question of human rights and national sovereignty, pitting them against each other in the post–World War II period.[12] This is part of the larger context within which the question of social control exercised through control of information must be considered. A systems approach to international communication also demands that it be considered.

Political and Economic Policies in Social Control

There are two other parts of this larger context that we must also consider. First, many countries have adopted political and economic policies ostensibly designed for ends other than controlling information, but that nevertheless have had impacts on the flow of communication across borders. Such policies include import restrictions, taxation and tariff policies directed at technologies crossing borders, and political decisions to centralize control of domestic communications systems, rather than leaving them open for private development. Various countries have adopted such policies, not only to control the import of technology itself, but also to tax or restrict the activities of transnational corporations operating within them. Some have acted for purely economic reasons: many countries in the developing world continue to be burdened with heavy debts, and thus look for any means to increase their access to hard currencies. Even industrialized countries sometimes use such tactics to protect domestic industries or to subsidize communications infrastructures. Other countries have acted more from political motives, attempting to continue their own domestic information

monopolies, regardless of the new opportunities created by the extension and development of the international system.

The Issue of Clandestine Communication

The second part of this larger context is the issue of clandestine communication, particularly broadcasting. Clandestine broadcasting is a type of "piracy," in the sense that the broadcasters are not using frequencies assigned to them by a national authority. International covenants therefore consider such broadcasts illegal. Clandestine broadcasting, however, is not merely pirate broadcasting, which has plagued many countries in Western Europe particularly. Rather, it is broadcasting aimed at the overthrow of a government by dissident or revolutionary elements, or by another state seeking to overthrow an adversary without armed intervention. The Soviet Union, for instance, considered the activities of RFE/RL to be clandestine in nature, particularly during crisis periods such as the 1956 Hungarian and 1968 Czechoslovak uprisings (see BBC Monitoring Service, 1988e). The Soviets also sometimes included the broadcasts of the BBC, Deutsche Welle, and VOA in the same condemnations. The West, however, rejected such claims, arguing that they clearly identified these stations and their respective target audiences.

2.6

Cultural Issues in Theoretical Perspective

Despite the fact that much international communication occurs through the activities of nongovernmental institutions, state administrations are still crucial to such activities. Besides such issues as social control, monopolies of knowledge, and political sovereignty, a systems analysis also provides the basis for examining two cultural issues: intellectual property, and cultural imperialism or hegemony.

Intellectual Property

The countries of the world have signed a number of agreements aimed at protecting intellectual property, that is, property such as patents, trademarks, and artistic works (protected by copyright). UNESCO and the World Intellectual Property Organization (WIPO), both agencies of the United Nations, are responsible for administering world copyright conventions subscribed to by most industrialized states, and increasingly by developing countries as well. UNESCO administers the Universal Copyright Convention (UCC), while WIPO administers the Berne Convention.

The UCC was adopted at the behest of the United States in 1952, although the U.S. Congress did not ratify the treaty until 1954, making it effective in 1955. The Berne Convention for the Protection of Literary and Artistic Works already existed, having been completed in 1885.

The logic undergirding such conventions is that, by providing protection to artists, and thus a claim on just compensation from those who use their products, other artists will be encouraged to produce. Additional reasons exist, however, particularly for art produced by collaborative efforts, such as films, television programs, and musical recordings, and owned through contract by large corporations. Simply stated, corporations seek to maximize profit and to dominate markets. Disputes have thus erupted between those who see these protections as

merely means to continue the long-standing domination of smaller and poorer countries by the larger and richer ones, and those who argue in favor of a "free flow" of information. The United States, which dominated both international patents and copyrighted works between the end of World War II and the mid-1980s, became the focus of much complaint (see Fortner, 1978b, 1991b). It is thus worth examining in some detail the U.S. position in these disputes.

The United States and Copyright Issues

The first question is why the United States did not sign the Berne Convention until 1989. First, the United States saw the Berne requirements as being contrary to U.S. interests in certain technical respects. For instance, Berne did not require inclusion of a copyright notice in the work itself, nor the deposit of the work in a national depository library, to gain copyright protection. The United States required both, largely because of the desire to have a national depository, the Library of Congress, contain copies of all artistic, literary, scientific, and architectural works produced in the country.

Second, the United States still had a "manufacturing clause" in its copyright law. This required that books be published in the United States to receive protection, a clause originally inserted to protect the infant book publishing industry from trade originating in Great Britain (Public Law 94-553, Section 601).

Third, U.S. publishers had taken advantage of what was called "backdoor protection" under the simultaneous publication clause of Article 3 of the Berne Convention, and saw little further benefit to be gained by actual signature. This clause extended protection to any work published in a Berne signatory country within 30 days of its original publication. A book published within this time limit was construed to be simultaneously published, and could be copyrighted. Most U.S. publishers simultaneously published in the United States and Canada (a Berne signatory) to gain international protection, and thus benefited from the requirement that countries extend protection to works published in other signatory countries equal to that provided to works published in their own. Nonadherence to Berne actually gave U.S. publishers an economic advantage: they could gain protection throughout the developed world by publishing in Canada, while the United States itself was not obliged to protect works published outside its own territory.

Finally, and most importantly, there was the issue of "moral rights." Berne (Article 6bis)[13] required recognition of two of these rights: the right of an author to be acknowledged as such and not to be identified as an author of another's work, and the right of paternity. U.S. courts, however, did not recognize these "moral rights" as enforceable under law. The U.S. entertainment industry was divided on the issue, with people taking one side or the other depending on whether they thought of themselves as authors.[14] The moral rights protection under Berne resulted, for instance, in the anomaly that U.S. filmmakers could successfully prevent the screening of "colorized" versions of their original black-and-white films in France, but could not prevent the colorization, or the screening of these versions, in the United States.[15]

Adherence to the Berne Convention, then, while it would have extended important protections to U.S. artists, also would have provided economic disincentives to the corporations that controlled most exportable U.S. art. Since film, recording, and video software has been an important component of U.S. exports since the end of World War II, the government refused to consider, until the mid-1980s, the question of Berne ratification.

The UCC, however, was another matter. This convention merely required that any contracting state afford protection to works published in other contracting states equal to that provided to those published in its own territory. Since U.S. copyright law required registration and publication of the copyright notice, any state not having such requirements would not be afforded protection in the United States. Most countries had no such requirement, since neither Berne nor the UCC required it.

When the United States finally joined Berne, it was largely as a result of pressure from domestic producers of television programs, films, records, audiotapes, books, and so on, faced with huge losses due to international piracy of their intellectual property. The economic disincentive they had tried to forestall by avoiding the Berne Convention finally worked to their disadvantage, mainly due to the development of inexpensive recording and dubbing equipment (the audio- and videocassette recorders) that allowed wholesale pirating of such products. Only then was ratification a serious possibility. The system for protection of intellectual property, part of the larger international communications system, was thus compromised by U.S. economic interests until those interests were themselves threatened by changes in technology. Even then, however, U.S. ratification did not extend "moral rights" protection to authors.

WIPO and Intellectual Property Protection

WIPO administers several intellectual property treaties, including the Berne Convention, the International Convention for the Protection of Performers, Producers of Phonograms and Broadcasting Organizations (Rome Convention, 1961), the Convention for the Protection of Producers of Phonograms Against Unauthorized Duplication of Their Phonograms (Geneva Phonogram Convention, 1971), and the Convention Relating to the Distribution of Programme-Carrying Signals Transmitted by Satellite (Brussels Satellite Convention, 1974) (see Ploman, 1982, p. 299). Each of these treaties extended protection to a new form of intellectual property, with even the Berne Convention (Article 11bis) protecting "a comprehensive right [of public performance] applicable to traditional broadcasting, wire diffusion, retransmission, rebroadcasting and public communication of broadcasts" (prepared statement of Donald C. Curran; see United States Congress, 1987, pp. 69–70). There are still serious questions, however, about how adequate the protection is, particularly of broadcast and satellite signals, given the necessity of achieving even minimal enforcement through application to the World Court (see Hondius, 1984; and Ospina, 1986).

The necessity for WIPO to administer an increasing number of treaties is itself an indication of the existence of an international communications system. As new technologies have extended the access to such property to greater portions of the world's population, and as the nature of the property itself has extended into newer forms of reproduction, new agreements have had to be signed and enforced.

DBS Transmissions as Intellectual Property

One major issue in direct broadcast satellite (DBS) communication, insofar as copyright is concerned, is the calculation of the audience size for purposes of determining the licensing fee for programs. Satellite broadcasters have argued that they should only be accountable for the audience they intend to reach, since they derive no benefit from other people who watch. Copyright holders have claimed that the entire audience of any satellite's "footprint" should be used, even if across an international border, since the broadcasts thus diminish the value of their property in the neighboring country (see Glenn, 1987, p. 144).

Again, DBS has demonstrated the inappropriateness of considering only one or another aspect of international communication. The technology creates problems for the trade relations, and the protection of intellectual property, among different politically sovereign countries. If copyright holders are compensated for what may be called spillover audiences, this will, in turn, create demands for compensation from those who worked on the original production: actors, musicians, scriptwriters and so on. Failure to compensate for such audiences, however, may result in lower revenues for a given product, and a disincentive to further production or sale to companies that are "guilty" of the spillover. Yet they cannot technically avoid the spillover.

Cultural Imperialism and Hegemony

A related but broader issue than intellectual property is the problem of domination of one country's culture by another. This issue is often framed in terms of cultural sovereignty, that is, the right of a country to determine its own cultural destiny.[16] More recently, scholars have begun to use the term *hegemony*. Cultural sovereignty is discussed in ways that echo concerns about political sovereignty. Power (1985, p. 178) made this link when he wrote, "Like political sovereignty, cultural sovereignty involves the right and the capacity to develop and protect national culture from outside influences." This linkage, in essence, is the theoretical justification for the cultural imperialism debate.

Countries have raised specific sovereignty issues in various international meetings. Their concerns include the following:

- the control of information entering a country that the national leadership considers damaging to indigenous moral or political systems
- the control of information reported about countries that affect foreign perceptions of their political stability, development commitments, or responses to disaster or disease
- the distortion of a nation's history, culture, or values by mediated content (see Nordenstreng, Manet, & Kleinwächter, 1986, for resolutions passed by various assemblies; see Nordenstreng, 1984, for discussions conducted within the framework of UNESCO)

These concerns extend the more particular issues raised in arguments about cultural imperialism, that is, the domination of a country's media systems by foreign material. In essence, they are concerns raised by those who see the issue of information control as central to the continued existence of sovereign states, particularly to the extent that the legitimacy of states is dependent on the flow (and control) of information. The term *hegemony* has emerged as scholars acknowledged the continuing sovereignty of countries (thus denying the correctness of the term *imperialism)*, but saw the choices of culturally dependent states as circumscribed by the important hegemonic activities of an international culture industry largely centered in the United States.

Conclusion

Communication is sometimes seen as a palliative for the ills of the world. If there were more communication, the argument goes, people would understand one another better. Wars would be less likely. It's not so simple, however. Much of the communication that flows between countries is not aimed at increasing understanding: It is politically or economically motivated; it seeks power and control.

Sometimes people are successful at wresting control from the bureaucratic apparatus. As Innis argued, challenges on the periphery of the "metropolis" are possible. Demands that communication be construed as a "human right," however, must be weighed against legitimate demands for national sovereignty. Too often culture has been equated also with the interests of political and economic elites, particularly with corporate interest in profits, to the detriment of genuine individual, ethnic, tribal, or linguistic expression.

If people expect communication to contribute to the achievement of social justice in the world, then, they will have to confront its all-too-frequent use as a tool of social control. If they expect it to enable artistic expression, they must cope with the vested economic interests of a culture-exporting industry. If they see it as a vehicle for political expression and for the certification of human dignity, they will have to challenge those who use it for their own, often repressive, political ends.

Whatever ends one might wish to promote in international communication requires that the system be seen in its entirety. Its various dimensions, and the variations on those dimensions that have spun off as people have put communications to work for their own ends, can work to the advantage of those who would use it for other ends. The existence of piracy, private distribution networks for audio- and video-cassettes, and clandestine broadcasting, for instance, all suggest as much. The system, although it legitimizes certain activities, is so complex that there are always places where its weaknesses can be exploited, and alternative means of communication developed, for less accepted, although not necessarily less noble, ends.

Notes

1. Sacred and profane places refers to the distinction between identifiable spaces where people are to conduct specific activities. Sacred places, such as churches, synagogues, mosques, or temples, are set apart for the practice of rituals or rites of special significance. Profane places are other nonsacred sites, or locations where "unholy" acts occur. A cemetery, for instance, depending on the culture examined, might be either sacred or profane.

2. See the struggles that ensued over technological development in the 19th century in Marvin (1988, chapter 2); see also Beninger's analysis (1986, pp. 18–21).

3. Thomas L. McPhail calls the dependency relationship that has developed between countries exporting communications hardware,

software, expertise, and protocols to developing countries (mostly former colonies) "electronic colonialism," and says that it is "just as dreaded as mercantile colonialism of the eighteenth and nineteenth centuries" (see McPhail, 1987, p. 18).

4. Hugh Dalziel Duncan (1962, p. 63), arguing from the point of view of John Dewey, says that "we can agree readily enough that society exists in and through communication, and that the social arts of ceremony, festival, and rite, in which the community or an institution within the community presents itself . . . determine society." Communication is thus the central factor in the construction and maintenance of community and society. Control of communication provides a crucial component to efforts to control society.

5. McQuail (1983, p. 225) also argues, however, that media potency is what people fear, or hope for, more than a reality. While communications media are crucial, then, they are not necessarily decisive.

6. Schmitt (1972, pp. 406–408) suggests that there are three spheres of social activity (thus three spheres for the exercise of social control): the state, which exercises authority; the nation, a culturally homogeneous group; and the economy, or market. The boundaries of these three spheres, he says, do not necessarily coincide.

7. The ambiguity of research results testing the impact of propaganda and persuasive techniques is reported in Jowett and O'Donnell (1986, pp. 102–109).

8. Such changes have been expected since Daniel Lerner's seminal work (1958). Other works, such as Rogers (1969), have also suggested that widespread change should be expected.

9. The creation of truly national states, necessary to the full development of nationalism, passed through two stages. The first was the creation of national dynastic states, established, for instance, in England in 1485, Spain by 1556, France by 1589, Russia by 1698, and Prussia by 1713. The revolt of the "rising middle class" against arbitrary and repressive absolute monarchs, in turn, led to revolutions that resulted in "representative and parliamentary government." These revolutions occurred in England between 1645 and 1689, in the new world between 1775 and 1783, and in France from 1789 to 1795. Europe also experienced a series of revolts in 1820, 1830, and 1848, as did Russia in 1905 prior to the Bolshevik revolution of 1917 (see Barnes, 1965, p. 660; see also Rich, 1970, especially chapter 3).

10. Some systems they would hardly apprehend at all except in exceptional circumstances — such as wire services or the wireless telegraph. Public evaluations of such technologies, or their content, were more the province of experts than those with more "hands-on" characteristics — the telephone and the radio. See Marvin (1988, chapter 1) for a discussion of "experts" and the "popular press" in relation to general populations.

11. Many of these terms are used by Robins, Webster, and Pickering (1987, pp. 4, 5) to set the study of propaganda and communication within "broader political theory and political economy of communications."

12. Codding (1959, pp. 70–71) has written that freedom to listen to international radio broadcasts was assumed to be a right prior to World War II, but "codified" only after the war beginning with the Universal Declaration of Human Rights.

13. 6bis refers to Article 6½. *Bis* is the French term used to designate one half.

14. See Ralph Oman's written "Response to Questions from Senator Charles Grassley" (United States Congress, 1988, p. 168).

15. A French high court barred the broadcast of the *Asphalt Jungle* in 1988, protecting John Huston's "artistic moral rights to the film's integrity" (Feliciano, 1988).

16. Cultural destiny should be understood as indicating a concern both for the production of indigenous cultural materials, such as films, recordings, books, and so on, and for what Max Weber called the "web of meanings," or the methods of understanding and responding to everyday life that come from the symbolic systems that make up a culture.

3

TECHNICAL DIMENSIONS OF INTERNATIONAL COMMUNICATION

3.1

Introduction

It is easy to assume that the uses of international communication, and the ways in which it is practiced, are functions of technology. Certainly technological abilities are important to understanding international communication, but it would be unfair to say that they are decisive. The capacity of circuits available, for instance, limits the amount of international traffic (voice, broadcast, data, etc.) any system can carry. Knowing the capacity of circuits, however, would not lead to an understanding of the uses made of them. For instance, although the telephone was patented in 1876 and its use increased rapidly in both North America and Europe, the first transatlantic telephone cable was not laid until 1956. Until that time transatlantic telephony had to share the high-frequency (HF) circuits avail-

able with shortwave radio services, and used much of the same technology employed by international broadcasters. The functions of transatlantic voice traffic, however, were decidedly different from those of international broadcasters.

Likewise, the propagation characteristics of shortwave radio limit its quality, and its bandwidth reduces its fidelity. Wire service traffic carried on HF links to Africa is slower than that carried on telex circuits or in on-line electronic databases. How international broadcasters choose to cope with limited bandwidth, however, cannot be understood merely by knowing its limits, nor can the political and economic factors underlying HF radio use versus telex and data communication for news traffic be understood merely by reference to speed and reliability. Nevertheless, familiarity with the technologies used for international communication is important, since they provide certain capabilities, and carry certain disabilities, that affect the uses made of them.

International communication occurs, of course, among people on an interpersonal level: through the contact of private citizens, informal national representatives, scientists, and artists or performing arts companies. It also occurs through formal national representatives, such as diplomats stationed in foreign countries, the United Nations, or its sponsored agencies. Private citizens working for organizations such as the International Red Cross or Amnesty International, volunteers who travel to disaster sites in other countries (as people from many countries have done in response to earthquakes and volcanic eruptions), and people who flee from disasters (as in the mass exodus from Iraq and the 1991 Bangladesh cyclone and Philippine mudslides) or political upheaval or oppression (as thousands of Haitians did in 1991 and 1992) all engage in international (and intercultural) communication. Increasingly, however, people, governments, and companies have discovered new uses for international communications *technology:* radio and television transmitters, satellites, and both terrestrial and submarine cables. People also encode messages on audio- and videotapes and on film stock, which are shipped through international postal systems and then heard or shown on audio- or videocassette recorders, or on village movie screens and in cinemas.

Many obstacles impede the flow of information channeled through such technical systems. Some of these are embedded in the technology itself; others are erected in efforts to control communication, to gain competitive advantage, or to influence perceptions and opinions.

Important considerations in the application of a particular technology to a specific

communications need include the following:

- *Bandwidth.* This controls the amount of information that can be carried at one time—and thus its speed of delivery;

- *Direction of flow.* This can be one-way or two-way. Broadcasting uses one-way flow, as do some telecommunications applications. Other telecommunications services use two-way flow, on either half-duplex or duplex circuits. (These terms are defined later in this chapter.) Voice communication uses **duplex circuits.** Interactive video uses one-way or duplex video circuits, and duplex voice circuits.

- *Accessibility.* This refers to the ease with which people can make use of the technology. Radio is the most accessible technology worldwide, while both television and telephone services are often unavailable in many parts of the world. More exotic services, such as facsimile, telex, and data communication, require specialized terminals for access. Another aspect of accessibility is the necessity of employing *codes.* Voice communication is the most accessible form of communication, although the languages used for radio and television programs may not be understood by all possible recipients. Increasingly, 5-unit **Baudot code** for teleprinter, and binary codes, such as the 8-unit **Alphabet IA No. 5** for data traffic and the **photoelectric facsimile code,** are used. Binary codes are associated with the future of telecommunications, which will employ *digital* rather than *analog* transmission methods. Digital codes, and wider bandwidths available on satellites and fiber optic cables, will allow for increased **multiplexing** of information and more efficient use of the available communication channels. Negroponte (1991,

p. 78) has even predicted that by 2010 "it will be perverse, if not illegal to use satellites for broadcast television." This is because, as he explains, "broadcast spectrum is scarce, whereas fiber, like computing power, is something we can just keep making more of. Those facts mean that the channels for distributing different types of information . . . will trade places. Most information we receive through the ether today—television, for example—will come through the ground by cable tomorrow. Conversely, most of what we now receive through the ground—such as telephone service—will come through the airwaves."

- *Propagation characteristics.* Several significant influences affect the propagation characteristics of shortwave broadcasting, the dominant means of international radio communication. These include the siting and power of the transmitters, the type of antenna used, including its **gain,** and the condition of the ionosphere.[1] Ionospheric conditions, in turn, are affected by (1) the time of day of the broadcast (day or night), (2) the season of the year, (3) the frequency used for broadcasting, (4) the sunspot cycle, and (5) the amount of natural and man-made interference present.

- *Frequencies.* Shortwave broadcasting frequencies are not assigned to specific broadcasters, and each broadcast service changes its frequencies four times each year as the atmospheric conditions change. Broadcasters often coordinate their frequency use, and must register their frequencies with the International Frequency Registration Board (IFRB), a specialized board of the International Telecommunication Union (ITU), the organization charged with overseeing international communications activity.

- *Satellite communications organizations.* The principal international satellite communications organizations include Intelsat, Intersputnik, Eutelsat, Arabsat, Palapa, and Inmarsat. Commercial satellite ventures include PanAmSat and Luxembourg's Astra, while West Germany and France are jointly developing direct broadcast satellites (DBS) in the TV-Sat and TDF series.

- *The future of international satellites.* This is clouded by the advent of fiber optic cables, which have broadband capability, provide secrecy in communication, and are unaffected by interference. Fiber optic cables, like other forms of wired communication, use **international gateways** through which connections are made between domestic and international networks. This provides national telecommunications administrations with more control over access and revenue, since they can monitor the flow passing through the gateway.

The varieties of technology available for international communication prevent any one of them becoming decisive in determining the type of communication that travels through international channels, or in limiting the uses to which it is put. Nevertheless, technology is always an important consideration in understanding international communication. The nature of international communication, the international regulatory structure that has developed in response to it, and the ideological debates that have erupted as a result of its use, cannot be fully comprehended without basic familiarity with the technologies employed by individuals, companies, and nations to move information in efforts to communicate.

Nations adopt certain conventions to encourage, channel, or control communication. Countries adopt such conventions either on an ad hoc basis to apply to particular methods of communication or more formally by use of treaties and regulations. For instance, several incompatible television transmission systems are used throughout the world. There are a variety of reasons for this, but certainly one major reason is that certain countries, notably Great Britain, Germany, France, and the United States, had long-established colonial or politico-economic relations with other countries. These relationships limited (or channeled) the choice of smaller and less powerful countries, which adopted the system of their respective "benefactor states." Latin American countries usually adopted the "American" National Television System Committee (NTSC) standard, Anglophone African countries (including former German colonies in East Africa) the German-British Phase Alternate Line (PAL) standard, and Francophone African countries the French Sequence Coleur à Memoire (SECAM) system. Although some of the countries in these blocks adopted differing standards, the prevailing (or dominant) standard effectively extended the patent control of organizations that developed these technologies,

and thus increased both their profits and the degree of control they could exercise in the international system by exploiting these patents (see, for instance, Oliveira, 1988, pp. 44–45, on Brazil; Martin, 1988, pp. 187–188, on Kenya; Kitatani, 1988, pp. 175–176, on Japan; Kinner, 1988, p. 225, on Nigeria; and Alisky, 1988, p. 240, on Peru).

The advent of satellite communication required, however, that the incompatible television standards of various countries be rationalized if it were to fulfill its technological promise. Otherwise, multiple satellite systems would be required, one for each standard. (See Table 3.1.) The limited number of orbital slots available for satellites argued against this solution, however. If incompatible television signals were to function in a single worldwide system, international agreement was required. As satellites with transponders (electronic devices that receive, amplify, change the frequency of, and retransmit signals) for each type of television signal developed, an increasing number of signal conversions at points of up-link (ground to satellite) and down-link (satellite to ground) occurred, and eventually a movement to assure that

Table 3.1
Technical Dimensions of World Television Standards[2]

System	Lines of Resolution	Frames per Second*	Bandwidth Required (in MHz)	Audio Carrier	Video Carrier
NTSC	525	30	4.5	FM	AM
PAL	625	25	6.5	FM	AM
SECAM	625	25	6.5	AM	FM

*The frames per second is not truly accurate, since television, unlike film, does not broadcast in frames. The systems employ different scanning techniques that have the effect of providing frames dependent on the field frequency of the electrical systems employed. In the United States that is 60 Hz, and in Europe 50 Hz.

Source: Rainger, Gregory, Harvey, & Jennings, 1985, p. 170.

high-definition television (HDTV) be adopted using a single worldwide standard emerged. By 1992, however, even this movement seemed stalled as the Japanese began domestic satellite HDTV broadcasts using an analog transmission system, while U.S. and European companies continued to develop incompatible transmission schemes. (See Figure 3.1.) The compromise was only partial, however, since multiple satellite systems existed from the time of the Soviet Union's Intersputnik[3] system, and countries were struggling, despite their desire for a single HDTV system, to agree on such a single standard. Since the breakup of the Soviet Union and its formal application to join Intelsat in 1991, the future of Intersputnik is uncertain, however (see Burgess, 1991). Russia continued to operate Intersputnik as a separate system in early 1992, although it had also assumed the Soviet Union's membership in Intelsat. The other independent states formerly part of the Soviet Union

had declared their intention to use Intelsat facilities but not to seek immediate membership.

Another activity requiring international cooperation is terrestrial (land-based) broadcasting. Radio and television signals do not respect international boundaries, but rather flow outward from their transmitter until they attenuate (weaken) sufficiently to be overpowered by other signals on the same or adjacent frequencies (channels). Where many smaller countries exist, such as in Europe, some areas of Africa, Central America, and Southeast Asia, it would be difficult, or impossible, for any nation-state to prevent its transmitter signals from crossing its borders. Even when large countries are involved, such as the United States and Canada, near-border transmitters can penetrate deeply into another country and often cause disputes. Allocating the available frequencies to specified broadcast services is thus imperative if interference-free

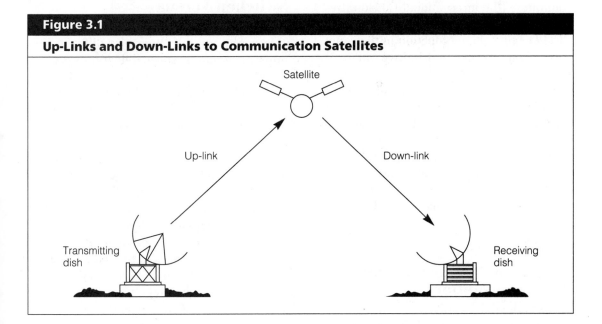

Figure 3.1

Up-Links and Down-Links to Communication Satellites

Satellite

Up-link

Down-link

Transmitting dish

Receiving dish

radio and television signals are to be of much use for communication. This situation means that often countries have to accept the penetration of their borders by outside broadcasts, although that challenges the information control they would otherwise have over their citizens. Countries have responded to their loss of control by employing a number of strategies: They have limited the channels that radios sold within their borders can tune in, adopted incompatible television standards, or demanded that international agreements limiting spillover of signals or condemning certain types of broadcast content be adopted. (These strategies are discussed in later chapters.)

International Telegraphy and Telephony

Although telegraphy and telephony are most easily discussed together, and fall under the auspices of the same ITU technical committee (the International Consultative Committee on Telegraphy and Telephony, or CCITT),[4] they do not function in the same way. Telegraphy uses a primitive binary code; that is, the current carrying the message is either "on" or "off," using long and short bursts of energy in intervals to represent letters. For instance, dot, dot, dot (···) is an "S" in Morse code, while dash, dash, dash (---) is an "O." Telephony, on the other hand, is an analog (or continually responsive) system that, like radio, uses modulated (altered) waves that fluctuate in response to the changing human voice.

Spark Gap Versus Continuous Wave Transmitters

Perhaps the most significant technological change, which made the shift from "wire-less telegraphy" to "wireless telephony" or radio possible, illustrates the difference. Early wireless telegraphy used what were called "spark gap" transmitters, which emitted bursts of energy into the air corresponding to a letter-based code. These transmitters used a spark shot across a small gap in the transmitter, which released the energy of the transmission. Longer and shorter bursts represented the dots and dashes of Morse code. During World War I continuous wave transmitters began to replace spark gap transmitters, and reduced interference between wireless telegraphy users. Early experiments with wireless telephony began. These continuous wave transmitters allowed voice (and eventually musical) fidelity to be achieved. The ability to change the amplitude (or power) of the wave in response to the changing amplitude of the source eliminated the need for energy bursts and thus the sparks (see Aitken, 1985).

Switched Versus Unswitched Systems

Telegraphy and telephony also differ in another important respect. Telegraphy was the first point-to-point electric communications technology. In wired telegraphy one station is connected with another directly, or serially, creating a star pattern around central stations of the telegraph system. (See Figure 3.2.) Telephony uses a more complex switched network system, however, allowing any user to dial up another user directly. (See Figure 3.3.) While telegraph messages can be "switched," or directed, from one station to another, individuals can dial others in telephony, rather than having a telegraph station and operator involved. Early telephony did require such operators, of course, and modern telegraphy, while it still requires human inter-

Figure 3.2

Unswitched Serial and "Star System" Telegraphy

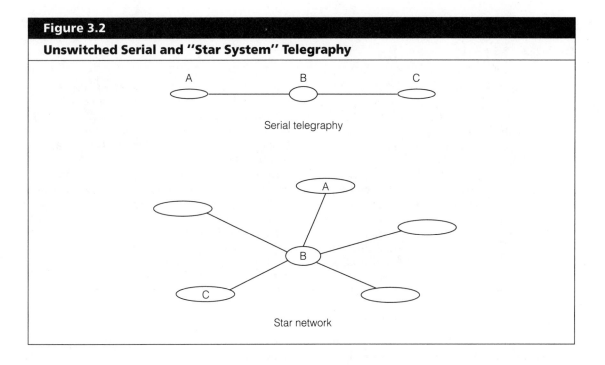

Serial telegraphy

Star network

Figure 3.3

Switched Network "Star" Telephone System

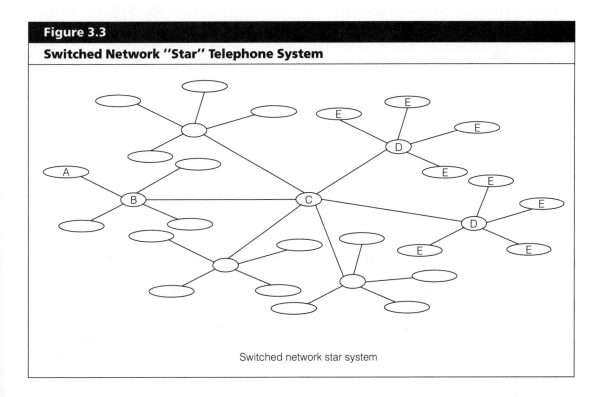

Switched network star system

Public Data Networks

In many countries the telecommunications administrations or private companies have created separate systems for data communication from those normally used for telephone (voice and facsimile) communication. They typically use dedicated data lines and require that users register and pay special fees (for both connection and time use) to allow access to on-line databases, electronic mail, user forums, or other information providers, as well as access to data terminals located within the same organization. In Great Britain, for instance, British Telecomm provides packet-switched data lines that allow high-speed transmission of data, but also access via normal telephone lines at low speeds. While such systems are used in various countries, most access to data information providers in the United States is provided through the normal telephone system, with speed of transfer affected by the type of telephone lines installed. For this reason the CCITT Protocol X25, a packet-switching protocol (or convention for communication) adopted to assure compatibility between systems in different countries has not come into widespread use in the United States.

vention, can provide its messages through the postal system once they have reached the city nearest to their final destination.

Switched networks provide more flexibility than unswitched networks (whether serial or star). As Figure 3.2 shows, people using an unswitched network are limited in the number of others with whom they can easily connect. As Figure 3.3 shows, using a switched network, however, allows the correspondent at point A to connect with another at any point E by using the intermediate switching apparatus at points B, C, and D. It is also easy to connect different switched networks together, since any switching station can serve as a convenient connector to a system centered in another country. While it is not difficult to add another line to an unswitched network, such lines must be connected to one of the limited connection points available on the serial/star system. Not all connection points are designed to handle the increased traffic generated by an entire system, however, so the connections are made into the main trunk line connector points.

In both types of systems (switched and unswitched) the capacity of the lines connecting different nodes is controlled. The main connector lines are trunk lines, capable of handling larger volumes of traffic than the smaller spur lines to outlying areas. In both cases, too, the points of connection from one national system to another would be international gateways, where communication could be *centralized* and *controlled* (for economic and political reasons) before being routed to its final destination.

Connecting these systems requires that countries adopt common technical standards. Not only do common standards allow the entire system to function, but they also prevent one national system from inflicting damage on another. Technical standards for voltage, speed, capacity, impedance, connection equipment, and switching are just some of those that must be negotiated between national administrations or through the ITU. As the complexity of these systems has increased, the number of standards has also had to keep pace. Countries have had to adopt more than 13 separate standards, for instance, to allow interconnection between differing national public data networks so that telephone lines could be used for data communication.[5] (See box, "Public Data Networks.")

Bandwidths

Each of the different uses made of wired systems also require channels of different bandwidths to operate. Simple telegraphy, for instance, can function on a bandwidth of only 2–3 kHz (continuous wave wireless telegraphy uses only 800 Hz), while voice communication requires 5 kHz for reasonable fidelity, AM-quality music 10 kHz, FM-quality music 200 kHz, and video signals between 6,000 and 10,000 kHz. Transatlantic telegraphy now uses voice grade circuits, because it no longer makes sense to dedicate such low-bandwidth circuits to telegraphy alone. Telephone voice grade circuits are being phased out in favor of broadband coaxial and fiber optic cables, which can provide all types of channels equally well. Satellite services can also combine voice grade circuits to provide for broadband needs, such as video signals. There are three principal categories of bandwidths,

each carrying different types of communication services. (See Table 3.2.)

Circuits for Telecommunications Traffic

Telecommunications, unlike broadcasting, depends on the use of *circuits*. These circuits can take various forms: one-way, half-duplex, and full-duplex. As the name implies, one-way circuits are those in which data can travel in only one direction. In half-duplex circuits data can travel in both directions, but only one way at a time. Full-duplex circuits can carry data in both directions at once. Remote monitoring uses one-way circuits, radiotelephony half-duplex circuits, and wired telephony full-duplex circuits. (See box, "Bandwidths.")

Codes for Telecommunications Traffic

Telecommunications traffic also uses several different codes, adopted by international convention to assure that devices in different countries could "talk" to one another. Morse code is an example. Another important code is the Baudot code, used for teleprinter traffic. The Baudot code is a 5-unit binary code now called the International Telegraph Alphabet (ITA) No. 2. Still another, used for data transmission, is an

Table 3.2

Bandwidth Categories and Appropriate Services

Bandwidth Category	Width (in Hz)	Services
Narrowband	0–300	Teletype and low-speed data
Voiceband	300–3,300	Voice and data
Broadband	over 3,300	High-speed data, facsimile, and video

Source: Blyth and Blyth, 1985, p. 107.

Bandwidths

International conventions establish bandwidths to accommodate the needs of particular services. As a general rule, the more complex the information to be carried, the wider the bandwidth assigned. Also part of the consideration is the degree of fidelity or comprehension necessary for the system to be useful, the nature of the signal to be carried (amplitude versus frequency modulation, or analog versus digital), and the speed of information transfer necessary (this last issue applies only to bandwidths in wired systems, since all electromagnetic waves travel at the speed of light). Each bandwidth is measured in hertz (or cycles per second). Each service requires different bandwidths to accommodate its signal, based on the above considerations. Any radio wave, if divided in half horizontally, has two sides that duplicate one another: The sides are redundant. (See Figure 3.4.) This means that a complete signal can be received by tuning in to only one side of the wave. Broadcasting using such a system is called "single-sideband" transmission and is to be implemented in international shortwave services after 1992 in an effort to increase the available frequencies in this congested service.

There are two important parameters of a radio wave, its frequency and its amplitude. The frequency, or the number of times per second that the wave passes a given point, indicates where on a radio or television the signal will be found. The amplitude, or height of the wave, determines the strength of the signal arriving at the receiver. The amplitude attenuates (or weakens) with distance; the frequency remains constant. The wave portion below the center line mirrors the portion above. Any receiver, then, that detects the frequency and amplitude of the wave from either the upper or lower portion will have all the information necessary to reproduce the original content.

8-unit binary code, Alphabet IA No. 5, formerly called the ISO code (for International Standards Organization), consisting of 7 information bits and 1 parity bit (even or odd). Facsimile transmission also uses a binary code. Its photoelectric scans are translated into electrical signals with only two conditions: black and white. The scanning is done line by line, which allows the receiving printer—also scanning line by line—to reproduce the original material based on whether the code shows a "black" or a "white" state (Wiesner, 1984, p. 48). All these codes are similar in the sense that they are binary, depending on registering an "on" or "off" state. They differ in the length of data strings used (3-signal strings for Morse, 5 for Baudot, and 8 for ISO), and thus in the speed and complexity of the data they can represent efficiently.

3.3

International Broadcasting

Besides the problem of standards development and adoption, other technical dimensions also affect the practice of international broadcasting. One of the most significant activities subject to technical difficulties is shortwave or high-frequency (HF) broadcasting.[6] (See Table 3.3.)

Many nations use shortwave broadcasting to communicate directly to populations in other countries. (It is still used in many parts of Africa and in Brazil for significant domestic services as well.) Such broadcasting, if it is not jammed, can provide information that might otherwise be censored by governments. Shortwave, however, has several peculiar propagation characteristics that broadcasters must take into account if they are to use it effectively.

Shortwave broadcasting is similar to AM radio broadcasting in the United States. For instance, it uses amplitude modulation (hence, AM) rather than frequency modulation (FM) to alter the carrier wave to carry information. Like AM radio, then, it is subject to atmospheric noise (such as lightning) that can make it difficult to listen to. (See box, "Modulation.")

Shortwave broadcasting uses sky waves as the means to reach its audience.[7] These waves are emitted upward from the transmitter, and bounce back to earth off the ionosphere, then back toward the sky, and then back toward the earth again. These bounces are called "hops," so an audience receiving the signal following its first bounce receives it on the first hop. Shortwave signals, however, travel much farther than domestic AM signals, so an audience

can be thousands of miles away. If this audience is within the signal path of one of the hops, and the signal is of sufficient strength to be picked up on radios, the audience can tune in a service emitted more than halfway around the globe.

Interference

Because shortwave signals travel so far, interference can be a major problem. This interference comes from four primary sources: (1) duplicative or adjacent channel broadcasting, (2) atmospheric noise, (3) inadvertent man-made interference, or (4) intentional man-made interference.

Duplicative or Adjacent Channel Interference

As with AM radio, signals of other broadcasters using the same frequency, or an adjacent one, can interfere with broadcasts. This is why many AM stations in the United States have to go off the air at dusk, or else lower their power to reduce the potential for interference. Shortwave broadcasters do

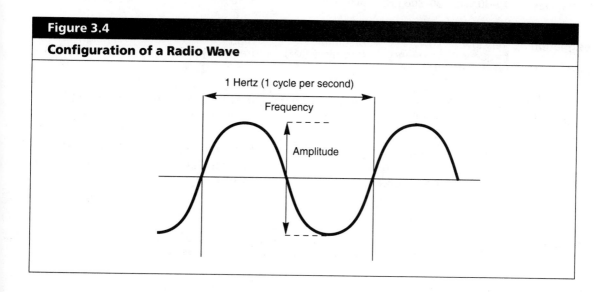

Figure 3.4

Configuration of a Radio Wave

1 Hertz (1 cycle per second)

Frequency

Amplitude

Modulation

Modulation refers to the practice of changing a characteristic (frequency or its amplitude) of a radio wave to have it match a characteristic of the sound or video source. If the amplitude (strength or height and depth) of a wave is changed, its frequency remains constant. If the frequency is altered, the amplitude remains constant. FM radio waves are subject to less interference because their bandwidth is 20 times greater than AM channels, and the constant frequency employed creates an "envelop" around the information that shields it from external interference. AM waves, by contrast, because their amplitude changes, create no "envelop," and this allows interference to "piggy-back" on the wave and be detected by receivers, resulting in crackling or booming noises.

Table 3.3

ITU Bands for the Electromagnetic Spectrum

Band Number	4	5	6	7	8
Frequencies*	10–30 kHz	30–300 kHz	300–3,000 kHz	3–30 MHz	30–300 MHz
Designation	Very low frequency (VLF)	Low frequency (LF)	Medium frequency (MF)	High frequency (HF)	Very high frequency (VHF)
Some Designated Uses	Long-distance point-to-point	Medium-distance point-to-point, Radio navigation, Aeronautical mobile, LF broad-casting	AM broadcasting, Short-range communication, International distress	International radio broadcasting, Air-ground, Ship-to-shore, International point-to-point	Line-of-sight communication, VHF–TV broadcasting, FM broadcasting, Aeronautical distress

*kHz = 1,000 cycles per second; MHz = 1 million cycles per second; GHz = 1 billion cycles per second not "power down" or go dark at dusk, however, as this is prime time. Also, since the signals travel so far, dusk at the transmitter site may be dawn at the target area (if the signals are traveling an East-West route), so the strategy applicable in the domestic case would not work for international shortwave.

Shortwave broadcasters have responded to this unintentional interference problem in several ways. Broadcasting services may coordinate their use of frequencies (that is, agree which service will use which frequencies) as a way of reducing the potential for interference. Western broadcasters such as VOA, the BBC, Germany's Deutsche Welle, RFE/RL, Radio Netherlands, and Radio Canada, for instance, do coordinate frequency use. Related to this is the work of the International Frequency Registration

Board (IFRB), which registers "demands" (i.e., registered frequencies) of broadcasters. This allows a broadcaster to learn what frequencies other services are using to reach a target, from what transmitter sites, and at what times of day. This provides information that can be used to attempt to minimize the potential for interference from other broadcasters. (See box, "The IFRB.")

Broadcasters have also installed more powerful transmitters. In an area where interference is common, the strongest signal is the one that will be heard. Putting a more powerful signal into a target area, then, can "drown out" the interference caused by other signals on a frequency, or its adjacent one. Shortwave broadcasters use much more power than U.S. domestic AM stations

9	10	11
300–3,000 MHz	3–30 GHz	30–300 GHz
Ultra high frequency (UHF)	Super high frequency (SHF)	Extremely high frequency (EHF)
UHF-TV broadcasting Space communication Radar Citizen's band radio	Microwave communication Space communication	Microwave communication Space communication Radar Radio astronomy

The IFRB

The IFRB is a specialized board functioning under the auspices of the ITU, which, in turn, is an agency of the United Nations. The IFRB has no power to demand that broadcasters use the frequencies assigned to them, or that they avoid using frequencies assigned to others. Its registration process, however, is designed to advise broadcasters concerning available frequencies in various parts of the world to make sure the electromagnetic spectrum is used efficiently and that interference is kept at a minimum.

The IFRB relies in great measure on the "good faith" of broadcasters (both state operated or sanctioned, and private) to follow the international agreements that condemn intentional interference with broadcasts, that certify that access to information is a "human right," and that guarantee to those broadcasters using a particular frequency "squatter's rights" — that is, that a "first come, first served" philosophy will prevail in any radio band until such time as its frequencies are assigned by international agreement to different services.

anyway, since their audiences are farther away. Shortwave broadcasters often use a 500-kilowatt (1 kw = 1,000 watts) transmitter, while U.S. domestic AM stations are limited to 50-kw (50,000 watt) transmitters. Shortwave transmitters can also be combined to provide more powerful signals than one transmitter alone, and antennas are designed to provide gain to the signals they emit, which means that a signal may leave its transmitter site with 1 million or more watts of power.

Shortwave broadcasters also negotiate agreements with other countries to set up new transmitter sites closer to their target audiences. Since broadcast waves attenuate (or weaken) the farther they get from their transmitters, the closer a site is to its audience, the higher the signal strength is when it arrives. Many shortwave broadcasters, for instance, have transmitters on islands in the Pacific Ocean to reach into the Asian land mass, or in the Mediterranean to reach into the Middle East and North Africa.

Finally, shortwave broadcasters transmit into a given target area from several sites si-

multaneously, often using several different frequencies. This allows the audience to search for the strongest signal. Broadcasters usually tell their audiences all the frequencies they are using during a program block; audiences can then tune in to the best one. Broadcasters also have signature tunes that allow listeners to recognize the service easily as they search their shortwave dials. (Information on available shortwave frequencies by service, including notes on signature tunes, can be found in the *World Radio-TV Handbook* or *Passport to World Band Radio*, both published annually.)

Atmospheric Noise

The second type of interference is atmospheric noise. Thunderstorms located anywhere in the path of a signal from its transmitter to its destination can interfere with reception. The closer a storm is to the listener, the more interference will exist (and the louder it will be). Lightning uses the electromagnetic spectrum just as do radio waves. A bolt of lightning, unlike radio waves, is not at a particular frequency, but is on all frequencies simultaneously, although most of its power is at lower frequencies. The lower a frequency in use, then, during a lightning storm, the more interference will exist.

Inadvertent Man-Made Noise

The third type of interference is man-made noise. All mechanical equipment generating sparks gives off electromagnetic energy, particularly that using DC current, such as automobile ignitions. Other sorts of equipment, however, such as electric razors, hair dryers, construction saws, and so on, also can cause interference with radio waves unless they are suppressed.[8]

Intentional Man-Made Interference

The fourth type is intentional interference, called "jamming." This is the practice of intentionally putting a signal on the same frequency as an incoming signal, but usually at a higher power, to drown out the incoming broadcast. Many Communist countries practiced jamming after World War II, although the Soviet Union and its allies in Eastern Europe ceased jamming in 1987 and 1988. In mid-1989 the Chinese began jamming incoming signals of both the BBC and VOA during the student protests in Beijing. Cuba jams the signals of Radio Martí broadcasting to Havana from Marathon, Florida.

Condition of the Ionosphere

Of the other phenomena that compound the problem of interference for shortwave broadcasters, the most important is the condition of the ionosphere. The ionosphere is the set of electrically charged layers of air that surround the earth. Their density, and hence the amount of refraction (or bending) they provide to radio waves striking them, depends on the sun.

Time of Day

During the day, for instance, three layers of the ionosphere affect radio wave refraction (or "bounce"), while at night a single layer functions. The amount of refraction, therefore, differs from day to night, since the target zone shifts as the refraction occurs at different altitudes, depending on the layer from which the waves bounce back to earth. The denser the ionosphere is, the higher the frequencies that can be used. At night, therefore, lower frequencies are used than during the day.

Sunspots

Sunspot activity, or the number of solar flares erupting on the sun's surface, also affects atmospheric density. The amount of sunspot activity is cyclical, rising and falling over an 11-year period. The higher the sunspot activity, the hotter the sun and the more dense the ionosphere becomes, thus allowing use of higher frequencies. In years with low sunspot activity, the ionosphere becomes less dense and lower frequencies must be used. The sunspot cycle reached its maximum in 1987, and its minimum in 1989–90; it will reach its maximum again in 1998.

Seasons of the Year

Finally, the seasons also affect the density of the ionosphere. As the year progresses, the tilt of the earth also changes. During the July–September period, when it is summer in the United States, the Northern Hemisphere tilts toward the sun, while during the winter, the Southern Hemisphere tilts toward it. The ionization of the atmosphere is greatest in each hemisphere during its winter months, while the spring and fall months are transitional ones. For shortwave purposes the seasons are unequal: Winter occurs between November and February, spring in March and April, summer between May and August, and fall in September and October. In the Southern Hemisphere, of course, the seasons are reversed.

Because of the distances covered by shortwave radio broadcasts, the waves can travel through both daytime and nighttime, or from summer to winter regions of the globe. The important geographical point, so far as the refraction of the waves is concerned, is the reflection point in the atmosphere where they bounce back toward the earth (Wheatley, n.d., p. 5).

Frequencies and Meter Bands

All the influences on the condition of the ionosphere provide the context for understanding another peculiarity of shortwave broadcasting activity. Unlike all other radio services, shortwave broadcasters do not use assigned frequencies. Any broadcaster can use any frequency in the defined bands (those between 3 and 30 MHz) subject to the interference created by other users.

Assigning specific frequencies in the shortwave bands would be a monstrous undertaking. For shortwave broadcasters to reach their audiences, the assignments would have to change based on the sunspot cycle, the hour of day, the season of the year, and the location of target audiences in relation to given transmitter sites.

Table 3.4

Shortwave Bands in Meters and Kilohertz and by Megahertz Band

Meter Band	Frequencies (in kHz)	Megahertz Band
11	25,600–26,100	26
13	21,450–21,750	21
16	17,700–17,900	17
19	15,100–15,450	15
25	11,700–11,975	11
31	9,500–9,775	9
41	7,100–7,300	7
49	5,950–6,200	6
60*	4,750–5,060	5
75*	3,900–4,000	4
90*	3,200–3,400	3
120*	2,300–2,495	2

*Known as "tropical bands," and reserved for use in designated tropical zones of Africa and Latin America.

Fortunately, the more sensible approach happens to be the one used: Broadcasters coordinate their frequency use whenever possible and register the frequencies used with the IFRB so that others will know the facts when they consider new frequencies.[9]

Rather than using specifically assigned frequencies, international shortwave broadcasters thus use "meter bands" within the electromagnetic spectrum. (The term *meter band* refers to the length of the wave used within the band.) These bands are also called megahertz (MHz) bands (one hertz is one cycle per second of frequency), and can also be referred to by their actual frequencies in kilohertz (kHz).[10] (See Table 3.4.)

As Table 3.4 indicates, the length of a radio wave (measured in meters) has an inverse relationship with its frequency. Thus, the shorter the wavelength, the higher the frequency of the signal. Also, the bands designated do not use all the frequencies between 2,300 kHz and 26,100 kHz. Broadcasters may broadcast using frequencies between the designated bands in what is referred to as "out-of-band transmission."

Relay Stations

Each shortwave broadcaster must decide, based on the available knowledge of other broadcasters' frequencies, where to place transmitter sites (called "relay stations"), and which ones to use at any given time to reach a given target area. VOA, for instance, uses relay stations on Ascension Island, and in Antigua, Belize, Botswana, Brazil, Greece, Honduras, the United Kingdom, Liberia, Morocco, the Philippines, Sri Lanka, Thailand, and Germany, as well as the United States. VOA also periodically considers other new relay sites, both for leasing and for building new facilities.

Every transmission site located outside a country's own territory, however, involves complex initial negotiations and then periodic renegotiation of agreements. Political friction between the host country and the transmitting country can affect broadcasters' plans, since a country can withdraw permission to use its territory. Because developing audiences depends on the ability to deliver a dependable signal, relationships between international broadcasters and their host governments are significant considerations. In this respect the Soviet Union, prior to its breakup, had a decided advantage: It was so large that all of its international service transmitters were located within its own territory. The United States, in contrast, had difficulties with the Greek government during the 1960s that threatened its relay stations at Marathon and Kavala. More recently, Israeli court action, based on environmental considerations, may have ended consideration of a proposed joint RFE/RL and VOA relay site in that country.

Although broadcasting organizations use shortwave to attempt to reach mass audiences, the distance from their transmitters to targets, and the need to calculate propagation patterns to these targets, suggests that such efforts share much with point-to-point communication. The broadcast antennas are "aimed," much like artillery, with portions of the antennas "excited" to direct signals in a particular direction. Newer antennas allow segments of the antenna to be excited in phase to allow for more precise aiming of signals. In all cases the antennas emit signals on all four sides, with the "front lobe" being the most prominent, and the "back lobe" and "side lobes" less so. People tuning in within the footprint of any of these lobes would be able to detect the signal. (See Figure 3.5.)

International broadcasters site their relay stations, too, to get as close as possible to target areas. The ideal situation is that signals would reach their target on the first hop (after one atmospheric bounce). Because of site limitations, however (as mentioned earlier), many signals reach their targets on the second or third hop. This means that signals often arrive weaker than desired, resulting in smaller audiences. The success of the broadcast is thus reduced by the inability to deliver high-quality, fade-free signals.

Multiple Language Services

Another complication is that broadcasters must transmit programs in multiple languages, sometimes even simultaneously, into adjacent target areas. Program relay sites therefore usually have multiple transmitters and antenna arrays. Broadcasters have also begun to use steerable antennas, which can be adjusted mechanically or electronically to aim signals at particular targets. The necessity of having multiple simultaneous transmissions, however, means that relay sites must be large, that great quantities of dependable electric power must be available, and that multiple **studio-to-transmitter links** (STLs) must be operational to assure that programs are delivered to audiences.

Availability of Shortwave Radios

One additional consideration further complicates the technical task of international broadcasters. Broadcasters are understandably concerned about their ability to reach a target area with a signal of sufficient quality to attract an audience. However, they must also consider the audience's ability to

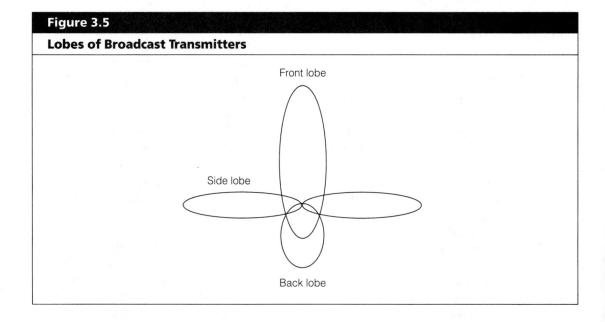

Figure 3.5

Lobes of Broadcast Transmitters

Front lobe

Side lobe

Back lobe

detect (or tune in) that signal. People obviously must have shortwave-capable radios to tune in, but all shortwave bands are not equally represented on shortwave radios. Research suggests that the 16- to 49-meter bands are the most prevalent, as a percentage of all shortwave-capable radios, throughout the world (Skoczylas, 1984, p. 34). Therefore, these bands are the most attractive to international broadcasters who seek the largest potential audience for their programs. This further complicates the interference problem caused by congestion on the shortwave bands. (See Figure 3.6.)

In 1979 the ITU-sponsored World Administrative Radio Conference (WARC) on high-frequency broadcasting expanded some of the bands to include new frequencies. These new frequencies are to become available in the early 1990s, and will result in several alterations. (See Table 3.5).

International broadcasters using shortwave frequencies, as mentioned before, register their intentions with the IFRB. The IFRB compiles these "demands" into a master registration list that broadcasters can use to locate frequencies potentially less subject to interference than others. The

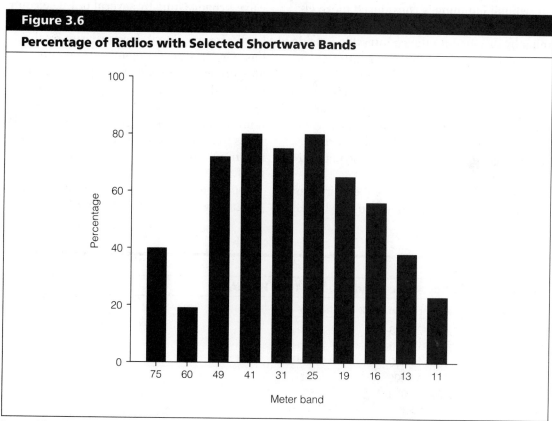

Figure 3.6

Percentage of Radios with Selected Shortwave Bands

Source: Skoczylas, 1984, p. 34; and BBC International Broadcasting and Audience Research, various in-country field surveys.

IFRB registration list considers a demand to be one frequency from one site into one target at a given time.

Jamming

Finally, some countries deliberately jam incoming radio signals, using one of two approaches. One is to set up horizontal or ground jamming transmitters that blanket a particular area with noise or other signals at higher power on the same frequency as incoming signals. The other is to use sky-wave jamming, which also uses a higher power signal aimed up to intercept incoming signals refracted by the ionosphere. Horizontal jamming is considered more effective, although people can escape the jamming by driving into the countryside outside the range of the jamming transmitters. Many Soviet and Eastern European listeners developed effective countermeasures during the period when Western broadcasts into their countries were consistently jammed, and RFE/RL published information designed to help people construct anti-jamming radio devices.

The crumbling of the Soviet "empire" in Eastern and Central Europe had two benefi-

cial results for shortwave broadcasting. First, as already mentioned, these countries stopped jamming incoming signals from the West. Several of them even invited Western services to set up news bureaus in their capitals. Following the failed Soviet coup, Boris Yeltsin, president of the Russian Republic, invited the BBC to begin broadcasting its Russian Service programs on Russian radio (Ljunggren, 1991). This followed decisions by Bulgaria, Hungary, Poland, and Czechoslovakia to allow Western programs, including both radio and television, to be broadcast locally (Konstantinova, 1991). Second, the end of the Cold War resulted in a reduction in the hours devoted to shortwave broadcasting by several of these countries, including Radio Moscow, and Radio Berlin International, formerly run by the East German government, ceased operation altogether. This freed up frequency spectrum and reduced unplanned interference, as well as decreasing the need for so many multiple signals and higher power transmissions to reach into these countries. This meant potentially lower operating costs in the future.

One consequence of the creation of the Commonwealth of Independent States

Table 3.5

Alterations to Shortwave Bands by the 1979 HF-WARC

Meter Band	Frequencies (in kHz)	Change
13	21,450–21,850	+ 100 kHz
16	17,550–17,900	+ 150 kHz
19	15,100–15,600	+ 150 kHz
22	13,600–13,800	+ 200 kHz
25	11,650–12,050	+ 125 kHz
31	9,500–9,900	+ 125 kHz
11*	25,670–26,100	− 70 kHz

*The 11-meter band is used principally by amateur radio operators.

(comprising most of what was the Soviet Union) was confusion within Radio Moscow itself. Many of its transmitting stations are actually in other republics, such as Ukraine and the central Asian republics, and Radio Moscow thus lost its guaranteed access. While Russia controlled the production of programs, it had to negotiate for the use of some transmitters and antennas.

3.4

Satellite Transmission Technology

Using satellites for communication depends not only on the ability of a transmitter 35,000 km (or 22,300 miles) in space to reach receivers on the ground, but on a number of other ingredients as well. First is the need to put a satellite into orbit and know its position thereafter, dependent on launch systems and telemetry technology. Second is the propulsion system of the satellite, needed to cope with what are called **"perturbations"** in its orbit. Even so-called geosynchronous orbit satellites are deflected off orbit and must use propulsion systems to steer them back to their proper positions. Eventually, their on-board fuel is spent, and they become uncontrollable and drift out of their proper orbit (see Rainger et al., 1985, p. 33). Third is the electrical system of the satellite, fueled either by nuclear power plants (in Soviet satellites) or by solar radiation (in U.S. satellites). The electrical system provides the power for the transponders and affects the radiated power that will reach receivers on the ground. Fourth is the transmitter technology itself, which uses transponders to receive, amplify, and retransmit signals, and to change their frequencies from the up-link (earth-to-satellite) to the down-link (satellite-to-earth) segment of the signal path. Fifth is the reception technology, with its associated antenna (or dish), which detects, collects, amplifies, and changes the frequency of the down-linked signal so that the information contained in the signal can be put to use.

Since satellites use radio waves that **attenuate** just as terrestrial signals do, the gain provided to the signal by both transmitting and receiving antennas is crucial to their success.[11] Early satellites were small and put out low levels of radiated power because the equipment was bulky and heavy, and launch vehicles were limited in the total amount of weight they could put into orbit. Later generations of satellites became lighter and more compact. This allowed them to be engineered to provide higher power output (both from the on-board electronics and from larger and more efficient solar panels that could be collapsed during orbit and extended in space). Early satellite dishes were larger (30 meters in diameter) because they had to collect weaker signals, and thus each one cost millions of dollars. As the power of satellites has increased, the size of earth stations has decreased, making them more affordable for poorer countries (see Hudson, 1990, p. 151).

The popularity of satellites for such applications as weather forecasting, storm tracking, precise terrestrial mapping, navigational positioning for ships and airplanes, military applications (including communication, navigation, and surveillance), and business (including linkage of distant sites for instantaneous transmission of financial quotations, interactive videoconferencing, and data linkage and control within transnational corporations) has resulted in a struggle for frequency spectrum and in efforts to exploit ever higher frequencies. This struggle mirrors earlier — and continuing —

struggles over terrestrial frequencies. The movement toward digital broadcasting applications, and away from analog techniques, has complicated this dispute, since digitally encoded information often requires wider bandwidths. This, in turn, has led to efforts to compress signals to save bandwidth, and to greater demand for international fiber optic cables, since these use not broadcast frequencies but light pulses to carry signals down glass "pipes" (see, for instance, "Broadcasters, Military at Odds," 1991; "Satellite Digital TV Coming into Focus," 1991; and "Short Future for Shortwave?" 1991).

Digital Transmission Technology

Broadcasting and telecommunications can occur using either analog or digital transmission schemes. Analog transmission carries a continuous signal composed of frequencies that mirror those of the source. Digital systems use **frequency sampling** to encode a source into discrete bits of information that can be decoded at a receiver to reconstitute the original set of frequencies and thus duplicate the sound.

Any sound can be encoded into digital form: telegraph signals, voice, music, or visual images. Western European countries began to experiment with digital television transmission using satellites in the mid-1980s. The signals use time division multiplexed bursts, called **packet switching.** The European Broadcasting Union adopted two principal packet systems for satellite television broadcasting. These were the C-MAC/Packet and D2-MAC/Packet systems using frequency modulation. The C-MAC/Packet system was developed for the 625-line television standard using a 27-

MHz-wide bandwidth satellite channel. The multiplexed carrier can carry a video channel, up to eight 15-kHz-wide audio channels, and data transmissions simultaneously, with the video picture time compressed and its three color elements carried in bursts in time sequence. The carrier also delivers its audio and data components in time sequence bursts (European Broadcasting Union Technical Centre, 1985a, 1985b).

For cable distribution the EBU also developed two packet-switching systems, the D-MAC and the D2-MAC (the same as for satellite distribution). These three systems (C-MAC, D-MAC, and D2-MAC) were designed to avoid the problems created by the multiple television standards used in Europe (PAL and SECAM). The EBU hoped that selecting standards before the services actually began would simplify pan-European television broadcasting.

The technical implications of these systems can best be understood by way of comparison. The 27-MHz bandwidth of the satellite packet systems, for instance, compares to the 4.5-MHz bandwidth of the standard NTSC television channel in the United States. So the satellite bandwidth is six times that of current U.S. television channels (and over three times that of HDTV channels).

Second, the stereo radio and television signals now used in the United States, which have more than one modulated signal carried within the same channel, use what is called frequency division multiplexing. The term *multiplex* simply means that multiple separate (or discrete) signals are carried within a specified channel, while *frequency division* means that the channel's total available bandwidth is divided into narrower bands, each of which carries a signal. A stereo signal using a 200-kHz channel, for instance, is divided into two 100-kHz portions, one of which carries the signal for the right-side speaker, and the other for the left-side speaker. Stereo receivers have dual tuners that can receive the separate signals within the same channel.

In time division multiplexing a similar division of the total signal occurs, but instead of the right and left sides being on different frequencies within the channel, their content arrives sequentially at the receiver in bursts, right side, then left side, then right side, and so on. The processing of these signals happens so quickly that there is room to include other packets of information as well, all of which is then sorted by the receiver and delivered to the appropriate device: a television set, a radio, a computer. In television the same process occurs, with the three separate color signals (red, green, and blue) delivered in rapid sequence. The information stream can also carry in packet bursts several different audio signals, allowing a single television picture to have multiple audio tracks for delivery of different languages.

3.6

Fiber Optic Technology

Fiber optics is a technology that picks up where coaxial cable leaves off. Instead of using copper wires to move signals from one point to another, fiber optics cables consist of strands of hair-thin "light pipes," or hollow tubes. Light pulses are used to carry the signals, and these signals can be time division multiplexed, carrying information in sequential bursts that are combined and then separated to reach different destinations. The actual upper limits of this technology, in terms of bits per second of information, is not known. Integrated services digital networks (ISDNs), for instance, are available that are capable of carrying

1.5–2 million bits per second of data, compared with the 19,200 bits per second that can be carried using a modem (modulator-demodulator) that converts digital signals (such as those used by computers) into modulated sound signals that can be carried by ordinary telephone lines. Synchronous optical networks (SONETs) have also been developed that have "transmission speeds ranging from 51 million to 2 billion bits per second. The SONET system allows data streams of varying transmission speeds to be combined or extracted without first having to break down each stream into its individual components. This system carries all information in digitized form, including voice, data, and video streams carried in packets (Cerf, 1991, pp. 47, 48).

3.7

Conclusion

The technologies used for the international system are only one part of it. Their development and use as part of the system, however, have contributed to its complexity and often made it controversial. Countries have found it necessary to participate in the system, and that has meant discovering means to integrate their domestic infrastructures with this international one. Since the major industrial powers have largely controlled decisions about technical standards, and are home to the corporations that dominate the manufacture of technological components for the system, many countries, particularly poorer ones, have had to participate suffering severe disadvantages. The system did not develop to serve their interests; its technical components were not designed to meet their needs.

Integration, then, has often been a double-edged sword. Sometimes it led to the means to establish alternative access to information. Sometimes it provided extended access via domestic systems to external sources of information and entertainment, but also exacerbated domestic inequalities (heightening the distinctions between the information rich and information poor), or provided the basis for those excluded from participation in the domestic communications system to gain access to the external system, and thus threaten the "monopoly of knowledge" vested in centrally controlled infrastructures.

Integration, exacerbation of inequality, and alternative access have all created domestic conflicts, and served as a catalyst for international disagreements over technology, regulation, culture, politics, and economics. Efforts to integrate, for instance, have led to disputes over technical standards, or to concerns about colonialism (or hegemony). Developing countries have been concerned since the beginnings of Intelsat with what they felt forced to accept as the price for participation. Manufacturers produce telecommunications technology to meet the needs of their major buyers. They use economies of scale in production to remain competitive. Developing countries, however, have objected to the fact that these manufacturers have not met their needs, or that they have been forced to purchase various equipment whose capacity exceeded their needs.

Domestic inequalities in access to information have also been exacerbated by integration. In many countries access to basic telecommunications services is restricted largely to urban areas due to a country's inability to afford the capital expenditure necessary to extend the systems more generally, or of its people individually to do so. Without such extensions, however, the increased access that urban areas gained with international integration merely increased the gap between urban and rural

areas. Some technologies, however, provided the basis for creating alternative, or parallel, networks by those disenfranchised by the centralized communications infrastructure. People have used audio- and videocassette and recorders and satellite dishes to bypass domestic systems, to gain access to entertainment materials from abroad, or to record their own material for distribution.

Disputes over technology often have contributed to conflicts in other issues, too, such as propaganda, human rights, or cultural sovereignty. Many of these disputes have erupted after the introduction of new technologies have created new conditions for communication to occur. The dispute over cultural sovereignty, for instance, was one that erupted when the colonial empires of the European states broke up, and when newly independent countries saw that their "freedom" to determine their own destinies was compromised by dependence on these same powers for news and entertainment. Complaints by African and Asian nations found sympathetic ears in Latin America, where countries saw their own dependency on the United States in a similar light, despite the fact that many of them had been politically independent for a century or more.

Understanding the technologies of international communication, then, contributes to increased discernment concerning some of these other issues, which can often be seen merely in ideological terms and thus are often more easily dismissed. They should not be dismissed, however, as they are indicative of the severe inequalities that exist in the communications system, and the difficulties that dominant economic and political paradigms cause for attempts to use the system as a means to encourage international cooperation, peace, and solutions to humankind's other serious problems.

Notes

1. "Gain" refers to the amount of increase in the signal strength added by components of broadcast transmitters or receivers. Whip or telescoping antennas, for instance, which gather a signal along their entire length, effectively combine what they gather into a single input that enters the receiver. The weak signal thus gains strength according to the efficiency of the antenna. The "ionosphere" consists of layers of electrically charged particles that surround the earth. These particles refract (or bend) radio waves at particular frequencies depending on their density (or how close together the particles are in a particular area).

2. The actual situation is even more complicated, since many countries have adopted variations on the three basic standards. CCIR Report 624-3, presented at the XVIth Plenary Assembly in Dubrovnik, Yugoslavia, in 1986, listed nine different color television standards then in use around the world (see "World Television," 1991, p. 353).

3. *Sputnik* is Russian for satellite. Intersputnik is thus an international satellite system.

4. The acronym CCITT is based on the French version, Comité Consultatif International Télégraphique et Téléphonique, not the English version. Both languages, among others, are official languages of the ITU.

5. CCITT recommendations (the basis for standards adoption) that apply to packet-switched data networks include: V3 — International Alphabet No. 5; V24 — lists of definitions for interchange circuits between data terminal equipment (DTE) and data circuit-terminating equipment (DCE); V25 — automatic calling and/or answering equipment on the general switched telephone network; V28 — electrical characteristics for unbalanced double current interchange circuits; V41 — code independent error control system; X3 — definition of packet assembler/disassembler (PAD) facility in a public data network (PDN); X20 — DTE–DCE interface for asynchronous transmission on PDNs; X21 — general purpose interface between DTE and DCE for synchronous operation of PDNs; X21bis — use on PDNs and DTEs, which are designed for interface to synchronous V series modems; X25 — DTE-DCE interface on PDN for packet mode operation; X28 — character terminal–PAD interface on a packet-switched PDN; X29 — procedures for exchange of control information and user data between packet mode terminal and PAD; and X121 — international addressing scheme for PDNs (see British Telecomm, n.d., p. 60).

6. HF refers to the nomenclature applied to waves of a particular length on the electromagnetic spectrum. Shortwave is the popular term applied to broadcasting using these waves, although engineers say that the proper way of using this word is "short-wave." This book generally will use the term *shortwave*, since it is concerned with the broadcasting service, and not the waves themselves. In the early part of this century, engineers thought that wavelengths shorter than those already discovered would attenuate, or weaken, so quickly as to be unusable for broadcast purposes. So they called these "last usable waves" short-waves.

7. Domestic AM broadcasting actually uses all three types of signal transmission: sky waves, direct waves, and ground waves. It is the sky waves that radios pick up from long distances at night, but that are not detected during daylight hours.

8. Suppression means that the ignition (or spark) systems of such devices are shielded so that the electromagnetic energy they emit is contained within the equipment itself, rather than being dispersed through the atmosphere.

9. European countries initiated the practice of coordination on the medium wave radio band following the 1927 Washington conference in which this band was divided into channels. The limited number of channels, and the large number of existing and planned European radio stations, required these countries to co-ordinate their activities (see Vyvyan, 1974, p. 206).

10. A kilohertz is equal to 1,000 cycles per second; a megahertz is equal to 1 million cycles per second. The wave of a broadcast signal operating at 6 MHz (or 6,000 kHz) is 50 meters long (about 162.5 feet), while one at 21 MHz (or 21,000 kHz) is nearly 14.3 meters long (or nearly 46.5 feet). A gigahertz, used for satellite communications, is equal to 1 billion cycles per second.

11. Satellites use higher frequencies so their attenuation is not precisely like that of terrestrial signals. Many factors affect the attenuation, including the elevation angle of the satellite and water in the atmosphere, particularly rain for frequencies at 12 GHz and higher (see Rainger et al., 1985, pp. 93–95).

4

THE BIRTH OF MODERN INTERNATIONAL COMMUNICATION: 1835–1913

Introduction

Many people eventually saw the development of the global metropolis either as an opportunity to exploit for economic or political gain, or as a threat to basic human rights or national cultural identity. The early years of the developing metropolis, however, did not evoke the same sense either of possibility or of danger. This was true for at least two reasons.

First, international communication initially was a problem to be solved. The earliest form of electric communication, the telegraph, required a good deal of international cooperation if transborder systems were to develop. Wires had to be connected, tariffs (toll charges) collected and distributed across national borders, operators speaking different languages trained to handle a common message coding system so that information would not be garbled in transmission, priorities established for han-

dling different classes of messages (railroad, governmental, business, and private), protocols adopted concerning confidentiality and use of **encryption,** and routes and technical standards determined. Solving these problems consumed much time and energy in the earliest period of international communication conducted over wires.

Second, these problems were addressed primarily in the European context. Most of the countries in existence in the late 20th century were either colonies or technologically unsophisticated and politically unorganized areas in the middle third of the 19th century. And the countries of North America (the United States and Canada) were large, with populations still settling in the West and immigrants usually learning a new common language, English.[1] Their wired communication could extend for thousands of miles without crossing a border. Cut-throat competition among various private companies assured rapid growth, limited (although sometimes crucial) government involvement, and creation of de facto single systems as companies established monopolies in these two countries. The result was that the United States and Canada (with only the former being fully politically independent in the early years) had little interest in the complexities of transborder European communication.

Imperial governments largely controlled the development of wired communication outside Europe and the Americas. Their interests were in centralizing control by assuring rapid communication with military, trade, and administrative outposts, and between themselves and their respective "mother" countries (see Betts, 1968; Peel, 1905). As Headrick (1981, pp. 163, 164) put it, "Cables were an essential part of the new imperialism. . . . [They] served to tie the European empires together," acting as lifelines of business communication in peacetime, tools of diplomacy during confrontations with other European powers in outlying regions, and "security itself" in times of war. They gave little or no thought to facilitating communication among the native populations of their territories.

To begin, it is appropriate to investigate how these networks formed, and how they related to one another. This examination encompasses not only their technologies, but also the visions of the people who considered investments in unknown networks, and the economic and political problems that infected them. Nations took advantage of the developing networks, or invested in creating them, to gain political and economic advantage. They used them as weapons of war and economic exploitation.

This brief explanation may be too Eurocentric. As Headrick (1981, pp. 4–7) points out, there are a variety of alternative expla-

nations for the imperialist impulse, some of which ignore the role of technology in opposition to those that make it central. There were, of course, a tangled set of motivations for technological change, and for its application to expansion of imperial power, both political and economic. "Whatever the motives of the imperialists . . . the territories they added to the Western empires were soon incorporated into the world economy" (Headrick, 1988, p. 6).

It is not just the motives of governments, either, that are at issue here. A variety of newly created corporate enterprises, bent on exploiting new technologies for profit, and often seeking monopoly control of these technologies on a global scale, also had what may be called imperial designs. They recognized the necessity of political stability, and of the projection of military power, to their own economic designs. They colluded with governments, received subsidies from governments, sought governmental intervention on their behalf with foreign powers, and even intimidated governments into providing for their own defined needs. The tangled tentacles of commerce that stretched outward until they confronted those extending from other countries, and with which they battled for control of international communication, were crucial in the creation of the international system.

The use and abuse of these early systems created a history that informed later commitments. Nations decided to build alternative systems, or to respond to communication abuse in kind, or to demand international treaties and regulations, based on what they saw occurring within this early international system. If the system worked, nations saw it as a model for subsequent developments; if it failed, as it often did, they saw the failures as reflections of a need for a new system or for new regulations and ideological commitments.

The debates of the 1990s about international communication are rooted in its early history. The remainder of this book thus takes a historical perspective as the best means to understand both the present and the future.

4.2

Early International Telegraphy and Telephony

Between 1835 and the beginning of World War I in 1914, various companies or state administrations introduced and applied three major technologies to international communication: the telegraph (1837), the telephone (1876), and the wireless (1899). Inventors in several countries, including Canada, France, Germany, the United Kingdom, and the United States, contributed to these developing technologies. These technologies also gave rise to some of the first transnational corporations, including the associated Marconi companies, which operated in several countries (with the parent company in the United Kingdom); Siemens and Slaby-Arco (Telefunken after 1903) in Germany; Thomson in France; Western Union, AT&T, and United Wireless in the United States; Philips in the Netherlands; and eventually Cable and Wireless in the United Kingdom; and General Electric and RCA in the United States. Attempts to use these technologies also led to the first international agreements in international communication.[2]

The Application of Telegraphy in Europe

Although electrical telegraphy was "invented" and tested both in the United States and Great Britain in 1837, Europeans quickly realized its potential as an international communications medium. Unlike in North America, where telegraphy could develop extensively as a domestic communications device, in Europe important economic and political considerations combined to encourage international applications (see Hall & Preston, 1988, chapter 4).

The first applications of electrical telegraphy even in Europe, however, were domestic (ITU, 1965, p. 29).[3] As in North America, Europeans quickly saw the potential of telegraphy to improve railway system operations and the coordination of government activities. Both of these activities also had international dimensions. European cities were tied together in an increasingly expanding rail network, which required coordination to meet time schedules, charge appropriate fares, and assure that passengers changing trains could continue their journeys across borders. In addition to helping improve international rail transportation, telegraphy allowed governments to communicate with embassies and consulates, and facilitated international trade (see Codding & Rutkowski, 1982, chapter 1). As the ITU's (1965, p. 29) own history of telecommunications put it, "The State saw [the telegraph] as an efficient means of establishing central control and government, the railways ensured by its use the safe and rapid functioning of their trains, and commercial users, as for example the newspapers, soon realised that rapid news of financial quotations from a foreign [s]ource or of political events, meant profits to them."

Countries first attempted to coordinate their activities with bilateral treaties, but this soon resulted in a hodge podge of arrangements.[4] What telegraph, rail, and diplomatic services needed was uniformity of technical standards, understandings about the use of codes and **ciphers,** and common application of message tariffs.[5] The confusion among state administrations had resulted, among other things, in many businesses developing private ciphers.[6] The British wire service Reuters, for instance, refined a system of telegraph codes so efficient that it could "transmit instructions for payment of money across the world more cheaply than its banking competitors." (Lawrenson & Barber, 1985, p. 37). While such tactics saved money, they also made it nearly impossible for telegraph operators or recipients to judge the accuracy of the message transmitted. National administrations also saw this tactic as an unfair means to avoid just and equitable treatment. This particularly vexed them since they depended on increasing commercial traffic to pay the cost for developing the system itself. Ciphers reduced tariff income, causing administrations to slow down development or to run operating deficits that they believed could be avoided with fair and equitable tariffs.

The Origins of the International Telegraph Union

In 1865 Napoleon III called a conference in Paris to draft a treaty to eliminate tariff policy discrepancies between two European telegraph groups, the Austro-German Telegraph Union and the West European Telegraph Union (see Savage, 1989, chapter 1, for a history of international telecommunications regulation). These two organizations themselves had brought order out of telegraphic chaos in the respective regions they served. The Paris conference was successful in (1) establishing international Morse code (a standardized version rather than variants that had emerged) as the basis for conducting international telegraphy, (2) reaching agreement on connections

between major European cities, hours of operation for reception of telegrams and mutual obligations to deliver messages originating in other countries and to dedicate network circuit capacity for international telegraph traffic, (3) creating an inter-European telegraph network, and most importantly, (4) creating an international body, to be known as the International Telegraph Union.

The Secretariat of the Telegraph Union, called the International Bureau, was set up in 1868. With its creation countries added substance to the Paris agreements of three years earlier. Kazansky (1897, pp. 6, 7) called the Union "one of the first treaties relating to the work of civilization ('culture treaties') which have attained world-wide scope. Its law constitutes one of the greatest chapters of the future world-wide Law of Nations. . . ."

In 1876 another conference was held, this time in St. Petersburg, Russia. It adopted a series of articles relating to responsibilities for transmitting encrypted messages and regarding uniform tariffs *(Documents de la Conférence Télégraphique International de St. Petersbourg, 1876).* These conferences served the economic and political interests both of governments and of corporate entities within their borders. Gradually, national interests were seen as being served by international agreements that standardized traffic flow and that protected diplomatic, military, and trade secrets. These agreements would eventually become the models for subsequent treaties that involved non-European states, and governed new technologies, such as the telephone, wireless, and radio, as they were incorporated into the international communications system.

These efforts to arrive at international agreements were complicated by two related conflicts. One was the struggle between state administrations and private interests, a dispute that could take a variety of forms. For instance, companies within countries expected their state administrations to buy equipment from them, but for various reasons (cost, quality, desire for standardization, patent disputes, etc.) administrations often objected to such desires. Also, many manufacturers expected their state administrations to protect their commercial and patent interests in international negotiations—they saw their country's national interests as identical with their own. In addition, commercial users of communications services expected their governments to protect their interests by forcing reduced rates and encouraging alternative routes or technologies. State administrations could not satisfy all these vested interests simultaneously, and often disagreed with these private commercial expectations.

The second struggle was between the competing private interests themselves. Cable companies' economic interests (high profits) conflicted, for instance, with those of newspapers, which wanted lower overall cable charges or special rates for transmission of news copy. Cable companies' interests also differed from those of the wireless companies that developed after the turn of the century. Governments were concerned that news from their colonies flow to the imperial capital. Such news helped maintain public support for their imperial policies and provided a sense of imperial identity. It also gave them an independent means to judge the efficiency of colonial administrations, and to consider military and economic needs. Many of them had subsidized submarine cable development, however, and were reluctant to undercut the economic viability of these systems, or to invest in alternatives, such as the wireless. Yet they were called on by the competing private interests to make judgments, with each company claiming that it represented the true interests of the empire.

The best documented example of these cross-pressures concerned the British government's relationship with the Marconi Company and users of its developing international communications system. The complicated tangle involved the British Post Office, which operated the state telegraph monopoly and represented the government at international communications conferences; the Colonial Office, responsible for relations with the dominions and colonies; British and colonial newspapers, major users of submarine cables; and British Marconi, which claimed that, if allowed the chance, it could undercut cable rates by over 90% (Baglehole, 1969, p. 15).

The Post Office wanted to extend its telegraph monopoly to wireless; Marconi wanted to break the domestic telegraph monopoly to increase its own business. The newspapers wanted wireless competition to drive down cable rates; the cable companies wanted to protect their monopoly and capital investment. Whose interests, then, were to be represented at international conferences? Could the Post Office adequately represent interests other than its own, even if instructed to do so by the cabinet (see Baker, 1970, pp. 85, 143–148; Hardman, 1909, pp. 90–92, 112–122, 157, 197, 319; Imperial Wireless Telegraphy Committee, 1923; and Ollivier, 1954, Vol. 1, pp. 21–71)?

In discussing the development of the submarine telegraph, Baglehole (1969, p. 9) wrote: "The turn of the century probably marked the zenith of the monopolistic power of the great cable companies as yet untouched by the early tentative experiments of Marconi. . . ." Sturmey (1958, p. 85) explained further that "the issue of monopoly was, and for many years remained, a crucial one in overseas communications. . . . The Post Office, in 1910, was not prepared to take the responsibility for organizing overseas radio services, largely because it believed that the Treasury would not make the funds available for such a purpose."

The Post Office found itself in the middle. Newspapers demanded relief from oppressive cable rates, while the cable companies' business was enhanced by the existence of the Post Office's domestic telegraph monopoly that fed their international cables. The Post Office's own business was likewise improved. The Marconi Company claimed it could lower rates, and newspapers jumped at the claim. Yet the Post Office coveted wireless; unlike submarine cables, which required bilateral agreements to land on foreign shores, the Post Office could use wireless within the confines of the empire, linking the colonies and dominions without messy foreign intervention.

The Post Office could also keep Marconi on a leash: Its domestic telegraph monopoly prevented Marconi from operating its wireless for commercial gain within the 3-mile territorial limit. Marconi eventually evaded the monopoly restriction by renting wireless equipment, including operators and the cost of messages, out to shipping companies (Baker, 1970, pp. 85–86). The telegraph law exempted intracompany messages from the Post Office's monopoly. Thus, by putting Marconi employees on ships and renting the equipment to the shipping companies, any communication between ship and shore became intracompany communication (Aitken, 1976, p. 234). This exemption also became part of Marconi's defense for its refusal to allow communication with non-Marconi-equipped ships: An agreement to communicate meant it ran the risk, if it received compensation, of running afoul of the Post Office monopoly; a refusal gave ac-

cess to rival companies without compensation (Baker, 1970, p. 95).

The British Parliament "resented the effective monopoly the Marconi Company had . . . achieved in British radiotelegraphy [by 1910]" (Aitken, 1976, p. 225). This struggle over control, a struggle among three prospective monopolists (the Post Office, cable companies, and Marconi), resulted in suspicion and duplicity between Marconi and the government, even when the Post Office chose to represent Marconi's interests at international meetings. It also carried over into the issue of how the British Broadcasting Company would develop an international radio service in the 1920s. (See chapter 5.)

Submarine Telegraphy and Imperial Communication

While pan-European telegraph efforts were progressing, many European states with extensive colonial possessions, particularly Great Britain, France, and Germany, were also busy planning and implementing imperial telegraph systems, linking the mother countries with their colonies. Britain, for instance, laid its first submarine cable in 1851 across the Straits of Dover to France, but quickly saw the telegraph as a means to tie its empire more closely together (see Kieve, 1973, p. 51). Britain completed its first direct cable to Bombay in 1870, and to Australia in 1872, only a few years after the successful transatlantic cable of 1866 (see Headrick, 1991, chapter 3, for a history of the expansion of the world's telegraph system up to 1890).[7]

Colonial governments and trading companies quickly recognized the value of the telegraph. The technology was at once a wonder and a means to centralization and control of power. It was filled with cultural promise—for good or evil. It "annihilated distance," its mythos resulting from expectations of "progress" and the first salvo in what would eventually lead to the vision of a "global village" (see Kazansky, 1897, p. 2). It gave "the power of supervision and control . . . binding, as it does, the isolated and distance dependencies of the empire to the mother country . . ." (Andrew, 1857, p. 140). Thus in 1887 the Canadian representative to the British Colonial Conference argued that "there can be no efficient intercourse nowadays without the telegraph. . . . [G]eneral mercantile business cannot be economically conducted without the telegraph; . . . in fact the telegraph is an indispensable auxiliary to all commercial transactions between persons separated by distance" (Fleming, 1887, p. 212). Furthermore, cable communication, as a report of a British

Royal Commission put it in 1914 (p. 40), "tends to quicken the pulse of nationality and forms an effective supplement to the broader, though slower, interchange of thought and sentiment by means of postal communication. It reinforces the feeling of joint life in a manner not possible by correspondence when two months or more are required for a reply to a letter" (see also Graham, 1967; Silburn, 1910, p. 278).

Such imperial communication links were important to colonial administrations for a practical reason: They sought to have consistent policies enforced across their worldwide empires (see Graham, 1967, p. 466; see also Newton, 1940, pp. 136–140, on the difficulties of imperial communication between England and India). This meant reducing the authority of colonial governors,

Table 4.1

Examples of International Submarine Telegraph Lines

Link	Date
England–Ireland	1851
England–France	1851
England–the Netherlands	1854
Denmark–Sweden	1860
England–Canada–U.S.A.	1866
England–Russia	1868
Malta–Egypt	1868
U.S.A.–Cuba	1868
Egypt–India	1869
Cuba–Jamaica	1970
Puerto Rico–Trinidad via Caribbean islands	1870
Singapore–Java	1870
Singapore–Saigon–Hong Kong	1871
India–Australia	1872
Jamaica–Puerto Rico	1872
England–Portugal–Madeira–Brazil	1874
Australia–New Zealand	1876
Aden–Zanzibar–Mozambique	1879
U.S.A.–Argentina via Chile	1890
Canada–Bermuda	1890
Zanzibar–Tanganyika	1890
Capetown–Ascension Island	1899
Mauritius–Australia	1901
Canada–Fiji–New Zealand–Australia	1902
Argentina–Ascension Island	1910
Brazil–U.S.A.	1920

Source: Kieve, 1973; and Baglehole, 1969.

and replacing it with control from imperial capitals (Knaplund, 1941, p. 371). The telegraph allowed centralized imperial governments to control sporadic crises more completely, and to implement changes in government policy uniformly and quickly (see Burt, 1956, p. 435).

The desire to administer from afar, however, coupled with the mutual distrust of these expanding empires (particularly during the so-called partition of Africa in the 1870s), also implied that each government had to control its own cable communications, leading to duplicate parallel systems on heavily traveled routes to Africa and across the Middle East to southern Asia (see Ensor, 1936, pp. 190–194, on the partition of Africa). Thus, "By 1880 nine cables crossed the Atlantic . . . and a total of 97,568 miles of cable traversed the oceans" (Kieve, 1973, p. 116). By 1898 there were 12 operational cables cross the Atlantic Ocean (Aitken, 1976, p. 240). By 1914 there were 350,000 miles of submarine cable connecting various imperial capitals with their far-flung empires, or over 3½ times the total cable mileage of 1880. Great Britain alone controlled over 40% (or 155,000 miles) of these cables (Graves, n.d., p. 9). (See Table 4.1.)

The value of imperial strategies became apparent at the beginning of both World War I and World War II. When Britain cut the German cables in the early hours of each conflict, Germany was unable to have its side of the story told in the Americas. The unhappy experience of World War I led the Germans to try to bypass the British stranglehold on cable communication during the 1920s. Germany began to establish a string of high-power wireless stations around the globe, including two on the east coast of the United States. The U.S. government confiscated both, however, at the be-

ginning of World War I. (See chapter 5 for a more complete discussion.)

These links were also consistent with a general intellectual premise of the 19th century: the idea of progress (see Royal Commission, 1914, p. 40). Those nations that were instrumental in extending the international communications system, and in contending with one another, both promoted and believed in this notion (see Andrew, 1884, p. xxxv, ci, 7, and 24, for conclusions about the role of communication as a "civilising power"). International telegraphy thus resulted in an early manifestation of its modern equivalent: the expectation of a global village. This idea, among others, justified (in the colonialists' eyes) the imperial extension that would later cause the new countries carved from these empires to reject their control of the international communications system.

Globalizing International Telegraph Agreements

The existence of these colonial empires also meant that the newly formed Telegraph Union could be global in its scope from the outset, even if its provisions were ratified only by the European states. Adherence to the convention by a given imperial capital implied adherence by the entire colonial empire. To gain additional leverage for its imperial interests, for instance, Great Britain insisted on sending multiple delegates to telegraph conventions, one for itself and one for British India. This step led to what became known as "colonial voting." Britain pressed an interpretation of previous agreements that allowed separate representation to telegraph conventions, arguing that identical language describing representation used in early wireless conventions allowed India to be considered a separate "Contracting Administration" (see International Conference on Wireless Telegraphy, 1906, pp. 28–29). By 1925 Great Britain, Italy, Portugal, and France each had seven votes to cast on convention business, obviously allowing them disproportionate influence on telegraph affairs compared with other states, such as Germany (whose colonies were stripped at the end of World War I). The United States was likewise granted six votes, despite its lack of official colonies, probably as a means to assure its participation. The United States was reluctant to be involved, however, in an organization dominated by countries with state-owned telecommunications monopolies due to its insistence on the superiority of privately operated systems. The grip of this handful of countries was so strong that the practice was not fully eliminated until 1973, nearly 30 years after the colonial empires began their slow dissolution (Codding & Rutkowski, 1982, p. 11).

The Telephone

In the 1860s and 1870s international submarine telegraphy came under the regulatory authority of the Telegraph Union. In 1885 countries began to discuss bringing the telephone under international regulation as well.

The telephone was first introduced in North America for domestic purposes. Its use among businesses quickly spread, followed by connections between doctors and patients, general stores, grain elevators and railway stations and their clients, even churches and parishioners in some cities. As with the telegraph, newspaper organizations also began to use it to gather the news. On the eve of World War I, two thirds of all telephones in the world were in the United States, which also accounted, not

surprisingly, for nearly 62% of all telephone wire in use and 65% of all telephone conversations. By that same date some 3.6 million telephones and 10.3 million miles of telephone wire were in use in Europe, which faced the same problems of interconnection, tariffs, and technical standards as had the rail and telegraph systems. Again, international regulation was required (The Statesman's Year-Book, 1914, p. lviii).

The basic obstacle to development of telephony as a significant international communications system was that the major European telecommunications administrations had made significant capital investments in telegraphy (see ITU, 1965, p. 103). Naturally, these state administrations did not want to see their investments threatened by a new method of communication requiring even more capital. Furthermore, they could not see the value of a medium that could not use an international language (such as Morse code) and that did not provide a written record.[8] Since at that time all telephone calls had to be routed through operators, they had to be able to communicate to complete the connections. No country could claim that its language was universal, however, and none was willing to accept another's as such. This problem was serious even within some countries, such as Canada, where the telephone connected French- and English-speaking Canadians (Fortner, 1980, pp. 90–95).

The problems of connection between countries could not be ignored forever. They could be postponed, however, since the first two decades of telephone development in Europe was largely confined to local, disconnected, urban areas (ITU, 1965, p. 103). The telephone was too valuable a tool for business, diplomacy, and social relations to allow incompatibility of systems, or squabbles about tariff sharing, to prevent its efficient use. These realities did not lead to detailed study of telephone problems, however, until 1925, when the Paris Telegraph Conference adopted a proposal to encourage the creation of a European telephone network. (See chapter 5.)

Early International Wireless Communication

Wireless communication was the brainchild of Guglielmo Marconi, who saw its applications originally as most significant where wired communication was not feasible, as in ship-to-shore communications. After failing to interest the Italian government in his invention, he went to Great Britain in 1896 where he was more fortunate. Britain, the greatest maritime power of that age, needed the communication capability promised by Marconi, for both military and commercial applications. Marconi successfully transmitted messages across the English Channel on March 27, 1899. He also transmitted signals across the Atlantic on December 12, 1901 (Vyvyan, 1974, pp. 19, 30), proving the feasibility of wireless for replacing submarine cables, and sent the first message across the Atlantic on December 15, 1902, demonstrating its long-distance potential and capability to deliver intelligible communication (Vyvyan, 1974, pp. 19, 30, 38; see also Sturmey, 1958, p. 78). In 1901 Marconi also signed a contract with Lloyd's insurance company to equip Lloyd's to provide marine information to ships, so long as the ships were equipped with Marconi apparatus (Aitken, 1976, pp. 235–236). He established the Marconi Wireless Telegraph Company and began installing his apparatus on British ships. To protect the invention, to increase its business, and to avoid the prohibition against competing

with the British Post Office telegraph monopoly, the company forbade any Marconi operator from communicating with stations using non-Marconi equipment.[9] Although Germany apparently tried to engineer an amalgamation of Slaby-Arco with Marconi, Marconi rebuffed the overture (Sturmey, 1958, pp. 53–54). This was the beginning of heated competition between Marconi and Slaby-Arco (Telefunken after 1903), and between the British and German governments.

Early International Wireless Conferences

In 1903 the German government called a conference in Berlin to deal with the Marconi noninterconnection policy. Both Germany and the United States objected to Marconi's practice, since each had wireless equipment manufacturers in their own countries and saw Marconi's practice as a threat to these companies' commercial viability (Sturmey, 1958, p. 60). The Germans were specifically outraged over the claim that Marconi operators had allegedly refused to communicate with the German liner *Deutschland* with the Kaiser's brother on board during a transatlantic trip in 1902. This was not just a petty commercial rivalry emerging, however. As Douglas (1987) points out: "Although the *Deutschland* incident appeared at first to be a petty confrontation between two rival companies and their respective countries, it was actually a watershed in the early history of wireless. The emerging problems surrounding the technology and its financing and regulation, and the sanctity of each country's territorial air, were embodied in the Marconi-German clash" (p. 120; see also Headrick, 1991, pp. 119–121).

The Marconi Company's official history claims that Marconi stations had been instructed to reply to any message from the *Deutschland,* but that no communication was attempted from the ship on the assumption that the Marconi stations wouldn't respond. Accusations were made that the ship's wireless apparatus had been jammed; "it is likely that . . . the *Deutschland*'s wireless was either partially or totally out of action because of a technical fault. Certainly the apparatus was removed from the ship shortly after" (Baker, 1970, pp. 95–96).

Whatever the truth of the matter was, the German government began a diplomatic effort to stop a possibly developing Marconi monopoly. "Germany feared that the activities of Marconi's and Lloyd's together would result in Britain establishing a radio monopoly" (Sturmey, 1958, pp. 53–54). As noted previously, Marconi was also working with the British insurance company Lloyd's, which was interested in applications of wireless to make shipping safer, and thus to protect its profits. Germany, in other words, saw a Marconi monopoly as a British one, although the British Post Office did not see it that way. As Aitken interpreted the situation, "The Marconi policy of nonintercommunication with competitive radio systems was not only well calculated to give it, as the leading firm in the industry, an effective monopoly; it was also the only way of circumventing the Telegraph Acts, the original purpose of which had been to assure monopoly by government" (Aitken, 1976, pp. 234–235).

The objective of the 1903 conference was to achieve an agreement requiring coast stations to communicate with all ships regardless of the type of equipment carried. Because Great Britain and Italy, two of the great maritime powers, refused to sign the protocol, however, it was worthless. The German government tried again in 1906, when 29 countries attended and drew up an international radio telegraph convention and regulations, but again it failed to break up the Marconi monopoly.

The 1906 conference did establish the principle that the electromagnetic spectrum could be divided into bands reserved for particular services (Codding & Rutkowski, 1982, p. 13). In this case frequencies below 188 kHz were to be used for long-distance communication by coast stations, while those from 188 to 500 kHz were to be used by government stations, which would take no public messages for transmittal. Stations were also required to avoid interference with existing wireless stations, and countries were required to give notice of (i.e., to register) their use of particular frequencies with the Secretariat of the Telegraph Union.

The conference also decided to adopt "SOS" as the international distress call, replacing the older "CQD" ("Safety of Life at Sea," 1932). The first record of "SOS," however, was not until 1909, when the U.S. ship *Arapahoe* used it ("The First SOS," 1933). And in 1910 the United States passed its first wireless law requiring any vessel using American ports, carrying 50 or more persons, and serving another port at least 200 miles distant to be equipped with a wireless set, and to have a skilled wireless operator on board. This act went into effect in 1911 (see Kahn, 1973, pp. 5–16, for reproductions of the Wireless Ship Act of 1910 and the Radio Act of 1912).

These three principles (reserved frequencies for services, avoidance of interference, and registration of frequencies) have formed the basis for regulation of international communication since 1906. They have also been the focus of dispute, however, when countries discuss new service allocations, or when such issues as jamming of radio signals or use of unregistered frequencies emerge in deliberations within the

International Telecommunication Union (the eventual successor to the International Telegraph Union).

The British Imperial Wireless Scheme

While the European and North American governments attempted to address regulatory and safety issues, Marconi continued building its monopoly: defending its patent rights, purchasing other companies, and signing agreements to establish wireless systems for various countries (see Baker, 1970, pp. 132–134, 156; Sturmey, 1958, p. 79). Germany was also active in beginning a wireless scheme to connect its colonies together (see Roscher, 1921, p. 71).

In 1911 the British empire's Imperial Conference approved a proposal to establish an imperial wireless telegraph system. The contract to build the system went to the Marconi Company in 1913.[10] World War I delayed the completion of the system, as did a dispute over ownership of the completed system (see Baker, 1970, pp. 143–148). The British Post Office saw wireless as an extension of its telegraph and postal monopoly, and claimed the right to own and operate the system. The Marconi Company, of course, disputed the claim. Despite this setback, however, the outbreak of the war left Marconi with "virtually a monopoly of marine installations" (Sturmey, 1958, p. 61).

Although another Imperial Conference in 1921 reaffirmed the commitment to an imperial wireless telegraph system, the dispute about ownership was not settled until 1924, when Marconi agreed that the wireless stations in England would be owned and operated by the Post Office (see Vyvyan, 1974, p. 74; see also chapter 5).

The Effect of the *Titanic* Disaster on International Regulation

In April 1912 the ocean liner *Titanic* struck an iceberg and sank within 3 hours. Fifteen hundred passengers and crew members perished. The ships closest to the *Titanic* had not responded to her distress calls, either because their wireless equipment was not manned in the middle of the night or because their engines were shut down, cutting electricity for wireless operations. The value of wireless in saving some 700 persons when one vessel did respond captured the world's attention. The public outrage and scapegoating that followed the disaster also caused the U.S. government to amend its 1910 act to require that ships using its ports have at least two wireless operators on board and maintain auxiliary power supplies to operate the wireless apparatus when the engines were shut down (see Douglas, 1987, chapter 7). Other countries, including Great Britain, passed similar requirements (ITU, 1965, pp. 138–139).

The magnitude of the *Titanic* disaster also led to another beneficial result. Although emergency communication between vessels, or between vessels and shore stations, had always been conducted regardless of the make of wireless apparatus used, at a wireless conference called in London, the Marconi Company finally agreed to end its practice of refusing to allow its operators to communicate with non-Marconi operators. The conference also drew up a new set of regulations regarding ship-to-shore communication that required that wireless apparatus on ships be manned full-time by experienced operators.

The United States had lagged behind the European countries in recognizing the value of wireless. During the 1903 Berlin conference, however, the United States realized its disadvantage: It had no national policy regarding wireless, and amateurs were largely responsible for developing the technology. The government thus began to take action during Theodore Roosevelt's presidency, first through the Bureau of Steam Engineering of the Department of the Navy, and eventually through the Department of Commerce, created in 1913. The government, however, found itself pitted against a formidable adversary in the amateur operators, who saw wireless as a technology developed without government assistance that the government now proposed to take over. They saw the "freedom of the air" being usurped by the government's preference for big "monopoly interests," despite the fact that, by 1910, amateur stations outnumbered commercial and government stations by over 4 to 1 (Douglas, 1987, p. 207).[11]

The United States had a wireless scheme underway by 1912. By 1914 it could use wireless to reach both Europe and Hawaii, and the following year it could reach Japan via Hawaii. In 1919 it could reach directly to Japan from the continental United States (Sturmey, 1958, p. 127). The United States or U.S.-based companies were also involved in a number of wireless schemes in Latin America, some to assist nations or companies there, and others to cement U.S. corporate hegemony in the region (see Schwoch, 1990, chapter 1).

The United States also refused to join the ITU during the decades when telegraphy, telephony, and then wireless were developing, arguing that it had no national administration to control these technologies, and could not sign agreements that it would be unable to enforce. Despite these claims European administrations sought U.S. participation in the conferences, even as they condemned the communications chaos they saw across the Atlantic, because they feared similar international chaos if they could not develop a scheme to include all broadcasting states in an international convention.[12]

4.4

Issues in Early Telecommunications Regulation

Private Companies and National Interests

Several issues animated early discussions on regulating international telecommunications. One difficult issue, touched on earlier in the chapter, was the relationship of private companies and national interests. The period up to World War I was one of rising nationalism, creation and consolidation of empires, and intense commercial rivalry. The tendency was to equate national interests with those of a country's major industrial concerns. The introduction of communications technologies led to efforts to protect domestic manufacturing firms in many countries, since governments were often dependent on these companies to construct and operate the transmission/reception stations that the state defined as crucial to its national or imperial interests. Increasingly, it became difficult to disentangle the interests of Telefunken from those of Germany, of Marconi from those of Britain, or of United Wireless or Anglo-American Telegraph from those of the United States.

Yet governments knew that separate interests existed. The press, as well as colonial and dominion governments, lobbied against monopoly submarine telegraph companies, claiming that these companies charged exorbitant rates. As already noted, the British Post Office resented the intrusion of Marconi into commercial telegraphy, which it considered should be a government monopoly. And Marconi in turn exploited loopholes in British telegraphy statutes to its own economic advantage.

The issue of private versus national interests became evident first in the position of Great Britain toward the Marconi Company in the 1903 and 1906 wireless conferences. It resurfaced when the U.S. and Canadian governments both denied that they could legitimately agree to regulations binding private commercial firms. Both countries' governments believed in limited intervention in private enterprise, and defined international conventions as inappropriately intrusive. Indeed, this problem—of whether governments could bind private companies to regulations they agreed to in international assemblies—hobbled many early efforts to rationalize wireless communication.

The Centralization of Power

Another issue was that of the centralization of power. All telecommunications systems developed as point-to-point systems. The telegraph developed to link city to city, imperial capital to colonial capital, and trading center to trading center. When overland lines were involved, the lines usually followed another point-to-point communications network, the railroads. These systems thus made access more difficult for people who did not live near system terminals, and served as methods for centralization of political and economic power as nation-states consolidated and imperial schemes developed.

One example of the significance of this issue involved the transatlantic cable. Although the cable crossing the Atlantic actually landed in Ireland and Canada, it

was immediately connected to cables that, in turn, connected London to New York, the terminus points of interest to commercial firms. Canadians could not actually use the cable directly, but had to send messages to New York to access it. Canada chafed because, even though part of the British Empire, it had to watch as all news or commercial information from London traveled to New York and then north again via Buffalo to Toronto (Fortner, 1978b, pp. 173–178). Another example was the development of imperial cable systems, which limited discretion of local governors, consolidating power in the hands of central governments.

Privacy

Still another issue was privacy. Both government and commercial interests wanted private messages to remain private. Sensitive diplomatic, military, or commercial information was often transmitted across international borders, sometimes even multiple times, before reaching its final destination. It was not unusual for messages to pass through the hands of telegraph administrations whose governments were hostile to the instructions contained in a diplomatic message, or for competing companies to bribe operators to pass along information about another's patents, products, or plans. Companies adopted various ciphers to guarantee secrecy of messages, although some administrations refused to carry messages in such form until international conventions guaranteed transit. Many administrations also objected to ciphers, believing them to be little more than means to avoid proper tariffs.

This problem of privacy was particularly acute in cases where messages had to be keyed and rekeyed as they crossed multiple borders, especially in Europe. Each operator involved in the transfer was another potential source of "leaks" to third parties, and another point of possible error in the keying process, since that operator couldn't verify the content of the message. The establishment of the European telegraph system and the adoption of international Morse code in 1865 helped to ameliorate some of these problems, but they did not eliminate them. While international Morse code provided a common alphabet, and thereby some way of checking the keying, it did not eliminate the language fragmentation of Europe. French telegraph operators would still not be sure they were keying an English or German message correctly, for

instance. Only new technologies could provide a further measure of relief.

Tariffs

The final issue had to do with tariffs. There were two major tariff concerns. One was how to share revenues generated by messages crossing the territory of multiple administrations, particularly those in which neither sender nor recipient lived. The second was how to assure that diplomatic and military cables between allies could cross other countries.

In the first case, telegraphy developed multiple routes, some of which were longer or shorter than original paths. To provide

Figure 4.1

The All-Red Route

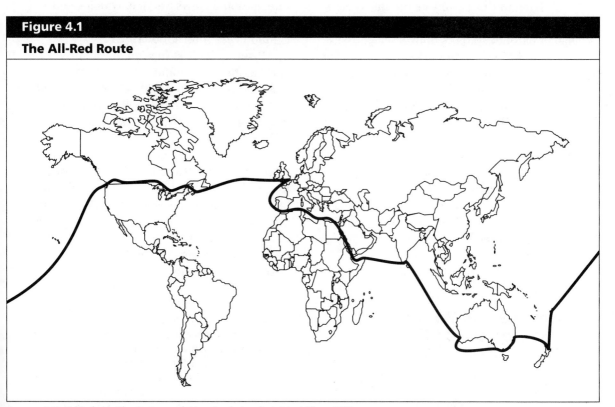

Source: J. S. Keltie (ed.), *The Statesman's Year-Book*. London: MacMillan, 1909, Plate 5.

flexibility in routing messages, and to assure their speedy arrival, countries had to standardize tariffs between major cities and apportion tariff revenue, regardless of the actual path traveled by the message.

Submarine cable installations heightened the difficulty created by multiple European administrations. The British had the most extensive cable network of any country, and often British cables were the only route by which other European countries could communicate quickly with their colonies. Rules adopted in the 1865 Paris Conference confirmed the obligation that all cable companies and administrations had to carry all messages, unless there was reason to believe that a message threatened a country's own security.

Related to this issue was the question of national control. Some countries established parallel systems to overseas possessions. In 1906 Germany's Telefunken began a wireless station in Nauen to reach both the United States and the western Pacific (Headrick, 1991, p. 129). It was the most powerful wireless station in the world when World War I began in 1914. And by 1909 Britain had established the "All-Red Route" a cable scheme that allowed London to communicate with its colonies around the globe without a message ever leaving British control (see Headrick, 1991, pp. 130–133).[13] (See Figure 4.1.)

4.5

International Wire Services and Information Flow

The first wire service was the French Agence Havas, established in 1835. The American Associated Press (AP) followed in 1848. Havas, like later European agencies, used a variety of methods to move its pro-

prietary information: mail coaches, carrier pigeons, couriers, and eventually the telegraph (Fenby, 1986, p. 28). AP was a cooperative association established by several New York City newspapers. It began as a telegraph agency and originally served only newspapers in the United States.

The Wolff agency, operating out of Berlin, joined Havas and AP in 1849, and the following year Reuters, headquartered in London, emerged. The European agencies all operated for profit, and began exchanging wire news copy in 1856. On the U.S. side the cooperative AP had a monopoly position until E. W. Scripps founded the United Press Association in 1907 as a profit-making organization. Other wire services soon emerged in the United States, such as the International News Service, which eventually joined the Scripps organization to form United Press International (UPI).

AP set up its first foreign news bureau as early as 1849 in Halifax, Nova Scotia, Canada. By 1900 it had 2,300 newspaper clients and was transmitting 50,000 words each day. It began supplying news to Cuba in 1902.

Many disputes erupted among the European agencies between 1856 and the beginning of World War I in 1914. These disputes led to new agreements among the agencies, established spheres of monopoly, and eventually a cartel, involving the principal European agencies and AP. Cooper (1942) describes this cartel:

> From these beginnings there arose the first, the greatest and the most powerful international monopoly of the nineteenth century. Its potentialities and its activities . . . were astounding. When Reuter, Havas and Wolff pooled their resources, established complete news agency control of international news and allotted to themselves the news agency exploitation in all the countries of the world,

they brought under their control the power to decide what the people of each nation would be allowed to know of the peoples of other nations and in what shade of meaning the news was to be presented. (pp. 7–8)[14]

AP's exclusive contract in North America ultimately led to the end of the cartel. It forced the Scripps' agency to establish its own foreign correspondents and bureaus to remain competitive, while the agreed-on monopoly spheres prevented AP from signing contracts with Latin American newspapers for "unbiased" news coverage of Germany at the outset of World War I. AP was forced by its contract to accept European coverage from Havas, but Latin American newspapers did not believe they were receiving full coverage via the French agency. While AP could not provide acceptable service under the contract with the cartel, the United Press Association began to provide news, beginning with *La Nacion* in Buenos Aires in 1914 (Read, 1976, p. 100).

4.6
Early Development of International Radio Services

Many dates could be selected to mark the beginning of international radio broadcasting. Even the earliest experimental broadcast, that of Reginald Fessenden from Brant Rock, Massachusetts, in 1906, was international, with reports coming from the West Indies that it had been heard (see Sivowitch, 1975, p. 24). Belgium began "grand concerts" using wireless on March 28, 1914, which European listeners could hear, and tried to reach its colony in the Congo, until World War I halted both experiments (Haslach, 1983, pp. 1–2).

4.7
Intellectual Property Protection Before World War I

In addition to conventions signed to govern use of the electromagnetic spectrum, to assure safety at sea, and to establish equitable tariffs and standards for wired communication schemes, countries during this period of history also signed two significant treaties to protect intellectual property. These were the Paris Convention for the Protection of Industrial Property, signed in 1883, and the Berne Convention for the Protection of Literary and Artistic Works, signed in 1886. These were the only conventions of their type signed prior to the end of World War II.

The Paris Convention only peripherally touched communications issues, as it was directed toward patent protection. The Berne Convention, however, clearly affected communication. It required that every signatory recognize minimum rights for copyright holders: a copyright duration of life plus 50 years; rights of translation, reproduction, public performance, adaptation, and arrangement; and control of motion picture production based on published works.

4.8
Conclusion

Although the period prior to World War I saw a variety of cooperative efforts among nations to facilitate international communication, it also witnessed developing rivalries, both political and commercial, based in the extension of the international communications system. Efforts to monopolize the international system were evident, even as countries attempted to solve problems involved in interconnection, frequency coordination, and use of new technologies to solve old problems.

Part of the difficulty lay in the suspicion with which European countries regarded one another in the period leading up to the war. Part of it emerged from the imperial obligations that they had assumed in partitioning the world during the last half of the 19th century. They struggled to hold these colonial empires together, saw the development of international communications as a means to assist in that effort, and objected to the possibility that commercial interests (particularly those outside their own country) might monopolize new means of communication.

During this period message-carrying capability was always minimal. Even the availability of multiple cables on heavily traveled routes was insufficient to keep up with demand. The North Atlantic cables were only operating at about half capacity in 1888, but peak hour traffic often had to be sent hours late. Their actual capacity thus did not match their potential, which was calculated based on a constant stream of messages 24 hours per day at a given rate of transmission. By this measure, there was over-capacity, but the reality of the situation — communicating immediately as demand occurred — meant that cables could not actually meet demand. Even after the arrival of the wireless in 1902–1903, the cable companies felt secure in their control of transatlantic communication (Sturmey, 1958, p. 76). Part of the reason for the underused capacity was the clog in the lines between New York and Glace Bay, Canada, that could delay messages up to 12 hours (Baker, 1970, p. 124). Not until 1923 "did the cable companies consider it necessary to reduce their charges on the trans-Atlantic service to meet the competition of

radio" (Sturmey, 1958, p. 80). This was only 3 years before the inauguration of transatlantic telephone service.

It was nation against nation, company versus company, suspicion opposing suspicion, in these early years of the international system: competition to control the means of communication and to establish commercial hegemonies and information monopolies. Yet it was also a period of cooperation, brought on by the necessity for interconnection and the desire to add value to capital investments made in creating domestic systems. Communication was a problem to be solved. Different imperial powers wanted to solve the problem on their own terms, of course, and inventor-capitalists wanted to exploit the developing solution for maximum profit. Yet cooperation was essential, as different uncontrolled events, such as the *Titanic* disaster, seemed to indicate.

Often domestic legislation prevented full-scale cooperation. Sometimes, it exacerbated the problem of competition between countries, or between state monopolies and commercial interests. Countries, however, were groping forward in an unfamiliar environment, trying to maximize their advantages and to prevent other rival states from gaining an edge, encouraging commercial development for both trade and military reasons, yet suspicious of having their communication in the hands of companies that might not be dependable in times of conflict. While the real conflicts and rivalries should not be ignored, neither should the substantial progress that was made in setting the stage for the continuing development of the international system.

While the European states struggled with one another, North Americans largely remained on the periphery. The United States and Canada were involved in the development of transatlantic submarine cables and wireless, and U.S. news organizations were becoming involved in international news flow, but most of that involvement was in the post–World War I era. As Cooper (1942) put it:

> The United States, completely isolationist through the nineteenth century, did not visualize the importance of international news. Broadly, the only foreign news they read was furnished by The Associated Press. . . . And the only foreign news that The Associated Press had, came from the great monopolistic European agencies headed by Reuters. (p. 12)

The advent of World War I rudely awakened the United States and its commercially driven corporations. War disrupted and distorted commerce; it required both government and corporate interests to see communication as a military tool, a conclusion reached long before by European governments. The ease of long-distance communication in North America, and the ability of U.S. firms to dominate Canadian companies, had allowed the country to consider its own needs first, and to assume that international connection would then follow on a U.S. model. In the aftermath of the war, the assumptions would be different, and the battles fought would find the United States a major player. But first things would have to return to "normal," that is, to their prewar condition.

Notes

1. The dominance of English in Canada caused major disputes on communication issues between English- and French-speaking Canadians (see Fortner, 1978a).

2. An international postal agreement preceded the earliest telegraph agreement but,

unlike the telegraph, did not set a pattern for subsequent communication agreements.

3. Europe's first telegraphs were actually visual telegraphs, using towers placed at distances that allowed signaling devices, such as semaphores, to be seen from one tower to the next. Claude Chappe completed a 15-station semaphore telegraph system between Paris and Lille (a distance of 144 miles) in 1794 (Garratt, 1958, p. 645).

4. The first international telegraph accord on record was signed on October 3, 1849, by Prussia and Austria (see ITU, 1965, p. 45).

5. A code is a standardized method of sending messages to take advantage of the possibilities offered by a particular medium. Morse code, for instance, used long and short electrical bursts in a prescribed order to represent letters of the alphabet. A cipher is essentially a secret code that is designed to be read only by those with its key. Each letter of the alphabet might be represented by another, for instance, or groups of words by a short sequence of letters that would otherwise be nonsensical.

6. The question of ciphers and the tariffs to apply to them were major issues at the St. Petersburg (1875), London (1879), Berlin (1885), Paris (1890), and Budapest (1896) conferences of the Telegraph Union. The dispute continued up to World War I, was discontinued because of the war, and then was taken up again. This was a contentious issue because countries expected one another to misuse ciphers to gain military, political, or commercial advantages in an age of suspicion, and because ciphers resulted — the delegates believed — in lost revenues, since they applied tariffs based on the number of words in a message. Ciphers telescoped words, allowing companies to avoid paying appropriate charges (see ITU, 1965, pp. 81, 86).

7. The first transatlantic cable was laid in 1858, but worked only a few weeks. Following the success of 1866, the earliest cable was re-

covered and repaired, and it became the second transatlantic link.

8. Morse code was considered an international language even though it allowed only letters of the Roman alphabet to be transmitted and did not guarantee that telegraph operators would understand the messages they received. The standardization did allow operators, however, to request that messages be repeated if the transmission was garbled, even when they could not translate the message into their own language. Standard three-letter messages — called "Q codes" — allowed key operators (both cable and wireless) to communicate even though they spoke different languages.

9. F. S. Hayburn told the delegates to the Madrid Radio Telegraph Conference in 1932 that in 1902 "they had a wireless Eden of their own into which no serpent of government authority had penetrated and in which there was no forbidden fruit, no apple of discord." Of course Marconi had just begun its nearly unchecked expansion (see Madrid Radio Telegraphic Conference, 1932, p. 7).

10. Vyvyan (1974, p. 71) claims the contract was signed in 1912. Post Office Archives, London, however, indicate that it was in 1913

(Imperial Wireless Telegraphy Committee, 1923, p. 1).

11. "Government stations" were those officially designated by federal agencies to carry official statements; they were not actually owned by the government.

12. C. A. Lewis, an officer of the BBC during its first year of operation (1922–23) claimed (1924, pp. 8–9), for instance, that it was fortunate that the British had not leaped into broadcasting during its initial year (1919–20). This could be seen, he said, "by glancing at the chaotic state of affairs on the other side of the Atlantic, where hundreds of transmitting stations are all giving out concerts on a narrow waveband, and no system of revenues or governmental control is yet in existence, as a result of which almost 50% have had to be closed down."

13. The route was "red" because of the practice of cartographers of coloring Britain and its colonies red or pink on maps showing European colonial possessions.

14. Cooper's account is not an unbiased one, as he spent a large portion of his career with the Associated Press.

5

EXPLOITING NEW POSSIBILITIES IN A POSTWAR ENVIRONMENT: 1914–1932

5.1

Introduction

The outbreak of World War I (1914–1918), the "war to end wars," came as a rude shock to the world. In the United States it confirmed the doctrine of isolationism, which argued for allowing the warring European nations to fight it out among themselves, and the "melting pot" mythology that suggested (at least to "Americans") that its ethnically mixed population, largely European and African in origin at this time, could live together in harmony. The 20 years prior to the war had seen North America absorb millions of immigrants, largely from Central and Eastern Europe. If the United States could assimilate these diverse immigrant groups into the societal mainstream, the argument went, why did Europeans continue their petty quarreling and warfare?

The war was also an interlude in the movement toward cooperation in constructing the international communications system. Politics, deep-seated imperial rivalries, the "groans" of European linguistic and ethnic groups seeking self-determination, the insistence by proud family monarchies on retaining power, economic inequalities, and a host of other influences had slowed the momentum toward an international communications system. Could that momentum be recaptured after the war?

During the war a new and important ingredient in world affairs emerged that would have to be taken into account in the post war environment. The Bolshevik Revolution (1917) ousted the Russian czar and seemed to confirm (despite the revolution's nonproletarian character) Karl Marx's interpretation of the movement of history.

The Marxist state that emerged in Russia, and that became the Soviet Union, saw itself in the vanguard of a more inclusive revolution that would shake off the imperial powers' grip on peoples' destinies and inaugurate a new epoch of equality, destroying the hereditary privilege and capitalist-based economic power that had led to exploitation of ordinary people (the workers or the masses) by the few. The Bolsheviks sought to export their revolution, and the means of communication were a tool to exploit for that purpose. In this context renewed cooperation after the war would be more difficult.

Despite its participation in the war during its final year, the United States would return to a kind of communication isolation at its conclusion.[1] Calls for continued government operation of the radiotelephone, for instance, which had been taken over during the war, were silenced by the desire to return to the prewar status quo. The U.S. corporations that had begun to develop technologies useful in wireless communication, and Marconi's U.S. subsidiary, American Marconi, had visions of exploiting a technology that had demonstrated its useful qualities in the war: Ground-to-air, ship-to-shore, and ship-to-ship communication had all proved valuable. The possibilities for knitting empires and spreading ideologies were too enticing to be long ignored or shelved in favor of government control. The U.S. Senate, too, refused to ratify the convention creating the League of Nations, even though it had been suggested originally as part of President Woodrow Wilson's 14-point peace plan to end the war, and as a vehicle to prevent subsequent armed conflicts. The U.S. government and its people wanted "normalcy," defined as limited government, noninvolvement in international affairs, and entrepreneurship in the private sector of the economy. The quest for profit would define "America" and provide for its citizens. Government, as the war had "proved," should not be trusted. Suspicion and fear of the Europeans, too, (particularly Great Britain) would result in policies to eliminate European domination of the international communications system.

In Europe reconstruction of the states "victimized" by the war, and heavy reparations from the losing Central Powers, led by Germany, were the orders of the day. Continuing national suspicions would affect the development of communications (particularly broadcasting), but so would realism: Cooperation was required if the interests of states, and their domestic industries, were to be met. More conferences and conventions would inevitably result.

5.2

Defining Propaganda

Propaganda was not an invention of the First World War, but rather, more than likely, is an activity that began with the institution of war itself.[2] Technology that became available in the 20th century did make a difference, however, in the way countries conducted propaganda campaigns. As Winkler (1978, p. 2) noted, "technological advances in the late nineteenth and early twentieth centuries opened up vast new possibilities. With world-wide communication now easily possible, the major powers all established programs to gain support from their own peoples and from the rest of the world, and to drive wedges between the powers they were fighting."

Conflicting Definitions of Propaganda

The term *propaganda* encompasses so much that it is difficult to say precisely what it means. Ellul (1965, pp. xii–xiii) says that people could "quote definitions for pages on end." His own definition embraces psychological action, psychological warfare, efforts to re-educate or brainwash, and both public and human relations. Ellul accepts such a broad definition because he believes that propaganda exists "in all 'civilized' countries and accompanies all 'progress toward civilization' in underdeveloped countries . . . ; it is an intrinsic part of the setting in which man finds himself in the technological society" (Ellul, 1965, p. 139). So, he (p. 9) argues, "Propaganda must be total. The propagandist must utilize all of the technical means at his disposal—the press, radio, TV, movies, posters, meetings, door-to-door canvassing."

Ellul thus suggests that propaganda is *unavoidable.* He should not be interpreted, however, as justifying propaganda. His remarks are descriptive, not prescriptive. Generally, all nations of the world condemn propaganda. The problem is that what any state justifies as legitimate communication, another state may decry as propaganda. Propaganda is thus often in the eye of the beholder.

Many scholars, however, do not define propaganda as broadly as Ellul. This is particularly true if the statements of those who see themselves as engaged in a battle with powerful (and usually, by definition, unscrupulous) adversaries for people's "hearts and minds" are examined. Many propagandists have been unwilling to acknowledge their activities as "propaganda." They have been eager to pin the label on others, however, because they typically see it as a "devil term" that will, once used, reduce the effectiveness of an opponent's information activities.

Propaganda as a Political Weapon

Propaganda is a term with obvious political connotations. Antagonists use it as a label to fling at those who adhere to different ideologies or who are on the opposite side of a conflict. Usually, scholars see propaganda as a set of methods to obfuscate the truth, whip up enthusiasm among the unwilling, or paint an adversary in the most unsympathetic and even evil terms. Lying is an accepted propaganda tool, as is the half-truth, or the interpretation that spins the truth to one's own advantage.

Propaganda, however, is not easily measured. The Nazis and Italian Fascists, for instance, saw the foreign language broadcasts of the BBC during the late 1930s as propaganda. The British saw them as an effort to administer a truthful corrective to fascist lies. The Soviet Union long considered the broadcasts of the Voice of America (VOA) and Radio Free Europe/Radio Liberty (RFE/RL) as propaganda. The United States defined them as antidotes to Communist subversion or disinformation campaigns impugning the United States. The North Atlantic Treaty Organization (NATO) members saw Soviet and Eastern bloc offers in the late 1980s to reduce conventional arms unilaterally at least partly as a propaganda ploy. The Soviets claimed the offers were sincere efforts to reduce the level of tension on the continent.

Obviously, different techniques may be used by those providing information or commentary to peoples of other lands. There were differences in both kind and degree between the activities of the Nazis and the BBC during the 1930s and 1940s. But often the distinctions are blurred, and the labels used dependent on the ideological posture of the observer. That is a conceptual problem in dealing with propaganda.[3]

Propaganda can be used within a country and outside it. It can be designed to placate a restless population or even to conduct legitimate democratic elections. When opposing political parties accuse one another of "partisanship" or "playing politics," they are simply using more polite terms for "propaganda." During the 1930s, for instance, pacifists in the United Kingdom used propaganda to try to stop rearmament and to advocate negotiation as the appropriate method of dealing with Hitler's increasingly aggressive posture in Europe (British Broadcasting Corporation, 1989).

The propaganda of concern here, however, is that directed from the government of one country to people in another. It often goes by a variety of names. As Whaley (1980, p. 339) suggests, it has been called "psychological warfare, political warfare, international political communication, or public diplomacy." Its characteristics are as follows:

- It is deliberately directed across an international border.
- It is directed not to a government, but to a population.
- It has predetermined aims: to convince people of the "rightness" of the propagandist's actions, interpretations of events, or opposition to the target population's government or leaders.
- It uses the various techniques of persuasion to accomplish this goal, and may include both truth and untruth as tactics toward this end (techniques of persua-

sion include logical, emotional, and ethical appeals or proofs).

- It approaches its audience as a "mass": not as individuals, but as people who have broad characteristics to which a propagandist can appeal.

As Ellul (1965) puts it, propaganda seeks not only

> to invade the whole man, to lead him to adopt a mystical attitude and reach him through all possible psychological channels, but, more, it speaks to all men. Propaganda cannot be satisfied with partial successes, for it does not tolerate discussion; by its very nature, it excludes contradiction and discussion. As long as a noticeable or expressed tension or a conflict of action remains, propaganda cannot be said to have accomplished its aim. (p. 11)

Propaganda is often accompanied by efforts to control the flow of information into a country, or to prove its genuineness by discussing matters that people experience every day, or to cast doubt on alternative explanations provided by a people's own leadership. It often creates or uses existing myths as a means of persuasion, thus adding credibility to its own messages and reducing that of opposing explanations that fall outside the mythic structure created. It avoids facts that contradict its myths or explanations, uses half-truths to add plausibility to its explanations, and elevates or denigrates events to focus the audience's attention on its agenda or to avoid unpleasant realities.[4]

The Cultural Implications of Propaganda

Propaganda uses the international system, to be sure, and is both a political and a cultural phenomenon. Its political orientation is obvious. It also has cultural implications, however, because it seeks to overwhelm ways of knowing, understanding, and interpreting experience within a population and to replace these with an alternative "universe of discourse." Propagandists want people to understand things from their point of view: to see victory or defeat as they define them, to see legitimacy as they define it. Symbols, icons, words, definitions, and ways of knowing are all part of the propagandist's arsenal; successful propaganda affects people's consciousness. Its impacts are thus cultural as well as political.

Propagandists see information and its context as a principal basis for power. As Nazi propagandist Eugen Hadamovsky (1972) put it,

> It must be emphatically pointed out from the very start that there is no such thing as propaganda *per se.* Propaganda is the will to attain power and can be victorious only as the tool of an idea. If the idea is robbed of its divine inspiration the most carefully contrived structure will collapse. The idea, propaganda and power are irrevocably connected. (pp. 2–3)

Attaining power ordinarily allows propagandists to use any means available. Thus, the propagandist claims as acceptable tactics distortions and lies, as well as specious interpretations of events, powerful symbolic constructs, and myths and vituperations attached to nations and their leaders. An examination of the historical legacy of propaganda in the broadcast media shows these characteristics.

Propaganda Versus Truthful Information

The difficulties of defining propaganda (and applying the definition to information activities) is twofold. The first problem is that any set of generalities used to define it (including those enumerated earlier) are likely to include various information strategies that attempt consciously to avoid being propagandistic. Both the British and U.S. information strategies of the Second World War (and Britain's during the 1930s) aimed to *avoid* propaganda. As Rolo (1942) put it;

> The very word "propaganda," in fact, had a distasteful sound to English ears, and was generally associated with the lies, bluster, and name-calling favored by totalitarian powers. It was considered undemocratic, ungentlemanly, something essentially "foreign." Further, the BBC was proud of the standards of truth, honesty, and good taste it has striven to maintain, and felt that these standards would go by the board if it were to embark upon high-pressure propaganda. (pp. 157–58)

British and U.S. strategies during the war were more in line with what Codding called the "general agreement" about the purposes of international broadcasting: "(a) to present the best of culture and ideas of the broadcasting country; (b) to present world news objectively; (c) to explain the broadcasting country's viewpoint on important world problems; and (d) to promote international understanding" (Codding, 1959, p. 61).

In the post–World War II period President Harry Truman continued the practice of a truthful information policy. He contrasted the policy not with that of the Nazis, however, but with that of the Soviet Union. He called propaganda "one of the most powerful weapons the Communists have" in the struggle for men's minds.[5] "Deceit, distortion and lies" were systematically employed, he said, "as a matter of deliberate policy." The U.S. approach was to be one based on truth, "plain, simple, unvarnished truth—presented by newspapers, radio

and other sources that the people trust."
(Truman, 1962, pp. 164–165).

The essence of this difficulty is the issue
of *intention*. Traditionally propagandists
manipulate. Their intention is, as Lasswell
and Blumenstock (1970, p. 9) put it, to control attitudes *"by the manipulation of symbols."* It is control they desire, and they are
willing to manipulate truth—exaggerating
victory, denying losses, never retreating, as
Lavine and Wechsler argue (1940, p. 7)—to
achieve it. They often have clearly stated
policies about how to conduct propaganda,
or deliberate and consistent practices that
can be judged to constitute propaganda.
Kenez (1985) says that the Soviet Union was
the first "propaganda state." Propaganda,
he continues (p. 1), "played a large role in
the 1917 victory of the Communists and an
even greater part in their ability to retain
power during the extremely difficult years
of the 1917–1921 Civil War." The Bolsheviks, he argues (p. 7), "were above all
propagandists."

When a country's leaders acknowledge
their strategies, as Hitler did in *Mein Kampf*
and Goebbels in his diaries, it is easy to
judge intention.[6] As White (1939, p. 13) said
of German and Italian propaganda, "the
main object aimed at is to turn the people
into a docile mass, obedient to the will, or
what is taken to be the will, of one man,
ready to believe and to feel whatever he
may wish them to feel and believe, and capable of entire disregard of their individual
and sectional interests."

Unfortunately, intention is not always so
explicitly stated. Often countries deny that
they use propaganda; the denial itself is
part of the propaganda strategy. Often the
urgency of "straight news" reports is such
that the information contained, particularly
if it comes from the point of view of a par-

ticipant in a conflict or event, takes on
the *flavor* of propaganda (in its rhetorical
power)—without actually becoming propaganda.[7] Hence the problem of making judgments is created. During the recent Persian
Gulf conflict Western reporters wondered
about being made into propagandists, for
instance, by the strict military censorship
exercised by the multinational force and by
the Iraqis, Saudis, and Israelis, although
they filed stories that were ostensibly
"objective."

The second difficulty is in the intended
audience for the information. Often international communication is directed not to the
entire population of a country, but to specific groups: "decision-makers," students,
members of a particular political movement
or language group. Such communication
would perhaps not be considered to be
aimed at the "mass," although it could still
be propaganda. Even Goebbels, Hitler's
propaganda minister, complained (Trevor-
Roper, 1978, p. 144) that Nazi propaganda
used late in the war was addressed to the
masses rather than individuals. So, although
the outline of general characteristics of
propaganda is useful as a method to search
for propaganda, it would still be necessary
to include strategies that might fall outside
the scope of the definition.

Propaganda Versus Information Distribution

These difficulties have led to particular
strategies to attempt to distinguish information dissemination from propaganda.
United States Information Agency (USIA)
public affairs officers, for instance, are expected to engage in "civilized advocacy" of
the U.S. point of view, not in propaganda.
The distinction, which is delivered in one of

the first lectures to junior officers, "is between manipulation and respect for the intellect and free choice of the audience. One might argue with a friend. One does not propagandize a friend. You will not always be speaking to friends, but the distinction nonetheless applies" (Burnett, 1989). Such distinctions deal with the issue of intention, but cannot guarantee that officers will not practice propaganda, or that other nations will not judge the efforts of officers as propaganda, regardless of their intention.

Much of what is known about the definition and techniques of propaganda emerged during the Second World War, and in the postwar assessment of it. The Nazis had claimed significant victories for their propaganda efforts, but Allied assessments were far less generous. In either event the use of propaganda did not stop with the end of the World War II. The realignment of power and shifting ideological focus occasioned by the end of the war led to new propaganda initiatives by both the United States and its allies on the one side, and the Soviet Union and its allies on the other. The United States quickly reversed its decision to de-emphasize international information dissemination activities in response to Soviet propaganda initiatives. Although politicians did not see propaganda as a particularly effective tool, it was something they believed they could not afford to ignore. That conclusion still holds. Even the fading Cold War in the post-Vietnam era and the crumbling iron curtain did not eliminate propaganda, nor information strategies and public diplomacy conducted via summitry, press release, or broadcast and newspaper monitoring and response. Each new conflict in the world, most recently the Gulf War, has resulted in countries using the communications system as a tool of war.

5.3

Propaganda in World War I

World War I was the first conflict in which the modern tools of mass communication were used for propaganda purposes. Although the war led many countries to fear this weapon of mass deceit and persuasion, the limited practical access to the products of propaganda actually restricted its use. Radio, for instance, was not available as a major weapon, since its development largely occurred following the war. Although broadcasting was a known possibility by the time of the war, the lack of radio receivers prevented widespread propaganda applications. The most famous uses of "radio," such as the delivery of President Wilson's "14-Points" speech from the United States to Europe, actually used the radio telegraph (wireless), with the content disseminated to the desired publics (government officials) by state monitoring stations through the press (Browne, 1982, p. 48).

A similar situation prevailed as far as film newsreels were concerned. Although the newsreel was a developed format by the beginning of the war, the military authorities in the field prevented cameramen from gaining access to front-line areas (Fielding, 1972, p. 115). Newsreels that were made near the front were heavily censored, which prevented the material from being of use to the enemy, but which also prevented "the circulation of news, true or false, which might have an undesirable effect upon morale at home" (Joseph Ward Swain, quoted by Fielding, 1972, p. 116).

The combatants did make efforts, however, to portray one another negatively to home publics. The Allied press was fond of printing "atrocity stories" about activities of the "murderous Huns," and stories predicting that, if the Allies won, this would be "the war to end wars."[8] The press gave special attention to the deaths of civilians and medical workers caught up in the land warfare through Belgium and France, and to the sinking of ships, particularly passenger ships such as the *Lusitania,* by German U-boats (see Read, 1941, p. 3; and Sanders & Taylor, 1982, p. 130). Artists, cartoonists, and traveling speakers, called "minute men" in the United States, portrayed the war to the public in ways designed to keep support for the war effort high (see Buitenhuis, 1987). The British also were active in the neutral United States, building on "ideas Americans already had concerning the belligerent nations" (Peterson, 1939, p. 5).

German objectives for propaganda aimed into the United States before and during the war, according to George Viereck (1930, p. 55), editor of the pro-German weekly *The Fatherland,* were threefold: "to strengthen and replenish Germany; to weaken and embarrass Germany's foes; and to keep America out of the War by spreading the truth as the Germans saw it" (see also Lasswell, 1927).

The slogans created by the Allied press and politicians, along with Germany's failure to respond in kind, were credited by Hadamovsky (1972, pp. 8–9) with breaking the spirit of the German people and contributing to the loss of the war. Knightley (1975, p. 82) argues that the Germans helped the Allied propaganda effort by their bungling of "human interest cases" and their failure to "efface the impression that they were the aggressors." The British, he argues, were so efficient in their propaganda efforts that Goebbels copied their techniques over a decade later (Knightley, 1975, p. 82).[9] Even Hitler mentioned British effectiveness in *Mein Kampf* (1939, chapter

6; see also Sanders & Taylor, 1982, p. 209), although his reason for doing so was at least partly to reinforce his claim that Germany had been "stabbed in the back" by its own leadership, and had not lost the war on the battlefield.

Clearly the British mastered the art of propaganda in this first world conflict: "Having entered the conflict with nothing that could even remotely be described as an official propaganda department, Britain finished the conflict with the most highly developed organisation of all the belligerents for influencing public opinion" (Sanders & Taylor, 1982, p. 1). The British manufactured posters, leaflets, pamphlets, postcards, and postage stamps by the millions, employed speakers with "lantern slides" to address theatre crowds, and produced films and books (Sanders & Taylor, 1982, pp. 104–112). They supplied information and publicity to newspapers and wire services, particularly Reuters (Sanders & Taylor, 1982, p. 37).

The German propaganda effort, however, was a lesson in futility (Martin, 1939). Its aim of keeping the United States neutral during the conflict failed, largely due, at least as the Germans interpreted it, to British cleverness (Lavine & Wechsler, 1940, pp. 332–335). As Viereck (1930, p. 125) saw it, "Our newspapers were helpless victims of circumstances. The German cable was cut, the German wireless was censored, while the British cables, going night and day, spluttered ceaselessly new tales of German atrocities." The German failures, and British successes, probably contributed to the stiff penalties exacted from the Germans by the victors at the war's conclusion. These penalties, in turn, contributed to Hitler's rise to power—one of his main themes was disavowal of the peace terms that had ended World War I.

The United States also had a propaganda agency during the war, the Committee on Public Information (CPI), headed by George Creel. Creel began a wireless cable service, a foreign press bureau, and a foreign film division. Some 650 local branches of U.S. exporters abroad also displayed CPI materials in their outlets (Green, 1988, pp. 12, 13). After the United States actually entered the war, CPI dropped propaganda from balloons over the trenches occupied by Central Powers troops and packed artillery shells with leaflets to fire over the troops. Creel's committee also engaged in disinformation and spread anti-German stories in neutral countries (Green, 1988, p. 14).

5.4

The International Communications System During World War I

When World War I began in 1914, both sides scrambled to protect their own vulnerable cables while attempting to disable the other's. The British were successful in dredging up German cables and cutting most communication between Berlin and its colonial possessions, as well as between Berlin and the United States, which Germany hoped might sympathize with it (Baker, 1970, p. 159). In fact, the British Royal Navy accomplished this within 4 hours of the declaration of war (Vyvyan, 1974, p. 126). As Peterson (1939, p. 13) explained the significance of this act, "The cutting of the cables between the United States and Germany was the first act of censorship and the first act of propaganda. These siamese twins of public opinion were from that time to dictate what the American people were to think." Germany was thus restricted to wireless communication

across the Atlantic. The German wireless communicated with German-operated stations in the United States until the U.S. government took these over. Germany also failed to damage most British cables, leaving Britain in a superior position vis-à-vis communication with its colonies and North America. It did cut the British Fanning Island (Pacific) cable on September 7, 1914, but the British were able to restore service on the cable by October 30 (Sturmey, 1958, p. 127).

The British also targeted German wireless stations outside the European theatre of war. In Africa, for instance, colonial troops were successful in eliminating the German wireless stations at Kamina in Togoland, at Dar-es-Salaam in Tanganyika, and at Windhoek in German Southwest Africa. The British also captured or destroyed stations at Yap in the Caroline Islands, in Samoa, at Nauru in the Marshall Islands, at Herbertshihe on New Pommern Island, at Duala in the Cameroons, and at Kiauchau (Baker, 1970, p. 160).

At the beginning of the war the German wireless station at Nauen (Germany) was the most powerful station in the world. When the war erupted, it communicated immediately with the other German stations, which (particularly the powerful Kamina station in Africa) then summoned German merchant ships into neutral harbors. As a result few German merchant ships were captured (Roscher, 1921, pp. 254–255). The governor of Togoland decided to destroy the Kamina station when British colonial troops advanced on it from the Gold Coast colony in August 1914 (Roscher, 1921, p. 260).

The French also attempted to jam the signals arriving in Germany from the Kamina station prior to its destruction. They sent out powerful jamming signals from their Eiffel Tower transmitter to inter-fere with the German transmissions, al-though they were apparently unsuccessful (Roscher, 1921, p. 256).

The antagonists in World War I also put communications technologies to more di-rect use in the conflict. They used direction-finding stations to pinpoint the source of radio waves emitted by their adversary as a way to locate U-boats and zeppelins (used in the war as bomb platforms), radio teleg-raphy to direct their fleets to targets and to communicate between spotter aircraft and artillery batteries, and telephony for com-munication between command and front-line troops, and between various fighting units in the trenches (see Dowsett, 1923, Vol. 1, pp. 2–15; ITU, 1965, p. 175; and Ra-diat, 1934, pp. 13–14). The telegraph was used "in the transportation of armaments, prisoners and soldiers and the regulation of traffic on field railways. It revolutionised military thinking and the planning of cam-paigns" (Kieve, 1973, p. 239). The telegraph was the "command and control" apparatus of the Great War.

Britain's ability to intercept German tele-graph and wireless traffic was also instru-mental in bringing the United States into the war on the Allied side. When the Ger-mans decided to inaugurate unrestricted submarine warfare, which made U.S.-registered merchant shipping targets of German U-boats, the Germans communi-cated a query to the Mexican government concerning the possibility of an alliance, if the United States gave up its neutrality. They promised Mexico U.S. territory in the southwest as bait. The British, however, in-tercepted the telegram, which became known as the "Zimmerman note." They held onto it until after the Germans actually began unrestricted submarine warfare, and then delivered it to the U.S. government. It

helped tilt the United States toward partici-pation in the war on the British side, partic-ularly affecting pacifistic elements in the U.S. West and Midwest. The U.S. press, in reporting its contents, omitted its most "sa-lient feature—that it was to apply only *in case of,* and *after,* the United States had declared war against Germany. The note turned out to be the 'overt act' for which the war hawks had been waiting" (Peter-son, 1939, p. 314; see also Radiat, 1935, p. 172; Schwoch, 1990, p. 45).[10]

5.5

The Postwar Environment: Political and Commercial Developments

In 1919 the Soviet Union used wireless to appeal to the "Working Class Organizations of France, England and Italy" to compel their governments to abandon the blockade of the Soviet state and enter into normal relations. International radio magazines reported other "revolutionary" radio mes-sages from Soviet stations in 1919, 1920, and the mid-1920s (Examples of propa-ganda broadcast from Russian stations, 1919–1924). These messages were appar-ently sporadic, and did not indicate the establishment of an international radio *service.*

Both the Netherlands and the Soviet Union engaged in more extensive interna-tional broadcasting beginning in 1927.[11] To the Dutch goes the credit for establishing the first continuous international radio ser-vice, while the Soviets get recognition for beginning the first "politically ideological" radio operation (Browne, 1982). By 1930 Holland was broadcasting in 20 languages, with regular services in Dutch, English, Spanish, Portuguese, French, and German

(International Broadcasting, 1930–1935a). Philips (the Dutch electronics company) operated the service with the call letters PHOHI, for **PH**ilips **O**mroep **H**olland-**I**ndie (Philips Holland-Indies Broadcasting). As the name implied, Philips saw its primary task as broadcasting to the Dutch East Indies (now Indonesia), and carried programs "devoted exclusively to matters of art, science, relaxation, sport, and news, while a certain proportion of religious matter is not excluded" (International Broadcasting, 1930–1935a). The Soviet Union broadcast programs in foreign languages during the 10th anniversary celebration of the Bolshevik Revolution, but ceased broadcasting when the celebration ended. In 1929 the U.S.S.R. began permanent international radio broadcasting on long wave, but eventually changed the service to shortwave (International Broadcasting, 1930–1935b).

Other countries soon followed the lead of Holland and the Soviet Union. Germany's Königswusterhausen, later renamed Deutschlandsender (1929), Radio France (1931), the BBC Empire Service (1932), and Radio Japan (1934) all began broadcasting to foreign audiences within the decade following these initial efforts.[12]

It was not only governments, however, that saw the potential of radio to reach across frontiers to distant people. Commercial radio began in 1921 with broadcasts from a state-run transmitter in the Eiffel Tower, and Radio Paris began operations the following year (Plomley, 1980, pp. 121–122). English-language broadcasts from Paris began in 1925, clearly aimed at an international audience in Britain. In 1933 Radio Luxembourg began operations.

Religious organizations, led by Radio Vatican (February 1931) and HCJB (Heralding Christ Jesus' Blessings), also known as the Voice of the Andes (December 1931), broadcasting from Quito, Ecuador, quickly followed the lead of government and independent international services. Radio Vatican used transmitters designed and built by Guglielmo Marconi. Its programs were designed to reach Catholics in remote places where churches and priests had not been established; discussions of the Catholic faith and radio masses were staples (see Browne, 1982, p. 299).

During the 1920s both Westinghouse (KDKA) and General Electric (WGY) experimented with international radio broadcasting, and their signals were picked up and "often rebroadcast by radio stations throughout the world" (Fejes, 1986, p. 50). NBC began international shortwave broadcasts in 1930, taking over an activity that RCA Communications, Inc., had conducted sporadically between 1925 and 1929 (Deihl, 1977, p. 4).[13] NBC's stated objective in its international operations, articulated in 1938, was to provide "a full service of uncolored world news and American news" and to present "as many phases of American life and culture as possible" (Deihl, 1977, p. 5).[14] CBS also began shortwave broadcasts to Latin America in 1930, with much the same objectives in mind. Both services were entertainment oriented, and the U.S. government "took little notice . . . of the potential role of radio as an instrument of propaganda" (Deihl, 1977, p. 7).

Both CBS and NBC had Canadian affiliate stations by the late 1920s. These affiliates, along with the powerful U.S. domestic stations whose signals reached into Canada (particularly the experimental 500,000-watt WLW in Cincinnati, which operated between 1934 and 1939), eventually caused an outcry that resulted in the creation of the Canadian Broadcasting Corporation (CBC) in 1936 and the elimination of Canadian affiliates of U.S. networks.[15]

Early International Radio Broadcasting

The Netherlands

The Dutch established a long-wave wireless telegraphy connection with the East Indies (Indonesia) on May 7, 1923, allowing messages to be sent between Holland and Java.[16] On June 13, 1925, they inaugurated shortwave telephony between Holland and the East Indies, and opened this circuit for private individual calls on February 28, 1928 (Haslach, 1983, p. 4). The first Dutch experimental radio broadcasts began in 1919 and could be heard across the English channel in Great Britain (Dowsett, 1923, p. 55). On March 11, 1927, Philips and six other Netherlands companies put radio station PCJJ on the air from Eindhoven, the corporate headquarters of Philips, planning to reach the East Indies (Haslach, 1983, pp. 5–17). This station, operated by Philips, became PHOHI.

When the Dutch government inaugurated regulation of broadcasting in 1930, it planned to treat international and domestic broadcasting identically. Both were to be "pillarized," a system by which the government had a monopoly on transmission, but provided organized groups, such as churches, labor organizations, and interest groups, with the funds to produce programs and guaranteed them broadcast time. This pillarization scheme resulted in the Philips-led group shutting down its international service to protest the government plans. The station returned to the air on Christ-mas Eve, 1932, after the Philips group reached a compromise with the government about operation of the station. This compromise, which left international broadcasting in private hands (thus treating it differently than domestic Dutch radio) provided other nonaffiliated groups with access to the Eindhoven station.

The Soviet Union

During the 10th anniversary celebration of the Bolshevik Revolution the Soviet Union provided the first known international broadcasts in foreign languages. The Soviets had used radio on and off before 1927, but most of the broadcasts had been in Morse code (Bumpus & Skelt, 1984, p. 7). On November 7, 1922, however, radio listeners outside the Soviet Union could hear broadcasts from the shortwave station Radio Komintern, ostensibly designed for domestic use (Bumpus & Skelt, 1984, p. 7). Reports on the anniversary of the October Revolution were aired in English, French, and German in November 1925 (Mehta, 1987, p. 59). Two years later, in 1927, foreign language programs on Soviet stations reported on the celebrations occurring in Moscow, but as soon as the festivities ended, as previously noted, so did the broadcasts. In 1929, however, the Soviet Union began continuous international broadcasting, starting Chinese, Korean, and English services from Khabarovsk, near Manchuria, and inaugurating Radio Moscow in German, French, and English soon thereafter. By 1930 the Soviet Union "was the only country . . . to have really grasped the significance of international broadcasting in foreign languages" (Bumpus & Skelt, 1984, p. 12).

Early Soviet use of shortwave was for domestic purposes, but the move from this limited service to an international one was easy. The very size of the Soviet Union seemed to require shortwave for domestic service. Shortwave, as many developing countries later discovered, was an inexpensive way to cover vast amounts of territory from a single site. Also, given the early Soviet desires to extend their revolution to other countries, and therefore the necessity of convincing the working class (the proletariat) of the necessity of revolution, the early move into international shortwave made perfect sense. Broadcasting to Germany's or Great Britain's working class was no different than using radio to appeal to Ukrainians or Byelorussians.

Germany

Germany began international shortwave broadcasting, directed to its own nationals and people of German origin abroad, in 1929. Until 1933, when Hitler took power in Germany, the Zeesen station (near Berlin) broadcast an average of only 200 hours of programming *per year,* all aimed at North America. All broadcasts were retransmissions of domestic programs (Bumpus & Skelt, 1984, p. 17).

The United States

Compared with many other major international broadcasters, the United States was slow to develop such operations. The United States did operate, however, what could be called an international point-to-point service between 1917 and 1919 when the government took over privately owned radio stations "to insure the proper conduct of the war against the Imperial German Government and the successful termination thereof" (Wilson, 1917). The messages car-

ried on these stations during World War I were in code, however, and not for general audience consumption. These U.S. stations carried President Wilson's proposed 14 points for ending the war to newspapers in Europe. The government-operated stations returned to private hands at the war's end, again by executive order, although the U.S. Department of the Navy argued that they should remain in federal hands.

The original U.S. decision to allow broadcasting to be operated by private enterprise caused several problems for any proposed international service. Some of these difficulties were foreshadowed by the earlier predicament the country had in signing international telegraphy conventions due to private ownership of point-to-point common carrier systems. Private ownership of broadcasting put the United States in a difficult diplomatic position during international discussions about regulating broadcasting. Also, the legitimation of private broadcasting organizations in the United States by federal decision provided them with a platform from which to argue convincingly against the international broadcasting plans of the U.S. government in the 1930s. This delayed the introduction of an American voice on the airwaves during the period when most major European services were inaugurated and during which they engaged in a "radio war" before World War II.[17]

5.7

Reintegration of the International System After World War I

While the suspicions of the First World War did not abate at its conclusion, the larger problems for reintegrating the international system were the reconstituted commercial rivalries of the prewar period and the development of separate imperial communications systems. The war had demonstrated to the warring powers the significance of communications and the necessity to control it.

Germany entered the postwar era burdened by heavy reparations payments to the victorious Allied powers, and bereft of her powerful wireless communications network. Great Britain, which controlled the largest empire in the world, sought to consolidate her position. France and Belgium had to rebuild. The United States wished to return to its isolation, but was suspicious of Britain and the British monopoly in international communications. Reconstruction of the international system would not be easy.

British Imperial Communications Development

The Marconi Scheme

The British government had signed a contract in 1912 with the Marconi Company to construct six high-power wireless stations in England, Egypt, East Africa, South Africa, India, and Singapore. The Parliament, however, refused to ratify the contract, claiming that the government had shown favoritism to Marconi (Sturmey, 1958, pp. 92–93). A new, less favorable contract was signed the following year, but when war erupted, only two stations in the chain were under construction and the scheme was abandoned (Imperial Wireless Telegraphy Committee, 1923, p. 2; see also Sturmey, 1958, pp. 96, 100). Marconi sued the government for losses, and eventually won a settlement of £590,000 plus expenses (Imperial Wireless Telegraphy Committee, 1923, p. 3).

During the war the British Admiralty placed a contract with Marconi for the construction and operation of 13 long-range wireless stations around the world that would allow the Admiralty to communicate directly from London to the British navy scattered throughout the empire. This chain was constructed, and by June 1915, all but one of the stations were operational (Baker, 1970, p. 161).[18]

Although this chain remained separate from any overarching "imperial wireless scheme" after the war, it demonstrated that such a scheme was possible, In 1919 the British cabinet authorized the completion of the England and Egypt stations. These were completed in 1921 and 1922, respectively, and opened for traffic between London and the Middle East (Imperial Wireless Telegraphy Committee, 1923, p. 3).

The impetus for the revived wireless scheme was the fact that many of the cables in existence during the war had been unable to handle the volume of traffic generated. An alternative means of communication seemed necessary. The British dominions and colonies also pressed for an alternative: "They felt that the British Government had not, so far as radio communications were concerned, played a distinguished role in the pre-war years" (Sturmey, 1958, p. 103).

By September 1918 Marconi was able to relay radio messages between England and Australia. It also undertook to establish wireless links between Great Britain and other European and Mediterranean basin countries, opening services to Madrid (1920), Paris (1921), Berne (1922), Barcelona (1923), Vienna (1924), Belgrade, Moscow, and Lisbon (1926), and Istanbul, Cairo, and Beyrouth (Beirut) (1928), as well as to Nova Scotia, in 1920 (Sturmey, 1958, p. 130).

The British Post Office Scheme

Meanwhile the British Post Office was also setting up radio telegraphy services into the Middle East, Italy, the Netherlands, Germany, Poland, and Czechoslovakia (Sturmey, 1958, p. 130). These services supplemented its extensive land and submarine telegraph system, tied into the services of other countries, and made the Post Office a potential competitor to Marconi.

In 1919–20 Marconi proposed to the British government an imperial wireless network based on long-wave propagation that would allow direct connection between London and Britain's most important imperial outposts.[19] The Imperial Wireless Committee set up by the Post Office rejected the proposal, although this committee did recommend that such a network be established (see Sturmey, 1958, p. 27).[20] The dominions and colonies, in turn, rejected the Post Office recommendations as inadequate. Beginning with Australia and South Africa, they contracted directly with the Marconi Company to erect high-power wireless stations capable of reaching Britain directly.[21]

Part of the dominions' rejection of the Post Office recommendations was undoubtedly due to their own struggle to make sense out of the empire: Was Britain committed to their welfare, or only her own? What did they gain or lose by continued imperial connection? Several of them had objected during the 1918 Imperial Conference to the indifference of the British government to providing adequate imperial communication, which they defined as alternative means to communicate, lower rates for messages, and news flow without "foreign" intervention.[22] They wanted inexpensive means to interact with London, to have their stories told there, and to receive up-to-date news reports about Parliamentary debates and decisions. In short, they

wanted involvement through interconnection. They did not accept the argument that an imperial network was too expensive; and they saw little rationale for an empire that valued them merely as a source of soldiers for European conflicts or of revenue for British-based manufacturing and service companies (such as monopolistic submarine cable companies). They seemed to be searching for purpose in the empire, purpose that would serve their interests as well as those of London, purpose that justified the continuation of the empire itself (see Baker, 1970, p. 213).

Marconi's proposal was also self-serving. Marconi knew, as Sturmey argues, that the British government would not license two wireless chains. Securing a license would eliminate potential competitors. Competitors outside the empire would also be at a disadvantage, given the limited number of wavelengths that, at the time, were thought to be usable for long-distance communication (Sturmey, 1958, pp. 88–89).[23]

The Marconi–Post Office Conflict

The Post Office acted to protect the British government's (and its own) investment in submarine telegraphy. It feared both a Marconi monopoly and loss of revenue for its cables.[24] Its fears had foundation, too, since the long-wave and shortwave telegraphy networks developed tended to follow the same routes as cables, and by 1927 nearly half of all cable traffic had migrated to the shortwave beam network where messages could be relayed nearly three times as quickly and at a cheaper rate (Committee on Imperial Defence, 1924; and Baker, 1970, p. 229).

A further complication in the relationship between the British government (including the Post Office) and Marconi was the development of radio. Marconi secured a license for an "experimental service" from the Post Office in 1920, but it was withdrawn in 1922. Shortly after withdrawing this license, the Post Office licensed the British Broadcasting Company (BBCo) to develop radio within Great Britain. This company was actually a consortium of manufacturing companies including Marconi and was the predecessor of the BBC. The complicated licensing scheme adopted for *listeners* to the new broadcasting organization was designed to protect the manufacturers from foreign competition.[25] It was at least a partial replay of the "protection" the British government had ostensibly extended to Marconi at the turn of the century.

Also in 1922 the British cabinet approved a contract with Marconi to establish direct wireless links with Australia and South Africa. The government itself would erect a station in India, which would then be turned over to the Indian government.[26] The following year the British government approved the entrance of private companies into the field of imperial communication, abandoning the idea of state monopoly that the Post Office had advocated.[27] In mid-July 1924 Marconi signed a contract with the British government to establish a shortwave beam system linking various parts of the empire. This was the first long-distance communication system to be based on shortwave technology (Sturmey, 1958, pp. 110–112).[28]

Essentially, the "beam system" of wireless communication used highly directional antennas, thus concentrating the power of the transmitters into a narrow path. This helped reduce interference between services, allowed frequencies to be reused on different paths, and provided additional security to wireless communication. The beam system rapidly developed, with links from England to Australia, South Africa, and India established by the end of 1927. Between November 1927 and May 1928, the links carried about 17 million words of communication (Sturmey, 1958, p. 117).

Beginning the British Imperial Radio Service

While this imperial wireless scheme was under development, the BBCo began to explore the possibilities of beginning a worldwide radio service, which British colonies advocated. Efforts to get the Parliament to provide funds for such a service, or to provide a greater portion of listeners' license fees to it so that it could afford to do so, were not successful. As late as 1927 a British writer denied that wireless could ever be a serious competitor to cables, as "it would be impossible for the Empire to rely on [wireless] in time of war" (Brown, 1927, p. 100). Sir John Reith, director-general of the BBC, addressed this issue as well. In a 1931 letter he complained that "other countries have taken a more intelligent view about the matter of short-wave broadcasting than this country." Nevertheless, because cable cutting during World War I had proved a valuable war strategy, the British did plan and implement a wireless radio Empire Service. The BBC inaugurated this program service with broadcasts in November 1927 (*B.B.C. Annual 1935,* 1935, p. 124).[29] The BBC took this action at least partly in response to the existence of Dutch and U.S. stations that people in the British dominions and colonies could hear (see "5SW Memorandum," 1929).[30] The BBC did not begin a full Empire Service, however, until 1932.

The Tangle of British Imperial Communication

The relations among the three separate wireless/radio entities during the 1920s in Britain were complex. The Post Office continued to operate its long-wave Rugby station, arguing for a state monopoly and questioning both the motives and tactics of the Marconi Company. The BBCo, and then the BBC, depended on Marconi to operate its 5SW experimental station used for the Empire Service programs, but its engineering staff chafed at the mismanagement that they claimed Marconi demonstrated (see "Empire Service Broadcasting," 1928, 1929a, 1929b). Marconi struggled with the submarine cable companies, pursued its wireless schemes in competition with foreign companies (particularly German and U.S.), and wooed those imperial territories that had been suspicious of private communications services, based on their experience with the cable companies.

The British government still desired to spread British culture, political philosophy, and economic power within the empire (see Heaton, 1890, for a historical view on using the penny postage stamp; see also Bennett, 1962, and MacKenzie, 1987, on propaganda in the Empire Service). It also wished, however, to accomplish these ends as inexpensively as possible. Private capital investment was therefore attractive. State engineers objected to what they saw as their "second-class" status, compared with Marconi engineers, and took every opportunity to denigrate Marconi. The BBCo/BBC, anxious to please the government during the period of uncertainty about its future in the 1920s, sharing the government's desire to spread British culture, and eager to establish itself as the premier broadcasting organization in the world, encouraged the dominions to use its programming and sought to establish a full-time service outside Britain. The first official broadcast of the BBC's Empire Service occurred on Christmas Eve, 1932, and was inaugurated by statements from Sir John Reith, director-general of the BBC, and King George V (see Mansell, 1982, p. 21).[31] The value of uniting the empire to confront new instability in Europe (partially caused by Allied demands for war reparations) contributed to creation of this Empire Service; however, the service was no longer "wireless," but radio.

The fortunes of the various participants were tangled. All desired to establish a monopoly of knowledge, based on control of the international communications system that still spun out in all directions from London, but none seemed able to shake its collaborative competitors. The British government wanted far more than it was willing to pay for; the dominions were largely unable to get what they were willing to pay for.

In 1928 the Imperial Wireless and Cable Conference recommended that all submarine cable and wireless radio services be amalgamated under a single enterprise. Despite the earlier desire of the dominions and colonies to see competition between these two technologies, they now wanted "unity of control and direction with subsequent economies" that would allow the company to resist "foreign encroachment" (Sturmey, 1958, p. 117). By this time Marconi was experiencing serious competition from International Telephone and Telegraph (a U.S. company), in addition to that from Telefunken and Radio Corporation of America. The result was that, in 1929, the Cable and Wireless Companies were formed, combining the British submarine telegraph and wireless radio companies into a single telecommunications enterprise (Sturmey, 1958, p. 121).

French, German, and U.S. Competition with Britain's Communications Hegemony

Britain's developing imperial communications system did not go unchallenged in the interwar period. Britain had an undisputed advantage in its worldwide empire so far as establishing and maintaining its wartime hegemony was concerned, but its commercial and political rivals had good reason not to acquiesce to its continuing hegemony. Not only did Britain's control give it military advantages, but the increasing spread of British telecommunications in the international system gave its companies commercial advantages that they could exploit in selling equipment to domestic firms in other countries (see Headrick, 1991, chapter 11). This increased the need for other countries to counter the British presence in (and dominance of) the international system.

During World War I France and the United States had cooperated in pioneering transatlantic wireless voice traffic. AT&T and the Western Electric Company were able to transmit speech and music from Arlington, Virginia, to Paris in October 1915 (see Baker, 1970, p. 184; Burrows, 1924, p. 45; or Sturmey, 1958, pp. 127–128). This breakthrough was based on the use of vacuum tube technology, or "valve transmitters," developed during the war for ground-to-air communication (Sturmey, 1958, pp. 25, 27). This startling experiment indicated that long-distance radio communication could be accomplished. Despite that, the British Imperial Wireless Telegraphy Committee denied in 1920 (p. 6) that the service, as "excellent and regular as it is," provided "a satisfactory commercial long-range ser-

vice as we have defined the term." Nevertheless, it did set up the struggle in the interwar years among U.S., German, and British corporations to monopolize the technology. In 1927 a regular transatlantic radio telephone service was begun between the United States and Britain, and all telephone traffic was carried via wireless from that date until 1956, when the first submarine telephone cable was completed.

In 1919, following World War I, the U.S. government forced American Marconi (a subsidiary of British Marconi) to sell its assets to a consortium of U.S.-based companies, which created an "all-American" organization, the Radio Corporation of America (RCA) (see Douglas, 1987, pp. 284–286). This action, taken to assure that the United States would not continue to be dependent on British-controlled submarine cables, and would be involved in international wireless, clearly escalated the conflict over this developing technology. It also continued the longer standing competition over control of communication across the Atlantic.[32]

By 1929 RCA was operating 42 international wireless circuits, mostly employing shortwaves (this compared to Cable and Wireless's 125 circuits). Other U.S. companies also operated services, mainly to Latin America (Sturmey, 1958, p. 131). By 1929, too, RCA had purchased the domestic broadcasting interests of AT&T and had begun the National Broadcasting Company (see Banning, 1946, chapter 19; and Bergreen, 1980, chapter 4). Through NBC, RCA cooperated with the BBC in radio experiments designed to determine the feasibility of sustained long-distance shortwave radio communication (Reith, 1928).

In the early 1920s the Germans, too, were busily constructing international wireless links, desiring to replace those destroyed in the war and to avoid dependence on British cables. They opened several wireless stations in East and Southwest Africa, and in the South Pacific (Roscher, 1921, p. 68). The Germans also examined the possibility of establishing a regular news exchange using wireless and set up communications service to the United States and Far East (see Roscher, 1921, p. 69; and Sturmey, 1958, p. 132). Finally, the Germans pioneered the use of wireless for communication from transatlantic passenger ships, inaugurating a service in 1925.

Competition and Collaboration

As Aitken (1976, p. 310) put it, and as these examples indicate, radio technology "appeared on the scene in a period of rising nationalism. Adoption and diffusion were accelerated by government sponsorship and government contracts." However, it was not just nationalism or political and military considerations that were instrumental. The desire for commercial monopoly and economic exploitation of the technology was also significant. In Britain, for instance, the Marconi Company's quest for monopoly was a continuing theme in reports of various Post Office committees, while in the United States and Germany rapid expansion was also prompted by the desire to prevent just such a monopoly (Imperial Wireless Telegraphy Committee, 1923, pp. 16–17).

By the late 1920s only four companies controlled nearly all the long-distance radio communication occurring in the world: Marconi, Cie Générale de Télégraphie sans Fils (France), Gesellschaft für Drahtlöse Telegraphie (Germany), and RCA. These companies formed the Commercial Radio International Committee in an effort to pool their patents, prevent overlapping services, and hinder the development of other com-

petitors. They turned to an old Marconi strategy to accomplish this last end: a refusal to interconnect with nonconsortium stations. As in the earlier era, however, other companies did develop, and eventually the consortium collapsed (see Sturmey, 1958, p. 132).

5.8

International Regulation in the Interwar Years

Despite the obvious rivalry between companies and between their respective countries, use of the radio spectrum continued to expand, particularly as various new services (long-distance wireless telegraphy, beam services, radio telephony, and high-frequency radio) claimed portions of the electromagnetic spectrum. Even the rising nationalism, as well as the subsidized services of the 1930s (whose competition, as Sturmey put it, was "jingoistic rather than economic or technical"), could not eliminate the necessity for cooperation (see Sturmey, 1958, p. 132).

The focus of cooperation in the interwar period was the International Telegraph Union. In 1925, for instance, the union created a Telephone Consultative Committee to study and make recommendations about telephony, including both technical and tariff matters, and a parallel Telegraph Consultative Committee (ITU, 1965, p. 72). These two committees were the precursors of the International Consultative Committee on Telegraph and Telephone (CCITT), at present functioning under the auspices of the ITU. These steps did not address the problems of international communication, however, particularly the rapidly developing new services and their hunger for assigned frequencies.

International Communications Conferences

In 1920 the United States, concerned about losing out on international commercial opportunities and about potential broadcast interference from neighboring countries, hosted its first international communications conference (see Schwoch, 1990, chapter 3). This 1920 conference proposed the creation of a single international communications organization. It would have a central bureau (secretariat), an administrative council, and an international radio technical committee, and would administer an allocation of frequency bands to dedicated services. National administrations discussed these proposals in Paris in 1921 and again in Washington in 1927, where the International Radiotelegraph Convention and Regulations were adopted and signed by all the major nations of the world with the exception of the Soviet Union. The Soviets were excluded from the meeting at U.S. insistence because of their avowed intent of fostering revolution in other countries. In deference to the private-industry-dominated systems of the United States and Canada, the adopted regulations included certain stipulations in a separate section so that these two countries could "take **reservations**" on it (indicating they did not intend to abide by it) and still endorse the remainder. All countries agreed on the principle of a single international communications body, and another conference finally created this organization in 1932, in Madrid, calling it the International Telecommunication Union (ITU). The Madrid conference also separated telephone from telegraph regulations for European countries, although the United States saw no reason to take a similar step for North America.

The 1927 conference also took steps to eliminate interference among the international communications services. It outlawed the use of **"spark gap" transmitters** for all communications over 300 watts, to be effective in 1940, and drew up the first frequency allocation table (ITU, 1965, p. 156; Sturmey, 1958, p. 63). This conference "might . . . be called the first of the truly modern telecommunication conferences." Eighty countries sent official delegates, and 64 private companies, broadcasting groups, and other international organizations also sent nonvoting representatives (ITU, 1965, p. 151). This set a pattern of participation that would continue to the present day.

European administrations saw the need to give up a measure of national control more clearly than did the United States or Canada. In 1925 the BBC hosted a preliminary conference to discuss possibilities for establishing an international bureau in Europe. The 10 conference participants agreed that a Union Internationale de Radiophonie, located in Geneva, should be set up, and a month later, at a meeting in Geneva, the first General Assembly was held to begin to frame the governing statutes *(The B.B.C. Handbook, 1928,* 1928, p. 285). The assembly agreed on a Plan de Genève to allocate broadcasting frequencies *(The B.B.C. Handbook, 1928,* 1928, p. 287); however, it did not cover all the European states. By 1929 more than 200 broadcasting stations were on the air in Europe, using 600 kilowatts of power. Two years later the number of stations had increased by 30% (to 261), but the power used had increased by more than 400%, to 2,860 kilowatts (Vyvyan, 1974, p. 207). While large countries, such as the United States and Canada, could easily handle this number of stations and amount of power, the smaller countries of Europe could not. Interference would have made the use of radio impossible. After the 1927 Washington conference, therefore, the European administrations met in Geneva and established a 10-kHz bandwidth for stations. Later they met in Prague to divide the broadcast band into 106 channels. The number of stations on the air, or under construction in Europe, however, required that the 10-kHz bandwidth be reduced to 9. With this adjustment the European states were able to agree on allocating 95 of the 106 channels for the exclusive use of individual countries. They reserved 11 for common use, "to be available to any nation for small stations of small range" (Vyvyan, 1974, p. 206). This agreement was the first one signed by all European broadcasting authorities.[33]

5.9

Control of International Communication Flow

The explosion of communication possibilities in the interwar period, as already discussed, resulted in commercially and politically inspired struggles over control of the emerging technologies. The new networks created by these technologies quickly supplemented, sometimes replaced, and always competed with the elements of the system already in place.

News Flow in the International System

As already noted, the development of submarine cables resulted in demands from British dominions and colonies for more efficient news flow (usually defined in terms of the rates charged to the press). During the Imperial Conference of 1917, the prime minister of New Zealand submitted a motion declaring that there was "a real necessity for improvement in the news service of the Empire and that it is essential that Im-

perial news should reach the various countries of the Empire through British rather than foreign channels" (Ollivier, 1954, Vol. 2, p. 255). The conference did not act on the motion, but in the 1918 Imperial War Conference a resolution declared that "an adequate news service should be available in all parts of the British Empire" and that "this service should be supplied through British sources" (Ollivier, 1954, Vol. 2, p. 273).[34] Such motions were undoubtedly prompted by World War I itself, but they also reiterated long-standing desires within the empire for stronger interconnection, with news being seen as a way of accomplishing that end.[35] In 1920 the British inaugurated a wireless telegraphy service using the Chelmsford station (Baker, 1970, p. 185).

The issue of news flow also affected decisions of Germany, France, and the United States to develop wireless. In 1901 the *New York Herald* became the first newspaper to own and operate a wireless station (Baker, 1970, p. 87). In 1921 the completion of the Paris Radio Center gave France, as one review ("The Paris Radio Central," 1921, p. 125) put it, "an incontestable superiority in the field of radio communications . . . [that] will enable the insufficiency of the cable communications to the French colonies and to other overseas countries to be overcome." That same year RCA opened a "high-power" wireless station on Long Island "to supplement the existing communication facilities from the U.S.A. and to provide direct radio services with Great Britain, France, Norway, Germany and other European countries as well as to South America." ("The Opening of the New York Radio Central," 1922, pp. 3–4). Marconi also opened a temporary wireless facility in Geneva, Switzerland, to report on the second assembly of the League of Nations. This facility allowed direct communication between Geneva and London, Denmark, Norway, Sweden, and Spain ("The Wireless Service for Press Messages from Geneva," 1921, p. 535).

Wireless and Military Intelligence Operations

During World War I the warring countries conceived the idea that wireless communication might be monitored for use as a counterintelligence weapon. This added a new dimension to the issue of control of communication. Although wireless stations could be established on a country's own soil, no country could control the radio waves themselves—they were no respecter of national boundaries. The idea for monitoring wireless messages apparently emerged from a newspaper article carried by the London *Daily Telegraph* on November 12, 1914:

> Wireless telegraphy conferred a boon on mankind, but it is not without its dangers in times of international complications. A representative of the *Daily Telegraph* was yesterday shown messages originating in Germany, France and the North Sea, which some time ago were received at a private wireless station in the West-end. Like the telephone when it was in its infancy, the wireless system attracted many amateurs and experimentalists, and numbers of aerials were erected. In time of war these installations may be used against the public weal. They may also be brought to serve in the best interests of the Empire by "catching" stray messages intended for the enemy. (quoted in West, 1986, p. 22)

Germany, Great Britain, and the United States all established services to decode encrypted messages. However, wireless intelligence was often subject to interservice rivalries between different branches of the military, each of which had a system it wished to protect.

Rivalry Among Wire Services

The wire services that had come into existence prior to the war were also active during the war attempting to consolidate their spheres of influence and profit-making potential. The Associated Press's ability to become a truly international wire service, however, was hobbled by the cartel restrictions that it began actively to fight as a result of the competition from United Press. AP had no illusions about why Reuters and Havas wanted to preserve the cartel arrangement following the outbreak of World War I. As Cooper (1942, p. 43) explained their motives: "(1) they kept out Associated Press competition; (2) they were free to present American news disparagingly to the United States if they presented it at all; (3) they could present news of their own countries most favorably and without it being contradicted." After extensive internal discussions AP decided to break free of the cartel. It convinced *La Nación* to switch to its service from UP, and in 1919 signed 25 Central American newspapers as clients.[36] It also began serving Japan in 1930, and in 1934 "signed a new contract with Reuter based on a policy of freedom of international news exchange" (Read, 1976, p. 101; see also Fenby, 1986, p. 49). In 1934 AP also began the world's first Wirephoto service, which its competitors then emulated over the next two years (Smith, 1979, p. 150). AP finally inaugurated a World Service in 1944, after being delayed by World War II.

Countries did address the question of imbalanced information flow in the interwar period. The League of Nations in 1925 recognized the press as "the most effective means of guiding public opinion towards that moral disarmament which is a concomitant condition of material disarmament" and invited its council to consider convening a panel of experts to determine how the press might contribute to world peace, particularly "by ensuring the more rapid and less costly transmission of Press news with a view to reducing risks of international understanding" *(Collaboration of the Press,* 1986, p. 105). This proposal was clearly aimed at both the technological issue of the speed of news distribution and its economic organization as controlled by a few Western news agencies. (The genesis of the League of Nations can be seen in Egerton, 1978, and Scott, 1973.)

The concern in the 1920s, however, was largely contained within the orbit of the "great powers." That orbit included the two thirds of the world now known as developing countries only tangentially, as they were then part of the Western European states' global empires. Only after the break-up of these empires, in the first stages of political stabilization in the 1960s, could developing countries themselves begin to argue that the control of information was an important element in achieving true sovereignty (see Nordenstreng, 1984, pp. 4–8, for another perspective on demands for a "new order").

`5.10`

Conclusion

The early struggle to control the news was, at least in part, the result of a growing recognition of a tension created by the expansion of the international communications system, and particularly the application of wireless. Until after World War I the system was, in each participant's national terms, containable. Although the communication

pace quickened and the system expanded globally, countries nevertheless largely defined their activities within more specific terms: Cables had to be physically connected; wireless had to be encoded; colonial or imperial systems had to be developed. Countries thought of communication as confined within their spheres of influence. This even affected the activities of the wire services that were clearly transnational in function, and yet which carved up the world into spheres of influence and pursued national interests in the presentation of news.

Radiotelephony, however, opened up the channels of the international system. Despite its technical limitations it allowed individuals to speak to others across borders, or expanses of ocean, directly—without intervention: No codes or physical connections were required. Radio accelerated the connection. As David Sarnoff (1931) put it:

> Radio is the medium by which we may learn to appreciate the thoughts and aspirations of other people. What we have already had in international broadcasting is but an indication of how the force unloosed by Marconi may bring the people of the world into a new and closer relationship. Long years of effort and the expenditure of hundreds of millions of dollars in the interests of world amity could not so readily promote the cause of lasting peace as the work of this one inventor. . . . Marconi annihilated the barrier of space and discovered the neighborhood of nations. (p. 31)

This was the vision of McLuhan's "global village" unleashed by radio. People took the idea of "progress," which was so crucial in the thinking of the 19th century, and the "romance" of modernity, and forged them into a dominating mythos, attaching them to radio (see Williams, 1907, on "romance").

It was the progress that necessarily accompanied technological development and the mythos that justified further advances.

Yet the lessons of World War I could not be forgotten. More realistic than Sarnoff (who had, of course, a vested economic interest in the fortunes of radio) were remarks from the BBC:

> Short-wave broadcasting stations are . . . springing up everywhere and some are under the direct control of Governments, having as their objects (1) the maintenance of touch with outlying nationals, (2) the world-presentation of the national view-point in terms of national culture. Neither of these objects is illegitimate, but the first assumes a principle that has already caused friction in Europe while in the second the boundary between cultural and tendenacious propaganda is, in practice, very indefinite. (Empire Service Broadcasting," 1929a, p. 6)

Pursuit of national objectives through the international communications system was legitimate; propaganda was not. People could be, as Wilfred Trotter had written during the war, moved to the "homogeneity of the herd" (Trotter, 1953, p. 114).

How, then, were countries to cooperate? The international system was to the advantage of all unless it was abused, or monopolized, or biased toward some countries. Yet how could such results be avoided? Could the system be neutral; would it inexorably be biased in its operations? What mattered most: control of the system, or its content? Could these two dimensions of the system be separated?

Disputes among countries on such questions would continue. The dynamics of the system, however, would not cease while nations sought answers. Continuing political upheaval, war, new technologies, the rise and fall of commercial fortunes, the break-up of colonial empires, the rise of new ideologies—all would affect the ability of the world's nations to answer them.

Notes

1. Baker (1970, pp. 179–180) argued that "the American national interest was furthered by neutrality. The European war created profitable new markets and also provided opportunities for entry into world markets which had hitherto been dominated by the European manufacturers.

This encouraged the rapid growth of American wireless manufacturers from an insignificant size to a point where they became serious rivals to the American Marconi Company."

2. Read (1941, p. 1) wrote that Sun Tsu's *The Art of War* described propaganda more than 2,400 years ago.

3. In Rome the Propaganda Palace is located on Via della Propaganda. The palace houses the offices of the Roman Catholic church responsible for *propagating* the faith, clearly indicating an entirely different understanding of the term than that discussed here.

4. Ellul (1965, pp. xi–xii) provides other definitions of propaganda as well. See also discussions in Davison (1965, pp. 183–185), Whitton and Larson (1964, pp. 8–11), Doob (1948, pp. 240–253), and Whitaker (1962, p. 5) among many others.

5. Griffith (1980, pp. 239–240) would suggest that Truman was correct in his assessment of the importance of propaganda to communists. As he put it: "The Marxist sense of certainty, its passion for conversion, and its emphasis on educating the masses predisposed its followers toward regarding propaganda as one of its most important tasks.

Marxist ideology thus inclined its propaganda toward elitism and manipulation of the masses. The communists were an elite, bearers of knowledge to the proletariat. Moreover, according to Marxist doctrine, true knowledge cannot be achieved by the process of cognition alone, but only by a combination of cognition and revolutionary activity — praxis."

6. Goebbels's diaries are sprinkled with references to propaganda campaigns, although their major topic is the actual conduct of the war (see Trevor-Roper, 1978).

7. Beachcroft (1942, p. 14) implies this in his work on the wartime BBC. When Britain faced Germany alone, he said, "News from Britain was of almost hourly emergency; and not only news, but information; personal stories and accounts of eye-witnesses; the real voice of the airmen and the citizens who were engaged in the struggle. People were thirsting for the true account of the strength at the heart of the Empire."

8. See Knightley (1975, chapter 5). In one paragraph that illustrates well the claims of the Allies, Knightley wrote, "The Kaiser was painted as a beast in human form. . . . The Germans were portrayed as only slightly better than the hordes of Genghis Khan, rapers of nuns, mutilators of children, and destroyers of civilization" (p. 82).

9. Sanders and Taylor, too, claim (1982, p. 1) that the British were responsible for opening the "Pandoran box which unleashed the weapon of propaganda upon the modern world." They elaborate with descriptions of propaganda aimed at "the bloated 'Prussian Ogre' proudly sporting his pickelhauber" (p. 137) and at the "so-called 'corpse-conversion factory'" where the Germans were supposedly "boiling down dead bodies to make soap" (p. 146), and discuss the impact of the Bryce Report purporting to summarize German atrocities (p. 143).

10. Radiat (1935, p. 172) went so far as to claim that "America declared war on Germany, solely on the strength of an intercepted telegram."

11. Baker (1970, p. 185) reports that PCGG began to broadcast concerts from the Hague, the Netherlands, on April 29, 1920, but regular broadcasting from Holland did not begin until 1927.

12. Marconi actually broadcast from the United Kingdom in 1920, with the signal reportedly reaching into Europe, Persia, and Newfoundland. The British Post Office, however, withdrew Marconi's experimental license for "interference with legitimate services" just as radio was getting off the ground in the United States (see Baker, 1970, pp. 185–187; see also Brunnquell, 1992, for a history of Radio France International).

13. Fejes (1986, pp. 51–52) concluded that RCA's initial involvement in international radio was part of a scheme to wrest control of U.S. broadcasting away from AT&T. RCA's first attempt at such broadcasting was a program exchange with the BBC on March 12, 1925. General Electric had begun its experiments in 1923.

14. The objectives were reported in *The New York Times,* December 11, 1938. Quoted by Deihl.

15. The first Canadian effort to establish national broadcasting began in 1932 with the creation of the Canadian Radio Broadcasting Commission. It was replaced by the CBC four years later (see Peers, 1969; and Weir, 1965).

16. "Temporary" communication between Holland and Java was achieved as early as 1919 ("Radiotelegraphy in the Dutch East Indies," 1921, p. 576).

17. The federal rejection of the navy's suggestion that shortwave stations be retained at the end of World War I, and the adoption of the Federal Radio Act in 1927, gave private stations a legitimacy by extending the umbrella of the First Amendment to their activities, and rejecting the option of "public service broadcasting" based on the British model.

18. The stations were located on Ascension Island, the Falklands (Malvinas), Bathurst, Ceylon (Sri Lanka), Durban (South Africa), Demerara (Guyana), the Seychelles,

Singapore, St. John's (Newfoundland), Aden, Hong Kong, Mauritius, and Port Nolloth (South Africa).

19. By 1920 Marconi had four high-power wireless links in operation (see Lewis, 1924, p. 6).

20. See also Imperial Wireless Telegraphy Committee (1923, p. 4): "The most important feature of the Committee's scheme was that they rejected . . . the Marconi proposals for direct communication between England . . . and India, Australia and South Africa . . . without any intermediate stations, and proposed instead a system of stations spaced at about 2,000 miles apart", and an unsigned memorandum: "the scheme would constitute a most serious encroachment upon the telegraph monopoly of the various Administrations."

21. A Post Office committee eventually claimed that the dominions were probably influenced by Marconi "propaganda" (Imperial Wireless Telegraphy Committee, 1923, p. 5). Sturmey concluded (1958, p. 123) that a number of things probably influenced the committee's original recommendation: opposition to Marconi per se, pressure from cable companies, complacency with Britain's place at the center of the world's cable network, and the appearance of adequacy in the international system without radio.

22. N. W. Rowell, a Canadian delegate, complained that news was selected for transmission across the Atlantic "for the consumption of the American public rather than the Canadian." Sir Joseph Ward, from New Zealand, rued the fact "that we are so far distant from the pulse of the Empire," and said that the need for "cheap and rapid communication" had "impressed itself upon the people out there"; Pike Pease, from Canada, objected that 13 of the 14 cables between Britain and North America were controlled by United States companies, and argued for more empire unity (see Ollivier, 1954, Vol. 2, pp. 308,

319, 320, and 341). The 1918 conference concluded that wireless stations should link the empire (see pp. 403–404). These concerns did not abate during the interwar period. The *Report* of the Imperial Wireless Telegraphy Committee (1924, p. 2) claimed that "the people of the Dominions were also disappointed to find that news and propaganda matter reaching distant British possessions and Far Eastern countries came from foreign services and that visitors sailing from the Antipodes had to rely on foreign wireless for news, until ships came within range of the British stations." The same sentiments were expressed at the Colonial Conference in 1927 (see "Wireless Communications and Broadcasting," 1927).

23. By the mid-1920s Marconi had financial interests in 60 companies operating in 20 countries (Baker, 1970, p. 227).

24. Aitken suggests (1976, pp. 226–227) that the bad feelings that developed between the Post Office and Marconi due to the failure in 1897 to establish a government wireless monopoly continued to plague relations between these two organizations.

25. The listeners paid a licensing fee on radio sets purchased based on the number of "valves" (or tubes) used in the radio. An exemption provided for those who purchased valves for radio experimentation later caused difficulties, and was part of the rationale for moving to an annual license fee based on ownership alone.

26. The Indian government apparently did not appreciate the idea that the British Post Office would erect its station. As the Imperial Wireless Telegraphy Committee (1923, p. 11) explained, "The Indian authorities, prompted no doubt by Marconi interests, desire a larger station and appear to have some preference for Marconi operation."

27. The Post Office had pressed the idea that it should control all wireless stations within Britain, and allow private companies to con-

struct those in the dominions and colonies. In one memorandum to the postmaster general in 1923, R. M. (probably in the Admiralty) said bluntly that "one of the strongest arguments against a Marconi Station here [in Britain] is that it would consolidate the virtual monopoly which they would otherwise obtain."

28. This agreement came despite the fact that the Post Office long-wave station at Rugby was powerful enough to reach all portions of the Empire (see Sturmey, 1958, p. 115; and Baker, 1970, p. 214).

29. The station used, located at Chelmsford, was opened on November 27, 1927 *(The B.B.C. Handbook 1929,* 1929, p. 406).

30. P. P. Eckersley, chief engineer, BBC, told the Colonial Office Conference in 1927 (p. 8) that "they have just started a [shortwave] station in Holland. . . . The essential basis of world linking is the short wave, and in America and in Holland there are short-wave stations, and they are the ones which are being received in the Colonies and Dominions and elsewhere. Britain is not possessed of a short-wave station, and, therefore, cannot relay programmes." Eckersley did not recommend a shortwave service, however, because he could not guarantee its quality, although he did ask for an experimental service "because other people are forcing our hands."

31. This service followed experiments between stations in Essex, England, and Schenectady, New York, in 1927, and broadcasts from the London Naval Conference of 1930, which involved telephone, broadcast, and directional

wireless telegraphy links around the world to about 242 radio stations (see *The B.B.C. Year-Book 1931,* 1931, p. 121; British Broadcasting Corporation, 1931, p. 12; and "Empire Service Broadcasting," 1929a, p. 3).

32. While the United States complained about the British cable monopoly, the British Post Office argued that most North Atlantic cables were, in fact, controlled by U.S. companies (see "Cable and Wireless Communications of the Empire," 1923, p. 1; see also Ollivier, 1954, Vol. 3, p. 118).

33. The final protocol of the Prague conference was signed by 27 European administrations on April 13, 1929 *(B.B.C. Year-Book 1930,* 1930, pp. 357–358).

34. See also the Memorandum Prepared on Behalf of the Empire Press Union and the Newspaper Proprietors' Association (Ollivier, 1954, Vol. 2, pp. 455–456).

35. Similar concerns were raised in the Imperial Conference of 1926 regarding the lack of empire-originated films (see Ollivier, 1954, Vol. 3, pp. 174–175).

36. As Kent Cooper of the AP explained it (1942, p. 34), the French control of South America prevented AP from serving *La Nación,* even though AP knew that "the French Government wished to prevent so far as possible the dissemination of Germany's war claims abroad. Likewise the French Government refused to permit newspapers in France to permit them." It was control of information, pure and simple.

6

THE TRIUMPH OF INTERNATIONAL PROPAGANDA: 1933–1945

Introduction

World War I had thrown international communications systems into chaos. Following the war the imperial powers strained to respond to new demands from their colonies for fast and low-cost connection. Wireless and cable companies vied for market share or monopoly. Wire services struggled to dominate one another, and then formed a cartel to protect regional markets. Manufacturing companies combined to drive competitors out of business. The losing powers of the war suffered under the weight of reparations payments, a burden that increased when the world economy crashed in 1929. The League of Nations, formed as part of the peace plan put forth by President Woodrow Wilson, attempted to provide nonmilitary options for settling disputes among nations, but suffered for lack of participation from the United States,

the only major power in the world that had not suffered physical damage in the war. The Soviet Union began the process of building a new state while struggling against expeditionary forces sent from the West to put down the Bolsheviks.

In 1922 Benito Mussolini became premier of Italy and began to construct a Fascist state. The communications media became vehicles to assist Mussolini's remaking of Italy, along with pageantry, physical conditioning, and other efforts to recapture "the glory that was Rome." Ten years after taking power, Mussolini declared that Italy was "fascistised": The Fascists had brought trade unions under their banner, balanced the budget, expanded both agriculture and industry, begun modernization, and cut in half the balance of payments deficit. "The successes of the regime were trumpeted through a propaganda machine that helped ordinary

123

Italians to identify with the goals of the movement, and with Mussolini in particular. He became *il duce,* the leader. Loudspeakers in the streets relayed his speeches to his people" (Overy, 1989, p. 151).

Mussolini's party, and the National Socialists who took power in Germany at the beginning of 1933, believed in the power of mass persuasion, both to motivate their own people and to demoralize their enemies. Mussolini's and Hitler's rise to power in Italy and Germany, respectively, also came while radio was still in its infancy and its potential uses largely unknown. Both of these dictators were able to turn radio to their own political advantage, disseminating ideologies, creating and sustaining myths, castigating scapegoats, and building personality cults, all to mass audiences enamored with this new means of communication. Mussolini and Hitler could also distribute these elements of their respective political movements beyond the borders of Italy and Germany, and speak through radio to other peoples in their own languages. In the Far East, Japan could disseminate its views in like manner throughout Asia.

Developing ideologies, resurgent nationalism, and rising militarism thus combined to create havoc with efforts to put international communications systems back in order following the First World War. The world's countries made some progress in addressing human rights and the conduct of war, and were able to work toward mutually satisfactory agreements for sharing the electromagnetic spectrum, establishing standards for telecommunications, and creating an established international communications organization, the ITU. Rapid development of technology, however, allowed countries to make new uses of it. Countries pursued political and economic advantages using communications systems, particularly after 1932, that made continued

cooperation either naive or dangerous. Countries began to define their friends and enemies; communications systems were to become weapons of war again. This time, however, their role could be decisive. If the period 1835–1932 was a period of accommodation and cooperation, 1933 saw the beginnings of conflict and politicalization in the international communications system. In the former period communication had been a problem to be solved; in the latter it rapidly became a danger to be contained.

Continuing Development of the International Communications System: The 1930s

Despite the war clouds forming over the world after Hitler became chancellor of Germany, international communications systems continued to develop. Commercial interests propelled the systems forward as companies continued to vie for market shares, patent new techniques and apply them to new services. The airwaves became more crowded as both commercial and state-owned broadcasters continued to go on the air. The growing tension in the world also suggested the necessity for redoubling efforts to link countries and empires together in preparation for war.

Commercial Developments

The Marconi Company, following the loss of its wireless network in the amalgamation that created Cable and Wireless Ltd., continued to build broadcasting stations around the world. By 1936 it had put more than 180 stations on the air in 32 countries ("Forty Years of Wireless," 1936, p. 3).

One of Marconi's main competitors, RCA, had consolidated a patent pool in the United States that, by the mid-1930s, controlled over 4,000 patents. This formidable barrier to competition was copied by companies in other countries and resulted in a "neat" division of the "world market for radio into distinct national markets, each ruled by the parties operating there" (Mirow & Maurer, 1982, p. 45).

This development was not necessarily a positive one for the international system, but other trends were more promising. By 1934 facsimile telegraphy made it possible for photographs to be "wirelessed" between Europe, North America, and Australia. Late that same year Cable and Wireless was able to fax motion picture film using Marconi wireless technology (Baker, 1970, p. 254; see also "Forty Years of Wireless," 1936, p. 3).

The British Imperial System

The British continued to develop communications as a means to unite the empire over the decade preceding World War II. Between 1929 and 1939 Imperial and International Communications Ltd. (part of Cables and Wireless Ltd.)[1] opened 60 new services, all of them routed so that cross-communication had to pass through London. This consolidated control of the system and increased its value at the outbreak of war. When war came, however, it was necessary to establish direct services that bypassed London, particularly between the United States and British colonies and dominions (Sturmey, 1958, p. 132).

The BBC's permanent external service made its maiden broadcast on December 19, 1932, in English, aimed at Australia and New Zealand, the most remote outposts of the British Empire. The broadcast opened with a message from J. H. Whitley, chair-

man of the BBC Board of Governors, who said, "This wireless, one of the greatest gifts of Providence to mankind, is a trust of which we are humble ministers. Our prayer is that nothing mean or cheap may lessen its value, and its message may bring happiness and comfort to those who listen" (quoted in Mansell, 1982, p. 2). This statement reaffirmed the idea of "public service broadcasting," which had been adopted as the original justification for the BBC. Here it carried into the international arena.

Following Whitley, Sir John Reith, director-general of the BBC, spoke (see Boyle, 1972, or Milner, 1983, for Reith's biography). He affirmed Whitley's remarks and presaged the difficulties that international shortwave radio was entering. Radio was, he said,

> an instrument of almost incalculable importance in the social and political life of the community. Its influence will more and more be felt in the daily life of the individual in almost every sphere of human activity, in affairs national and international. Now it becomes a connecting and coordinating link between the scattered parts of the British Empire. . . . The service as a whole is dedicated to the best interests of mankind. (quoted in Mansell, 1982, p. 2)

The BBC motto, adopted several years before the inauguration of the international service, was "Nation shall speak peace unto Nation."

On Christmas Day, 1932, the BBC prevailed on King George V to address the nation and the empire over its facilities. Thus, the dream of an empire radio service, which had surfaced briefly in 1913 and again in the Colonial Conferences of 1927 and 1930, came to pass.[2] In the early years, however, the audiences in the United States seemed largest of all, if the quantity of mail received by the BBC was any indication. The BBC would not inaugurate detailed audience research for many years (Mansell, 1982, p. 23).

The Empire Service carried programs in rotation destined for particular areas of the world. The daily programs for each area consisted of 2-hour blocks, beamed consecutively to Australia and New Zealand, India, East and southern Africa, West Africa, and Canada and the West Indies (also heard in the United States). The BBC discovered, however, that people did not necessarily listen to the block directed to them, but often heard other blocks at different times of the day, all of which were in English. This fact had a significant impact. As Mansell (1982) explained,

> It strengthened the BBC's resolve to speak only with one voice. Whatever regional emphasis was placed on any particular programme it could never be at the expense of overall consistency since it had to be assumed that it was likely to be heard almost everywhere. Thus not only did it come naturally to the BBC, as a matter of fundamental policy, to deal with its listeners with unwavering honesty, but it was also made imperative by the technical characteristics of short wave broadcasting. (p. 24)

From the outset the BBC kept track of its impact throughout the empire. It submitted a report to the Ullswater Broadcasting Committee in 1935 (set up to examine the issue of renewing the BBC's charter) indicating that it had received 11,250 letters and listeners' reports in 1933, 13,500 in 1934, and 12,800 during the first 17 weeks of 1935. It also noted that 65% of these had come from the United States, and 35% from the empire (Ullswater Broadcasting Committee, 1935, Paper No. 134).[3] It reported, too, that its programs were regularly rebroadcast by stations in Ceylon (Sri Lanka), India, Australia, Kenya, South Africa, and New Zealand—all areas that were part of the empire.

The Ullswater Broadcasting Committee, in its final report (1936, p. 36), noted that it attached "great importance to the maintenance and development of the Empire Service." Its conclusion was in accord with the position of the General Advisory Council of the BBC, as well as BBC management (Ullswater Broadcasting Committee, 1935, Paper No. 93, p. 5; see also *B.B.C. Annual 1937*, 1937, p. 131).

By the mid-1930s, then, Britain had again succumbed to the mythos of communication. Radio annihilated time and space; it bound the empire together.[4] Shortwave, according to one writer, "verily put a girdle around the earth" (Hunter, 1935, p. 136). As one British colonial administrator put it, the tribesmen of northwest India had received the BBC "with astonishment," and had named radio "with a native word meaning 'speech from Heaven.' I have never heard any listener in this country talk of the B.B.C.'s programmes as 'speech from Heaven'" (Strabolgi, 1935, p. 140).

By the late 1930s the BBC saw its task in somewhat less glorified terms. Its 1937 *B.B.C. Annual* (pp. 134–135) noted that "the general growth of short-wave broadcasting all over the world has been most marked, and the factor of world rivalry among the many nations now operating services cannot be lightly disregarded in considering the development of the Empire Service—as the voice, not of Britain only, but of the British Empire."[5]

The Crowded European Airwaves

The airwaves of Europe continued to become more crowded, too, as both new state and new commercial broadcasters took to the airwaves. One British radio magazine reported in 1932 that listeners should be able to hear, on long- and medium-wave bands, the following: Radios Barcelona and Catalana (Spain), Radios Cologne and Langenberg (Germany), Eiffel Tower and Radios Paris and Toulouse (France), Radio Hilversum (the Netherlands), Radio Katowice (Poland), Radios Milano, Roma, and Turin (Italy), Radios Stockholm and Motala (Sweden), Radio Prague (Czechoslovakia), and Radio Vienna (Austria) ("Radio Station Identification Guide," 1932, p. 2). This list only included stations where listeners could find popular entertainment programming and thus excluded most state broadcasters. By 1935 British citizens could also tune in to Italian medium-wave stations from Naples, Florence, Bolzano, and Trieste ("Italia on the Air!" 1935, p. 261). Even German stations received praise from Britain's *Radio Magazine*.[6]

The increase in commercially sponsored radio stations in Europe added to these numbers. A number of stations outside Britain began to broadcast in English with advertising support from British companies that could not use the BBC. Radio Luxembourg (1933), Radio Normandie (1934), Radio Lyons (1936), Radio Toulouse (1937), and Radio Athlone (Ireland) all carried English language programs, as did other stations for at least short periods of time (see Vinogradoff, 1945).[7] Such activities, many of which were sponsored by the International Broadcasting Company that operated from London, led to a series of protests from the BBC through the British Post Office to the governments of various countries, and to the International Radio Union (which represented various European broadcasting administrations). Some of the broadcasts eventually ceased, but several were silenced only by Hitler's aggression.[8] Radio Norman-

die, forced off the air on January 3, 1940, managed to return to the air using an aging transmitter in Fécamp, calling itself Radio International during the day, and the Czech Freedom Station or Austrian Freedom Station after 8:00 P.M. Eventually it, too, was silenced (see Plomley, 1980, pp. 166–167, 1972; and Briggs, 1970, pp. 126–127).

Still other broadcasters adding to the European mix during this period were Radio Sweden (1938), Radio Andorra (1939), Radio Vaduz (1939), and Radio Monte Carlo (1943). Radio Vaduz was sponsored by the British government and operated from Liechtenstein, but the principality withdrew authority for the station after a short time because the German government said "it regarded the activities of Radio Vaduz as a source of political irritation" (Lindahl, 1978, p. 83).

U.S. broadcasting organizations were also active in Europe. They could reach Europe via shortwave and also provided programs, or sponsored them, on continental stations broadcasting to Britain (see Vinogradoff, 1945, pp. 34–35).[9] The BBC, which had cooperated with RCA in transatlantic radio experiments, persuaded NBC and CBS not to cooperate with Radio Luxembourg in July 1934. U.S. programs continued to be carried, however, and CBS explained to the BBC that "it could not prevent direct negotiations with its clients such as the 'March of Time' sponsors": CBS itself did not own all its own programming (Vinogradoff, 1945, p. 36).

Japanese International Broadcasting

Nippon Hoso Kyokai (NHK), the Japanese Broadcasting Corporation, began its international radio activities by broadcasting to Machoukuo (Manchuria), Formosa (Taiwan), and Chosen (Korea) in 1935 (see Ryō, 1983, p. 319). These broadcasts also reached both North and South America, Hawaii, and Australia. By mid-1935 NHK was broadcasting an "overseas" program designed for Japanese citizens living abroad. This 1-hour program included news in Japanese and English, music, entertainment, lectures, and the Japanese national anthem (Ullswater Broadcasting Committee, 1935, Paper No. 89). By 1941 NHK was broadcasting in 16 languages, for a total of nearly 25 hours daily. By November 1943 the Japanese were broadcasting in 24 languages over three transmitters for over 32 hours daily (Ryō, 1983, p. 320). A committee composed of members of Japan's army, navy, and Foreign, Home, Great Asian, and Communications ministries, along with representatives from NHK and the Dōmei news agency, controlled NHK's wartime broadcasts (Ryō, 1983, p. 322).

6.3

The "Radio War" in the 1930s

Battle Lines of the Radio War

The Soviet Union apparently was the first country to employ radio as an offensive weapon in a conflict with another state, using it against Romania in 1926 in a dispute over Bessarabia (Bumpus & Skelt, 1984, p. 10). Radio Moscow went on the air in 1929, and by 1930 the Soviet Union had grasped the significance of broadcasting in foreign languages (Bumpus & Skelt, 1984, p. 12). Almost immediately complaints came to the British Foreign Office about the broadcasts, which were, according to one letter to the Foreign Office, "in English and urging Revolution repeatedly" (quoted by West, 1987, p. 22).

Although Germany also began broadcasting in 1929, it limited its broadcasts at first to its own nationals living abroad or to German-born nationals of other countries (particularly the United States), a pattern followed by Italy's foreign broadcasts, which began in 1930. With the inauguration of the British Empire Service in 1932, the "radio war" that erupted in the mid-1930s by these ideological adversaries became a possibility. Germany and Italy were ideological allies, with both the Soviet Union and Great Britain in opposition, although from differing ideological perspectives.[10]

The Soviet Union and Nazi Germany began propaganda broadcasts attacking each other following the National Socialist election victory in 1933 and the establishment of the Third Reich (see Lukes, 1988, pp. 79–81). By that time both the Soviets and the Nazis had had opportunity to test propaganda strategies on their own people, and the Soviet Union had even begun a permanent "politically ideological" program service in 1929 (Browne, 1982, pp. 49–50). The Nazis had used propaganda to good effect during the 1920s as they struggled for power, adopting a multifaceted appeal that included anti-Semitic and anti-Bolshevik diatribes. Many characterized the Jews as the scapegoats of Germany's misfortunes, both for losing the First World War and for the economic deprivations that followed it (see Bytwerk, 1983).[11] Others emphasized the need to restore Germany's greatness and Hitler's ability to accomplish it.

Nazi Initiation of the Radio War

The "radio war" began when the National Socialists (Nazis) took over Germany in 1933. The Nazi government established a *Propagandaministerium* to coordinate its activities. Both Hitler and Goebbels believed that radio could stir their own population to sacrifice for a greater Germany and to discourage Germany's enemies. Goebbels claimed that "real broadcasting is true propaganda. Propaganda means fighting on all battlefields of the spirit, generating, multiplying, destroying, exterminating, building and undoing. Our propaganda is determined by what we call German race, blood and nation" (quoted in Hale, 1975, p. 2). And, as Martin (1980, pp. 274–275) has argued, radio "was the ideal instrumentality of the international propagandist. With the invention of radio and the cheap wireless receiver, the international propagandist could address himself to a receptive audience without fear of his own physical detention or of the censorship of his message."

By 1935 both Nazi Germany and Mussolini's Fascist state in Italy were broadcasting a constant barrage of aggressive messages into Europe, North Africa, and the Americas. They aimed either to whip up support for their causes or to discourage interference with their plans, mainly by undermining British and French influence in North Africa and the Middle East through appeals to Arab national sentiments. It was the Italian broadcasts into North Africa that prompted the BBC to begin foreign language broadcasting and, after the beginning of the war, to expand its language services and to initiate a department to provide "intelligence reports" about the nature of the propaganda that was being broadcast to other countries.[12] In 1941, for instance, one of these reports summarized German propaganda broadcasts to the United States during February (several months before U.S. entry into the war). This report observed, among other things, the following:

> Almost every day the U.S.A. was told that her intervention had been made too late. The guarantors of England's doom are the German air force and the German submarines.
>
> Terrible pictures were drawn of life in English slums and these were contrasted with conditions in Germany. The wretched lot of British working class children was also stressed. Social service organisations make it impossible in Germany for any child to live in need. "That is the practical Christianity of the new Germany — of the Nazis." It is the Nazi creed itself and not merely the natural German way of life that is identical with Christianity. "Germans *today* live closer to Our Lord's rule than *ever before*."
>
> Berlin admits that most Americans now hate Germany. This antipathy is attributed to Anglo-Jewish lies and propaganda. When, some time in the future, Jews have been expelled from the U.S. the American and German people may understand each other better. They have much in common and are the youngest and most vitally promising nations today.
>
> That Germany has no designs outside Europe came to the fore again towards the end of the month. . . . After the war, Germany and America will be the two big countries and their interests will be complementary to one another. (BBC Overseas Intelligence Department, 1941a, pp. 4–5).

Both Hitler and Goebbels believed, as Hale put it, that propaganda should be aimed at the masses, that appeal to the emotions (both to subvert and create faith) was central, and that there was no need to tell the truth. Lying was, to Goebbels, a tactical weapon; Hitler believed in the "big lie," a lie based on tactical truths but made into a lie by interpretation (Hale, 1975, chapter 2).[13] The "first targets" of external Nazi broadcasts were the *Volksdeutsche* (German people) living abroad, particularly in Austria, which was to be the site of the *Anschluss* (annexation) in 1938 (see Zeman, 1973, pp. 50–51).

By 1934 the Germans were broadcasting in foreign languages to Asia, Africa, and

South America, in addition to North America. By the end of 1935 they were broadcasting on seven frequencies in German, English, Spanish, Portuguese, and Dutch (Bumpus & Skelt, 1984, p. 18). In 1936, during the Berlin Olympics, the Nazis broadcast commentaries in 25 languages; by 1938 their international output had climbed to 5,124 hours (Bumpus & Skelt, 1984, p. 19).

Nazi broadcasts were notorious for their propaganda content. Martin (1980, p. 280) claims that Nazi Germany itself was "essentially the product of propaganda: it was the first country to develop an effective worldwide propaganda organization, and it put tremendous resources into its unique propaganda organization" (Kenez, 1985, p. 1, argues, however, that the Soviet Union was the first "propaganda state," and introduced "a new approach to politics"). Even the early pre-Nazi broadcasts to the United States were designed to elicit sympathy from German-Americans for the plight of the country suffering under the war reparation requirements imposed at the end of World War I. After the Nazis took power, the broadcasts were more pointed, directed at keeping the United States out of the conflict in Europe by putting indirect pressure on the U.S. government through the large German-American population.

Nazi and Fascist propaganda flowed worldwide through a variety of channels. In Germany and Italy public addresses and rallies, print media, and film were used in addition to radio and loud-speakers (see Hay, 1987, Ellwood, 1983, and Rondolino, 1983, concerning Italy's use of film as propaganda; see Brady, 1937, chapter 3, concerning Germany's use of the arts; see Welch, 1983, on Nazi newsreel propaganda; see Kershaw, 1983, "Introduction," for discussion of the Nazi *Weltanschauung;* see Golomstock, 1990, chapter 3, on Nazi art; and see Strebel, 1983, on film propaganda

by the Vichy government in France). International radio carried the message abroad, and people in other countries who sympathized with these causes picked up the themes, slogans, symbols, and stereotypes characteristic of Axis propaganda, and used them in their own publications. The effect of the propaganda thus spread internationally through domestic publication in many other countries.

The United States was not immune to such tactics. NBC, for instance, eventually removed Father Charles Coughlin of the "Shrine of the Little Flower" from his Sunday evening time slot on American network radio for his sympathetic remarks about fascism. Also, William Dudley Pelley formed an organization modeled on the Nazi brownshirts (called the "silvershirts") and published *Pelley's Weekly,* a newspaper that claimed in 1936 that the governor of Minnesota, who had been "raised" and "surrounded by Jews," was attempting to make that state "the first Communistic political unit in the American union," and later that a revolution aimed at "setting up an open Jewish dictatorship" was only "a matter of months away and maybe only weeks" ("Minnesota Close to Red Abyss," 1936; "Silvershirts Instructed to Prepare," 1936). Fritz Kuhn, too, began a similar organization, the German-American Bund.

The British Response to Fascist Radio

The Italians joined the radio war in 1935, "attacking British Mideast policies in . . . [their] Arabic broadcasts to the Middle East from Radio Bari" (Browne, 1982, p. 50).[14] This caused the British government to begin to rethink its external broadcasting policy, specifically the issue of allowing the BBC to engage in foreign language broadcasting. Finally, in 1938, the BBC inaugurated foreign language services, beginning with Arabic in January, then Spanish and Portuguese to Latin America in March, and, following the Munich crisis in September, German, French, and Italian (see Bumpus & Skelt, 1984, p. 27; Mansell, 1982, chapter 3; or Browne, 1982, p. 50).[15] "By the summer of 1939," Bumpus and Skelt wrote (1984, p. 31), "some twenty-five countries were broadcasting internationally in foreign languages. Most were European with the United States, China, Japan, and Australia. The only Latin American country to have an international service was Brazil which broadcast in English and Spanish as well as Portuguese." U.S.-based broadcasts were still commercial, unlike the others, which were government-funded or -directed. U.S. propaganda was therefore more "commercial" than "political."

When World War II began in 1939, Nazi Germany was broadcasting in the most foreign languages, 26, followed by its ideological ally, Italy, with 23. Allied services included the French with 21 languages, the Soviet Union with "around thirteen," and the BBC with 10 (Bumpus & Skelt, 1984, p. 31). Nazi broadcasts quickly jumped from 26 to 39 languages at the outset of the war (see Grandin, 1939, for an analysis of international broadcasting a few weeks prior to the onset of World War II; see also White, 1939).

British and Nazi Foreign Language Broadcasting

The principal assumption that underlay this "radio war" was that foreign language broadcasting was propaganda simply because it provided programs in a language other than a country's native tongue. This was the main issue in the British debate over the propriety of such services.[16] The decisions of governments to begin foreign

language services, then, can be seen as conscious attempts to use radio as a propaganda tool, even if the decisions were couched in other terms, such as the desire to respond to an adversary's propaganda.[17] The approach of the belligerents to the medium of radio, however, was fundamentally different.

In 1935 Fascist Italy began broadcasting in Arabic into the Middle East, a politically sensitive region for the British, and an area on which Mussolini had military designs. This led quickly to discussions within the BBC, and between it and the British government, on a proper response to an emerging threat. No action was taken, however, until 1937 when the BBC sought Parliamentary approval to begin foreign language broadcasts to counteract Nazi and Fascist propaganda. On January 3, 1938, the BBC inaugurated its first foreign broadcast service, in Arabic, also directed into the Middle East and North Africa. This broadcast began with a story about the execution of an Arab for carrying a concealed weapon that "proved to be the most famous and perhaps the most controversial in the history" of the BBC (Partner, 1988, p. 17). Although the broadcast caused consternation in the British Foreign Office, which feared such broadcasts would incite rebellion in the region, it also contributed significantly to the BBC's prestige as a service that would tell the truth, even when it hurt (see Partner, 1988, pp. 17–22, for a discussion of this broadcast).

Two months after this initial broadcast the BBC began services to Latin America in Spanish and Portuguese. Following the Munich crisis later that year, the British added programming in German, French, and Italian.

After the Foreign Office objected that BBC news would inflame passions in the Middle East against the British involvement (following the first BBC broadcast in Arabic), the BBC agreed only to hold "regular consultations" with the Foreign Office to hear its position on controversial issues (see Partner, 1988, pp. 17–22). As Lord Reith had earlier explained the BBC position,

> the effect of a news service carried out by the BBC in any language would be based on telling the truth. Prestige depended on truthful and comprehensive broadcasts. People should feel that because they have heard a statement on the British wireless it was correct; and conversely that if it was not included in the British broadcasts it was incorrect. (quoted in Mansell, 1982, pp. 50–51).

Reith's opinion contrasted sharply with that of Goebbels, the Nazi propaganda chief, and his allies. Hadamovsky and Raskin, two of the early organizers of Germany's overseas broadcasting service, both claimed that true broadcasting was propaganda (Sington & Weidenfeld, 1943, p. 139). Goebbels himself asserted, "News is a weapon of war. Its purpose is to wage war and not to give out information" (quoted in Hale, 1975, p. 10).

It would be easy to suggest that, because the Nazis thought of their broadcasts as propaganda while the British did not, the Nazis were propagandists and the British weren't. Such a conclusion, however, would be too facile.[18] Ellul, for instance, would conclude that both were propaganda. Propaganda, he argued (1965, pp. 118, 139), was not just the work of "evil men, seducers of the people, cheats and authoritarian rulers," but also included approaches to people taken in "all civilized countries." Others would assert that the efforts of the Nazis were so blatantly manipulative, so obviously an effort to deny choice to their listeners, that they must be understood as propaganda. The British broadcasts, by contrast, with their emphasis on accuracy and dispassionate reporting—despite the military setbacks of the early war years—should escape the opprobrium of such a label.

If both are propaganda, they are certainly of two different sorts. Ellul would refer to them as "black" and "white." The British approach (white propaganda) was based on the dissemination of unvarnished truth, the Nazi (black) on the strategic use of lies or the selective presentation of truth.[19] While the end sought in each case was similar, winning the battle for people's minds and thus the war, the choice of tactics was crucial to the distinctions drawn.

British Monitoring Services

After a series of complaints from members of Parliament, the BBC, British listeners, and the Post and Foreign Offices about Soviet propaganda broadcasts, the British government established a monitoring service in 1930. This service reported in 1938, for instance, that the Soviet shortwave services had begun to broadcast "war songs, which listeners all over Russia are learning to sing, at the rate of one new song a week" ("Russia's Martial Music," 1938).[20]

To conduct the radio war many countries found it necessary to monitor and analyze one another's broadcasts.[21] Shortly after inaugurating its German, French, and Italian broadcasts in 1938, the BBC began examining the situation created by its foray into "propaganda." M. A. Frost circulated a memo (1938) saying that "in view of the reorganisation of the Empire Programme Department and the assumption by heads of Home Programme Departments for responsibility for Empire programmes, it is now highly desirable for this Department to pay greater attention to the analysis of Empire correspondence and press reaction." Sir S. G. Tallents suggested (1939) that "the monitoring and digesting of foreign broadcasts is likely to prove the most important source about the outside world in the present War." Although this suggestion was not taken up immediately, in 1940 recommendations were made to establish an "Empire Intelligence Service" that would provide "reliable information" for BBC external programming. This information was to be obtained by using "intelligence representatives" in each broadcasting area, "scientific audience research," and "'intake' reports from the Propaganda Research Section." All these sources were "vitally necessary if we are to compete successfully with our opponent." These recommendations recognized, too, the strength of the adversary, continuing,

> We are up against an opposition which has been studying the power of ideas for the last fifteen years and exploiting that power to its own ends, which has spared no effort and no expense for the last seven years in order to perfect its technique, and which as a result has already reaped an enormous harvest. We simply cannot afford to let our opponents' machinery and technique be better than our own, nor is there any reason why we should if once we realise the power of ideas if properly used is greater than the power of all the armed forces in the world and if we then act accordingly. (British Broadcasting Corporation, 1940, p. 2)

The eventual result was the creation of this service and the publication of "Monthly Intelligence Reports" on different regions, including Europe and the "Empire Countries and the U.S.A." In 1941 one of these reports on Europe suggested the importance that the BBC had in the British war effort: "Germany's second Spring campaign may have fallen short of its objectives, but it has driven Britain out of Europe once more, so that broadcasting is Great Britain's only bridgehead in Europe—a bridgehead held

not in a corner of Europe but in a corner of many million Europeans" (British Broadcasting Corporation, 1941b, p. 1).

Nazi Propaganda

As BBC reports suggested, Axis propagandists were skilled, having had the opportunity to practice their craft for many years. The first Nazi use of radio as a propaganda weapon against an external foe had been against Austria in 1933. The following year Germany had launched a "systematic propaganda campaign" to the Saarland, aimed at influencing the plebiscite on the future of the Saar scheduled to occur in 1935.[22]

> The local Nationalist Socialist circle of listeners looked after the supply of the *Volksempfanger,* cheap [people's] receivers produced in Germany; in the months between January 1934 and April 1935 some 4,000 sets were distributed in the Saarland, and the number of listeners went up from 28,000 to 40,000. In addition, the National Socialist listeners' associations organized community listening to transmissions of important party events; about fifty such meetings were organized during the Saar campaign, and the total of listeners attending meetings throughout the area often exceeded 100,000. . . .
>
> There can be no doubt that broadcasting played the decisive role in the success of the National Socialist campaign. The Germans were of course unlikely to lose the plebiscite: but they would never have one by such a clear majority without an effective propaganda campaign. (Zeman, 1973, pp. 51, 53)

In 1938 Hitler himself defined the propaganda aspects of the impending assault on Czechoslovakia:

> Propaganda warfare must on the one hand intimidate the Czechs by means of threats and wear down their power of resistance; and on the other hand it must give the national racial

groups indications as to how to support our military operations and influence the neutrals in our favor. Further instructions and determination of the appropriate moment are reserved to me. (quoted in Delfiner, 1974, p. 5)

Nazi propaganda was multifaceted.[23] The Nazis used it both in specific campaigns, such as those already mentioned, and as part of the broader effort to appeal to potential allies, to maintain order in occupied areas during the war, to demoralize their enemies and castigate enemy leaders for the benefit of third parties, and to pin blame for the war and wartime suffering on their enemies. They also used it to justify Nazi actions, to deny sympathy for Nazi victims, and to portray the Jews as parasitic nonhumans who deserved the Nazi "final solution." As Baird wrote (1974, p. 7), "Although public mention of the 'final solution' was avoided, every means short of an announcement of the mass liquidations were taken to prepare the nation psychologically for the fait accompli." Nazi propaganda was simple and repetitive. It used a few themes, adopted slogans that could be easily reproduced on posters or used as guidelines for newspapers and radio programs, and concentrated on emotional appeals, such as loyalty to the fatherland or führer, the need for sacrifice to win the war, and so on (see Research and Analysis Reports, 1942c, for a comparative analysis of propaganda themes from Germany, Italy, Japan, and the United States during the war; see also Cruickshank, 1981).[24]

One major figure of German radio propaganda aimed at Britain was "Lord Haw-Haw." His real name was William Joyce, but Jonah Barrington of the London newspaper *Daily Express* gave him the name "Haw-Haw" on September 18, 1939 (Barrington, n.d., p. 9). One British member of Parliament told a news reporter in 1940 that "radio listeners are believing a lot of what Haw-Haw says," and suggested that the BBC reply "each night to Haw-Haw, pointing out to the British people the lies he has been spreading" ("M.P. Wants an Answer to Haw-Haw," 1940). But the BBC's response, based on a "superficial study of several hundred spontaneous comments on the German broadcasts," was that most British listeners regarded Haw-Haw as "entertainment" (Silvey, 1940).

Audience research did indicate to the BBC, however, that Haw-Haw had a following, particularly among lower income citizens. In light of the statistics, Briggs says, "it is not surprising that the BBC decided deliberately to switch some of its most popular programmes to the period immediately after the 9 o'clock news" when Haw-Haw was on the air (Briggs, 1970, p. 149; see also pp. 140–159). Barrington claimed that, although Joyce's early broadcasts into Britain were "pure poison," once the name "Haw-Haw" had stuck, "however cleverly he may twist his news (and he can be very clever at times) you can't take it seriously when you remember him as 'Lord Haw-Haw of Zeesen'" (quoted in Briggs, 1970, p. 149). The British convicted Joyce, an Irish nationalist, of treason at the conclusion of the war (see also Rolo, 1942, chapter 6, or West, 1985, chapter 8, for a discussion of Haw-Haw).

Other important Axis propaganda figures ("renegade Americans") broadcasting to the United States from Germany were "Paul Revere," Jane Anderson, and Fred Kallenbach (introduced as "Lord Hee-Haw"), and from Italy, Ezra Pound. None of them had the "billing" of Haw-Haw, however (see Research and Analysis Reports, 1942c, pp. 21–22, 24; and Shirer, 1943).

Each program in the Nazi broadcasts to the United States, as Rolo put it (1942, p. 95), was designed to put across "one single idea; only the simplest reasoning is used and long terms are laboriously elucidated. All arguments are vividly connected with Americana." The broadcasts were transmitted by "a motley crew of men and women, some fanatics, some frustrated, embittered misfits — the counterparts of Berlin's British and French radio traitors — only too willing to sell their American accent and knowledge of American life for Nazi ration cards" (Rolo, 1942, p. 96).

Japanese Propaganda

Belligerents in the Pacific theater of the war also used propaganda. *Newsweek* reported in 1942 ("U.S. Takes Over Short Waves") that

> immediately after Pearl Harbor the Japanese radio beamed a propaganda barrage at the Philippines. Gen. Douglas MacArthur urgently asked for American programs to combat those of the Tokyo stations. We had the programs, but the problem was to get them on the air. KGEI, San Francisco, tried to broadcast; Japan effectively jammed the wave length. Apparently, no other American facilities were available to do the job. As a makeshift, the government finally leased three RCA transmitters on the West Coast which were used for telephonic communications. These were put into service, beamed at the Philippines, and the programs were rebroadcast in the islands. (p. 30)

The Japanese, like their German and Italian allies, had become adept at using propaganda during the 1930s (see Research and Analysis Reports, 1944). Japanese propaganda conducted using Tokyo Radio, the Dōmei News Agency, and the Japanese press was credited with helping deceive both America and Britain in the months preceding the attack on Pearl Harbor (see De Mendelssohn, 1944, p. 9). The Japanese also used propaganda effectively to "soften up" points of resistance in their consolida-

tion of power in the Pacific in the early years of World War II, and to help pacify their conquered territories, all with little interference from the Allies, who were unprepared to fight a propaganda war in the Pacific theater (see De Mendelssohn, 1944, p. 11). The Japanese first directed their propaganda against Britain, "which was considered Japan's greatest opponent," but later against both the United States and the Netherlands, which controlled the Dutch East Indies (Netherlands East Indies Government, 1942, p. 35).

Japanese propaganda was an important strategy in the period between the invasion of Manchuria in 1931 and the attack on Pearl Harbor a decade later. Although both Japan and China directed propaganda toward neutral countries to enlist their sympathy, the Japanese efforts, in hindsight, were more important. Japanese propaganda directed toward the United States emphasized the trade relations between the two countries, used fear appeals as well as those that offered hope for "international harmony," and attempted to identify Japan's approach to Asia with America's Monroe Doctrine for the Americas (see Lasker & Roman, 1938, pp. 35–58).

Naokichi Horikawa of *Asahi*, a Tokyo newspaper, explained Japan's approach to propaganda in a speech. It was, he said, "to promote good feeling and co-operation" among allies, to justify to neutral countries "the sincerity of one's own country in making war," and "to enlist the support of the peoples in occupied regions and induce them to share the prosperity of one's own country" in areas where war was being waged (quoted in De Mendelssohn, 1944, p. 13). Japan's two main propaganda themes were aimed at inducing other Asian peoples to join in their "Greater East Asiatic Co-Prosperity Sphere," by ending "Anglo-American hegemony" in Asia. The principal slogan adopted was "Asia for the Asiatics" (see De Mendelssohn, 1944, pp. 133–143).

Japanese propaganda also denied that it was propaganda, denouncing the "mischievous uses of propaganda devices by their opponents" (Lasker & Roman, 1938, p. 94). Some Japanese authors even complained that Japan "was ignorant of the value of propaganda" and "inept in presenting her case to the world." This was traceable, one writer said, to the fact that the Japanese "have not been mentally trained in the art of propagandizing but were taught on the contrary, that even presenting one's case by word of mouth amounted to superfluity" (quoted in Lasker & Roman, 1938, p. 95).

6.4

Broadcasting During World War II

British Broadcasting

When the British Expeditionary Force deployed in France in 1939, the BBC began a special broadcast to the troops (General Post Office, n.d.). The BBC struggled to define the nature of this alternative program, and ultimately concluded that its decidedly sabbatarian approach to Sunday programming should not be followed in broadcasts to the troops, who were in "special circumstances" (Briggs, 1970, p. 132). By May 1940 BBC Listener Research reported that "there is no doubt that the Programme for the Forces is immensely popular" (Briggs, 1970, p. 136). The program proved to be equally popular with British civilians as well.

In its international service to other countries, the BBC took the position that the best antidote to Axis propaganda was to tell the truth. Its first Arabic language broadcast epitomized this strategy. In that instance, as Mansell (1982, p. 53) put it, the Foreign Office did not "appear to appreciate the danger to the BBC's credibility of omitting uncomfortable items of news which other hostile radio stations might be making much of. It was a lesson which Whitehall was to learn the hard way in the first two years of the war."

Britain did engage in propaganda, however, although it was reluctant to admit it. Britain not only allowed transmitters on British soil to be used by governments in exile, but also became masters of "black" propaganda: "Not only was the [propaganda] work secret, it was not even recognized by the government. The government was not responsible for it, and yet it was carried out by a government department" (Bennett, 1966, p. 218).

U.S. Broadcasting

By 1933 the U.S. expectation that international shortwave radio had a commercial future had ended: "American shortwave broadcasting did not fill any conceivable function or role in the commercial broadcasting system, nor did it offer any special advantages to the companies with shortwave transmitters. Indeed, it seemed that the shortwave activities were beginning to become a burden" (Fejes, 1986, p. 59). Nevertheless, William Paley, who headed CBS, did appear to be interested in continuing activities in Latin America. Although Paley turned down an offer to become coordinator of inter-American affairs for Franklin Roosevelt, he did pursue the idea of signing up Latin American affiliates for CBS. "'Our plan,' Paley said, 'was to offer these network affiliates exclusive rights to rebroadcast free of charge our Latin American programs created by a special program department in [the United States]; they in turn would build up programs for retransmission throughout the U.S., thus affording a true exchange rather than a one-sided dumping of cultural achievement and ideas.'" He intended that this service be commercially funded (Paper, 1987, p. 80).

U.S. manufacturers had begun to have some success in promoting their products abroad by buying time on foreign stations in the mid-1930s. Radio Luxembourg grossed $1 million from U.S. firms in 1935; U.S. commercial interests began buying time in Shanghai; and companies such as Parker, Quaker, Standard Oil, and Ford, among others, had advertisements on 47 radio stations in 16 Latin American and Caribbean countries (Fejes, 1986, p. 84). U.S. stations were still denied the right to sell commercial time, however. In Europe in 1935 the BBC was so concerned about U.S.-sponsored programs broadcast to the United Kingdom from Radio Luxembourg that it attempted to have them stopped (Vinogradoff, 1945, pp. 34, 35). The BBC also pressed the U.S. networks, CBS and NBC, not to cooperate with Radio Luxembourg, but this did not stop the supply of programs or advertisements, since these were often controlled by advertisers themselves, not the networks (Vinogradoff, 1945, p. 36) By 1937 the BBC concluded that shortwave broadcasting had grown so rapidly throughout the world, and had become such a source of "world rivalry," that it could not be avoided in discussions about developing an "Empire Service" (B.B.C. Annual 1937, 1937, pp. 134, 135). Much of this development was sponsored by commercial interests.

In 1939 five U.S. broadcasting organizations—NBC, CBS, Westinghouse, General Electric, and Crossley—controlled 38 stations using international shortwave frequencies. Their programming consisted largely of rebroadcasts of domestic material, including commercials. On June 1, 1939, the FCC changed course and lifted the restriction that had prevented the two U.S. networks from actually selling commercial time on their international programs (it had denied earlier requests from CBS and NBC to allow such sales). United Fruit became the first U.S. international advertising customer, purchasing time from NBC for commercials broadcast to South America (Barnouw, 1968, p. 128). NBC and CBS subsequently set up program interchanges with affiliates in Latin America (Deihl, 1977, p. 9; see also Fejes, 1986, pp. 116–120). In 1941 General Electric also began to include advertising directed specifically to foreign audiences. This commercial activity was short-lived, however, as the U.S. government, by executive order, assumed control of private shortwave stations on March 7, 1942 (see Fejes, 1983; and Schwoch, 1990). This act created a network known as the Voice of America (VOA) (Green, 1988, p. 16; see also Shulman, 1990, chapter 3). By the end of the war, the interest of the major U.S. broadcasting corporations in shortwave operations had waned, leaving the field open for smaller companies to develop international radio as a commercial activity.[25]

By 1940 CBS, NBC, Westinghouse, and Crossley all had international services, in addition to their domestic U.S. services. Unlike the European and Asian powers, however, the United States had neither a state-controlled broadcasting apparatus nor a public service corporation to carry out psychological warfare.

The U.S. government had considered establishing an international radio service in the 1930s. It had proposed at the Pan-American Conference in Montevideo in 1933 that a shortwave station be inaugurated in the United States to carry news and entertainment regularly to Latin America. President Franklin Roosevelt set aside five shortwave frequencies for this service. The idea was scuttled, however, in the face of opposition from U.S. commercial broadcasters, who saw a government-directed service as a competitor, and international broadcasting as a logical adjunct to their domestic operations (see "Extracts from article PAN-AMERICAN PEACE CONFERENCE," n.d.).

The United States thus not only entered World War II late, it also began the war at a propaganda disadvantage (see Shulman, 1990). The other warring powers had been engaged in a psychological war for nearly a decade. Nearly a year after the U.S. entry into the war, *The Nation* calculated the difference in the capabilities of the United States and its adversaries in reaching foreign audiences. It concluded that, while the United States was using a total of 23 transmitters (9 only occasionally), the Axis powers in Europe used "close to ninety" and Japan "about fifty." "Even when all English shortwave transmitters are counted," *The Nation* claimed (see Rundt, 1942, p. 210), "the enemy in Europe maintains a superiority of at least three to two. With Japan . . . included, the Axis powers outnumber the united nations two to one in high-powered, long-range senders. For short-wave transmitters of various power the ratio is at least five to three (this includes Allied international stations in Australia, India, Chungking, and the Soviet Union)." By the end of the war the United States was operating 36 transmitters on eight sites.

U.S. overseas government propaganda commenced in February 1942 when 11 privately owned shortwave stations broadcast a program called the "Voice of America" to Europe (see Green, 1988, p. 16; and Soley, 1989, pp. 48–68, 81–93). In June 1942 the government created the Office of War Information (OWI), which would come to be the most important of the government's infor-

mation dissemination and propaganda departments. OWI negotiated operating contracts with privately owned U.S. shortwave station owners, but the existing owners remained as licensees, due to fear that government control "could lead to . . . control of domestic broadcasting" (Weldon, 1988, p. 83). By November 1942 the government had put all U.S. private international stations under federal supervision. Demands that the federal government declare its intention to return all stations at the conclusion of the war delayed the adoption of the plan for federal wartime control by several months.

The purpose of the VOA, forged in debate over the role of propaganda and appropriate activities for a democratic country, was to "spread the gospel of democracy throughout the world" (debate chronicled in Winkler, 1978, pp. 16–23, 29–50). Robert E. Sherwood's belief that "truth is the only effective basis for American foreign information," which mirrored the BBC commitment, became the operational principle (quoted in Winkler, 1978, p. 26). Sherwood, who had created the Foreign Information Service (FIS) under orders of President Roosevelt in 1941, was responsible for inaugurating VOA as part of the overseas operations of OWI. Elmer Davis, appointed head of OWI at its creation, was given his mandate: to "formulate and carry out . . . information programs designed to facilitate the development of an informed and intelligent understanding, at home and abroad, of the status and progress of the war effort and of the war policies, activities, and aims of the government" (quoted in Winkler, 1978, p. 34; see also Shulman, 1990, chapter 1).

OWI continued to wage political battles throughout the war: against the State Department, which claimed that OWI's information activities were diluting its authority; against the military, which wanted to conceal war difficulties, casualties, and losses; and against the Congress, where certain members objected to the domestic political implications of some of OWI's overseas information activities. By 1943 President Roosevelt had to act "to restore the prestige and strength of OWI": An internal struggle between Sherwood and Davis resulted in Sherwood's leaving the agency for a new assignment (see Winkler, 1978, p. 103).

The international radio activities of OWI grew, however, despite the domestic difficulties, largely as a result of Allied capture of Axis transmitting facilities. In time the propaganda activities of the Psychological Warfare Branch (PWB) of Allied Force Headquarters, which was able to capture enemy newspaper plants, radio studios, and movie theaters in North Africa in late 1942, supplemented those of OWI. The PWB operated in military theaters of operation, and during the Tunisian campaign "dropped twenty million leaflets that had some effect in contributing to the demoralization of the enemy. Leaflets with such themes as 'You Are Surrounded' and 'Drowning Is a Nasty Death' rained on Axis territory from Royal Air Force planes" (Winkler, 1978, p. 117).

David Sarnoff, president of RCA, was drafted and put in charge of the broadcasting in Europe under the Supreme Headquarters of the Allied Expeditionary Force (SHAEF), under Eisenhower's command. Preparing for D-Day, his job was to oversee a broadcasting station directed to Allied troops in the European theater of operations, evaluate the military communications system set up for use between headquarters and the invasion forces, and coordinate all print and broadcast communications from the battle zones on the continent for U.S. and British correspondents (Lewis, 1991, p. 292). On the first day of the invasion, Sarnoff's system relayed 570,000 words across the Atlantic reporting on the military operation (Lewis, 1991, p. 294).

By the end of the war, U.S. propaganda activities had earned some respect, despite their late start and errors made throughout the war. When Italy surrendered to Allied forces, the Japanese government "warned its people that the Italian collapse 'could partly be ascribed to British and American propaganda aimed at the disintegration of the home front'" (Green, 1988, p. 17).

Dutch Broadcasting

During the so-called radio war of the 1930s between the Nazi/Fascist and democratic governments of Europe, the Netherlands maintained a policy of strict neutrality in its programming. Once Holland was overrun by the German armies, however, Dutch radio was also on the run. It operated briefly as Vrij (Free) Nederland from Radio Paris, and then from BBC transmitters in England as Radio Oranje. Radio Oranje broadcast from July 28, 1940, until June 2, 1945, and "the first shortwave broadcast from liberated Holland was relayed from the Philips Eindhoven studios of Herrijzend Nederland via the transmitters of the BBC, on May 24th, 1945" (Haslach, 1983, p. 72).

Soviet Broadcasting

During World War II the Soviets, like the Dutch, found themselves broadcasting *into* their own occupied territory. Between 1941 and 1945 Soviet radio programmers prepared special broadcasts for guerrilla fighters and those living in German-held Soviet territory (Mehta, 1987, p. 59).

Clandestine Broadcasting: "Black Propaganda"

During the war openly acknowledged broadcasting, such as that practiced by the BBC and VOA, became known as "white propaganda."[26] Radio stations set up clandestinely and claiming to be located inside another country, and often operated by dissidents, were referred to as "black propaganda" operations. Black propaganda stations, if they existed as claimed, would have been illegal under the domestic laws of the affected state. Since the war a further distinction has been drawn: "Gray propaganda" operations include those whose purposes are overt but whose source is hidden, or those with both overt source and overt purpose but operated by actual revolutionary or subversive organizations.[27]

During World War II both sides operated overt and clandestine (or black propaganda) stations. The clandestine stations (some of which have already been mentioned) included those that claimed to be representing anti-Nazi or anti-imperialist sentiments within Germany or Britain, or that surreptitiously interfered with broadcasts by breaking in with programming to replace the actual material using more powerful transmitters, or that were designed not to be noticed.[28]

Clandestine broadcasting occurred in a number of places prior to and during the war: broadcasts of Radio Free Spain during the Spanish Civil War, the first armed conflict pitting Fascist and Communist sympathizers against one another; Irish Republican Army broadcasts in Northern Ireland; secret Communist radio broadcasts in Czechoslovakia; and broadcasts by anti-Nazi Germans. Such radio activities all began in the 1930s (see Soley & Nichols, 1987, p. 3). Rudolf Wormys ran the first anti-Nazi

clandestine station, beginning in Germany in September 1934. He eventually left the country, but continued broadcasting until his death at the hands of the Gestapo in January 1935.

The British began a clandestine operation aimed at Germany on May 26, 1940, which claimed (untruthfully) to be broadcasting from within Germany. The Soviet Union, France, Austria, and Spain all operated clandestine stations during World War II.[29]

The Dutch also operated a clandestine station that, while actually aimed into the Netherlands from England, claimed to be within Holland during the Nazi occupation. The station, *de Flitspuit* (the bugbomb), "managed to give the impression of Netherlands origination through the highly efficient British 'parrot' service, which gathered all Netherlands newspapers and transmitted their contents to London, via Stockholm, within 24 hours. So [Meyer] Sluyser [the controller] was able to take items, not only from major urban papers, but also from the least likely rural journal," which gave the impression "that every detail was known" (Haslach, 1983, p. 59).

The Nazis also operated clandestine stations during the war. They began one aimed at Britain in February 1940, under the organization Büro Concordia, called the New British Broadcasting System. There is no evidence, however, that it ever attracted much of an audience, in contrast to known audiences attracted by the British clandestine operations (see Briggs, 1970, pp. 157–159). The Nazis used clandestine broadcasting against the Soviet Union as well, but it was ineffective because the Soviet people knew about German atrocities committed during the invasion of their country. In addition, the Nazis directed clandestine broadcasting against the United States through Radio De-Bunk, which claimed to broadcast from the

American Midwest. There is no evidence of any effect from its operations.

The operation of "black" stations was perhaps a form of disinformation (see Whaley, 1980, p. 340). Certainly such operations shared characteristics with disinformation, practiced using BBC transmitters by the British Directorate of Military Intelligence. This directorate, which aired a program called the "German Forces Programme" that was aimed at the Wehrmacht (German armies), was "an obvious channel for calculated indiscretions" (White, 1955, p. 59).

The Political Warfare Executive, which directed the propaganda activities of the British government, considered the broadcasts of the BBC to be white propaganda, along with other means of disseminating acknowledged information, such as leaflets dropped behind enemy lines (White, 1955, p. 64). The Allies did supplement their white propaganda, however, from time to time with other tactics, such as jamming enemy radio signals to isolate an area to increase the impact of their own broadcasts (White, 1955, p. 65).

Propaganda in various forms became a staple in the arsenals of the various powers during the war. Although assessments of its effectiveness conducted after the war failed to indicate any major success among the populations to which it had been directed, there was also evidence that people did listen to enemy broadcasts. As the fortunes of war shifted in favor of the Allied powers, the Nazis saw their propaganda job as more difficult, because people's hardships caused them to be more inclined to believe enemy broadcasts. The information monopoly that each country hoped to exercise to protect home front morale was broken when people listened to the enemy. The broadcasts must be judged successful, then, simply because they broke this monopoly and pro-vided information that was not otherwise available to either soldier or citizen.

6.6

Control of Information During World War II

Countries used a variety of techniques to control information flow during World War II. Most obviously, the effort to reach across an enemy's borders with information was an effort to control. But there were other less obvious approaches available as well. Some of these techniques were designed to prevent people from hearing broadcasts from enemy radio services or to otherwise stem the flow of outside information to them. Others were designed to "eavesdrop" on enemy communications traffic — that is, to deny control of information to the adversary. Still others were aimed at poisoning the information that the adversary provided to its own citizens.

Jamming

The first of these techniques was jamming, or the deliberate interference with incoming radio signals.[30] Jamming was first used as early as 1922 in Argentina; and in Europe in 1923 a French radio station purposely broadcast on the same frequency as a German station that was protesting French occupation of the Ruhr (see Schwoch, 1990, chapter 5). The German station ended its operations after a few days. In 1938 the Austrians jammed Nazi broadcasts, in accordance with a 1936 international convention that banned radio propaganda "aimed at undermining a state's political system" (BBC Monitoring Service, 1987b).

Jamming intensified with the outbreak of the war. The Germans eventually tried to jam BBC signals in 17 different languages, and directed jamming at other services as well. Italy jammed incoming signals from the Allied powers, too, and both the French and Soviets jammed German broadcasts into their territories. A BBC Intelligence Paper remarked about the jamming of signals into Germany in 1943:

> Very little indeed is known about the effectiveness of jamming of our broadcasts inside Germany. All our advertised wavelengths have been reported, at one time or another and in one district or another, to have been heavily jammed, and observations here and in countries bordering Germany have borne out these reports. Local jamming transmitters of short range have been described as numerous in southern Germany at least, and more powerful jammers operating on our wavelengths can be heard all over Europe. (British Broadcasting Corporation, 1943a, p. 3)

Interference with Information Reception

Another weapon involved confiscating radios or passing legislation that made it illegal to listen to foreign broadcasts. Such tactics were aimed at foiling the strategies of external propagandists who wanted to affect the morale of local populations or their faith in their leaders.[31] This was the principal reason the Nazis required Germans to listen to domestic propaganda (it would inoculate them from the external "lies"), and appointed radio officers whose task was to encourage listening to Nazi broadcasts and who led discussions of them to promote "correct" thinking. This concern also "justified" both the laws making it illegal to listen to foreign broadcasts and the confiscation of radios, particularly in the occupied areas.[32] One BBC report remarked, for instance, that "one menace to our audience is the confiscation of sets. Till lately,

except in Poland, the Germans confined the confiscation of wireless sets almost entirely to sets belonging to Jews. But now in occupied France they have begun to confiscate sets 'as a disciplinary measure'" (BBC Overseas Intelligence Department, 1941c). The Nazis prohibited listening to foreign radio broadcasts in a regulation issued September 1, 1939. Nazi authorities confiscated receiving sets, and violators were imprisoned or sentenced to hard labor. Those who listened and then spread information from the broadcasts faced hard labor or even execution. Italians were likewise forbidden to listen to foreign radio transmitters.

The Nazis also forbade people in occupied territories to listen to such broadcasts. A regulation issued by the Nazis in Belgium in August 1940, for instance, specifically banned listening to the BBC. This was expanded to include all broadcasts not originating in Germany or German-occupied territory on December 23, 1941. In Poland by the end of 1941, following the repudiation of the Soviet-German nonaggression pact and the German advance into eastern Poland, "there was, officially, no Polish audience for broadcasts other than those provided by the Germans and made accessible to the public by means of loudspeakers in the streets" (British Broadcasting Corporation, 1943b, p. 2). Discovery of Poles with radio sets was "immediately followed by the summary execution not only of the owners or users of the set but of all persons of either sex occupying the building in which the set was located" (British Broadcasting Corporation, 1943b, p. 5).

Related to this strategy was another used by the Nazis. As Thomas (1935) put it,

> To ensure that the German mind, secure from defilement within the Reich, shall not be sul-

lied from without, strenuous efforts have been made to market a cheap and efficient receiving set, the *Volksempfänger* (People's Set), one of whose objects is apparently to get German stations satisfactorily but nothing else— though amazing claims for its receptivity are sometimes made. (pp. 494–495)

The belligerents used yet another strategy to deal with the ability of governments to communicate using point-to-point systems: cables and wireless. As in the First World War, both sides attempted to cut submarine cables to halt telegraph traffic. Italy severed all five Gibraltar-to-Malta cables in the Mediterranean, and Britain cut all the Italian cables to South America and Spain (Baglehole, 1969, p. 23). And in the Far East the Japanese quickly overran all the Cable and Wireless Ltd. stations, leaving 11 cable facilities and over 18,000 miles of cable routes in Japanese hands until the end of the war (Baglehole, 1969, p. 24).

Despite such reverses the traffic on British cable routes increased by 400% within a short time following the outbreak of the war, and the war resulted in some reductions in the charges for cable messages that the dominions and colonies had been requesting for years. Special low cable rates were introduced for armed forces personnel, a penny per word press rate was instituted, and all evacuated children and prisoners of war were allowed free use of the cables. The volume of radio pictures also increased. In 1938, the year prior to the war, Cable and Wireless had carried 231 million words; in 1944 the company carried 705 million (Baglehole, 1969, pp. 23–24).

Ghost Voicing

Another aspect of information control was the use of "ghost voicing." This involved breaking into a speech or newscast surreptitiously and broadcasting false statements or news reports, and then returning the frequency to its original controllers to end the program. Also, broadcast engineers could impose hoots, jeers, and laughter on the original signals, "piggybacking" them onto the carrier wave. Both the British and Germans used such techniques, although the British were apparently more successful, particularly in piggybacking onto the broadcast speeches of Adolf Hitler.

One principal reason for the relatively greater British success using such techniques was the availability of native German speakers in England. Refugees provided ready sources of such speakers to work on clandestine operations, and these speakers seemed authentic because of their language facility. By contrast, the Germans had difficulty finding English speakers whose accents would not give them away: Native English speakers were almost nonexistent in Germany, and English-speaking Germans were too easy to detect.

Code Breaking

Both sides during World War II used radio in another way as well: as a source of foreign intelligence. Countries set up listening services and analysis units to monitor and analyze radio broadcasts for information on civilian morale, food shortages, transportation problems, casualties, damage inflicted in bombing raids, political and military announcements, new laws passed to deal with domestic problems, or even troop, ship, and submarine movements inadvertently broadcast by careless operators. Both military and civilian services conducted these activities (see Headrick, 1991; Renier & Rubenstein, 1986; West, 1986, 1988; and Winterbotham, 1974). They monitored both military communications and nonmilitary international and domestic stations that carried reports about the war.

Both the British MI5 and the U.S. Federal Communications Commission kept track of enemy communications traffic. MI5 established the Radio Security Service, using amateur radio operators to monitor German radio services known to include coded messages for frontline troops and warships. Also, the British Secret Intelligence Service (SIS) spent the war breaking military codes to allow the Allied navies to mount an effective defense against the German U-boats, which were sinking thousands of tons of Allied shipping (see Kahn, 1991). The United States conducted similar operations, centered in the Signal Intelligence Service and the navy's Communications Security section. Both the British and U.S. services worked on cracking German and Japanese military ciphers created by Enigma encryption machines once the war began, building on work originally begun by the Poles in 1930 (see Modelski, 1986, chapter 1, and Welchman, 1982, pp. 14–16). Intelligence services referred to the different Enigma codes by colors—red, purple, blue, brown, violet—the result of early British efforts to track the different discriminants used by the Germans to indicate how the receiving operators were to set the machines to decipher the scrambled messages (see Welchman, 1982, p. 54). Luftwaffe traffic was "Red" at the beginning of the war, but this color came to designate all the operational traffic of the German ground and air forces as the war got underway. "Chaffinch" and "Light Blue" were used to designate the traffic of the army and air force during the German offensive in North Africa under Rommel (Welchman, 1982, pp. 88, 123).

The Wire Agency Cartel and Control of Information

Meanwhile, the news gathering and dissemination agreement among the three European agencies—Agence Havas, Reuters, and Continental-Wolff—also strained and eventually broke. Although the three agencies had struggled with one another from the early days of the cartel arrangement as each tried to dominate the others, the slide toward dissolution—exacerbated by AP demands—was prompted by the rise of National Socialism (Nazism) in Germany. The Nazis saw the Continental-Wolff agency as a possible propaganda tool, and heaped blame on the old Prussian government for its failure to conduct effective propaganda during the First World War. The Germans saw the British propaganda of the First World War as more successful than their own in "undermining enemy morale and keeping up spirits at home." They criticized Reuters for cooperating with the government during the war (and particularly for its director acting as advisor on cable and wireless propaganda to the British government) (Lawrenson & Barber, 1985, p. 44). The German newspaper *Berliner Tagesblatt* suggested that "mightier and more dangerous than Fleet and Army is Reuter. We, too, must have a Ministry of Propaganda unless we are to be deprived of the fruits of our sacrifices, sufferings, and achievements" (Lawrenson & Barber, 1985, p. 44). Hadamovsky (1972, p. 8) argued that "the German people were not beaten on the battlefield but were defeated in the war of words and because their spirit was broken." As the Nazis turned Continental-Wolff increasingly to propaganda, both Havas and Reuters chafed at their contractual agreements. Hadamovsky's conclusion that "it is only the more naive persons who still believe that any news item itself, and consequently the manner in which it is reported by the press, could be objective" increasingly seemed to govern the activities of Continental-Wolff (Hadamovsky, 1972, p. 112; see also Fenby, 1986, p. 51). In 1938 the political conflict about to engulf the continent heated up. Both Germany and Italy began to offer free news services, and the British government "offered Reuters the use of official radio facilities to send out two daily news services, which the agency was paid state money to produce" (Fenby, 1986, p. 53). Winston Churchill also persuaded the "Fleet Street" newspapers of London to bail Reuters out of its difficult financial position by purchasing shares in it and signing a trust agreement guaranteeing Reuters' independence (Lawrenson & Barber, 1985, p. 13). When the Nazis overran France in 1939, they disbanded Agence Havas, thus dissolving the European remnants of the cartel.

Whereas the German press agency never did rise from the ashes of war, the two U.S. agencies were able to strengthen and consolidate their international clientele outside the theaters of war while the carefully constructed cartel division of world markets crumbled. This left Reuters at a decided disadvantage, and AP and UPI emerged as the dominant news powers in 1945. This was at least partly due to intervention of the U.S. government. AP enlisted the help of the U.S. State Department to "break the cartel" and allow the American company to expand (see Renaud, 1985). During the war the slogan of "freedom of information," originally used to argue for the end of European-dominated worldwide news services, was resurrected "as the panacea for all of the world's ills, as the only way to prevent the recurrence of war" (Blanchard, 1983, p. 60).

Although the U.S. government was not necessarily being cynical in focusing on the value of freedom of information as an instrument of peace, it was at least convenient, economically and politically, for the government to champion the cause.

6.8

Regulation: Small Victories

The Madrid Radio Telegraphic Conference of 1932 was successful, as already indicated, in providing a permanent international organization to "regulate" radio: the International Telecommunication Union. Given the U.S. refusal to allow the Soviet Union to attend the 1927 conference, it is perhaps not surprising that, when the United States proposed English as the official language in Madrid, the Soviet delegation objected. The seeds of politicalization, planted in 1927, were sprouting. The Soviet delegate proposed French as the official language, and gave force to this proposal by saying that he was "speaking for a nation of some 180,000,000 people." He was followed by the Chinese delegate, who supported the U.S. proposal, "remarking that he was speaking for a nation of 450,000,000." The conference was carried on in both languages ("International Conventions: Address by Mr. W. Platt," 1935, p. 6).

The 1930s saw two other international conventions address problems of using radio waves. The first, in Lucerne, Switzerland, in 1933, adopted a frequency allocation table for Europe. The second, in Cairo, Egypt, provided frequency allocations for intercontinental air route traffic (ITU, 1965, pp. 164–165).

The Lucerne Plan for frequency allocation did not solve the difficulties of interference in Europe. In 1934 representatives of 20 countries' broadcasting organizations, CBS, NBC, and 13 European state administrations met in London and declared it "insufficient to permit a national service of satisfactory quality." It recommended that governments and broadcasters "take all possible measures to stop the . . . interference" (International Broadcasting Union, 1934, p. 7). The increasing political and military tensions of Europe, however, rendered that impossible.

6.9

Conclusion

The international communications system was both consolidated and broken by the ideological conflicts of the 1930s and the war that followed. The application of communication as an ideological weapon required that other countries concentrate their efforts, both to protect the material substance of the system (its cables, relay stations, and broadcasting facilities) and to assure that the world understood their political, economic, and cultural values.

The politicalization of the system that resulted from often strident ideologies demanded that countries take steps that they had previously rejected. The United Kingdom took up foreign language broadcasting. The United States put all private international stations under government supervision and began a government-directed international radio service. The Czechs attempted to stop inroads from German propaganda by banning listening to foreign stations. Other countries began to jam signals or to protest the nature of program content.

Gradually during the 1930s the international communications system became a potential (and then an actual) weapon of war. Propaganda became the order of the day,

and control of information a necessary adjunct to military conflict. Private companies found their capital investments swallowed up by aggression, their networks severed, their surviving assets applied to the business of war.

Between 1939 and 1945, in addition to waging massive ground, air, and sea wars throughout Europe and Asia, countries battled for the minds and allegiances of people using the international communications system. They struggled to establish and maintain monopolies of knowledge, and to break through these monopolies with their "truth." As the BBC put it, "it has been the special duty of the BBC's service in German, as also in Czech and Polish, to bring . . . people [under Nazi domination] the truths which the Nazi Government has deliberately withheld from them" (*B.B.C. Handbook 1940,* 1940, p. 51).

The promise of communication had been distorted by evil. Its mythos had been tarnished. The outcome of the war would determine which powers would reconstitute the system at war's end, and on what terms. Victorious powers would reap the commercial and political rewards that came with continuing control of communication.

The post–World War II world, however, would not be business as usual. The United States would not be protected by oceans in a ballistic missile age, an age that had been presaged by Nazi V-1 and V-2 rockets fired at Britain. The Soviet Union would not be a weak power, subject to intervention from capitalist states. The empires, which had seemed so important in European thinking into the 1930s, would crumble under the demands of the peoples of the Southern Hemisphere. Reconstructing the international system in the aftermath of war would be accomplished within new realities. The "tried and true" approaches to rationalizing, controlling, and using the international system would be inadequate in the postwar environment.

Notes

1. Originally the company was Cables and Wireless Ltd. Later it was changed to Cable and Wireless Ltd.

2. As Baker (1970, p. 231) put it, Marconi's "life-long ambition," a "Marconi-controlled Imperial Wireless Chain, ended almost as soon as it had been realized in the beam system." Marconi developed the chain, but then watched it slip through its fingers.

3. The BBC continued to tally listeners' responses. By the end of December 1938 it had received 99,000 letters and reports (see British Broadcasting Corporation, 1939, p. 5).

4. The BBC was aware of the counter arguments to this mythos. In its 1935 annual it carried an essay by Ernest Barker (1935, p. 145), who warned, "These new inventions of our day—the aeroplane, the radio, the film—are all escaping, like so many birds, from what seem to be the ancient cages of the nations. . . . And yet the bird has not altogether escaped from the cage. The nation is like nature; you may drive it out with a pitch-fork, but it will always return."

5. Martin (1980, p. 282) argues that the "British had to maintain rather than to develop their world power in the post–World War I era that saw the rise of institutionalized international propaganda. The British were appealing not to publics that already had national allegiances of their own, but mainly to peoples who were economically, if not culturally, tied to the British Empire. . . . The British were frankly elitist from the start. They catered to the head on the assumption that the body and tail would follow."

6. "Germany is once more on the map for the listener who wants a variety of good musical programmes. . . . It is unfortunate that propaganda now occupies a large part of the programmes from Vienna, but in between talks and news bulletins the transmitter is maintaining—and even enhancing—its reputation for first-class musical programmes" ("Radio from Foreign Fields," 1934, p. 23).

7. Other stations listed include E.A.Q. Madrid, Radio Ljubljana (Yugoslavia), and Radio Méditerranée (France).

8. Radio Luxembourg largely ignored the Post Office objections. The French promised to act, but did not. Italy and Spain stopped English language advertising programs in 1934 and 1935, respectively. The UIR said it had no power over private stations or nonmember states (see Vinogradoff, 1945, pp. 32–34). Radio Athlone, renamed Radio Eireann in 1938, was the only European station to continue to air sponsored programs after the outbreak of war (Vinogradoff, 1945, p. 42). Radio Luxembourg became one of Germany's propaganda stations after the Nazis overran Luxembourg in 1940 (see Barnouw, 1983).

9. Only 3% of the United Kingdom's population was reported to be listening to U.S. stations in November 1939 (Vinogradoff, 1945, p. 50).

10. Rolo wrote (1942, p. 11), "Radio went to war on five continents shortly after the Nazi Party came to power in Germany. In eight years it has been streamlined from a crude propaganda bludgeon into the most powerful single instrument of political warfare the world has ever known." The British Foreign Office expressed concerns about the Soviet's use of propaganda in 1932, particularly aimed toward Palestine and the Persian Gulf. The BBC responded to the concern by saying that there was nothing it could do directly. One memo said, "The B.B.C.'s Empire Service could not conceivably start fighting the Russians with their own weapons, nor could the Empire programmes be made use of for direct political propaganda" (E.S.D., 1932).

11. Martin (1980, p. 281) suggests that, while both communism and nazism saw their "source of power stemming from the masses, the nazi philosophy was disdainful of their intellectual capacities and for that very reason appealed directly to them whereas communism, which, at least overtly, did not look upon the masses as simple-minded, believed in a multistep flow of propaganda through highly trained and motivated elite cadres."

12. The 1940 *B.B.C. Handbook* noted that services in Czech, Romanian, Serbo-Croat, and Turkish were added because of the war and that the Empire Service "was modified so as to make it virtually a World Service" *(B.B.C. Handbook 1940,* 1940, pp. 49, 50).

13. Two explorations of Nazi propaganda strategy, written just prior to the war, are Martin (1939) and Wilson (1939). The Research and Analysis unit of the Office of War Information (OWI) in the United States also analyzed Nazi propaganda techniques, based partly on monitoring reports provided by the Federal Communications Commission. (See, for instance, Research and Analysis Reports, 1942a–e, 1943a–b.)

14. The belief that such broadcasts were coming from Radio Bari, a medium-wave station, were mistaken, says Mansell (1982, p. 47).

15. Browne, (1983, p. 425) claims that the growing German and Italian broadcasting in the mid-1930s had "no immediate effect in terms of spurring the government to take a serious interest in expanding and improving British international broadcasting." But Mansell (1982, pp. 40–41) says that, despite lack of evidence as to whether the impetus for foreign language service came from the BBC or the British government, attention to this possibility, based on the German and Italian activities, was raised at least as early as 1935.

16. A March 1937 BBC paper objected that "to introduce foreign languages into the Empire Service broadcasts would . . . inevitably prejudice the integrity of the Service . . . it would *pro tante* be indulging in propaganda" (quoted in Partner, 1988, p. 2).

17. The BBC's decision was, in fact, prompted not by the desire to engage in propaganda — which the BBC found anathema — but to tell the truth when the air was full of lies.

18. A number of perspectives on the nature and role of propaganda can be found in Smith (1989); see also Martin (1958, chapter 2).

19. A lengthy examination of both British and German propaganda can be found in Balfour (1979).

20. The report included excerpts from some of the songs. One, "Song of the Tachanka," was about a four-wheeled vehicle outfitted with machine guns and presumably drawn by horses. The last stanza of the song, which was monitored on February 18, 1938, included references to "thunder tanks," "aeroplanes," the "fighting chariot," and the "machine-gunner."

21. The German monitoring system was used by the Allies as a means of propaganda itself: "Allied broadcasters were fairly sure that even if they couldn't reach a large audience in Germany, they would have the attention of the influential group of German government officials who read the monitoring reports. After the war, it was found that this assumption was correct" (Davison, 1965, p. 54).

22. The Saar is an area along the German-French border. It was administered by the League of Nations from 1919 until 1935, when a plebiscite (or indication of preference) was conducted to determine whether its people wanted to become a part of Germany. The people of Saarland voted to join the Third Reich.

23. A number of scholars have examined Nazi propaganda (see, for instance, Baird, 1974; Childs & Whitton, 1942; Kris & Speier, 1944; Rolo, 1942; Sington & Weidenfeld, 1943; see also United States Congress, 1935).

24. Goebbels decided toward the end of the war (noted in his diary for March 23, 1945), after noting the increasing success of Allied propaganda with the German people, to publish a series of slogans "which are much in

vogue among the people at present. Propaganda by sticker and chain-letter will also be stepped up" (Trevor-Roper, 1978, p. 214).

25. The United States actually began testing broadcasts in February, and in the effort to pinpoint the actual inauguration of VOA during its 50th anniversary celebration located what appears to be its first officially scheduled broadcast. This German-language program was aired on February 24, 1941, but was carried into Europe on BBC transmitters.

26. This typology uses the terms *black* and *white* differently than before, when they referred to persuasive tactics. These two terms are used in both ways throughout the literature of propaganda, much of which is written by practitioners rather than scholars.

27. All of these distinctions are discussed by Soley and Nichols (1987, p. 11).

28. Soley (1989, p. 2) defines clandestine radio stations as "illegal political stations that advocate civil war, revolution or rebellion. Clandestine stations provide misleading information as to their sponsorship, transmitter location, or raison d'être."

29. Soley (1989, pp. 8–35) describes clandestine radio operations during the 1930s and 1940s by Germany, Italy, France, the United Kingdom, and the United States.

30. Various forms of jamming used in 1940 included mechanical Morse code, another voice, artificial static, and noises, including sirens, bangings, and bells. "The last named system is most frequently resorted to by Germany, the purpose being to enable conscientious National Socialists to denounce their subversive brethren: the noises issuing suddenly from the loud-speaker would in principle discover an unpatriotic listener to his neighbours, and even to the police" (A Listener, 1940, p. 242; see also Grandin, 1971, p. 25).

31. The Czechs used this strategy to counteract German propaganda in the mid-1930s. They prohibited "public reception of political programmes from foreign stations; the owner of a wireless set may not invite friends to listen to such programmes" (Thomas, 1935, p. 495).

32. Winkler (1978, p. 19) wrote that Joseph Goebbels "was single-minded in his approach, for he saw propaganda as a means of control over an entire way of life. . . . The truth, for Goebbels, was not important, for propaganda, he declared, had 'nothing at all to do with the truth.' Rather, the real aim was success."

7

A NEW POSTWAR ENVIRONMENT: DEVELOPING AND CRUMBLING HEGEMONIES: 1946–1969

7.1

Introduction

At the conclusion of World War II in 1945, the muddled geopolitical composition of the world suddenly clarified. The sometimes strained relationship between the United States and Great Britain on the one side, and the Soviet Union on the other, broke down completely as the Allies split Germany and Berlin into sectors, and the Soviet Union occupied Eastern and Central Europe. Confrontations between the United States, which assumed the mantle of "leader of the free world," and the Soviets began. The Communist coup in Czechoslovakia in 1948, the Soviet blockade of West Berlin and the formation of the North Atlantic Treaty Organization (NATO) in 1949, the outbreak of the Korean War in 1950 — all served to heighten tensions between East and West. The Soviet devel-

opment of the atomic bomb, the recriminations in the Rosenberg spy scandal that followed, and the McCarthy period of "witch-hunting" and "red-baiting" between 1950 and 1954, also contributed to the mood of suspicion.

The European empires began to break apart. New countries were created from former colonies in Africa and Asia. Both sides in what came to be called a "bipolar world" began to court the allegiance of these new "third world" nations. These countries developed into a majority in international organizations in the 1960s, particularly in the United Nations and its specialized agencies. East and West put together foreign aid packages designed to establish economic and political ties with these countries, and to influence their votes in these organizations. Information agencies organized communication activities, such as establishment of libraries in embassies, distribution of films, student and faculty exchange programs, and lecture tours, to introduce the people of these new countries to the "superpowers" and their allies. The battle for the "hearts and minds" of foreign peoples gradually developed into a multi-faceted adjunct of traditional diplomacy (known as "public diplomacy") and military alliances.

When the war ended, it might have been reasonable to hope that the "radio war" would end, and that the destructive application of national interests to news flow, which had led to its use as a propaganda agent and to news manipulation, would die away. The old newswire cartel had crumbled; the Allied broadcast apparatus had overcome the campaign of lies with a strategy of truth on the airwaves. New applications of technology for communication purposes, particularly the microwave and satellite, would soon be discovered. A new United Nations would shortly be born, and with it would come new condemnations of abusive communication (such as propaganda) and affirmations of human rights. Perhaps the international communications system, which had fragmented in the First World War, had been partly reconstructed in the 1920s, and then had suffered the hammer blows of ideological conflict and then another world war, could be reconstituted.

This transitional period did see many of the old formulas for operating the international system of communication strained. Whatever expectations may have existed, however, about the possibilities for new harmony among nations were soon dashed. The United States did dismantle its international radio service at the end of the war, but soon thereafter it decided to restart it and to build new ones to battle the Soviet Union over the airwaves. The new nations that were created by the break-up of empires began to view the international system, which had developed before and during the war, as being contrary to their own political and economic (and eventually cultural) interests. The political climate itself, fueled by the revelations about Nazi atrocities that emerged at the end of the war, elevated new aspects of human rights to world consciousness. This led not only to overtures to incorporate these rights into international treaties, but also to new conflicts over appropriate access to information across international borders.

The new technologies, some of which had been applied for the first time in the war, obviously had applications for both domestic and international communications. The microwave (originally developed for radar systems) could carry information; the ballistic missile, developed by the Nazis in the V-1 and V-2 rockets, could possibly carry satellites into space. Microwave communication between continents using such satellites was predicted. Arthur C. Clarke wrote in *Wireless World* in 1945 that satellites placed 36,000 kilometers above the equator (22,300 miles) would rotate at the same speed as the earth, making them essentially "stationary," and enabling communications to occur 24 hours a day (see also Hudson, 1990, pp. 2, 3). This was the only distance, too, at which this phenomenon worked, making the **orbital slots** at that altitude extremely valuable for uses that required stable space platforms, such as communications. These satellites were in **"geo-synchronous orbit."** Countries began to question whether their needs would be accounted for as these new methods of communication emerged, however. They complained that the patterns of domination, which had developed under the old imperial system, were continuing in the postwar period.

The ITU

The ITU, as Savage (1989, chapter 1) explains, "sets the 'rules of the road'" for international telecommunications. The ITU is responsible for three main elements of international telecommunications: (1) coordinating radio frequency assignments, including the assignment of bands for specific types of services, and the division of the geostationary orbit, including orbital slots, for satellites; (2) recommending technical standards for international communications, including standards for wired connections, bandwidths for particular radio and television services, and other technical parameters for services; and (3) regulating international "common carrier" services — telegraph, telephone, data transfer, and other new services.

7.2

Postwar Reconstruction of the International System

The dynamic nature of the Second World War resulted in far more damage to the communications infrastructure of Europe than did the static trench warfare of World War I. The French government, for instance, detailed the damage to French telecommunications systems shortly after the war:

> Two hundred buildings were seriously damaged, 90,000 km of overhead wire were down, 60 relay stations had been destroyed, 30 cities had their underground cable networks cut, 110 telegraph offices lay in ruins, tens of thousands of telephone sets had to be replaced, 50 submarine cables had been cut, and of the original 42 French national broadcasting transmitters, only four were useable. (ITU, 1965, p. 183)

Cable and Wireless Ltd. (United Kingdom) faced the problem of reconstructing its overseas system, too, which had fallen into Japanese hands in Asia after Pearl Harbor. As various territories were retaken, Cable and Wireless personnel landed and began using the system to carry press dispatches and military traffic (see Graves, n.d., chapter 12).[1] Germany, Japan, and the United Kingdom had to dig out from the rubble of massive bombing attacks: Britain from the "Blitz," Germany from carpet bombing that had utterly leveled major cities, and Japan from both atomic and incendiary weapons (Tokyo, a city built of wooden structures, was subjected to an incendiary bomb attack that left it in smoldering ruins). The Soviet Union and Eastern and Central Europe had been devastated, too, by the seesawing battles along the "eastern front" and the stubborn, but destructive, defense of cities such as Stalingrad.

Constructing the Postwar Regulatory Environment

Nevertheless there were reasons to hope that the international communications system would be rebuilt. In 1945 representatives of 50 countries met in San Francisco at the United Nations Conference on International Organization. On June 26 these representatives signed the charter of the United Nations (UN), which officially came into existence on October 24, 1945, following ratification by the required number of states. In 1947 the International

Telecommunication Union (ITU) became a specialized agency of the UN, which also created the International Frequency Registration Board to operate under the ITU (ITU, 1965, p. 196) (see box, "The ITU"). In 1949 the United States finally signed the international telegraph regulations, although it still left the telephone regulations unsigned (ITU, 1965, p. 111). The international regulation of cable, wireless, and radio communications seemed to be gaining credibility.

In 1956 the two bodies created to deal with telegraph and telephone matters within the ITU were merged into a single organization, the International Consultative Committee for Telephone and Telegraph (CCITT). Over time the members of the ITU created various study groups under CCITT to deal with technical issues. These came to include study groups devoted to such ares as telephone switching, telegraph apparatus, data transmission, telephone circuits, worldwide automatic telephone networks, telephone operation and tariffs, definitions, and symbols (ITU, 1965, p. 220).[2]

The British imperial network was also moving toward greater consolidation and central control during the postwar years. In 1945 the Commonwealth Telecommunications Conference "recommended the acquisition of the [cable and wireless] services in the United Kingdom, the Dominions and Rhodesia by the Governments involved, and the establishment of a unifying Commonwealth Communications Board" (Baker, 1970, pp. 232–233). London implemented the recommendation in 1946 and nationalized Cable and Wireless on January 1, 1947. By June 1950 all the company's assets in these areas of the Commonwealth had been taken over by the respective governments (Baglehole, 1969, pp. 28–29).

Postwar Telecommunications Development

In 1956 the telecommunications carriers of three North Atlantic nations—AT&T in the United States, the Canadian Overseas Telecommunication Corporation, and the British Post Office—completed the first submarine telephone circuit between Europe (Scotland) and North America (Newfoundland). It used two cables, one for carrying information in each direction, each with 51 repeaters and each capable of handling 36 simultaneous conversations (see Baglehole, 1969, p. 33; see also ITU, 1965, p. 101). This was the first transatlantic telephone (TAT) link. In 1961 direct telephone connection was made between London and Vancouver, and on December 2, 1963, a Pacific communications cable (COMPAC) joined the Canadian-transatlantic telephone organization (CANTAT) to link London with Australia via Vancouver, New Zealand, Suva, and Hawaii.[3]

In July 1962 the Atlantic TAT link was supplemented by Telstar, the first active communications satellite, which linked 23 cities in Europe with 23 cities in the United States, and which could carry 80 simultaneous conversations (ITU, 1965, p. 101). Telstar was a **low-orbit satellite,** however, and thus was useable for transatlantic links for only a few hours each day (it had such a low orbit that one could stand outside at night and watch it cross the sky). A year later Syncom I briefly linked the United States, Europe, and Africa with satellite telephone, teletype, and facsimile transmission capability, until its electrical system failed; the United States launched the more successful Syncom II a few months later (ITU, 1965, p. 239). Syncom III, launched in 1964, demonstrated the commercial viability of geosynchronous satellites and carried live coverage of the Tokyo Olympics to the United States (Hudson, 1990, p. 19).

Broadcasting Developments

Despite the lack of technical compatibility between the world's various television systems, television exchange also began to occur during this period. In April 1961, for instance, the Intervision system, operated by the International Radio and Television Organization (OIRT) in Eastern Europe, and Eurovision, operated by the European Broadcasting Union (EBU) in Western Europe, began exchanging television programs on a link across the Gulf of Finland between Finland and the Soviet Union (ITU, 1965, p. 198).[4] The number of programs exchanged between the two organizations increased from 84 in 1961 to 239 in 1969. (See Figure 7.1.) By 1975 these exchanges amounted to over 1,100 news feeds from Western to Eastern Europe, but only 34 in the other direction (Varis & Jokelin, 1976, pp. 82–88).

Although Vatican Radio and HCJB (Heralding Christ Jesus' Blessings) had been using international radio for religious purposes since the 1930s, the post–World War II period saw a rapid increase in the number of Protestant "missionary radio" organizations on the airwaves (see Bernardoz & Haney, 1978; King, 1973; and Robertson, 1974). The first addition was the Far East Broadcasting Company, Inc. (FEBC), established in California in 1945, and clearly anti-Communist in tone during its early years. FEBC's first transmitters were located in the Philippines. In 1951 missionaries began the Pacific Broadcasting Association to evangelize the Japanese, and in 1954 the Voice of Tangier began in Morocco.

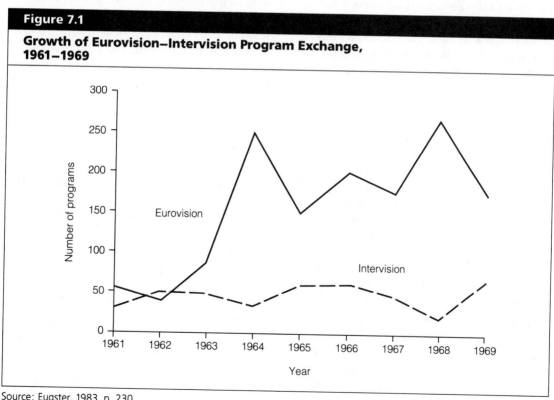

Figure 7.1

Growth of Eurovision–Intervision Program Exchange, 1961–1969

Source: Eugster, 1983, p. 230.

Voice of Tangier became Trans World Radio (TWR) in 1960 (brief descriptions of several religious broadcasting organizations can be found in Browne, 1982, chapter 11; the history of Trans World Radio can be found in Freed, 1979; of HCJB in Cook, 1961; of FEBC in Ledyard, 1963). In 1967 the Far East Broadcasting Association (FEBA) was begun in the United Kingdom, the first non-U.S.-based Protestant missionary radio organization. Its transmitters were, and continue to be, in the Seychelles, in the Indian Ocean.[5]

In 1954 two missionary organizations, the West African Broadcasting Association and the Sudan Interior Mission, set up ELWA (Eternal Love Winning Africa) in Liberia. (This station was destroyed in the Liberian civil war in 1990.) The following year a Swedish evangelical group began the International Radio Broadcasting Association (IBRA), and put its first programs on the air from Tangier. In 1962 the Lutheran Federation put Radio Voice of the Gospel (RVOG) on the air from Ethiopia, but it was shut down by government troops in 1977 (see Kennedy, 1979, pp. 71–77; and Lundgren, 1983, pp. 1–2, 67). In 1974 WYFR-Family Radio, operating from Oakland, California, began international radio broadcasting, and in 1985 WHRI-World Harvest Radio began its international shortwave broadcasts. Adventist World Radio, operated by the Seventh Day Adventist church, began international broadcasting in 1971.

"Free Flow" of Information Under Western Control

Another important element in the reconstruction of the international system was its intellectual context. One key aspect of this context, pursued vigorously in the postwar period by the United States, was the argument in favor of a "free flow" of information. The United Nations itself had endorsed this idea in 1948, when its Conference on Freedom of Information declared such freedom to be a "fundamental right of the people," and resolved "that everyone shall have the right to freedom of thought and expression," and that news media personnel should have "the widest possible access to the sources of information," to be able to travel unimpeded, and to transmit copy without unreasonable or discriminatory restrictions ("Final Act," 1986; see also Spiegel, 1984).

The United States was the principal champion of the free flow ideology applied to communication. Although the U.S. government had itself managed the news in times of crisis (during wartime, for example), its "official" posture was to deny the legitimacy of attempts to restrict the free flow of information (see Knightley, 1975; Steele, 1985; and Washburn, 1985; for criticism of U.S. "posturing" see Mehra, 1985). Part of the rationale for the U.S. position was the philosophical underpinning of the American press: classical liberalism, which argued that truth would emerge in any "equal contest" with falsity, and that truth was more likely to be quashed by censorship than falsity (see Siebert, Peterson, & Schramm, 1956, chapter 2). Another important consideration, however, was that in the post–World War II world, companies in the United States quickly seized a significant degree of control of the world's communication system. U.S. firms dominated the international film and recording industries, television program distribution, and wire services, and eventually satellite communication. By 1939, for instance, U.S. companies already owned about 40% of cinema houses worldwide (Taylor, 1983, p. 33). Many of the U.S.-owned foreign cinema houses, which were concentrated in Europe, were destroyed in the war. The U.S.

film industry emerged from the war stronger than ever, however, and quickly moved to dominate the major foreign markets in Canada, Europe, and Australia, and to provide the bulk of films to the smaller number of cinema houses in Latin America and within the European colonial empires (see Guback, 1969, for a worldwide perspective of the international film industry in the postwar period, and Usabel, 1982, chapter 12, on U.S. film distribution in Latin America). The United States was also a principal member of the Western industrial cartel that dominated telecommunications: telegraphy, telephony, and data communication.

The freedom envisioned by the United Nations in 1948, however, turned out also to reinforce the hegemony of the Northern Hemisphere industrial powers. Developing nations had not had a major hand in adopting the freedom of information standard (most of them were not yet created in 1948), and the call for such freedom from the United States had become muted as the client base of the U.S. news service agencies had reached parity with, and then surpassed, that of the European agencies. By 1970 the so-called big four agencies — AP, United Press International (UPI), Reuters, and Agence France-Presse (AFP) — dominated international news flow. Some minor competition (at least ideologically) came from the Soviet agency TASS. Developing countries' interests in news were, however, minor issues to the dominant agencies, which depended on domestic client bases, news exchange agreements with their competitors, and foreign subscribers on either side of the North Atlantic for their livelihood. News flow reflected the industrial powers' economic relations, the relative expense of news coverage within developing countries, and the differing ways the wire services saw their primary focus of business. Reuters, for instance, increasingly saw its profits come

from its Northern Hemisphere–based "Monitor" service, which provided financial services information to more than 15,000 clients in 112 countries by 1983 (Lawrenson & Barber, 1985, p. 12). The U.S. services' source of profit was primarily the thousands of local newspapers and radio and television stations in North America. Coverage of developing countries was limited, as the proverbial wisdom suggested, to reports of "coups and earthquakes." Even then, however, as electronic journalism, based in lightweight ENG (electronic news gathering) equipment, became easier, television news programs could carry live reports, with video, which undercut the traditional form of wire agency reporting. Competition for audiences, in other words, also contributed to decisions about coverage in the so-called Third World.

The "Right to Communicate" as a Human Right

Related to the advocacy of free expression was another idea: that of a "right to communicate," which, along with the right to freedom of information, has been enshrined in several international agreements since the end of World War II. The UN General Assembly in 1946 declared that "freedom of information is a fundamental human right and is the touchstone of all the freedoms to which the United Nations is consecrated." The Universal Declaration of Human Rights, adopted by the General Assembly in 1948, stated, "Everyone has the right to freedom of opinion and expression" (quoted in Fisher, 1982, p. 11). Jean d'Arcy, credited with being the first to articulate the idea of a right to communicate, wrote (1969, p. 14) that "the time will come when the Universal Declaration of Human Rights will have to encompass a more extensive right than man's right to information, first laid down

21 years ago in Article 19. This is the right of man to communicate." The MacBride Commission endorsed this right, although it admitted that "its full implications have yet to be explored" (MacBride, 1980, p. 138; see also Harms & Richstad, 1977; and Harms, Richstad, & Kie, 1977).

As a result of rapidly developing U.S. dominance of the world's communication content (the software delivered by the international communications system), the U.S. government sought protection for U.S.-produced products. In the field of intellectual property this meant a new international agreement on copyrights: the Universal Copyright Convention (UCC). According to Article I of the UCC (1945), one of the purposes of the UN was that it would "recommend such international agreements as may be necessary to promote the free flow of ideas by word and image." This purpose accorded with both the United Nations Charter (1945) and the Universal Declaration of Human Rights, Article 19 (1949). The U.S. desire was thus in accord with avowed principles endorsed by the world's nations at the end of World War II (see World Intellectual Property Organization, 1988, pp. 19–25, 37–38).

7.3

Wire Services, Newspapers, and Broadcast Networks

The wire services and the news distribution system also underwent major changes following the war. The old cartel of Reuters, Continental-Wolff, and Havas had been broken by a convergence of events in the 1930s. The Nazis had made the German agency, Continental-Wolff, a vehicle for propaganda, and had dismantled Havas when they defeated France. Reuters had suffered financial problems requiring a bail-out from London's "Fleet Street" newspaper barons. The two major U.S. agencies, AP and UP, had become financially stronger during the war by acquiring new clients made available by the dissolution of the cartel. They also enjoyed the protection of the U.S. government.

In the war the international wire services had had to learn to use a variety of technologies to facilitate the flow of information around the globe. For instance, because many of the cables had been cut early in the war and it was often difficult to repair them during the hostilities, radio waves with shortwave frequencies had been used to move copy through much of the world. Also, the rapid movement of armies during the war had often made it difficult to send reports from the front using wired systems, so correspondents had become accustomed to reporting with a microphone. As the competition from radio networks—the BBC and the United States' CBS, NBC, and Mutual—intensified during the war, wire service reporters had found it necessary to file their stories as quickly as possible, which also meant an increasing dependence on shortwave radio. In addition, the wire services (as their name implies) used telegraph and telephone lines to facilitate information flow between reporters and **stringers** and their bureaus, and among the various bureaus that served particular regions of the world, when they were available.

The activities of wire services were perhaps more obvious after World War II, largely as a result of the rapid growth in the number of independent states. Before the war wire services could function almost unnoticed, since they could operate within large empires and report events to a population that shared the assumptions of empire. After the war, however, as newly independent African states began to question their operations, the services became more visible. These questions, prompted by the emphasis of the news agencies on political instability, corruption, poverty, and rebellions in these states, which many of them saw as implicit colonial bias, eventually led African countries to demand a new world information order (after 1970). This new order, they claimed, not only would balance the flow of news and provide more reporting sympathetic to the African condition, it would also separate news reporting from its continual focus on the ideological conflicts between the Western alliance and the Soviet bloc, and the implications of that conflict for states attempting to be "non-aligned" (see Picard, 1991, pp. 74–75; and Laïdi, 1990, chapter 1, on rivalry of the United States and the Soviet Union in Africa).

The enhanced visibility of wire service practices, prompted by the removal of the cloak of colonialism that subjected them to indigenous criticism from formerly voiceless peoples, was an unexpected turn of events. Although they had worked hand-in-glove with the Western powers through two world wars, they had continued to define their role as that of independent disseminators of news. Now, what they had defined as news was being criticized as politically biased. As Righter (1978, p. 37) explains, developing countries see these agencies as prejudiced, culturally biased, indifferent, and neglectful in coverage of their affairs (see Tunstall, 1981, 258–267, for other criticism of international news agencies, and "News Agencies and the Issues," 1981, pp. 268–282, for rejoinders).

Agence France-Presse (AFP) was created following the liberation of France in 1944, but neither it nor the British service, Reuters, had the extensive network of foreign bureaus or clients that the two U.S. agencies enjoyed. All the wire services, regardless of their national origin, however,

gradually adopted common reporting styles, stressing political neutrality (objectivity) and the provision of news as a profitable commodity worldwide. This led to the five agencies' products looking increasingly similar, even though they operated on different principles: AFP was subsidized by the French government, Reuters and AP functioned as cooperatives (owned by newspapers), and UP operated as a profit-making enterprise (Fenby, 1986, p. 62). In 1958 the United Press took over the International News Service (controlled by the Hearst newspaper group) and became United Press International (UPI).

The "big four" news agencies — AFP, AP, Reuters, and UPI — gradually built up their news-gathering operations, developed new methods of distributing their products, initiated language services aimed at particular world markets, and consolidated their activities into those that each one found most profitable (see Tunstall, 1977, chapter 1). They used a variety of technologies to distribute their news services around the globe, including submarine cables, radio teletype (RTTY), and eventually satellite and fiber optics networks.[6] In 1968 Reuters introduced a computerized news distribution system, called automatic data exchange, or ADX. This system allowed multiple dispatches to be sent simultaneously to coded addresses throughout the world. It also eliminated the previous necessity of re-entering the same news story for different destinations, and allowed news to flow uninterrupted from source to client without intervention from the central news desk in London (Boyd-Barrett, 1980, p. 81). UPI introduced a similar service in 1971.

The news agencies also began to develop other services: newsphoto, newsfilm, and video news. AP was the first wire service to begin newsphoto transmissions in 1927, but

only within the United States. In the early
1950s it began distributing photos abroad
by radio, and by 1964 was sending them to
15 European countries, and to the Soviet
Union and Latin America.

UPI began newsfilm operations shortly
after the end of World War II, working with
Fox Movietone and then British Movietone.
Reuters began international newsfilm distribution in 1960 when it bought into the British Commonwealth International Film
Agency that, four years later, became Visnews, owned jointly by Reuters (33%), the
BBC (33%), and the broadcasting networks
of Australia, Canada, and New Zealand. In
1967 UPI began a newsfilm venture with
Britain's Independent Television News,
known as UPITN.

> During the 1960s and 1970s, Visnews and
> UPITN came to dominate the flow of film cov-
> erage of foreign events to television stations
> outside the United States. Visnews supplied
> 200 subscribers in 98 countries in the early
> 1980s, while UPITN had 120 subscribers in
> 70 nations. Each provides regular feeds of
> film delivered increasingly by satellite and
> electronic circuits instead of by the original
> method of air freight. In Western Europe, 40
> to 50 percent of material in the regional film
> exchange system, Eurovision, originates from
> the two agencies. Most television stations
> elsewhere in the world depend on one or both
> of the services for international coverage, and
> each agency has exchange agreements with
> major U.S. networks. (Fenby, 1986, p. 108)

Another significant international wire
service agency, TASS, the Telegraph Agency
of the Soviet Union, was established on December 1, 1917.[7] It was originally part of the
official "propaganda apparatus" of the Soviet state, and was directed by officials with
close ties to the Communist party.

Besides TASS, a smaller, "semiofficial"
news organization, the Novosti Press
Agency (APN), also operated from the So-

viet Union beginning in 1961. Its correspondents attempted to provide commentary,
features, and cultural material to news organizations as independent contributors
(Roxburgh, 1987, pp. 57–58). Novosti was to
be "independent" of direction from the
Communist party in the Soviet Union, although its journalists received the same
training (including ideological indoctrination) as other Soviet journalists. Novosti
correspondents abroad worked out of the
public affairs offices of Soviet embassies, as
did their TASS counterparts. Their reporting and commentaries, however, in addition
to being sent back to the Soviet Union, were
also submitted to domestic news organizations for publication, independent of TASS
distribution. Novosti journalists therefore
saw themselves as being truly "objective"
writers in these countries, since they judged
that Western journalists had to meet the
demands of economic necessity imposed by
their editors and publishers—that is, to attract readers for advertisers.

7.4

International Radio Broadcasting During the Cold War

By 1946 the United States and its European
allies saw the Soviet Union, which had been
their ally in World War II, as a potential military threat. The Soviets revived their aggressive anticapitalist ideology advocating
revolution by the working class, muted during the war by their struggle for survival.
The United States feared that Europe, economically and militarily devastated by the
war, was ripe for Soviet domination. Thus,
in response to the perceived threat, it
passed a new National Security Act in 1947
to re-establish U.S. intelligence operations,
dismantled in 1945 by President Truman. By

1948 the newly established Central Intelligence Agency (CIA) was active in the Italian election campaign, attempting to stem what the United States saw as a tidal wave of communism threatening to overrun Western Europe.

The focus of the media war shifted as a result of the reorientation of world power. The stage was no longer only Western Europe, but the world, and the struggle of the two "superpowers," the United States and the Soviet Union (see, for instance, Aronson, 1970; Liebovich, 1988; and Sayre, 1982). Each sought allies for its ideological cause and began to court newly forming countries in Africa and Asia (see Laïdi, 1990).

Voice of America

At the conclusion of the war the United States cut back on the budget of its international broadcasting operation, just as it did in all sectors of its wartime propaganda efforts. The Voice of America (VOA) also kept its criticism of the Soviets to a minimum, even controlling its rhetoric during the Berlin crisis and airlift in 1948 (the Berlin airlift is discussed in Tusa & Tusa, 1988). Finally in 1948 the Congress passed the Smith-Mundt Act, creating a permanent international information agency, and providing operating funds for VOA. When the Korean War broke out in 1950,

> attempts to limit criticism of the Soviet Union and Communism stopped. President Truman launched a "Campaign of Truth" in April 1950, in which he called upon the media to "promote the truth about America in order to combat Communist distortions. . . ." In September 1950 . . . he issued a classified message to the State Department instructing it to combat Communism and Communist media output "by exposing its lies . . . and subjecting it to ridicule." Thus began the "hard line" era in which "tough" and even highly dramatic

> VOA prose called attention to perceived Communist deficiencies. . . . (Browne, 1982, p. 98)

Congress appropriated $121 million for Truman's "Campaign of Truth" (an enormous sum at that time, equivalent to over $1 billion in 1991), and Truman himself set up a Psychological Strategy Board to advise the National Security Council about conducting propaganda. "In 1953, President Eisenhower appointed a personal advisor on psychological warfare. Although this appointment lapsed after only one year, propaganda had now established itself as a top priority in the Cold War strategy. The stridently anti-communist tone of the Voice reflected this priority" (Hale, 1975, p. 34). Eisenhower also created an Operations Coordination Board (OCB) that was to centralize and direct the government's overseas propaganda efforts. This board was unable to implement its ideas, however (Green, 1988, p. 29). The U.S. Advisory Commission on Information, and an independent expert committee created by Eisenhower and headed by William Jackson, a New York businessman, both recommended in 1953 that an independent organization be established to coordinate U.S. information initiatives abroad. These recommendations resulted, on August 1, 1953, in the creation of the United States Information Agency (USIA). USIA's first director, Theodore S. Streibert, after restoring morale damaged by large-scale layoffs in the federal government, moved VOA's operations from New York to Washington, and began to direct its activities (Green, 1988, pp. 30, 31).

VOA was the "official" voice of the United States, although U.S. citizens were not to be part of its audience. Under its charter, originally written in 1960, revised in 1963, and codified into law under the Ford administration in 1976 (Public Law 94-350), three basic principles governed the broadcasts of VOA: (1) VOA would serve as a consistently reliable and authoritative source of accurate, objective, and comprehensive news; (2) VOA would represent *all* of U.S. society, not merely selected elements, and would present a balanced and comprehensive projection of significant U.S. thought and institutions; and (3) VOA would present the policies of the United States clearly and effectively, and would also present responsible discussion and opinion of these policies (for an analysis of VOA's early "propaganda" broadcasts, however, see Rathkolb, 1987; and Shulman, 1990, pp. 53–73; for later broadcasts, see Alexandre, 1988, pp. 81, 82). The delay in codifying the charter seems to have resulted from disagreements within the government about the role of VOA, and particularly of its news organization. Was it to be, as Hobart Lewis, former chairman of the U.S. Advisory Commission on Information, put it, a "surrogate for the U.S. government" (Alexandre, 1988, p. 82)? Or was it an autonomous agency (see Alexandre, 1988, pp. 81–94, for a full discussion of the 1976 passage of the Charter)?

Radio in the American Sector, Radio Free Europe, and Radio Liberty

Besides VOA, the United States also established three other services in Western Europe. The first, Radio in the American Sector (RIAS), was set up in West Berlin in 1946, ostensibly to serve the Allied occupation forces in Berlin, although obviously the signal would reach into East Germany, which surrounded the city (see Browne, 1986). Radio Free Europe (RFE) was next, established in 1949 as a "private" organization dedicated to reaching Central and Eastern Europe, by then annexed into the Soviet bloc, and the three Soviet Baltic states,

which the United States did not recognize as part of the Soviet Union. It began broadcasting on July 4, 1950, from West Germany, and gradually added various language services between then and May 1952 (see Holt, 1958). The third operation was Radio Liberty (RL), established in 1951 on lines similar to those of RFE, with broadcasting aimed into the Soviet Union beginning in 1953. It broadcast in Russian and other indigenous languages of the Soviet Union (see Alexeyeva, 1986).

For more than 20 years the CIA secretly provided most of the financing for RFE/RL. Suspicions of CIA involvement grew over time, however, and in 1973 the Presidential Study Commission on International Radio Broadcasting ended this practice and recommended that a separate board be established to oversee operations on the two services. This recommendation resulted in the formation of the Board for International Broadcasting (BIB) (see Hale, 1975, pp. 39–40).

The programming of RFE/RL had a fundamentally different character than that of VOA. It was not intended to represent the United States, but the regions and peoples it served. These services were to portray to their target populations the opinions of their countrymen not otherwise heard over their official domestic communication services. They broadcast news about the countries that were their targets and engaged in "psychological warfare," originally seeking to "roll back" communism in Europe and destabilize the Soviet Union (see Mickelson, 1983, chapters 2 and 3).

The Soviet Union objected to the activities of RFE/RL, RIAS, and VOA. It saw the programs of these services as propaganda directed against itself and its allies in Central and Eastern Europe. In particular, it objected to RFE/RL and RIAS broadcasts, citing instances in which these stations fomented disturbances, or even incited insurrection in some countries. RIAS, for instance, was labeled a "main factor" in disturbances in East Germany in June 1953, while RL was seen by the Soviets as "increasingly provocative in [its] insinuations, openly instigating listeners to violate Soviet law" (Alov & Viktorov, 1985, pp. 58, 71).[8]

Probably the best known instance in which these services were accused of "provocation" was in 1956, when RFE broadcasts were viewed as incitement to the Hungarian uprising.[9] As Hale (1975, p. 41) put it, "The first thing to be said about incitement is that the crude and insensitive propaganda that led to accusations of stirring up the 1956 revolt is a thing of the past. Despite the lack of documentary evidence that there was any direct call to take to the street, even RFE officials now admit that the total effect of the broadcasts was such that an excited and frightened audience might have been expected to overreact." Soley and Nichols (1987, p. 64) more directly accuse RFE, writing, "The CIA-financed station did its best to propagandize against any peaceful settlement of the Hungarian revolt. Radio Free Europe demanded that all Communists resign from the government. After Nagy [a popular Communist leader in Hungary] asked rebels to lay down their arms, Radio Free Europe carried a conflagrational message. . . ."

7.5

Propaganda in the Cold War Between East and West

Nazi Germany and Great Britain dominated the ideological struggle of World War II. After 1945, however, as these examples suggest, the focus of ideological struggle shifted and the principal actors also changed. Following the war the Soviet Union and the United States took up the principal roles in the new battle of ideas. As already stated, the United States did not immediately begin propaganda activities directed to the Soviet Union. OWI's funding was greatly reduced at the end of the war, and President Truman terminated the agency in 1946, reserving only a small fraction of its previous activities within the State Department, and cutting the personnel from the wartime high of 11,000 to 3,000, including both VOA personnel and staff stationed at U.S. embassies.

The following year, however, Winston Churchill, in a speech in Fulton, Missouri, warned that the free nations of Europe were slipping behind an "Iron Curtain," and the United States began to re-examine its foreign policy (see Harbutt, 1986, especially chapter 7). "Nobody 'declared' the Cold War; it just grew, with the belated American resistance to Soviet imperialism. The need had again arrived for an overseas propaganda mechanism to serve America's geopolitical strategy" (Green, 1988, p. 18).[10] While the United States may have wanted to believe that such activities were unnecessary in peacetime, it faced the same problems whether war existed or not: The adversary could have an information monopoly, or it could be denied one. If the Soviet Union believed in an international information strategy, then the United States would have to have one, too. The 1948 Smith-Mundt Act (the U.S. Information and Educational Exchange Act) directed the secretary of state "to provide for the preparation and dissemination abroad of information about the United States, its people and its policies" (Daugherty, 1962, pp. 29–30). In 1953 the government created the United States Information Agency (USIA), an agency separated from the State Department.

During the period from 1945 to 1953 the United States struggled to determine how it should conduct its official international communication activities. During this period the government moved from an assumption that U.S. propaganda activities would be "demobilized" (just as the armed forces were doing), to a recognition that a permanent information agency would be required. But what sort of agency—one that advocated democracy or an "American" way of life, or one that merely told "America's" story?

The international political situation helped answer that question. The confrontation over Berlin, the rising fortunes of Communist-inspired political parties in Western Europe, the failing grip of the old European powers over their empires (leaving newly forming countries adrift to confront aggressive communism), the loss of China to Mao Tse Tung's forces, and the invasion of South Korea by the North all led U.S. international broadcasting to adopt an increasingly virulent anti-Communist tone. Even with this shifting emphasis, VOA found itself under investigation by the House UnAmerican Activities Committee headed by Senator Joseph McCarthy (Kretzmann, 1967, p. 27; see also Sarnoff, 1955). Hunting for Communists and detailing Communist propaganda activities became a type of "cottage industry" in the United States (see, e.g., Clews, 1964).

The defining act of this period became President Truman's "Campaign of Truth," a propaganda offensive begun in 1950 to "combat Communist distortions" by promoting the truth about the United States. This offensive, and the lukewarm support of the State Department, is what led to the creation of the United States Information Agency in 1953 (Alexandre, 1988, pp. 10, 11).

Gradually, the United States developed a multipronged propaganda and information service. The Soviet Union joined the United States in a propaganda battle.[11] International broadcasting networks (including Radio Moscow, Radio Peace and Progress, and Radio Kiev on the Soviet side and VOA, RFE/RL, and Radio Martí on the American side), summitry, activities in international organizations (including the United Nations, military alliances, Intelsat, Intersputnik, councils and committees of various organizations, etc.), public affairs activities conducted in embassies and with the press in foreign capitals, and humanitarian and development assistance projects—all were used to spread the two countries' respective ideologies.[12]

Much of this activity went under the name "public diplomacy," indicating that it went beyond obvious efforts to persuade, such as occurs in broadcast editorials or commentaries, while still occurring in public (see Abshire, 1976). It was still another form of "white" propaganda, although it eschewed the manipulative elements of traditional propaganda.[13]

Both the United States and the Soviet Union also used "black" or "gray" propaganda.[14] The Soviet Union was adept at establishing "revolutionary" movements in the developing world that often undertook broadcasting activities to support their cause, and using "agents of influence"—journalists, labor leaders, government officials, academics, students, and so on—to argue their case in other countries (see Kirkpatrick, 1956; Lendval, 1981; and Schultz & Godson, 1984, pp. 132–135). The United States also used similar tactics, particularly clandestine radio, such as the CIA-funded "Radio Swan" directed at Cuba, as well as covertly funding RFE/RL, broadcasting organizations that were ostensibly financed by private interests, for 20 years (see Frederick, 1986, chapter 2; Mickelson, 1983; and Soley & Nichols, 1987, chapters 7 and 9).

In addition, both the Soviet Union and the United States were allied with other countries that shared their basic ideological stance, and that often operated their own external broadcasting stations espousing similar values. Such stations served to reinforce the propaganda of their ideological leader, because they helped legitimize the messages, or interpretations, provided by a dominant country. Besides the Soviet's own radio operations, for instance, Bulgaria, Czechoslovakia, East Germany, Hungary, Poland, and Romania all operated external radio stations broadcasting in multiple languages. In the West, significant allied stations (at least from the Soviet point of view) included Deutschlandfunk, Deutsche Welle, and the BBC, in addition to the U.S. operations (see Fraenkel, 1986b; Heil & Schiele, 1986; Kirsch, 1986; Reiss, 1986; Short, 1986; and Whitaker, 1962).

7.6

Jamming of Broadcast Signals

The major means available to countries that wanted to stop unauthorized broadcasts to their citizens, and thereby reassert their own information monopoly, was jamming. Jamming is a rather simple activity. Countries jam by broadcasting a second signal on the same frequency as an incoming but unwanted broadcast. The second signal can be ordinary broadcast programming, or simply a "wall of noise," as VOA has called it. Jamming signals can be directed into the path of a broadcast wave bouncing to the earth from the ionosphere (sky jamming), or they can blanket an area where the incoming

signal would "land" (ground jamming). Ground jamming is the more effective and more often utilized form.

There is some question about who first practiced jamming. Some evidence suggests that the French tried to jam German radio telegraph signals during World War I from the Eiffel Tower. Browne accuses the French, too, but identifies a radio station as beginning it, and in 1923 (Browne, 1982, pp. 16–17).[15] Schwoch (1990, chapter 5) credits an Argentinian radio station that jammed the signals of another station operated by an international syndicate trying to dominate South American broadcasting in 1922. Radio Moscow blames the Austrians, saying they began jamming Nazi broadcasts in 1938, thus denying "the popular belief in the West" that the Soviet Union was the first to jam radio signals (BBC Monitoring Service, 1987a). Both Austria and Romania were also early jammers.[16]

At the end of World War II jamming quickly became a major source of controversy between the Soviet Union and the Western democracies. The Soviets first jammed Western radio signals in 1946. In 1948 the Soviets began jamming on a large scale, and "by 1949 the Soviet Union was using over 1000 stations to jam Russian-language programs originating in the West. . . . In June, 1949, Assistant Secretary of State Allen admitted that this jamming was 70–75 percent effective" (Whitton & Larson, 1964, pp. 210–211). A UN Sub-Commission on Freedom of Information and the Press and the UN General Assembly both condemned jamming in 1950 (Whitton & Larson, 1964, pp. 204, 211). Nevertheless, by 1962 the Soviets had doubled the number of jamming transmitters (up to 2,000), and "an estimate in *The Economist* put the number of transmitters used for this purpose in the Soviet Union and eastern

Europe at 3,000" (Hale, 1975, p. 133; see Lisann, 1975, chapters 2–4, for a history of jamming).

The Soviet Union and its Eastern European allies did not jam Western signals consistently; from time to time they stopped jamming the BBC and VOA, though not RFE/RL.[17] In 1987 and 1988, however, jamming of all such services into these countries was halted, beginning with the BBC in January 1987, VOA in May, and then in late 1988 RFE/RL, KOL Israel, and West Germany's Deutsche Welle. By this time only Czechoslovakia and Bulgaria were still jamming (Ottaway, 1988b). This, too, ended as liberalization, and then democracy, hit Eastern Europe. Until the jamming ceased, the Soviet Union was reportedly spending more money jamming signals than the United States was spending to broadcast into the country (see Shanor, 1985, p. 145).

The international conventions administered by the ITU oblige countries not to interfere harmfully with radio signals of other member states. Obviously, jamming qualifies as harmful interference. The ITU, however, was unable to prove that willful interference was occurring, despite protests from the United States and other countries, until the 1984 World Administrative Radio Conference (WARC) instructed the IFRB to "organize monitoring programmes in the bands allocated to the high frequency broadcasting service with the view to identifying stations causing harmful interference" (quoted in Sowers, Hand, & Rush, 1988, p. 109; see also "A New Approach to Radio Jamming Abroad," 1986). These monitoring programs indicated that, for the June 1986 period, 95% of VOA programs into the Soviet Union were jammed, while 100% of RL, 98% of RFE, 96% of KOL Israel, and 95% of BBC and Deutsche Welle broadcasts in various languages into the Soviet Union and in their Bulgarian, Czech, and Polish ser-

vices into these countries were jammed (Sowers, Hands, & Rush, 1988, p. 113; see also "IFRB Backs U.S. Claims of Soviet Jamming," 1986).

Other countries have practiced jamming, too. The Nazis, for instance, jammed Allied signals during the war. Spain jammed Soviet radio signals in 1946, just as the Soviets began jamming Spanish signals that year. Both France and the United Kingdom have jammed radio signals, and Iraq and Iran jammed one another's radio signals beginning in 1980 when the two countries went to war. The BBC even found that Iraq was jamming its Pashto and Dari language broadcasts aimed at Afghani refugee populations in Pakistan, although it suspected that the Iraqis had misunderstood the purpose of the broadcasts. The jamming ceased following a protest to the Iraqi government. In 1989 the Chinese government jammed the signals of both the BBC and VOA to prevent students from judging the effectiveness of their Tiananmen Square protests by reports from other Chinese cities carried on these two services. The South Korean government also reportedly considered jamming a Pyongyang (North Korea) FM radio station broadcasting "anti-Seoul" propaganda in 1989 (BBC Monitoring Service, 1989b). During the Persian Gulf conflict Iraq also reportedly jammed BBC broadcasts into the region. And Cuba routinely jams Radio and Television Martí signals aimed into Havana (for a discussion of international law on jamming, see Price, 1984).

7.7

Radio Communication in the Developing World

As these struggles were occurring in Europe, other world events were also changing the world's political complexion: The clamor of the peoples of Africa, the Middle East, and Asia for independence, often punctuated by riots, uprisings, and wars of liberation, gradually caused the dissolution of the great empires constructed by Britain, France, Holland, Portugal, and, to a lesser degree, the United States. As new countries were created, beginning with Ghana in 1957, they, too, inaugurated domestic communication systems, sometimes inheriting colonial networks, but often attempting to construct communication networks from scratch (for a history of All India Radio, for instance, see Masani, 1976, chapter 5). These countries came to see domestic communications as a means to hasten economic, political, and social development, and international communications as a method of participating in world economic and political life (see Lerner, 1958; Pye, 1963; Rogers, 1969; and Schramm, 1964).

The Impact of Communication Technologies

U.S. communication researchers began suggesting in the 1950s that investment in communications infrastructures was linked to modernity and economic progress. Based on his work in the Middle East, Lerner, for instance, claimed (1958, p. 55) that "no modern society functions efficiently without a developed system of mass media. Our historical forays indicate that the conditions which define modernity form an interlocking 'system.' They grow conjointly, in the normal situation, or they become stunted severally."[18] Schramm (1964, p. ix) echoed the claim: "Without adequate and effective communication, economic and social development will inevitably be retarded, and may be counter productive. With adequate and effective communication, the pathways to change can be made easier and shorter." And Rostow identified investment in com-

munications as one of the "preconditions for take-off" of national economies (1960, pp. 7, 19).

Such statements meshed well with the expectations of many leaders of new countries, who, as Lawrenson and Barber (1985, p. 113) put it, "wanted the status symbols of independence, . . . above all a government radio station and a news agency. These were the symbols of progress, but also real instruments of power because they gave the new leaders the ability to control the news and information flow within their own countries." Whether the implied link of modernity and communication was accepted by developing countries because of their need to believe that they could "catch up" with the industrial states, or was merely a convenient rhetorical weapon to justify their own grab for political power depended on the specific country. Undoubtedly, both conclusions were true in many instances.

The arguments for investment seemed convincing on their face. The development of the transistor radio seemed to make it economically feasible: Large numbers of radio receivers could be imported and dispersed if national radio systems could be put into place. Money was spent, and technicians, journalists, and audiovisual educators were trained (largely in U.S. universities). The results, however, were disappointing. The gap between wealthy and poorer countries remained as wide as ever (scholars have produced a variety of works on this problem; see, for instance, Driscoll & Wellender, 1974; East, 1983; Graff, 1983; Granger, 1979; Jéquier, 1984; Jussawalla & Lamberton, 1982; Mowlana & Wilson, 1988; Prasad, 1986; Renaud, 1987; Rogers, 1983; Saunders, Warford, & Wellenius, 1983; Stover, 1984; and Turner, 1973).

Even as developing countries invested in communications, problems arose. Opening societies to mediated communication also opened them up to both capitalist and socialist propaganda, and the tyranny of rising expectations in societies that could ill afford to meet them (see Horowitz, 1972, p. 19). Scholars began suggesting that developing countries were being made even more politically, economically, and culturally subservient to countries that produced large quantities of media material and technology, engaged in significant foreign propaganda activities, or developed new technologies for export (see Fortner, 1978a; and Schiller, 1971). Technology itself came to be seen as a threat to indigenous cultures. Multinational corporations, as major vehicles for technology transfer, were found arguably to be the cause of ever more dependency on industrialized countries (see, for instance, Barnet & Müller, 1974; and Goulet, 1977, pp. 243–244). Even media controlled within countries were subject to indirect control by foreign production styles. These styles were so potent, the argument went, that producers in developing countries simply copied them (see Elliott & Golding, 1974, p. 236; and Waterman, 1988).[19] The payoff from investing in communications technologies thus might be far less than had been supposed.[20]

Africa

In Africa most newly formed nations' initial broadcasting systems used shortwave, inherited from colonial authorities as these administrations were dismantled (see Mytton, 1983). This was the least expensive form of broadcasting, since shortwave signals were capable of covering larger amounts of territory than medium-wave (AM) signals using the same power. African nations, however, have continued to lag behind other nations of the world in terms of development of communications, due both

to political instability and to lack of economic capability (see, for instance, Guttman, 1986).

The adoption of shortwave as a technology also allowed other nations access to African audiences using the same technology and beaming signals into target areas. The BBC, for instance, initiated broadcasting in native languages in 1957, followed by VOA in 1959 and Deutsche Welle in 1962 (Browne, 1974, pp. 184–187). Radio Moscow began broadcasting to Africa in 1958, using more African languages than any of its competitors; Radio Peking and Radio Berlin also began broadcasting, in 1959 and 1960, respectively (Browne, 1974, pp. 177–178). And under Gamal Nasser, Egypt became active in broadcasting in indigenous languages to sub-Saharan Africa as well.

Asia

In Asia the same forces were at work as colonial empires crumbled and indigenous populations fought for political control. France, followed by the United States, was engaged in fighting off a "war of liberation" in southeast Asia. In China a civil war eventually resulted in a Communist government on the mainland and the establishment of the "Republic of China" on Taiwan; on the Korean peninsula a United Nations force stalled a military offensive from the northern half aimed at toppling the government in the south.

Broadcasts in indigenous languages aimed at the native populations, while existing before World War II, were not very significant until 1942. Nazi Germany, Japan, the United States, Britain, and Australia all had services in Asian languages by the end of that year (Browne, 1978, pp. 318–319; Ryō, 1983, p. 320). In 1950 the nationalist Chinese on Taiwan began broadcasting both to the Chinese mainland and to the world, and by 1951 Radio Peking was broadcasting in 13 Asian languages. Also in 1951 the CIA set up the Asian equivalent of Radio Free Europe, operating out of Manila, called Radio Free Asia. It went out of operation two years later, but was replaced by the Radio of Free Asia, which operated until 1966. Radio Japan, forced off the air at the end of the war and throughout the Allied occupation, reinstituted international broadcasting in 1952 (Browne, 1978, p. 319). Radio Deutsche Welle, West Germany's international service, began the following year.

These services to developing countries joined the broadcasts that already existed, directed both into Europe and the Americas. The propaganda battles of the 1930s had resulted in significant foreign language broadcasting by the European powers directed to one another, and both North and South America also were prime targets for the services of the BBC and Germany's "Weltrundfunksender." During the war the United States also began broadcasting into Europe, and took over its private broadcasters' stations that had reached into Latin America. Gradually, through the expansion of radio broadcasting directed into developing countries, they became a part of the geopolitical turmoil that affected the Northern Hemisphere. They had gained independence from colonial masters only to find themselves subjected to new demands: to take sides in a bitter ideological struggle that increasingly defined the political relations of states. What they had gained in legitimacy by having programming directed to them in their indigenous languages was often more than offset by the refusal of the cold-warring states to assist them in development if they were on the wrong side of the ideological divide. Radio had again become one of the tools in the arsenals of political and military adversaries.

The Beginning of International Satellite Communication

Intelsat I, also known as "Early Bird," was the first commercial geosynchronous orbit satellite. It was launched in 1965, following experiments with passive—Echo 1 (1960) and Echo 2 (1964)— and active—Courier (1960), Telstar 1 (1962), Telstar 2 (1963), Relay 1 (1962), and Relay 2 (1964)—satellites in orbits between 600 and 6,000 miles. The first geosynchronous satellite, Syncom 1, was orbited in 1963 (see Rees, 1990, pp. 8–10).

The vehicle for providing satellite circuits worldwide was an international common carrier organization, Intelsat. Intelsat was formed in 1964 at "American instigation" among 19 "mostly industrialized countries" (Rees, 1990, pp. 10–17; Snow, 1986, p. 34). It provided telephone, broadcast-quality radio, television, facsimile, and data communications circuits to member countries. It delivered its services via satellite earth stations, which at first required standard earth stations 30 meters in diameter for low-power C-band links. By the end of the 1980s dish sizes had shrunk and satellite power had increased. The smallest dishes then in use were 60 centimeters in diameter for high-power links used in high-speed data transmission (basic information about satellite communications can be found in Hollis, 1984; or Sutphin, 1986).[21]

Nineteen countries signed the original treaties in 1964 that created the International Telecommunications Satellite (Intelsat) organization. This was the first international satellite system, and it became operational—that is, capable of handling satellite traffic—in 1965 with the launch of Early Bird. Membership has since grown to over 110 countries, with a total of 170 nations using Intelsat facilities by 1988, many through up-links in neighboring countries. Early Bird was capable of carrying 240 telephone conversations simultaneously. Since then the capacity of satellites has increased significantly, with Intelsat VI capable of handling 80,000 simultaneous voice conversations (Hudson, 1990, p. 3). (See Table 7.1.)

Intelsat was organized as a nonprofit cooperative organization. It operates commercially, charging members and nonmembers alike for its services, but has consistently reduced its rates since 1965. It serves members and nonmembers on an open and nondiscriminatory basis. Intelsat owns only the space segment of international circuits, with the earth stations necessary to up- and down-link signals owned and operated by telecommunications authorities, usually post, telegraph, and telephone administrations (PTTs), although in the United States the designated authority is Comsat, the Communications Satellite Corporation, a private entity set up by Congress in 1962. Comsat's largest participant is AT&T.

Intersputnik was created in 1968 by the Soviet Union, and became operational as an international system in 1971. That year it was registered as a United Nations organization, and several socialist European countries and Cuba joined it. Intersputnik began its telecommunications services to Eastern Europe, Cuba, and Mongolia, using Soviet MOLNIYA 2 and 3 satellites in the mid-1970s, and since then has expanded the system to provide worldwide coverage using Statsionar-T and 1-10 series C-band satellites (see Downing, 1986; and Howell, 1986, p. 180).

7.9

Inequities and Injustice in the International Communications System

The inequalities in access to the international communications system were obvious in the decades that preceded the two world wars. After the end of World War II, two trends offered hope that these inequities might be ameliorated. One was the break-up of the European empires. In south central Asia, for instance, Mahatma Ghandi's successful nonviolent resistance to British rule succeeded in convincing Britain to leave the Indian subcontinent, with both India and Pakistan achieving independent sta-

Table 7.1

Circuit Capacity of Intelsat Satellites

Year	Satellite	Telephone Circuits		TV Circuits
1965	Intelsat I	240	or	1
1968	Intelsat III	1,200	and	1
1971	Intelsat IV	5,000		—
1976	Intelsat IV-A	6,000		2
1980	Intelsat V	12,000	and	2
1985	Intelsat V-A	15,000		2
1989	Intelsat VI	100,000*		2
1992	Intelsat VII	100,000 +		2

*33,000 circuits are available, but using compression techniques allows this total to be tripled.

Source: Rees, 1990, pp. 34–48.

tus within the Commonwealth in 1947. In 1950 India became a republic, and in 1957 Pakistan was proclaimed an Islamic republic. And in Africa similar forces were at work. In northern Africa Libya (1951), Ethiopia (1952), and Sudan and Tunisia (1956) all became independent. Former French colonies, such as Niger and Senegal (1960) and Mali (1961) also achieved independence. In eastern and southern Africa, South Africa and Tanzania (1961), Uganda (1962), and Kenya (1963) achieved independence, as did Nigeria, the Congo, Ivory Coast, and the Central African Republic (1960), Sierra Leone (1961), and Lesotho and Malawi (1966) in the central and western portions of the continent.

While such a trend might have resulted in fragmentation of the highly centralized international communications system, newly independent states, pursuing their own objectives, might also have demanded a system more responsive to their needs. Their economic capacities and infrastructures were weak, however, and their political institutions fragile. They were unable successfully to demand that the old colonial structures for international communication

be altered. Communications traffic, like air travel, continued to flow through the hubs of former imperial capitals.

The other trend was the establishment of international organizations, most obviously the United Nations, and the flurry of declarations that followed in their wake. In addition, the efforts were made to rationalize the international communications system by bringing various organizations, such as the ITU, WIPO, and UNESCO, under the aegis of the UN. (See Figure 7.2.)

Under the UN, treaties or conventions were to be adjudicated by the International Court of Justice—the World Court. The court's own statute (adopted in 1945) allowed it to apply (1) international conventions, (2) international custom, (3) general principles of law recognized by civilized nations, and (4) "judicial decisions and the teachings of the most highly qualified publicists of the various nations, as a subsidiary means for the determination of rules of law" (Article 38). The court was given no official sanctions to impose on countries against which it ruled, however. It had to rely on "world opinion" or "moral authority" as the basis for nations to abide by

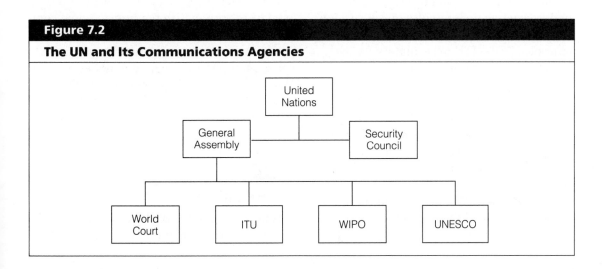

Figure 7.2

The UN and Its Communications Agencies

its decisions. Regulations implementing treaties could also be adjudicated by the court, but they were to be treated in like manner, so far as sanctions are concerned. A country winning a case before the court could take a grievance to the UN Security Council should the losing party fail "to perform the obligations incumbent upon it." The Security Council, however, could only "make recommendations or decide upon measures to be taken to give effect to the judgment" (Ploman, 1982, p. 8). Also, when the court ruled against the permanent members of the Security Council (the United States, the United Kingdom, France, the Soviet Union, and People's Republic of China), these members could veto any suggested actions.

Regulations could also be "enforced" by the weight of world opinion during meetings of the international agency entrusted with their implementation. Meetings of the ITU, for instance, were sometimes bogged down by ongoing contentious issues, such as jamming of radio signals or assignment of frequencies. Although all nations agreed that the radio spectrum was an international resource, and that agreements had to be made and adhered to by all, the sanctions available to the ITU and its constituent bodies were again limited to moral suasion (see Levin, 1971, p. 3). As a result, the approach of the ITU to regulatory issues has been categorized as laissez-faire, although as Leive suggests, the ITU's approach gradually evolved into one more sympathetic to "planning," as pushed by developing countries, than to the traditional "first come, first served" approach favored by industrialized countries (Leive, 1984, p. 74).

The rationalization to be achieved, then, by development of the ITU, or of the UN generally, was limited. The requirements of reaching, and enforcing, international agreement still tended to favor some (more powerful) countries over others. This problem would persist, too, even after new countries began to achieve independence in the late 1950s.

Such agreements, too, had limited effects on the activities of transnational corporations or corporately controlled networks that were part of the international communications system. In 1965, for instance, when the Zenith Corporation was sued by Hazeltine Research Inc., "which had been formed to handle the patent pools administered by RCA," the suit "exposed the network of patent pools in Canada, Great Britain, and Australia, involving subsidiaries of General Electric, Philips, RCA, AT&T, and the English companies EMI and Marconi," all of which had adopted measures designed "to seal off these markets from imports" (Mirow & Maurer, 1982, p. 45). Such organizations, in other words, protected their own economic interests by supplementing the international system's protection with their own.

Neither law nor international agreement nor intellectual context nor the changing geopolitical relations of countries altered the tactics of corporations, or aspirations of states, to monopolize the international communications system. Both countries and corporate interests continued to press for, or to maintain existing, monopolies of knowledge, struggling to impose their versions of history and methods of interpretation on the world's peoples.

7.10

Conclusion

From the beginning of the development of the international communications system through the 1960s, the major military, economic, and political powers in the world had defined the system as they saw fit. They created the networks, decided the cost of using them, chose when to compete and when to cooperate. The European imperial powers, particularly Britain, had extended their influence through developing and using communications networks, had used those networks through two world wars, and had successfully exploited them for their own economic and political ends. The United States had reluctantly abandoned its isolationist posture and, after World War II, embarked on an ideological battle with the Soviet Union using this international system.

Most of the peoples of the world had not benefited from the development of the international system. The system had allowed imperial governments to centralize control over extensive territories and their peoples, but it had not liberated them. By the end of the 1960s, however, the number of independent countries in the world had more than doubled from that in 1946. The 1970s would be the test of their independence, insofar as the international communications system was concerned. Could they, by sheer weight of numbers or moral suasion, convince the entrenched interests to consider their interests? Or would it be business as usual, haves versus have-nots, the continuation of colonialism?

Notes

1. As Graves explained of the war (n.d., p. 163), "Throughout the six years, the Company's staff were subject to all the risks of War Correspondents, and many more. Cable stations were priority targets all over the world for enemy aircraft. Time and again the staff remained at their posts until the last minute in the best traditions of wireless operators in sinking ships. They were bombed, machine-gunned, shelled and torpedoed."

2. The International Consultative Committee on Radio (CCIR) also had several study groups, including transmitters, receivers, fixed services, space systems and radio astronomy, tropospheric and ground-wave propagation, ionospheric propagation, broadcasting, television, mobile services, and vocabulary (see ITU, 1965, p. 230).

3. This link was proposed by the June 1958 Commonwealth Telecommunications Conference (see Baglehole, 1969, pp. 33, 34).

4. Eurovision and Intervision also negotiated jointly for the rights to broadcast the 1960 Rome Olympics, with Intervision taking feeds from Eurovision for the Olympics in September 1960. The formal, or "permanent," link was established the following year (see Eugster, 1983, p. 108). Le Duc (1981, p. 136) claims the 1960 beginning.

5. The history of FEBA can be seen in Winter (1971) and Cousins and Cousins (1978). FEBA was originally a group of British associates who supported the work of FEBC. When the Seychelles site became available, however, FEBA took on a separate existence to operate the site, since the Seychelles were, at that time, a British colony. Test transmissions from the Seychelles commenced on October 18, 1969 (see Cousins & Cousins, 1978, pp. 38–45).

6. RTTY communication shares the shortwave bands with international broadcasters, and also uses satellites for transporting messages in Baudot code, or encrypted codes that prevent nonsubscribers from using the information. Baudot code uses transmitters that shift the frequency of the wave or emit audio tones (called audio frequency shift keying). The United States Information Agency (USIA) and various governments also use RTTY to communicate with their foreign missions (see Pritchard, 1989, p. 51).

7. The Soviet news agency originally went under the acronym ROSTA. In 1935 it was renamed TASS (Taylor, 1983, p. 29).

8. One example of instigation cited by Alov and Viktorov (1985, p. 71) occurred on May 5, 1973, when "a Radio Liberty programme in Ukrainian incited Soviet citizens to perform religious rites in public places, where they would interfere with the normal pace of life and inconvenience the majority of people contrary to Soviet laws which limit the performance of religious rites to their appropriate places such as churches, chapels, temples, etc."

9. Such accusations were still being made as late as 1988 (see BBC Monitoring Service, 1988e).

10. In 1947, while the United States was still considering how to deal with the question of an international shortwave service, 34 other nations were broadcasting 3,200 program hours per week across their borders. Marjorie Foulkrod argued (1947, pp. 12, 16) that it would be shortsighted to scrap VOA as some in Congress were urging be done.

11. During the 1920s, Kenez says (1985, p. 1), "the revolutionary leadership [of the USSR] attempted to transform man and society through mass indoctrination." Griffith wrote (1980, Vol. 2, p. 243) that "Leninist propaganda . . . is totalistic. It is intended to dominate and control not only all means of elite and mass communication but also all history, social science, literature, art, and music" (see also Remington, 1988).

12. Both superpowers are involved in so many international organizations and activities that they cannot all be listed. Both countries use cultural and scientific exchanges, conferences on such concerns as the "peaceful uses of outer space" and "law of the sea," involvement in assistance projects in developing countries, negotiations—such as those which led to the Helsinki accords in 1975 or which are aimed at the reduction of military forces

or tensions in Europe—distribution of literature and films, trade fair exhibits, Olympic competition, and so on, to demonstrate the superiority of their ideas to those of their ideological competitors. To see a discussion of only part of these activities, see Bittman (1988a, pp. 3–10) and Green (1988, pp. 98–119).

13. The development of public diplomacy itself was a result of the experiences of World War I. As Sanders and Taylor (1982, p. 1) put it, the principal lesson of that experience was that "public opinion could no longer be ignored as a determining factor in the formulation of government policies." A good example of Soviet use of U.S. media for public diplomacy was seen in Mikhail Gorbachev's visit to the United States for the Washington summit in December 1987. Tom Brokaw interviewed Gorbachev on Sunday, November 29, prior to the summit, and Gorbachev held an American-style news conference prior to leaving Washington (see "NBC Gets Gorbachev," 1987). Public diplomacy going both directions can be seen in the "space-bridges" between the United States and the Soviet Union (see "ABC News Show Links U.S.-Soviet Officials," 1987).

14. Soley (1989, pp. 6–8) provides a number of examples of Soviet and Eastern European sponsorship of clandestine radio stations.

15. Browne's information was taken from an article in the New York Times (March 6, 1923), "German Station Broadcasting Ruhr News and Music Is Drowned Out by Eiffel Tower."

16. Whitton and Larson (1964, pp. 210–211) cite the Austrian jamming of 1934. Biro (1932) discusses Romanian jamming of Soviet radio signals in 1932.

17. Soviet jamming of VOA stopped between June 19 and August 21, 1963, when the Soviets invaded Czechoslovakia and started it again, and between September 10, 1973, and August 20, 1980, when it "resumed in response to

VOA coverage of the Solidarity labor movement in Poland" (Read, 1986, p. 92).

18. It is worth noting here, too, that the promise of communications technology became well known in developing countries, with information passed on by the researchers performing field work, by students from these countries who studied in the United States, and by papers presented at various meetings with representatives of developing countries present.

19. Waterman argues (1988, p. 145) that foreign audiences watch U.S. television programs for their production values, not their cultural content.

20. The original promises were not made cynically; they were more likely a reflection of U.S. technological optimism — what some have referred to, in other contexts, as the "technological mythos."

21. Earth station sizes are expressed in terms of their diameters.

8

PERIPHERY VERSUS CORE IN THE GLOBAL METROPOLIS: 1970–1985

Introduction

By 1970 the nature of the world and the community of nations had changed fundamentally. Developing countries outnumbered industrialized countries. Their populations dwarfed those of their richer brethren. They questioned whether the independence they had achieved in the postwar era had resulted in true freedom from foreign domination. They demanded that they be accorded full equality in the international arena, and that their needs and philosophies be treated seriously by other nations.

Throughout the 1960s developing countries had been pressing for the imbalance in communication flow between Northern and Southern hemispheres to be addressed. They had sought assistance from the ITU in solving propagation problems in tropical regions. They had sought development assistance from the International Monetary Fund (IMF), the World Bank, the United Nations, and both government and private agencies to develop telecommunications infrastructures. They had raised the question of whether the ideology of "free flow of information" adequately addressed their needs, and had even proposed a new model for news writing: developmental journalism, or journalism in the service of development.

Although there were some positive responses by the industrialized countries and international agencies to the plight of developing nations, no fundamental changes were made in the operation of the international system. The system, as it existed, continued to serve the needs of the developed world. Its intricate networks of parallel technical systems continued to grow, linking Europe, North America, and selected other countries (former British colonies, such as Australia and New Zealand; countries with large U.S. military bases, such as the Philippines and South Korea; major trading partners, such as Taiwan and Mexico) with larger capacity, less expensive, and more reliable means of communication. These countries, too, continued to dominate international radio communication, sound recording, film distribution, and, increasingly, television and data communication. Their wire services controlled international news flow, both in words and pictures. The United States and the Soviet Union dominated satellite technology and its associated launch systems. The continuing inequality of access to the international communications system, and the inability of developing countries to manage their own communications destiny, was not an issue of major concern to those who held the reins of control.

In the Northern Hemisphere the ideological battle between East and West continued. The Soviet bloc accused Western radio stations of conducting "psychological warfare" against the Soviet state. The Soviets drew on some of the same international treaties used by the West to condemn jamming as the basis for their own condemnations. These treaties, designed to protect the rights of humankind to communicate, thus continued to play an equivocal role in world politics.

Between 1970 and 1985, however, developing countries were able to begin to press their demands on the world stage (see Agarwala, 1983; Gifreu, 1986; Horton, 1978; Lozoya & Birgin, 1981; and Nordenstreng, 1984). Their concerns about communication flow began to be heard. Both UNESCO and the ITU released significant studies about the state of world communication, which served as the focus of continuing debate. Developing countries worked together to begin new wire services oriented to their own needs, and to improve their telecommunications infrastructures and methods of cooperating to gain access to new technologies.

The difficulties faced by developing countries were exacerbated, however, by a shift in the dominant paradigm governing the vision that Western societies had of the international communications system. Developed societies had seen communication first as a problem to be solved, then as a danger to be contained. With the growth of technologies that could be employed within the international system, the perception changed again. Communication, and its multifaceted international system, became a possibility to be exploited for either economic or political gain.

Consumer electronics technology also had a major impact in helping people in developing countries to enlarge their access to information. This increased access threatened the monopolies of knowledge based both in centralized domestic communications infrastructures of developing countries and in the centralized international distribution systems of U.S. and European recording, film, and television companies.

In the East-West struggle, too, changes occurred. Mikhail Gorbachev introduced restructuring (perestroika) and publicity, or openness (glasnost), into Soviet society, leading ultimately to the dissolution of the Soviet sphere of influence in Eastern and Central Europe. The Cold War began to wind down, causing a rethinking on the part of Western propaganda radio services. For the first time since the Second World War, the question of what programming should be aired on such stations, as well as on more "neutral" stations, began to be considered. "Winning hearts and minds" from communism was no longer going to suffice.

8.2

The State of Communications Flow: Contending Forces

After countries began to achieve their political independence from the great colonial empires in the 1960s, the developed world often rebuffed their attempts to exercise that independence. Southern Hemisphere countries were still economically tied, or even dependent, on their former "mother countries," or else found themselves in need of assistance from others, particularly the United States and the Soviet Union, both of whom were eager to develop client relationships with them (see, for instance, Laïdi, 1990, chapter 1).[1] Such economic ties, as well as their own domestic political weakness, compromised their political sovereignty. Their ability to exercise true independence, to have their needs addressed in the international arena, was thus seriously weakened.

Also questionable was their "cultural" sovereignty: their ability to use indigenous symbolic structures to define their own paths to nationhood, political structure, and social and economic justice, or their ability to make sense out of the world, to understand it on their own terms, to participate in world affairs without accepting one of the two dominant ideologies, capitalism or communism. Sauvant and Mennis (1980, p. 277) argued that the long period of imperial domination had resulted in "sociocultural colonization. The values and behavioral patterns of important segments of Third World societies had been transformed to reflect those of metropolitan countries." Kumar (1980, pp. 14, 34) suggested that the long period of subjugation to foreign powers left developing nations feeling inferior and inadequate, and that transnational corporations (TNCs) "not only facilitate movements [of goods] across national boundaries, but also the underlying ideas, philosophies, values, and behavior patterns" (see also Biersteker, 1978; Dagnino, 1980; Mirow & Maurer, 1982; Solomon, 1978; and Vernon, 1977).

Not only did the developed countries of the Northern Hemisphere dominate political organizations, such as the United Nations, or set the agenda for international politics by waging the Cold War and shaping the bipolar world, they also dominated the globe's symbolic apparatus, its communications system. Increasingly during this period this domination came to apply to the content of communication: its software. Control of the international market for software — television programs, films, sound recordings, data, and advertising copy — became as significant as control of the hardware — that is, the technologies — of the international system. The international communications system thus continued to be an arena of symbolic, or cultural, conflict, not only in propaganda, but also in entertainment, news and advertising copy, music, trademarks and patents, and proprietary data. As Schramm put it in 1980 (p. 297), "it is the size and pace of information flow . . . that typifies human communication today. More information is coming, faster, at cheaper rates per unit, from farther sources, through more channels, . . . with more varied subject matter, and with focus and content that are ever briefer and more rapidly shifting." Yet the size, flow, direction, and content continued to be dominated by industrialized Western countries, especially, increasingly, by the United States (see Legum & Cornwell, 1978, pp. 19–71).

Television

Television entertainment programming became an important international communication activity. Commercial network programming from the United States soon came to dominate the international market for such material, but other countries also provided significant quantities, particularly the United Kingdom. Many of the same concerns about Western domination of entertainment material emerged as had been argued about news flow, although the language of the debate was somewhat different. As with news exchange, the trend toward alternative programming provided through regional and bilateral agreements among nations bypassing the dominant Western producers accelerated in the 1980s.

Although international television program exchange began in 1950 between England and France, the United States quickly became the major program supplier, based largely on the vitality of its domestic television industry (see Nordenstreng & Varis, 1974, p. 31). "Until the beginning of the 1960s, the United States alone had more television sets than the rest of the world together; it was only in 1962 that the 53 million sets owned outside the United States for the first time surpassed the American

total of 50 million" (Nordenstreng & Varis, 1974, p. 31). By the mid-1960s the United States was providing twice the total hours of programming as all other countries combined. And by the end of that decade U.S. exports earned nearly $100 million per year (Tunstall, 1977, p. 142; see also Nordenstreng & Varis, 1974, p. 12). For the years 1972–73 Nordenstreng and Varis (p. 12) estimated the following:

- One half of Latin America's television programs were of foreign origin.
- One quarter to one third of Western European programs were imported.
- Several countries in Asia imported more than half of their programs.
- In the Near East, countries imported approximately half of their programs.
- In Africa, excluding Egypt, half of all programs were imported, with some countries, particularly Zambia and Nigeria, importing two thirds of their television programs.

A study conducted in seven countries for UNESCO in 1979 (UNESCO, 1981b)

Table 8.1

Foreign Television Programming as a Percentage of Total Program Hours, 1979*

Country	Total Foreign Programming	Amount from the United States
Belgium	79.1	12.4
Bulgaria	24.4	—
Canada	52.7	44.3
France	8.3	6.7
Hungary	31.8	3.4
Italy	17.7	11.5
Japan	9.4	6.7

*This study did not examine all on-air stations in each country, but concentrated on particular cities, or channels available in each country.
Source: UNESCO, 1981b.

reconfirmed the large discrepancies in the amount of television programming imported by various countries, even in industrialized countries. This study indicated that foreign productions made up between 8.3% (France) and 79.1% (Belgium) of total program output. (See Table 8.1.) Other major suppliers of programming varied from country to country. (See Table 8.2.) Several years later Varis again studied the international flow of television programs. He concluded that imported programming still constituted a large percentage of total program hours in many countries around the world. (See Table 8.3.)

The changes over the 11-year period (1972–73 to 1983–84) encompassing these three studies occurred largely within individual countries. Western European television became a more important source of programming for some regions. Eastern European countries began to engage in greater program exchange, reducing dependence on the Soviet Union. Arab countries also began to share their programs to a greater degree, reducing dependence on the United States (see Varis, 1986). Throughout the period, however, the two countries that stood out as anomalies were the United States and the Soviet Union, which were the most "closed" societies to foreign television programming.

There were several reasons for the dominance of the United States as a supplier of television programs internationally. One obvious one was that the United States, for most of the history of television, produced the most total hours of television programs. It had more national networks producing or purchasing programs, and more hours per day of on-air television to fill.

A second contributing factor was the willingness of U.S. program suppliers to provide television shows for significantly less money than they could be produced elsewhere. In 1982, for instance, 30-minute programs from the United States could be purchased for between $30 and $15,000. Prices rose considerably following 1982, but by 1989 they were still low, ranging from $200 to $3,000 for a half-hour program in South America, $300 to $18,000 in the Far East (including Australia), $400 to $20,000 in Europe, and $3,000 to $35,000 in Canada. Half-hour programs cost $250–300 in Botswana, $300–400 in Iceland, $550–650 in Israel, and $1,100–2,000 in South Africa ("Global Television Prices," 1989, p. 156).

Table 8.2

Principal Foreign Television Program Suppliers, 1979

Country	Principal Supplier	Percentage Supplied
Belgium	France	52.6
Bulgaria	Soviet Union	15.0
Canada	United States	44.3
France	United States	6.7
Hungary	Soviet Union	7.0
Italy	United States	11.5
Japan	United States	6.7

Source: UNESCO, 1981b.

The price depended on the size of market, the length of time that a foreign audience had been "cultivated to consume" U.S. programs, and the ability of the client to pay for the programs (Pendakur, 1985, pp. 57–58; see also Cascino, 1989; and Schneider, 1989). Such prices were far below what it would cost for an organization to produce its own programs, which encouraged countries to supplement their own production capabilities with imports (see Hoskins, Mirus, & Rozeboom, 1989).[2]

Another contributing element was the long-standing political and economic relationship that Western nations cultivated with developing countries, often the result of colonial ties broken only after World War II. In Africa, for instance,

> nearly all . . . the television stations have been introduced with the assistance of Western advisors and capital. The Thomson Organization . . . set up the Kenya station in 1962, the Sudan one in 1963, and a new station in Ethiopia in 1964, while the Overseas Rediffusion in London did the same job in Liberia. Most of the French-speaking African countries have used OCORA (L'Office de Coopération Radiophonique) to set up the stations, train staff and assist in administration. (Nordenstreng & Varis, 1974, p. 29)

All three U.S. broadcasting networks also had relationships with broadcasters in other countries: NBC in Italy, Rhodesia (now Zimbabwe), Kenya, Mexico, Argentina, Peru, Venezuela, Hong Kong, and Australia; CBS in South America and in Japan and Bermuda (Read, 1976, pp. 80–81). All these relationships involved economic investments and, in ABC's case, an international network: WorldVision. Most of these arrangements were abandoned, however, because of poor financial returns, or difficulty with national government ministries. Many countries also called in RCA, the par-

Table 8.3

Percentage of Television Programming Imported, 1983–84

Country/Region	Amount Imported*	Main Source
United States	2	United Kingdom (25%)
Canada	22–54	United States (70%)
Latin America	25–67	United States (77%)
Western Europe	30–67	United States (44%)
Eastern Europe	27	Soviet Union (24%) / Western Europe (43%)
Soviet Union	8	Western Europe (55%)
Asia and Pacific	3–75	not reported**
Arab countries	33–50	United States (32%) / other Arab countries (33%)
Africa	31–83	United States (47%)

*Ranges refer to the percentage of imports for different countries. For Canada, it refers to French and English programs.
**Varis did not report the sources of imported programs into Asia and the Pacific as he did with other regions. He did report that a total of 35% of programs in the region were imported, with 90% of the programs aired in the Philippines originating in the United States.
Source: Varis, 1985, pp. 22–48.

ent of NBC, to provide **turn-key installations** of television production studios and transmitters, a service that RCA alone was able to provide until the early 1970s when both Japanese and West German companies developed such capabilities (Boyd, 1984, p. 384). The BBC, too, actively worked with nascent broadcasting organizations in sub-Saharan Africa to help them in providing national program services to their countries (see Armour, 1984).

Satellites

Development of the International Satellite System

Besides Intelsat, one other international and several regional satellite organizations were organized to carry both common carrier and television signals. More recently, privately owned international satellite companies developed. The Soviet Union's Intersputnik system, in addition to its common carrier service, handled the television exchanges of Intervision, operated by the International Organization for Radio and Television (OIRT) for European socialist countries. Regional organizations included Arabsat, the Western European Eutelsat, and the nationally owned systems of Indonesia (Palapa), India (Insat), Brazil (Brazilsat), Canada (ANIK), and Japan (NHK), all of which could be picked up by satellite dishes in adjacent or nearby countries, as could U.S. domestic satellites by Canadians, Central American, and Caribbean island citizens or broadcasting and cable organizations. (See Appendix 3.) Programs selected from satellites that were not designed for foreign distribution were not calculated, of course, in the totals used to determine foreign programming percentages within countries, since they were not under contract.

Another important satellite agency created during this period was the European Space Agency (ESA), devised in 1975 as a means to foster inter-European cooperation in space. Western European countries, Austria, and Canada (through a cooperative agreement) were members.[3] The ESA developed the Ariane satellite launch vehicle. Beginning in 1979 it began to cooperate with Eutelsat by providing satellites, launch vehicles, tracking systems, and satellite maintenance to establish a pan-European satellite telecommunications system. The first Eutelsat satellite was launched in 1983 and provided 10,000 telephone circuits for Europe, the Middle East, and Africa. Since that time Eutelsat has also begun to provide satellite television distribution, and from 1985 on was able to lease 22 transponders for television, two of which went to the third European communications organization, the EBU (Rees, 1990, p. 64). All Eutelsat satellites carry transponders for both PAL and SECAM television systems. Eutelsat I satellites each have 19 transponders, 13 of which are devoted to television. Eutelsat II satellites were designed to duplicate the high-power transponder services, and thus reduced earth station sizes, available using Luxembourg's commercial Astra satellites (Rees, 1990, p. 66).

Also in Europe, the German and French governments began operating a joint space venture that deployed German TV-Sat and French Televisione Diffusion de France (TDFL) satellites. These satellites were planned during this period, but failures of the early satellites to deploy properly delayed inauguration of the services. TV-Sat 2 was finally successfully launched in August 1989. Both the German and French models were designed to employ digital encoding of both audio and video programming, which required using special receivers that could decode the digital signals for use by analog-based radios and televisions in people's homes.

Arab League ministers created Arabsat in 1976, but its first satellite was not launched until 1985. Its two satellites each have a capacity of 8,000 telephone voice circuits, seven television channels, and a single channel for community television (Rees, 1990, pp. 68, 69). Arabsat's goals included the expectation that it would provide the mechanism to "exchange broadcast and television programmes among administrations and specialized organizations of Arab states through the channel of Arab space telecommunications, and regulate the use of television transponders to satisfy the local and community needs of the Arab states" (United Nations General Assembly, 1982, p. 17). By 1988, however, it was operating at only 30% of capacity, and by 1989 was running a deficit of $60 million (BBC Monitoring Service, 1989d). The league excluded Egypt (potentially its largest user) until 1989 because of its peace agreement with Israel.

Indonesia began its satellite service in 1976. It launched the first Palapa satellite in 1984, which carried both broadcast and telephony services to serve communication needs throughout southeast Asia. By 1990 it also was not yet operating at full capacity.

A number of other regional satellite projects were delayed as countries considered the experience of Arabsat, the failure of several satellites to reach orbit or deploy properly, and the apparently lackluster performance of certain satellite applications (notably DBS in the United States and the United Kingdom). The possibilities offered by fiber optic technology, too, which appeared to offer more predictable connections, also eroded some of the enthusiasm for satellites.

Finally, another international satellite organization, Inmarsat, was founded in 1976, but it had no satellites to start operations. This international marine satellite organization, whose satellites were designed to allow ships of all sizes to fix their locations and send distress signals as needed, was also used for other purposes as well, including telephone, telex, data, and facsimile services (Rees, 1990, p. 58). The United States Armed Forces Radio and Television System (AFRTS), for instance, began using Inmarsat in November 1988 to deliver its radio programs to the U.S. Pacific fleet, and in

Table 8.4

Capacity of U.S.-European Submarine Telephone Cables

Cable	Installation Date	Number of Channels
TAT-1	1956	36
TAT-3	1963	138
TAT-5	1970	840
TAT-6	1976	1,976
TAT-8	1988	8,000
TAT-10	August 1992	8,000 +
TAT-11	August 1993	to be determined
TAT-12	1995	to be determined

March 1989 to its Atlantic fleet (BBC Monitoring Service, 1988n).

Intelsat was so successful in fostering international cooperation that it carried 75% of common carrier (telegraph, telephone, telex, facsimile, data) traffic by the middle of the 1980s. Its success, however, also contributed to the clamor for competition in providing satellite services, which the U.S. government began to argue for successfully in 1984. Still, undersea cables to carry this traffic continued to be developed, with the latest U.S.-European cable, TAT-8, installed in 1988. The development of the submarine cable's capacity itself was an indication of the increased demands placed on this method of communication. (See Table 8.4.)

Satellites and the International Flow of Information

The geosynchronous orbit satellite affected the flow of information around the globe in several significant ways. Some news services that had originally used older technologies gradually shifted to satellites, other services were delivered more quickly and inexpensively, and still others were introduced more widely than before. However, although satellites still seem to many to be a "new" technology, by the late 1980s they were threatened by even newer ones, and many services carried by satellites began to shift to these. Satellites are expected to continue to provide basic communications services to some areas of the world (for geographic or economic reasons), but in others they are likely to become a more specialized means to deliver new services, some of which are not necessarily welcome in all countries.

The original promise of satellites for international communication was to provide inexpensive voice circuits between pairs of countries. This allowed for the rapid expansion of telecommunications services between nations, and gave an incentive for domestic telecommunications development. Domestic service development was known to be correlated with economic growth. Satellites were thus a principal means to help developing countries' economic progress.[4]

Intelsat owned and operated its own satellites, which increased in capacity enormously from the first generation put into orbit. By 1990 a single Intelsat VI satellite carried 100,000 telephone circuits and two color television channels. These circuits could be combined or subdivided to provide the proper capacities for the other communications services available.

Although Intelsat originally served industrialized countries, it gradually expanded its services to less developed nations. The cost of a satellite voice channel dropped from its original price of $32,000 per year to below $5,000 between 1964 and 1985, largely due to the treaty obligation to use "globally averaged pricing." This obligation meant that the profits from high-density routes were used to subsidize the costs of low-density ones, which allowed poorer countries to participate in the international system (Snow, 1986, pp. 35, 47). Thus, Snow concludes (1986, p. 48), despite its original genesis, "INTELSAT is regarded by most of its member countries and proponents as the embodiment of an apolitical, nonideological international organization that has harnessed a new technology for the good of mankind."[5]

Although the Soviet Union began using the Intelsat system in 1974, it had already created, along with several Eastern European countries, its own international satellite system, Intersputnik, in 1968, which became operational and was registered as a United Nations organization in 1971. Several countries in the developing world, including Algeria, Burma, India, Mozambique,

Nicaragua, and Sri Lanka, also joined Inter-sputnik. Its first operations were conducted using polar-orbit MOLNIYA 2 and 3 satellites in the mid-1970s, but later the Soviet Union began to provide worldwide service via Statsionar-T and Gorizont 1-10 series C-band satellites (see Howell, 1986, p. 180). Intersputnik satellites carried both telephone-telex and radio-telephone circuits. They were also the vehicle for the exchange activities of OIRT, the Soviet and Eastern European equivalent of Western Europe's European Broadcasting Union (EBU).

The U.S. government's decision in 1984 that separate satellite systems were in its national interest resulted in a third international satellite organization. The decision opened the door for competition with Intelsat, although the Intelsat agreement required that any new satellite system be "coordinated" to assure technical compatibility and to avoid "significant economic harm" to Intelsat ("President Extends Free-Market Doctrine into Space," 1984; see also Pelton, 1986b; Staple, 1984; and Trezise, 1987). The outcome was a new organization, founded in 1985, PanAmSat, the Pan-American Satellite Corporation. PanAmSat (also called Alpha Lyracom) provided satellite links between countries in the Americas, and between North America and the United Kingdom. In addition, 38 U.S. and 6 Canadian satellite networks providing transborder services were approved in Intelsat's "coordination" process ("President Extends Free-Market Doctrine into Space," 1984; "Intelsat Board Pases [sic]," 1984).[6]

Satellites carry a large part of the television programming crossing international borders. Intelsat carries the bulk of such programs, although Arabsat is an important carrier of Arabic language programming, Intersputnik of programs shared among OIRT members (through Intervision), and Eutelsat among EBU members (through Eurovision). OIRT and EBU member countries also exchange programs via satellite. This allows them to provide live coverage of sports and to exchange news and other programs across the former ideological divide (by 1991 largely an economic divide) separating Europe (see Eugster, 1983, chapter 7; Jakubowicz, 1988, and Quester, 1990, chapter 7).

The United States, through the United States Information Agency (USIA), also began global television broadcasts in 1983 via "Worldnet" (see Roach, 1987, p. 41). It was designed originally as an interactive system, allowing journalists in other countries to interview, or discuss topics with, U.S. policymakers and other representatives on matters of mutual interest (see "Worldnet Begins South, Central America Service," 1986). Its programming increased to include other types of material, including news and commentary, but eventually it returned to its original forms. This cutback resulted from USIA's inability to convince Congress that the expense was justified by total audience size (see Randolph, 1989b; and "Worldnet's Funding Dilemma," 1989).

8.3

International Communications Flow: An Assessment

Developing countries' views of impediments to their development began by the early 1970s to center first on the world economic order and then on its sociocultural dimensions, including the imbalance in information flow between the Northern and Southern hemispheres (see Nordenstreng & Varis, 1973; Pavlic & Hamelink, 1985; Ravault, 1981; Schement, Gonzalez, Lum, & Valencia, 1984; and Wert & Stevenson, 1988). Their objections to the state of economic and information relationships (eventually expanded to include communication relationships more generally) remained fairly consistent since being first officially declared in Algiers in 1973.[7] The leaders of developing countries have amplified their objections since then, and their concerns have informed debates in a variety of international arenas (see Aziz, 1978). These include not only the Non-Aligned Movement but also the United Nations General Assembly, UNESCO, the ITU and its various world and regional conferences, and other specialized meetings.

The focus of developing countries on the information-communication order as a principal cause of their inability to progress economically by comparison with the industrialized West had two primary roots, one intellectual and the other technological. The intellectual roots of this conflict can be found both in the optimism of some U.S. communications experts about a positive link between communications infrastructure development and economic progress, and in the historical position of the West, led by the United States, in favor of a free flow of information.[8] The technological roots lay in the developing competition among communication technologies, and in the new interpretations of the significance of this competition in a post–Cold War world. The debate initiated on the information and communication order heated up just as the United States was pulling out of Vietnam, the angry rhetoric of the superpowers was being toned down, and new strategies were being developed for relationships between East and West, and for the Northern Hemisphere countries' relationships with the developing world. The timing was propitious for developing countries to press their demands.

By 1970 developing countries saw that neither intellectual base for the existing world information order worked in their best interests. For one thing, massive investments and dependence on communications technology had not spurred economic and political development. For another, the traditional practices of international news coverage and distribution had allowed their interests to be ignored and often had served to reinforce existing negative stereotypes about the nature of their societies and cultures. Radical action seemed to be required to create a new information and communication order.

Also by 1970 new technologies were beginning to appear, or were on the horizon, that might provide the basis for organizing this new order. The United States and the Soviet Union had orbited the first communications satellites; countries had formed an international communications satellite organization, experimented with coaxial cable distribution systems, and discussed direct broadcasting satellite applications; and engineers were making predictions about the future of optical fibers, lasers, and digital transmission as communications devices. By 1975 competition was beginning to crack the U.S. telephone monopoly held by AT&T; Japanese and West German companies, such as Toshiba, Sony, and Telefunken, had become major telecommunications equipment suppliers, joining U.S., British, Dutch and French companies; and the formation of the Organization of Petroleum Exporting Countries (OPEC) had demonstrated the potential power of developing countries to use their natural resources as the basis for new economic relationships with industrialized countries.

The turmoil created by the development of new communications technologies, and their possible competitive consequences for existing communications systems and their expensive infrastructures, which began in the mid-1970s, has yet to be resolved, and is not likely to be until well into the next

century. The debate over a number of issues—satellite applications in both telecommunications and broadcasting, the use
of optical fibers and their implications for
engineering in developing countries, the
emergence of high-definition television, the
reconfiguration of international shortwave
services, the potential movement of news
wire services to newer transmission
methods—will likely continue indefinitely
(see Fortner, 1988b). Even the long-term
impacts of videocassette recorders, audiotape recorders and playback units, and the
piracy of television programs are as yet unknown (see Boyd, 1988; Ganley & Ganley,
1987; and Ogan, 1988).

Developing countries are anxious that
their needs and future uses of such technologies not be ignored, particularly by the
United States, Japan, and Western European nations, which are pushing the application of new communications technologies.
They raised the question about communication flow during this period because of their
sense that the political sovereignty they had
achieved had not resulted in equality in the
international community. They raised two
fundamental issues. First was the economic

order of the world, an order that still rele-
gated Southern Hemisphere countries to a
status as supplier of raw materials, and allowed Northern Hemisphere countries to
continue their dominance in manufacturing,
product development, research, and technology. Developing countries proposed a
"new world economic order" to redress this
imbalance. Second was the information order of the world, one that followed the same
pattern as the economic order, with Northern Hemisphere countries dominating the
nations south of the equator. As a result of
pressure applied by developing countries on
organizations such as the ITU and UNESCO,
these organizations undertook studies of the
state of the world's information flow.

The first study occurred under the auspices of UNESCO. The study, completed by
the International Commission for the Study
of Communications Problems, had a broad
mandate: "to study the totality of communication problems in modern societies" (see
MacBride, 1980, p. 16). The commission
concluded that by the late 1970s North
America accounted for over 45% of the
world's annual mail traffic, and that it, along
with Europe and the Soviet Union, ac-

Table 8.5

**Distribution of Communication Materials, as Percentages
of World Totals, 1980**

Region	Daily Newspapers	Radio Receivers	Book Titles Published	Percentage of World Population
Africa	1.0	1.9	1.4	9.9
North America	16.2	44.9	15.4	7.5
Latin America	5.6	8.8	5.2	10.5
Asia	21.8	11.2	16.4	43.8
Arab States	.7	1.9	1.0	4.5
Europe	28.2	16.5	45.6	4.5
Oceania	1.7	1.5	.8	8.1
Soviet Union	24.8	13.3	14.2	8.1

Source: MacBride, 1980.

counted for over 82% (MacBride, 1980, p. 68). Telephony was equally concentrated, with 80% of all telephones concentrated in 10 North American and Western European countries (MacBride, 1980, p. 68). Developing countries, by contrast, with 70% of the world's population, produced only 20% of the books each year. The national libraries of the Soviet Union, the United States, and Western European countries contained over half of the books of all national libraries worldwide combined (MacBride, 1980, p. 71). In short, the distribution of communication materials, the commission said (p. 89), regardless of the type examined, was grossly uneven, particularly when compared with the percentage of world population living in each region of the world. (See Table 8.5.) The commission concluded that

> in most cases the developing countries are not yet in a position to meet their basic communications needs. . . . The fact that the poorer countries can invest less than the richer countries and that their populations are growing at a much faster rate goes to explain why the gap between the two groups continues to widen. It will be narrowed only by a mighty co-operative effort far in excess of anything being attempted at present. (MacBride, 1980, pp. 91–92)

The second study, completed by the Independent Commission for World Wide Tele-communications Development for the ITU, agreed with the previous commission, saying that "two-thirds of the world population has no access to telephone services. Tokyo has more telephones than the whole of the African continent" (Maitland, 1984, p. 13). Efforts to redress imbalances through tele-communications development projects had not significantly changed the situation, the commission determined, and research and development activities in telecommunications conducted in industrialized countries was not directed to producing equipment responsive to the particular needs of developing countries (Maitland, 1984, pp. 18–20, 47). Progress, therefore, in exploiting advances in telecommunications, from satellites to solar-powered two-way radios, "has been painfully slow" (Maitland, 1984, p. 8).

Other studies reached similar conclusions. The annual BBC estimate of worldwide radio and television receivers (BBC International Broadcasting and Audience Research, 1991) consistently showed wide discrepancies between developed and developing countries. (See Table 8.6.) And a study completed for the Voice of America and the United States Information Agency in 1986 (Fortner & Durham, 1986) concluded that the penetration of radio re-

Table 8.6

Radio and Television Receivers, Developed Versus Undeveloped Regions of the World, 1990 (in thousands)

Region	Population	Radio Sets	Television Sets	VCRs
World	5,284,000	2,124,000	1,020,000	211,000
Europe	848,000	568,500	352,900	71,200
Arab world	276,000	73,500	36,100	10,200
Southeast Asia and Far East	2,907,000	611,900	316,100	40,900
North America and Caribbean	287,000	608,000	203,500	71,400
Latin America	428,000	164,000	83,800	10,200
Australasia and Oceania	28,000	26,600	9,700	4,300

ceivers in some developing regions was actually worsening in the early 1980s and would not recover until near the turn of the century. The reasons were twofold: (1) Population growth was outstripping the economic ability of developing countries to import radio sets, resulting in reduced penetration; and (2) many countries had placed import restrictions on radio sets, or taxed them at exorbitant rates, to reduce the outlay of hard currency necessary to purchase these goods for import.

All available evidence, then, pointed in the same direction: The developing countries had reason to be concerned about the distribution of communications capability. This inequality of capability, too, was a major reason for the inability of such countries to stem the flow of media materials, particularly television programs, wire news copy, and sound recordings, into their countries.

Across all the media (except for film) the dominance of industrialized countries could at least partially be explained by the fact that the domestic media base (the number of newspapers published, the number of television sets in use, etc.) provided the economic base for production and distribution activities. In cinema several developing countries, notably India, Mexico, Egypt, and Brazil, along with Hong Kong and other Asian nations to lesser degrees, were able to produce significant numbers of feature length films (see MacBride, 1980, pp. 77–78). Attendance at cinema houses, however, began to fall in most areas of the world (MacBride, 1980, p. 78).

8.4

International News Flow

A variety of other specific indicators also suggested that the concerns raised by the developing countries were valid. These in-

cluded statistics on the flow of television and film, sound recordings, and printed literature of various sorts; on the existence of technologies used for communication, from telephones to computers; and on the dominance of the flow of news by wire services.

Wire Services

The AP delivery system, by the early 1970s, used

> radio teleprinter transmitters in New York, San Francisco, London, and Tokyo [to] reach every part of the world continuously with AP news. Where the foreign news and newsphoto flows are the heaviest, more reliable means of telecommunications are used. Leased cables, operating around the clock, link the United States and Europe. Satellite circuits and cables provide connections with key points in Asia. Two-way service for parts of Latin America is furnished via satellite, microwave, and cable. The gathering and distributing of news pictures follows the same pattern. (Read, 1976, p. 101)

By 1980 each of the U.S. agencies had about 1,500 newsphoto clients, half within and half outside the United States (Fenby, 1986, p. 104). In 1984 Reuters took over UPI's foreign newsphoto distribution operation (one symptom of UPI's financial problems) and in 1985 launched its international photographic service. Later NBC purchased part of the Reuters organization. In 1981 the American Broadcasting Company (ABC) joined UPITN (a newsfilm organization jointly operated by UPI and Independent Television News); the following year UPI left the service.

The four major news agencies were estimated to provide about 80% of the immediate international news circulating throughout the world every day (Fenby, 1986, p. 7). They provided up to 300,000 words per day of news copy in English,

French, Spanish, German, and Arabic (Fenby, 1986, pp. 8–9). In 1983 AP, for instance, served the news media of 115 nations, and Reuters 158. AP maintained bureaus in 65 countries, and Reuters in 93 cities (103 in 1985, with 10 in the United States) (Boyd-Barrett, 1989, p. 109).

These services, however, were oriented toward North America and Western Europe, where they are headquartered and where they earn most of their profits. The few studies completed studying their content indicated that these two areas of the world received the most coverage by the wire services, followed by (in order) Asia and the Far East, Latin America, the Middle East, Africa, and Eastern Europe. Approximately half of all wire service stories, however, originated in the United States and the NATO countries (see Adams, 1964; Harris, 1977; Hester, 1974; and Weibul, Olsson, & Lundquist, 1971).

Dissatisfaction with the perceived bias of Western and Soviet news services led to alternative wire agencies being established by developing countries. These regional wire news exchanges allowed countries to have news focused on their own country and neighbors, and to communicate with one another through news without the intervention of major world powers. Most of these agencies were begun after the debate over the new world information and communication order (NWICO) started in the early 1970s. One of the major agencies of this sort was the Non-Aligned News Pool, established in New Delhi in 1976 by information ministers from developing countries who desired to improve and expand "mutual exchanges of information and dissemination of correct and factual information about non-aligned countries" (Mankekar, 1986, p. 32). This pool began with about 30 members, but by the late 1980s had more than 80. It exchanged over 60,000 words daily, compared to the major agencies' 40 million words each day. Another regional wire exchange was the Pan-African News Agency (PANA), which began operations on May 25, 1983. At that time its 6 members received 7,000 words per day, but by the late 1980s its membership had grown to 44 members and it was carrying 20,000 words daily (BBC Monitoring Service, 1987c). Other significant news agencies are Tanjug (Yugoslavia), DPA (West Germany), and the Middle East News Agency (MENA) (see assessments of success in Giffard, 1985; and Jakubowicz, 1985).

Despite such efforts, however, scholars continued to express concern. Matta (1980, p. 204) argued, for instance, that "examples of news dependence . . . are innumerable. Latin American countries, although territorial neighbors, communicate the news between themselves according to decisions made by international agencies outside the region." In 1990 PANA was on the verge of collapse, too, as a result of nonpayments of dues (studies on news values and flow include Altschull, 1984; Arno & Dissanayake, 1984; Harriman, 1987; Kariel & Rosenvall, 1984; Sreberny-Mohammadi, Nordenstreng, Stevenson, & Ugboajak, 1985; and Sussman, 1977; see also Article 19, 1988, for a worldwide survey of information flow within countries).

Newspapers

Although not as prominent as wire services, some newspapers also distributed news internationally, and provided significant amounts of international news—at least in selected countries. Probably the most prominent papers in this respect were the *International Herald Tribune* (jointly owned by the *Washington Post* and the *New York Times,* and published in Paris), the *Times* and *Financial Times (London),* the *New*

York Times, the *Christian Science Monitor* (Boston), and the *Wall Street Journal* (New York). Increasingly, too, *USA Today* became available outside the United States, and the *Washington Post* and *Los Angeles Times* became significant primarily because of their joint operation of a wire service available to foreign clients (see Boyd-Barrett, 1989, p. 109). Major newspapers and news magazines *(Time, Newsweek, U.S. News & World Report, The Economist)* also maintained foreign correspondents to cover news in other countries. For instance, in 1983, 286 foreign media organizations from 61 countries maintained 480 accredited journalists in Washington, DC, while in 1979, 46 countries maintained 182 journalists in Moscow, and in 1982, 25 countries employed 103 correspondents in New Delhi (Ghorpade, 1984, p. 667). These print organizations, however, like their wire service brethren, were principally concerned about news of interest in countries bordering the North Atlantic.

Television News

Television networks, too, provided stories to countries outside their domestic bases of operation. The U.S. broadcasting networks—ABC, CBS, and NBC—provided

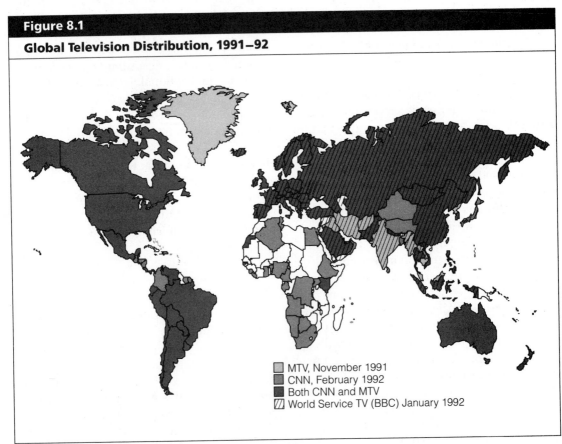

Figure 8.1

Global Television Distribution, 1991–92

■ MTV, November 1991
■ CNN, February 1992
■ Both CNN and MTV
▨ World Service TV (BBC) January 1992

Source: "MTV's Reach Around the World," 1991, p. 11; and Cable News Network (CNN).

video news stories or international sports coverage to countries contracting for such service, or had their signals pirated by countries in the Caribbean when they began to use satellites for news distribution in the early 1980s. The Cable News Network (CNN) began distributing its news service to Europe in 1985, and, like its domestic cousins, had both its **news feed** and its **back-feed** (from the news location back to Atlanta, GA, where the news is processed) pirated by countries that fall within the domestic U.S. satellite footprint. CNN gradually extended its international services so that it was available on a global basis by the late 1980s. In 1989 Vietnam became the 83rd country to receive CNN service ("Jimmy Carter Tells Journalists," 1989). By 1990 CNN's service reached a total of 95

countries, and by February 1992, 130 countries and territories, although largely confined to hotels and limited-distribution cable systems. (See Figure 8.1.)

In 1987 both CBS and NBC began distributing their U.S.-produced evening news programs in Western Europe, CBS through the French Canal Plus UHF-TV national subscription channel, and NBC on AngloVision, a satellite channel aimed at hotels on the continent ("Network News Going International," 1987). By 1990, too, Visnews was distributed to over 400 broadcasters in 85 countries (Wilhelm, 1990, p. 65). The French company Canal Plus also began distributing news programming around the world in the 1980s, and Rupert Murdoch's News Corp. Ltd. began distributing "Sky News" in Europe (see Schrage, 1985). In

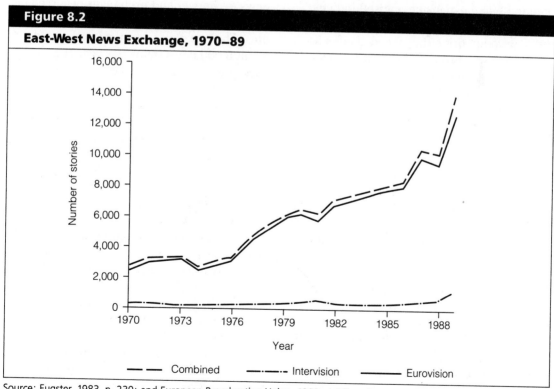

Figure 8.2

East-West News Exchange, 1970–89

Source: Eugster, 1983, p. 230; and European Broadcasting Union, 1988, p. 37, and 1990, p. 23.

1991, as a result of the Persian Gulf conflict, 24-hour news channels planned by Japan's NHK and Europe's EBU both received major boosts. EBU's "Euronews" was scheduled to begin broadcasting in the fall of 1992, while NHK was looking for a U.S. or European partner (see Jones, 1991; and LaFranchi, 1991). NHK planned to spend $1 billion to launch its service, and to have "news in equal parts from Asia, Europe and North America" ("Japan's NHK Details Plans for Global News Network," 1991, p. 14). Also in 1991 the BBC began broadcasting to Europe and Asia. The Asian service was scheduled to be available to 38 countries, and included both news and current affairs, as well as the best of the rest of BBC's domestic programming ("BBC Launches Satellite TV Services to Asia," 1991b). BBC's service, along with CNN's planned Asian expansion, caused indigenous Asian broadcasters to acknowledge the new competition they faced. Jaafar Kamin, the new president of the Asia-Pacific Broadcasting Union (ABU), conceded that Asia's broadcasters would have to find a way to peacefully coexist with the new direct satellite services (Tat, 1991).

The flow of television news between East and West continued to be dominated by Western European countries. (See Figure 8.2.) The principal reason for the large disparity via the Eurovision-Intervision link, as Le Duc (1981, p. 140) suggested, was the difference in news values between East and West. Whereas Western stories were "ideally suited" for Eastern portrayals of the flaws in Western society, the heavily political nature of Eastern reports were of little interest to Western news organizations. "Thus, although a quantitative survey of this situation would indicate the existence of a serious imbalance, it is possible to argue that the Eurovision-Intervision exchange is in reality meeting the needs of all broadcast systems involved, even though not operating at parity in terms of number of news units received and delivered."

The EBU and OIRT organizations also cooperated with U.S. television networks. They served, too, as models for the creation of regional electronic news exchanges in other areas of the world (see Fisher, 1980). In 1980, for instance, joint EBU-OIRT operations received 230 hours of coverage of the Winter Olympics from Lake Placid, New York, from the ABC television network (Eugster, 1983, p. 187). In Asia several countries cooperated to establish the AsiaVision News Exchange, which had members from all ideological camps in the region, including the People's Republic of China, South Korea, Japan, India, and Indonesia, and several other countries. AsiaVision was divided into two zones to facilitate television news exchange, and exchanges occurred using both air freight exchange and satellites. The two zones together exchanged about 5,000 news items per year (Lansipuro, 1987). Officials of Japan's NHK said that the "idea has not worked very well since most television in Asia is government controlled. 'We get a lot of royal ceremonies, and that's it,' says NHK official Tomoyuki Kanagawa" (quoted in Jones, 1991).

Increasing Complexity of News Flow

The postwar development in international news, then, was characterized by increasing complexity arising from two sources. First, new technologies gradually became significant in international news flow. Shortwave, telegraph, and telephone were supplemented by the satellite, and wired and voiced reports were challenged by increased distribution of newspapers and video pictures, including live coverage of significant international events (e.g., funerals, coronations, inaugurations, the Olympics, natural disasters, terrorist incidents, etc.). Second, the nature of the primary ideological battle changed from a simple East-West confrontation to one in which North and South collided, countries formed regional cooperatives, and the democratic-communist state differences were narrowed and, in many cases, confused.

This led to more news reports, and different kinds of reports, filed and available to people.[9] It led to greater degrees of competition among news agencies of all types and an increasing amount of "positioning" as different companies followed various strategies to improve their competitive edge: buying and selling services, moving into new markets, and so on. It led, too, to heated argument about the role of information flow, and its control, among the nations of the world.

8.5

The NWICO Debate

The Industrialized Capitalist Countries

Western countries, which took the lead in "defending" the old information order, did not suggest that the discrepancies in communications capability were illusory, or that developing countries were closing the gap in access to technology.[10] They did point to the gains made by developing countries, however, particularly through membership in Intelsat, and to the commitment of the World Bank, the ITU, and both government-sponsored and privately funded foreign aid programs to addressing their technical needs. The United States, too, asserted that the development of technology itself would make it possible to address developing

countries' needs in the future, especially in satellite communications. This argument, however, was merely a continuation of the original articulation by Lerner and Schramm, one that had not resulted in developing countries closing the information gap with more developed nations.

The "old information order" was dominated by the idea of a free flow of information. Other articulated aspects of the Western position included faith in eventual technological development to a level at which communication problems would be solved and the belief that, when scarce spectrum resources (such as orbital slots for satellites, or the shortwave frequency bands) were allocated, preference should be given to those countries prepared to make use of them immediately; they should not be reserved for future users.

The position of the West stemmed from several underlying beliefs. Probably the most obvious of these was the belief in the value of information per se. "One of the central arguments for the U.S. position on DBS [direct broadcast satellites]," Luther (1988, p. 89) writes, "is that the free movement of information is an objective force that 'injures no nation' and that an 'open marketplace of ideas and information is essential to the well-being of the international community'" (see also Twentieth Century Fund Task Force, 1978, pp. 1–12). Western democracies shared the classical liberal view of information as an antidote for error, truth as a goal best achieved by allowing free play in the "marketplace of ideas," and humankind as sharing a fundamental right to freedom of expression.[11]

The right to communicate, while its genesis arguably began with the idea of free expression, had not served to bolster the Western defense of the existing information order. On the contrary, as a result of the obvious disparities between the ability to communicate in developed versus developing worlds, many critics, including the MacBride Commission (MacBride, 1980), claimed that this fundamental right had been violated. In their view this right became meaningless when so much of the world's population was denied access to the basic tools to exercise it (see Cocca, 1988; and MacBride, 1980, pp. 136–138).

The Socialist and Developing Countries

Although the interests of Socialist countries (the so-called Second World) and developing countries were not identical, their approach to the dominance of Western countries (the First World) in information flow coincided in many respects. Until the advent of *glasnost* in the Soviet Union, and the subsequent acceptance of the concept by many Eastern and Central European countries in the Socialist orbit, these countries (including Albania, Bulgaria, Czechoslovakia, East Germany, Hungary, Poland, and Romania) had sought to limit the flow of information from the West to their citizens. Various tactics—including jamming of radio signals, installation of wired radio sets that could carry only official state programming, registration of typewriters, and decisions not to import Western technology, such as computers, VCRs, and high-quality shortwave radios, or publications—had all been used to accomplish this end.

When the NWICO debate erupted, then, the developing countries, which desired, among other things, to control the flow of information across their borders, found allies among Socialist countries. The ideologies underlying the positions of the two groups of countries were not identical, but the implications of the respective coincident

ideologies on this issue for the flow of information were. The result was to put the outnumbered "free flow" advocates on the defensive.

Socialist countries had long denied the premise of the Western position on the free flow of information, and had rejected its claims that the Socialist media were controlled while Western media were free. The news agencies, newspapers, and domestic broadcasting stations in Western countries, the Socialist critique began, were controlled by vested economic interests, banks, transnational corporations, and advertising interests, and could not offer the "objective" news that was the linchpin of professional journalistic ideology. In contrast, media in Socialist countries were seen as free from such pressures.

On the issue of "state control" the Socialist position in this period was that in their countries the state was the embodiment of the wishes of the people (see Marhold, 1987). Socialist advocates rejected Western claims that a state-controlled press was not free. This position developed from the Marxist understanding of history, which saw the dominant elements in society working to support and legitimate one another. The press in Western countries, therefore, was seen as supporting its own interests by legitimizing capitalism and its ruling class. The arrival of socialism, however, heralded the onset of the classless society in which the state acted for the interests of all citizens. The principal mission of the Soviet media system, for instance, was "the socialization of the person receiving the message." Because Marx's vision that revolution would occur when the workers' consciousness had achieved a "common ethos, and common bonds would unite them" had not occurred when Lenin led the Bolsheviks to victory in the Russian revolution, the media were assigned two principal tasks:

First, the media must change the ethical and moral outlook of the population. The psychological orientation underlying the society of the future, when full communism has been achieved, requires cooperation and collectivism and eschews selfishness, careerism, greed, and, in general, the development of an individual that might supersede the societal collective. Second, the media must rouse the population to contribute to the economic goals of the leadership. (Mickiewicz, 1988, pp. 26–28)

The expectations that the media were to serve a common socialization function provided the ideological basis for Socialist governments to side with developing countries for a new information order. Like Socialist governments, developing countries wanted to use the media to help meet their economic and political goals. But their efforts, they thought, were impaired by the serious imbalances in the old information order. These imbalances, articulated by Mustapha Masmoudi of Tunisia (1981, pp. 79–81), affected the news and information flow between the developed and developing worlds, and the availability of indigenous information resources and radio spectrum to developing countries. Their impacts were exacerbated by the "marked indifference" of Western media "to the problems, concerns, and aspirations of the developing countries," the technological and cultural power of the West and its transnational media that "imposed their own way of seeing the world upon the developing countries." The result was the survival of colonialism, alienation in economic, social, and cultural spheres, and "messages ill-suited to the areas in which they are disseminated." Developing countries rejected the Western "populist doctrines like liberty and freedom of expression and the press which, in their experience, are divisive and disruptive in their impact on politically immature and

unstable societies, to whom survival and national unity and security are the supreme goals at their present stage of political evolution" (Mankekar, 1981, p. 2).

Developing countries saw the old information order as one in which their own legitimate political and economic aspirations were thwarted by the dominance of Western media over both the quantitative and qualitative dimensions of information flow: the channels of communication (such as wire services), and the decision structures that define what is news. They sought to correct the imbalance by suggesting that journalists be licensed, that alternative news gathering and distribution systems be established to provide for greater variety of product, and that their future needs for communication channels be accommodated in plans reserving spectrum and satellite orbital slots for their eventual use.[12] Such suggestions were anathema to Western governments. Nevertheless, spokespersons in developing countries have contended that "information balance is at the root of the controversy over international communication" (Rao, 1981, p. 141).

At issue in the controversy between Western countries, on the one hand, and Socialist and developing countries on the other, then, was the question of information control. Western governments argued that state control or intervention into the flow of information was an evil. They made such arguments, too, although their post, telegraph, and telephone administrations themselves often attempt to protect their own monopolies, rather than facilitating communication (see Hirsch, 1986, p. 120; and Martin, 1984, p. 225). They made them, as well, even when they were willing to censor news flow for political reasons (see Hannan, 1988). Socialist and developing countries' governments argued that the old order provided not for "free flow," but rather for a directed flow, one that followed inappropriate criteria for news selection in that it was designed to satisfy the demands of Western information clients, newspapers, and radio and television stations for new audiences to maximize profits.

Both sides in the dispute saw the ideological position of their adversary as resulting from vested political or economic interests, and their own position as being objectively correct. While the West was accused of simply trying to protect its current information monopoly, Socialist governments were accused of trying to control information flow to stifle dissent and continue repression, and developing countries of trying to avoid the political and economic consequences of poor planning, mismanagement, and political corruption. Accusations, however, did not contribute to constructive dialogue on the issues.

The one shared perspective across all three "camps" in this dispute was that information was powerful—too powerful to ignore. The problem was that the adversaries could not agree on who should control this power. The Western industrial countries, while acknowledging information's political power, chose (usually selfishly) to see information as a commodity, an item of economic value. Both Socialist and developing countries saw it more as a social good, one that should be shared freely and commonly, although with a particular kind of "political correctness" that was anathema to industrialized countries.

8.6

Culture: Imperialism and Sovereignty

Another aspect of the information flow issue was cultural imperialism. Although part of the larger issue of new versus old infor-

mation and communication order, it also often functioned more as a parallel than an integrated concern.

As with international news flow, developing countries criticized Western industrialized states, particularly the United States, for their domination of media cultural products. They also complained about the implications of that dominance for their own cultural values. Mushi (1966, p. 13) remarks that "one could hardly visualize the existence of a nation without culture—or, if such a nation were to exist it would merely be a disunited group of people living together simply because there existed geographical boundaries and some political authority to control them from above." Western technology, social and political institutions, and ideologies, Coleman (1954, p. 410) wrote, had been "violently disruptive of the old familistic order" of African societies, creating "new values and symbols, new techniques for the acquisition of wealth, status, and prestige, and new groups for which the old system had no place" (see also Mazrui, 1980, p. 208).

Western European states created many developing countries by imposing arbitrary geographical boundaries, particularly in Africa. The result was often severe difficulty in building political institutions, implementing economic development projects, and developing national cultural policies, because tribal animosities, linguistic differences, and sociocultural dynamics interfered with these processes. One cultural manifesto adopted in Africa acknowledged that "culture starts with the people as creators of themselves and transformers of their environment. Culture, in its widest and most complete sense, enables men to give shape to their lives" (quoted in Dumila, 1976, p. 2; see also Adeyinka, 1977, pp. 39–40; and Archampong, 1977, p. 53). The leaders of developing countries, however, had difficulty seeing how culture, in the sense outlined by this manifesto, could develop in nations swamped with Western cultural imports: films, television programs, music, newspapers, and magazines.

The term *cultural imperialism* implied not only that cultural products were at issue, but that other nations had imposed these products on countries too weak to resist. Schiller (1971, pp. 3, 8), one of the leading proponents of the "cultural imperialism" thesis, wrote in 1971 that the United States' "powerful communications system" constituted an "emerging imperial network." This network was reflective, he said, of its "technologically powerful economy," which was linked to "economically feeble" and "recently independent states" at the bottom "of a power pyramid dominated by the United States." Elliott and Golding (1974, p. 230) claimed, too, that "the *international media system* is one mechanism by which developing countries are brought within the common cultural hegemony of western capitalism" (italics added).

Claims of cultural imperialism continued in the work of Schiller (1976) and others (Nordenstreng & Schiller, 1979; Servaes, 1986; and Tunstall, 1977; see also studies of specific countries, such as Antola & Rogers, 1984 (Latin America); Astoroff, 1987 (Puerto Rico); Boonyaketmala, 1986 (Thailand); Chapman, 1987 (Europe); Izcaray & McNelly, 1987 (Venezuela); Kang & Morgan, 1988 (Korea); Mattelart & Piemme, 1982 (Belgium); and McAnany, 1987 (Chile), not all of which reach the same conclusions). Other analyses, however, suggested that such claims may have overstated the case (see Bornschier & Chase-Dunn, 1985; Lee, 1979; and Righter, 1978, pp. 212–232).

Clearly the Western industrial powers, especially the United States, dominated the production and distribution channels for media materials. There was little doubt,

too, that Western cultural materials were becoming increasingly popular worldwide. That, however, was not the entire story. One issue clearly was dominance per se, but another was the assumption (or implication) that this dominance was the result of coercion by more powerful states. The dominance, however, was the result of commercial, not political, intent, based in the belief that information (and cultural products) were commodities to sell. The tangle of countries' political motives with those of private companies located within them was reminiscent of long-standing problems in the international system. Yet often the dominant states' power over the companies they "represented" in the international arena was limited. In many cases they may have been more servant than master, yet unable to see the negative aspects of their dependency.

It was not difficult to find examples of efforts by Western business enterprises to implant themselves where they were not wanted. For instance, NBC was forced to withdraw from television investments in both Ireland and Italy (Read, 1976, pp. 79–80). ABC and Time-Life, which both attempted to secure footholds in Latin American television markets, eventually withdrew from most of their ventures, which turned out to be poor investments (Lee, 1979, pp. 84–86). It was difficult, however, to find clear instances of Western coercion, particularly following the peak of U.S. media influence abroad in the mid-1960s.

Usabel (1982) suggests that the zenith of U.S. film dominance in Latin America actually occurred in the late 1940s. Schiller (1989, p. 33) continued to argue, however, that "the influence of the informational-cultural sphere of American capitalism shows little sign of diminishing—if anything, it continues its global mastery." Sepstrup (1989, p. 101) criticizes such conclusions as "generally not very convincing as to methodological approaches and the reliability of results." This is thus as much an ideological conflict itself as it is a description of the situation it seeks to explain.

The International Flow of Cultural Materials

U.S. media products attained global popularity during this period, as did materials produced in several Western European countries and in Japan. The formidable task of quantifying this popularity is further complicated by audio and video bootlegging, piracy, secondhand readership, group listening and viewing, all of which make it difficult to specify the exact effects of foreign cultural materials (see, for instance, Hoffman-Riem, 1987; and Johnson, 1981). Available statistics should be interpreted as being indicative guideposts, then, not definitive (or inclusive) parameters.

Interpreting Measures of Cultural Imperialism

A study published by UNESCO in 1986 also illustrates a problem in claiming, based on global exports, that cultural imperialism exists. This study, based on 1980 data, listed the five largest exporters of books, newspapers and periodicals, and records and tapes (pp. 17, 27, 37). (See Table 8.7.) As this table shows, the five largest exporters in these categories of materials constitute 67.5% of book, 75.3% of newspaper and magazine, and 75.8% of record and tape exporters, suggesting not only dominance of these media materials, but seemingly clear evidence of cultural imperialism by industrialized countries.

A different picture emerges, however, when the major partner countries for these exports are examined. In books, for instance, only two developing countries, Mexico and Brazil, were major partner countries of the United States, receiving 6.2% of U.S. book exports. Nigeria received 12.7% of U.K. book exports; the African countries of Algeria, Cameroon, Gabon, Ivory Coast, Libya, Madagascar, Morocco,

Table 8.7

Top Five Exporters of Books, Newspapers and Magazines, and Records and Tapes, with Values in Millions of U.S. Dollars, and Percentages of Total World Exports, 1980

Country	Books		Newspapers and Magazines		Records and Tapes	
	Value	Percentage	Value	Percentage	Value	Percentage
United States	183.3	24.3	76.6	19.8	599.5	21.6
United Kingdom	112.6	14.9	43.0	11.1	244.6	8.1
Federal Republic of Germany	86.9	11.5	66.0	17.0	354.0	12.8
France	70.6	9.3	55.7	14.4	239.9	8.7
Italy	—	—	50.5	13.0	—	—
Japan	—	—	—	—	682.5	24.6

Source: UNESCO, 1986.

Senegal, and Tunisia received 18.4% of French book exports; and no developing countries were listed as major partners of the Federal Republic of Germany (West Germany). Only Spain exported significant numbers of books to the developing world, with 68.2% of its exports going to the Latin American countries of Argentina, Mexico, Venezuela, Chile, and Colombia. And only Mexico appeared twice as a major trading partner on two lists—those of the United States and Spain (UNESCO, 1986, p. 20).

The same pattern reappears in examination of newspapers and magazines, and records and tapes: No developing country received as much as 6% of any developed country's total exports of any media commodity, and only Nigeria and Saudi Arabia appeared on more than two lists. (See Table 8.8.)

The primary trading going on, then, in all three sets of media commodities—books, newspapers and magazines, and records and tapes—was occurring among developed countries themselves. The result was that, while the developing countries' percentage of literate adults and school age populations was dramatically increasing, their share of both book production and international trade in cultural materials was declining. The developed nations of the world were not so much pushing their culture on devel-

Table 8.8

Major Exporting Countries' Partner Countries in the Developing World, in Percentages of Commodity Exported Going to Each Partner, 1980

Exporter	Newspapers and Magazines		Records and Tapes*	
	Country	Percent of Export	Country	Percent of Export
United States	Venezuela	5.8	Mexico	5.7
	Hong Kong	2.0		
France	Morocco	4.9		
	Algeria	4.1		
	Ivory Coast	3.1		
	Tunisia	2.2		
	Guadeloupe	2.0		
	Senegal	1.7		
United Kingdom	Nigeria	2.7	Nigeria	1.9
	Saudi Arabia	2.0		
Japan			Singapore	4.8
			Saudi Arabia	3.6
			Kuwait	3.6
			Hong Kong	3.2
			Libya	2.3

Source: UNESCO, 1986.

*Neither West Germany nor Italy appears using these commodities.

oping countries as they were "imperially" discounting their significance, a result of profit orientation and increasing prices (see Smith, 1980, p. 172). Although the UNESCO study did confirm the almost nonexistent South-to-North trading in media commodities, it hardly suggested that developed countries were swamping the developing world with cultural products (see also Kanocz, 1989).

An even more complicated picture emerged when the statistics relating to television, film, and processed data were examined, but the general conclusion is much the same. The United States was clearly the world leader in television exports. In 1983 Varis examined the sources of television programs in representative countries throughout the world. His analysis of the pattern of imported programs showed the United States to be the major supplier of foreign television programs in most regions of the world. (See Table 8.9.) He did not calculate the major foreign suppliers for countries in Asia.

Again, however, the effect of the U.S. programs on the cultures of other countries, particularly in the developing world, could easily be overstated by these statistics. The same study showed, for instance, that 10 countries in North America and Europe, along with Japan and Brazil, had among them almost three quarters of all the television sets in the world (Varis, 1985, p. 89). In sub-Saharan Africa, in 1988, there were only 11 million television sets to serve a population of 430 million. "So the influence of television is largely confined to the more educated and wealthier members of African communities" (Wilkinson, 1989, p. 154).

Programming imported by developing countries, then, reached relatively few people. This conclusion was bolstered by the fact that most television service in developing countries was limited to urban areas where the most compatible environments for imported television existed: the homes of elites. Also, if the percentage of total transmission time of domestic systems was

---

Table 8.9

Percentage of Foreign Television Imports Provided by the United States, and the Next Largest Supplier, 1983

Region	Percentage from the United States	Percentage from Next Largest Supplier
Canada	70	8 (France)
Latin America and the Caribbean	77	12 (other Latin American countries)
Western Europe	44	16 (United Kingdom)
Eastern Europe*	5	24 (Soviet Union)
Soviet Union**	6	23 (Federal Republic of Germany)
Arab countries	32	13 (France)
Africa	47	25 (United Kingdom)

*The United States is the fifth largest supplier of programs to Eastern Europe, following the Soviet Union, West Germany (16%), France (11%), and the United Kingdom (8%).
**The United States is the fourth largest supplier of television to the Soviet Union, tied with Mongolia and Yugoslavia. Larger suppliers, following West Germany, are France (22%) and Czechoslovakia (14%).
Source: Varis, 1985, pp. 26–27, 33, 36, 38, 47–48.

taken into account, the presence of U.S. television programs shrank dramatically in many cases. (See Table 8.10.) Finally, as countries increase their own production, enter into agreements for program exchange, and participate in international television coproduction, the percentage of time devoted to foreign television decreases.[13]

Film

"U.S. feature-length films were also among the most popular in the world. It is difficult, however, to measure precisely the extent of the popularity, due to the methods of reporting their relative success (often based on box office receipts), or the imprecision with which countries report information about foreign film screenings. Also, the introduction of the VCR caused the number of films distributed on pirated videotapes to increase dramatically. Panama, for instance, reportedly exported between 20,000 and 30,000 pirated videotapes *per month* into other Central American countries (Ganley & Ganley, 1987, p. 55).

The import of U.S. films into various regions of the world, as a percentage of total imports, was apparently not much lower than that of television programs (although global surveys are all dated). Tunstall (1977, pp. 280–281), for instance, reported, based on UNESCO's 1975 *World Communications,* that U.S. films made up between 26% and 61% of imports into 54 countries across all regions of the globe.[14]

Obvious changes occurred following Tunstall's report, which was based mostly on 1970 data. For instance, although they remained convinced of the domination of U.S. film companies worldwide, Mattelart, Delacourt, and Mattelart (1984, p. 78) noted that foreign rentals of U.S. films, which provided 30% of revenues in 1977, had fallen to 17% by 1982. They attributed this not to a lessening U.S. influence, but to a restructuring in the film industry (part 3, chapter 3, and part 4). Another factor was the increasing flow of videocassettes, which reduced revenue from screenings (see Ganley & Ganley, 1987, chapters 6 and 7). Still another was the debt crisis and lack of hard currency in developing countries, which

---

Table 8.10

U.S. Television Programs as a Percentage of Total Program Output, 1983

Region	U.S. Percentage of Total Program Output
Canada	29
Latin America and the Caribbean	12 (including Canadian imports)
Western Europe	not calculated
Eastern Europe	negligible
Soviet Union	negligible
Asia and the Pacific	35 (including ALL imported programs)
Arab countries	14
Africa	17

Source: Varis, 1985, pp. 25, 29, 35, 37–38, 46, 49.

prevented them from obtaining the rights to air/screen U.S. theatrical film and television products. In 1988 alone, developing countries paid their creditors $50.1 billion in interest and capital repayments (see Ganley & Ganley, 1987, chapters 6 and 7).

By 1984 the U.S. motion picture industry earned over $5.3 billion from worldwide theatrical sales. Of this total, $1.2 billion came from videocassette sales, $600 million from pay television sales, and $500 million from U.S. network, syndication, and foreign television rentals; foreign revenues amounted to $1.7 billion, or about 32% of the total (Wildman & Siwek, 1988, pp. 26, 28). In 1988 U.S. feature-length films earned the U.S. production companies $929 million (see "The International Movie Marketplace," 1989, p. 67).

Data Communication

The information available to quantify U.S. or developed country domination of data communication is even more difficult to obtain than for film. This is due both to the proprietary nature of much of this form of communication and to the fact that a large measure of it occurs within transnational corporations (TNCs) themselves and has only recently assumed global proportions.

Mowlana (1985, p. 50) concluded that transborder data flow (TBDF) both threatened developing countries' economic advance and held out potential to help it. While it could provide the basis for alternative approaches to resource allocation, he suggested, it also reinforced the traditional division of labor between developing countries, which provided raw materials, and the industrial states, which provided finished goods (in this case, information). Jussawalla and Cheah (1987, p. 17) argued, too, that "the operations of TNCs make it difficult in terms of costs for Third World countries to access the international data market or to enforce national regulations which would widen participation in the gains of TBDF." One major U.S.-based TNC with a major impact on the distribution of computer *hardware,* of course, has been IBM, which holds significant market shares in mainframe computers across the globe (see DeLamarter, 1986).

The number of industrialized countries using international voice and data circuits to carry telex, facsimile, and computer information increased rapidly over this period (see Russell, 1981, on fax). Many countries in Europe began to set up Datel (data transmission using the telephone and telex network) and Datex (data transmission using public data networks) systems (see Dizard, 1986). By 1982–83, for instance, Sweden's Datex network was connected with those of West Germany, Denmark, Finland, and Norway. The Datex traffic between Sweden and these four countries amounted to over 208,000 messages in the fiscal year 1982–83. Between 1978–79 and 1982–83 in Sweden, the number of computer modems used for data communication increased from 19,000 to nearly 50,000 (Televerket, 1985).

In 1978 Radio Austria established an international node in Vienna to connect with the North American public data networks, TYMNET and TELENET. The system was subsequently expanded to allow communication with other European systems, Australia, and Japan, and to serve as the entry point for the Soviet bloc CONECOM countries, principally Hungary, Bulgaria, Czechoslovakia, and the Soviet Union. Hungary's public data network, NEDIX, was connected to Radio Austria's (RADAUS) node (Sint, 1988, pp. 12–13; and 1989). By 1988, too, the Yugoslav press agency, Tanjug, linked up with major Western database services, including Dialogue (United States), Data Star

(United Kingdom), Echo (European community), and Scan-a-Bid (international database on projects in developing countries) (BBC Monitoring Services, 1988l; see also Endrödi, 1989; Marinov, Trichkov, & Todorov, 1989; and Smirnov, 1989).

Unfortunately, the cost of such systems put them out of the reach of most people in the world. Even in the rapidly developed European data market, access charges and connection fees remained far higher than was the case in the United States. While U.S. data users could connect with several on-line databases using local exchanges, and paid line charges only for connection, in the United Kingdom users had to pay the equivalent (in U.S. dollars) of a $60 sign-up fee, a $3 connection fee for each use, and data retrieval and line charges for both domestic and international connections (various studies on the role of international data communication include Jusswalla, 1985; Olenick, 1979; Renaud, 1986; Rutkowski, 1979; Sauvant, 1986a; United Nations, 1983; and Wigand, Shipley, & Shipley, 1984).

8.8

The Role of International Broadcasting

International broadcasting, although dominated by Western countries, the Soviet Union, and more recently China, escaped much of the criticism associated with other means of international communication. There were two principal reasons for this.

First, since the frequencies used for international radio broadcasting are unassigned, countries were free to use them for either domestic or international purposes. While this often resulted in interference between radio services, developing countries at least had access to the spec-

trum on the same basis as other nations. They were not precluded from using the frequencies because other broadcasters were there first, and the spectrum, while crowded, nevertheless had the flexibility to accommodate them. Although the "big powers"—the United States, the Soviet Union, China, West Germany, and the United Kingdom—used the lion's share of frequencies, many developing countries began international radio operations after achieving their independence. By 1990 over 80 countries provided international radio services.

Second, international radio's most rapid growth occurred during the 20 years after the end of World War II, when many developing countries were just beginning their domestic services. Many such countries received assistance in establishing their systems from U.S., British, and French companies, and those expanding international services were able to "piggyback" onto their domestic counterparts. Also, many developing countries' domestic services were originally located on shortwave, for two reasons: (1) They inherited the shortwave systems established by colonial authorities, and (2) shortwave allowed domestic broadcasting to develop with the least capital investment, since the waves would travel farther than those of medium-wave stations.

Creation and expansion of such domestic systems, then, encouraged people to purchase radios, but economic and political problems usually resulted in poor-quality domestic services in developing countries. The existence of multiple broadcast signals, however, may have encouraged people to purchase radio sets. While this fact benefited both domestic and international broadcasters, the dissatisfaction with domestic services encouraged people to look for alternatives, which benefited the major international services. Finally, by the end of the war, international broadcasting already had a long history. It would have been difficult for developing countries to protest the continuation of radio services that predated their own independent existence.

These historical circumstances, then, to a great extent insulated international radio from the criticisms raised in the NWICO debate (see Maeda, 1981, on the role of international broadcasting). Also, since many developing countries, such as Cuba, Egypt, India, Iraq, Nigeria, North Korea, and Turkey, began to engage in international broadcasting, criticizing it per se would not have been as potent as directing complaints to other services from which developing countries seemed to be excluded. Furthermore, the fact that most countries conducted international broadcasting using languages indigenous to the areas to which they broadcast helped mute criticism, since this practice usually required that the services employ fluent speakers (normally foreign nationals) to broadcast in these languages. This at least gave the appearance of cultural sensitivity (BBC International Broadcasting and Audience Research, 1989a).

The objections to international broadcasting raised in the debate over cultural imperialism were therefore largely directed to television, specifically direct broadcast (DBS) television. Both cultural and political sovereignty were at issue in discussions about DBS. The ITU, for instance, adopted regulation 428A in 1971, requiring that "in devising the characteristics of a space station in the Broadcasting Satellite Service [BSS], all technical means available shall be used to reduce, to the maximum extent practicable, the radiation over the territory of other countries unless an agreement has been previously reached with such countries" (Luther, 1988, p. 84; see also Savage, 1989, chapters 2 and 3, for a discussion of different approaches to regulating the radio frequency spectrum and of free flow versus prior consent; and Konstantinov, 1989).

8.9

Problems for the International System: Propaganda

International radio, although it escaped most of the criticism of the cultural imperialism and NWICO debates, did have to contend with another recurring issue: propaganda. The Cold War continued through this period, only slowly beginning to thaw after the mid-1980s.

In 1984 the Novosti press agency released an article that attacked American "piracy" on the airwaves (see Bannov, 1984). It quoted Konstantin U. Chernenko (who was named Soviet general secretary, but who died after only a few months in office) before the Central Committee of the Communist party saying that "we are dealing with attempts to organize a true information and propaganda intervention against us, to turn radio and television channels into a weapon for interfering in states' internal affairs and conducting subversive actions." The article singled out for criticism VOA, as a "mouthpiece for anti-Soviet mobs"; the BBC, whose broadcasts "abound with forgeries, slanderous fabrications and tendentious treatment of public opinion"; and Deutsche Welle, "another powerful propaganda center of imperialist reaction" whose programs were "devoted to cock-and-bull stories about imaginary USSR preparations for war." Such criticisms continued the tradition of superpower rivalry, a hallmark of this period in the development of the international communications system. This rhetoric notwithstanding, Griffith (1980, Vol. 2, p. 248) claims that the Soviets, under premiers Kosygin and Brezhnev, reformed their propaganda, targeting more specific audiences, emphasizing Soviet achievements, particularly in science and technology, and reducing their use of "agitation."[15]

Developing countries have raised similar claims of bias by Western shortwave broadcasts. Middle Eastern countries have complained about the bias of both U.S. and British broadcasts directed into the region. Two specific instances concerned alleged bias against the shah of Iran, and subsequently against the Khomeini government, and later alleged pro-Iraqi broadcasts during the Persian Gulf crisis (see Fortner, 1991a; Larson, 1986; Mowlana, 1984; and Tusa, 1990, pp. 85–94).

8.10

The Impact of Trade Restrictions on the International Communications System

People's abilities to exercise the freedom of expression and information "guaranteed" them by various international resolutions are tied to their access to the technologies necessary to participate in the international system. Many countries around the globe have adopted strategies, however, to discourage such access. Sometimes they aimed specifically to deny access, and sometimes to accomplish other ends, such as protecting limited hard currency reserves or allowing nationally established economic priorities to be met.[16]

The Soviet Union

The Soviet Union and its allies in Eastern Europe adopted several policies to restrict the flow of Western communications technology into their countries.[17] Some of these strategies were designed specifically to restrict public access to Western media content. Others, however, perhaps had other intentions, although their effect was the same.

One Soviet strategy was to install wired radio sets in cities throughout the country. Since wired radio sets were incapable of receiving off-air signals, their effect was to allow people to hear Soviet radio signals while denying them access to outside signals. By 1985, 97% of the Soviet population had access to wired radio sets, with over 600 cities included in the system (Mehta, 1987, pp. 60–61). By 1987 Moscow alone had 6 million wired radio receivers in operation, and a new six-channel system was being installed and tested to replace the three-channel system already in use (BBC Monitoring Service, 1987b).

Another strategy was to limit the number of imported communication devices, whether shortwave radio receivers, PAL-standard television sets (SECAM is the standard in what was formerly Socialist Europe), videocassette recorders, satellite dishes, or personal computers, each of which could provide increased access to Western information (see Boyd, 1983, concerning the results of this for the "two Germanies"). As Kissinger (1985) put it, "Where the control of information is considered the key to political power, cassettes, video machines and computers become threats, not technological opportunities." However, the Soviet Union had difficulty controlling the spread of these technologies. A lively business existed throughout Socialist Europe for engineers willing to alter domestically produced radios to receive Western signals (see Shanor, 1985, p. 161). By the mid-1980s Polish dissidents were using VCRs to distribute banned plays and films, and Soviet citizens were watching Western films that found their way into the

Soviet Union through various unofficial and diplomatic channels (see "Beware of Fresh Ideas," 1987, pp. 17–22; Diehl, 1986a, 1986b, 1988, pp. A1, A26; Echikson, 1987, pp. 88, 90, 163; "Hungarian Shoppers Beat a Path to West," 1989; and Taubman, 1985). Poland was flooded with half a million video recorders "privately imported and a black market in video cassettes began to thrive in the country" (Mojkowski, 1987, p. 22). By the late 1980s Poland was granting licenses to citizens for satellite television receivers, and Hungary was admitting that its broadcasting would have to "fight harder for [the] attention" of its audience, since satellite television was about to become a reality (BBC Monitoring Service, 1987f, 1988c, 1988s). Warsaw's *Tryuna Ludu* claimed in 1987 (BBC Monitoring Service, 1987g) that "computers, video and satellite television are attacking the collective unconscious. . . . Satellite television will demolish the existing structure of information and communications, to the clear advantage of the greatest industrial and most highly technologically developed powers. It will cross national, cultural and political borders." By the late 1980s the difficulties of controlling information in Eastern Europe under the deluge of new technologies and content had reached seemingly unmanageable levels (see BBC Monitoring Service, 1988j, 1989j, 1989w). Gradually the Eastern bloc began to open up (see BBC Monitoring Service, 1987e, 1988h, 1989a, 1989e, 1989f, 1989h, 1989m, 1989s, 1989v).

A third strategy was to manufacture radio receivers with limited frequency coverage. Until 1989, for instance, the Soviet Union manufactured no shortwave receivers for domestic use that could receive signals below 25 meters (see BBC Monitoring Service, 1989y). The Soviet practice made it easier for them to jam signals of Western broadcasters. It also prevented

people from listening to all broadcasts in the upper frequency bands (11, 13, and 19 meters) unless they altered their sets. There was, in fact, a lively set-altering activity in Communist countries that allowed these bands to be received and lessened the effect of jamming. RFE/RL also published information designed to help people with these problems.

Developing Countries

Developing countries, too, adopted various approaches to control the flow of information and technology across their borders. Their reasons for doing so, however, were often aimed not at stopping the programming flow, but at protecting their economic and political sovereignty. Jussawalla (1982) argued, for instance, that

> communication technology and its planned input to development encounter certain restrictions in developing countries, such as shortage of capital, vague perceptions of the country's communication goals, undefined criteria for service quality, and unsatisfied and unexpressed consumer demand. Under such limitations, the import of new technology is likely to have mixed consequences. The transfer of technology through trade is costly and creates a burden on the balance of payments. (p. 93)

Developing countries often saw new technologies, too, as potentially disruptive of the "delicate balance" they had constructed in the arenas of politics, culture, and social development (see Powell, 1985, p. 6). They also saw these technologies (and the cultural products that inevitably flowed in their wake) as continuing the old colonial relationships, in which they sold raw materials to developed countries in exchange for manufactured products. What they got back, as Somavia and Reyes-Matt (1981, p. 83) said, was their own raw material processed "by agencies that are alien to our environment." In 1988 Nigerian President Ibrahim Babangida issued a decree requiring that all foreign news agencies operating in his country pass their material through the News Agency of Nigeria (NAN). He claimed (BBC Monitoring Service, 1988p) this was necessary because of the "lopsided patterns" of world news flow, which resulted in information about Third World countries being "scanty and deliberately inaccurate."

Like the former Socialist European countries, developing nations tried to restrict the import of communications technologies. They accomplished this by restricting imports of specific types of technology and by imposing various duties, tariffs, and miscellaneous taxes on imports. Some countries, of course, restricted imports of nearly all "nonessen-

tial" goods to protect what little hard currency reserves they are able to develop. Often their debt problems were so severe that these measures were necessary (or required by lenders) as part of mandated austerity programs. Many countries also defined certain types of technologies as "luxury goods," which made them subject to higher taxes than would be the case otherwise.

To illustrate the results, radio receivers were subject to no taxation when they entered Singapore, but up to 400% entering Morocco. Egypt taxed combination radios, those incorporating tape or phonograph systems, at 100%, but all other types at 50%. In addition, however, Egypt also imposed a 1% statistical tax, a 10% consolidation of economic development surcharge, a

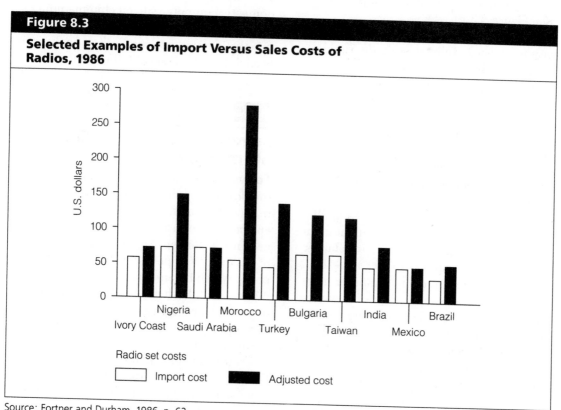

Figure 8.3

Selected Examples of Import Versus Sales Costs of Radios, 1986

Source: Fortner and Durham, 1986, p. 62.

3% of total duty imposed pier handling charge, a .2% CIF (value of product plus costs, insurance, and freight) marine duty, and a 20-, 30-, or 40-piasters per metric ton of imports porterage duty. Iran levied a duty of 30% on radios, plus a 70% commercial benefits tax (CBT), a 1–1.5% municipal tax, a 6% ministry of interior tax levied on the duty and CBT, and a 1.5% red lion and sun society tax levied on duty and CBT. All shipments into Mehrabad Airport also incurred an additional 15 rials per kilogram tax. Other countries imposed merchandise circulation taxes, commercial transaction taxes, stamp duties, customs surcharges, and consumption taxes. Such charges provided hard currency to the taxing authority, but also drove up the prices of radio and television receivers at sometimes alarming rates (Fortner & Durham, 1986, pp. 50–64). (See Figure 8.3.)

Developing countries also attempted, largely unsuccessfully, to stem the rapidly growing number of VCRs in their citizens' hands, and established various barriers to reduce the trade in data flows and processing (see Ganley & Ganley, 1987, chapter 10; and Pavlic & Hamelink, 1985, p. 37). Brazil, for instance, restricted the importation of computer equipment to protect fledgling Brazilian computer manufacturers, although the results were somewhat less favorable than anticipated (repeating Brazil's unfortunate experiences in audio equipment manufacture) (see Edfelt, 1986; and Mattelart & Schmucler, 1985, pp. 17–19 and 101–112). In 1991 Brazil reopened its computer market after failing to satisfy domestic demand for fast and dependable computers, fax machines, and other electronic equipment (Belsie, 1991). South Korea's domestic computer manufacturing, too, added little to the capability of its citizens, since it directed 70% of its production toward export to foreign markets (Kim, Lee, & Lee, 1987).

Some notable successes, however, were reported (although anecdotal in nature), such as the manufacture of satellite dishes by villagers in Tonga and Peru.[18]

These efforts to control technology were part of a long tradition in international communication. The British government's claimed inability to demand interconnection with non-Marconi apparatus by British Marconi, and its restrictions on the import of foreign-made radio tubes in the 1920s, both protected domestic manufacturers. The fixed-frequency radio receivers sold in Nazi Germany did as well. More recently, France's efforts to build a domestic electronics industry protected from outside competition through development of the SECAM television standard, and U.S. attempts to restrict import of digital audiotape (DAT) players and to protect its domestic computer silicon chip manufacturers, stemmed from the same basic nationalistic impulses (see Crane's analysis of French impulses on color TV, 1979).

8.11

Sovereignty and the Control of Information

The various strategies adopted to control the flow of information or to circumvent that control, as discussed here, all revolved around the central concern for political sovereignty, a concept legitimizing the exercise of authority and power by the state.[19] Sovereignty can be enhanced or degraded by information. Both governments and their oppositions recognize that, which is why they seek to control the flow of information within societies.

Controlling information, according to Shanor (1985, p. 1), was "one of the three basic instruments of rule in the Soviet system" a system, he says, where "foreign broadcasts play such an important part in informing people . . . that some Soviet citizens call them the 'University of the Millions.'" Whether the Soviet Union was, by the mid-1980s, abandoning this instrument became an issue. Clearly it had begun to open its borders to Western information. Such openness, however, could end as quickly as it began, as it did in China in the middle of 1989 (see Vines, 1989).

Before it changed its policy, the Soviet Union was perhaps the most significant apologist for controlling information. It had argued consistently that practices such as jamming were justified when external broadcasters attempted to meddle in internal affairs of a country. Radio Moscow, for instance, had claimed (BBC Monitoring Service, 1987a) that "the Soviet Union, in accordance with the international convention on broadcasting, has been jamming those radio broadcasts that are aimed at undermining national security, spreading anti-Sovietism, ethnic antagonisms among our people and broadcasts that may be considered war propaganda or that offend our people's dignity."

Other countries, however, argued for different measures. The sovereignty issues that concerned them included the rights discussed here: restricting technology imports, protecting scarce hard currency reserves, restricting programming imports that could lead to discontented consumers, or controlling the activities of TNCs that could move profits from country to country to avoid making their proper tax contribution to a country's economy. Since information was a commodity itself, subject to manipulation to serve the economic interests of states or corporations, countries intervened increasingly to protect their own sovereign authority over it (see Feketekuty & Aronson, 1984; Ganley, 1987; Neumann, 1987; Robinson, 1985; Stevenson, 1988,

pp. 6–8; and United States Congress, 1979, for discussion of information trade).

Such intervention was legitimized, too, in the international arena. The Helsinki Accords, signed in 1975, acknowledged the necessity for all signatory states to "respect each other's right freely to choose and develop its political, social, economic and cultural systems as well as its right to determine its laws and regulations" (Conference on Security and Cooperation in Europe, 1975, p. 324). The Maitland Commission (Maitland, 1985, pp. 37–38) also acknowledged the sovereignty of states to "define the financial framework within which [telecommunications systems] operate," and concluded, "It is for individual governments to decide whether telecommunications should be wholly state-owned and operated, or wholly or partly privately-owned; whether telecommunications should be operated as a monopoly; or whether competition should be admitted." Such political sovereignty was also extended to cover the cultural sovereignty of states. Powell (1985, p. 178) made this link when he wrote, "Like political sovereignty, cultural sovereignty involves the right and the capacity to develop and protect national culture from outside influences." This was, in essence, the theoretical justification for the cultural imperialism debate that emerged.

Specific sovereignty issues also arose in various international meetings, including the following: (1) the control of information entering a country that the national leadership considers damaging to indigenous moral or political systems, (2) the control of information reported about countries that affect foreign perceptions of their political stability, development commitments, or response to disaster or disease, and (3) the distortion of a nation's history, culture, or values by mediated content. These concerns extended the more specific issues raised in arguments about cultural imperialism: the domination of a country's media systems by foreign material. In essence, they were concerns raised by those who saw information control as central to the continued existence of sovereign states, particularly to the extent that the legitimacy of states was dependent on the flow (and control) of information.

Conclusion

The introduction of a variety of new communications technologies in the 1970s and early 1980s increased the complexity of the international system. The content of the system diversified, the competition intensified, and the nature of control over the system exercised by Northern Hemisphere countries shifted away from its traditional base in hardware to encompass both distribution and content control as well.

The system was also complicated by the maturing of concern about the international system within developing countries, which were able to assess the implications of the system for their own priorities, and to begin the process of demanding full equality for their interests. This led to disputes over the system itself and over its underlying philosophical underpinnings established both by history and by postwar agreements that had largely failed to take account of developing countries' needs in the initial period of independence.

By the middle of the 1980s developing countries' complaints were being heard, but not necessarily responded to effectively. Many long-standing issues that had haunted the international system continued: propaganda, private versus public ownership, pricing and tariffs, free flow versus control of information, protection of vested economic interests and established monopolies of knowledge, and so on. Coincidentally, new means of communication, and new strains on the resources of the international system, were developing. The complexities of this period would continue, and even be exacerbated, by such changes. While each new development held promise that the international system could finally become fully accessible to all global citizens, the increasing complexity also suggested that inequalities would continue. The division between the information rich and information poor would likely grow; the global metropolis would expand even while failing to meet the basic communication needs of all its citizens.

Notes

1. One major debate concerned the relationship between developing countries and transnational corporations. A number of authors have examined this issue. Opposing arguments may be seen in two contrasting works, Barnet and Müller's *Global Reach* (1974) and the Committee for Economic Development's *Transnational Corporations and Developing Countries: New Policies for a Changing World Economy* (1981), and in Jenkins, (1987).

2. Australian broadcasting networks could purchase U.S.-made hour-long series episodes, for instance, for $12,000 each in 1980. The same length program produced in Australia, however, cost $70,000 (see Breen, 1981, p. 389).

3. Austria is listed separately from Western European countries because it is not a member of either the European Economic Community (EEC), commonly known as the Common Market, or NATO.

4. The correlation between the number of telephone sets per 100 inhabitants and the gross national product is close to 1.0 (see

Pelton, 1986a, p. 40; see also O'Brien, Cooper, Perkes, & Lucas, 1977).

5. Snow continues (1986, p. 48), "Developing nations have gained access to telecommunications services they could not otherwise afford, and the industrialized world has shared in the technology and aerospace contracting needed to maintain the system."

6. "Coordination" is the term used to require that any new international satellite systems be coordinated (technically and economically) with Intelsat.

7. The Fourth Conference of Heads of State of the Non-Aligned Countries called for developing countries to reorganize existing channels of communication "which are the legacy of the colonial past and which have hampered free, direct and fast communication between them," to "initiate joint action for the revision of existing multilateral agreements with a view to reviewing press cable rates and facilitating faster and cheaper inter-communication," and to "take urgent steps to expedite the process of collective ownership of communication satellites" (Action Programme, 1973, p. 275). A UNESCO meeting of experts on communication policies and planning had brought the issue up in 1972, focusing on aspects of "cultural neo-colonialism" in international communication practices (see Pavlic & Hamelink, 1985, p. 13).

8. The expectation of "take-off" in national economies continued through this period, although the "dependency school" of economic relations also began to emerge (see Bornschier & Chase-Dunn, 1985, p. 27).

9. How much is available to people is dependent both on their own abilities (literacy) and access to reception technology (radios and televisions), and on the area of the world in which they live. The world continues to be divided into information rich and information poor countries, and countries varying in degrees of access.

10. Pye (1963, p. 440) suggested, however, that the emphasis of the governments of develop-

ing countries was "generally one of providing (latent) propaganda in support of government policies."

11. Basic historical documents articulating the Western philosophical position include John Milton's *Aereopagitica* (1951) and John Stuart Mill's *On Liberty* (1947). Other principal advocates include Thomas Jefferson and James Madison (primary architects of America's Declaration of Independence, Constitution, and Bill of Rights), Thomas I. Emerson (1970) and Isaiah Berlin (1969).

12. Eight equatorial countries claimed segments of the geosynchronous orbit over their territory in 1976 in the Bogota Declaration, but their claims received little support in the United Nations (see Gorove, 1984, p. 4).

13. U.S. film and television libraries are already becoming foreign-owned (see "Going Hollywood," 1989, pp. 40, 41). On the issue of international coproduction see Renaud and Litman (1985, pp. 245–261).

14. Tunstall also reported that France, Italy, the United Kingdom, and West Germany were virtually tied with the United States in exports into the European Economic Community and actually exceeded the U.S. percentage into other developed countries in both Eastern and Western Europe, and elsewhere, as well as into Africa. The largest Eastern European film exports into the European Socialist countries were the Soviet Union (19%), East Germany (7%), and Czechoslovakia and Poland (6% each). India was also a significant exporter of films into the Far East, providing 17% of total imports.

15. The *Great Soviet Encyclopedia* (1973, Vol. 1, p. 137, and Vol. 21, p. 269) differentiated propaganda from agitation. The former was designed to convey many ideas to a few people, while the latter concentrated on a single or a few ideas, conveying them to the "great mass" of people. Propaganda was more theoretical and ideological, agitation more popularized and demanding of mass action.

16. Hard currencies are those accepted worldwide as payments for goods and services. They include, as examples, the U.S. dollar, British pound sterling, French and Swiss francs, German Deutschmark, and Japanese yen. Currencies of developing countries are typically not accepted as hard, and neither is the Soviet ruble.

17. Western technology here includes products of Japan and other Far Eastern technology producing states, even though, strictly speaking, they are not "western."

18. The manufacture of such dishes in Tonga was related by Reinhard Keune of Freidrich-Ebert-Stiftung, Bonn, West Germany. The Peruvian case was reported by Graham (1988, pp. A37, A38).

19. "Men do not wield or submit to sovereignty. They wield or submit to authority or power. . . . Although we talk of it loosely as something concrete which may be lost or acquired, eroded or increased, sovereignty is not a fact. It is a concept which men in certain circumstances have applied—a quality they have attributed or a claim they have counterposed—to the political power which they or other men were exercising" (Hinsley, 1986, p. 1).

9

POLITICAL AND ECONOMIC TURMOIL IN THE GLOBAL METROPOLIS: 1986–PRESENT

9.1

Introduction

Nearly three decades have passed since the world began to expect the arrival of the global village. Despite continuing references to it as fait accompli, it has still not arrived: It is a myth, albeit a powerful one. Certainly profound changes, even in the past 5 years, have caused a reconfiguration in elements of the international communications system; yet its basic structure remains. The control of the system is still vested in the governments of, and private corporations housed within, the major industrial nations (see McQuail, 1989, p. 207). Yet new challenges to this control have also been mounted from the periphery of the global metropolis, often from the least expected places.

The most significant change of this brief period was the breakdown of Soviet politi-cal and military hegemony in Eastern and Central Europe, the reunification of Germany in 1990, the independence movements within the Soviet Baltic States, and finally, the dissolution of the Soviet Union itself. Another important change, at least to some observers, was the "revitalization" of the United Nations as a peace-keeping organization, and its sanctioning of military action against Iraq in the Persian Gulf crisis.

Developing countries continued to press for change in the international system, but their demands were not as insistent as before. A major worry for them was that development assistance might be rechanneled by the Western industrial democracies toward rebuilding Eastern and Central Europe, and away from their own pressing problems. This may have contributed to their more temperate tone in criticisms of the international communication and information order.

On the economic front the continued popularity of U.S.-produced entertainment throughout the world resulted in non-U.S. companies taking over U.S. entertainment firms. New forms of international cooperation in coproducing television and cinema material also developed, partially due to the rising cost of such material, partly to efforts to avoid programming quotas that were introduced into the European community, and partly because of increasing competition coming from new deregulatory moves in many countries.

A related problem was the increasing concern about the extent of piracy of recorded material, including audio and video products, and feature-length films. U.S. firms, which dominated the world markets in all three of these commodities, began to press for revitalized protection for intellectual property, and particularly for the adoption by developing countries of international conventions designed to protect such assets. Their concerns, however, first required that the United States ratify the Berne Convention.

On the technology front fiber optics began to be a viable alternative to satellite communication on some of the world's major point-to-point telecommunications routes (e.g., across the North Atlantic and between the United States and Japan). New bands were also made available to expand shortwave broadcasting, and single-side-band transmission was to become a reality in 1992. Japanese, U.S., and European firms also competed directly to establish an international standard for high-definition television (HDTV), and trade disputes between the United States and Japan over communications equipment, including cellular technology, consumer electronics, and new

generations of computer chips, continued to strain their relationship.

Ideology and Communication in East-West Relations

The arrival of Mikhail Gorbachev did not result in immediate changes in the complexion of East-West broadcast communication, but by the middle of the 1980s the possibility of significant change seemed real. By 1990 profound change had occurred, although within the Soviet Union itself some were reporting that progress in escaping state censorship was becoming more difficult as the political and economic condition of the country deteriorated (various opinions can be seen in Kilpatrick, 1987; Lee, 1987a, 1987b, 1987c; Remnick, 1989a, 1989b; Remnick & Diehl, 1988; Szeseckö, 1987, on Hungary; and Trusov, 1987).

Changing U.S.-Soviet Communication Flow

The ideological line followed by U.S. and Soviet state services began to unravel in the late 1980s, leading to policy changes and to emerging differences in the treatment of news and commentary. One indication of change was the acceptance by the Soviets of external broadcasts directed at their citizens. In January 1987 the Soviets, as part of Gorbachev's *glasnost* initiative, stopped jamming BBC broadcasts, and in May 1987 ceased jamming operations against VOA. Poland stopped its jamming in January 1988, and in November 1988 the Soviets and Hungarians stopped jamming altogether, followed soon after by the Bulgarians and Czechs. By December 1, 1988, all jamming in Europe and the Soviet Union had stopped for the first time since the end of World War II.[1]

In 1990, in talks between the United States and the Soviet Union on improving communication flow between the two countries, the Soviets did continue to complain about some broadcasts by VOA and Radio Liberty. Vladimir F. Petrovsky, Soviet deputy foreign minister, claimed ("U.S. and USSR Continue to Find Communications Common Ground," 1990, p. 60) that these two services were broadcasting "nonobjective, distorted, tendentious information about events occurring in the USSR" and reporting the actions of the Soviet Union "in a biased manner . . . in the foreign policy arena." His remarks were aimed at broadcasts in January 1990 about the interethnic unrest in Azerbaijan. Both U.S. services did admit to errors in their coverage.

Other significant events contributed to easing of tension on communication issues between these two superpowers, however. "Space-bridges" linking various audiences in the two countries, such as journalists, legislators, and university students, provided opportunities for conversations and reduction of misunderstanding between citizens in the two societies. U.S. radio stations began sending crews to the Soviet Union to broadcast live back into the United States (see "Back from the USSR," 1989). The Soviet Union also began to ease restrictions on its citizens' use of international telecommunications networks, looking for ways to provide easier access to international telephony, and opening up both fax and electronic mail services to the United States (Dixon, 1990, p. v). Commercial non-state-controlled radio stations also began operating in the former Soviet bloc, led by stations in Hungary and Poland, and in the Soviet Union itself in 1990. The Atlanta-based Ca-

ble News Network also began distributing its news programs through Gostelradio, the Soviet state committee for radio and television, and in hotels in both Poland and Hungary (see "New Kids on the Bloc," 1990, p. 101).[2] Even U.S.-based religious broadcasting organizations, such as Robert Schuler's "Hour of Power" television program, the Christian Broadcasting Network (CBN), and Trans World Radio, announced plans to distribute programming or open production facilities in the Soviet Union (see "Religious Broadcasters Clean House," 1990, p. 72). In 1990 the World Christian Broadcasting Corporation began distributing a Nashville-produced weekly religious radio program on the Soviet Union's state radio network.

Although the Gorbachev years saw the introduction of *glasnost* and the cessation of jamming, the Soviet accusations about Western intervention in the internal affairs of Socialist states continued, though perhaps on a less strident note. *Pravda,* for instance, carried a report in early 1989 (BBC Monitoring Service, 1989l) about the elimination of jamming, but claimed that

> it would be naive to think that with our restructuring and new thinking, the tasks of certain foreign "voices" have changed and they now operate exclusively in the interests of the struggle for peace, freedom and mutual understanding. As before, alongside honest, objective and well-intentioned broadcasts, one can encounter lies, falsifications and distortions on the air. All these methods from the "psychological warfare" arsenal do not, of course, promote trust between countries.

On the U.S. side, too, suspicion remained. In its 1989 *Annual Report,* Radio Free Europe/Radio Liberty (Board for International Broadcasting, 1989, p. 5) claimed that "in short, [RFE/RL] remains the most powerful instrument the United States has for influencing the course of developments in Eastern Europe and the Soviet Union in a positive and peaceful manner." VOA, too, along with RFE/RL, planned to install sixteen 500-kw transmitters and 37 curtain antennas in Israel to broadcast in 29 languages to the south and central portions of the Soviet Union, Asia, and Africa (see "U.S. Shortwave Station in Israel," 1990, p. 66; see also Buell, 1986; and Mainland & Pomar, 1986). Israeli court action eventually stalled this project.

Television Martí

One controversial U.S. television initiative was Television Martí, which followed on the heels of Radio Martí, created in 1983 as a specialized surrogate service to Cuba. Television Martí was to provide television programming from a transmitter carried aloft on an aereostat (blimp) moored off the southern Florida coast. The National Association of Broadcasters (NAB) raised objections to the scheme, however, fearing Cuban retaliation on U.S. radio frequencies that would interfere with U.S. domestic broadcasters. In addition, feasibility studies showed that assumptions underlying the scheme contained serious flaws. In spite of all this, things went ahead as planned, and the federal government funded Television Martí as part of the fiscal 1990 budget (see "TV Martí Bill Approved by House," 1989).

Cuba quickly condemned U.S. plans for Television Martí, in April 1989 calling them "a grave aggression against the sovereignty of our country by the United States."[3] According to "Tele Rebelde" in Havana, the 10th Conference of the Intergovernmental Council of Non-Aligned Countries for the Co-ordination of Information and Communications passed a resolution in August 1989 (BBC Monitoring Service, 1989z) also calling the project "an aggression and an in-admissible precedent which constitutes intervention in the internal affairs of a state" (see also BBC Monitoring Service, 1988v). A VOA report admitted, too, that the U.S. Advisory Commission for Public Diplomacy had raised questions about the project (BBC Monitoring Service, 1989c), asking whether it was "consistent with US obligations under international law" (see also Frederick, 1986, United States, 1982, and Youm, 1991, pp. 95–103, for earlier discussions about the U.S.-Cuban broadcasting situation).

Cuba and the United States sparred over the issue, too, at the 1989 ITU Plenipotentiary Conference in Nice. The Cuban delegation recalled its denunciation of U.S. plans for Radio Martí at the 1982 Plenipotentiary Conference in Nairobi, and claimed (ITU, 1989a, p. 8) that since the inauguration of the station, the United States had been "carrying out an aggression which represents, without any doubt, a gross and crude interference in the internal Cuban affairs." The Cuban delegation also claimed (ITU, 1989b) that U.S. activities constituted a breach of the North American Radio Broadcasting Agreement (NARBA) and a violation of the ITU's Radio Regulations for medium-wave (AM) radio services.[4] Cuba promised a "vigorous response," while regretting "the unintended effects which may be produced" (ITU, 1989c, p. 8). The delegation also denounced the plans for Television Martí, calling the project "an even more harmful, insulting and unscrupulous aggression" (ITU, 1989c, p.8).

The United States responded to the Cuban assertions by accusing the delegation (ITU, 1989d) of attempting to politicize the conference, and of "making numerous unsubstantiated and false charges against the United States." The U.S. delegate denied that Radio Martí violated NARBA, and countercharged that Cuba was operating stations "unregistered with the IFRB" or stations "operating outside their registered parameters" that had been "causing harmful interference to United States commercial medium wave stations since 1959. Since Cuba totally disregards its obligations under the International Telecommunication convention and associated Radio Regulations and, in 1981 abrogated [NARBA], Cuban threats to renounce its obligations are redundant."

The Cuban delegation responded to the U.S. charges in a later plenary meeting in Nice, and reminded the U.S. delegation that it could not invoke the Universal Declaration of Human Rights as a justification for its broadcast activities unless it took into account Article 29, "to the effect that these rights cannot be exercised in a manner contrary to law, morality, respect for the rights and freedoms of others in accordance with the purposes and principles of the United Nations" (ITU, 1989e, p. 1). In its signing of the Final Acts of the conference, the Cuban delegation also denounced (ITU, 1989f, p. 63) "the interventionist escalation by the Government of the United States in establishing radio and television transmitters directed against the people of Cuba, using the radio frequency spectrum and the geostationary-satellite orbit in frank and malicious violation of the principles and provisions that govern international telecommunications."

A U.S. delegation traveled to Cuba in 1990 to discuss this U.S.-Cuban war of words. Cuban officials warned the delegation that it had options other than jamming as means of retaliation against U.S. broadcasting, which they considered a violation of Cuban sovereignty:

> Interruption of the U.S.-Cuban immigration agreement seemed one option. . . . But while the Cubans did not specify interference with American AM stations members of the [U.S. delegation] — sensitive to the interference American stations as far from Cuba as Minnesota and Utah have suffered from Cuban AM outlets over the years — said that was clearly implied in the Cuban's remarks. ("U.S. Group Has 'Jam' Session," 1990, p. 94)

In early 1991 the aerostat transmitter for Television Martí broke free and fell into the Everglades, temporarily ending its broadcasts. It was out of commission for about two months, but then VOA was able to relaunch it, and it began broadcasting again on April 21. Nothing had been resolved. In June 1991 a House appropriations subcommittee voted to end funding for TV Martí, with one spokesperson calling it a Cold War "relic," an "ineffective . . . disaster" ("House Subcommittee Votes," 1991, p. 80). Although the full House Appropriations Committee restored the funds a week later, it did so in the face of criticism from a U.S. Advisory Commission on Public Diplomacy report calling TV Martí's budget a "disproportionate allocation of television resources" when its funding was compared with that of Worldnet, USIA's effort to provide a global television service ("U.S. Urged to Increase Spending," 1991, p. 26). In December 1991 the President's Task Force on U.S. Government International Broadcasting recommended that Television Martí change or extend its hours of operation, since it was "forced to broadcast during a time period when there are few viewers." If that could not be done, the task force said, "the service should be terminated" and its resources transferred to other U.S. government international broadcasting services (p. 15). The point was not necessarily to condemn the service per se, but to assure that U.S. government broadcasting to Cuba was as effective as possible during what the task force called a "potentially dramatic time in the history of Cuba." The task force asserted (p. 15) that 1992 was "no time . . . to limit or diminish our broadcasting efforts toward Cuba if they are effective."

In a related development, in October 1991, Turner Broadcasting System filed a suit against the U.S. Treasury Department for blocking its plans to distribute CNN and its entertainment channel, TNT South, to Cuban hotels. Although Turner and Capital Cities/ABC had been granted permission to air the Pan American games from Havana in the summer of 1991, a continuing program service to Cuba would have violated the Trading with the Enemy Act. This dispute was an indication of the unwillingness of the U.S. government to shut down the Cold War as it applied to U.S.-Cuban relations, despite the collapse of communism in Europe (see "TBS Sues Treasury," 1991, p. 42; see also De Marco, 1991, p. A3).

Worldnet

By 1987 USIA had expanded through its satellite-fed television service Worldnet to include a daily 2-hour news program and a feature program. In 1988 the system was serving 81 cable television systems in 13 European countries, as well as hotels and American embassies and consulates throughout the world. USIA had installed 95 TVROs (television-receive-only antennas) for Worldnet, 46 in Europe, 27 in Latin America, 9 in Africa, and 13 in Asia and the Middle East (Tuch, 1990, p. 103). The service provided programming in English, Spanish, French, and Arabic. However, in late 1988 the news and features programming was forced off the air by Congress when USIA was unable to show that it had 2 million regular viewers in Western Europe; a commissioned survey of Worldnet's European audience had indicated a regular audi-

ence of only 234,000 (Randolph, 1989b). The interactive "Dialogue" programs were continued, but other "active" programs were not. The service supplemented "Dialogue" by carrying passive services, such as C-Span and the Cable News Network (CNN). By 1991, however, Worldnet was a much-reduced operation, with inadequate budget, an unclear mission, and small audiences. As Tuch (1990, p. 105) put it, "Until the fall of 1988, USIA management had been too involved in the creation of the new medium to be expected to regard its brainchild critically and determine how to employ it effectively. Now, budgetary necessities have mandated rationalization of Worldnet's advantages over other media in its ability to focus on specific audiences and specific objectives at a specific time."[5] The President's Task Force on U.S. Government International Broadcasting (1991) also addressed Worldnet, saying that its interactive programming, by which journalists and others in foreign countries could question U.S. government spokespersons, "is and will continue to be a useful tool for providing U.S. views on issues to elites in foreign countries" (p. 36).

Soviet and Russian Information Activities

The Soviet Union's international wire service, TASS, provided both wire copy and photo services to over 1,000 clients in 115 countries. It provided its copy in seven languages, and claimed to process more than 4 million words per day (BBC Monitoring Service, 1987h) and more than 6.5 million photographs per year (BBC Monitoring Service, 1989q). TASS had correspondents in 128 countries and provided "hard news," commentaries, and official government materials (texts of speeches, reports on official visits and meetings within the Soviet Union,

Soviet government appointments, etc.) to its clients (Roxburgh, 1987, p. 57). In January 1992 TASS announced that it was to be merged into a new wire service established by the Russian Republic. The new agency was to be the Russian Information Telegraphy Agency (RITA), and would incorporate both TASS and Novosti. TASS was to handle only domestic wire service for Russia, while RITA would handle the international services. RITA thus joined the independent service, Interfax, which had been started after Soviet President Gorbachev's *glasnost* initiative in the mid-1980s (see "RITA Ousts TASS," 1992).

The Soviet Union did not usually appear as a prolific exporter of cultural materials, but it did export a significant number of books. In 1987, for instance, the Soviet Union exported the following:

- to Poland, 14.8 million rubles worth of books[6]
- to India, 1.5 million rubles worth of books
- to the United States, 1.3 million rubles worth of books
- to West Germany, 900,000 rubles worth of books
- to France, 800,000 rubles worth of books
- to Japan, 700,000 rubles worth of books
- to the United Kingdom, 400,000 rubles worth of books[7]

In 1986 the Soviets exported 449 different book titles to Latin America, amounting to 134,619 books. This compares to the USIA's distribution of 800,000 copies of 300 different titles *worldwide* each year.[8]

Disinformation

Disinformation, or *dezinformatsia,* is part of what are referred to in Soviet ideology as "active measures." Such measures include efforts to influence another government's policies, undermine confidence in a country's leaders or institutions, disrupt relations between countries, and discredit opponents of a given country. These measures may be pursued using means to deceive or distort perceptions of reality, and may be practiced using both overt (officially sanctioned) channels and covert (or clandestine) means (Schultz & Godson, 1984, p. 2).

Researchers have found several instances of the use of disinformation, and a growing number of studies have been published about it. Soviet ideology acknowledged that disinformation is a valid tactic, while U.S. ideology rejects such an approach, even though instances of its use by the United States exist. For instance, in 1986, the United States released reports just before the U.S. air strike that Libyan leader Moamar Ghadaffi was about to be overthrown. VOA reports and calls for a popular uprising were the subject of an ABC television news report. The *New York Times* editorialized (quoted in Rubin, 1988, p. 59) that the effort of the White House to spread disinformation through the U.S. press was unjustified. "There is no place in America," the *Times* said, "for those who envy the Communists and their deceptions. There is no place in America for disinformation." In 1988, too, the *Washington Post* carried an article (Parry & Kornbluh, 1988) accusing the Reagan administration of attempting "to manipulate American views of the war in Nicaragua through an unprecedented, covert propaganda bureaucracy." This bureaucracy "attempted to manipulate the media, the Congress and public opinion to support the Reagan administration's policies" (see also Wallis & Baran, 1990, pp. 135–136).

On the Soviet side, the most notorious recent disinformation campaigns linked the

United States with the outbreak of AIDS, claimed by Soviet propaganda to be the result of American biological warfare tests, and accused the United States of "baby-organ trafficking" to allow U.S. children to have organ transplants from babies purchased for this purpose in developing countries (see Bittman, 1988b, pp. 24–25; Godson, 1988; and "U.S. Says Moscow Spread Lies," 1988; see also Bittman, 1985). The Soviets also conducted other disinformation campaigns using forged U.S. documents, and published false military statistics and technical data (see Deacon, 1986, chapters 7 and 9; Ottaway, 1988b; and Rubin, 1988).

Disinformation as a form of propaganda is not only more difficult to detect, but also harder to attach to its source. This is particularly true when the propagandists make the effort to "plant" the information in a source unconnected to the originating organization. This is a standard approach, allowing the propagandists to deny plausibly their involvement, and allowing them to use the information as though it comes from an unbiased source.

9.3

The Soviet Interpretation of the Role of International Propaganda

The Cold War Period

It should come as no surprise that during the Cold War the Soviet Union and the United States interpreted the value of propaganda differently, or that each country condemned distortions or disinformation from its adversary even while using such tactics itself. It is useful, however, to examine briefly the specific value that these two countries saw in international broadcasting and public diplomacy, and how they differed in their interpretations of the role of radio propaganda and disinformation (see Remington, 1988, for an analysis of changing Soviet perspectives on communication; see Volkogonov, 1986, for an examination of "business as usual" under Gorbachev).

Two stated purposes of Radio Moscow in its North American service were to (1) "communicate a cross section of true information about the Soviet people to people in the U.S. and Canada," and (2) "build a favorable attitude toward the U.S.S.R." (statement by Joseph Adamov, Radio Moscow, quoted in Howell, 1960, p. 263). More recent programming strategies of Radio Moscow confirmed that these purposes were still operational until the disintegration of the Soviet Union. During the 2-week period surrounding the December 1987 Washington summit, Radio Moscow carried a variety of programs about the meetings between Mikhail Gorbachev and Ronald Reagan: commentaries, interviews with U.S. and Soviet scientists, man-on-the-street interviews in Moscow and Washington, excerpts from statements and speeches made by the two summit principals, and so on. The desire to communicate *true* information about the Soviet Union could be seen in a curious Radio Moscow program, however. This was the slightly delayed broadcast of the Tom Brokaw–Mikhail Gorbachev interview on November 29. Brokaw's questions were unedited, but Radio Moscow used a different translator than that used by NBC. The effect of the different translator, coupled with the 15-minute delay, was that Gorbachev's answers were presented, although almost word for word, with greater assurance than was the case in the live interview. Pauses were eliminated; Gorbachev never seemed to grope for words. The impression given was that Gorbachev was more confident, and more in control of the interview, than it seemed on NBC, where the two men conversed as equals, with all the awkward and normal pauses of any conversation.[9]

Radio Moscow's actual summit coverage also provided clues about the service's approach to major world news. The number of stories filed and the amount of time devoted to summit coverage by Radio Moscow actually peaked the day before and the day after the summit, suggesting an apparent desire to provide a context for summit events, rather than depend on unpredictable events themselves to make a point. This accords, too, with the stated purpose of building goodwill toward the Soviet Union, since the degree of control Radio Moscow could exercise over the summit broadcasts was inversely related to the amount of freedom the events and actors had to "speak for themselves." Radio Moscow covered little of the actual summit, choosing instead to screen all reporting using an interpretive framework.

The basic pattern of Soviet news coverage remained consistent, too, during the 1988 Moscow summit, although there were indications of a less ideological tone in the coverage. On matters of serious U.S.-Soviet disagreement, however, such as President Reagan's decision to meet with dissidents, Radio Moscow's coverage remained critical (see Fortner, forthcoming, chapter 5).

Soviet writers also criticized the activities of Western radio operations, particularly those of the United States. Contrary to Western explanations of the beginnings of the Cold War, the Soviet interpretation claimed that "imperialism launched a cold war against the Soviet Union" and that in the 1950s "Western powers (especially the United States) began constructing a network of powerful radio transmitting and relay stations to blanket the entire territory of the socialist community" (Alov & Viktorov, 1985, p. 11; and Artemov, 1981, p. 5). The Cold War "seriously impedes, if not completely rules out, the flow of truthful information about socialism and breeds negative stereotypes of the Soviet Union," Soviet commentary claimed, and in a clever turn of phrase attempted to exploit a Western symbol: "Detente, on the other hand, breaks down the iron curtains erected by diehard anti-communists, and enables objective information about the USSR and other socialist countries to reach the capitalist world" (Artemov, 1981, pp. 8–9).

The Soviets saw the role of propaganda, too, as increasing, emerging "as one of the most important means of the class struggle." In that struggle they identified radio as a premier instrument: "the most effective peacetime weapon of psychological warfare" (Artemov, 1981, p. 13). The Western dominance of wire services, the Soviets also claimed, and their control of radio, through VOA, the BBC, and Deutsche Welle, and television distribution resulted in most of the world having a distorted view of the Soviet Union (Artemov, 1981, p. 33).

Propaganda itself received some commentary by the Soviets. They claimed that it was Western "bourgeois theoreticians" who have defined it as "a purely mechanical manipulation of 'impulse situations' that should provoke an equally mechanical reaction." In contrast, "Marxist theoreticians," they said, demanded that propaganda "be *truthful*, and they consider the propagandist's main talk to be the *enlightenment* of the selected audiences, especially by *rational* methods for influencing their consciousness." The difference, according to the Soviet explanation, was that Western theorists based propaganda on manipulation using emotional and irrational methods, while Marxists based it in understanding using rational thought processes (Panfilov, 1981, p. 79; see also Downey, 1984, on the problems of regulating propaganda).

In addition, Soviets often interpreted statements by Western leaders about the Soviet Union, or its Socialist ideology, as interference in their internal affairs or as psychological warfare aimed at the Soviet Union (Alov & Viktorov, 1985, chapter 2). The Soviets even defined radio activities of VOA, or other U.S. international radio operations, as "radio war" or "radio aggression" (Alov & Viktorov, 1985, p. 49). Proof, they said, came from the programming of U.S. stations, "prepared and presented with the help of emigres, turncoats, defectors, renegades, war criminals and other 'experts' hostile to the Soviet Union." These programs, the Soviets claimed, aimed to "undermine the unity of Soviet society and discredit the Soviet social system," and they provided the example of "programmes about so-called dissidents, the 'persecution of Jews,' discrimination against believers and other slanderous reports about the alleged violation of human rights in the Soviet Union" (Alov & Viktorov, 1985, p. 71). Through its propaganda, the Soviets claimed, the United States had "exposed itself to the world public as both a perpetrator of lies and slander and an organiser of overt subversion" (Panfilov, 1981, p. 137).

The Soviets argued such conclusions strongly because of their belief in the power of information. As Artemov (1981) put it,

> information is a powerful ideological and political weapon and can be used to subvert sovereign nations. The ideological enemies of socialism maintain that today everything has changed and that they no longer call for revolt or preach violent overthrow of the Soviet system. But the absence of counterrevolutionary war cries and blacklists prove nothing. Ideo-

logical interference by propaganda, and especially by radio, has become much more versatile and sophisticated. (p. 154)

The Post–Cold War Period

Much of this strong condemnation has faded with the end of the Cold War. Boris Yeltsin "welcomed" Radio Liberty to Russia, inviting it to open a permanent bureau in Moscow in the wake of the failed 1991 coup (Feldmann, 1991). Both Radio Liberty and its counterpart, Radio Free Europe, found their access to Soviet politicians expanded as a result of changes in the Soviet Union (Thorson, 1991). In late 1991 the BBC World Service reached agreement with Radio Russia to put two Russian language current affairs programs on the air beginning early in 1992 (Ljunggren, 1991).

Both Soviet opinions—those critical of Western communication practices and those welcoming them—as disparate as they are, shared a common base: the belief in the power of information. Under the old interpretation the Soviets saw "raw" uninterpreted information as infected by a bias devised by those who created it. If true understanding of events, movements, or history was to occur, then, the relevant information had to be processed for it to make sense. Understanding was created through the application of rational methods that were, themselves, ideologically based. Western propaganda, they argued, was often slanderous, subversive, and aggressive. It was dangerous because it claimed to be "value-neutral" but in actuality used psychological warfare tactics to make its information appealing. It was based on the experience gained "in manipulating the minds of people at home." (Artemov, 1981, p. 154)

The advent of *glasnost* under Gorbachev resulted in several changes in Soviet communications and journalistic policy. Even in domestic television, one Soviet commentator said, *glasnost* had eliminated "off-limit themes," and "objectivity and access to information" had become a function of a journalist's own convictions and tenacity, not state control (BBC Monitoring Service, 1988m). The influence of *glasnost* and *perestroika* on Soviet external services was not as quick, however, as one of Radio Moscow's German language commentators had written in *Sovetskaya Kultura* (BBC Monitoring Service, 1988o).

Although Radio Moscow began to offer time for advertising, a claimed result of "restructuring," TASS also chose to criticize the operations of a Panamanian clandestine radio station (Radio Constitucional) that it said was operating "under the direction of the United States," and had much in common with Radio Swan (directed to Cuba at the time of the Bay of Pigs invasion in 1960), RFE/RL, Radio Free Kabul, and Radio Free Afghanistan. TASS commented, "The CIA voice is now easily recognized by the people on all continents" (BBC Monitoring Service, 1988e, and 1988q).

The Soviets also decided to disband "Krestyaninova Service," which formerly jammed foreign radio signals directed into the Soviet Union. Pravda (BBC Monitoring Service, 1989l) explained that "the majority of radio listeners are capable of deciding for themselves what is true and what is a lie, what is information and what is the cunning manipulation of 'facts.'" Joseph Adamov, presenter of "Moscow Mailbag" on Radio Moscow, commented, however (BBC Monitoring Service, 1989g), that he had listened to Radio Liberty after the jamming stopped. He complained that it contained "not a positive or friendly word. It is rabidly anti-Soviet, unfortunately. . . . [I]t seems that the aim of Radio Liberty is to deride us, or to jeer even the things positive."

It is worth discussing the role of the international communications system as it operated during the Soviet coup. As Hoffman (1991) put it in the *Washington Post*.

> Antennas and telephones, satellite dishes and fax machines became the tools by which the United States and other countries let Russian Federation President Boris Yeltsin and others resisting the coup in Leningrad, the Baltics and elsewhere know they were being supported in the outside world. In turn, the channels let Yeltsin and his backers provide important advice to the outside. . . . Moreover, the blanket of global communications made it impossible to hide the public opposition to the coup leadership, although authorities had shut down much of the Soviet media. . . . The global network is also reflected in the willingness of many Western leaders and now the Soviets to use the telephone for immediate consultations that in the past would have required hours or days.

Western radio services worked overtime during the coup to reach into the Soviet Union (Britt, 1991; Goshko, 1991; and Sinai, 1991). Gorbachev himself indicated that these stations were his link with the outside world while he was detained by the military (Roberts, 1991a; see also "VOA, RFE/RL Victorious," 1991, p. 37, and "VOA and the Soviet Coup," n.d.).

It was not merely radio, however, that provided crucial links between the Soviet Union and the rest of the world. An official in Yeltsin's office notified the United States about the beginning of the coup by using a fax machine to contact the Center for Democracy in Washington ("Coup Alert by Fax," 1991, and "Make It Known," 1991). Other information arrived in the United States via electronic mail that was retrieved by computer (Blumenfeld, 1991). CNN also continued to be delivered via satellite to hotels in the Soviet Union, allowing foreigners there to keep abreast of what was happening in the streets (Roberts, 1991b, pp. B1, B9; and "Soviet Coup Worries," 1991, p. 3).

In the aftermath of the coup the serious deficiencies in the communication links between the United States and the Soviet Union also began to receive more attention. AT&T applied to the FCC for additional circuits to the Soviet Union to be provided by the Soviet Intersputnik system; the FCC approved its application, along with that of IDB Telecommunications Services Co., on August 22 (Skrzyski, 1991). This opened up 48 new telephone circuits to the Soviet Union, providing a total of 115 (Naylor, 1991). Despite this increase AT&T estimated that over 90% of all calls to the Soviet Union were never completed, and that a total of 2,300 circuits were required to meet demand. Charles Meyers, AT&T's manager of federal government affairs, noted that his company has more circuits from the United States to Iceland than it has to the Soviet Union (Skrzyski, 1991; see also Nelson, 1991). Sprint, another U.S. long-distance carrier, also applied to the FCC for approval to supplement its 12 Intelsat circuits with 43 leased from Intersputnik.

Nevertheless, change did occur, fallout from the failed Soviet coup. The Soviets still believe in the power of information, although they may have decided to pursue their international information objectives using different tactics.[10] Their rhetoric has toned down somewhat, but the old criticisms of Western information activities could still erupt. This will continue to be a problem through at least the early 1990s because of both the general political instability in Eastern and Central Europe, and the precarious understanding of the idea of free expression and its application in countries where such an approach has not been fully legitimized. For instance, while the ra-

dio station Moscow Echo, which went on the air in August 1990, "stubbornly, courageously and conscientiously informed its listeners around the clock about what was going on in Lithuania in January 1991 (when Soviet tanks entered Vilnius), a conservative communist newspaper, *Soviet Russia*, reacted: 'What are we to think about the fact that in the heart of the capital of a great power there operates a radio station whose voices slander our constitution, incite and coordinate illegal acts? For Moscow Echo, to call a spade a spade, engages in provocation'" (Krutogorov, 1991). Even after the Soviet coup, the Russian government threatened two independent newspapers with closure for violating the press law, while Eastern European broadcasters were finding it difficult to switch from state ownership to commercially based operations (Hift, 1991b; and Sneider, 1991; see also Vita, 1990, on the role of U.S. surrogate stations during the Azerbaijani crisis in January 1990).

9.4

The U.S. Interpretation of the Role of International Propaganda

Standard U.S. journalistic practices form the basis for the U.S. approach to propaganda. Although the orientation of VOA is different in some respects from that of Radio Martí or RFE/RL, all services rely on these standard practices as the basis of their activities: "objective news" reporting, a "news event" orientation, and a clear separation of news from editorial commentary.[11] U.S. coverage of world events, therefore, often seems merely reactive: a searchlight scanning the globe for an event that can be succinctly reported for a limited period of time before the searchlight moves on to its next event. Often little context is provided for the reports, although they may serve as the grist for separate commentaries.

The expectations that U.S. government radio services will adhere to these standard practices can best be seen when they are violated. In 1987, for instance, Radio Martí created a flap because it presented an "interview program" with Ronald Reagan as though it were live, with Reagan's answers translated into Spanish by an interpreter. It was not live, however. Reagan had been presented with the questions in writing, but his written answers had been altered by the White House and the National Security Council (NSC) staffs. Reagan had then recorded only the first sentence or two of each answer, and left the translator to work from a script for the remainder. A translator was reading a script. The criticism was that this program was a violation of journalistic standards (see Kurtz, 1987, p. A4). That same year the *Washington Post* (Goshko, 1987b) carried a story about a VOA editorial that had praised Iran and told the story of VOA officials voicing suspicion about it that had resulted in direct intervention with Charles Wick, director of USIA, by State Department officials. This problem was created by a long-standing practice of the State Department, which many journalists at VOA question. The VOA carries "official statements of U.S. policy" as editorials that precede some of its newscasts. Although the editorial is separated by official announcement and a musical bridge from the actual newscasts, and is written by State Department staff (not VOA itself), journalists at VOA have objected that its existence taints the claim that VOA is independent of the government in its news coverage. This particular editorial seemed questionable

because of the enmity between the two countries that VOA often reported, and that itself was the result of U.S. policy. The editorial thus was, at best, confusing, and at worst, cynical and disinformative.

The U.S. approach to propaganda, however, was not uncoordinated by comparison with the Soviets. It was simply organized differently. All products of the USIA, for instance, are examined to determine the possible policy implications of their release.[12] Ronald Reagan stated in 1981 that the objectives of U.S. international broadcasting would be "to foster the infrastructure of democracy—the system of a free press, unions, political parties, universities— which allow a people to choose their own way, to develop their own culture, to reconcile their own differences through peaceful means" (quoted in Tyson, 1983, p. 95). And Wick claimed in 1985 that the United States was winning "the hearts and minds of people around the world" ("The War of Words," 1985, p. 38).

This approach to propaganda could be seen clearly in the 1987 Washington and 1988 Moscow summits. It both cases the National Security Council, with input from the USIA and other federal agencies, constructed "themes" or "talking points" that were to guide U.S. statements during the summits. At the Washington summit, for instance, U.S. spokespersons were to emphasize, in addition to the obvious "peace themes" occasioned by the signing of the INF treaty, human rights, regional conflicts, Soviet disinformation efforts, and the lack of reciprocity in "media access" between the two countries.[13] These themes were directed to perceived weaknesses in the Soviet image before the world; the strategy was designed to place the U.S. position on such matters in a positive light, and to force the Soviets to respond to U.S. criticisms of their record in these areas. Radio Moscow did, in fact, comment on these areas during the summit, although not extensively. After the Washington summit, too, jamming of all Western broadcasts ended. In addition, U.S. periodicals began to appear regularly on Soviet newsstands, and the Soviets made new overtures on the Helsinki Accords, conventional forces and short-range nuclear weapons reductions in Europe, and reductions in strategic nuclear weapons.

The United States under Reagan also began to put more emphasis on the role of information in appealing to the world's people. *Newsweek* claimed in 1981 ("A Hot New Cold War at ICA," 1981, pp. 36, 37) that Reagan was "revitalizing" the U.S. information service, which had begun distributing a monthly Soviet Disinformation Alert to all U.S. embassies. *U.S. News & World Report* said ("The War of Words," 1985, pp. 34–39) that a public relations battle had erupted between Reagan and Gorbachev. And the United States Advisory Commission on Public Diplomacy claimed in its 1986 *Annual Report* that

> public diplomacy is part of a worldwide transformation in the conduct of international affairs. Traditional secret government-to-government communications have become less important as world leaders compete directly for the support of citizens in other countries. . . . Put simply, instant global communications are breaking down rigidities and isolation, and public opinion is increasingly influential in shaping foreign policy. (1986, p. 10)

Despite the changes in the Soviet Union and its former client-states, the United States continued to develop its international public diplomacy assets. This included funding for Radio Free Afghanistan and renewed emphasis on broadcasting to developing coun-

tries (see "Radio Free Afghanistan to Air in Pashto," 1987; and Wasburn, 1988).

Surrogate Broadcasting in the Post–Cold War Era

In 1991 U.S. Representative Helen Delich Bentley (Republican from Maryland) proposed that the Congress create Radio Free Asia on the model of RFE/RL (Bentley, 1991, p. 19; see also Sibley, 1991, p. 4). This proposal came after the crumbling of the Iron Curtain, the reunification of Germany, and the aborted Soviet coup. The RFE/RL model of surrogate broadcasting seemed a success. Russian President Boris Yeltsin had even suggested that Radio Liberty might be allowed to broadcast using domestic medium-wave (AM) frequencies in his country (Feldmann, 1991, p. 3).

The two questions that emerged, however, were these: (1) If RFE/RL had succeeded, was their task over—could they be disbanded? and (2) If they were successful, could the same techniques be applied in other parts of the world? Elliott argued that what the United States needed was a single voice (Elliott, 1989/90, 1991). Leaders from Czechoslovakia, Hungary, and Poland wrote to President Bush, Secretary of State James Baker, and RFE/RL Director Eugene Pell "imploring them to keep the service going" (Feldmann, 1991, p. 3). Such questions were not easily answered in Congress, although the Senate Foreign Relations Committee held hearings that resulted in a former ambassador to China, Winston Lord, criticizing President George Bush's "'steady double standard on human rights and democracy,' one for China and another for the rest of the world" (quoted in Lardner, 1991, p. A23). Exiled Chinese dissidents joined in the clamor for a Radio Free China, bills were introduced into both houses of Congress to create such a station, and President Bush appointed a task force to inquire into the future of U.S. government international broadcasting. The task force addressed issues such as continuing RFE/RL, creating an Asian surrogate station, and reorganizing the fragmented U.S. international broadcasting activities that were governed by two separate organizations, USIA and the Board for International Broadcasting (see Hughes, 1991, p. 19; and Hutzler, 1991, p. 13).

The push for consolidation of U.S. international communication activities, particularly from the United States Advisory Commission for Public Diplomacy (1991a, 1991b, p. 9), caused some newspaper columnists to decry the "raid" on Radio Free Europe (see Safire, 1991, p. A11; see also Evans & Novak, 1987, p. A23, for similar arguments about Radio Liberty during an earlier debate). The Advisory Commission also recommended (1991b) that Radio and Television Martí be removed from USIA/VOA oversight and join BIB, but doubted the wisdom of creating a Radio Free Asia within the RFE/RL structure, arguing (p. 37) that it would not necessarily "be necessary, cost-effective, or realistic in the current budget climate."

The President's Task Force (1991, p. 21) recommended against the consolidation proposed by the Advisory Commission. It also concluded (p. 16) that RFE/RL had "helped move the world toward freedom," and that "creation of a surrogate radio for Asia at this time would . . . be shrewd: We will not only be on the right side, but on the winning side." Surrogate radio, the commission said (p. 17), promotes freedom and nurtures democracy, and "is the best mode for providing domestic news of internal affairs in China to the people of China. That is precisely the kind of news which is scarce in China" (see also Safire, 1992, p. A15; and Smith, 1991, p. A10).

Unquestionably, Western radio stations were seen in the former Soviet bloc as important mechanisms for information and perspective. The accolades that flowed from leaders of Eastern European countries, particularly after the August 1991 coup attempt, were testimony to that fact (see Board for International Broadcasting, 1992, pp. 1, 19, 27–28).

As of March 1992, no new surrogate service had been voted into existence by the Congress. Neither had President Bush acted on the recommendations of his task force. Although U.S. international broadcasting is unlikely to continue without change for very long, it is difficult to know precisely what changes are in store for its international broadcasting activities.

United States–CIS Communication Activities

As the government debated the future of surrogate services, other changes were overtaking U.S. communication relations with the Commonwealth of Independent States (CIS). The flow of information among these countries increased significantly compared with what had been possible with the Soviet Union, even under *glasnost*. A variety of private enterprise initiatives, too, supplemented the activities of the governments in encouraging freer communication.

A number of joint enterprises began to spring up between CIS-based enterprises and U.S.-based companies. In January 1992, for instance, a Russian-U.S. joint venture, Radio Maximum, started operation in Moscow, and in February a Ukrainian-U.S. FM radio station was started in Kiev (see BBC Monitoring Service, 1992c, p. A9, and 1992d, p. A9). In addition, a new Russian company, Ostankino Teleradio, replaced the All-Union Television and Radio Broadcasting

Company (or Gostelradio, the state-operated monopoly), after the dissolution of the Soviet Union, and allowed foreigners to invest in its stock (see BBC Monitoring, 1992b, p. A9).

Warner Brothers International Television also donated U.S. television programs to Russia to be carried on its television system. These programs included the films *Bonnie and Clyde, Superman,* and *Being There,* the television programs "Murphy Brown" and "Perfect Strangers," the miniseries "Napoleon and Josephine," and Bugs Bunny cartoons (Friedman, 1992; see also "Former President Jimmy Carter Has Joined NAB," 1991, p. 7; Weinraub, 1992, pp. C1, C5; and "Worldwide TV Network Planned," 1991, p. 7, for discussion of cooperative ventures prior to January 1, 1992).

On the telecommunications side, GTE Spacenet Corporation became the major contractor to install new long-distance lines between the United States and the Soviet Union in July 1991 for a new joint venture company, Sovintel. It planned to increase the number of international lines available from 550 to 790 ("GTE Spacenet in Soviet Venture," 1991). AT&T, too, began to contract with various republics to install new telephone lines, and already by October 1991, had put into operation the first digital switching system in the Soviet Union (Py, Sams, & Aluise, 1991, p. 9; and Ramirez, 1991, pp. C1, C4). Despite the low telephone density in the Soviet Union (9.7 lines per 100 population, compared to 49 lines per 100 in the United States, 45 per 100 in the old West Germany, and 23.3 per 100 in the old East Germany), the telecommunications traffic between the United States and the Soviet Union increased so rapidly following the start of the Soviet coup that AT&T and IDB Communications applied for permission to use the Soviet Intersputnik system to ease congestion. Less than one

call out of every 100 from the United States to the Soviet Union was being connected (Bradsher, 1991, p. C2; see also "Linking Lines in Europe," 1989, p. 38). The FCC granted the application. In October 1991 Lithuania applied to join Eutelsat, and in December Romania became the first Eastern European nation to install a Eutelsat earth station. Use of Eutelsat satellites would allow new members access to Western European television and additional telephone links to the West ("Lithuania Applies to Join Eutelsat," 1991; and "Romania to Host," 1991). By January 1991 AT&T had entered into a joint venture with the government of Ukraine to modernize the Ukrainian telephone system (Mintz, 1992, pp. F1, F2).

9.5

Major International Broadcasters

Despite the enormous growth in the system of international communication, a process that incorporated such technologies as satellites, fiber optics, facsimile and data transfer via both wired and wireless networks, audio- and videocassette player/recorders, and so on, international radio conducted using both medium-wave and shortwave transmission continues to be a significant form of international communication. During the Persian Gulf conflict VOA, for instance, carried "airmail" from the families of U.S. hostages held in Iraq and of persons hiding in Kuwait for broadcast over its transmitters aimed into the region (see "Letters to the Hostages," 1990). In 1991 the BBC's budget for current affairs programming was increased by the largest amount in its long history, allowing it to add new programs, more correspondents, and increased hours of broadcast in several languages.

Table 9.1

Estimated Total Program Hours per Week of Major Government-Funded External Broadcasters*

Country	1950	1960	1970	1980	1992**
Soviet Union	533	1,015	1,908	2,094	1,317
United States	497	1,495	1,907	1,901	2,317
China	66	687	1,267	1,350	1,555
West Germany	—	315	779	804	673
United Kingdom	643	589	723	719	808
Egypt	—	301	540	546	593
North Korea	—	159	330	597	370
East Germany	—	185	274	375	—
India	116	157	271	389	541
Albania	26	63	487	560	196
Iran	12	24	155	175	358
Cuba	—	—	320	424	251
Australia	181	257	350	333	320
Spain	68	202	251	239	263
Nigeria	—	—	62	170	126
Netherlands	127	178	335	289	294
France	198	326	200	125	401
Turkey	40	77	88	199	346
Bulgaria	30	117	164	236	308
Japan	—	203	259	259	336
Poland	131	232	334	337	110
Czechoslovakia	119	196	202	255	143
South Africa	—	63	150	183	184
Israel	—	91	158	210	388
Canada	85	80	98	134	188
Sweden	28	114	140	155	130
Italy	170	205	165	169	159
Romania	30	159	185	198	209
Portugal	46	133	295	214	214
Yugoslavia	80	70	76	72	61
Hungary	76	120	105	127	57

*East Germany's Radio Berlin went off the air after the reunification of Germany (see "New Factors in Bid to Rule the (Air) Waves," 1990). Several former Soviet client states in Eastern Europe also reduced their hours of broadcasting after the "crumbling" of the Iron Curtain, as has Radio Australia. Radio Canada's future was also threatened in 1990 as a result of a budget crisis at the Canadian Broadcasting Corporation. Even VOA faced budget cuts between 1987 and 1990 that resulted in significant reductions of program services (see McAllister, 1987a, 1987b; and "VOA Cuts Services," 1990, p. 32; see also Wallis & Baran, 1990, chapter 6). After German reunification Deutschlandfunk became a domestic broadcaster for its German-language broadcasting.

**As of February.

Source: BBC International Broadcasting and Audience Research Library, 1989, 1990, 1991, 1992.

State-Controlled or -Funded International Broadcasting

Over 80 countries use shortwave broadcasting to reach populations in other countries. Shortwave, however, is not the only transnational media vehicle for reaching these audiences. Many international broadcasters use medium wave (MW or AM) in some parts of the world. They also put their programs on VHF-FM stations, or provide program feeds to domestic broadcasters, which then select the programming they will relay to their own audiences. In February 1992, for instance, 120 radio stations in 17 countries (plus Gibraltar) in Europe were re-broadcasting the BBC World Service, and 48 cable systems in Austria, Belgium, Denmark, Finland, France, Germany, Hungary, Ireland, the Netherlands, Norway, and Switzerland were also carrying it. These radio stations and cable systems were downlinking the signals from European satellites (BBC International Broadcasting and Audience Research, 1992).

By 1988 VOA-Europe was being broadcast in Munich on medium wave, and cable and VHF-FM stations in more than 40 countries carried the service. Altogether, radio or television stations in 103 countries were carrying VOA programs (*Voice of America 1989,* 1989, p. 3). On a slightly different front, in Poland the state-operated radio system began broadcasting excerpts from Western radio stations in 1987 under the title Mowi Zachod, or "The West Calling." And Romania began doing so in 1991. By 1992 BBC, VOA, RFE, and RL were all operating freely in Eastern Europe, with many domestic services carrying their programs.

In 1986 more than 40 countries directed broadcasting into the United States, including the Soviet Union, several Eastern European countries, U.S. European allies, Israel, and several Asian, Middle Eastern, African,

and Latin American countries. Religious broadcasters and U.S. private shortwave broadcasters, including WYFR, KUSW, and WRNO, could also be heard, as could VOA in some areas. Some private U.S. broadcasters, such as WYFR in Okeechobee, Florida, also leased out their transmitters to allow foreign countries better signal quality into the United States (see *World Radio TV Handbook 1992,* 1992, pp. 586, 587).

Government-sponsored (or -funded) broadcasters continued to play a major role in international communication. (See Table 9.1.) In this table the 1992 totals for the United States include 1,139 hours per week for VOA, 978 for RFE/RL, and 200 for Radio Martí and Radio Free Afghanistan. Totals for Russia include those only for Radio Moscow, and totals for West Germany include 585 hours for Deutsche Welle and 257 hours for Deutschlandfunk's language services (not including German).[14] The table does not attempt to include international commercial or religious broadcasters (BBC International Broadcasting and Audience Research Library, 1992).

The volatility of the international radio environment, particularly as related to the rapid end of the Cold War, can be seen in the changing output of selected broadcasters. (See Figures 9.1 and 9.2.) In these figures the reduction in broadcast output by Eastern European countries is evident, compared with the steady, or even slightly increasing output, of the West.

Nongovernment International Broadcasting

Major nongovernment services, such as the BBC, commercial operators, Europe No. 1, Africa No. 1, Radio Sud, and others, as well as international religious organizations such as Radio Vatican, Trans World Radio

(TWR), Far East Broadcasting Company (FEBC), and Association (FEBA), Voice of the Andes (HCJB), Radio Veritas, and so on, also broadcast using shortwave bands (see Mayo, 1980, on international radio services; see BBC Monitoring Service, 1988a, 1988b, 1989n, 1989aa, on the recent activities of Adventist World Radio). The *Christian Science Monitor* also began broadcasting on shortwave, although not as a "religious" or missionary radio service (see "Christian Science Church Launches International Broadcast," 1987; and "'Monitor': Reaching Around the World with Radio," 1989). Finally, clandestine and pirate radio stations may be heard in some areas of the world, particularly in Europe, the Middle East, and Southeast Asia, using these bands (see Soley, 1982; and Soley & O'Brien, 1987).

International evangelical Christian broadcasters are major users of shortwave bands, providing over 20,000 total hours per week, in over 100 languages. After religious broadcasters the Soviet Union broadcast in the most languages, 64, but this was reduced dramatically in 1992. In January 1992 VOA used 46 languages, and the BBC 37 (Heil, 1992). VOA's 47th language, Kurdish, will air beginning in April 1992. International religious broadcasters are rapidly increasing the number of languages used for programming. The four largest

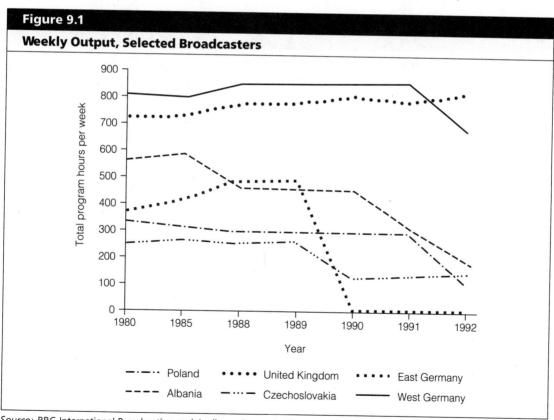

Figure 9.1

Weekly Output, Selected Broadcasters

Source: BBC International Broadcasting and Audience Research Library, 1989, 1990, 1991, 1992.

organizations have a goal to provide Christian broadcasting in all languages spoken by at least 1 million people by the year 2000.

Government-financed broadcasters select their programming languages for a variety of reasons. Among them are the realities of long-standing political and economic relationships, efforts to establish influence in particular parts of the world, response to their own domestic constituencies' demands for broadcasts in particular languages, and strategies to show that they recognize the importance of a country (see Shakespeare, 1986).[15] Although the total worldwide audience for shortwave radio broadcasts is unknown, both VOA and the BBC claim sizable regular audiences, defined as those people who tune in at least once a week. (See Figures 9.3 and 9.4.) Each organization claims weekly audiences of roughly 120 million people worldwide, although both admit that the BBC has more regular listeners. (The U.S. Advisory Commission actually claims VOA's regular audience is 127 million worldwide.)

There was also resurgence of interest in international commercial broadcasting among U.S. companies beginning after 1980. WRNO (Radio New Orleans) was the first to seek a license from the FCC. In that year there were only 4 privately licensed U.S.

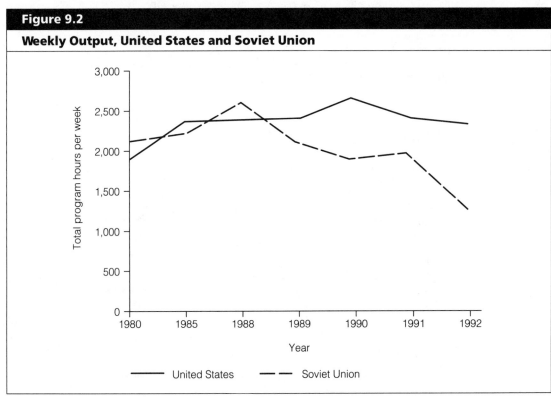

Figure 9.2

Weekly Output, United States and Soviet Union

Source: BBC International Broadcasting and Audience Research Library, 1989, 1990, 1991, 1992.

shortwave broadcasters; by 1988 there were 15 (Jacobs, 1988, p. 87). U.S. companies engaged in international commercial shortwave broadcasts by the end of the 1980s included World International Broadcasters Inc. (also a religious station), WRNO Worldwide, KCBI International, KUSW, and Radio Earth International (see *World Radio TV Handbook,* 1989, pp. 270–272). WRNO simulcast its sister New Orleans FM station, and its owner contended that "foreign audiences are just as fascinated by American domestic advertising as they are by rock music" (Head, 1985, p. 373). By 1991, however, WRNO-AM was for sale. In 1982 KYOI began operating in Saipan, an

island in the Mariana Islands, a U.S. trust territory (Head, 1985, p. 373). None of these stations, however, had the presence in Latin America that the French international commercial broadcasters had in Europe and Africa, perhaps because Latin America had its own commercial stations, and commercial radio was therefore not such a novelty.

The commercial radio picture in Europe grew complicated during the 1980s. In Europe major international commercial broadcasters include Radio Luxembourg, Radio Monte Carlo, Europe No. 1, and two French-owned stations. All concentrate their programming on popular music. Radio

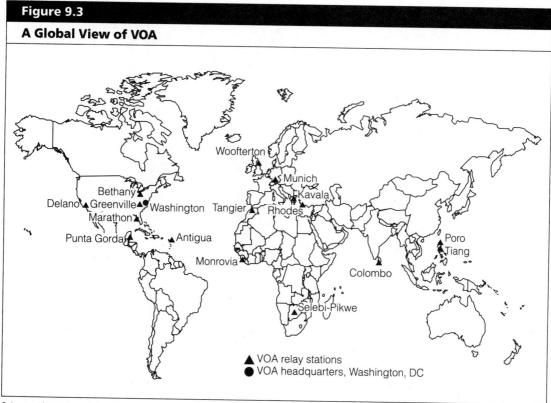

Figure 9.3

A Global View of VOA

▲ VOA relay stations
● VOA headquarters, Washington, DC

Source: The Voice of America.

Luxembourg also carries religious programming after 10:00 P.M., and Radio Monte Carlo turns its transmitters over to Trans World Radio during the late evening hours. There have been several changes in the French-owned stations since 1981, and new competitors have emerged, such as the newly purchased Europe No. 1.

SOFIRAD, the Société Financière de Radiodiffusion, controls a network of French-owned commercial radio stations. It operates what are called *périphériques,* or peripheral radio stations, so named because they are located

along the periphery of France and yet broadcast into France. This arrangement was required by the French ban on commercial stations (since lifted). SOFIRAD, despite the French government's apparent distaste for commercial media (given its ban on commercial radio), is now a state-directed public enterprise. It has stakes in two *périphériques,* Radio Monte Carlo and Radio Télé-Luxembourg (RTL), both of which broadcast popular commercially sponsored programming into France (Boyd & Benzies, 1983, p. 59; see also Howell, 1986, p. 91). SOFIRAD,

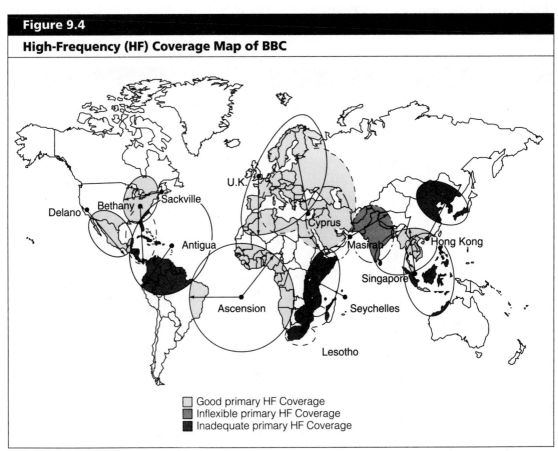

Figure 9.4

High-Frequency (HF) Coverage Map of BBC

Good primary HF Coverage
Inflexible primary HF Coverage
Inadequate primary HF Coverage

Source: BBC World Service.

which had majority voting rights in Europe No. 1 in West Germany, has since sold off this station to other investors. The Andorran government closed down another former SOFIRAD station, Radio Sud, under a ban on foreign broadcasters.

SOFIRAD also participates in other commercial radio stations located in, or directed to, regions outside Europe. It would perhaps be fair to say that, as SOFIRAD's European operations have shrunk, its other international interests have grown. SOFIRAD operates stations for the Middle East, central West Africa, and the Caribbean. Radio Monte Carlo Moyen Orient, headquartered in Paris but with transmit-

ters on Cyprus, is directed into the Middle East, and broadcasts "mostly popular Western and Arab music, news, and talk." It has a large following in its target region (Boyd & Benzies, 1983, p. 63). SOFIRAD also has minority interests in Radio Méditerranée Internationale (RMI, popularly known as Médi 1), begun in 1981 and operating from Morocco (51% owned by Moroccan State Enterprises and 49% by SOFIRAD), Africa No. 1 in Gabon (West Africa, also begun in 1981), and Télé-Liban in Libya (Boyd & Benzies, 1983, pp. 64–65). Médi 1 also carries religious programs produced by the Swedish International Broadcasting Association (IBRA). (See Figure 9.5.)

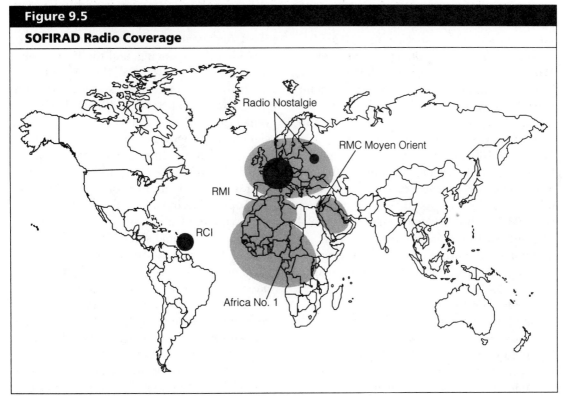

Figure 9.5

SOFIRAD Radio Coverage

Source: SOFIRAD.

Beginning in 1986 Europe No. 1's programs began to be carried into the Caribbean. The programs were up-linked to France's Telecom-1 satellite, and then down-linked for broadcast by Radio Caribbean International (with controlling interest since 1982 in the hands of SOFIRAD) in Dominica. Other stations in Tahiti, French Guyana, and Reunion Island in the Indian Ocean also carried the programs (BBC Monitoring Service, 1987d).

Africa No. 1, besides providing its own programming, also relays programs for other international services, including Radio France Internationale (30 hours per week), Swiss Radio International (3 hours per week), Radio Japan (11.5 hours per week), and Adventist World Radio. It carries programs for its own audience in French (its primary language) and English, and a news headline service only *(World Radio TV Handbook,* 1989, p. 153; see also *World Radio TV Handbook,* 1990, p. 148). It has large audiences through West and central Africa, with its regular adult listeners varying between 15% and 59% in the countries of central West Africa (Mytton & Forrester, 1988, p. 468). Africa No. 1 also broadcasts 18 hours per day of its own programming, and operates five 500-kw transmitters. In 1988 the station's gross revenues were 58.5 million French francs (about $9.4 million), up 16% from the previous year, and it earned a profit of 4.2 million French francs (about $672,000) (BBC Monitoring Service, 1989t).

Besides Africa No. 1, another privately owned international radio station on the continent is Radio Syd, which began operating on the Canary Islands in 1964, but moved to The Gambia the following year. It was begun by a Swedish entrepreneur, Ms. Britt Wardner, and carried, in addition to its own programming and advertising,

"news and programs of national importance from Radio Gambia." Its programs were received not only in The Gambia, but also in Senegal, until the Senegalese authorities passed a law requiring that external broadcasters using commercials have prior approval to cross their border (Cohateh, 1974, pp. 97–98). Although some feared that the station would fold due to financial difficulties, it was still operating in 1989, providing programming in English, French, and Swedish (in the winter for tourists), and the African languages of Wolloff and Mandinka, and still relaying programming from Radio Gambia *(World Radio TV Handbook,* 1989, p. 153; see also *World Radio TV Handbook,* 1990, p. 148).

France was also active helping countries in Francophone West Africa with television technology and programming in the 1980s. In 1988, for instance, the French government provided the financing, and the French electronics firm Thomson CSF the technology, to establish two television stations in Benin (BBC Monitoring Service, 1988f). The same year France's Canal Plus television network signed an agreement to provide TV service in Gabon, to be called Canal Plus Afrique (BBC Monitoring Service, 1988k). This station was to join another commercial television operation in Gabon, financed jointly by the Swiss and Gabonese, Tele-Africa. This station, operational since May 1988, airs Italian, French, and American feature films, CNN news, and other material. It does not have its own studios (see Mytton, 1988, p. 9). Canal Plus also announced that it had reached agreements to provide similar services in Cameroon, Senegal, and Algeria (Mytton, 1988, p. 9). (See Figure 9.6.) In addition, France International (CFI) provides French language television programming to Africa. The French cabinet was also considering a proposal to create a Conseil de l'Audiovisuel Exterieur de la France (CAEF) to create a "TV programme bank throughout the world so that within five years the whole world can be covered by French-language programmes" (BBC Monitoring Service, 1989u).

Such relationships facilitated the sale of U.S., French, and British television programs to countries throughout the world (see Tunstall, 1977, pp. 39–40; and Wells, 1972). Although they do not explain the dominance of these countries' (particularly U.S. and British) programming, they do suggest that established broadcasting organizations would be a starting point as potential sources for programming, which, indeed, they were.

Two other countries with broadcasting interests in Africa are Spain and Cuba. Spain provided financing to set up radio station Africa 2000 in Equatorial Guinea in October 1988. The aim of this station was to secure "the Spanish language in the only country in Africa which uses it as its official language" (Mytton, 1988, p. 12). Since 1986, too, Cuba has been feeding television programs via Intersputnik to Angola.

New satellite services also changed the "information environment" of the societies in which they exist, often providing live video images of distant events that international radio broadcasters can only talk about. They bring popular music and other forms of entertainment as well, and do so

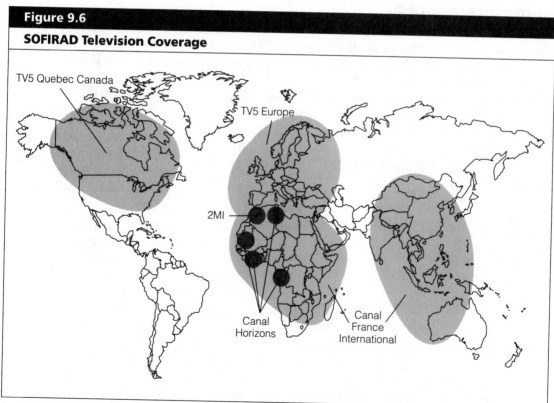

Figure 9.6

SOFIRAD Television Coverage

TV5 Quebec Canada

TV5 Europe

2MI

Canal Horizons

Canal France International

Source: SOFIRAD.

with greater fidelity than shortwave can. Already the audiences for shortwave radio have shrunk where the information environments have been enriched by new technologies, not only satellites, but VCRs, radio cassette players, and hi-fis as well. In short, these services have begun to compete with traditional ones, both domestic and international, and will force reappraisals of the program strategies (in terms of both content and presentation) by the older services (see Fortner, 1989, for a discussion of the changing information environments into which shortwave broadcasts are directed).

9.6

Pirate Broadcasting in the International Communications System

Broadcast piracy is a difficult phenomenon to classify. Pirates establish broadcasting stations to reach a specific (usually youthful) population within a given country. They would therefore not strictly qualify as international broadcasters. However, many pirates do locate over a border, or broadcast from ships anchored offshore from their given target country, to avoid being closed down by the domestic regulatory authority of the country to which they broadcast. Whether these floating radio stations are international or not, then, depends on the distance from their anchorage to the shore, and whether the target country has claimed a 3-mile, 12-mile, or 200-mile territorial limit over the ocean adjacent to its shore.

Many countries have found their domestic media systems under siege from pirate radio, and more recently, television operations, particularly those in Western Europe. The United States' most notorious experience with pirate radio broadcasters was during the 1930s, when John Brinkley, the owner of radio station KFKB in Milford, Kansas, was stripped of his license by the Federal Radio Commission (FRC). Brinkley had become a popular radio figure, providing "medical advice" and selling a "goat gland" sexual rejuvenation operation and patent medicines to his listeners. But he had run into conflict with the American Medical Association (AMA), and was found by the FRC not to be broadcasting in the public interest. After losing his license, however, he purchased station XER in Mexico and continued his broadcasting via a telephone hookup from Kansas until U.S. authorities persuaded the Mexican government to shut down his station (see Barnouw, 1966, pp. 258–259).[16] Periodically, since then, U.S. authorities have had to shut down other pirate radio operations, including one in 1987 off the Atlantic coast. Two men had anchored their ship offshore to put "Radio New York International" on the air, only to be shut down by the U.S. Coast Guard (Yen, 1987).

Western European countries have had much more trouble with pirate broadcasting, however, largely because they have had a limited number of stations and programming choices. Pirates believed that youthful audiences wanted more pop/rock music. Most of the pirates have therefore concentrated on alternative musical forms, at first American rock and roll, then reggae and other music appealing to both youth and ethnic immigrant markets. As Hind and Mosco (1985, foreword) put it, "Pirate radio in the 1980s emerged out of two basic commitments—a belief in the freedom of the airwaves and a belief in the music."

The early development of sea piracy in Europe began in 1958 when Radio Mercur began broadcasting off the coast of Denmark. Radio Veronica broadcasting to Holland and Radio Nord to Sweden followed soon after. In 1961 the Commercial Neutral

Broadcasting Company began transmitting to England from Radio Veronica's ship, and in 1964 Britain's most famous pirate station, Radio Caroline, began operations. "Radio Caroline was followed nine months later by more pop stations, including, amongst many others, Radio Atlanta, Radio 270, Caroline North, Radio Scotland, and 370. Some of the stations lasted until 1968, others were short-lived — new stations appeared and disappeared" (Hind & Mosco, 1985, p. 12). Radio Veronica was eventually incorporated into the Dutch "pillarized" system of broadcasting, becoming a legitimate Dutch broadcaster.[17] Sweden's pirate station, Radio Caroline, eventually became Radio Syd in The Gambia.

Sea-based pirates broadcasting into the United Kingdom disappeared after 1968, following a crackdown by authorities, but re-emerged in 1983 and 1984 with the broadcasts of Radios Caroline and Laser (Hind & Mosco, 1985, p. 17). Most of the 1980s pirates in England, however, are land-based, operating in large cities, particularly London, using small-power transmitters and moving frequently to elude authorities.[18] As before, the programming is pop/rock/reggae, tastes that have still not been addressed sufficiently by the BBC to squelch the desire for "alternative music." Many of the pirates now are recent arrivals from the Caribbean, who provide music from their homelands to other immigrants.

9.7

The Role of "Personal Technology" in the International System

The transfer of communication materials via "personal technologies" — VCRs and audiocassette player/recorders — is assuming an increasingly significant role around the world. People buy these technologies both through official import and distribution channels, and through unofficial or "black market" channels (see Boyd, Straubhaar, & Lent, 1989, pp. 67, 185—186; and Ganley & Ganley, 1987, chapter 3). While such technologies have opened possibilities for indigenous production of media materials, and there is a thriving bootleg and pirate market in both audio- and videotapes in many developing countries, these countries' governments have raised the specter of cultural threats posed by them (see Boyd & Straubhaar, 1985; and Fortner, 1986a, 1987, and 1991b).

Access to Communication Through Personal Technology

In developing countries, too, the "personal" technologies provide the means to communicate to many groups that have been otherwise excluded from access to communications technology. The historic shift from interpersonal to mediated communication has changed the dominant means by which people gain access to information. Furthermore, it has expanded the worldview of people by providing external sources of information, and has involved greater numbers of people in global economic and political structures (see Boyd, Straubhaar, & Lent, 1989, pp. 9, 20, 70). The new, relatively inexpensive, battery-powered lightweight technologies have provided a new basis for inclusion.[19] People have also been left behind in this shift, however, excluded from participation largely for economic or political reasons.[20]

In Eastern and Central Europe new opportunities for inclusion in the worldwide information order began to develop with the spread of the videocassette recorder and satellite dish. USIA published a study concerning the penetration of new communications technologies in 1990. (See Table 9.2.)

The difficulty with such technologies is that governments see themselves as the guarantors of citizens' fundamental freedoms (including the right to communicate), and expect to control the flow of information that enables people to exercise their freedoms in particular ways. Although this is as true of Western industrialized countries as of any other, these countries have argued that it is people who have these freedoms, and this fact limits the authority of the state to intervene. This is another manifestation of the Western value placed on the free flow of information, defined as flow outside the control of the state. The introduction of these personal technologies, therefore, has complicated the issue for developing countries' governments, since people could exercise their "right" apart from state control, which they did not see as an advantage given the control over the international communications system by Northern Hemisphere countries.[21] These technologies have therefore exacerbated the "fundamental conflict about the nature of man and society," which was the historical basis for the ideological struggle between East and West on this question (see Fisher, 1982, p. 24).

The governments of developing countries thus see the spread of these technologies as a further extension of technological and cultural dependence on developed countries. The Japanese, for instance, control the patents on VCRs and on the cameras and most other ancillary equipment, so it is difficult for developing countries to manufacture these machines themselves, unless TNCs with rights to the patents operate within them. Also, since much (if not most) of the software people use on these machines is imported (and pirated) from Western sources, developing countries see the cultural hegemony of the West continuing.[22] Although each new technology seems to offer possibilities to break the "old communication order," they conclude, each actually tightens the control exercised by the developed world on the cultural products consumed by citizens of developing nations. When freedom is the result, it turns out to loosen not the "shackles" of external domination, but the influence of developing countries' governments themselves on

---

Table 9.2

Penetration of New Communications Technologies in Eastern and Central Europe, 1990

Country	TV Households	Satellite Dishes	VCRs	Cable
Poland	10.0 million	18,000	1.1 million	—
Hungary	2.6 million	15,000	0.86 million	18%
Soviet Union	86.0 million	15,000	2.2 million	—
Bulgaria	3.9 million	1,000	0.55 million	—
Czechoslovakia	4.3 million	30,000	0.8 million	—
Romania	3.8 million	‹100	0.46 million	—
Yugoslavia	5.5 million	30,000	2.0 million	0.2 million MATV*

*MATV is an acronym for Master Antenna Television.
Source: "USIA Publishes Guide," 1990, p. 58.

their own citizens. The rationale for video-cassette piracy, for instance, is the right to choose external television and film materials over those produced within one's own country (see Alvarado, 1988, for a discussion of video piracy's significance in various countries).

The basic question for many developing countries continues to be their sovereignty. As the minister of posts and telecommunications of Niger put it at an ITU meeting in Nice (ITU, 1989b, p. 8), "The concept of 'national sovereignty' is another matter that must be taken into account in the development and evolution of telecommunication services, particularly as far as the developing countries are concerned. A final solution to this problem should be sought with a view of harmonization of national and international activities in the telecommunication field." The Final Acts of the World Administrative Telegraph and Telephone Conference, held in Melbourne in 1988, also began (ITU, 1989a, p. 3): "While the sovereign right of each country to regulate its telecommunications is fully recognized, the provisions of the present Regulations [aim to promote] the development of telecommunication services and their most efficient operation while harmonizing the development of services for world-wide telecommunications."

The Views of the Industrialized Countries

Western countries also recognize the political implications of a free flow of information. They believe that unfettered communication will result in greater democratization within totalitarian countries and serve as an antidote to ideological communication practices or propaganda that they claim to be practiced routinely by many countries, whether Communist or

not.[23] Sometimes, they say, restricting information flow is a way to maintain Communist rule—as in China, North Korea, or Vietnam. Sometimes it is to prop up or maintain military dictatorships or corrupt regimes. They point to countries such as Myanamar (Burma), Iraq, or Libya. As Rupert Murdoch put it in 1988, "The benefits of global communications know no boundaries. It is democratic in nature, premised on freedom—freedom of communication, freedom of access. It will bring down barriers between nations" (quoted in "More Freedom Sought for World Media, 1988, p. 49).

Developed countries, too, recognize the trade implications of a free communications environment. Not only are they the major suppliers of communications and telecommunications equipment, but the TNCs headquartered in their countries seek the freedom to move information at will across international borders. This ability simplifies the production scheduling, marketing, funds transfer, and inventory control activities of the TNCs, and provides the means to maximize profits by coordinating the efforts of people scattered in multiple sites around the globe (see Jussawalla & Cheah, 1987, pp. 29–30).

Finally, industrialized countries have succumbed to a techno-economic mythos that values efficiency as a primary justification for technological change. The belief in the efficacy of technology to resolve long-standing problems in communication is profound. Western European countries, for instance, have pioneered the effort to deal with language fragmentation by developing packet transmission systems that allow multiple audio signals to accompany a single video broadcast. This system allows for true pan-European broadcasting in real time. The Japanese have taken the lead in developing direct broadcast satellites to solve the problems of mountainous terrain and the necessity of maintaining thousands of remote transmitters for nationwide television coverage. The United States has led Western delegations at ITU-sponsored conferences in championing an evolutionary "first come, first served" approach to orbital allotments, thus providing maximum flexibility in developing new generations of geosynchronous communications satellites (see discussions of ITU meetings, especially World Administrative Radio conferences, in Fenkell, 1979; Hudson, 1985; Kavanaugh, 1986; Possner, 1979; Rutkowski, 1979, and 1981; United States Congress, 1983; and Valerdi, 1985).

It must be recognized, too, that Western countries, and companies located within them, had vested economic interests in the old communication order, whatever its benefits or deficiencies. Not only did they dominate the development and application of new communications technologies, they also controlled the international flow of news, sound recordings, television programming, data, record services, and voice communication. It would have been unrealistic to expect them to ignore the value of existing structures, and naive to expect them to endorse a new order that not only would bring few added benefits to them, but also appeared to risk the considerable investments, and attendant advantages, provided by the existing order. Also, they saw no reason why their own experience could not be duplicated by other countries that adopted their approach to developing communication infrastructures and exploited them freely.

9.8

Audio Piracy and Bootlegging

Personal technologies provided a capability to people both to create and to duplicate communications materials. One result of this new capability was piracy: illegal copying of recorded materials. This piracy represents the efforts of individuals and entrepreneurs to enlarge communication flow (or to make money) at the least organized levels of the global metropolis. Those who control intellectual property see the impacts of piracy as negative: It distorts international trade, deprives artists and copyright owners of rightful compensation, and impedes the development of new intellectual property. From the perspective of those who use personal technologies for illegal duplication, who distribute such materials in their societies, or who use this material, piracy is a means to participate in international information flow. It is, in fact, a type of flow, even if it represents the "underside" of the international system.

A large amount of the communication material flowing in international channels, particularly audio and video software, does not necessarily have to use broadcasting channels. Often this material moves around the globe in nonbroadcast form, conveniently packaged in cassettes. In the case of audio, too, many of the tape cassettes are duplications of "bootlegged" material, usually surreptitiously recorded rock concerts or rehearsals.

Audiocassettes provide musical material to audiences that do not have easy access to it from their own country's domestic radio operations. Pirated audiocassettes provide it more cheaply than it might be obtained through legal distribution outlets, and more conveniently to people who do not live in large cities where shops are available that carry legitimate copies. Bootlegged tapes provide material that may not otherwise be available at all.

The phenomenon of international audiotape piracy is one that arose largely after the mid-1960s. By that time the number of audiocassette players, as well as player/recorder, had begun to rise dramatically in many countries. This provided an increasingly profitable market for audiotapes as the numbers of playback units increased.

The sale of audio hardware products by the Japanese (far and away the dominant manufacturing power in such products) showed a steady increase between 1965 and 1977. Sales then showed a slight decline to 1980, when sales began to drop significantly (although they remained higher than color television sales, usually seen as the premiere mass medium) (see Fortner & Durham, 1986, p. 123). The number of tape players themselves sold by the Japanese, however, showed an increase from over 63 million units in 1983 to a peak of nearly 75 million units in 1985, and then a decline, undoubtedly fueled by the economic difficulties of developing countries, to about 59 million in 1988 (see *Japan Electronics Almanac 1985,* 1985, p. 173; and *Japan Electronics Almanac 1990,* 1990, p. 20). In contrast, the manufacture and sale of radios without tape playback capability dropped precipitously between 1951 and 1975, before plateauing at a low level of annual production (about 4% of the tape recorder, and 3% of combination stereo sales) (Fortner & Durham, 1986, pp. 123, 138).

The market for audiocassettes produced by changing consumer audio technology provided the basis both for profitable legitimate distribution and sale of audiocassettes, and for its illicit counterpart. As but one indication of this, in 1984 the International Federation of Producers of Phonograms and Videograms (IFPI) estimated ("Nigeria: Problems and Opportunities," 1984, p. 6) that in Nigeria, 30 million illicitly obtained audiocassettes were sold annually, largely for illegal largescale copying of the local music repertoire. Also, although 3.5

million prerecorded cassettes were legally sold annually in Nigeria, the number of illegally recorded cassettes sold was estimated at 17.5 million. Indeed, the number of pirated audiocassettes worldwide is enormous. In 1977, for instance, over 38% of the audiocassettes sold in the United States were pirated. Approximately 10 million pirated audiocassettes were being shipped annually from Singapore to Saudi Arabia. In 1989 the markets in several countries, especially in the developing world, were dominated by pirated audiocassettes, LPs, and CDs.[24] (See Figure 9.7.)

The International Federation of the Phonographic Industry (IFPI) divides the illegal activities of pirates into three categories. First are pirates who copy not only the recording itself, but also its label, sleeve, trademarks, and other details. IFPI refers to these pirates' products as "counterfeits." Second are those who record an artist's performance, either from a concert or from a radio or television program, and then reproduce it without authorization. These are "bootleggers." Third are those who record only the contents of a legally distributed product, and then reproduce it for sale, but package it themselves. These are "pirates" (World Intellectual Property Organization, 1981, p. 2).

IFPI claims that the nature of law enforcement within a given country is what determines the form in which audio piracy will occur. Where copyright laws and their enforcement are adequate, John Hall, director general of IFPI says, counterfeiting will dominate. Where laws or law enforcement are inadequate, however, piracy itself will prevail, because the pirate does not have to go to the trouble of counterfeiting. IFPI finds, therefore, according to Hall (World Intellectual Property Organization, 1981, p. 3), "that in Western Europe, subject to certain exceptions, a high proportion of pirate product is counterfeit. On the other hand, in Greece, India, Indonesia, Singapore and Thailand ... the pirate market is 100 percent or almost 100 percent pirate ... product."

The difficulties involved in obtaining exact figures on illegal activities notwithstanding, IFPI estimated that, in 1980, Asia and Australasia led the world in the number of units of pirated audio products, followed by North America. (See Table 9.3.) The International Labour Office (ILO) claimed (statement in World Intellectual Property Organization, 1981) that in that year, 33% of the European cassette market was accounted for by pirate products; "in the Mid-

dle East and North Africa between 50 and 70 percent of the cassette market; in Asia between 60 and 80 percent of the cassette market; in North America ... 14 percent for cassettes; and in Latin America between 15 and 30 percent of the cassette market."

Due to international pressure several countries where pirated products are produced have initiated crackdowns. In Italy, for instance, between 1978 and 1981, 70 clandestine pirating operations were closed down and more than 1.6 million cassettes seized (statement of Luigi Conte, chairman of the Executive Bureau, International Confederation of Societies of Authors and Composers [CISAC], Rome, World Intellectual

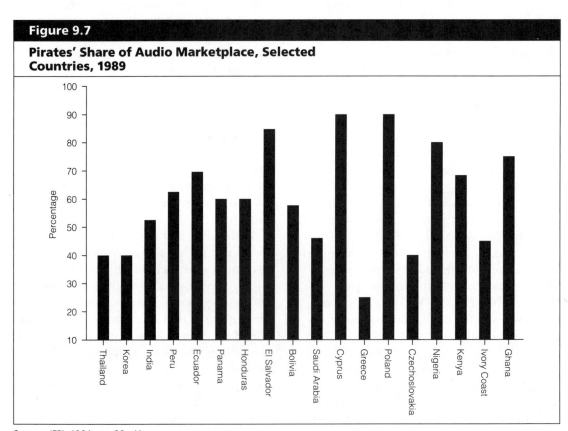

Figure 9.7

Pirates' Share of Audio Marketplace, Selected Countries, 1989

Source: IFPI, 1991, pp. 39–41.

Property Organization, 1981, p. 2). In February 1981, 1 million pirated cassettes imported into Cairo were seized by Egyptian customs agents (statement of Mohamed Gouma, Sub-President, Sono-Cairo Record Company, Cairo, World Intellectual Property Organization, 1981, p. 2). During 1981 and 1982, in 22 different cases, Spanish authorities seized nearly 92,000 audiocassettes and 52,000 covers (statement of W. Woodring, International Criminal Police Organization [INTERPOL], World Intellectual Property Organization, 1983, p. 7). The ultimate success, however, in stopping the trade in illegal cassettes is difficult to assess. In 1985, one report claimed (Brown, 1985; see also Harrington, 1986), pirates manufacturing pirated audiocassettes in Indonesia and selling them in the Middle East were still making millions of dollars.

The unit sales in 1982 translate to 16% of total retail LP and audiocassette sales in North America; 14–15% in Western Europe; 60–80% in the Mediterranean, Middle East, Africa, Asia, and Australasia; and 30–50% in Latin America. The type of material pirated, however, varies from country to country. Even in Western Europe different countries' experiences may vary. Of the pirated music in Belgium, for instance, 95% comes from the international repertoire, as does 100% of Denmark's and 60% of Italy's. Of the Netherlands', however, 90% is from the national repertoire, as is 65% of Greece's and 75% of the United Kingdom's. The amount of classical music pirated in Western Europe varies from 3 to 10%, and the amount from the pop-ethnic repertoire from 2 to 40%. France has the most diverse mix of pirated material, with 10% of its classical, 30% of its national, 20% of its international, and 40% of its pop-ethnic musical repertoires provided by pirates (Davies, 1986).

Pirates obviously practice their "trade" to make large profits. In 1980 worldwide sales of pirated audio products were estimated at over $1 billion (Hall in World Intellectual Property Organization, 1981, p. 4). This figure has remained fairly constant since then, rising only slightly to $1.1 billion in 1989 (IFPI, 1991, p. 41). The most significant areas of loss in 1989 were North America ($423.4 million), Southeast Asia ($322

Table 9.3

Number of Units of Pirated Phonograms (Records and Tapes), in Millions

Region	Number of Units		
	1980	1982	1989
North America	74	60	46.5
Western Europe	26	33	21.6 (EEC)
Mediterranean, Middle			2.4 (non-EEC)
East and Africa	50	50	46.6
Asia and Australasia	120	102	288.5
Latin America	44	25	71.7

Source: Figures for 1980 from International Labour Office, World Intellectual Property Organization, 1981, p.4; figures for 1982 from Davies, 1986; 1989 from IFPI, 1991, p. 41.

million), and countries in the EEC ($147.8 million). Much of this profit occurred in the industrialized countries where counterfeit products (commanding higher prices) were sold, but there were still significant profits worldwide, except for Asia and Australia, where cheap pirated copies were sold at a loss. Even there, however, as Indu Chuda Menon, Director of Program Services for the Asia-Pacific Broadcasting Union (ABU) put it (World Intellectual Property Organization, 1981, pp. 1–2), there were reasons for it to continue. "Piracy is like prostitution," he said. "As long as there is a demand for it, it will exist. . . . For the consumer in a developing country to pay US$41 for a genuine recording, unless it is something like classical music, is a big amount of the budget. Popular music is the most pirated and it is, we must admit, the most ephemeral of any creative work."

9.9

Piracy of Videocassettes

The sources of material for pirated videocassettes include both off-air television programs and legitimate videocassettes (and occasionally film masters), which may include television programs, feature-length films, and other material. As with audiocassettes, no country is immune from piracy. In the United States, for instance, films such as *Star Wars, Close Encounters of the Third Kind, Apocalypse Now,* and *The Living Daylights* were all available in pirated videotape form before they were released to cinemas (statement on behalf of the International Labour Office, World Intellectual Property Organization, 1981, pp. 2–3).

As with audio, reliable figures on the extent of videocassette piracy are not available. There are estimates, however, for

several countries throughout the world, which may be taken to represent the global problem in this area. (See Table 9.4.) This situation can be understood more fully by examining specific countries about which more information exists. In the United Kingdom, for instance, the number of new video releases pirated rose from 88 in 1985 to 130 in 1986 and 223 in 1987. At the same time, however, the number of English language tapes seized by authorities declined from 18,993 in 1985 to 15,025 in 1987, the number of Asian film tapes from 1,748 in 1985 to 885 in 1987, and the number of Chinese language tapes from 14,901 in 1986 to only 1,100 in 1987. The number of prosecutions under the Video Recordings Act and the Copyright Act remained steady over the 3-year period, suggesting that the pirates were managing to evade detection, and avoid prosecution, more successfully as time passed (figures from *Screen Digest,* 1988, p. 72). Despite their efforts, then, the United Kingdom's ability to escape from the "dubious honor of being the world centre for the duplication and sale of illegal video recordings" was questionable (Norris, 1983, p. 25).

As the list of films where pirated versions were available before authorized versions attests to, the U.S. film industry is a major victim of international video piracy. Dennis Patrick, chairman of the FCC, claimed in 1987 ("Patrick Condemns International Program Piracy," p. 78) that the U.S. film and video industry was losing $2 billion per year to video pirates (see also Burgess, 1987).

In general, developing countries have higher percentages of pirated videocassettes than do the more developed countries. Even in Western Europe (with the exception of Spain) the more affluent countries have the lowest percentages of piracy, and the poorer ones the highest. In South America the low figure for Colombia is probably an indirect result of the drug trade, which provides massive amounts of cash to purchase videotapes in the United States. It may also be an error.

In Hong Kong in 1981, 8 illegal video manufacturing centers and 25 retail outlets were raided by Customs and Excise authorities, netting cassettes valued at over $1 million in Hong Kong dollars (US$130,000), and in 1982, 7 more manufacturing centers and another 18 retail outlets were raided, resulting in additional seizures

Table 9.4

Estimated Percentage of Videocassettes Pirated in Various Countries, 1986 and 1987

Region/Country	Amount Pirated
Asia and Australasia	
Australia	20
Indonesia	95
Japan	25–30
New Zealand	25
Philippines	90
Singapore	90
Taiwan	60–70
Western Europe	
Austria	25
Belgium	25
Cyprus	70
Denmark	2
Finland	10
France	25–30
Greece	50
Ireland	40
Italy	50–60
Netherlands	35
Norway	10
Portugal	90
Spain	25–35
Sweden	2–5
Switzerland	15
United Kingdom	25
West Germany	20–30
Latin America	
Brazil	75
Colombia	10
Mexico	25
Venezuela	60

Source: **Screen Digest,** 1987, p. 275, and 1988, p. 48.

worth $900,000 in Hong Kong dollars (US$116,000) (statement of Suen Wing-yiu, head of Copyright Division, Customs and Excise Department, Hong Kong, World Intellectual Property Organization, 1983, p. 2). France "reported the seizure of 1,500 counterfeit video cassettes in the Ile de Reunion resulting in the destruction of a distribution scheme which reached to Mauritius." The French estimated that the losses to legitimate video producers amounted to 2 million French francs per year (US$500,000) (statement of W. Woodring, World Intellectual Property Organization, 1983, p. 1).

In Cameroon, which in 1983 did not yet have television, the number of video clubs had risen from 2 to 35 between 1980 and 1982. Authorities had determined "that the videocassettes circulated by these video clubs have not been lawfully procured and that in most cases, they are recordings that have been copied without authorization from television broadcasts put out by European stations" (statement of Samuel Nelle, Director, Cameroon Copyright Society, World Intellectual Property Organization, 1983, p. 1).

The Asia-Pacific Broadcasting Union, headquartered in Kuala Lumpur, Malaysia, surveyed its members in 1982 and found that 30% reported their programs as having been pirated and sold both domestically and internationally (statement of Indu Chuda Menon, World Intellectual Property Organization, 1983, p. 1). Even in India, which is so poor that only 10% of households are estimated to have radio sets, the penetration of VCRs had reached a level (even though still far less than 5% of households) at which it became profitable to distribute pirated films and foreign programs, including pornography, illegally (Agrawal, 1986, p. 35).[25]

Since the collapse of communism in Central and Eastern Europe, piracy of a variety of materials has also become a major problem for owners of intellectual property. Rapid Associates, an organization of Polish authors, estimates that 60% of videotapes rented in Poland are pirated; computer software goes for the equivalent of US$1 per disk, with even a program such as WordPerfect selling for about US$6 in Warsaw's outdoor computer software bazaar (Harden, 1991). The Motion Picture Association of America (MPAA) has also called Soviet behavior on film "state-condoned piracy." In the Soviet Union "operators, including organizations run by the state, appear to have no qualms about distributing and exhibiting pirated films. . . . Even Soviet television has aired pirated United States pictures" (Hift, 1991c, p. 12).

The Motion Picture Association of America (MPAA) has a program to combat film, video, and satellite theft in the United States, and its counterpart, the Motion Picture Export Association of America (MPEAA), has cooperative programs in a variety of countries around the world. In 1990 MPAA investigators seized over 180,000 illegally duplicated videocassettes in the United States. During the same year MPEAA assisted 40 other countries initiate over 6,600 raids against pirate operations. Altogether such raids removed over 855,000 videocassettes from distribution (Motion Picture Export Association of America, 1991).

In addition to the piracy of cassettes, piracy of television signals also occurs. This is particularly a problem where the footprint of a satellite used for domestic purposes by one country can also be picked up in another. The footprints of U.S. domestic communications satellites, including pay-TV channels, for instance, also cover the Caribbean and part of Central America, allowing pirates there to pick up the signals and record feature-length films for later resale (see Owens, 1986).

9.10

Piracy of Computer Software and Databases

While the losses to firms producing audio and video materials are difficult to document, losses due to the piracy of computer materials are even more problematic to assess. Piracy of computer software and databases is a relatively recent phenomenon, brought on by the rapid spread of personal computers. As previously noted, however, most personal computers in use are in the United States, so the computer piracy problem is still in its infancy. Future Computing Inc., a U.S.-based information service firm, estimated that between 1981 and 1984 U.S. business software producers lost US$1.3 billion in revenues to piracy, and in 1985 another US$800 million.[26] These were losses calculated from a survey distributed only in the United States.

The extent of computer software and database piracy outside the United States is even more difficult to calculate. Estimates suggest that U.S. software vendors lose between US$500 and $800 million per year overseas due to piracy, that in only nine developing countries U.S. firms lose US$128 million per year in software sales due to piracy, and that piracy costs software-producing firms US$137 million per year in the countries of Brazil, Egypt, Indonesia, South Korea, Malaysia, the Philippines, Singapore, Taiwan, and Thailand.[27] All intellectual property losses together, including films, sound recordings, television programs, computer software, databases, printing and publishing, suffered by Amer-

ican companies was estimated by Ambassador Clayton Yeutter, U.S. trade representative, to be over US$6.3 billion in 1986 (United States Congress, 1988, p. 101). By 1988 the losses to U.S. firms on computer software in Western Europe alone, according to the Software Publishers Association and the Business Software Alliance, were $2.81 billion. This increased to $3.38 billion in 1989 and $4.46 billion in 1990 ("Software Piracy Costs Firms Billions," 1992, p. 8). Based on available statistics, then, the total costs to U.S. firms in 1990 in audio, video, film, and software piracy is approximately $6.56 billion.

One obvious technique that could be used to protect computer software from piracy is copy protection. Many popular programs originally carried copy protection, and various schemes for bypassing such protection were also developed. The trend in the late 1980s, however, was to remove copy protection, since the principal buyers of software objected to it. For one thing, many of the schemes made the software cumbersome to install. For another, users objected to difficulties created when hard disk drives crashed and all the allowable installations on the software were used. Although companies typically would provide new installation capability to registered users, valuable time was lost waiting for these new installation disks to arrive. Thus, both data and software protection are problematic (see Bing, 1984).

9.11

Intellectual Property Protection and the Piracy Problem

Several international conventions have been signed to protect both industrial and artistic property. The cumulative force of these conventions governs the relations of various states in protecting intellectual property. These conventions are the following:

- the Paris Convention for the Protection of Industrial Property, signed in 1883
- the Berne Convention for the Protection of Literary and Artistic Works, signed in 1886
- the Rome Convention for the Protection of Performers, Producers of Phonograms and Broadcasting Organizations, signed in 1971
- the Geneva Convention for the Protection of Producers of Phonograms Against Unauthorized Duplication of Their Phonograms, signed in 1972
- the Brussels Convention Relating to the Distribution of Programme-Carrying Signals Transmitted by Satellite, signed in 1974
- the Universal Copyright Convention, negotiated in 1952 (and signed by the United States in 1955) and administered by UNESCO (see Statement on behalf of the International Bureau, World Intellectual Property Organization, 1981, p. 1; see also Wildman & Siwek, 1988, chapter 8)

While the number of conventions (treaties) signed may seem an impressive list, these treaties simply have not been effective in curbing international piracy. The effects of piracy have lessened in some cases, although largely as a result of stricter domestic legislation in some states or of greater effort to enforce existing laws, not from application of these conventions (a description of intellectual property laws in the developed world can be found in Organisation for Economic Co-operation and Development, 1989).

Attempts at international intellectual property protection have failed for a variety of reasons. Perhaps the most obvious one is changing technology. For audio, video, and computer materials, current technology makes piracy simple: The technological capability that makes cassette recorders and computers useful also provides the ability to pirate the intellectual property these devices use (see statement of Kenneth W. Dam, United States Congress, 1988, p. 254; see also statements of Barbara Ringer, United States Congress, 1987, p. 42; and of Allen Wallis, United States Congress, 1988, p. 111). In addition, many countries where pirate operations are located (such as South Korea, Singapore, and Taiwan) are not members of any of the intellectual property conventions. And other countries do not adequately protect rights, even though they are signatories of one or more of the conventions.[28]

Another problem is that the conventions provide different levels of protection to copyrighted works. The Berne Convention, for instance, offers a higher level of protection than the Universal Copyright Convention (UCC). Berne requires that minimum rights be recognized by its signatories—such as copyright duration of life plus 50 years, as well as rights of translation, reproduction, public performance, adaptation, and arrangement, and rights regarding making motion pictures from other published works. The UCC requires merely that signatories provide equal protection to foreign creators as to their own citizens (referred to as "national treatment"), but many countries afford little protection to anyone (their own nationals included), thereby making their adherence to the UCC almost meaningless (see statements of Arpod Bogsch, director general, WIPO, United

States Congress, 1987, p. 9; and of Carlos J. Moorhead, United States Congress, 1988, p. 60). Also, conventions are rewritten, but signatory countries to earlier versions may choose not to ratify later ones. This makes the levels of protection worldwide for a given work variable and difficult to enforce. Most of the conventions listed as protecting intellectual property are actually rewrites of earlier agreements, adopted in an effort to extend protection to newer forms of property.

The United States has the greatest stake in international copyright protection of any country in the world. As U.S. trade representative Clarence Yeutter has said (United States Congress, 1988, p. 117), "because [the United States has] more intellectual property to protect than anybody else in the world does, . . . we have more to be pirated than anybody else does." U.S. companies, besides providing the lion's share of sound recordings, films, and videocassettes in world distribution, also control 70% of the world's software trade (statement of Kenneth W. Dam, United States Congress, 1988, p. 262).

"There are countries," as David Brown of the Motion Picture Association of America (MPAA) put it (United States Congress, 1988, pp. 342–343), "where it is extremely difficult to find a legitimate copy of a prerecorded cassette of an American film. . . . Moreover, in a number of foreign markets U.S. films are often available within days of their U.S. theatrical release." The film *E.T.*, for instance, was rated consistently across the globe as the most popular videocassette available to people — years before it had even been released in that form. In response to the pirate threat the MPAA had established, by the mid-1980s 18 film and security offices around the world, which as-

sisted in the operation of nearly 60 anti-piracy programs across the globe (United States Congress, 1988, p. 366). In 1990 the MPAA began planning a satellite movie service for Latin America in an effort to preempt the piracy of Hollywood films. This service would be encoded using the B-MAC scrambling system. MPAA also initiated lawsuits in Latin American countries, beginning with Panama and Costa Rica, in an effort to establish copyright protection for its members' products ("Latin American Movie Plan," 1990, p. 39).

The ability of the United States to respond to global piracy of its intellectual property, however, is limited. The United States did not become a member of the Berne Convention, for instance, until 1989, which complicated bilateral antipiracy negotiations with other countries (United States Congress, 1988, p. 114). Also, certain countries, such as the United Kingdom, do not approach all aspects of intellectual property the same way. English computer software entrepreneurs, for instance, don't depend on copyright to protect their products; rather, they aim to develop new products quickly enough that piracy is not a problem (statement of Fred W. Weingarten, United States Congress, 1985, p. 102). This means that the United States has difficulty from time to time developing sympathy for its position on intellectual property protection.

Also troublesome to music copyright holders has been Japan's attitude toward a widespread practice there, the operations of CD rental stores. Under Japan's copyright law, Japanese CD producers could ban CD rental, and demand rental fees from the stores for their products. Foreign firms, however, which accounted for one-third of the rental market in Japan (or about $1 billion annually in lost sales), were not covered by this law. In response to this inequity, the United States began pressing at the GATT talks for a 50-year moratorium on rental of intellectual property. In 1992 the Japanese government agreed to initiate new legislation to ban CD rentals for one year after their release. But, as *The Economist* put it, "given Japan's dire record for protecting intellectual property, [that] may not be good enough to stamp out CD bootlegging for good" ("A CD Business," 1992, p. 80).

Developing countries also claim extenuating circumstances in their posture toward protecting intellectual property. "Protection of computer software is not merely a commercial issue," as Vitthya Vejjajiva, Thailand's ambassador to the United States, has put it (1989), "but is essential to modernization in developing countries. An equitable balance must be struck between the need to reward the creators and the need for the products to be accessible to the developing world." The same logic has been applied to Thailand in its regulations on pharmaceutical patents — to meet "the urgent need to make medicine affordable to the people."

Although not technically a piracy problem, satellites have also introduced new difficulties for copyright protection, particularly in the pan-European environment. In 1986 the Council of Europe Committee of Ministers agreed to a Recommendation on Principles relating to Copyright Law Questions in the Field of Television by Satellite. This agreement required that all states distinguish between fixed satellite services (FSS) and direct broadcast satellites (DBS) for copyright purposes. FSS was used principally for broadcasting organizations to transmit among themselves; it was not intended for audiences. DBS services, on the other hand, were directed to general reception (see Pichter, 1987, p. 97).[29]

The Realities of Information Flow in the International Communications System

Statistical Measures of Information Flow

The differences in the relative communications capabilities of various countries are staggering. The United States, for instance, has over 37% of all the telephones in the world. It also has 16% of all radio transmitters, 27% of all radio receivers, 21% of all television sets, over 21% of daily newspaper circulation, and 49% of global advertising expenditures (Kurian, 1984). (See Figure 9.8.)

The Japanese Ministry of Posts and Telecommunications suggests that the growth of telephone traffic between developed countries, especially the United States and Japan, has largely been the result of the rapidly expanding use of fax machines by businesses linked in trade relations (see Ministry of Posts and Telecommunications, 1988, pp. 31, 33).[30] Japan uses over 27% of all television transmitters in the world, and the top 10 countries (none of which are from the developing world) account for 67% of all television transmitters (Kurian, 1984, p. 399). The United States and Canada together provide over 15,000 hours of television programs to their citizens *each day,* while most countries provide fewer than that *per year* (Kurian, 1984, p. 414). The developed countries also account for over 95% of the world's computer capacity, measured by value of equipment installed (MacBride, 1980, pp. 91–92).

On the telecommunications side, the TAT-8 cable between North America and Europe, installed in 1988 with digital circuit multiplication equipment, could carry 40,000 conversations simultaneously.[31] A similar fiber optic cable was laid under the Pacific (Coy, 1989).[32] The total fiber optic cable expected to be installed worldwide in 1988 was 625,000 miles (Burgess, 1988a). In 1991 the TAT-9 fiber optic cable was laid, capable of handling 80,000 telephone calls simultaneously, or more than 1.1 billion bits of information per second. This meant, for instance, that the entire contents of the 24-volume *Encyclopedia Brittanica* could be transmitted across the Atlantic in less than 1 second (Young, 1991, p. 12). By 1995 capacity is expected to rise to 2.4 billion bits

per second ("Group Agrees to Merge," 1991, p. 11).

Such statistics need to be put into context. Despite the large number of telephone conversations that could be handled between the United States and Europe, and between the United States and Asia, these capabilities were restricted mainly to developed countries. Developing countries were still largely left with far less capability to use such systems than the industrialized nations. An example is Brazil, one of the most advanced of the developing countries. Using cable alone, the United States has over 120,000 circuits available for telecommunications to Europe and Asia. By contrast, in 1985 Brazil had a total of only 700 circuits, with plans to in-

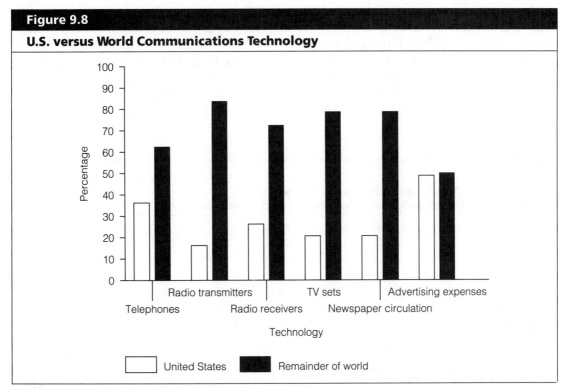

Figure 9.8

U.S. versus World Communications Technology

Source: Kuman, 1984.

crease the number to 3,500 by 1993 (Hobday, 1985).

The ITU's secretary-general also reported to the Nice Plenipotentiary Conference (ITU, 1989b, p. 3) that the Administrative Council's report

> shows that there is no significant improvement in the availability and distribution of telecommunications in most of the developing countries, even in regard to what is universally recognized as a basic service. The situation in respect of the many new services including telematics, is far worse. In general, the disparity between the industrialized and developing countries continues and with the technological strides being made in the former, the stage appears to be set for further deterioration.

His statement was echoed by Malaysia's minister of Energy, Telecommunications and Posts, who remarked (ITU, 1989b, p. 7) that "in international trade, as in other spheres of international relations, the countries that are strong tend to dominate those that are not as strong." He thus was concerned about trends in deregulation that could tend to widen the gap between industrialized and developing countries. (See Table 9.5.)

The capacities of the cables being installed for developing countries can also be understood by reference to the proportions of telephones available within them, compared with the remainder of the world. In the mid-1980s, for instance, Organization for Economic Cooperation and Development (OECD) countries (the developed world) had 12.5% of the world's population, but 90% of its telephones (Pelton, 1984, p. 77). In 1990 the world telecommunications market was estimated to be around $500 billion. Investments in Western Europe, North America, and Japan accounted for 95% of this total (Bond & Jones, 1990, pp. 2–3).

Similar statistics exist for the volume of telecommunications traffic worldwide. In 1987 the number of international calls placed by different countries varied from 1,477,000 from Paraguay to 566,998,000 from the United States. North America, Western Europe, and Japan accounted for more than 2.2 billion calls, compared with almost 94.5 million from Latin America,

Table 9.5

Comparisons of Telecommunications Capabilities of Industrialized, Developing, and Less Developed Countries

	Industrialized Countries	Developing Countries	Less Developed Countries
Main lines	355.3 million	——— 84.5 million ———	
Access*	100%	50%	24%
Unmet demand	0.5%	——— 14.4% ———	
Call completion rates	90%	——— 50–60% ———	
Telephones			
1987	355 million	84 million	0.59 million
2000	499 million	181 million	0.82 million

*Defined as the availability of a telephone within 5 kilometers (one hour's walk).
Source: ITU, 1989b, pp. 227, 229.

65.9 million from Australia, 51.8 million from Hong Kong, 6.8 million from both Indonesia and Malaysia, 8.3 million from the Philippines, 57.6 million from Saudi Arabia, 33.7 million from Singapore, 16.6 million from South Africa, and 2.2 million from the Soviet Union *(International Telecom Statistics,* 1989, p. 24).[33] The U.S. telephone company AT&T alone channeled more than 1 billion overseas telephone calls in 1988, nearly doubling the previous year's total (Burgess, 1988b; see also comparative statistics in "Siemens Releases World Telephone Stats," 1990, p. 5).

The realities of information flow in the international communications system are more complex than such comparisons suggest, however. Each type of information within the system flows following a somewhat different dynamic (discussions of various types of international telecommunications services can be seen in Goldey, 1986; Kincaid, 1986; McKnight, 1987; and Mestmächer, 1988). Each has resulted in varying amounts of control exercised by industrialized nations over developing countries.

Transborder Data Flow

The threat posed by transborder data flow (TBDF) to developing countries may come more from the structure of the marketplace than from domination of domestic systems. The current problem is denial of access, rather than an overwhelming presence. Most developing countries do not have sufficient capability to participate in global TBDF, except in highly specialized arenas. Nor do they have the hard currency reserves required to buy access to the databases created mostly in Northern Hemisphere countries. The result may be that as the global economy accelerates with the expanding use of electronic data flow, developing countries will again be left behind, dependent on others in yet another area of economic development (see Cole, 1986). Although Intelsat has experienced a dramatic increase in the number of small-aperture business service earth stations using its satellites worldwide, these generally belong to TNCs that are building their own privately owned international gateways to use digital, data, voice, voice conference, fax, and telex services without using the expensive infrastructures of developing countries' PTTs.[34]

The introduction of geosynchronous orbit satellites originally raised the possibility of dependable high-speed international digital communication. The introduction of relatively inexpensive personal computers and high-quality telephone lines and modems further encouraged the process of data communication. By 1984 companies were making proposals to extend fiber optic cables between Europe and North America, which would be followed by global fiber optic networks. The enormous capacity of optical fiber perhaps made the widespread global use of digital communications inevitable. It certainly increased the feasibility of such schemes since these cables provided features far beyond those of coaxial cables or satellites: (1) bandwidth and signal capacity and fidelity, (2) speed and dependability, and (3) privacy, since such cables cannot be tapped (see other advantages in Podmore & Faguy, 1986). The principal impediment to global implementation was that the system was optical, not electromechanical. The problem created by this shift in technology largely affected developing countries. They did not have the trained engineers or financial resources to allow them to shift quickly from standard telephone technology, employing electrical impulse circuits and electro-mechanical switching apparatus, to the new optical systems (see Senior, 1985, for an explanation of the basics of fiber optics). Another obstacle was that optical fibers, like the twisted-pairs and coaxial cables they were to replace, were not usable for point-to-multipoint or multipoint-to-multipoint distribution (see Hudson, 1990, p. 6).[35] Nevertheless, such systems became increasingly important during the 1980s. As one UNESCO study (Mowlana, 1985) put it,

> An important trend in international economic activities during the past decade has been the increasing role of data communication. Information-sensitive industries such as banking, insurance, airlines, multinational businesses and news agencies are heavily dependent on the instantaneous availability and dissemination of data around the world. . . . [T]o transmit vital management information, manufacturing and trading firms operating in more than one country must facilitate reliable lines of data communication between the parent organization and its subsidiaries. Governments also rely on data links via satellite and cable for military, diplomatic and technical communication and decision-making. (p. 45)

The United States was the leading actor in the increasing use of international data communication, largely because it was the first country to recognize the importance of the service sector in international trade, the economic area in which TBDF is included. During the 1980s the United States was the world's largest exporter of services, including data services. It used its position to press the international community for an open global environment for service transactions, particularly data services (Sauvant, 1986b, pp. 293–294). The world market in telecommunications and computer services was estimated in 1984 to be $300 billion, and was predicted to rise by 1990 to $560 billion, an increase of nearly 87% in 4 years

(see Robinson, 1985, p. 311). By 1990 information technology alone was a $200 billion worldwide industry, and U.S. companies accounted for more than half of that total. The single largest market for information technology firms remained the United States (ITAA, 1991).

The use of domestic satellites for telecommunications in the United States also suggests the rapid movement toward broadband services (data and video) as opposed to more traditional voice communication. The number of domestic communications satellite transponders devoted to voice communication in the United States has been declining since 1987, while the number devoted to data communication has been increasing. By 1989 voice channels used only 20% of the total, data 30%, and video 50% (Space Applications Board, 1989, p. 26).

In Europe countries began establishing public data networks, and then integrating them on a regional basis. The Nordic countries of Finland, Sweden, and Norway set up such a regional system, and Austria served as an interaction point for data flow between Eastern and Western Europe (see Sint, 1988, pp. 12–13, and 1989, pp. 216–232). Although quantitative information about the significance of international data communication remains difficult to find, some examples can be cited. Sweden's international telecommunications packet (telepak) and data exchange (datex) services with other countries increased, for instance, from 277,000 messages in 1982–83 to 441,000 messages just one year later. In Norway, between 1982 and 1985, the number of leased lines for data telecommunications (datel) services increased from 10,217 to 17,512 (an increase of 71%), and for datex services from 800 lines to 7,531 (up 841%), while the number of packet data systems went from 75 in 1984 (the year the service was introduced) to 601 only a year later (Norwegian Telecommunications Administration, 1982–1985; Televerket, 1985; see also Cyprus Telecommunications Authority, 1980–1986; Instituto Nacional de Investigacion y Capacitacion de Tele-comunicaciones, 1985, 1986; and *Memoria Anual,* 1986).

Most international data communication still occurs among developed countries (only 5,755 of Sweden's 441,000 datex messages in 1983–84 were sent to nations in the developing world). However, this communications capability still affects nonindustrialized countries. As Mowlana (1985) has suggested:

> To the extent that information is the basis of power, access to information and ability to utilize it can give some nations political, economic and social advantages over others. Third World nations fear that underdeveloped computer technology and lack of access to the international data market will block their participation in the growing information-based world economy, and perpetuate their dependence on the developed world. (p. 50)

Satellite Communication

The operations of Intelsat have caused developing countries a different concern. Two elements determine the price of satellite services: the space segment cost and the earth station cost. In Intelsat's case, as Vizas (1986, pp. 81–82) argues, the space segment cost has been minimized (thus the drop in annual transponder costs), but this has resulted in higher earth station costs. The reason, he says, is that the space segment is designed for high-volume, public-switched traffic. Therefore, he concludes, "earth station investment (not to mention operating costs) averages twice as much per half circuit for developing and newly industrializing nations as it does for industrialized nations." The implication here is

that low-volume traffic would use simpler, and less expensive, earth stations, which would serve the needs of developing countries better than the current system, although it would raise the annual transponder cost.

The impacts of satellites on the communication activities of developing countries can be viewed from a variety of angles. Vizas's argument is one. Another has to do with historical development. From this point of view, for instance, the decision to implement active, rather than passive, satellites for international communication, and to move from low- to medium- and then to high-power satellites, had the effect of reducing the size of earth stations, thus working to the advantage of developing countries. (See Appendix 3 for technical characteristics of satellites.) Still another angle is to acknowledge that the high-volume traffic in some corridors of Intelsat's total service have subsidized the lower volume traffic in corridors that have primarily served developing countries.

Evidence for the historical argument can be seen in the increasing membership in Intelsat by developing countries since the mid-1960s, and by the increasing numbers of countries served by the system. By 1989 Intelsat was using 13 satellites, connected by over 2,000 earth-station-to-earth-station links, using over 800 antennas at 600 earth station sites. One hundred seventeen nations were members of Intelsat, and 170 used the Intelsat system (Intelsat, 1988–89, p. 7). (See Appendix 4 for a list of Intelsat, and other satellite organization, members.) As one report to the ITU (ITU, 1989b, p. 1) put it, "In the period 1982–1988 space telecommunications continued to develop towards a better use of the frequency spectrum and less expensive earth stations. Digital technologies have allowed the introduction of [various techniques that have resulted in decreased] per channel costs."[36] There is likewise evidence of consideration of the needs of developing countries in the creation of Intelsat, and in the pricing policies adopted by the organization (see Hudson, 1990, chapter 3). Despite such gains, however, telephone systems in many developing countries, including even Asia's "superstar economies" remains "pitiful" ("No Connection," 1992, p. 76).

It is difficult to know, however, which strategy best serves the needs of developing countries in the long run, or how their needs should be balanced against those of countries that require high-volume capability for such services as video and high-speed data transfer. Although developing countries have joined Intelsat, or use Intel-

sat, despite such economic constraints, their continued ability to do so may be in jeopardy. The new entrants in satellite communication, such as PanAmSat, are unlikely to have a positive impact on this problem, as their primary markets will be the high-volume corridors already served by Intelsat and developing fiber optic networks.

Intelsat has also been classified by some, especially those who view it as an obstacle to competitive systems, as a monopoly seeking to "squash innovative and new niches." The criticism echoes that directed at the British cable and Marconi wireless monopolies prior to the First World War, at European wire services between the wars, and at U.S. film, television, and wire service companies since the end of World War II.

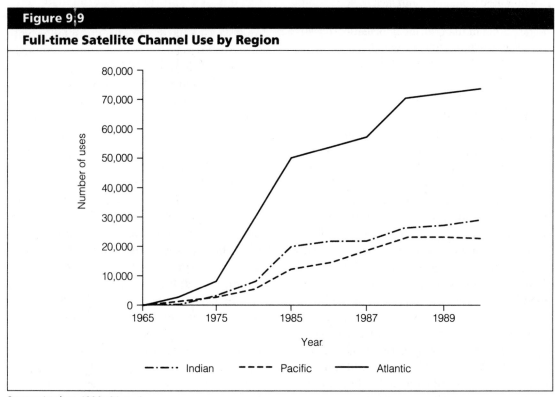

Figure 9.9

Full-time Satellite Channel Use by Region

Source: Intelsat, 1990–91, p. 4.

John Puente, chairman of Orion, claimed at a satellite conference in 1990 (Chase, 1990, p. 32) that "Intelsat has become a profit center selfishly exploited by its major users . . . and a profitable center it is." Rene Anselmo, chairman of Alpha Lyracom (PanAmSat), echoed Puente's remarks. The Intelsat treaty, Anselmo said (Chaise, 1990, p. 32), was "an agreement among thieves." Intelsat itself had "stolen a technology that it did not invent, and it has kept it from the world instead of bringing it to the world." All monopolies, he continued, "turn out to be rotten in the end."

Despite such criticisms Intelsat has come to play an increasingly significant role in the international communications system, both for telecommunications and broadcasting applications (see Colino, 1986). Intelsat satellites carried only 80 hours of television programs in 1965, for instance, but 55,778 hours worldwide in 1987. During the 1988 Bush-Gorbachev Moscow summit meeting, Intelsat carried over 19,000 minutes of transmissions of summit news, and provided 20 simultaneous television channels to various broadcasting organizations around the world (Intelsat, 1988–89, pp. 22, 24). Intelsat also provided 32 simultaneous television channels for use during the Seoul Olympics in 1988 (Intelsat, 1988–89, p. 24). Intelsat set new records for providing continuous service, too, during the 1990 Bush-Gorbachev Malta summit meeting, which was outside the major telecommunications trunk networks for global communication (see Meyers, 1990). By any measure countries have been making increasing use of

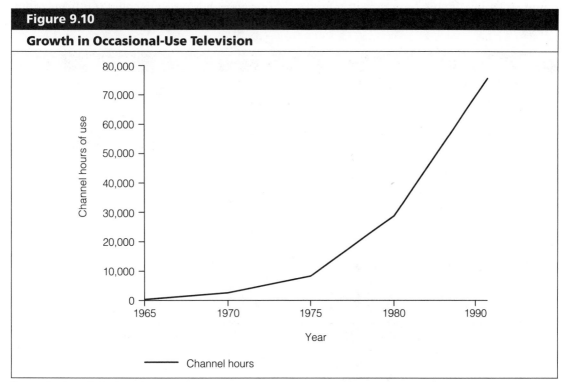

Figure 9.10

Growth in Occasional-Use Television

Source: Intelsat, 1990–91, p. 7.

Intelsat since its creation. Full-time satellite use has increased annually in all three regions served by Intelsat (see Figure 9.9), occasional-use television has increased over 900-fold since it began in 1965 (see Figure 9.10), and the Intelsat business service (IBS) has increased from only 14 channels in 1984 to over 10,000 only six years later (see Figure 9.11). By 1990 Intelsat offered IBS (including digital data, voice, fax, electronic mail, remote printing, picture transfer, audio feeds, and videoconferencing) in 52 countries using 225 earth stations.

Intelsat has been joined, however, by other international satellite carriers, such as PanAmSat, Orion, Brightstar, and Inmarsat. Inmarsat, one of whose principal functions is satellite communications for ships, also provides its signatories telephone, telex, high-speed data, telex, and telephony group calling, and compressed video signal communication. Its total minutes of tele-

phone service carried between 1982 and 1987 increased nearly four times, from 2.25 million minutes to 9.5 million. Telex increased nearly as fast, from 3.5 million minutes in 1982 to 12 million in 1987 (INMARSAT, 1987/88, pp. 32–33). The various satellite systems also provided an increasing number of television transponder leases, from only 5 full-time international leases in 1985 to 28 by 1988. The U.S. television networks, CNN, the EBU, Japanese and Australian broadcasters, and Visnews all had one or more leases by 1988 (Marshall, 1989, pp. 264–265).

Television

The United States still dominates the world of international television entertainment, for four primary reasons: (1) It produces more television than any other country and therefore has more to sell; (2) it licenses its

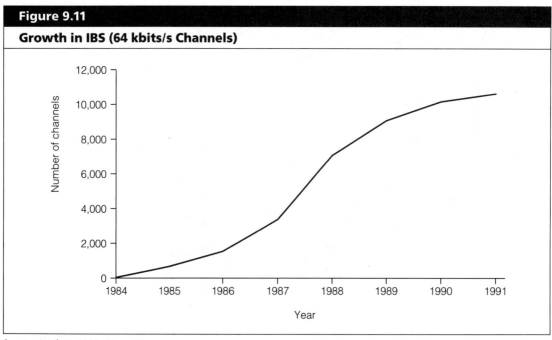

Figure 9.11

Growth in IBS (64 kbits/s Channels)

Source: Intelsat, 1990–91, p. 14.

programming for far less money than it costs other countries to produce programs of the same length; (3) its networks capitalize on long-standing economic relationships with foreign countries; and (4) its programs are culturally compatible with the idea of a global television marketplace. The fourth factor, cultural compatibility, was explained by Read (1976, p. 12): "In sum, American mass media during the first third of the twentieth century invested themselves with a bland ideology compatible with various cultures. Thus they were being prepared, albeit unwittingly so, to venture into foreign countries" (see also Liebes & Katz, 1990; Schwarzkopf, 1989; and Thomsen, 1989). As but one example, MTV, by 1991, was available nearly worldwide, with the exception of a few countries in northern South America, the Caribbean, and Central America, and most of sub-Saharan Africa. Europe, mainland Asia, Australia, North and South America, the Indian subcontinent, Southeast Asia, the Middle East, Malaysia, and Indonesia—over 200 million households in all—could receive MTV ("MTV's 'Cultural Colonialism,'" 1991, p. 11) (see Figure 8.1).

The BBC and France are also active in promoting licensing of their television products abroad, particularly in Africa. France also has begun to extend its television program accessibility via satellite to other Francophone regions, such as the Caribbean. Other countries, too, have begun exchange relationships to allow them more control over the content of their domestic television channels, and to save money in producing television programs.

As already suggested, the dominance of Western (and particularly U.S.) television has begun to erode. Increasingly, other countries are developing significant indigenous production capabilities, and countries sharing basic cultural values and languages

have begun to share their programming. Two areas where this has become important are Latin America and the Middle East (see Straubhaar & Viscasillas, 1991).

Countries in South and Central America, for instance, exchanged 12% of their total program output in 1983–84. This total, while not large by comparison with the amount of programming purchased from the United States, nevertheless constituted the second largest source of foreign programming within the region (Varis, 1984, p. 27). One primary vehicle for this exchange was the *telenovela,* or soap opera, which was one of the most popular forms of television in the region. In Brazil, for instance, the *telenovela,* along with national news, is the highest rated form of programming available (see Kottak, 1990, 1991). Major producers of *telenovelas* for exchange in the region are Brazil, Mexico, Venezuela, and Argentina.

The Arab countries of the Middle East have also increasingly cooperated to exchange television programs, beginning in 1985. One third of all programs imported by Arab countries come from their neighbors, with the United Arab Emirates and Egypt providing about half of imported programs in the region (Varis, 1984, pp. 45, 47). By 1989, too, Arabsat provided capability through two satellites for 8,000 simultaneous telephone circuits and seven television channels. The satellites could also be used for equivalent electronic traffic, such as electronic mail, facsimile, computer links, picture and text transmissions, and audio links for radio, telex, or teleconferencing (Ryan, 1989, p. v). Arab countries were using the system to provide a daily pan-Arab television news package to Arab League members, and could link with Intelsat to provide news feeds in the same way as CNN, Visnews, or Worldwide Television News.

By the late 1980s many countries were seeking partners with whom to establish bilateral radio and television exchange agreements. The advantage of such agreements was twofold. First, the programs exchanged would allow each country to stretch its production budget by supplementing it with culturally compatible programs free of charge from the other. Second, the exchange, by increasing the total number of hours of television available for each state, would allow them to avoid purchasing so many hours of inexpensive Western television programs. The two gains together would allow the countries to exercise more national control over the content of their respective television systems. In 1988 Egypt and Pakistan signed such an exchange agreement, for instance, to provide each other with programs "reflecting the cultural, social and economic aspects of both countries" (BBC Monitoring Service, 1988r). Iran and Hungary signed a similar agreement, as did Poland and Turkey, Cyprus and the Soviet Union, West Germany and the Soviet Union, and Egypt and the Sudan, among others (BBC Monitoring Service, 1988u, 1989k, 1989n, 1989w).

In western Europe similar arrangements were initiated between various countries and U.S. companies, despite the long-standing concern about U.S. encroachment in European television. By 1989 a number of U.S. companies were making production, investment and distribution arrangements with European partners ("The New World of International TV Programming," 1989). Television was taking on a "transfrontier character" as it gradually transformed from a vehicle of national identity to a cultural industry (see European Television Task Force, 1988, pp. 4–6). As television developed, first from terrestrial to satellite transmission, then from analog to digital, and now from "low" to "high" definition, the stakes for participation have seemed to get higher. Countries have seen their participation as part of their "quest for communication equality" (Anawalt, 1984; see also d'Arcy, 1978).

Privatization of Domestic Communications Systems

Many countries, particularly in Europe, are beginning to "privatize" their national radio and television systems. France and Spain, for instance, are joining Italy and the United Kingdom in adding private broadcasting to supplement state-operated systems, or selling off part of the state system to allow private broadcasting to begin. Some countries, such as the United Kingdom, have also privatized state-controlled telecommunications networks. Internationally, this process is known as deregulation, although it is a different process than what happened in the 1980s in the United States under the same name (see Palmer, 1988, for a discussion of the European situation).

This process has also resulted in anxiety in many other countries, which fear that new profit-centered private corporations will arise seeking the same type of system control that other companies sought earlier in this century. Paul Quile, minister for Posts, Telecommunications and Space of France, argued (ITU, 1989b) that this phenomenon must be controlled to assure that its impacts were favorable over the long term, both to consumers and to the international community.[37] Egbon (1989, pp. 46, 55) has also expressed fears that technology and economics have outstripped the ability of countries to control them, leaving the system to develop without clearly defined national goals or priorities. "The heavy concentration of communications technology in the hands of the few developed nations and their multi-national corporation agents," he argued, "does not seem to auger well for the well being of the less privileged nations. It seems likely that there will be a virtual monopoly or at least a preponderance of commercialization in international communications."

Despite such criticism the trend toward a privately controlled and largely deregulated system has continued, leading, among other things, to new opportunities for international communication. In television program licensing, for instance, privatization brought competition, and competition brought pressures for new broadcast and cable television channels. U.S. program suppliers were already doing approximately $2.5 billion per year in business with foreign companies and governments by 1989 ("Signs of Truce Between Europe and U.S.," 1989; see also "MIP-TV Convenes in Cannes," 1988). The 1990s will see even greater revenues generated by international program sales, both for the United States and for other major producing countries (see Dunnett, 1990, for an economic analysis of television production and distribution).

Although cable penetration of Western Europe is low, with the notable exceptions of Belgium, Denmark, and the Netherlands, both private companies and state administrations were developing pan-European satellite television systems by the late 1980s ("Expanding Opportunities in the Unfolding European Market," 1987; see also European Television Task Force, 1988, p. 6).[38] France, Germany, and Britain were developing domestic DBS systems, and Luxembourg's Societe Europeen Des Satellites (SES) was expanding its long-standing commercial radio and television operations into satellites with ASTRA, a pan-European DBS venture ("Expanding Opportunities in the Unfolding European Market," 1987). By early 1989 ASTRA was carrying seven channels of tele-

vision to the whole of Europe, including FilmNet, Sky Channel, Eurosport, Sky News, Sky Movies, Scansat TV3, and MTV Europe (BBC Monitoring Service, 1989d). These channels joined the 19 that were already available via satellite (although not DBS) by 1986 (see European Television Task Force, 1988, p. 18; "The Sky's the Limit for Broadcasters," 1986; and "Wie Phoenix aus der Asche," 1986). The French satellite TDF-1 was operational by 1988, but the German TV-SAT 1, although launched, failed to deploy one of its solar panels and had to be abandoned. Rupert Murdoch was also operating Sky Channel and Radio Music Box as DBS services for Britain, and had plans for moving into new pay channel services (see "Disney Forges New Alliance with Murdoch," 1988).[39] He had lost over $120 million (£75 million) by 1989, however, and nearly $340 million a year later (Henry, 1989; "Murdoch Takes Big Hit," 1990). By 1991, however, Murdoch's Sky TV operation had absorbed British Satellite Broadcasting (BSB) and was airing Sky's programming via two satellites to the United Kingdom (see "Britain's Satellite TV Up in Air After Merger," 1990, p. 32).

The BBC also began looking into a television world news broadcast in 1987. The Foreign and Colonial Office, which underwrites the external broadcasting of the BBC, did not fund the project, however, and the corporation began looking for private funding. A British consulting firm was retained to seek support from British financial houses. The BBC was able to inaugurate the service, along with documentaries and entertainment, as a subscription channel, BBC World Service Television, for Europe and Asia in 1991, and planned to have it available worldwide by 1993 (see Figure 8.1).

By 1991 a number of other broadcasters were also considering the possibilities of new broadcast satellite applications.

Germany planned to use its 3SAT-TV to provide a German-language "linguistic and cultural bridge" into Eastern Europe, and China announced that its Huayi Broadcasting Company would begin to cover Asia and Europe from Fuzhou (BBC Monitoring Service, 1991b, pp. A2, A3, 1991d, p. A4). By early 1992 India had also announced that it was planning a 14-hour-per-day satellite-delivered Hindi television service to cover 50 countries from Nigeria to Japan, beginning in January 1993 (BBC Monitoring Service, 1992a, p. A8).

DBS Services

The development of international news and entertainment programming via satellite, particularly via DBS, has important consequences for broadcasting, both domestic and international. On the domestic side these new services have broken the monopolies established within many countries that controlled their citizens' access to both information and entertainment. For instance, in Belgium citizens have access to the television programs of seven different countries on their cable system, and an increasing number of satellite services. In Holland, besides Dutch programs, television from West Germany, Belgium, France, and the United Kingdom is carried on cable systems. One estimate suggested that Britain alone would require an additional 100,000 hours of programming per year over the next several years as a result of the TV "boom" in Europe ("U.S. Film Industry Is Big Winner," 1989). Another was that 200 new channels may soon be created in Europe (Neher, 1989).

National communications administrations (or state broadcast monopolies) have had to begin competing for audiences. They have also seen much of the justification for funding them through the vehicle of license fees evaporate. At the same time, the provision of new services has resulted in fears that ideas such as public service broadcasting, pioneered in the United Kingdom, will be trampled by commercial pressure, and the result will be vulgarization, commercialism, and the loss of national cultural presence on television.[40] These fears led the European Economic Community to search for means to stem the rising tide of U.S. television programs in Europe by requiring that a majority of programs on national television stations be of European origin (see "EC Tentatively Adopts Curbs," 1989; see also Bencivenga, 1991, p. 14; Hift, 1991a, pp. 10, 11; Holmstrom, 1991, p. 9; and Sterritt, 1991, p. 13).

Arguments over the role of DBS have occurred in many international organizations, including the General Assembly of the United Nations, the ITU, UNESCO, and the Committee on Peaceful Uses of Outer Space (COPUOS, created by the UN General Assembly).[41] Traditional arguments about the threat to cultural and political sovereignty have been raised. The Soviets, too, threatened to consider any efforts to use such satellites to cross their borders as "ideological aggression" (see "Television Too," 1985).

Much of the difficulty with international DBS is that using satellites for broadcasting directly into people's homes was originally conceived of as a *domestic* (or national) service (see Tydeman & Kelm, 1986, p. 102). Therefore, the restrictions built into agreements for its use (such as satellite beam width and power flux densities) were adopted under the assumption that satellites would provide domestic television services. Applications for international services not only violate these assumptions, but lead to complaints that developed countries are taking advantage of early agreements to push for new services that will further entrench their dominance of international communication. Also, even though digital transmission schemes would allow for the same video signal to have multiple audio signals, developing countries know that providing them would deny broadcasters the economy of scale they would otherwise achieve using satellites. They conclude, therefore, that broadcasters are not likely to provide them.

Many problems still must be solved, then, before such satellites will be generally applied in international communication. Japan, Germany, France, and the United Kingdom have begun to apply DBS for domestic purposes, however, and Europe is quickly becoming a test case for international DBS, with both Luxembourg and private companies based in other countries competing for a European audience through satellite (see Fortner, 1988b).[42] One estimate suggested that the potential DBS audience in Europe (excluding Greece and Portugal) would be nearly 50 million households (about 45% of the total) by 1990 (Tydeman & Kelm, 1986, p. 119). By 1988 the majority of Eutelsat's income was already coming from full-time television leases: "[S]atellite television channels on EUTELSAT were reaching over 14 million cabled homes and thousands of SMATV . . . and domestic TVRO . . . installations" (Eutelsat, 1988, p. 8).

9.13

News via Satellite

Increasingly, both private and public broadcasters are making use of satellites to collect and distribute news. Perhaps the best-known such operation in the United States is CNN, but there are other important news broadcasters, such as Sky News, Visnews, and BBC World Service Television. *Time* magazine calls CNN the "world's largest

global TV network" ("Prince of the Global Village," 1992), and by 1992 it had over 1,700 employees, reached 75 million homes in over 100 countries, and was earning a profit ($134 million in 1990) (Zoglin, 1992, p. 31).

The various global news operations have exchange relationships that allow them to feed one another's coverage automatically when events break that require immediate broadcast. When the Gulf War broke out in January 1991, Intelsat immediately began to operate five TV channels: CNN from Riyadh, Saudi Arabia, and Baghdad, Iraq; CBS News from Tel Aviv, Israel; a British TV pool (BBC and ITN) from Riyadh; and ABC News from Amman, Jordan. These signals all were relayed around the globe for clients to pick up for domestic broadcast, or were carried on satellites to feed cable systems or satellite dishes in subscribing countries. The British Riyadh signal, for instance, was down-linked to the BBC World Service Television dish, fed via microwave to London's British Telecom's international teleport to the United States, and again up-linked to cross the Pacific to Japan ("War News by Satellite," 1991, p. 23).

Audio feeds for live reports are up-linked to the international maritime satellite system (Inmarsat) to link directly into domestic telephone systems. These feeds use transportable "flyaway" earth stations with dishes, generators, or battery-packs that take 15 to 20 minutes to set up for broadcast. The dishes are between 85 and 100 centimeters in diameter ("War News by Satellite," 1991, p. 24).

In April 1991 BBC TV Europe (a subscription service) was replaced by BBC's World Service Television (WSTV), which inherited 700,000 household subscribers, and quickly built its client base to 1.1 million. WSTV could be seen from Northern Africa through Europe almost to Moscow. It is carried on the national domestic television services of Poland, Czechoslovakia, Hungary, Romania, and Yugoslavia (Hickman, 1991, p. 19). In late 1991 WSTV began broadcasting to 38 countries from the Red Sea (in the Middle East) to the Yellow Sea (between the Korean peninsula and the Chinese mainland) via HutchVision's Star TV headquartered in Hong Kong ("BBC Launches Asian News Channel," 1991, p. 58; Tomaru, 1991, p. 18). In January 1992 the Chinese government (PRC) banned hotels in Peking from receiving signals from Star TV. One hotel manager said the authorities may have been concerned about the BBC news programming. Another expected that negotiations between the government, hotel operators, and satellite broadcasters would result in the service being cleared, but that this would probably require new regulations to be drafted (Brown, 1992).

Other broadcasters have also been interested in beginning similar services. NHK planned a 24-hour news service to compete with the BBC and CNN by providing an "Asian counterpoint to Western-dominated broadcasts," but abandoned the project for lack of financial resources (Sanger, 1991, p. C8). In February France, Italy, Spain, and Belgium agreed to provide $4 million to launch Euronews, a satellite news channel to compete with CNN in Europe. The channel would be operated by the EBU ("European Governments to Back Euronews," 1992). The channel was scheduled to begin operations in January 1993. Germany announced, too, in March 1992 that it would begin a German-language magazine format satellite television program. Deutsche Welle would operate the service, using staff it inherited from a television allocation for RIAS TV that had been folded into its operations. Deutsche Welle planned to produce the program in English and Spanish as well, and would broadcast the program three

times each day to Asia, Europe and Africa, and North America (BBC Monitoring Service, 1992e, p. A3, and 1992f, p. A5).

Visnews, jointly operated by Reuters, NBC, and the BBC, applied to the Cuban government in late 1991 for permission to set up a news bureau in Havana. The Cubans, however, delayed responding to the request. If granted it would make Visnews the first Western television network to have a permanent bureau in Cuba (see "Cuba Says Still Considering," 1991).

AP also began satellite delivery of its news and photo services to Latin America in 1991 via the Pan American Satellite, and to Europe in October 1991 via a network operated by British Telecom. AP planned to have 250 down-link sites in Europe by the end of 1993 ("Europe Satellite—AP," 1991).

9.14

Conclusion

The 1990s witnessed an explosion of potential in the international communications system. The "global village" had perhaps never seemed so near. But several trends also continued, particularly one that maintained the discrepancies between information-rich and information-poor countries. Despite the fact that "adequate telecommunication [was] more and more recognized as one of the key infrastructures in economic and social prosperity," developing countries had become ever more cynical about their ability to share equally in an increasingly complex and expensive system (ITU, 1989b;[43] see also Hanson & Narula, 1990, pp. 5–10, chapters 4 and 5).

Some countries almost seemed to plead for the opportunity to claim a place in the international system. As Dr. Pedro Martin Leyes Hernandez, minister of communications of Colombia, put it, all the nations of the earth, whether rich or poor, large or small, developed or underdeveloped, have a place in the present and a space in the future. Let us recognize their rights, whether human, geographical or orbital, without violating the balanced designs of nature and of God who created us. A man with galactic ambitions while countenancing poverty must not bring to extra-terrestrial space the same imbalances, contradictions and imbalances that bedevil mankind. (ITU, 1988)[44]

Despite such pleas the industrialized countries of the world during this period continued to reject the idea that orbital slots for satellites or frequency assignments for new communications services should be reserved for future use (ITU, 1989b).[45] They also continued to employ ever newer technologies and to invest increasingly heavily in plant, equipment, and transmission corridors for international communications services (see Kellaway, 1990; Knight, 1990; McCartney, 1990; "World Public Switching Expenditure," 1990; and "World Transmission Equipment Expenditure," 1990).

Also during this period efforts to develop and integrate a truly international communications system as a nonfragmentary entity faltered. Even while the ideological wall between East and West was beginning to crumble, the economic divide between the Northern and Southern hemispheres grew wider. The simple Intelsat-dominated international satellite network began to fragment; new pressures for privatization within Europe and commercialization across the components of the international system emerged. Even the dominance of the United States in the various softwares used in the system (recorded music, television, film, data, and so on) began to be threatened by corporations based in other countries. The system seemed to have entered an era of constantly shifting reconfigura-

tions. Competition could come from any side; the dynamics of the system speeded up to a point where no single locus of control existed.

This fragmentation and dynamism possibly could have resulted in greater equality in the system. That, however, did not happen. Dynamism was still centered in the historically dominant industrialized countries of Europe, North America, and Japan. Only a few new entrants, such as Hong Kong, South Korea, Taiwan, and Singapore, joined these countries, and Australia and New Zealand, as significant centers of regional or international control.

What, then, would the future hold? If history had a lesson, it was that the centrifugal force of an increasingly complex and dynamic international system would continue to widen the gap between the haves and have-nots. New technologies would continue to expand the possibilities for international communication, but fail to provide a true right to communicate to all the world's citizens. The global metropolis would not devolve into a village.

Notes

1. The West German international wire service, DPA, reported that on March 8, 1989, all jamming of Western radio stations by Eastern Bloc countries had ceased (see BBC Monitoring Service, 1989i).

2. See also "East Europe Looking to U.S. for Help" (1990, p. 34) for a report from a U.S. task force assessing broadcasting and telecommunication needs in Hungary, Czechoslovakia, Romania, and the German Democratic Republic (now part of the reunited Germany). The task force estimated that an investment of between $400 and $800 million was needed to bring telecommunications in Eastern Europe up to developed country levels.

3. Statement by Carlos Aldana, secretary of the Community Party of Cuba's Central Committee, carried on Radio Rebelde, Havana, on April 14, 1989 (BBC Monitoring Service, 1989p).

4. The minister also called U.S. actions "a saddening manifestation of illegality and a violation of international regulations, whereby a strong country exploits its economic and technological power in telecommunications to attack a neighbouring country [which] clearly constitutes an example of the use of force in international relations."

5. Tuch concluded (1990, p. 105), "Thus Worldnet joins other USIA media as an innovative, imaginative, highly effective tool serving the U.S. government's overall public diplomacy effort." This is as much wishful thinking, however, as demonstrable fact.

6. The figure for Poland is not directly comparable to those for Western countries listed. Poland pays in soft currencies, such as the Polish zloty, while Western countries pay in hard currencies (dollars, pounds sterling, francs, Deutschmarks, etc.). The Soviets provide more books per unit of hard currencies than soft, so the Polish figure here is inflated.

7. Statistics provided by the United States Department of Commerce, U.S.S.R. Desk, 1989.

8. Unfortunately the two countries do not break down their book products in the same way, and comparable figures are therefore not available. These statistics are provided by the United States Information Agency, Washington, DC, August 16, 1989.

9. The Soviet news program "Vremya" also carried the Brokaw-Gorbachev interview, but it was delayed until December 1, and lasted 57 minutes rather than 60. Several additions and deletions were made to the script on this broadcast to the Soviet people, however. Gorbachev's positive remarks concerning relations between the two countries, for instance, was changed to "relations between our peoples," and several passages were reworded

("Moscow TV Comparison of Gorbachev Interview," 1987, p. 12). Also in the Moscow rebroadcast, references to his wife Raisa, with whom Gorbachev had said he discussed "everything," were cut (see Anderson, 1987; and Grenier, 1987).

10. Leonid Petrovich Kravchenko, general director of TASS, said in an interview that "information is our main product. It affects millions of people in our country and billions of people in the world. The quality of information and the problems with it should be discussed publicly and openly. Moreover, so to speak, Tass is the eyes and ears of the country. Tass is also the official mouthpiece" (BBC Monitoring Service, 1989q).

11. Steve Salerno claimed in 1987 (p. 28) that VOA, RFE, and RL shared a mission: "to fill the gaps and to objectively clarify the distortions put out by Soviet state-controlled news services" (see also Goshko, 1985).

12. Green claims (1988) that "all Washington-generated products of USIA except books must faithfully reflect foreign policy." Stanton Burnett (1989) former counsellor of the agency at USIA, denies flatly that any such faithful reflection is required, and that books escape policy considerations.

13. The Soviets did call for increased competition (carrying each other's programming on domestic outlets to compete with existing content) between the two countries in information, culture, and ideas at the Reykjavik summit. Gorbachev accused the United States of becoming a "closed society" (see Carnes, 1986; and "Excerpts from Gorbachev Speech," 1986).

14. Totals prior to 1992 for the Soviet Union include Radio Moscow, Radio Peace and Progress, and regional stations (such as Radio Kiev). Following the break-up of the Soviet Union, the various republics took over transmitting facilities in their territory, leaving Radio Moscow to lease them as necessary. The Supreme Soviet of the Russian Federation passed a resolution on January 20, 1992, to

transfer Radio Moscow to the All-Russian Teleradio Broadcasting Company and to rename the service *Golos Rossii,* or the Voice of Russia, effective on March 29, 1992 (BBC Monitoring Service, 1992g, p. A8).

15. In 1988, when VOA announced the termination of its Thai language service, a Bangkok newspaper criticized the decision, saying, "When a national radio broadcasts programmes in other languages, this means that the country attributes importance and value to its relations with those countries, on a bilateral basis as well as within the framework of international relations." VOA's decision had apparently been taken as an affront to Thailand's importance (BBC Monitoring Service, 1988g).

16. Sterling and Kittross (1990) report that Brinkley moved to Del Rio, Texas, to continue his operation from Mexico, and that he was forced off the air in a frequency reallocation in 1940, when the United States, Mexico, Canada, and Cuba adopted the North American Radio Broadcasting Allocation (see also Fowler & Crawford, 1987).

17. The Dutch system gave the Netherlands Broadcasting Company (NOS) the monopoly over transmission, but provided a vehicle for groups, such as churches, labor unions, and other organized constituencies, to qualify for airtime on both radio and television, based on the size of their membership (see Browne, 1989, chapter 3).

18. A brief interpretation of the impact of the pirates on British radio can be found in Tunstall (1983, pp. 45–48).

19. What is "relatively inexpensive" varies from region to region. Electronic technologies are less expensive in the United States, for instance, than just about any place in the world, and U.S. residents have more disposable income to purchase these technologies than do people in the vast majority of countries.

20. Boyd, Straubhaar, and Lent (1989, pp. 16–17) report that prices for videocassette recorders in 1984 varied from $350 in Kuwait

to over $2,000 in Cameroon, Egypt, Jamaica, Jordan, the Sudan, and Tanzania.

21. The major impact of VCRs in developing countries has been on their broadcasters: Boyd, Straubhaar, and Lent report (1989, p. 22) that their audiences have been "decimated."

22. Developing countries still object to the control of the international communications system. At an ITU conference in 1988 the delegate from the Islamic Republic of Iran said, for instance, "We are of the belief that this Conference cannot expect Member States to place their telecommunication sectors, and with them, their economic, commercial and industrial future, in the hands of telecommunication corporations with the sole assumption that competition among them shall guarantee their national interest, and that such action shall in the long run meet the needs of the international telecommunication community as a whole" (ITU, 1989a). Michael Egbon (1989, p. 50) of Nigeria argued in a similar vein: "No matter how alluring the benefits to be derived from the new technologies of communication may be, this is not enough. Unless Africans have the capability to be an active recipient and have ability to participate meaningfully on an equal basis, the African nations are simply doomed to an era of electronic imperialism."

23. News flow in many developing countries is highly restricted. Many westerners therefore argue that allowing them to control news flow across their borders would subject news to such questionable journalistic standards, or to such volatile political and/or economic forces, that the result would be less information, or at the least less reliable information, about these countries than is currently available. As one diplomat put it to me, "The only thing worse than AFP's coverage of Zaire is Zaire's coverage of Zaire."

24. Much of the data available on pirated materials is unfortunately dated. Global studies of this phenomenon are conducted infrequently,

leaving only aggregate estimates available for the periods between them.

25. Cassettes would be distributed both to individual households and to "video parlors," which have sprung up by the thousands in India and which show tapes, often to fewer than 10 persons at a time.

26. Information provided by ADAPSO, the Association of Data Processing Service Organizations, based on a press release of Future Computing Incorporated, January 17, 1985.

27. Gorlin provided (1987) the annual $500 million figure; Kenneth W. Dam of IBM provided the $800 million figure in testimony (United States Congress, 1988, p. 255); Vico E. Henriques, president of the Computer and Business Manufacturers Association, claimed the $128 million figure in testimony before the same committee (United States Congress, 1987, p. 245); the $137 million figure came from a written response to questions provided by C. William Verity, U.S. secretary of commerce (United States Congress, 1988, p. 122).

28. Countries mentioned as failing to protect intellectual property rights include Argentina, Brazil, Chile, Costa Rica, Egypt, India, Mexico, Pakistan, the Philippines, Portugal, Sri Lanka, Thailand, Turkey, Uruguay, Venezuela, and Yugoslavia—nearly all in the developing world. See the testimony of Donald J. Quigg (United States Congress, 1987, p. 117), the statement of Donald C. Curran (United States Congress, 1987, p. 52), and the submission of the Coalition to Preserve the American Copyright Tradition, based on a report of the Office of Technology Assessment in 1986 (United States Congress, 1988, p. 443).

29. Pichter also writes (1987, pp. 34–35) that broadcast satellite services (BSS) trigger copyright protection because the decisive act is the emission of a signal, not its reception.

30. The MPT also suggested (1988, p. 30) that the rapidly increasing level of telephone traffic between Japan and Europe, the Americas, and Asia paralleled, "although not in exact proportion, the increases in Japan's overseas investment by region."

31. The voice channels referred to here are duplex, or simultaneous 2-way, circuits.

32. A further fiber optic link between Japan and China is planned for completion in 1993. It will be capable of handling 35,000 calls simultaneously, and will connect, via the transpacific cable, China with North America (see Quimpo, 1990).

33. Western European countries included were Belgium, West Germany, Denmark, Finland, Greece, the United Kingdom, Iceland, Italy, Switzerland, and Spain; Latin American countries included Argentina, Brazil, Colombia, Mexico, Paraguay, Peru, Uruguay, and Venezuela.

34. The number of privately owned IBS earth stations grew from 6 in 1985 to 85 by 1987 and an expected 128 by 1988 (see Stephens, 1987, p. 15). These operations often use very-small-aperture terminals (VSATs) that provide two-way data applications using packet switching networks. "Packet switching is a data transmission process utilizing addressed packets [or bursts], whereby a channel is occupied only for the duration of the transmission of the packet" (Stratigos, 1990, p. 22). Intelsat began to provide VSAT service through Intelnet in 1988. It has also provided the Intelsat Business Service (IBS) since 1983, using small- and medium-sized earth stations, to provide an integrated business communication system including voice, data, telex, facsimile, and videoconferencing (see Intelsat, 1988–89, p. 21).

35. Point-to-multipoint distribution is the configuration of broadcasting, while multipoint-to-multipoint distribution is used for such activities as telex, facsimile, data, and wire service distribution.

36. Document 47-E. 10 April 1989. Report of the Administrative Council of the Plenipotentiary Conference.

37. Document 119-E. 1 June 1989. Minutes of the Opening Ceremony, 23 May 1989, page 4.

38. Only 12 million of Europe's 120 million homes were passed by cable systems in 1987.

39. The Murdoch-Disney alliance fell apart in 1989 before the channel was launched.

40. Rupert Murdoch, speaking at the Edinburgh TV Festival in 1989, "put . . . much effort into denigrating the public service broadcasting values that, he said, have corrupted British television for 50 years" (quoted in Henry, 1989).

41. Good explorations of the debates surrounding DBS can be found in Luther, (1988) and Powell (1985; see also American Society of International Law, 1975; *Direct Broadcasting by Satellite,* 1981; *Direct Broadcast Satellite Communications,* 1980; and Gibbons, 1985, pp. 131–134).

42. Several U.S. companies also want access to the European market via transatlantic television services. In the mid-1980s Orion Satellite Corporation, International Satellite Inc. (ISI), Cygnus Satellite Corporation, and RCA Americom all applied to the FCC for permission to launch and operate satellites to provide business and video entertainment across the Atlantic (see Tydeman & Kelm, 1986, pp. 96, 97).

43. Document 47-E. 10 April 1989. Report of the Administrative Council to the Plenipotentiary Conference, page 3.

44. Document 112-E. Minutes of the First Plenary Meeting, 20 August 1988. Annex 3. Statement of the Minister of Communications of Colombia, Dr. Pedro Martin Leyes Hernandez, p. 13. Hernandez also suggested (p. 11) that the "first come, first served" approach that traditionally governed ITU frequency and orbital slot assignments provided "equality of rights but inequality in practice."

45. Document 523-E. Declarations and Reservations made at the end of The Plenipotentiary Conference of the International Telecommunication Union, Nice, 30 June 1989, page 110.

10

THE FUTURE OF THE INTERNATIONAL COMMUNICATION SYSTEM

10.1

Introduction

This book has focused on the system of international communication. It has introduced the technologies that constitute the system, or systems, and that provide the channels for international communication. It has also examined the history of the development of the system, including several of the principal disputes in which nations struggled to shape the system to their own political, economic, cultural, and social ends.

The current system of international communication resulted from several historical conditions: (1) the technology and scientific knowledge available at a given time, (2) the political dynamics of relations between nations, (3) the economic conditions of the world's countries, (4) the ideological commitments of states, and (5) the culture and social relations of the world's constituent peoples. There was no inevitability about this evolution: It could have taken many different turns.

The result of the struggle between nations, and the cooperation they often achieved for common ends, was a dynamic system characterized by complex interrelationships among technologies, politics and ideologies, and economics. This historical complexity should inform the forecasts made about the future of the system. These forecasts should acknowledge that what is known today about technology could change tomorrow, that ideological commitments could suddenly turn on their head, that the relations between peoples may suddenly improve or worsen. Certainly such changes have occurred before, and are even now shaping the future. This system is still evolving, perhaps toward an intelligent one that itself controls the flow of communication through application of computer intelligence rather than the individual commitments of sovereign states.

Whatever changes occur, whether incremental or abrupt, they will affect the configuration of the world communications system, and its constituent elements in the United States. The fortunes of U.S. television program producers and filmmakers depend partly on the evolving role and control of broadcasting in other countries, the extent of their tolerance for piracy, and the continuing spread of consumer technologies. The ability of U.S. journalists to function without interference depends on the value other peoples and their governments place on the role of the press or the idea of a free flow of information. The ability of the U.S. government to use international broadcasting as a tool of public diplomacy depends on the availability of frequencies, the atmospheric conditions, the decisions of adversaries about jamming, and the force of world opinion manifesting itself in international meetings to discuss communication issues. U.S.-based communication activity does not exist in a vacuum: It is dependent on the events, commitments, and economics of its global environment. Neither do the activities of other countries using the international system occur in a vacuum: They, too, must respond to the changing contours of the international system, and the changing information context of the world's peoples.

10.2

Communication: A Basic Human Right?

The significance of communication, and of international communication more specifically, has increased as the system has be-

come more complex and more crucial to the practice of politics and economics. "Information," Paul Quile, minister for posts, telecommunications and space of the French Republic, said (ITU, 1989b), "has now become the third production factor after work and capital. . . . The telecommunication networks now constitute the veritable nervous system of a modern economy, which means that they are of vital importance to the development of trade and goods."[1] Schramm explained in 1980 (Vol. 3, pp. 297–298) that the world had entered the "Age of Information." He suggested that "information may truly bulk larger in social control and social change than will armies or explosives. We have long said that knowledge is power, but now we are going to experience it in its full complexity and difficulty."

Communication is significant, information is power, control is crucial. The difficulties that the people of the world have faced historically, then, in actually achieving equal access to the means of communication (for both transmission and reception), or to information itself, will continue. Ironically, even as the means of both communication and information creation, distribution, and reception have multiplied, the efforts to centralize control over technology and content have likewise intensified. Some decentralization has occurred, but as Innis predicted, this has been on the fringes of society, where control is weakest. The metropolis has grown, in other words, with power concentrated in its center (the industrialized countries of the Northern Hemisphere), even as the means of communication have increased.

The mythic expectations of communication, however, remain. As Pekka Tarjanne, the latest secretary-general of the ITU, suggested (quoted in "Guiding ITU in a Brave New Telecommunications World," 1989), "it is my firm conviction that a well-developed telecommunications network around the world is the best hope for world peace." Intelsat continues to quantify its successes in helping "accommodate global, time-sensitive demand involving television, two-way digital data, telephone, facsimile and telex communications"; "global television" continues to provide "choice" for viewers (Marshall, 1989, p. 263; Meyers, 1990, p. 18). Often major world events claim potential audiences of 1 billion or more. The "global village" then seems a realistic possibility.

Yet the conflicts remain. There are conflicts, for instance, between the communication ideology of the West and that of developing countries. As Egbon (1989, p. 50) put it, "There are contradictions which will inevitably result in a confrontation between the western dominant model of *communication development,* usually characterized by global transnational control, as opposed to *development communication* of the developing nations." What is needed, he says, is a reorientation of the international system to "generate participation and . . . reinforce the cultural identity of all the participating groups, countries and regions." Tarjanne, despite his optimism, also recognizes that "policymakers are now required to ensure that the enhanced power of the media is used wisely and well" (quoted in "ITU-COM Explores Problems," 1989).

The extent to which communication can be affirmed as a basic human right will likely continue to depend on the particular society. Reportedly, for instance, prior to its political break-up, the openness of Soviet society *(glasnost)* had been trimmed in response to the ethnic unrest in various areas of the Soviet Union.[2] During the attempted coup in the Soviet Union in August 1991, the hard-liners who organized it shut down all but one television channel, and all the independent newspapers that had sprung up since the advent of *glasnost* (Remnick, 1991, p. A29). Even after the demise of the Soviet Union, the Russian government threatened two newspapers with closure for violating the press law. As Vitaly Tretiakov, editor of *Nezavisimaya Gazeta,* put it, "The democrats very quickly start to manifest the same intolerance of any kind of criticism as their predecessors the Communists did. The democrats loved us when we criticized the Communists, but they can't stand it when we go after them" (quoted in Schneider, 1991, p. 3; see also Sedykh, 1992, p. 19). During the Persian Gulf crisis Arab state complaints about the broadcasts of both the BBC and VOA led to a number of independent assessments of their newscasts. Arab coalition members had claimed that the BBC and VOA stories were not neutral, but "pro-Iraqi." These complaints said as much about the differing news values of Arabic and Western societies as they did about the broadcasts themselves. I was involved in one of these independent studies, and I saw little evidence to indicate that the complaints were valid (see Fortner, 1991). Even the news values in VOA, however, were questioned, and defended, within the pages of U.S. newspapers. The dispute, however, reflected the continuing confusion about the role of VOA in international communication as much as its news judgments (see Greenberger, 1991; "Speaking for America," 1991; "VOA 'Does' Journalism," 1991; and "Voice of America Defends Role in Gulf War," 1991).

The international communications system per se will not provide equality of access to the peoples of the world, however great its capacity, complexity, or completeness. Technological possibility alone will not inaugurate a global village. There are too many disparities in economic and political power, and in ideology, and too much desire to control for the system to bring about this condition merely because the technological potential exists for it to happen. One example of this is included in an International Institute of Communications report in January 1992: "Far from turning into cultural colonies of America, most places are interested only in themselves." The news coverage aired in the 55 countries studied was heavily biased toward events in their own areas of the world. "Since broadcasters are state-controlled in most places, television news often reflects less what viewers want to watch than what governments think they should" (Each Man an Island," 1992, pp. 92, 94). By this account the world remains a disparate group of villages, each primarily concerned about its own well-being. Despite the development of global news distribution systems, fiber optic cables, high-speed digital communication systems, and satellites, the boundaries that people and governments erect to protect their own views of the world remain largely intact.

Individual countries, too, will continue to see communication and information flow as potential threats. No government is immune to the tendency to control information; the United Kingdom, for instance, has an Official Secrets Act (see Evans, 1990, pp. 192–195). Many countries license journalists, own most or all the means of communication, censor the press, or simply choose not to expand the domestic networks needed to connect to the outside world. Germany has estimated, for instance, that it needs six times the current number of telephone lines between "east" and "west," although the government has increased the

number of lines from 8,000 to 30,000 since reunification (Veale, 1991). Prior to reunification East German citizens waited up to 30 years for telephone service once they requested it; the German government has promised to meet all current demand for telephones by 1998. In the United States the General Accounting Office estimated that, between October 1, 1989, and March 31, 1990, federal agencies conducted screenings of over 10,500 articles, speeches, and miscellaneous writings by federal employees to determine their "suitability" for release. "The GAO found that during the six-month period studied, 143,531 federal employees and 98,093 contractor employees signed nondisclosure agreements" (Flesher, 1991). The United States Constitution, of course, guarantees "freedom of speech and of the press."

10.3

International Communication and Public Diplomacy

One of the principal uses of international communication since 1946 has been to conduct public diplomacy. Public diplomacy aims to affect the policies of other nations by appeals to its citizens through means of public communication. Traditional diplomacy, taking place between official representatives of governments, is either supplemented or bypassed by public diplomacy, which seeks to create or alter perceptions of a country's actions, or to affect public opinion about that country's political or economic system, its ideology, or the lives of its citizens, within the population of another country (see Fisher, 1987, on U.S. international relations; Mowlana, 1986, on international relations; and United States

Advisory Commission on Public Diplomacy, 1986b, on the Soviet use of U.S. media for public diplomacy).

Techniques of Public Diplomacy

Public diplomacy uses a variety of techniques: publication of books, distribution of films or television programs, tours by performing arts ensembles or theatrical companies, art exhibitions, participation in trade fairs, establishment of student exchange programs, and lecture tours by members of a country's intellectual, political, or academic establishment. One form of public diplomacy is, of course, propaganda (which fact may suggest that public diplomacy began as early as the 1920s).

Of principal concern here is the use of two other means of conducting public diplomacy. The most obvious one is the use of international radio or television broadcasting: It is here where nations have contended across borders, where ideologies have clashed, where propaganda is practiced. The second is the staging of what Daniel Boorstin called "pseudo-events" to attract press attention and coverage. These events include press conferences, summits, meetings between foreign or economic ministers, and meetings that occur within international organizations, such as the United Nations, the ITU, the World Bank, or the International Monetary Fund (IMF).

Radio and television broadcasting provide a means to reach audiences without depending on intermediaries. International radio broadcasting allows countries to program directly to mass audiences. Television, at least at present, is largely a means to reach more elite audiences, such as journalists or government officials. USIA's World-

Net, for instance, allows reporters in other countries to participate in live press conferences with U.S. government officials. World-Net uses a one-way video link from the United States, and an interactive (two-way) audio link via satellite. Gradually, international television will be used as radio traditionally has been. Rebroadcast of satellite-delivered programs produced in one country by domestic stations in another has already begun, pioneered by the French. Direct broadcast satellites (DBS) will increasingly supplement them with services designed for pickup in other countries (see Rogers, 1988).[3]

Another technique for reaching foreign audiences is to schedule press conferences, summit meetings, state visits, or other official functions that will attract media attention, and then attempt to influence the media's perception of the event such that the coverage achieved is favorable. During summit meetings between the United States and the Soviet Union, for instance, the principals negotiated in advance about the scheduling of events, operation of press pools, and nature of public statements to be made to the press. The host country also set up a media center, accredited journalists and news organizations wishing to cover the event, provided technical support (telephones, photocopiers, fax and telex machines, audio and video production facilities, satellite up-links, etc.) and personnel support (guides and escorts, typing pools, etc.), and provided spaces for press conferences, press release distribution, and interviews.

Summits provide opportunities for maximum exposure of the policies of the participating countries. The policies of countries can also be examined side by side, as they share the same media spotlight. As the

United States Advisory Commission on Public Diplomacy put it (1989, p. 31), "World opinion is the dominating characteristic of summit diplomacy. Indeed, it is the public attention given to summit meetings, particularly those involving the superpowers, that makes them unique and distinguishes them from traditional forms of public dialogue. How summits are perceived fundamentally shapes their outcomes with important consequences for the policies at stake."

USIA accredited over 1,700 journalists for the Reagan-Gorbachev Washington summit of December 1987, which provided ample opportunity for worldwide press coverage. The summit merited over 250 news stories on VOA, Radio Moscow, and major European international broadcasters (BBC, Deutsche Welle, and Radio Netherlands) in a 14-day period bracketing the summit, with over 700 minutes of airtime on these services' major daily news programs devoted to the summit (out of approximately 1,700 total available minutes). The United States' National Security Council, the State and Defense Departments, and USIA prepared for the summit (and anticipated the press coverage) by outlining a set of themes that were to guide all U.S. spokespersons in their remarks. Policymakers hoped that the media would pick up these themes as they reported the substance from different angles. The themes emphasized, besides the INF (intermediate nuclear forces) treaty's significance to reduction of world tensions, the importance of human rights, Soviet involvement in regional conflicts, and the discrepancy in access to information afforded to citizens of the Soviet and Western blocs. The effort was not altogether successful, however, at least according to the reports of the international radio broadcasters examined (see Fortner, 1988a).

Other means of reaching the press with information are also employed as tools of public diplomacy. USIA, for instance, uses data transmission and teletype facilities to deliver five regional editions of its "Wireless File" to 125 foreign posts for distribution to journalists and news organizations. In 1987 it also initiated Express File, which goes directly to news organizations in Western Europe, Turkey, and Israel without passing through USIA foreign posts, and is carried on wire service facilities leased from UPI and the International Foreign Correspondents Association. The next step in distribution will be delivery of such material via subcarriers on Worldnet's satellite channels, which already carry 500 interactive programs each year.

Concerns About Public Diplomacy

Two principal concerns affect public diplomacy efforts. The first is the problem of propaganda and interference in a country's internal affairs. Various international resolutions condemn propaganda, particularly that designed or likely to incite violence. Also, any communication that interferes with the internal affairs of another state is "illegal" under international law. Public diplomacy, by definition, aims to influence the public opinion in another country (see Cohen, 1986). Clearly, however, various states are likely to judge differently whether particular information or communication strategies constitute interference or propaganda. Antagonisms between states will almost inevitably lead to charges that public diplomacy efforts constitute interference or propaganda.

To return to one example of this difficulty, the turmoil in the People's Republic of China in mid-1989 was a media event. VOA, as well as other international broadcasters, reported on the disturbances and the difficulty of the government in containing the spreading student "prodemocracy" movement. There were reports that the students listened to VOA to determine how people in different areas of China, particularly in other major cities, were responding to their demands. In response to VOA's reporting, on May 22, 1989, China began jamming several daily broadcasts, reinitiating a policy abandoned in 1978. The government apparently saw the VOA broadcasts as interfering in its affairs, and thus took steps to limit further damage. Later it saw fit to justify its actions with accusations. A "Beijing Ribao" commentary on June 12, 1989, on VOA reporting about the student uprising in China, for instance (BBC Monitoring Service, 1989r), accused the service of using "provocative, demagogic, offensive, malicious language" and said that its "ability to fabricate lies and spread rumours to confuse people's minds alone has really reached the peak of perfection and [to] an alarming degree." China also expelled journalists for reporting about unrest, and used ABC backfeeds of interviews with Chinese dissidents to identify them and bring them to trial in the aftermath of the Tianenmen Square crackdown (see "China Expels Reporters," 1989; "China: The Weeks of Living Dangerously," 1989; "China vs. Press," 1989; Hoagland, 1989; "Interview Aftermath," 1989; and Randolph, 1989a).

The tension between the United States and China about VOA broadcasts has continued. In late 1991 a new book was released in China accusing the U.S. government of waging "'psychological warfare' against socialist countries and instigating political turmoil in China" ("China-VOA," 1991). The U.S. government, according to the *Beijing Daily,* in recommending the

book, uses the VOA as a "war wagon to topple a city wall. . . . The article repeated accusations that VOA tried to 'instigate and even fan the flames and mastermind' the 1989 pro-democracy demonstrations in Beijing that led to the government's violent crackdown at Tiananmen Square. 'The many examples in the book make readers clear that a foreign radio station airs all inciting propaganda toward a country that has diplomatic relations with its country, which is nothing but interference in a country's internal affairs,' the article said" ("New China Book: VOA Waging War on Socialism").

The second problem for public diplomacy is the shifting tide of relations beween the superpowers (and later between the United States and the Commonwealth of Independent States (CIS). Mikhail Gorbachev's *glasnost* initiatives complicated the strategies of the West in dealing with the Soviet Union. The Soviet Union stopped jamming Western broadcasters, and made new proposals on arms reductions that influenced European public opinion to be more positive toward it. The historical rift between the Soviet Union and China was apparently on its way to being healed by Gorbachev's visit to Beijing in May, 1989. The content of Radio Moscow obviously reflected the changes. "Moscow Mailbag," for instance, a program in which listener's questions about the Soviet Union were answered on the air, became more self-reflective, made new admissions of past mistakes, and openly discussed the disagreements among various parts of the Soviet political establishment and the citizenry. The old, staid, colorless, and clearly ideological service became more lively (see Kagan, 1989). At the same time, however, some observers advised caution, perhaps thinking that the Soviet initiatives themselves were part of a "disinformation" campaign, designed to lull the West into complacency about the Soviet Union's true designs (see Ebon, 1987, pp. 1–106; Pincher, 1985; and Rose, 1988).

Such changes required, in turn, alterations to the strategies of Western public diplomacy. Western radio services could not afford to be dealing with the "old thinking" when "new thinking" was fundamentally altering the approach of the Soviet Union to communication activity, both foreign and domestic. New information strategies of the Soviets in dealing with their own population, and in presenting themselves to the world, required that Western services reassess their information strategies not only toward the Soviet audience but toward other audiences who would hear both Soviet and Western portrayals of events.

In 1981 Kenneth L. Adelman, who had been a member of Ronald Reagan's foreign affairs transition team, argued (1981, p. 913) that an "evolving global communications network" had made "public diplomacy a more powerful instrument." He said that "the American mood is one of pride, not shame. The national desire is to exalt America's virtues, not to veil them. Gone is the self-deprecating temper of the 1960s and 1970s, when many Americans, particularly the intellectual establishment, shrunk from the advocacy of what they deemed a flawed, even sick society." In its place, he said, was a temper that "may appear a little chauvinistic, even jingoistic." By the end of the decade, however, Kim Elliott, a VOA researcher, was arguing that there were "too many voices of America": U.S. international broadcasting services, he said, should be consolidated (Elliott, 1989/90, 1991). Ted Koppel, too, reported ("The Democratization of Television News," 1989) that "the U.S., that fountainhead of public relations and advertising savvy, of marketing skill and production talent, is failing to use those abilities in telling its story abroad. Deputy

Secretary of State Lawrence Eagleburger acknowledged in an interview with Koppel that 'public relations has not yet become an integral part of the [U.S.] foreign policy establishment.'"

The role and practice of public diplomacy will change as newer technologies provide different capabilities for information distribution and as the political climate between adversary states alters. Change will bring increasing complexity to the system of international communication as applied in the diplomatic context. If the current trends continue, which seem to suggest that tendencies toward military confrontation may subside and that the differences between states will be argued in international forums, the role of the international communications system will become increasingly significant. As nations discover that by cooperating in the maintenance and extension of the international communications system, they further their own political, economic, and cultural commitments, the speed of its development may increase (one commentary on the future of public diplomacy may be seen in Webster, 1990, pp. 219–227).

10.4

The Future of Communications Technology

Several technological changes are likely to affect the practice of international communication over the next two to three decades. Personal technologies—the audiocassette player, compact disc player, videocassette recorder, satellite dish, personal computer, and fax machine—are likely to continue their slow penetration of the global population, particularly in developing countries where most of the world's people live. Fiber optic cables will also continue gradually to replace the world's complex network of submarine coaxial cables. Also, they will increasingly compete with satellites as the means to carry an expanding number of communications services, including broadband services such as television and data. New versions of old technologies, such as high-definition television, will be introduced, and the question of putting old services, such as international shortwave broadcasting, on newer technologies (satellites) will continue to be addressed.

Radio Technology

The worldwide annual production of radio sets is not expected to grow beyond its current level of 150 million units. What will happen, however, is that manufacturers will struggle to hold their current market share, or to improve on it, rather than take advantage of an increasing market for their products. This will mean an increase in competition within this stable market, the likely addition of more features ("bells and whistles") to radio sets, and a decline in production of inexpensive radio-only sets.

The trend toward incorporation of cassette tape players within radio receiving units has several implications. First, since cassette players consume more energy than do radio receivers, they shorten battery life, and in areas of the world where batteries are the only source of energy for such devices, operating them is a financial burden that may result in decreased use. Also, the purchase of such units has already meant that the potential audiences for international broadcasting have diminished, since the radio reception portion of the sets cannot be used while people use the tape mechanisms for playback purposes. The principal market for radio/cassette players is the young, who will remain a significant portion of the world's population, partic-

ularly in developing countries. The popularity of Western music on inexpensive cassettes also will serve as an ongoing barrier to the further development of audiences for international shortwave services, unless broadcasters develop programming strategies that appeal to this population.

Second, the higher cost of more elaborate radio/cassette players and digital display receivers will slow their penetration in areas of the world where demand for personal technologies is elastic, that is, price-driven. This may result in decreased household penetration levels. Predictions are that this will occur in some parts of the developing world (notably Africa) during the 1990s (see Fortner & Durham, 1986, p. 155). The era of "cheap" transistor radios is ending, not because they cannot continue to be made, but because demand for them is beginning to drop, and the principal manufacturing companies are not so interested in committing production capacity to making them. Some countries, such as India and certain sub-Saharan African nations, will continue to manufacture inexpensive radios for domestic consumption. The dominant trend, however, will be to ever more sophisticated and expensive units.

Third, the trend in many regions of the world, including Pacific Rim countries, Western Europe, and parts of Africa, is to move domestic services to VHF (FM) radio. This trend is part of a larger movement toward increased fidelity, occasioned by the audiocassette and compact disc, and suggests that low-fidelity shortwave broadcasting will have to provide extraordinarily high-quality programming to continue to draw the large audiences that it has attracted in the past. Delivery of near-compact-disc-quality audio signals from satellites is already a possibility. The frequencies under discussion for this service, however, are not within the tuning range of existing radio receivers. So the movement to higher fidelity is not likely to involve satellites at least until after the turn of the century.

The other problem created for shortwave broadcasters by the high-fidelity trend is that countries sometimes import receivers with only the frequencies employed by domestic broadcasters included. If they do not use shortwave for domestic broadcasting, they may not import shortwave-capable receivers. In South Africa, for instance, the domestic radio service designed for blacks is all on VHF. This purposely provides an economic disincentive to purchase radio sets with amplitude-modulated (AM) shortwave frequency bands. This strategy slowed the penetration of shortwave into black townships of South Africa, and although a majority of sets there may now have these bands, they are still underused because the populations are unfamiliar with how to use them. In South Korea import of shortwave receivers is illegal, while in some areas certain portions of the shortwave bands must be made "untunable" by manufacturers of imported sets, largely to protect military frequencies.

Related to this is the push of UNESCO toward local radio service and use of indigenous technological capability to produce low-power VHF (FM) radio services in developing countries. UNESCO's effort to foster community radio, and its strategy of providing solar-powered click-stop radios with only one or two tunable frequencies, should the process proceed beyond the experimental stage, will also provide disincentives to people to acquire shortwave radios.

Yet another technological problem for shortwave is the introduction of sets with programmable memories, which allow people to avoid the "band scanning" that often led them to listen to a service not heard before. This means that there will be less oc-

casional listening to international services, and fewer "accidental" listeners who just happen onto these services. This may result in smaller, but more committed, listeners for international shortwave.

The most recent developments in radio are proposals to begin direct audio broadcasting from satellites. Although questions about applications of DBS for audio have been around for some time (this question was the focus of work I did for VOA in 1985–86, and of the National Academy of Sciences and Engineering panel I joined in 1987), the developments of 1990 and 1991 have had a distinctly different focus. Two specific proposals have emerged suggesting that DBS-audio services be employed to increase the communication flow among developing countries. Afrispace planned broadcasts in the 1.5- to 2.5-GHz frequency range, requiring receivers with special chips that it claimed could be sold for about US$50 ("N. Va. Company to Build Satellite," 1990). It was not at all clear, however, in 1992, that the project was truly feasible. Its planned frequencies had already been allocated for terrestrial (land-based) transmissions, and a variety of other radio-based point-to-point services were arguing that such frequencies should be reallocated for their use. No satellite radio receivers were in production, and the requirement that all satellite feeds be up-linked from the United States created potential political difficulties with a variety of countries that might otherwise be interested in the project. Afrispace, a U.S.-based company, did succeed in 1991 in gaining FCC approval for proposed up-links necessary to relay programming to Africa. The Kenya TV network reserved an audio channel aboard the AfriStar 1 satellite, which was to be launched in late 1993 or early 1994. Afrispace also contracted with a U.S. engineering firm to design a US$100 hand-held radio, called the "Starman," to receive the signals from AfriStar 1, but the price per unit had increased to US$100 (see "Swahili by Satellite," 1991, p. 64). The second proposal, emerging from Radiosat International, another U.S.-based company, was for an international common carrier DBS-sound system that would allow national radio systems to replace their terrestrial transmitters with leased satellite transponders to reach directly to portable and automobile radios (Radiosat International, 1991). At the end of 1991, however, this proposal was still on the drawing board.

The technological trends, then, in radio are the movement toward greater fidelity, user-controlled content (cassettes as opposed to radio services), and programmable and solar-powered limited-frequency sets. By the middle of the 1990s, scanning radios will be available that can search for coded signals embedded in services, allowing for further reductions in band scanning. Also, by then, the digital-processing radio receivers developed in Europe for the German and French digital audio services will be more widely available, allowing for radio services to move from analog to digital broadcasting (discussions of digital broadcasting can be found in Le Floch, Halbert-Lasalle, & Castelain, 1989). By the end of the century single/double-sideband switchable receivers (already available) will begin to be more widely available, although mainly in developed countries, and shortwave broadcasters may be able to begin using single-sideband broadcasting. At first, however, such efforts will have to duplicate the signals of double-sideband transmissions, which will mean that expectations for reductions in the congestion (and interference) experienced on the shortwave bands will not be immediately apparent. Research I have completed for the BBC indicates that the number of radio receivers

capable of picking up single-sideband transmissions will rise very slowly, particularly in developing countries; it will be 20 or more years before those audiences could conceivably be large enough to compete with those available from terrestrial shortwave transmitters (see Fortner, 1991c).

In the WARC meeting held in Torremolinos, Spain, in 1992, the question of single-sideband shortwave broadcasting was a major issue. Some broadcasting administrations were in favor of a switch from double- to single-sideband to open up frequencies for new services, while others, including most developing countries, were opposed. The BBC was opposed for fear that such a change would mean a drastic reduction in their worldwide audience, while developing countries objected because of the additional costs it would impose of them to alter their transmitters. Despite resolutions proposed by some broadcasting administrations, the consensus among engineers was that SSB was not a reasonable alternative to the current double-sideband modulation. BBC and VOA research suggested that a more feasible alternative was the application of digital audio broadcasting (DAB) techniques to shortwave, and the attempt to compress the digital signals into the same bandwidth as SSB would occupy. Actual application, however, would still not occur until after the turn of the century (Wheatley, 1992, p. 1).

Television Technology

The economic stakes for nations and manufacturing companies in television technology are much higher than for radio. Television sets will have a higher value-added component, and can be coupled with other image technologies (such as VCRs and computers) to perform a variety of tasks besides delivering entertainment and news programming.

Also, the cost of setting up, maintaining, and operating a television production and transmission system is much higher than a comparable radio one, so countries tend to be more concerned about video's technological future.

Two major developments will eventually have an impact on television: (1) digital television with signals carried using time division multiplex bursts (packet switching) and (2) high-definition television (HDTV). These developments are not mutually exclusive; either one or both could occur within the next decade. Both are used in domestic systems, but their applications in the international sphere have been slower.

Digital Television

This technology was designed to allow for the most efficient use of available frequencies for television services and to allow single video channels to be enhanced with multiple language sound channels and data communications capability. Time division multiplexing also allowed for the use of digital signals, thus enhancing the interface of new production and signal storage devices with transmission systems.

Receiving digital television signals requires a microprocessor (computer)–controlled decoder that translates digitized transmitter code into usable code for the audio and video processors. These two processors allow the signals to actually be heard and seen on television sets. The audio processor, for instance, controls the power output amplifiers to transmit the sound (Prentiss, 1985, chapter 5).

High-Definition Television

HDTV is the second possibility for international television communication. It enhances current television standards by providing increased resolution in the television picture (see Schneiderman, 1988). As Wassiczek, Waters, and Wood put it (1990, p. 321), "There is no doubt that HDTV will be the most important medium of the next century. It will have an impact on a wide range of facets of life: broadcasting, computing, medicine, printing, etc."

HDTV also requires wider bandwidths than conventional television, between 1.5 and 2 times that used by NTSC, PAL, or SECAM signals (Nickelson, 1990, p. 304). If a single international standard could be adopted, however, it would simplify international television transmission, which currently depends not only on the three principal standards, but on some 16 variations of these (Nickelson, 1990, p. 303).

The most dramatic improvement from inaugurating HDTV would occur in the Americas and Japan, where the NTSC color standard is prevalent, since it provides the lowest resolution of any color television standard. Various countries, including Japan, the United States, and numerous European nations, are promoting several high-definition television standards. Not only is an anticipated lucrative market at issue, but also the question of compatibility with existing color television sets. The United States is pushing a system that would allow current television sets to receive HDTV signals (showing about half the available picture, equivalent to current picture quality). Europeans, however, see the increased resolution such a system would provide to their own televisions as insufficient to justify the investment in new production, transmission, and reception technologies; they want a higher resolution system (one that would provide 1200+ lines, rather than the 1000+ lines promised based on the NTSC standard). The Japanese have yet another perspective, for they see HDTV as an entirely new system, not one that must be compatible with terrestrial television systems.

The Japanese-developed HDTV system provides 1,125 scanning lines with 30 frames per second (60 Hz), while the European Eureka system provides 1,250 scanning lines with 25 frames per second (50 Hz). Although the Japanese were the first country to begin actual HDTV broadcasting, in November 1991, the high cost of equipment necessary to receive the signals, delivered by satellite, severely restricted the audience available for the programs. HDTV units were selling for $35,000, and high-definition videocassette recorders for $154,000 when broadcasts began (see Thurber, 1991). The Eureka system is also compatible with the MAC packet systems developed by the EBU. Study Group 11 of the CCIR is studying the two systems to propose a single international standard of HDTV ("International HDTV Progress," 1987). Even as this activity progresses, however, U.S. broadcasting interests are promoting other standards more completely compatible with U.S. terrestrial television, and the Japanese have begun talking about a new era of three-dimensional television employing 2,000 scanning lines (see "NBC Unveils New HDTV Standard," 1988; and "Twelve That Would Be HDTV," 1988).

The U.S. Congress and the Commerce and Defense Departments all are interested in the standard eventually adopted. HDTV arguably will enable a more complete interface between communications and information technologies. In addition, it will provide a large export market for new electronics technologies—Nickelson estimates (1990, p. 311) that HDTV will lead to a multibillion dollar market in new equipment. Congress and the Commerce Department thus are concerned about the U.S. trade position, and about how HDTV may revitalize American consumer electronics exports (see Rich-

ards, 1989). And the Defense Department is concerned that loss of HDTV technology to foreign developers and manufacturers will endanger U.S. defenses, which are increasingly dependent on imported electronics technology (see Richards, 1988).

By 1991 the three-way race that had developed, pitting Japan, Europe, and the United States against one another, had taken, like other technological races before, some unusual twists. The Japanese had begun satellite HDTV delivery. The Europeans, who had earlier attempted to standardize incompatible analog-based television delivery (PAL and SECAM) through application of packet-switched satellite and cable delivery, seemed to have reached a compromise position in negotiations sponsored by the European Commission. New services started after 1995 would use D2-MAC as a compulsory interim standard for wide-screen and other satellite programming prior to implementing HDTV. Existing services would continue to use current standards for broadcasting. This might eventually mean even more incompatible standards for European broadcasting, with PAL, SECAM, D2-MAC, and an HDTV standard all used simultaneously until the older systems could be phased out after the turn of the century. Still, this compromise did not entirely satisfy the Germans or French, who have invested heavily in the D2-MAC technology, but who could see its lifetime shortened as a result of its designation as an interim solution (see "All EC Countries but France Support HDTV Strategy," 1991; and Perry, 1991). Meanwhile, AT&T and Zenith received final approval from the FCC to test their all-digital television system that promised to "deliver the same cinema-quality pictures promised by HDTV plus a wide range of other services—at a much lower cost. The two firms said their technology would send interference-free signals to a significantly larger geographic area than is possible through either conventional broadcasts or any proposed HDTV system." The FCC is scheduled to approve a U.S. HDTV standard in 1993. "A successful digital system would most likely sound the death-knell for European HDTV and the more advanced Japanese system, both of which are satellite-delivered and based on a national standard." Digital television could be delivered either by satellite or terrestrial broadcasters, and would be easily converted to compatibility with any national system (Arnst, 1991c).

As with other new communications technologies, the expense of HDTV means that it will be introduced first in Western industrialized countries, and only slowly find its way into the developing world. The large-screen displays, required tuners, processing electronics, and sound and recording system to be employed will all be too expensive to expect rapid adoption in the poorer countries. Nickelson estimates (1990, pp. 311–312) that at least a decade of HDTV broadcasting compatible with existing color receivers will be required before the technology can stand on its own, even in wealthy countries.

Compression Technology

Coupled with these two technologies is a third, the result of the increased bandwidth needed to enhance the signals (as in HDTV) or to carry digital signals: **compression** technology. As with HDTV, however, there are a variety of incompatible compression systems under development, which may delay the introduction of this technology as broadcasting and satellite organizations wait for a common standard to emerge (see "Cablevision Tests Digicable and Digisat," 1991, p. 52). As Jeffrey Sudikoff, chairman of IDB Communications, explains the signif-

icance of this technology, however, "Compression is the single most important thing that's happening right now. It's going to change the economics, and it's potentially going to change the way everything is handled aboard satellites and on the ground" (quoted in "Video Compression," 1991, p. 34). Compression ratios ranging from 3 to 1 to as high as 8 to 1 are under development.

International Telecommunications Technology

Perhaps the most significant questions about international telecommunications technology involve (1) the future of Intelsat and (2) the relative use that countries will make of satellites and fiber optic cables. Satellites and cables, like high-frequency radio waves, are both capable of carrying a variety of communications content: telegraph, telex, voice, facsimile, audio, video, and data. Although these technologies are not necessarily mutually exclusive, nor do they necessarily provide inherently unique services, each has certain advantages, over its competitors. Satellites, for instance, can cover portions of the earth with beams that enable "senders" to deliver a message simultaneously to thousands, or millions, of "receivers." Fiber optic cables provide secrecy difficult to match with a satellite, and offer transmission unaffected by normal electromagnetic interference as well as enormous bandwidth. High-frequency radio is an accessible technology compared to either fiber optics or satellites. It provides most nations with communications capability that they can replace only at great expense (which many countries can ill afford).

Intelsat, which once enjoyed a monopoly on international satellite communication, began to experience competition in 1988 from PanAmSat. This competition was the result of decisions made by the Reagan administration that competition with Intelsat was in the United States' national interest, and by Intelsat's Assembly of Parties (its governing authority) that coordination of other international systems with Intelsat was possible. The assembly's decision reflected a conclusion of the Board of Governors that competition for some services on some routes would not cause economic harm to Intelsat (see "Intelsat Approves System Coordination," 1987; Schrage, 1984; and "White House Sees No Problem," 1985). PanAmSat began providing service between the United States and South America (beginning with Peru) in 1988, and with Western Europe (beginning with the United Kingdom) in 1989. In 1989 the Intelsat Assembly of Parties also authorized the Orion satellite system for transatlantic communication to proceed, despite its conclusion that Orion would "cause significant economic harm to Intelsat," because of strong U.S. and British assurances of continued support for Intelsat ("Intelsat Approves Orion Plan" 1989). Orion will not launch its competitive satellite system for transatlantic service, however, until 1995 (Lambert, 1992, p. 100).

In 1986 another small company, Columbia Communications, was granted permission by the FCC to launch a satellite to provide transpacific telecommunications service. In 1989 it bid on spare capacity on two NASA satellites, but the space agency leased the capacity to Intelsat despite the fact that Columbia's bid was $10 million higher. In January 1990 Columbia won a lawsuit filed against NASA, which required that the capacity be leased to it instead of Intelsat. It was not until September 1991, however, that Columbia could actually begin to sign up customers, because Intelsat had used the economic harm argument to pre-

vent competition (see "Intelsat Upon," 1992, p. 65).

The long-range implications of fiber optic technology for satellite communication are probably more significant than are competitive satellite systems. Besides their role as major carriers of voice traffic, satellites were seen during their initial development as providing a means for inexpensively distributing broadband communications—at that time, television. Data communication and other digital communication signals could also take advantage of this capability. Coaxial submarine cables represented a more expensive channel for such purposes, and television shot in other countries and returned to the United States, for instance, normally used film that was carried back by air transport. Fiber optics, however, provides capacity similar (or superior) to that of satellites. This new technology has the additional advantage of providing a protected channel that may help eliminate signal piracy and secure links for data traffic. Its reliability may also lessen the amount of redundancy necessary in data communication flow over wireless channels, thus further reducing total transmission costs.

Many countries, particularly in North America and Europe, have already installed fiber optic cables in their domestic telecommunications systems. Submarine fiber cables are also being used in transatlantic and transpacific voice, telex, fax, and data traffic services, and will be used increasingly in other areas of the world as well. The problem from developing countries' points of view, however, is that they will not have trained engineers to allow them to use the technology effectively. Fiber is an optically based technology, fundamentally different from the electromagnetic technology in which these countries have invested and on which their engineers are trained. Adopting fiber, then, leads developing countries once again into dependence on the United States, Europe, and Japan, something many of them are leery of. Also, many applications designed to take advantage of the characteristics of fiber (speed, bandwidth, and security) will be data applications, using digital rather than analog transmission. Again, this puts developing countries at a disadvantage, requiring investments in international gateways capable of handling digital information. Many are unsure just when they would be able to use the larger capacities and new capabilities, such as ISDN, which fiber cables provide (see Wigand, 1988, on ISDN).

Comsat and several consulting organizations have concluded that, for the period 1995–2005, satellite and fiber optic technologies will be complementary, each with the potential to be optimized for particular routes. International telecommunications traffic, they estimate, will grow at a rate of 9.5% per year, and will be stimulated by increasing data communication and television traffic. "By the year 2005, the total number of international TV channels in the Atlantic and Pacific Ocean regions is projected to be five times 1986 levels. And, the amount of business service traffic is projected to more than double its growth rate on both satellites and cable" ("Satellite Versus Fibre," 1989, pp. 18–19). Despite an annual 7.5% growth rate in satellite traffic over this period, these organizations also project that satellite's share of total telecommunications traffic will drop from 50% in 1995 to about 44% in 2005 ("Satellite Versus Fibre," 1989, p. 19).

Many countries are also considering mobile and **cellular communications** systems as part of their approach to meeting telecommunications needs. In areas of the world where several small countries cluster together, these technologies, which have dedicated frequencies assigned, can use lower power transmitters, and allow countries to reuse frequencies regularly, could provide new methods of conducting some international communication and avoiding costly wired telecommunications infrastructure development. Again, however, movement to such technologies does require new investment, as such systems are not merely enhancements of existing switched network capability, but employ new technologies in old configurations (see Carlsen, 1991, pp. 1, 2).

From the perspective of many developing countries, which wish either to control access to communication or to have the means to tax it, the use of cables is also advantageous. Cables must use the international gateways that people and businesses have bypassed as the **power flex density** (or signal strength) of satellites has increased and the commensurate size of receiving dishes has shrunk. Eventually fiber optic links may carry most point-to-point communication, with satellite use restricted to broadcast applications. Although Intelsat's primary role has been to provide voice channels, it will see that role diminished by fiber. The erosion of its voice traffic will occur first on the most heavily used paths, such as that between the United States and Western Europe. Traffic on less heavily used paths will lag significantly until developing countries have sufficient engineering expertise to begin to employ the new optical technology, and sufficient resources to finance the import of necessary technology.

Integrated Services Digital Networks (ISDN)

Another trend is the interface of technologies into a new integrated system. Telecommunications networks, digital computer technologies, and video systems are increasingly being combined to provide new communication capabilities. As the Administrative Council of the ITU put it (1989b), the "unprecedented growth of technology and the fusion of telecommunications and information technologies even leading to the creation of intelligent networks" have "enabled the provision of new and ever expanding telecommunication-based services" and the introduction of "many new uses of telecommunications for communication and information transfer for specialized needs and applications."[4] One instance of this is the retrieval of newspaper and wire service copy via computer modems (see Markoff, 1991).

The result of this amalgamation is twofold. First, it creates difficulties for international regulation that, until now, has operated on the principle that there is a clear separation between telecommunications and broadcasting activity. As Richard Stursberg, assistant deputy minister in Canada's Department of Communications, put it,

> The problem presented by such new media [based in digitized forms] is that they do not fit the two basic premises of communications regulations, that of common carriers, with its strict separation of content and carriage, and that of broadcasting, film and publishing, which are centered on content issues. The emerging integration [of services] carries with it an emerging policy vacuum. . . . As the two areas converge, the tensions between them will become evident. ("ITU-COM Explores Problems," 1989, p. 64)

Richard Butler, former secretary-general of ITU, joined Stursberg in this analysis, suggesting ("ITU-COM Explores Problems," 1989, p. 63) that "it is often the ad hoc way in which the user takes advantage of innovations that have thrown the process of regulation into disarray. For no matter how quickly laws are enacted, developments in the marketplace will easily make them superfluous."

The second result is the role of this integrated system in people's lives. As Jin Ku Kang, vice chairman of Samsung, put it,

> We're now entering a period in which electronics are becoming an integral part of people's lives, requiring increasing levels of intellectual sophistication. The fundamental transformation of telecommunications networks, which are now one of the most important parts of the social infrastructure, is starting to turn the electronics industry into a genuine social innovator.
>
> The question . . . is basically how to deal with new social phenomena; the interfacing between the technology and society, as well as between man and machine. ("ITU-COM Explores Problems," 1989, p. 65)

The requirements placed on the international communications system by organizations demanding video, high-speed data, and high-resolution image transmission had created, by 1990, enough demand (and thus the economic incentive) to improve digital communications capability to handle these needs. The basic requirement was an international system that could carry several types of communication materials simultaneously, quickly, and cheaply from point of origin to destination(s), often moving from one type of transmission system to another—for example, from a domestic telephone system into an international fiber link or satellite path, and then into another domestic telephone or data communication system.

Two crucial technical problems had to be solved. First, the information had to be easily altered from electrical impulse (which travels in three possible states: zero voltage, positive voltage, and negative voltage) to optical impulse (which travels in only two states: on or off), and back again. Otherwise, signals originating in one type of structure would be restricted to using that portion of the international system that could carry it, even when that might delay transmission, drive up costs, or restrict possible destination points.

Second, the problem of timing error had to be solved. Digital systems depend on transmission of information within tight parameters of timing error: a 125-microsecond error limit between the two end points. Otherwise, the information transmitted becomes garbled because the receiving node will process the decoding information incorrectly: It expects 8 bits of information in each frame and will process accordingly, even if part of the data was lost in transmission or arrived too late to be included in a given frame. This problem is exacerbated by the switch between 2-state and 3-state data (or electrical and optical data), by the use of satellites in orbits that fluctuate (as all do), and by the existence of alternative routes between two points in the international system (see Thomas, 1991, pp. 29–35).

These problems required that international standards organizations adopt time references, based on international atomic time, that would allow all the components of the international system to be synchronized and monitored, and for distribution of timing signals throughout the networks that are linked. This has spurred the development of a synchronous optical network (SONET) for providing these timing signals, standards that would allow equipment produced by different vendors to be compatible within the same international system, and rationalization of the differing national systems adopted by various countries operat-

ing domestic telecommunications systems (see Warr, 1991, p. S4).

The development of this internationally synchronized and rationalized system has also been made more difficult by the trend toward privatization of telecommunications systems. As new organizations have become part of the international system, they have also had to be incorporated into the standardization process (see Whittle, 1992, pp. 31–36). So have computer companies that increasingly provide the end-point equipment for connecting into the system, state-operated PTTs, and video-conferencing vendors that provide private companies with satellite dishes, television cameras, signal processors, and the like for intracompany video communication (see, for instance, Appleton, 1991, pp. 80, 81; Dixon, 1991, p. 35; and Py, Sams, & Aluise, 1991, pp. 7, 8).

Despite such complexities, says Ivor Knight of Comsat World Systems, global ISDN, based in the use of fiber optic technology, must be compatible with satellites. Without satellites, "there will simply not be enough of a world market for narrow-band and broadband ISDN to be cost-effective. . . . [R]egional and global standards organizations will have to join forces to meet several standardization challenges: broadband ISDN, advanced audiovisual systems, intelligent networks, telecommunications management networks and universal personal telecommunications (UPT)" ("Special Report: Toward Liberalized, Global Communications," 1991, pp. 4, 5).

The idea of UPT is, of course, another manifestation of the notion of the "global village," and the technological mythos that surrounds the development of ever more sophisticated communications devices. As one reporter put it in describing a newly proposed low-orbit satellite system to link "pocket-sized phones anywhere on Earth . . . a person standing in a field in Kansas could call someone in a Mongolian tent using a phone network that would be based entirely in space" (Burgess, 1992, p. B1). Despite developing country support for the idea as an inexpensive means of providing telephone service to remote villages, it is unlikely that such a system will make a large difference in access to telecommunications in poorer countries unless their economic condition improves significantly.

The developing and increasingly complex international system, then, despite the access that it seems to offer poorer countries, will more likely result in an increasing gap between haves and have-nots. The future of international telecommunications, particularly developing technologies and improving interfaces among these technologies, will continue, if history is a guide, to offer the greatest improvement in interconnection to the industrialized countries, whatever speculations exist to the contrary. If this gap does, in fact, continue to widen, this will further complicate the task of developing countries that attempt to take advantage of the international system: They will be continually trying to catch up to technological capability, continually trying to put it to work to assist in their development goals.

10.5

International Broadcasting

Although some international broadcasting uses medium waves, most of it still occurs on the shortwave bands. It might seem inevitable that a more dependable and higher fidelity means of communication, such as the satellite, will replace this low-fidelity, sometimes unpredictable form of broadcasting. In fact, many international broadcasters, including VOA and the BBC, inquired into this possibility during the late 1980s. Their research indicated, however, that shortwave still had a long life ahead of it. Two studies concluded, for instance, that the anticipated major competitor to shortwave, audio-DBS, is an expensive alternative to continued use of terrestrial relay facilities (see Bachtell, Bettadapur, Coyner, & Farrell, 1986; and Federal Systems Division, 1985).

Other reports have concluded that international shortwave broadcasting will be a viable technology well into the next century. A study I completed for Academy for Educational Development, under contract to VOA, for instance, found that replacing terrestrial shortwave with DBS delivery systems would not be feasible until 2020 or later, primarily due to the lack of radios capable of receiving the frequencies necessary to use satellites, and the global economic and political conditions that would make the move toward this technology a long-term prospect (see Fortner & Durham, 1986, 1988; Mytton, 1988). Although some engineers have suggested that there are ways around some of these problems, the consensus is that, while audio-DBS and their respective radio receivers are technically possible, it will be many years before international broadcasters begin to use satellites for delivery of programs directly to individuals.[5] As another group that I worked with, the Technical Operations Study Committee for the VOA, put it (Committee on Antennas, Satellite Broadcasting and Emergency Preparedness for the Voice of America, 1989, p. 2), "After examining the various broadcasting techniques available, the committee concludes that shortwave will remain the primary means of international broadcasting into the twenty-first century." Still a third study I completed, this one for the BBC, found the same results for the ITU-suggested move toward single-sideband shortwave broadcasting (Fortner, 1991c, pp. 40, 41).

Several international broadcasters already use satellites to link their terrestrial transmitter sites together, to feed cable systems, and to provide content for rebroadcast by the domestic radio services of other countries. VOA, for instance, uses Intelsat V to connect its up-link at Greenville, North Carolina, to down-links in Belize, Morocco, and Botswana. (See Figure 10.1.) It has relay stations in Bethany (Ohio), Greenville,

Dixon and Delano (California), and Marathon (Florida), besides those scattered around the globe. (See Appendix 2.) The BBC feeds all its overseas relays by satellite, including those in Cyprus, Oman, the Seychelles, Singapore, Hong Kong, Lesotho, Ascension Island, Antigua, and so on.

Rebroadcasting is also becoming an increasingly important option for international broadcasters, particularly in areas, such as Western Europe, where privatization of radio facilities is rapidly occurring. Some of the most popular programs provided by international broadcasters can be picked up from satellites for rebroadcast by medium-wave or VHF-FM stations hungry for programming. The programs can be

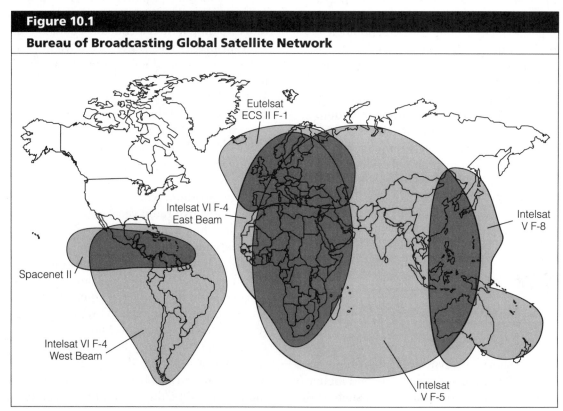

Figure 10.1

Bureau of Broadcasting Global Satellite Network

Source: Voice of America, 1992a, p. 80.

picked up without cost in some cases, or for the cost of the down-link alone in others. Such programs can also capitalize on audiences already built up by the shortwave broadcasts of the originating service.

The most significant problem for international shortwave broadcasting is the erosion of its audience due to increasingly sophisticated and high-fidelity domestic services, increases in the availability of television, and the rapid growth of personal technologies, particularly audio- and videocassette recorders, which give people unprecedented control over their information/entertainment environment. Major U.S. and cable programs are becoming available throughout Western Europe, for instance, and personal technologies are spreading through most of the world, even to areas where the economic capability would seem to be insufficient to support them. As the VOA-2001 Committee put it (1987; see also Flint, 1992, p. 30);

> even . . . authoritarian regimes will demonstrate a new and more sophisticated use of their own media. VOA and other international broadcasters flourish when people do not trust what they hear from their own government. Yet, even those governments in information-deprived societies are becoming increasingly sophisticated in the handling of their own media. . . . Besides the assumed, intensified international competition, increased competition will also come from national media attempting to hold and to augment their audience share. . . . These changes will require VOA to become more sophisticated than ever in its reporting, more astute and more aggressive while still maintaining its reputation for credibility and accuracy.

International broadcasting has become an important tool in the public diplomacy efforts of an increasing number of countries. The number of international broad-

casters (both public and private) increases every year, leading to more and more crowding of the shortwave bands. This trend shows no signs of abating, making the engineering problems ever more acute. The significance of international broadcasting, however, is such that it will not be abandoned or scaled back, although alternative delivery systems to reach new audiences, or to hold existing ones, will continue to be explored, and applied where feasible.

Countries have examined two options for increasing the efficiency with which the shortwave bands could be used. One was to assign particular frequencies to individual broadcasters (reviving an old idea), but this approach suffered from the difficulties to which shortwave propagation is subject. Experimentally, however, the ITU is assigning a few frequencies on this basis. The second option was to authorize broadcasters to begin using single- rather than double-sideband transmission. Since any radio wave, if divided in half horizontally, has two sides that duplicate each other, using only one side of it would allow, at least theoretically, for twice as many frequencies in a given broadcasting service without loss of information.

Two problems do exist with single-sideband transmission, however. First, most radio receivers do not have single-sideband reception capability, so any broadcaster using this transmission could reach only a fraction of its current audience. Second, the single-sideband system does not actually save half of the available frequencies, but only about one third. Far fewer new services can be accommodated, therefore, than was originally assumed. The actual significance of single-sideband transmission will be to reduce the interference among existing users, rather than to accommodate new ones. Nevertheless, all new shortwave allocations are scheduled to use single sideband as they become available (see Pritchard, 1989, p. 47).

These problems have convinced major international broadcasters to be cautious in planned applications of single-sideband transmissions. Broadcasting using this technology will probably result at least in the short term in more congestion of the short-wave bands, since broadcasters will have to duplicate their signals in both single- and double-sideband transmission modes on different frequencies to reach their total audiences.

Another "new" development with possible application to international broadcasting is DBS, for both radio and television. While DBS technology is not expected to replace shortwave radio broadcasting, it will likely prove to be a new competitor for the international audience. VOA, for one, continues to be interested (see Sukow, 1991, p. 60). However, since ITU conventions require that any application of such a satellite in television first have the permission of the receiving country's government before signals are directed into it, and that any spill-over of satellite television signals be limited as much as possible, any application on a global scale in the near future is unlikely. Only in cases where countries are of like mind about its use will it become a competitor before the end of the century. This has already happened in Western Europe, and increasingly the signals supplied there are finding their way into Eastern European homes as well. The requirement of "prior consent" has stalled many other potential applications of the technology, however. With radio, countries have not yet agreed to assign exclusive frequency space for international satellite applications. Apparently, satellites will not be used in international

radio broadcasting until sometime in the next century.

Some hesitancy in the application of DBS for international purposes is probably the result of mixed results in domestic applications. DBS experiments in the United States, for instance, did not yield the results necessary for continued investment in this technology. The more recent effort in the United Kingdom to introduce satellite television has also been less successful than predictions suggested. Satellite difficulties delayed German and French plans, too. Japan was thus the only country by 1989 with enough experience in DBS to allow any judgments to be made.

One possible application of DBS technology, but one that has not received the attention afforded to television, is audio-DBS. Although no major international broadcasters have immediate plans for implementation of satellites for direct audio/radio broadcasting, Afrispace let a contract in 1990 to build and launch the first satellite for audio-DBS application to serve Africa and the Middle East. By early 1992 Afrispace had signed CNN and the Kenyan Broadcasting Corporation as client broadcasters.

A variety of research studies have examined the prospects for DBS devoted to audio (see CCIR Study Groups 10 and 11, 1987; Chaplin, Fromm, & Rosetti, 1984; European Broadcasting Union, 1987; Thomson-CSF, 1982; and U.S.A., 1986a, 1986b, 1986c). Generally, they have agreed that it is technically feasible to use satellites for this purpose, provided that the financial and regulatory aspects are adequately addressed (including the assignment of suitable frequencies). Such frequencies might be shared with some terrestrial services (see Sullivan & Miller, 1987).

10.6

International Communications Law and Regulation

It is difficult to say what the future holds for international law in communications. Law is affected by the international political climate, which changes dramatically as alliances shift or as new ideas emerge. The emphasis on human rights (particularly the right to communicate) is likely to continue, given the ideological convictions of the United States, and the cultural and economic concerns of developing countries. Sometimes the position of the Western democracies will coincide with that of developing countries, as seems probable in the application of satellites for international communication. This process will build on the successful Intelsat experience, and offer clear economic advantages to poorer countries that can use international service satellites to develop more sophisticated domestic broadcasting services without the expense of building expensive terrestrial limited-range VHF-FM services. In addition, the desire of Western countries for continued expansion of fiber optic capability seems likely to find a positive reception in many countries. Some of these countries do have concerns, however, about the expense of yet another new communications technology. Despite economic reservations, the fact that fiber cables will have to make use of international gateways will allow countries to maintain control over the passage of information through them, and many will see this as advantageous compared to the alternative — widespread satellite use.

The interests of many countries, in other words, may be similar: The technological and economic interests of industrialized

countries may coincide with the political and economic interests of developing countries, as well as with the political interests of totalitarian or other closed countries. This could result in decreased tension on communication issues in the United Nations and its specialized agencies.

The coincidence of interests between North and South, or between free and closed societies, however, does not extend across all issues. Developing countries continue to be concerned about trade issues, about domination of their cultures, and about the ways in which Western news agencies portray them to the world's peoples. Their concerns may lead to further initiatives, such as efforts to control information flow or to license journalists, that are anathema to Western countries. The extent of the differences in information access between North and South may widen. Bridging that gap may depend on whether developing countries see the historical imbalance in information flow being redressed by the application of new technologies. It may depend, too, on how quickly the developed world pushes to inaugurate new services that take advantage of its technological superiority, or whether the wealth in information resources (technology, software, and information itself) begins to be shared more equitably among the world's nations.

The inability to achieve greater equity in access to and use of the international communication system continues to be highlighted in assessments of its impact, however. In 1989 the 25th General Conference of UNESCO, for instance, adopted a new strategy for communication, aimed at achieving free flow of information, wider and better balanced distribution, and removal of obstacles to free expression. These goals mirrored concerns that have been part of the discussion of international communication from its earliest days. It also reflected the concerns of developing countries as expressed beginning in 1970, and of the International Program for the Development of Communication adopted in 1980 (see "Communication in the Service of Humanity," 1990, pp. 23–24; and Hamelink, 1990, pp. 27–28).

Mowlana (1990) has criticized the UNESCO document on two counts. First, he says, the new world information and communication order that has evolved since the NWICO debate erupted is quite different from the one envisioned by developing countries. What exists, he says, is an order constructed by the advanced industrialized nations partially "to limit and block the original demands put forward by the Third World." Second, he argues that since the original MacBride Commission report, "a desire and indeed a quest for a new cultural order which goes beyond the simple notion of communication and information" has evolved.

> This new discourse, which has a potential for a major international and world-wide debate, makes communication and information concepts subservient to the broader notion of culture and social ecology. This discourse proceeds with the notion that although the early advocates of NWICO rightly recognised and acknowledged the inter-relationship between information and culture, they nevertheless made technological, economic and political factors the focuses of their demands. The underlying assumption was that once the nation states and the peoples acquired independence, sovereignty, and communication infrastructure on some equal basis, the cultural questions that were being debated would automatically be resolved. (p. 25)

While Mowlana's analysis is correct, it does not go far enough. Mowlana neither separates the elites/governments of developing countries from their peoples, nor acknowledges that part of the reason for the failure of the "underlying assumption" is that the developing countries have never been able to acquire communication infrastructures "on some equal basis." The first issue merits attention since the governments of many developing countries clearly have chosen not to invest in domestic infrastructures designed to involve their people in communication activity. Rather, they have concentrated on infrastructures that meet the needs of business and corporate interests, and of their own political interests in centralized control of information. They have thus duplicated the inequalities of the international system controlled by the state apparatus and corporate entities of the industrialized nations. They have fulfilled Innis's "prophecy."

Second, even in their attempts to meet the more limited needs developing countries' governments have identified, they have failed to bridge the gap in infrastructure. This is because the technology, and its various complex interfaces, has developed far more rapidly than their limited economic resources could handle. Thus the political "sovereignty" many countries thought they had achieved in the 1960s and 1970s, when the European empires broke apart, has seemed hollow. Few developing countries could afford to devote themselves to cultural issues, even when they were intimately interrelated to the technological, political, and economic questions of the NWICO debate, because they were rapidly slipping back into a dependence based in the international communication system itself that they thought they had escaped with independence. As Mwaffisi (1991, p. 89) put it, "the ability to broadcast signals from satellites into household receivers has increased the threat of developed nations to the culture and ideology of developing countries and thus the urgent need for new world information order [sic] to reverse the one-way flow of international communications from the developed to the developing countries." Although Mwaffisi identifies a number of control measures that developing countries could adopt to deal with this threat (such as jamming, government-controlled community receivers, and other technical means), he doubts that these countries have the economic means to use them, and continues to worry about the use of powerful media "for propaganda [that] causes what has come to be called 'cultural imperialism'" (p. 91; see also Tsui, 1991, pp. 69–93; and Winseck & Cuthbert, 1991, p. 196).

Other events suggest, too, that the question of information flow and cultural imperialism will become more complicated, not less. In late 1991, for instance, while Africa No. 1 announced that it would begin a broadcasting service in Paris, putting "an end to the north-south monologue . . . ," Nigeria was calling on other African states to help salvage PANA, which had been hit with staff departures, debt, and rapidly deteriorating equipment as a result of countries not paying their dues (BBC Monitoring Service, 1991a, p. A1, and 1991c, p. A14).

These varying perspectives will all have an impact on the laws adopted for or applied to communication in the international arena. On the one hand, growing disparities might lead to contentious and potentially divisive relations among countries that could stall applications for new international services, allocation of frequency spectra, adoption of technical standards, or agreements on protection for intellectual property. On the other, convergence of ability and access could have an ameliorating effect on rela-

tions among countries, which will lead to cooperative relations and facilitation of communication.

International Audiences

The role played by international communication depends on those who make use of it: audiences. Every technology used for international electronic communication—whether broadcasting, satellites, wire services and their client organizations, data transfer, voice, facsimile, or telex—requires users: an audience. This term obviously does not refer to audiences in the traditional sense: those who read, listen, or watch. The audiences in question are those that participate with the international communications system. Some do indeed only read, listen, or watch. Many others initiate communication, however, using telephones, fax machines, or computers, or seek out new methods of fulfilling more traditional roles, such as investing in personal technologies.

Some technologies, Schramm argued (Vol. 3, 1980, p. 296), are "sender-related," while others are "receiver-related." Sender-related technologies include high-speed printing and duplicating technologies, phototypesetting, the telegraph, the telephone, radio and television, cable, satellites, and laser and waveguide systems. All of these are "dedicated to circulating more information faster and more widely." They are, in Innis's terms, space-biased. Receiver-related technologies, such as libraries, summary news services, information retrieval systems, abstracting services, microfiche, recording devices, and the computer, have "lagged behind" their sender-related counterparts. In a sense, they are time-biased, for they allow people to incorporate information at their own pace, ignoring it when they choose, engaging with it continuously if necessary.

Relatively few studies have been done on the actual audiences for various forms of international communication, with the obvious exception of audiences for international and domestic shortwave radio services (see, for instance, Delauzun, Mytton, & Forrester, 1988; Mytton, 1986; and "Shortwave Radio Tunes More Americans," 1987). Figures reported earlier on such issues as VCR penetration and video piracy might be used to extrapolate possible audiences, but such figures would be subject to criticism. Audiences around the globe, too, would differ in composition, sophistication in media use, and reasons for participation (see Gryspeerdt, 1985, on the European audience; see also Maletzke, 1986).

The future of a comprehensive international audience using these various technologies is dependent on several particulars. How quickly or extensively countries develop their domestic communications infrastructures, and which technologies they favor, will affect people's ability to use different portions of the international system, and thus their engagement with certain types of information. Without basic telephone voice service it is difficult for people to access newer fax, telex, or data communication services, for instance. Without extension of national power grids, it is difficult to extend television or satellite services, because the power demands deplete batteries too quickly for people to depend on them to access the international system. Favoring one or the other will determine, however, the "bias" of a given society's international participation and the degree of dependency or sovereignty it enjoys in using the international system.

Whether countries develop these infrastructures depends on whether they have the political will and the economic ability to do so. Political will is a function of both domestic political realities and the view that governments take of the significance of participation in the international communications system. Some countries will be content to assure only government or government and business connections to certain portions of the system. Others will desire full citizen participation. Even such desires may not be enough to assure such involvement, however. As Mattelart (1991, p. 218) argues, "the democratic marketplace so beloved by the heralds of this new 'human right of commercial free expression' is in no way the same as the democracy of the defenders of human rights, the rights of the citizen and of nations. Between them there lies the immense abyss with which the new and inegalitarian rationality has bisected a planet that is pierced by social exclusions." The trends toward privatization and commercialization, in other words, are likely to continue to exclude large portions of the world's population from participating in the global communications system, and continue to mock the technological mythos that claims creation of a global village.

Economic ability is a function of the ability both to raise funds domestically and, in many cases, to attract foreign investment capital and loans. Again, different countries have differing abilities to locate adequate financing, or even to seek it out (see "Poor Man's Burden," 1989). Also, whether countries spend money for infrastructure development will depend on the priority they establish for it. In some countries other needs (extension of health services, adequate housing, water supplies, even food) will have to take precedence, particularly in times of environmental crisis (drought, floods, earthquakes, etc.).

One reality affecting the extension of the international system is population growth itself. This has two separate but related results. First, some regions of the globe have such high rates of population growth that even major commitments to communications development will not be able to keep up. For instance, population growth in sub-Saharan Africa will be so great between 1990 and 2000 that the expected increase in the number of radio receivers (from approximately 60 million to 72 million) will actually result in fewer households having access to this basic technology. This is the result of a predicted increase in the number of households in this region from 100 million to nearly 150 million over the same period. Most countries in sub-Saharan Africa will not have the economic ability to import the number of radio sets to keep up with population and subsequent household growth (Fortner & Durham, 1986, p. 178).

This problem applies even more acutely to technologies requiring extensive capital investments: those with wired connections or satellite earth stations. Those portions of the international system that require sophisticated user-interfaces, such as personal computers, will also likely result in decreased participation (on a per capita or household basis) as the world's population in poorer countries increases more rapidly than the ability of governments to respond adequately to it.

The second effect of population growth affecting international communication participation is the resultant distribution of population across age groups. The proportion of these larger total populations who are (and will be) age 14 and younger is expected to remain fairly stable. In developing areas the percentage varies over time from

between 33% (in Asia) to over 47% (in sub-Saharan Africa) (Fortner & Durham, 1988, p. 18). Young people cannot participate in many portions of the international communications system (due to lack of either economic capability, literacy, or technological sophistication). They tend, too, when they are able to invest in a technology that allows participation, to buy personal technologies, primarily audiocassette players. This means that a large portion of the world's total population is likely to exist on the fringe of international communication activity, participating in a highly selective way with a small portion of the information available. This implies a difficult task for information providers to involve these audiences, and undercuts the philosophical arguments in favor of a "right to communicate" as part of humankind's basic rights. The right to communicate is difficult to apply to those who cannot participate due principally to their age. This right will not apply in any real sense, then, to between a third and nearly a half of the population in different parts of the world.

Trends in the International Communications System

Increasing trade and commerce, banking, and development efforts have encouraged expanding transnational communication systems. Lending and development agencies see domestic telecommunications infrastructures as significant in efforts to help economic expansion and as reflective of positive social and political change. Also instrumental as catalysts to communications infrastructure development and international linkages are the rapid increase in the number of independent countries since the end of World War II, the military alliances and conflicts, and the search for political stability in a world fractured by competing ideologies, religious strife, and severe economic disparities. Both communication and telecommunication among peoples and countries have increased enormously as a result of such factors.

The system of international communication will become increasingly sophisticated as new technologies add further dimensions to it. The result will be, for part of the world's population, increased opportunity to control their information environments, to seek information, and to participate in sophisticated interconnections across a broad range of technologies. They will be the information rich (or at least potentially rich) if they take advantage of the opportunities provided. For most of the world's population, however, broad-ranging increased participation is unlikely, even though they will be able to access some new services as television is extended, basic telephone service becomes more prevalent, and they discover consumer technology and software. These populations' participation will remain limited, however, by the economic and political problems that affect their countries, even in the face of privatization of industry and liberalization of governments (assessments of citizen access to the international system in developing countries can be seen in Crossette, 1990, and Singh, 1991).

The system itself does not function on technological possibility alone, but is directed by nontechnological demands: political, economic, cultural, demographic, topographical. Although knowing the technologies available, the extent of their use and application, the history of their development, the laws and understandings that govern them, the disputes that arise over them, and the ways they are abused, is all valuable as a means to complete the picture of international communication, even that is insufficient. The system operates within a complex environment that itself must be understood if the functions of communication on a global scale — and the problems that beset it — are to be made meaningful.

The nature of this environment is undergoing change, as it has done from its infancy. The reduction in tension between East and West dominates the thinking in the early 1990s. Other significant changes, however, are also taking place. Intersputnik, at one time the Soviet Union's response to the U.S.-dominated Intelsat system, may become a member of Intelsat itself, essentially merged the two competitors into a single global service. Around the world privatization of media is occurring. "Public service" broadcasters and state-owned telecommunications entities are straining under government initiatives to turn their activities over to profit-making entities, or even to introduce profit-making into government-owned organizations.

The outcome of this change will have potentially explosive consequences for international communication. It will affect the purchase of media products, international law and regulation applied to communication, trade and intellectual property issues, and fears about cultural imperialism. In the European community alone, for instance, a 1983 report on television led to recognition that privatization might cause an annual program deficit of as much as 245,000 hours, which would have to be met with extra-European imports (see Hirsch, 1986, pp. 121–122). The likely results will be competition, rapid increases in the total information available, and further debate about cultural imperialism.

Another change is the increasing participation of countries in international copyright conventions. Major exporters of media products, such as the United States, see more universal adherence as a blessing. However, some critics point to difficulties, such as the Soviets' alleged use of the Universal Copyright Convention to prevent the foreign publication of works of dissidents (see Newcity, 1980, p. 2). Nevertheless, the United States and other major publisher/producer/exporter countries do expect, as a result of continuing pressure exerted bilaterally and through such international vehicles as the General Agreement on Tariffs and Trade (GATT) negotiations, that more universal adherence to copyright conventions will be forthcoming. Developing countries, concerned about cultural imperialism, may discover, too, that adherence to such conventions will allow them to control more easily the distribution of Western cultural materials. Many will have to choose the lesser of two evils: paying for information that they think should be more widely shared, and more inexpensively, by Western producers, or increasingly being deluged with Western cultural material illicitly produced and distributed by bootleggers and pirates.

Another international legal issue that will be confronted over the next decade is that of privacy. As an increasing number of countries become fully integrated into the international data network, this issue, which has largely been discussed among OECD countries so far, will gradually become more globalized. The full-scale introduction of ISDN, too, will exacerbate the concerns of many countries, as its intelligent network control software will perhaps remove some of their abilities to protect sensitive information. ISDN, at least in its domestic form in the United States, does not have database protection capability.

Since the value of global data communication to its users increases with the number of information providers that can be accessed, the system will "demand" that the greatest possible set of databases be made available. Database providers and users alike also recognize that the greatest economy of scale will be realized as the system becomes more universally available. Both technological and economic logic, then, will argue for universality. That, in turn, will raise further fears about the protection of privacy.[6]

Finally, the system will continue to be subject to the debate about the international communication order: The East-West dimension of this debate will remain muted, while its North-South dimension will dominate. The terms of the debate, however, are likely to change. Already some privatization is occurring in developing countries. Nigeria, for instance, is introducing commercialism into its radio network. This may reduce some of the philosophical difference between North and South, if significant numbers of countries follow Nigeria's lead. Developing countries are also likely, however, to continue to build alternative regional news agencies to assure a flow of news of particular interest to them and to demand some control over the information flow across their borders. This aspect of the debate will likely continue.

One barometer indicating the respective stakes of countries in the international communication order are the attitudes toward UNESCO. Both the United States and the United Kingdom withdrew from UNESCO, in late 1984 and late 1985, respectively. Both objected to "mismanagement" in UNESCO, with the U.S. official announcement followed by a new conference where Gregory J. Newell, assistant secretary of state for organizational affairs, claimed (quoted in Giffard, 1989, p. 107) that "extraneous politicization continues, as does, regrettably, an endemic hostility toward the institutions of a free society — particularly those that protect a free press, free markets and, above all, individual human rights." The thrust of this explanation had already been contradicted, however, by Leonard Sussman, vice chairman of the U.S. National Commission for UNESCO, in testimony before two subcommittees of the House Foreign Affairs Committee earlier in 1984.[7] Both the United Kingdom and the United States have re-examined their positions on UNESCO, but neither had decided to rejoin by the end of 1991 (see Wells, 1987, for another version of this history). UNESCO itself has examined its own activities in communication, and has promised major changes (see Unesco Executive Board, 129th Session, 1988; and Schwartz, 1989).

Ironically, Mowlana argues (1990, p. 25), the refusal of the United Kingdom and United States to rejoin UNESCO came after drastic changes in world and global politics had resulted in greater democratic participation and cultural resurgence, so that the objections to "conspiracies and tendencies in UNESCO and elsewhere to curb the freedom of the press" are no longer (if they were ever) valid. Also, as Roach suggests (1990, p. 29), a significant part of the U.S. strategy concerning UNESCO was to force it to "curtail its communication research activities, since these were viewed as providing the conceptual and empirical bedrock for the NWICO movement." By the end of the 1980s, she says, "Unesco's role as a research organisation in the field of communications, like its previous position as an intellectual catalyst, is being undermined."

In many respects, then, the United States and United Kingdom got what they wanted from UNESCO. As Jakubowicz puts it (1990, p. 33), "As a political issue, NWICO is no doubt dead." But UNESCO, in its efforts to

"reform" and to woo these countries to rejoin (and thus again to provide the lion's share of funding for the organization," "pleased no one" (Jakubowicz, 1990, p. 33). While UNESCO remains a potential forum where the differences between the various participants in the international communications system can engage one another on political, economic, cultural, and social issues, the absence of the United Kingdom and the United States from its deliberations makes them largely irrelevant. These two countries, as should be apparent, are too crucial to the operation and future of the international communications system to be "left out" of such debates. They continue to dominate the system, despite the growth in the number of independent states, their larger populations, and efforts to press their concerns (or demands) on the international communication agenda. In 1991 the American Society of Newspaper Editors (ASNE), a leading critic of UNESCO's communication policies, withdrew its opposition to the United States' rejoining the organization, indicating the truth of Jakubowicz's assertion.

On some fronts, including technology (such as satellites and fiber optics, including ISDN), intellectual property, standards development, and privacy, the interests of North and South may come to coincide. Northern Hemisphere countries are likely to pursue technological change more vigorously than their Southern Hemisphere counterparts, since they control the technologies and will earn the profits. The chance to participate in the information age more fully, however, will be enticing to developing countries, and their choices will not be easy ones. Participation implies allocation of often scarce resources and the exacerbation of existing tensions between haves and have-nots. Nonparticipation, however, will also be a dangerous and possibly more damaging alternative. Many developing countries will recognize this consequence, and choose the route to full participation.

Still another change affecting the relations of countries in the last decade of this century is the increasing globalization of control of the communications system. The first indications of significant change were the buy-out of Columbia Pictures and CBS Records by the Sony Corporation. In 1990 Matsushita bought MCA Inc., the largest purchase ever of a U.S. company by a Japanese firm ("Hollywood's Biggest Ever," 1990, pp. 36, 37). And in 1991 Sony acquired the U.S. domestic production assets of New World Television, planning to revive TriStar Television (Tyrer, 1991, pp. 1, 31). In March 1992 the British conglomerate Thorn EMI reached agreement to purchase Virgin Music Group, one of the last remaining independent record labels, further concentrating the ownership of audio production (records, audiocassettes, and CDs) into the hands of the so-called Big Six: Time Warner, Sony, Thorn EMI, Matsushita, Philips Electronics, and Bertelsmann. (See Table 10.1.)

10.9

Conclusion

What all these potential changes will likely lead to is an increasingly problematic debate over information control. Some trends in the development of the international system demand increased access; others offer increased opportunities to control that access. Some threaten to unleash even more difficult forms of cultural imperialism; others hold out the opportunity to offset cultural imports or to control the unbridled flow of pirated cultural materials. The evolving system, then, will not solve the problems that have bedeviled international communication since the mid-1800s. It will, however, provide ever more sophisticated technologies: Some offer control, some threaten to demolish it.

Whatever the changes in the international system, McLuhan's vision of a "global village," for most of the world's population, will likely remain as remote a possibility in the year 2000 as it was in the 1960s. Though the system of interconnection among the world's peoples has become increasingly sophisticated — and will grow even more so — it has not been able to involve a large

Table 10.1

International Music Market Control

Company	National Home	Market Share (percentage)
Time Warner	United States	29.7
Sony	Japan	17.0
Thorn EMI	United Kingdom	17.0 (est.)
Matsushita Electric	Japan	14.0
Philips Electronics	Netherlands	10.8
Bertelsmann	Germany	8.2
Independents	various	3.1 (est.)

Source: Farhi, 1992, p. C1

portion of the world's peoples, nor will it do so anytime soon. The percentage of the world's people who are active participants in the global communications system may actually decline as the world's population soars. A more accurate vision of the future continues to be that of a global metropolis, where the means of communication provide a network of interconnection (a technological nervous system) that bypasses many of the citizens even as it affects them indirectly through the activities of their governments and industries.

Prospects continue to be bleak for developing countries. The African continent remains in "pitiful condition" in terms of telephone access, with Nigeria, Africa's most populous country, having a line density of 0.2 per 100 people, compared to the U.S. density of 50 lines per 100. (Throughout the developing world the penetration is only 2.3 lines per 100 people.) In some countries, such as Botswana, the situation is more favorable, but, as Kigng'eno arap Ng'eny, head of Kenya's telecommunications authority put it, "it is inconceivable that the developing countries with their limited resources will be able to benefit" from technological changes affecting telephony in the West (Arnst, 1991b). "At current levels of population and main line growth, it would take more than 40 years for the Third World to match Western countries' penetration rates" (Arnst, 1991a). As Dertouzos put it (1991), in evaluating the prospects that new technologies would more fully integrate developing countries into the international communications system,

Will these new technologies widen the gap between rich and poor? I suspect so. . . . Unless wealthy countries see it as their duty to help developing nations make good use of the evolving technologies, the information age will likely widen the rift between the haves and have-nots.

Rich nations must also remember that if they become enamoured of and blinded by the glamour of the information era and neglect to produce and improve tangible wealth . . . the information colossus will lead to nothing and so will collapse. (pp. 32, 33)

Notes

1. Document 119-E. 1 June 1989. Minutes of the Official Opening Ceremony, 23 May 1989. Opening Address, page 4.

2. Although Oleg M. Poptsov, chairman of the All-Russian Committee for Radio and Television, had claimed that "glasnost has taken hold," the Soviet State Broadcast Committee under Leonid P. Kravchenko had increasingly criticized the Soviet media since the military crackdown on the Baltic republics in 1990, and President Gorbachev's attempt to suspend the law guaranteeing freedom of the press. Kravchenko had also attempted to shut down Interfax news agency, the successor of Novosti, which operated from Radio Moscow but which then moved to the offices of Boris Yeltsin, leader of the Russian Republic (Bryan Brumley, Associated Press Report, April 20, 1991).

3. Worldnet produced daily programs for distribution to domestic television stations until October 1988 when funding for the programs was cut by the Congress due to the low audiences attracted to them. Canal France Internationale and Canal Plus Afrique are already delivering French language programs to parts of Africa and the Caribbean. French and German DBS also allow citizens of these two countries to see programs produced by the other. Luxembourg's Astra satellite will soon carry international television across Europe, and people in some Eastern European countries can now purchase satellite-receiving

equipment to allow them access to Western European programming.

4. Document 47-E. 10 April 1989. Report of the Administrative Council to the Plenipotentiary Conference, page 3.

5. Thomas Rogers, an advocate of the introduction of audio-DBS, has set out his views (1985). A Technical Operations Study Committee for VOA, operating under the auspices of the Board on Telecommunications and Computer Applications of the National Academy of Sciences and Engineering, of which Rogers was a member, agreed, however (1986, pp. 11, 12, 86), that such a service would not be introduced until "the early 2000s" (see also CCIR, 1986; Committee on Antennas, Satellite Broadcasting and Emergency Preparedness for the Voice of America, 1988; Fortner, 1988b; and Stott, 1985).

6. Eventually the concerns raised on this issue may themselves lead to more fundamental issues, related to the "human rights" questions that already animate much debate about international communication issues. The human rights will be those of dignity and identity (see Fortner, 1986b).

7. Sussman argued that, although the U.S. media "reported communication debates at UNESCO as though the ultimate goal was censorship: by licensing journalists, establishing codes of journalistic practice, monitoring reportage, and penalizing those who broke the code," none of these elements had ever been approved by UNESCO. "'Not a single resolution, not a single statement of a top official at Unesco ever called for licensing, governmental codes for journalists, monitoring of journalistic output, or censorship. On the contrary, Director General M'Bow and his deputy for communications repeatedly decry censorship, even as they call for improved communications infrastructures and better coverage of social and economic developments in the Third World'" (quoted in Giffard, 1989, p. 79).

APPENDIX 1

RADIO WAVES
AND THE IONOSPHERE

Radio waves sent from the ground toward the sky "bounce" off the E, F_1, and F_2 layers. The lowest layer, the D layer, is too thin to cause refraction. At night the E layer thins out and the F_1 and F_2 layers merge into a single one.

As can be seen in Figure A.1, the higher a wave travels before it is refracted, the farther from the antenna it will strike the earth. This also varies depending on the frequency of the signal: the higher the frequency, the more chance that the signal will not bounce back but will escape through the ionized layers. "This is because," as Wheatley (n.d., p. 3) explains, "of the shorter wavelength possessed by the higher frequencies, giving the electrically charged air less time to act on each cycle as it travels through the ionized region." Also evident is the multiple hop of the radio waves. Waves that refract from the lowest ionized layer

achieve the least distance on each bounce and provide a weaker signal at point X than any waves that arrive at the same point on the first or second hop.

As Figure A.2 illustrates, at night the waves travel farther because they are refracting from the ionosphere at a higher altitude, thus achieving more distance. They are not refracting from the E layer because it has thinned out in the night.

Finally, as Wheatley explains (n.d., p. 5), these aspects all affect not only the placement of stations, and the frequencies chosen to broadcast, but the choice of the paths of the waves themselves. "It is a general rule," he writes, "that north-south or south-north transmission paths provide the best reception, day and night, but if this is not possible the station on the sunny side of the target area will have the advantage" (see also Judd, 1987).

Figure A.1

Illustration of Radio Wave Refraction, Daytime

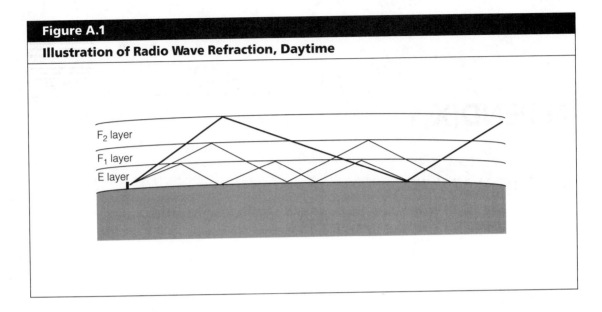

Figure A.2

Illustration of Radio Wave Refraction, Nighttime

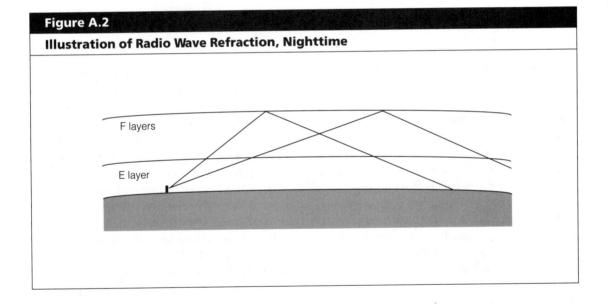

APPENDIX 2

VOA BROADCAST TRANSMITTERS AND ANTENNAS, JANUARY 1992

Relay Station	Number of Antennas	Transmitter Power (kw)	Target Areas
Bethany, OH	22	1,500	Latin America West Africa
Delano, CA	15	1,750	East Asia Central America
Greenville, NC	66	6,500	Latin America Western Europe North and West Africa
Bahrain	1	50 (MW)	Persian Gulf
Bangkok, Thailand	1	1,000 (MW)	Southeast Asia
Selebi-Phikwe, Botswana	1	200 + 200 (April 1992)	Northern South Africa, southern Zimbabwe
Kavala, Greece	23	3,000 (MW & SW)	**Medium wave:** Eastern Europe **Shortwave:** Central, southern, and western Soviet Union Eastern Europe
Rhodes, Greece	8	600 (MW & SW)	Middle East
Monrovia, Liberia	27	1,600	Sub-Saharan Africa
Munich and Wertachtal, West Germany	85	2,700 (MW & SW)	Eastern and Western Europe Western Soviet Union North Africa

(continued)

Relay Station	Number of Antennas	Transmitter Power (kw)	Target Areas
Poro and Tinang, Philippines	56	1,420 (MW & SW)	**Medium wave:** Vietnam **Shortwave:** China, Southeast Asia East Africa Far eastern Soviet Union
Colombo, Sri Lanka	19	115	China, southern Asia Middle East South and East Africa
Tangier, Morocco	32	640	Eastern Europe North Africa
Punta Gorde, Belize	2	200 (MW)	Northern Central America
Wooferton, England	37	2,700	Western Russia Eastern Europe
TOTAL	395	24,175	

Source: Voice of America, 1992b.

APPENDIX 3

CHARACTERISTICS OF SELECTED TELECOMMUNICATIONS SATELLITES

Satellite	Voice Circuits	TV Channels	Transponders	Total Bandwidth (in mHz)
Intelsat IVA	6,000	2	20	800.0
Intelsat V	12,000	2	29	2152.2
Intelsat VA	15,000	2	30	2250.0
Intelsat VA (IBS)	18,000	2	30	2750.0
Intelsat VI	35,000	2	48	2972.0
Intelsat VII-A*	22,500	3	—	—
Eutelsat-I F1**	—	12	12	864.0
Eutelsat-I F2**†	—	12	14	947.0
Gorizont 7††	—	7	6	204.0 + 1 Ku-band transponder
Gorizont 15††	—	8	8	204.0 + 2 Ku-band transponders
Arabsat F2††	—	25	25	100 gHz
Palapa B1	—	24	24	864.0
AsiaSat 1	—	24	24	864.0

*This satellite is scheduled for launch in 1995. In 1991 Intelsat had a total of 454 transponders operating on 15 satellites (13 V/V-As and 2 VIs). There were 370 C-band, 81 Ku-band, and 3 L-band transponders operating (Intelsat, 1990–91, p. 22).

(continued)

**Eutelsat satellites were designed to carry video services for Eurovision, operated by the EBU.

†This satellite carries two 12.5–12.583 gHz transponders for Eutelsat's Satellite MultiServices network, designed for "high speed digital telecommunications [transmitting] a variety of point-to-point and point-to-multipoint services on behalf of European businesses and government. These services include teleconferencing, computer-to-computer transfers, remote printing, facsimile, telexes, and electronic mail" (Long, 1987, pp. 118–119).

††Gorizont satellites carry 6 C-band transponders and experimental Ku-band transponders. The Ku-band transponders are used only occasionally. The C-band transponders carry television, telephone, and telegraph signals interchangeably, as do most satellites. Intelsat satellites are the only ones that classify voice channels separately from broadband channels.

Source: Long, 1987, pp. 63–127; *World Radio TV Handbook*, 1992, pp. 427–442.

APPENDIX 4

MEMBERSHIP IN SELECTED TELECOMMUNICATIONS ORGANIZATIONS

Arabsat (1987)

Algeria
Bahrain
Djibouti
Iraq
Jordan
Kuwait
Lebanon
Libya
Mauritania
Morocco
Oman
Palestine Liberation
   Organization
   (PLO)
Qatar
Saudi Arabia
Somalia
Sudan
Syria
Tunisia
Yemen Arab
   Republic*
People's Democratic
   Republic of
   Yemen*
United Arab
   Emirates

*These two countries have since combined into one, Yemen.

Eutelsat (1987)

Austria
Belgium
Cyprus
Denmark
Finland
France
Germany (FRG, now
   including GDR)
Iceland
Ireland
Italy
Liechtenstein
Luxembourg
Malta
Monaco
Netherlands
Portugal
San Marino
Spain
Sweden
Switzerland
Turkey
Vatican City
Yugoslavia

Inmarsat (1987)

Algeria	Italy
Argentina	Japan
Australia	Korea
Bahrain	Kuwait
Belgium	Liberia
Brazil	Malaysia
Bulgaria	Netherlands
Canada	New Zealand
Chile	Norway
China (PRC)	Oman
Denmark	Pakistan
Egypt	Philippines
Finland	Poland
France	Portugal
Gabon	Saudi Arabia
German Democratic	Singapore
Republic (now	Spain
Germany)	Sri Lanka
German Federal	Sweden
Republic (now	Tunisia
Germany)	United Arab
Greece	Emirates
India	United Kingdom
Indonesia	United States
Iran	USSR (now CIS)
Iraq	

Intersputnik (1987)

Afghanistan	Laos
Bulgaria	Mongolia
Cuba	North Korea
Czechoslovakia	Poland
German Democratic	Romania
Republic (now	USSR (now CIS)
part of the unified	Vietnam
Germany)	Yemen
Hungary	

Palapa (1992)

Palapa is actually a domestic Indonesian telecommunications satellite. However, it provides telecommunications services for other countries. These include:

Australia (the Topaz
   network)
Malaysia
Philippines
Thailand

Intelsat (1992)

Afghanistan	Cyprus
Algeria	Denmark
Angola	Dominican Republic
Argentina	Ecuador
Australia	Egypt
Austria	El Salvador
Bahamas	Ethiopia
Bangladesh	Fiji
Barbados	Finland
Belgium	France
Benin	Gabon
Bolivia	Germany
Brazil	Ghana
Burkina Faso	Greece
Cameroun	Guatemala
Canada	Guinea
Cape Verde	Haiti
Central African	Honduras
Republic	Iceland
Chad	India
Chile	Indonesia
China (PRC)	Iran
Colombia	Iraq
Congo	Ireland
Costa Rica	Israel
Côte d'Ivoire	Italy

Jamaica
Japan
Jordan
Kenya
Korea (ROK)
Kuwait
Lebanon
Libya
Liechtenstein
Luxembourg
Madagascar
Malawai
Malaysia
Mali
Mauritania
Mauritius
Mexico
Monaco
Morocco
Mozambique
Nepal
Netherlands
New Zealand
Nicaragua
Niger
Nigeria
Norway
Oman
Pakistan
Panama
Papua New Guinea
Paraguay
Peru
Philippines
Portugal
Qatar

Romania
Rwanda
Saudi Arabia
Senegal
Singapore
Somalia
South Africa
Spain
Sri Lanka
Sudan
Swaziland
Sweden
Switzerland
Syria
Tanzania
Thailand
Togo
Trinidad and Tobago
Tunisia
Turkey
Uganda
United Arab
    Emirates
United Kingdom
United States
Uruguay
Vatican City
Venezuela
Vietnam
Yemen Arab
    Republic
Yugoslavia
Zaire
Zambia
Zimbabwe

Sources: Long, 1987, pp. 83, 106–107, 117, 123; Intelsat, 1990–91, pp. 37–40; *World Radio TV Handbook,* 1992, p. 440.

GLOSSARY

Advanced television (ATV) A reference to any television broadcasting standard that uses more than the 525 or 625 lines of visual resolution provided by NTSC, PAL, and SECAM standards in use throughout the world. See also **high-definition television (HDTV), NTSC, PAL,** and **SECAM.**

Alphabet 1A No. 5 An international standard alphabetic code for the transmission of data using telecommunications devices. See also **ASCII.**

Amplitude Modulation (AM) A method of changing the peak values of a wave carrying information so that they vary with the strength (or loudness) of the information signal, thus causing a receiver to detect and amplify the signal to match that of the originating transmit-

ter, and reproducing that signal so that it can be heard accurately over a speaker. This form of broadcasting is used by both shortwave and medium-wave transmitters, and for the audio or video signals of some television standards. See also **frequency modulation (FM).**

Analog broadcasting The form of broadcasting used since the early days of radio. It requires that the radio waves that carry the information from transmitter to receiver, and the electrical signals that travel from microphone, tape player, or compact disc to transmitter, and from receiver to speaker, each reproduce faithfully the original signal in both strength (amplitude) and frequency within the limits of the channel used. See also **digital broadcasting.**

Sources: The definitions in this glossary were adapted from several sources, including Bittner, 1985, pp. 462–472; Fortner and Durham, 1986, pp. 244–256; Graham, 1983, pp. 9–187; and Head, 1985, pp. 403–420.

Antenna A device used to transmit or detect radio waves. Shortwave broadcasting uses several different types of transmitting antennas, the most common one being a curtain antenna using cables strung between towers to create a curtain effect. Receiving antennas also are of several types: telescoping whips, loops, long wires strung between houses and other objects, towers, and so on. All antennas are designed to increase the gain (or power) transmitted or received.

ASCII The standard U.S. code for information interchange, a version of the International Alphabet No. 5 code. It is a 7-bit code (plus a parity bit) used for data transfer within or between computers.

Attenuation Reduction in quality of signals, often as a result of distance. In wired systems, repeaters are used to compensate for attenuation. In wireless systems, broadcasters increase power or reduce frequencies to compensate.

Back-feed Raw news copy that is fed from on-site locations back to central news rooms for processing into news feeds. Back-feeds are not designed for audience consumption. See also **news feed.**

Bandwidth The width of a channel or signal carried between a transmitter and receiver. Bandwidths are measured in hertz (or multiples of hertz, such as kilohertz, megahertz, and gigahertz). The wider the bandwidth of a channel or signal, the more information it can carry. Television signals thus use wider bandwidths than do radio signals, and radio signals use wider ones than do telephone signals.

Baudot code A 5-digit code named for Emile Baudot, who discovered that signals could be coded and decoded based on the number of pulses per second used.

Bootleg An unauthorized recording, often made during a live concert, that is then duplicated and sold by recording pirates.

Broadband A channel using a wide bandwidth capable of carrying complex signals, such as video signals. Coaxial cables (capable of bandwidths of up to 60 mHz), waveguides (capable of bandwidths of up to 11 gHz), and satellite channels (typically using bandwidths for video signals and data communication between 34 and 72 mHz) are all broadband technologies.

Broadcast satellite service (BSS) The ITU designation for broadcasting signals delivered to audiences directly from satellites. See also **direct broadcast satellite (DBS).**

C-band A dedicated satellite band of frequencies between 3,700 and 4,200 mHz, used by the satellites manufactured in the United States and the Commonwealth of Independent States for both telecommunications and broadcast services.

Cellular telephony/cellular communication A form of telecommunication using radio waves to increase use of mobile telephones. The system is based on the use of low-power transmitter/receivers and computer-controlled switches located in cells, generally between 2 and 10 miles in diameter, that handle all the cellular communication within them and then relinquish control of communication as users pass into an adjacent cell. The system is also capable of handling data communication, and is designed to allow large numbers of users to use the same radio frequencies without interfering with one another.

Ciphers Coded transmissions between senders and receivers that prevent other users of a telecommunications system (whether wire-based or wireless) from reading information they intercept. Such codes are widely used by the military, and to a lesser extent by private corporations, to protect secrets. See also **encryption.**

Clandestine radio Secretive radio stations that desire to keep their actual identity unknown. They represent political movements, guerrilla organizations, or a country at war with another that attempts to broadcast into a country under false pretenses. They also operate without license, or authorization, from the target country.

Coaxial cable A cable with two transmission layers on a single axis. These layers consist of a central copper core and a woven copper tube under a covering of insulating material. They are capable of broadband transmissions, and are used in the United States to deliver cable television signals to homes and internationally for submarine cables.

Compression A technique to reduce the bandwidth required to move a signal between transmitter and receiver. It is based in digital signal processing. The signals are squeezed into a narrower bandwidth by eliminating redundant information, for instance by transmitting only the differences between one image and the next, allowing the second image to be constructed on the basis of the first, rather than by transmitting each complete image independently.

Convention A term applied in international law to a treaty or other ratified agreement.

Cultural imperialism The belief that the indigenous values, mores, or ways of life of the people in one country are supplanted by those of another through control of cultural artifacts, such as radio and television programs, news copy, recorded material, and books. Since the world's production and distribution of such cultural materials is dominated by Western industrial countries (particularly the United States and the United Kingdom), they are said to be exercising hegemony over the world's peoples in a manner akin to that exercised by the former empires of Britain, France, Germany, and so on from the 18th to the middle of the 20th century.

Currency exchange The interchangeability of the currency of one country for that of another. This term is used mostly in the context of the interchangeability of local currency for what are called "hard" currencies — that is, those that are accepted globally as media of exchange in international trade, including the U.S. dollar, British pound sterling, French franc, Swiss franc, German deutsche mark, and Japanese yen. See also **hard currency.**

Digital audiotape (DAT) A recording technology using signal processors to convert the analog signals produced by phonographs, microphones, or conventional tape recorders into digital form, or to duplicate the digital signals of compact discs, for recording on tape. This system provides the capability to reproduce recordings without loss of quality from one recorded medium to another. Record producers have objected strenuously to its introduction, arguing that it will enable audio pirates to produce illegal recordings of the same quality as those of legitimate companies.

Digital broadcasting A form of broadcasting using digitally encoded signals rather than analog signals. Digital signals use binary (on or off) digits to encode information, and are based on sampling the original sound or image to process it into digital form. Digital signals have lower error rates than analog signals, and thus require less redundancy in the transmission system. This means that such signals can be compressed into narrower bandwidths without loss of information. They can also be regenerated easily, require less complex interfaces, and can be multiplexed using time division methods that increase the speed of transmission, thus saving transmission costs.

Direct broadcast satellite (DBS) A satellite designed to deliver signals directly to audiences without redistribution by a terrestrial system, such as cable or radio rebroadcast. Viewers use their own satellite dishes for video signals, some of which are less than 3 feet in diameter, and may be able to use helical antennas (figure 8s imposed on short tubes) or even whip antennas to pick up satellite radio signals.

Disinformation The process by which one country surreptitiously releases information designed to mislead another, usually either about its own intentions or about the activities or motives of a third country.

Down-link The signal path from a satellite to a terrestrial satellite dish. Using satellites for point-to-point or point-to-multipoint distribution requires the use of both up-links and down-links. Specific separate frequencies are assigned for both legs of a satellite path, which allows the same dish to be used as both transmitter and receiver for telecommunications applications. See also **up-link.**

Duplex circuit A circuit that allows for two-way simultaneous conversations. It carries signals between two terminals in both directions simultaneously.

Economy of scale The phenomenon that allows the per unit cost of producing a commodity or service to decline as the total production volume increases. Certain fixed costs of administration, capital investment, borrowing, and so on, when spread over a larger number of units of production, allow certain economies to be made, thus producing what is called an economy of scale.

Electromagnetic frequency Any light or radio wave broadcast through the air uses a particular detectable frequency. Such waves are referred to as electromagnetic waves, since they use a portion (or frequency) of all the known frequencies. The total of known frequencies for all light or radio wave transmission makes up what is called the electromagnetic spectrum. The radio waves for broadcasting use frequencies in this spectrum between 30 kHz and 3gHz.

Electronic funds transfer (EFT) The practice of moving money from one site to another by electronic means. Although the money itself does not actually move, funds are removed from one account and added to another electronically on demand.

Encryption The practice of transmitting information using codes that must be deciphered before the recipient can make sense of the message. Encryption is designed to prevent unauthorized persons from having access to sensitive information, such as military or trade secrets. See also **ciphers.**

Facsimile (fax) A machine and transmission system (based on facsimile telegraphy) that allows graphic images, including letters, photographs, maps, and so on, to be transmitted over wired or wireless telecommunications systems. It uses an optical scanning device that converts an image into electrical signals representing the presence or absence of image (i.e., ink, line, or letter) that are then transmitted to a similar device that reproduces the image based on these signals. Facsimile devices are rated according to the speed with which they will transmit a standard A4-size document (similar to the U.S. letter size $8\frac{1}{2} \times 11$). Group 1 machines require 3 to 6 minutes for such transmission; group 2, 3 minutes; and group 3, 1 minute.

Fiber optics Transmission systems using light pulses traveling down hollow glass tubes the diameter of a human hair. The light pulses are reflected off the outer sheath inside these tubes to carry the information with very little degradation of the signal. Each fiber is capable of carrying an enormous amount of information, including multiple video signals or high-speed data.

Frequency The number of oscillations (or cycles) per second of a radio or light wave. Radio channels are designated by their center frequency (i.e., 550 kHz or 104.6 mHz). The width of such channels is also calculated using designations, with voice telephone channels occupying 3.0 to 3.4 kHz, AM radio waves 9 or 10 kHz width, FM radio waves 200 kHz, and television signals 5 to 8 mHz, including the audio feed.

Frequency modulation (FM) A method of changing a carrier wave's frequency around a constant reference point in response to the low-frequency signal transmitted. Broadcasting in FM also uses wider bandwidths than do AM signals, and thus has higher fidelity. In addition, FM signals are less susceptible to atmospheric interference, or static, than are AM signals. See also **amplitude modulation (AM).**

Frequency sampling The practice of periodically taking a sample of the frequencies used in a communication activity, such as a conversation or concert, as the basis for recording signals using digital encoding. Frequency sampling is the basis of compact disc recording and playback.

Gain The increase in the power of a signal accomplished in the process of amplification. Gain is provided by transmitting antennas, receiving antennas, and amplification circuits.

Geostationary satellite A satellite put into an equatorial orbit at a distance of 35,000 kilometers. At this distance from the earth, the satellite's orbital speed will match that of the earth's rotation, so that it will appear to be motionless in the sky. This allows satellite dishes to be trained on it 24 hours per day, thus providing full-time transmission and reception of signals. See also **geosynchronous orbit.**

Geosynchronous orbit The orbit of satellites at a distance of 35,000 kilometers (22,300 miles) from the surface of the earth. At this distance the satellites' orbits are synchronous with that of the earth's rotation, making them appear to remain stationary. Such satellites reduced the cost of earth stations by making it possible for satellite dishes to be trained at one point in the sky rather than have to track a moving satellite. See also **geostationary satellite.**

Gigahertz (gHz) A reference to the frequency of a radio signal, expressed in billions of cycles per second. Satellite communication occurs at gigahertz frequencies. See also **kilohertz (kHz)** and **megahertz (mHz).**

Hard currency A reference to the currency (money) of a few economically powerful countries that can be readily exchanged (or converted) in almost any other country of the world. Goods are bought and sold using these currencies, and international debts must be paid using them. The U.S. dollar, the British pound sterling, the French and Swiss francs, the German deutsche mark, and the Japanese yen are the currencies most widely used as hard currencies. Prior to the demise of the Soviet Union, the ruble was widely used within the Soviet bloc as a hard currency, but it had no status outside the countries of Soviet-dominated Eastern and Central Europe.

High-definition television (HDTV) An advanced television standard that increases the lines of resolution available on television screens. The best HDTV systems allow television sets to approximate the detail (or definition) of 35 mm film. HDTV increases the current 525- to 625-line broadcasting standard to 1,000 or more lines. HDTV broadcasting will allow wide-screen television with an aspect ratio similar to that of movie theaters.

High-frequency radio (HF radio) Another name for shortwave broadcasting, so called because it uses that portion of the electromagnetic spectrum referred to as "high frequency"—frequencies between 3 and 30 mHz.

Impedance The measure of resistance to the passage of a signal through a recording or transmission system, such as a coaxial cable.

Intellectual property Products of the mind, such as books, newspaper stories, films, and sound and video recordings. Intellectual property can be protected by copyright and trademark statutes.

Internal affairs A reference to the activities that occur within the borders of a nation-state and are construed by international law not to be subject to interference by other states. Sovereignty refers, among other things, to any country's control over its internal affairs.

International gateways Points of connection between the domestic telecommunications infrastructure of any country and the international system, such as those between domestic telephone systems and international fiber optic cables or satellite links.

International public opinion A reference to the existence of world opinion on particular issues. Although various countries refer, or appeal, to world opinion, it is not a measurable phenomenon.

Jamming The practice of deliberately transmitting a signal on the same, or very nearly the same, frequency as another radio or television signal to interfere with the reception of that signal. Jamming can be accomplished by simply putting another broadcast program on the frequency to garble or confuse it for the listener, or by broadcasting tones, noises of various kinds, or "static" on a frequency to make it so difficult to listen to that audiences give up. Jamming is usually employed by governments to prevent their citizens from hearing the broadcasts of external (or nondomestic) broadcasters and thus to maintain a monopoly of information.

Ka-band A dedicated band of satellite frequencies between 18 and 20 gHz.

Kilobit A reference to the speed of data transfer. A kilobit is 1,000 bits of information, and will transfer via a digital transmission system (such as a fiber optic cable, or through use of a computer and modem over a telephone line) at so many kilobits per second. A gigabit, when used to describe the capacity of optical fibers, refers to the transmission of one billion bits of information per second.

Kilohertz (kHz) A reference to the frequency of a radio wave. The channels used for radio transmission are assigned particular frequencies within the electromagnetic spectrum. The transmitted signal travels within a band centered on the assigned frequency, and radio and television receivers tune in the assigned

center frequency to detect the program sought. These frequencies are designated by the number of hertz (or cycles per second) that they use: the higher the frequency, the higher the hertzian designation. One kilohertz indicates 1,000 cycles per second.

Ku-band A dedicated band of satellite frequencies between 10.9 and 12.75 gHz. The Ku1-band, between 10.9 and 11.75 gHz, is dedicated to fixed satellite services (FSS); the Ku2-band, between 11.75 and 12.5 gHz, is dedicated to direct broadcast satellite service (DBS); and the Ku3-band, between 12.5 and 12.75 gHz, is dedicated to telecommunication services.

Low-orbit satellite Any satellite operating in less than a geosynchronous orbit. Such satellites must be tracked, and are available for a limited amount of time to any given earth station. See also **geosynchronous orbit.**

MATV Master antenna television. A type of cable television operation used within apartment buildings or other dense living facilities that allows a single antenna to receive broadcasting signals for distribution within the entire complex.

Medium wave (MW) Also called medium frequency. A portion of the electromagnetic frequency spectrum used for what is usually called AM broadcasting. Medium-wave signals use frequencies between 300 and 3,000 kHz.

Megahertz (mHz) A reference to the frequency of a radio wave. One megahertz is equivalent to one million cycles per second. See also **kilohertz (kHz)** and **gigahertz (gHz).**

Mobile communication Communication that occurs between a moving object, usually a vehicle such as an automobile, and a fixed-point base station, or between two such vehicles. This term is often applied to cellular radio systems. See also **cellular radio.**

Multiplexing The practice of mixing signals from two or more channels into a single path by using frequency division (for analog signals) or time division (for digital signals) to increase the efficiency of transmission. Multiplexed paths carry denser streams of signals, allowing for higher transmission rates or increased complexity. Stereo broadcasting signals are multiplexed, for instance, which allows the separate signals for left and right speakers to be carried on the same FM channel.

News feed The processed news product carried from a central newsroom to a distribution system (affiliated station, cable operation, or satellite) for delivery to an audience. News feeds are packaged final products designed for audience consumption. See also **backfeed.**

NTSC (National Television Standards Committee) The broadcast television standard adopted in the United States in 1951, and used primarily in the Americas, the Philippines, and Japan. It includes a 525-line video field and a single color subcarrier, and is broadcast using amplitude modulation for the video signal and frequency modulation for the audio signal, in either monaural or stereo.

Orbital slot The assigned spot occupied by a satellite in geosynchronous orbit.

Packet switching The practice of bundling various types of information (conversations, radio and television signals, data) into smaller bits (or packets) that can be transmitted over a packet-switching exchange. These packets can be transmitted out of sequence or can follow different transmission paths, and are reconstructed by receiving stations based on transmitted identifiers and sequencing information that travels with each packet. This allows each transmission path to be used more efficiently, as packets can be inserted into a data stream as openings become available.

PAL (phase alternate line) The television standard originally developed by Germany's Telefunken Company, and adopted throughout Western Europe (except France) in the post–World War II era. It is also widely used in other parts of the world, particularly in areas that were colonial possessions of the British. It uses a 625-line video field and a single color subcarrier, and is broadcast using amplitude modulation for the video and audio signals. Variations on the PAL standard have been adopted by various countries, including PAL M (Brazil), and PAL N (Argentina).

Perturbations Variations in the orbit of a satellite. Satellites carry booster rockets that allow ground control stations to correct such perturbations to keep them in their proper orbital slots.

Photoelectric facsimile code A binary code indicating the presence or absence of ink on paper that the optical scanner of a fax machine uses to transmit that image over a telecommunications path.

Pirate broadcasting Radio or television broadcasting conducted without a broadcasting permit or license from the country where the broadcaster is operating, and without official registration with the IFRB. Such broadcasts can be aimed at domestic audiences in the country where the pirate's transmitter is located, or at audiences in adjacent countries. Often pirate broadcasters use low-power transmitters that can be easily moved to prevent governments from locating them.

Power flux density Measurement of the power of a satellite's delivered signal to the earth.

Propaganda A term usually applied to the political information provided by any country's perceived "enemy" in a dispute. Such information is often considered untrue or biased, and is designed to destabilize the recipient country's government, interfere in its internal affairs, or illegitimately question its policies. See also **internal affairs** and **psychological warfare.**

Psychological warfare The practice of a state using communication, particularly the mass media, as a weapon in disputes with other states. The term typically is confined to the media activities of states that are ideological adversaries or are clearly involved in a military conflict.

Public diplomacy The practice of explaining the policy of a government by using the mass media, including media operated or funded by the government, and independent media. Many governments have official "voices," such as the Voice of America or the Voice of Baghdad, that express official views, but that also attempt to influence the independent press or broadcast media to report particular stories or to provide the government's views on events they report.

Radiotelegraph Another term for wireless telegraphy; the transmission of telegraph signals using radio waves.

Record service Any transmission system that provides a written record of the actual content of the communications transmitted. Telegraph, telex, teleprinter, and facsimile systems are all record services, whereas telephone systems are not.

Reservation A statement made by a government when signing an international agreement or treaty that it does not intend to follow particular clauses or requirements of the document. By taking a reservation the government exempts itself from that portion of the agreement, and cannot be held accountable under international law for that provision.

Right to communicate The declared right of individual people to seek out information and to communicate with others as a defensible and basic human right. This right, enshrined in a variety of international agreements and declarations, supersedes the right of the state to control access to information or the ability

of people to communicate with others domestically or across international frontiers.

Satellite dish A concave antenna designed to collect and amplify the transmitted signals from satellites sufficiently to allow them to be decoded and used in radio and television receivers.

Satellite orbital slot The parking space assigned to each satellite as it is put into orbit. Satellite orbital slots have been assigned at closer and closer intervals as the beams have become more tightly focused and methods of polarization have improved. Some satellites are now parked as close as 1 degree apart.

S-band A dedicated satellite band of frequencies between 1,700 and 3,000 mHz.

SECAM (Séquence Coleur à Mémoire) The television broadcasting standard developed by the French, and used in France and more than 20 other countries, mostly in Eastern Europe. It uses a 625-line video field and two color subcarriers (red and blue), and is broadcast using a frequency-modulated video signal and amplitude-modulated audio signal.

Shortwave (SW) In engineering terms, shortwave or high frequency. This term is usually applied to broadcasting services, both domestic and international, that make use of the high-frequency portion of the electromagnetic frequency spectrum.

Spark gap transmitter Early wireless radiotelegraph transmitters operated by pulsing powerful radio waves into the atmosphere. They operated by completing an electrical circuit and gave off sparks as the two elements of the transmitting device neared each other. They had to be replaced by continuous wave transmitters before radio could develop, since they emitted only bursts of energy corresponding to various binary codes, such as Morse code.

Spillover A reference to the footprint of a satellite crossing the border of a target country into neighboring countries. Since the actual footprint, or reception area, of a satellite signal cannot easily be made to conform to the exact boundaries of a country, spillover is a normal result of the application of communication satellites, although ITU regulations on DBS television require that it be kept to a minimum wherever possible.

Standard Any agreed upon technical requirement applied to a communications system. Standards are adopted to ensure that the domestic communications systems of countries can be interconnected without damaging one another, and to provide manufacturers with technical specifications for the production of communications equipment. Standards are adopted and ratified by countries that are members of various international organizations, such as the International Standards Organization (ISO) and the International Telecommunication Union (ITU).

Stringer A journalist who provides occasional copy to a news organization, including newspapers, wire services, and news broadcasters. Stringers are usually paid on a per story or per word basis for the copy used by the recipient organization.

Studio-to-transmitter link The transmission link between the studio in which a program originates and the transmitter that sends the signal to the audience. Such links can be telephone lines, microwave links, or even satellite paths.

Submarine telegraph An underseas cable capable of carrying telegraph signals. Early transatlantic telegraph links, for instance, were referred to as submarine telegraphs.

Technical standards The requirements adopted by countries or international agreements that govern the manufacture and installation of equipment as part of telecommunications or broadcasting systems. See also **standard.**

Telecommunications Long-distance point-to-point communication conducted using either wired or wireless electrical or electronic means.

Telex A telegraph exchange. A communications service based in the use of teletypewriters and switched telecommunications networks, such as telephone lines. Telex signals use the International Alphabet No. 2.

Transponder A transmitter/receiver used in a communications satellite.

Turn-key installation A completed communications facility, such as a broadcasting station, satellite transmitting and receiving station, or telecommunications switching station, constructed and tested by a contractor and turned over ready to be operated. All phases of the construction and implementation are handled by the contractor, leaving the final user only the job of operation.

Up-link The path of a signal from a terrestrial satellite dish to a satellite.

Very high frequency (VHF) The frequency used for frequency modulation (FM) radio transmission and VHF television (channels 2–13); frequencies between 30 and 300 mHz.

Voice circuit Two voice channels, each with a 3 to 3.4 kHz bandwidth, that allow a conversation to move in both directions between terminals. See also **bandwidth** and **duplex circuit.**

Voltage Measure of the motive power of an electrical circuit, calculated by dividing the wattage of the connected device by its amperage.

VSAT (very small aperture terminal) A type of satellite receiving dish, usually 60 cm or less in diameter, used for high-speed data communication.

WARC (World Administrative Radio Conference) Meeting called under the auspices of the ITU to consider specific international regulatory issues, such as broadcasting standards, assignment of portions of the electromagnetic spectrum to specific services, satellite orbital positions, and so on. WARC meetings usually result in conventions and/or regulations to govern specific practices of countries engaging in international communication. See also **convention.**

REFERENCES

A $3 Billion International Program Market. (1982, September). *Video Age International,* 41.

ABC news show links U.S.-Soviet officials. (1987, September 28). *Broadcasting, 113,* 64, 65.

Abshire, D. M. (1976). *International Broadcasting: A New Dimension of Western Diplomacy.* Beverly Hills, CA: Sage.

A CD business. (1992, January 3). *The Economist, 321,* 80.

Action Programme for Economic Cooperation of the 4th Summit Conference of the Non-Aligned Countries. (1973). In K. Nordenstreng, E. G. Manet, & W. Kelenwächter (Eds.), *New International Information and Communication Order Sourcebook.* Prague, Czechoslovakia: International Organization of Journalists, 275.

Adams, J. B. (1964). A qualitative analysis of domestic and foreign news on the AP TA wire. *Gazette, 10,* 285–295,

Adelman, K. L. (1981). Speaking of America: Public diplomacy in our time. *Foreign Affairs, 59* (Spring), 913–936.

Adeyinka, A. A. (1977). The impact of foreign culture on African education. *Universitas, 6.*

Agarwala, P. N. (1983). *The New International Economic Order: An Overview.* New York: Pergamon Press.

Agrawal, B. C. (1986). Cultural response to communication revolution: Many modes of video use in India. *Gazette, 38,* 29–41.

Aitken, H. G. J. (1976). *Syntony and Spark — The Origins of Radio.* New York: Wiley.

Aitken, H. G. J. (1985). *The Continuous Wave: Technology and American Radio, 1900–1932.* Princeton, NJ: Princeton University Press.

Alexandre, L. (1988). *The Voice of America: From Detente to the Reagan Doctrine.* Norwood, NJ: Ablex.

Alexeyeva, L. (1986). *U.S. Broadcasting to the Soviet Union.* New York: Helsinki Watch Committee.

Alisky, M. (1988). Peru. In P. T. Rosen (Ed.), *International Handbook of Broadcasting Systems.* New York: Greenwood Press, 237–242.

All EC countries but France support HDTV strategy. (1991, December 18). Reuters report.

Alov, G., & Viktorov, V. (1985). *Aggressive Broadcasting: Evidence, Facts, Documents.* Moscow: Novosti Press Agency.

Altschull, J. H. (1984). *Agents of Power: The Role of the News Media in Human Affairs.* New York: Longman.

Alvarado, M. (Ed.). (1988). *Video World-Wide: An International Study.* London: John Libbey.

American Society of International Law. (1975). *Direct Broadcasting from Satellites: Policies and Problems.* St. Paul, MN: West.

Anawalt, H. C. (1984). Direct television broadcasting and the quest for communication equality. In *Regulation of Transnational Broadcasting.* In *Michigan Yearbook of International Legal Studies 1984.* New York: Clark Boardman, 361–377.

Anderson, L. (1987, 7 December). Raisa-watching nears its summit. *Chicago Tribune.*

Andrew, W. P. (1857). *Memoir on the Euphrates Valley Route to India: With Official Correspondence and Maps.* London: Wm. H. Allen.

Andrew, W. P. (1884). *Indian Railways as Connected with British Empire in the East.* (4th ed.). London: Allen.

Antola, L., & Rogers, E. M. (1984). Television flows in Latin America. *Communication Research, 11,* 183–202.

Appleton, E. L. (1991, November 1). Solving the international networking blues. *Datamation, 37,* 80, 81.

Archampong, K. (1977). The problem of cultural identity and individualism. *Universitas, 6.*

Armour, C. (1984). The BBC and the development of broadcasting in British colonial Africa 1946–1956. *African Affairs,* 359–402.

Arno, A., & Dissanayake, W. (Eds.). (1984). *The News Media in National and International Conflict.* Boulder, CO: Westview Press.

Arnst, C. (1991a, October 7). World telecommunications industry eyes developing world. Reuters report.

Arnst, C. (1991b, October 14). Africa need phone, must travel. Reuters report.

Arnst, C. (1991c, December 1). Europe's struggles over HDTV eclipsed by new technology. Reuters report.

Aronson, J. (1970). *The Press and the Cold War.* Indianapolis, IN: Bobbs-Merrill.

Aronson, J.D., & Cowhey, P. F. (1988). *When Countries Talk: International Trade in Telecommunications Services.* Cambridge, MA: Ballinger.

Artemov, V. (1981). *Information Abused: Critical Essays.* Moscow: Progress.

Article 19. (1988). *Information, Freedom and Censorship.* London: Longman.

Astoroff, R. (1987). Communication and contemporary colonialism: Broadcast television in Puerto Rico. *Studies in Latin American Popular Culture, 6,* 11–26.

Ayish, M. I. (1987). The VOA Arabic service: A study of news principles and occupational values. *Gazette, 40,* 121–130.

Aziz, S. (1978). The new international order: Search for a common ground. *International Development Review, 20,* 6–15.

B.B.C. Annual 1935. (1935). London: BBC.

B.B.C. Annual 1937. (1937). London: BBC.

The B.B.C. Handbook 1928. (1928). London: BBC.

The B.B.C. Handbook 1929. (1929). London: BBC.

BBC Handbook 1940. (1940). London: BBC.

The B.B.C. Year-Book 1930. (1930). London: BBC.

The B.B.C. Year-Book 1931. (1931). London: BBC.

Babcock, C. R. (1988, 12 June). Allegations delay contract on U.S. broadcast station near Dead Sea. *Washington Post.*

Bachtell, E. E., Bettadapur, S. S., Coyner, J. V., & Farrell, C. E. (1985). *Satellite Voice Broadcast Final Report* (Contract No. NAS3-24233) (Executive Summary). Martin Marietta Denver Aerospace.

Back from the USSR. (1989, 4 September). *Broadcasting, 117.*

Baglehole, K. C. (1969). *A Century of Service: A Brief History of Cable and Wireless Ltd. 1868–1968.* London: Cable and Wireless.

Baird, J. W. (1974). *The Mythical World of Nazi War Propaganda: 1939–1945.* Minneapolis: University of Minnesota Press.

Baker, W. J. (1970). *A History of the Marconi Company.* London: Methuen.

Balfour, M. (1979). *Propaganda in War 1939–1945: Organisations, Policies and Publics in Britain and Germany.* London: Routledge & Kegan Paul.

Banning, W. P. (1946). *Commercial Broadcasting Pioneer: The WEAF Experiment 1922–1926.* Cambridge, MA: Harvard University Press.

Bannov, B. (1984). Piracy on the airwaves: evidence points to the CIA [*Novosti press agency release,* monitored by the BBC from Moscow on December 4].

Barker, E. (1935). International broadcasting: Its problems and possibilities. In *B.B.C. Annual 1935.* London: BBC, 145–155.

Barnes, E. B. (1965). *An Intellectual and Cultural History of the Western World* (3rd rev. ed.) (Vol. 2). New York: Dover.

Barnet, R. J., & Müller, R. E. (1974). *Global Reach: The Power of Multinational Corporations.* New York: Simon & Schuster.

Barnouw, E. (1966). *A Tower in Babel: A History of Broadcasting in the United States to 1933.* New York: Oxford University Press.

Barnouw, E. (1968). *The Golden Web: A History of Broadcasting in the United States, 1933–1953.* New York: Oxford University Press.

Barnouw, E. (1983). Propaganda at radio Luxembourg: 1944–1945. In K. R. M. Short (Ed.), *Film and Radio Propaganda in World War II.* London: Croom Helm, 192–197.

Barr, P. (1986, February/March). Who needs the most can afford it the least. *Asia-Pacific Broadcasting & Telecommunications,* 31–33.

Barrington, J. (n.d.). *Lord Haw Haw of Zeesen.* London: Hutchinson.

BBC International Broadcasting and Audience Research. (1983, July). *Survey in the United States November 1981 to April 1982.*

BBC International Broadcasting and Audience Research. (1988, 6 January). *BBC Rebroadcasts Using European Satellite Circuits.* London: BBC, IBAR.

BBC International Broadcasting and Audience Research. (1989a, February). *BBC and Competitors: External Broadcasting Languages.* London: BBC, IBAR.

BBC International Broadcasting and Audience Research. (1989b, June). *World Radio & Television Receivers.* London: BBC, IBAR.

BBC International Broadcasting and Audience Research. (1991, June). *World Radio and Television Receivers.* London: BBC, IBAR.

BBC International Broadcasting and Audience Research. (1992, February 28). BBC European Satellite Rebroadcasts.

BBC International Broadcasting and Audience Research Library. (1989 June). League Table.

BBC International Broadcasting and Audience Research Library. (1990, January). League Table.

BBC International Broadcasting and Audience Research Library. (1991, June). League Table.

BBC International Broadcasting and Audience Research Library. (1992, February). League Table.

BBC Launches Asian News Channel. (1991a, October 21). *Broadcasting, 121,* 50.

BBC Launches Satellite TV Service to Asia. (1991b, October 14). Reuters report.

BBC Monitoring Service. (1987a, March 20). USSR: Radio Moscow comments on the jamming of international broadcasts. [Second Series]. *WBI: World Broadcasting Information* (No. 12), A9.

BBC Monitoring Service. (1987b, May 15). USSR: Six-channel wired radio system on test in Moscow. [Second Series]. *WBI: World Broadcasting Information* (No. 20), A8.

BBC Monitoring Service. (1987c, May 29). Senegal: PANA announces plans for commercialisation and computerisation. [Second Series]. *WBI: World Broadcasting Information*] (No. 21), A12.

BBC Monitoring Service. (1987d, October 9). France: Europe No. 1 relayed via satellites to Caribbean Commonwealth countries. [Second Series]. *WBI: World Broadcasting Information* (No. 41), A4.

BBC Monitoring Service. (1987e, November 13). Poland: Polish radio starts programme of excerpts from Western broadcasts in Polish. [Second Series]. *WBI: World Broadcasting Information* (No. 46), A5.

BBC Monitoring Service. (1987f, November 27). Hungary: Hungarian television comments on satellite TV. [Third Series]. *WBI: World Broadcasting Information* (No. 48), A4.

BBC Monitoring Service. (1987g, November 27). Poland: Newspaper comments on the challenge of satellite television. [Third Series]. *WBI: World Broadcasting Information* (No. 48), A6.

BBC Monitoring Service. (1987h, December 4). USSR: Profile of Tass on agency's 70th birthday. [Third Series]. *WBI: World Broadcasting Information* (No. 49), A10.

BBC Monitoring Service. (1988a, January 15). AWR-Asia transmitters now fully operational. [Third Series]. *WBI: World Broadcasting Information* (No. 4), A3.

BBC Monitoring Service. (1988b, March 25). AWR-Latin America and its future plans. [Third Series]. *WBI: World Broadcasting Information* (No. 14), A1.

BBC Monitoring Service. (1988c, March 25). Interest in satellite TV continues to grow in Poland. [Third Series]. *WBI: World Broadcasting Information* (No. 14), A9–A10.

BBC Monitoring Service. (1988d, April 22). Director general of Egyptian radio interviewed on broadcasting developments. [Third Series]. *WBI: World Broadcasting Information* (No. 18), A3.

BBC Monitoring Service. (1988e, June 10). US accused of operating anti-Noriega radio. [Third Series]. *WBI: World Broadcasting Information* (No. 24), A5.

BBC Monitoring Service. (1988f, June 17). France to finance TV stations at Parakou and Natitingou. [Third Series]. *WBI: World Broadcasting Information* (No. 25), A1.

BBC Monitoring Service. (1988g, June 17). VOA criticised for replacing Thai HF service with satellite feed. [Third Series]. *WBI: World Broadcasting Information* (No. 25), A6–A7.

BBC Monitoring Service. (1988h, July 8). Foreign TV crews to be permitted to film without Foreign Ministry authorisation. [Third Series]. *WBI: World Broadcasting Information* (No. 28), A3.

BBC Monitoring Service. (1988i, July 15). PLO programme temporarily carries only Koranic verse and patriotic songs. [Third Series]. *WBI: World Broadcasting Information* (No. 29), A1.

BBC Monitoring Service. (1988j, July 10). The reception of Hungarian radio and TV in Romania. [Third Series]. *WBI: World Broadcasting Information* (No. 29), A2.

BBC Monitoring Service. (1988k, July 22). Canal plus signs agreement to provide TV service to Gabon. [Third Series]. *WBI: World Broadcasting Information* (No. 30), A1.

BBC Monitoring Service. (1988l, August 26). Tanjug links with international data banks. [Third Series]. *WBI: World Broadcasting Information* (No. 35), A8.

BBC Monitoring Service. (1988m, September 9). The influence of "glasnost" on Estonian TV. [Third Series]. *WBI: World Broadcasting Information* (No. 37), A7–A8.

BBC Monitoring Service. (1988n, October 7). AFRTS end short-wave transmissions. [Third Series]. *WBI: World Broadcasting Information* (No. 41), A5.

BBC Monitoring Service. (1988o, October 14). Perestroyka "slower" on external services. [Third Series]. *WBI: World Broadcasting Information* (No. 42), A6.

BBC Monitoring Service. (1988p, October 14). President announces decree to regulate foreign news agencies. [Third Series]. *WBI: World Broadcasting Information* (No. 42), A7.

BBC Monitoring Service. (1988q, October 21). Radio Moscow offers advertising on external services. [Third Series]. *WBI: World Broadcasting Information* (No. 43), A4.

BBC Monitoring Service. (1988r, October 28). ERTU signs co-operation agreement with PBC. [Third Series]. *WBI: World Broadcasting Information* (No. 44), A3.

BBC Monitoring Service. (1988s, October 28). Satellite TV gaining popularity. [Third Series]. *WBI: World Broadcasting Information* (No. 44), A6.

BBC Monitoring Service. (1988t, November 4). Religious broadcasting on TV and radio. [Third Series]. *WBI: World Broadcasting Information* (No. 45), A3.

BBC Monitoring Service. (1988u, November 25). Co-operation agreement between Iranian and Hungarian radio and TV. [Third Series]. *WBI: World Broadcasting Information* (No. 48), A4.

BBC Monitoring Service. (1988v, December 2). "All available means" to be used to respond to anti-Cuban TV. [Third Series]. *WBI: World Broadcasting Information* (No. 49), A5.

BBC Monitoring Service. (1989a, January 13). Jamming transmitters to be dismantled or used for broadcasting. [Third Series]. *WBI: World Broadcasting Information* (No. 2), A5.

BBC Monitoring Service. (1989b, January 17). Pyongyang FM radio accused of "anti-Seoul" propaganda. [Third Series]. *WBI: World Broadcasting Information* (No. 3), A4.

BBC Monitoring Service. (1989c, February 3). US commission raises questions over TV Martí project. [Third Series]. *WBI: World Broadcasting Information* (No. 5), A5.

BBC Monitoring Service. (1989d, February 24). MTV starts transmission via Astra satellite. [Third Series]. *WBI: World Broadcasting Information* (No. 8), A9.

BBC Monitoring Service. (1989e, March 10). RFE correspondents accredited to Hungary. [Third Series]. *WBI: World Broadcasting Information* (No. 10), A2.

BBC Monitoring Service. (1989f, March 10). Short-wave broadcasting of Union Republics' radios to begin in Moscow. [Third Series]. *WBI: World Broadcasting Information* (No. 10), A6.

BBC Monitoring Service. (1989g, March 17). Comment on the former jamming of Radio Liberty. [Third Series]. *WBI: World Broadcasting Information* (No. 11), A5.

BBC Monitoring Service. (1989h, March 17). Details of republican broadcasts to Moscow: Former jamming transmitters used. [Third Series]. *WBI: World Broadcasting Information* (No. 11), A5.

BBC Monitoring Service. (1989i, March 17). DW reports all Eastern block jamming has ceased. [Third Series]. *WBI: World Broadcasting Information* (No. 11), A2.

BBC Monitoring Service. (1989j, March 17). Subscription cable TV service in Volgograd. [Third Series]. *WBI: World Broadcasting Information* (No. 11), A6.

BBC Monitoring Service. (1989k, March 24). CBC signs co-operation agreement with Gostelradio. [Third Series]. *WBI: World Broadcasting Information* (No. 12), A2.

BBC Monitoring Service. (1989l, March 24). "Pravda" report on the disbanded jamming service. [Third Series]. *WBI: World Broadcasting Information* (No. 12), A7.

BBC Monitoring Service. (1989m, March 24). Review of first six republican broadcasts for listeners in Moscow. [Third Series]. *WBI: World Broadcasting Information* (No. 12), A8.

BBC Monitoring Service. (1989n, April 7). Polish and Turkish broadcasters cooperate. [Third Series]. *WBI: World Broadcasting Information* (No. 14), A3.

BBC Monitoring Service. (1989o, April 7). Review of AWR transmissions from Portugal. [Third Series]. *WBI: World Broadcasting Information* (No. 14), A3.

BBC Monitoring Service. (1989p, April 21). House of Representatives approves TV Marti budget. [Third Series]. *WBI: World Broadcasting Information* (No. 16), A6.

BBC Monitoring Service. (1989q, April 21). Tass general director discusses agency's plans. [Third Series]. *WBI: World Broadcasting Information* (No. 16), A8.

BBC Monitoring Service. (1989r, April 24). VOA accused of "rumourmongering" and "lies" to aid "counterrevolutionary rebellion." [Third Series]. *WBI: World Broadcasting Information* (No. 24), A2.

BBC Monitoring Service. (1989s, August 4). Action taken against unlicensed broadcasters in Fergana oblast. [Third Series]. *WBI: World Broadcasting Information* (No. 31), A6.

BBC Monitoring Service. (1989t, August 4). Africa No. 1 announces profits; fifth transmitter to be commissioned soon. [Third Series]. *WBI: World Broadcasting Information* (No. 31), A2.

BBC Monitoring Service. (1989u, August 4). CFI project to be extended to whole world. [Third Series]. *WBI: World Broadcasting Information* (No. 32), A8.

BBC Monitoring Service. (1989v, August 4). Domestically-produced equipment to enable reception of satellite TV. [Third Series]. *WBI: World Broadcasting Information* (No. 31), A8.

BBC Monitoring Service. (1989w, August 4). Programme exchange between Sudan and Egypt; reestablishment of Nile Valley Radio discussed. [Third Series]. *WBI: World Broadcasting Information* (No. 31), A6.

BBC Monitoring Service. (1989x, August 4). Reception of foreign satellite TV by individuals. [Third Series]. *WBI: World Broadcasting Information* (No. 31), A9.

BBC Monitoring Service. (1989y, August 18). Domestic radios to cover shortwave bands below 25 metres. [Third Series]. *WBI: World Broadcasting Information* (No. 33), A6.

BBC Monitoring Service. (1989z, August 18). Non-aligned conference calls for cancellation of TV Marti project. [Third Series]. *WBI: World Broadcasting Information* (No. 33), A6.

BBC Monitoring Service. (1989aa, December 16). AWR-Asia completes antenna construction. [Third Series]. *WBI: World Broadcasting Information* (No. 51), A3.

BBC Monitoring Service. (1991a, October 25). Africa no. 1 to broadcast in Paris. [Third Series]. *WBI: World Broadcasting Information* (No. 43), A1.

BBC Monitoring Service. (1991b, November 8). China Huayi Broadcasting Company to cover Asia and Europe from Fuzhou. [Third Series]. *WBI: World Broadcasting Information* (No. 45), A2, A3.

BBC Monitoring Service. (1991c, November 15). Nigerian minister of information calls on African leaders to salvage PANA. [Third Series]. *WBI: World Broadcasting Information* (No. 46), A14.

BBC Monitoring Service. (1991d, November 22). Radical changes to 3SAT TV to cater for information need in Eastern Europe. [Third Series]. *WBI: World Broadcasting Information* (No. 47), A4.

BBC Monitoring Service. (1992a, January 3). International satellite channel in Hindi to start on 1st January. [Third Series]. *WBI: World Broadcasting Information* (No. 1), A8.

BBC Monitoring Service. (1992b, January 10). "Izvestiya" reports on takeover of the former Gosteleradio Organisation. [Third Series]. *WBI: World Broadcasting Information* (No. 2), A9.

BBC Monitoring Service. (1992c, January 17). The Radio Maximum Network to be similar to that of NBC in the USA. [Third Series]. *WBI: World Broadcasting Information* (No. 3), A9.

BBC Monitoring Service. (1992d, February 14). Joint Ukrainian-American enterprise starts experimental FM service in Kiev. [Third Series]. *WBI: World Broadcasting Information* (No. 7), A9.

BBC Monitoring Service. (1992e, February 21). Deutsche Welle to start daily satellite TV service this year. [Third Series]. *WBI: World Broadcasting Information* (No. 8), A3.

BBC Monitoring Service. (1992f, February 28). Deutsche Welle TV for Europe to start in April on Eutelsat satellite. [Third Series]. *WBI: World Broadcasting Information* (No. 9), A5.

BBC Monitoring Service. (1992g, February 28). "Voice of Russia" to replace Radio Moscow world service (Russian) on 29th March. [Third Series]. *WBI: World Broadcasting Information* (No. 9), A8.

BBC Overseas Intelligence Department. (1941a, March 12). *Monthly Intelligence Report: Empire Countries and the U.S.A.* Caversham, England: BBC Written Archives Centre.

BBC Overseas Intelligence Department. (1941b, June 17). *Monthly Intelligence Report: Europe.* In *European Intelligence Papers: Series IA.* Caversham, England: BBC Written Archives Centre.

BBC Overseas Intelligence Department. (1941c, August 16). *Monthly Intelligence Report: Europe.* Caversham Park, England: BBC Written Archives Centre.

Beachcroft, T. O. ([1942]). *Calling All Nations.* London: BBC.

Bebey, F. (1974). UNESCO. In S. W. Head (Ed.), *Broadcasting to Africa: A Continental Survey of Radio and Television.* Philadelphia: Temple University Press, 254–258.

Belsie, L. (1991, April 5). Brazil opens computer market. *Christian Science Monitor*, 9.

Bencivenga, J. (1991, May 9). Brazil opens computer market. *Christian Science Monitor.*

Benge, R. C. (1972). *Communication and Identity.* London: Clive Bingley.

Beninger, J. R. (1986). *The Control Revolution: Technological and Economic Origins of the Information Society.* Cambridge, MA: Harvard University Press.

Bennett, G. (Ed.). (1962). *The Concept of Empire: Burke to Atlee 1774–1947* (2nd ed.). London: Adam & Charles Black.

Bennett, J. (1966). *British Broadcasting and the Danish Resistance Movement 1940–1945.* Cambridge: Cambridge University Press.

Bentley, H.D. (1991, October 28). Radio Free Asia. *Christian Science Monitor*, 19.

Bergreen, L. (1980). *Look Now, Pay Later: The Rise of Network Broadcasting.* New York: Doubleday.

Berlin, I. (1969). *Four Essays on Liberty.* London: Oxford University Press.

Bernardoz, C. E., & Haney, W. E. (1978). Religious broadcasting in Asia. In J. A. Lent (Ed.), *Broadcasting in Asia and the Pacific: A Continental Survey of Radio and Television.* Philadelphia: Temple University Press, 338–349.

Betts, R. F. (1968). *Europe Overseas: Phases of Imperialism.* New York: Basic Books.

Beware of fresh ideas—your control is slipping. (1987, August 29). *TV Guide,* 17–23.

Biersteker, T. J. (1978). *Distortion or Development? Contending Perspectives on the Multinational Corporation.* Boston: MIT Press.

Bing, J. The Council of Europe Convention and the OECD guidelines on data protection. In *Regulation of Transnational Communication.* In *Michigan Yearbook of International Legal Studies 1984.* New York: Clark Boardman, 271–303.

Biro, S. S. (1932). The international aspects of radio control. *Journal of Radio Law, 2.*

Bittman, L. (1985). *The KGB and Soviet Disinformation: An Insider's View.* Washington, DC: Pergamon-Brassey.

Bittman, L. (Ed.). (1988a). *The New Image Makers: Soviet Propaganda and Disinformation Today.* Washington, DC: Pergamon-Brassey.

Bittman, L. (1988b). The new image-makers: Soviet propaganda and disinformation under Gorbachev. In L. Bittman (Ed.), *The New Image Makers: Soviet Propaganda and Disinformation Today.* Washington, DC: Pergamon-Brassey, 11–34.

Bittner, J. R. (1985). *Broadcasting and Telecommunications* (2nd ed.). Englewood Cliffs, NJ: Prentice-Hall.

Blanchard, M. A. (1983). The crusade for worldwide freedom of information: American attempts to shape World War II peace treaties. *Journalism Quarterly, 60,* 583–588.

Blumenfeld, L. (1991, August 21). The computer link, plugged into the news. *Washington Post,* B1, B2.

Blyth, W. J. & Blyth, M. M. (1985). *Telecommunications: Concepts, Development, and Management.* Indianapolis, IN: Bobbs-Merrill.

Board for International Broadcasting. (1982). *Eighth Annual Report.* Washington, DC: BIB.

Board for International Broadcasting. (1983). *Annual Report.* Washington, DC: BIB.

Board for International Broadcasting. (1985). *Annual Report.* Washington, DC: BIB.

Board for International Broadcasting. (1989). *Annual Report on Radio Free Europe/ Radio Liberty, Inc.*

Board for International Broadcasting. (1992). *1992 Annual Report.* Washington, DC: BIB.

Bobrow, D. B. (1972). Transfer of meaning across national boundaries. In R. L. Merritt (Ed.), *Communication in International Politics.* Urbana: University of Illinois Press, 33–61.

Bond, R. B. & Jones, W. G. T. (1990, April). British Telecom in the developing global information network industry. *British Telecommunications Engineering, 9.*

Boonyaketmala, B. (1986). Influence of the transnational media in Thailand. In U. Kivikuru & T. Varis (Eds.), *Approaches to International Communication: Textbook for Journalism Education.* Helsinki, Finland: Finnish National Commission for UNESCO, 249–261.

Bornschier, V., & Chase-Dunn, C. (1985). *Transnational Corporations and Underdevelopment.* New York: Praeger.

Bortnick, J. (1986). Information technology and the developing world: Opportunities and obstacles. *The Information Society, 4,* 157–170.

Boyd, D. A. (1983). Broadcasting between the two Germanies. *Journalism Quarterly, 60,* 232–239.

Boyd, D. A. (1984). The Janus effect? Imported television entertainment programming in developing countries. *Critical Studies in Mass Communication, 1,* 379–391.

Boyd, D. A. (1988). Third world pirating of U.S. films and television programs from satellites. *Journal of Broadcasting & Electronic Media, 32,* 149–161.

Boyd, D. A., & Benzies, J. Y. (1983). SOFIRAD: France's international commercial media empire. *Journal of Communication, 33,* 56–69.

Boyd, D. A., & Straubhaar, J. D. (1985). Developmental impact of the home video cassette recorder on third world countries. *Journal of Broadcasting & Electronic Media, 29,* 5–21.

Boyd, D. A., Straubhaar, J. D., & Lent, J. A. (1989). *Videocassette Recorders in the Third World.* New York: Longman.

Boyd-Barrett, O. (1980). *The International News Agencies.* Beverly Hills, CA: Sage.

Boyd-Barrett, O. (1989). Multinational News Agencies. In P. Enderwick (Ed.), *Multinational Service Firms.* London: Routledge, 107–131.

Boyle, A. (1972). *Only the Wind Will Listen: Reith of the BBC.* London: Hutchinson.

Bradsher, K. (1991, August 22). A. T. & T. and IDB to use Soviet satellite on trial basis. *New York Times,* C2.

Brady, R. A. (1937). *The Spirit and Structure of German Fascism.* London: Victor Gollancz.

Branigin, W. (1989, April 29). U.S. move in Panama called inept. *Washington Post,* A1, A22.

Branscomb, A. W. (Ed.). (1986). *Toward a Law of Global Communications Networks.* New York: Longman.

Breen, M. P. (1981). The flow of television programs from America to Australia. *Journalism Quarterly, 58,* 388–394.

BRF — Gorbachev — Radio. (1991, August 22). Associated Press report.

Briggs, A. (1970). *The History of Broadcasting in the United Kingdom. Vol 3: The War of Words.* London: Oxford University Press.

Briggs, A. (1985). *The BBC: The First Fifty Years.* Oxford: Oxford University Press.

Briggs, C. F., & Maverick, A. (1858). *The Story of the Telegraph, and A History of the Great Atlantic Cable.* New York: Rudd & Carleton.

Britain's satellite TV up in air after merger. (1990, November 12). *Broadcasting, 119,* 32–33.

British Broadcasting Corporation. (1929, November). Empire Broadcasting. In *Empire Service Policy 1928–1929.* E4/2. Caversham Park, England: BBC Written Archives Centre.

British Broadcasting Corporation. (1931). *Fourth Annual Report 1930.* London: HMSO.

British Broadcasting Corporation. (1939). *Receiving the Empire Station.* London: BBC.

British Broadcasting Corporation. (1940, November 27). Recommendations for an Empire Intelligence Service [Memorandum]. Caversham Park, England: BBC Written Archives Centre.

British Broadcasting Corporation. (1943a, June 28). European audience estimates. In *European Intelligence Papers.* In *European Audience Estimates 1943–1944. E2/184* [Series 5, No. 1]. Caversham Park, England: BBC Written Archives Centre.

British Broadcasting Corporation. (1943b, August 4). European audience estimates: Poland. In *European Intelligence Papers.* In *European Audience Estimates 1943–1944. E2/184* [Series 5, No. 3]. Caversham Park, England: BBC Written Archives Centre.

British Broadcasting Corporation. (1982). *BBC External Services: 50 Years of Broadcasting to the World*. London: BBC.

British Broadcasting Corporation. (1985). *Annual Report and Handbook 1986*. London: BBC.

British Broadcasting Corporation. (1986). *Annual Report and Handbook 1987*. London: BBC.

British Broadcasting Corporation. (1989, September 6). *The Road to War* (Part I) [Television program]. London: BBC.

British Telecomm. (n.d.). *First Steps in Packet Switching: The Public Data Network*.

Britt, D. (1991, August 21). The Voice of America, keeping the channel open. *Washington Post*, B1, B2.

Broadcasters, military at odds over DBS as WARC approaches. (1991, October 7). *Broadcasting, 121.* 60–61.

Brown, A. (1992, January 21). Star TV banned from hotels in Chinese capital. Reuters report.

Brown, F. J. (1927). *The Cable and Wireless Communications of the World: A Study of the Present Day Means of International Communication by Wireless Containing Chapters on Cable and Wireless Finance*. London: Pitman.

Brown, M. (1985, 1 December). Bootleg tapes cash in on Live Aid. *Sunday Times (London)*, 9.

Brown, R. (1986). Computers and the information industry. In A. W. Branscomb (Ed.), *Toward a Law of Global Communications Networks*. New York: Longman, 49–54.

Browne, D. R. (1974). International broadcasts to African audiences. In S. W. Head (Ed.), *Broadcasting to Africa: A Continental Survey of Radio and Television*. Philadelphia: Temple University Press, 175–198.

Browne, D. R. (1978). International broadcasting to Asia. In J. A. Lent (Ed.), *Broadcasting in Asia and the Pacific: A Continental Survey of Radio and Television*. Philadelphia: Temple University Press, 318–337.

Browne, D. R. (1982). *International Radio Broadcasting: The Limits of the Limitless Medium*. New York: Praeger.

Browne, D. R. (1983). Going international: How the BBC began foreign language broadcasting. *Journalism Quarterly*, 423–430.

Browne, D. R. (1986). Radio in the American sector, RIAS Berlin. In K. R. M. Short (Ed.), *Western Broadcasting over the Iron Curtain*. New York: St. Martin's Press, 185–203.

Browne, D. R. (1989). *Comparing Broadcast Systems: The Experiences of Six Industrialized Nations*. Ames: Iowa State University Press.

Brunnquell, F. (1992). *Fréquence Monde: Du Poste Colonial à RFI*. Paris: Hachette.

Buell, W. A. (1986). Radio Free Europe/Radio Liberty in the mid 1980s. In K. R. M. Short (Ed.), *Western Broadcasting over the Iron Curtain*. New York: St. Martin's Press, 69–97.

Buitenhuis, P. (1987). *The Great War of Words: Literature as Propaganda 1914–18 and After*. London: Batsford.

Bumpus, B., & Skelt, B. ([1984]). *Communication and Society. Vol 14: Seventy Years of International Broadcasting*. Paris: UNESCO.

Burgess, J. (1987, December 6). Fighting trespassing on "intellectual property." *Washington Post*.

Burgess, J. (1988a, August 21). The evolving symbiosis of optical fiber, satellites. *Washington Post*, H1, H5.

Burgess, J. (1988b, December 27). The battle for long-distance dollars. *Washington Post*, A1, A6.

Burgess, J. (1989, April 20). "Global office" on rise as firms shift service jobs abroad. *Washington Post*, E1, E2.

Burgess, J. (1991, June 19). Soviet Union prepares to join Western satellite consortium. *Washington Post*.

Burgess, J. (1992, March 4). International group backs global satellite phone plan. *Washington Post*, B1, B2.

Burke, K. (1966). *Language as Symbolic Action: Essays on Life, Literature, and Method.* Berkeley: University of California Press.

Burnett, S. H. (1989, February 27). Personal communication.

Burns, T. (1977). *The BBC: Public Institution and Private World.* London: Macmillan.

Burrows, A. R. (1924). *The Story of Broadcasting.* London: Cassell.

Burt, A. L. (1956). *The Evolution of the British Empire and Commonwealth from the American Revolution.* Boston: Heath.

Bytwerk, R. L. (1983). *Julius Streicher.* New York: Stein & Day.

Cable and Wireless communications of the empire. (1923). In *Memorandum of the Post Office for the Imperial Economic Conference, April 1923. Post 33.* Post Office Archives, London.

Cablevision tests digicable and digicast as Cablelabs issues compression RFP. (1991, August 19). *Broadcasting, 121.*

Canada. House of Commons. (1911). *Parliamentary Debates* (11th Parliament, 3rd session).

Carey, J. W. (1989). *Communication as Culture: Essays on Media and Society.* Boston: Unwin Hyman.

Carlsen, C. (1991, December 6). PacTel explores cellular overseas. *San Francisco Business Times, 6,* 1, 2.

Carlsson, U. (Ed.). (1986, January 27–30). *Unesco Consultation on Collaborative Research into the Impact of the New Communication Technologies at the University of Gothenburg.* In *Final Report.* NORDICOM-Sweden.

Carnes, L. (1986, 5 November). Open airwaves: Call the Soviets' bluff. *Washington Post.*

Cascino, A. (1989). The experience of Americanization in Italian TV-programming within twelve years of non-regulated competition. In C. W. Thomsen (Ed.), *Cultural Transfer or Electronic Colonialism? The Impact of American Television Programs on European Television.* Heidelberg, Germany: Carl Winter Universitätsverlag, 57–70.

CCIR. (1986). Report 955 (MOD F). In *Satellite Sound Broadcasting with Portable Receivers and Receivers in Automobiles.* In *XVI Plenary Assembly* [Document 10-11S/238].

CCIR Study Groups 10 and 11. (1987). Satellite sound broadcasting with portable receivers and receivers in automobiles in bands 9 and 7. In *Document 10-11S/94-E* [Report 955-1].

Cerf, V. G. (1991, September). Networks. *Scientific American, 265,* 42–51.

Chalfont, L. (1976, August 30). Why the Kremlin pours out millions to jam the voices of freedom. *The Times (London).*

Chaplin, J., Fromm, H. H., & Rosetti, C. (1984). Broadcasting of sound radio programmes by satellite direct to portable and vehicle receivers: A proposal for Africa. *Space Communication and Broadcasting, 2,* 3–11.

Chapman, G. (1987). Towards a geography of the tube: TV flows in Western Europe. *InterMedia, 15,* 10–21.

Chase, S. (1990, May). Future scenarios: Separate systems proponents spar over role of Intelsat. *Via Satellite, 5,* 32.

Childs, H. L., & Whitton, J. B. (Eds.). (1942). *Propaganda by Short Wave.* Princeton, NJ: Princeton University Press.

China: The weeks of living dangerously. (1989, June 12). *Broadcasting, 116,* 29–30.

China expels reporters. (1989, June 19). *Broadcasting, 116,* 46.

China: VOA. (1991, November 16). Associated Press Report.

China vs press: Attempted censorship. (1989, June 5). *Broadcasting, 116,* 34.

Christian Science church launches international broadcast. (1987, March 16). *Broadcasting, 112,* 68.

Clark, A. C. (1945, October). Extra-terrestrial Relays: Can rocket stations give worldwide radio coverage? *Wireless World.*

Clemmensen, J. M., & Wallenstein, G. D. (1986). Innovation paradox in telecommunications. *Telecommunication Journal, 53,* 694–703.

Clews, J. C. (1964). *Communist Propaganda Techniques.* London: Methuen.

Cocca, A. A. (1988, May). Human condition and communications — the right to communicate. *Transnational Data and Communications Report, 11,* 15, 26.

Codding, G. A., Jr. (1959). *Broadcasting Without Barriers.* Paris: UNESCO.

Codding, G. A., & Rutkowski, A. M. (1982). *The International Telecommunication Union in a Changing World.* Dedham, MA: Artech House.

Cohateh, S. J. S. (1974). The Gambia. In S. W. Head (Ed.), *Broadcasting in Africa: A Continental Survey of Radio and Television.* Philadelphia: Temple University Press, 97–98.

Cohen, S. S., & Zysman, J. (1987). *Manufacturing Matters: The Myth of the Post-Industrial Economy.* New York: Basic Books.

Cohen, Y. (1986). *Media Diplomacy: The Foreign Office in the Mass Communications Age.* London: Frank Cass.

Cole, S. (1986). The global impact of information technology. *World Development, 14,* 1277–1292.

Coleman, J. S. (1954). Nationalism in tropical Africa. *American Political Science Review, 48.*

Colino, R. R. (1986, September). Global politics and INTELSAT: The conduct of foreign relations in an electronically interconnected world. *Telecommunications Policy, 10,* 195–208.

Collaboration of the Press in the Organisation of Peace [League of Nations] (25 September 1925, Geneva). (1986). K. Nordenstreng, E. G. Manet, & W. Kleinwächter, Eds. Prague, Czechoslovakia: International Organization of Journalists, 105.

Colonial Conference. (1887). *Proceedings* (Vol. 1). London: Harrison.

Committee for Economic Development. (1981). *Transnational Corporations and Developing Countries: New Policies for a Changing World Economy.* New York: Committee for Economic Development.

Committee of Imperial Defence. (1924). *Report* [Post 33. Minute 15959/1924. Imperial Communications Committee. Sub-Committee on Colonial Wireless System] (March 28, 1927). Post Office Archives, London.

Committee on Antennas, Satellite Broadcasting, and Emergency Preparedness for the Voice of America. (1988). *Antennas, Satellite Broadcasting, and Emergency Preparedness for the Voice of America* [Board on Telecommunications and Computer Applications. Commission on Engineering and Technical Systems. National Research Council]. Washington, DC: National Academy Press.

Committee on Antennas, Satellite Broadcasting and Emergency Preparedness for the Voice of America. (1989). *International Audio Broadcasting for the Twenty-first Century* [Board on Telecommunications and Computer Applications. Commission on Engineering and Technical Systems. National Research Council]. Washington, DC: National Academy Press.

Committee on Imperial Defence. (1927, March 28). *Report* [Post 33. Minute 15959/1924, Appendices A and B]. Imperial Communications Committee. Sub-Committee on Colonial Wireless System]. Post Office Archives, London.

"Communication in the service of humanity"—Unesco's new plan. (1990). *Media Development, 37*, 23–24.

Conference on Security and Cooperation in Europe: Final Act (Part 1(a), par. I). (1975, September 1). *Department of State Bulletin.*

Cook, F. S. ([1961]). *Seeds in the Wind.* Oka Locka, FL: World Radio Missionary Fellowship.

Cooper, K. (1942). *Barriers Down: The Story of the News Agency Epoch.* New York: Farrar & Rinehart.

Coup alert by fax. (1991, August 20). United Press report.

Cousins, P., & Cousins, P. (1978). *The Power of the Air: The Achievement and Future of Missionary Radio.* London: Hodder & Stoughton.

Coy, P. (1989, April 18). Trans-Pacific fiber-optic cable begins Far East service today. *Washington Post*, D3.

Crane, R. J. (1979). *The Politics of International Standards: France and the Color TV War.* Norwood, NJ: Ablex.

Crossette, B. (1990, December 2). Talk of tuned-in Pakistanis' Cable TV news. *New York Times*, 6.

Cruikshank, C. (1981). *The Fourth Arm: Psychological Warfare 1938–1945.* Oxford: Oxford University Press.

Cuba says still considering bureau request by TV agency. (1991, November 7). Reuters report.

Cyprus Telecommunications Authority. (1980–1986). *Annual Reports.*

Czitrom, D. J. (1982). *Media and the American Mind: From Morse to McLuhan.* Chapel Hill: University of North Carolina Press.

Dagnino, E. (1980). Cultural and ideological dependence: Building a theoretical framework. In *Transnational Enterprises: Their Impact on Third World Societies and Cultures.* Boulder, CO: Westview Press, 297–322.

d'Arcy, J. (1969, August). Direct broadcast satellites and the right to communicate. *EBU Review*, 14–15.

d'Arcy, J. (1978). Broadcasting in the global age. In *Symposium on the Cultural Role of Broadcasting* [Summary Report]. Tokyo: Hōsō-Bunka Foundation, 124–130.

Daugherty, W. E. (1962). Psychological warfare: Organization and personnel in the United States since World War II. In U. G. Whitaker, Jr. (Ed.), *Propaganda and International Relations* (rev. and enlrg. ed.). San Francisco: Chandler.

Davies, G. (1986). *Piracy of Phonograms* (2nd ed.). Oxford: ESC.

Davison, W. P. (1965). *International Political Communication.* New York: Praeger.

Dawidziuk, B. M., & Preston, H. F. (1979, 24–26 September). International communications: Network developments and economics. In *Third World Telecommunication Forum* (Part 2). Geneva, Switzerland: ITU.

DBS crucial for European industry. (1984, August). *Cable & Satellite Europe*, 43–44.

Deacon, R. (1986, Fall). *The Truth Twisters.* London: Future.

Deihl, E. R. (1977). South of the border: The NBC and CBS radio networks and the Latin American venture, 1930–1942. *Communication Quarterly, 25*, 2–12.

de Kadt, E., & Williams, G. (Eds.). (1974). *Sociology and Development.* London: Tavistock.

DeLamarter, R. T. (1986). *Big Blue: IBM's Use and Abuse of Power.* New York: Dodd, Mead.

Delauzun, F., Mytton, G., & Forrester, C. (1988). International broadcasting: A voice in the desert? *RTV: Theory and Practice, 3*, 48–67.

Delfiner, H. (1974). *Vienna Broadcasts to Slovakia 1938–1939: A Case Study in Subversion.* New York: Columbia University Press.

DeMarco, E. (1991, November 4). Turner, U.S. wrestling over Cuba. *Atlanta Business Chronicle, 14,* A3.

De Mendelssohn, P. (1944). *Japan's Political Warfare.* London: Allen & Unwin.

The democratization of TV news. (1989, 18 September). *Broadcasting, 117,* 53.

Dertouzos, M. L. (1991, September). Communications, computers and networks. *Scientific American, 265,* 30–37.

Dewey, J. (1926). *Experience and Nature.* Chicago: Open Court.

Diedriks, V., I. H. Ph. Current issues in remote sensing. In *Regulation of Transnational Communication.* In *Michigan Yearbook of International Legal Studies 1984.* New York: Clark Boardman, 305–316.

Diehl, J. (1986a, March 12). Dissident Poles exploit VCR boom. *Washington Post,* A1, A24.

Diehl, J. (1986b, August 19). Polish peddlers make a market. *Washington Post.*

Diehl, J. (1988, April 17). VCRs on fast forward in Eastern Europe. *Washington Post,* A1, A26.

Direct Broadcasting by Satellite: Report of a Home Office Study. (1981). London: Her Majesty's Stationery Office.

Direct Broadcast Satellite Communications: Proceedings of the Symposium. (1980). [Sponsored by the Space Applications Board and the Board on Telecommunications-Computer Applications. National Research Council]. Washington, DC: National Academy of Sciences.

A dish too small. (1985, May). *Cable & Satellite Europe,* 49–50.

Disney forges alliance with Murdoch. (1988, November 28). *Broadcasting, 115,* 127.

Dixon, H. (1990, April 19). The paranoia eases. *Financial Times (London),* v.

Dixon, H. (1991, October 12). Global telephone cartel begins to show cracks. *Financial Times (London),* 35.

Dizard, W. P. (1986). International public service data systems. In A. W. Branscomb (Ed.), *Toward a Law of Global Communications Networks.* New York: Longman, 185–190.

Dobbs, M. (1989, January 10). What's your sign, comrade? *Washington Post.*

Documents de la Conférence Télégraphique Internationale de St. Petersbourg. (1876). Berne, Switzerland: Bureau International des Administrations Télégraphiques.

Doob, L. (1948). *Public Opinion and Propaganda.* New York: Henry Holt.

Dougan, D. L. (1987, January). An international policy perspective on the information age. *IEEE Communications Magazine, 25,* 18–23.

Douglas, S. J. (1987). *Inventing American Broadcasting 1800–1922.* Baltimore, MD: Johns Hopkins University Press.

Downey, E. A. (1984). A historical survey of the international regulation of propaganda. In *Regulation of Transnational Communication.* In *Michigan Yearbook of International Legal Studies 1984.* New York: Clark Boardman, 341–360.

Downing, J. D. H. (1986). Cooperation and competition in satellite communication: The Soviet Union. In D. A. Demac (Ed.), *Tracing New Orbits: Cooperation and Competition in Global Satellite Development.* New York: Columbia University Press, 283–304.

Dowsett, H. M. (1923). *Wireless Telephony and Broadcasting.* London: Gresham.

Driscoll, R. E., & Wellender, H. W. I. (Eds.). (1974). *Technology Transfer and Development: An Historical and Geographic Perspective.* New York: Fund for Multinational Management Education.

Dumila, F. ([1976]). *For Love of Our Culture.* Nairobi, Kenya: no publisher.

Duncan, H. D. (1962) *Communication and Social Order.* London: Oxford University Press.

Duncan, H. D. (1969). *Symbols and Social Theory.* New York: Oxford University Press.

Dunham, C. B., & Hering, B. G. (1986). The global television market. In A. W. Branscomb (Ed.), *Toward a Law of Global Communication Networks.* New York: Longman, 95–104.

Dunnett, P. (1990). *The World Television Industry: An Economic Analysis.* New York: Routledge.

Dymond, A. (1987, June). Reducing the number of missing links: Regional cooperation and telecommunications development in Southern Africa. *Telecommunications Policy, 11,* 121–134.

Each man an island. (1992, February 8). *The Economist, 322,* 92, 94.

East, H. (1983). Information technology and the problems of less developed countries. *The Information Society Journal, 2,* 53–64.

East Europe looking to U.S. for help in broadcasting and telecommunications. (1990, March 19). *Broadcasting, 118,* 34.

Ebon, M. (1987). *The Soviet Propaganda Machine.* New York: McGraw-Hill.

Echikson, W. (1987, September). Video free Europe. *Video,* 88–90, 163.

Eckersley, P. P. (1927, May 20). Wireless communications and broadcasting [Post 33. Minute 15959/1924. Imperial Communications Committee. Sub-Committee on Colian Wireless System].

EC tentatively adopts curbs on foreign TV programming. (1989, March 15). *Washington Post,* D3.

Edfelt, R. (1986). Telematics, public policy and economic development with special reference to Brazilian protectionism. *The Information Society, 4,* 187–203.

Egbon, M. (1989). Promises of new communications technologies and the African dilemma. *Space Communication and Broadcasting, 7.*

Egerton, G. W. (1978). *Great Britain and the Creation of the League of Nations: Strategy, Politics, and International Organization, 1914–1919.* Chapel Hill: University of North Carolina Press.

Eisenstein, E. L. (1979). *The Printing Press as an Agent of Change* (Vols. 1 and 2). Cambridge: Cambridge University Press.

Elliott, K. A. (1989/90, Winter). Too many voices of America. *Foreign Policy, 77,* 113–131.

Elliott, K. A. (1991, May 23). *New Structures and Strategies for United States International Broadcasting* [Unpublished paper].

Elliott, P., & Golding, P. (1974). Mass communication and social change: The imagery of development and the development of imagery. In E. de Kadt & G. Williams (Eds.), *Sociology and Development.* London: Tavistock, 229–254.

Ellul, J. (1965). *Propaganda: The Formation of Men's Attitudes.* (K. Kellen & J. Lerner, Trans.) New York: Vintage Books.

Ellwood, D. (1983). Italy: The regime, the nation and the film industry. In K. R. M. Short (Ed.), *Film and Radio Propaganda in World War II.* London: Croom Helm, 220–229.

Emerson, T. I. (1970). *The System of Freedom of Expression.* New York: Random House.

Empire Broadcasting. (1928, December 6). [Memo from chief engineer to director-general, BBC. E4/2. Empire Service Policy 1928–1929]. Caversham Park, England: BBC Written Archives Centre.

Empire Broadcasting. (1929a, November). [E4/2. Empire Service Policy 1928–1929]. Caversham Park, England: BBC Written Archives Centre.

Empire Broadcasting, (1929b, February). [E4/2. Empire Service Policy 1928–1929]. Caversham Park, England: BBC Written Archives Centre.

Endrödi, G. (1989). Co-operation between Hungarian and Western European/American Databases. In J. Becker & T. Szecskö (Eds.), *Europe Speaks to Europe: International Information Flows Between Eastern and Western Europe.* New York: Pergamon Press, 259–274.

Ensor, R. C. K. (1936). *England 1870–1914.* Oxford: Clarendon Press.

E.S.D. (1932, September 29). [B.B.C. Internal Circulating Memo to F.D. Subject: Meeting with Mr. [R.A.] Leeper [Foreign Office]. E4/6. Empire Service Policy 1932–1933]. Caversham Park, England: BBC Written Archives Centre.

Eugster, E. (1983). *Television Programming Across National Boundaries: The EBU and OIRT Experience.* Dedham, MA: Artech House.

European Broadcasting Union. (1987). *EBU Studies on an Advanced Digital System for Satellite Sound Broadcasting in the UHF Band* (Document No. 10-11S/2-E). Geneva, Switzerland: Study Groups 10 and 11, CCIR.

European Broadcasting Union. (1988, May). Statistics of Eurovision Programmes and News Exchanges, 1.1.1987 – 31.12.1987. *EBU Review: Programmes, Administration, Law. 39.* 37–39.

European Broadcasting Union. (1990, May). Statistics of Eurovision Programmes and News Exchanges, 1.1.1989 – 31.12.1989. *EBU Review: Programmes, Administration, Law. 41.* 23–25.

European Broadcasting Union Technical Centre. (1985a). *Frequency Modulation Parameters of the D2-MAC/Packet System for DBS* (Reference CT/III-A). Brussels, Belgium: EBU Technical Centre.

European Broadcasting Union Technical Centre. (1985b). *Television Standards for the Broadcasting Satellite Service Specification of the C-MAC/Packet System* (Reference CT/III-C) (4th rev. ed.). Brussels, Belgium: EBU Technical Centre.

European broadcast satellite still waiting to beam down initial programs. (1989, February 8–14). *Variety,* 104.

European governments to back Euronews. (1992, February 14). Reuters report.

European Television Task Force. (1988). *Europe 2000: What Kind of Television?* Manchester, England: The European Institute for the Media.

Europe Satellite – AP. (1991, September 30). Associated Press report.

Eutelsat. (1988). *Annual Report.*

Evans, H. (1990). The Norman conquest: Freedom of the press in Britain and America. In S. Serfaty (Ed.), *The Media and Foreign Policy.* New York: St. Martin's Press, 189–201.

Evans, R., & Novak, R. (1987, March 25). Don't cripple Radio Liberty. *Washington Post,* A23.

Examples of propaganda broadcast from Russian stations. (1919–1924). In *File on the Soviet Union.* London: BBC, IBAR.

Excerpts from Gorbachev speech on the Reykjavik talks and "Star Wars." (1986, October 23). *New York Times.*

Expanding opportunities in the unfolding European market. (1987, October 19). *Broadcasting, 113,* 32.

Extracts from article PAN-AMERICAN PEACE CONFERENCE – EXCHANGE OF PROGRAMS PLANNED (n.d.). In *File on the United States of America.* London: BBC, IBAR.

Farhi, P. (1989, April 9). Heritage to the highest bidder. *Washington Post.*

Farhi, P. (1992, March 7). Thorn EMI to buy Virgin music group. *Washington Post,* C1, C4.

Federal Systems Division. (1985). TRW Space and Technology Group. *Satellite Voice Broadcast Study. Vol. 1: Executive Summary.* (Contract No. NAS3-24232).

Fejes, F. (1980). The growth of multinational advertising agencies in Latin America. *Journal of Communication, 30,* 36–49.

Fejes, F. (1983). *The U.S. in Third World Communications: Latin America, 1900–1945. Journalism Monographs* (No. 86).

Fejes, F. (1986). *Imperialism, Media and the Good Neighbor: New Deal Foreign Policy and United States Shortwave Broadcasting to Latin America.* Norwood, NJ: Ablex.

Feketekuty, G., & Aronson, J. D. (1984). Restrictions on trade in communication and information services. In *Regulation of Transnational Communication. In Michigan Yearbook of International Legal Studies 1984.* New York: Clark Boardman, 145–167.

Feldmann, L. (1991, September 4). Yeltsin welcomes Radio Liberty's presence in Russia. *Christian Science Monitor, 3.*

Feliciano, H. (1988, 24 November). Colorized films barred by French. *Washington Post.*

Fenby, J. (1986). *The International News Services.* New York: Schocken Books.

Fenkell, D. B. (1979). U.S. preparation for ITU conferences: WARC '79, a case study. In *Regulation of Transnational Communication. In Michigan Yearbook of International Legal Studies 1984.* New York: Clark Boardman, 319–338.

Fielding, R. (1972). *The American Newsreel 1911–1967.* Norman: University of Oklahoma Press.

Final Act of the United Nations Conference on Freedom of Information. (1986). In K. Nordenstreng, E. G. Manet, & W. Kleinwächter (Eds.), *New Information and Communication Order Sourcebook* (1948). Prague, Czechoslovakia: International Organization of Journalists, 115–118.

The first SOS. (1933, September). *Radio Intelligence, 48,* 5.

Fisher, D. (1982). *The Right to Communicate: A Status Report.* Paris: UNESCO.

Fisher, G. (1987). *American Communication in a Global Society* (rev. ed.). Norwood, NJ: Ablex.

Fisher, H. A. (1980). *Journalism Monographs* (No. 68). *The EBU: Model for Regional Cooperation in Broadcasting.*

5SW. (1929, September 26). [Memorandum. E4/2. Empire Service Policy 1928–1929]. Caversham Park, England: BBC Written Archives Centre.

Fleming, S. (1887). Statement. In *Proceedings of the Colonial Conference, 1887.* London: Harrison, 212.

Flesher, J. (1991, April 20). Associated Press report.

Flint, J. (1992, February 24). After 50 years, the voice is loud and clear. *Broadcasting, 122,* 30.

Foreign Broadcast Information Service. (1987, December 3). Moscow TV comparison of Gorbachev interview. In *Report* [Soviet Union, 87-232].

Foreign ownership: Salvation or selling out? (1991, July 15). *Broadcasting, 121,* 36–37.

Former President Jimmy Carter has joined with NAB in support of effort to link U.S. broadcast facilities with those in Soviet Union. (1991, November 25). *Television Digest, 31,* 7.

Fortner, R. S. (1978a). Strategies for self-immolation: The third world and the transfer of advanced technologies. *Inter-American Economic Affairs, 31,* 25–50.

Fortner, R. S. (1978b). *Messiahs or Monopolists: A Cultural History of Canadian Communications Development 1846–1914* [Dissertation]. University of Illinois.

Fortner, R. S. (1980). The Canadian search for identity, 1846–1914, Part III: Communication and regional/provincial imperatives. *Canadian Journal of Communication, 6,* 32–46.

Fortner, R. S. (1986a, June 5–7). The geopolitics of technology transfer: Culture access and circumvention of state control in the developing world [Paper presented at the Canadian Communication Association annual meeting, Winnipeg, Manitoba].

Fortner, R. S. (1986b). Physics and metaphysics in an information age: Privacy, dignity and identity. *Communication, 9,* 151–172.

Fortner, R. S. (1987, November 4–8). New technologies and national sovereignty: The illusion of state control over communication and culture [Paper presented at the Speech Communication Association annual meeting, Boston].

Fortner, R. S. (1988a). News coverage of the Washington summit: A cross-national comparison of international radio services [Paper presented to the 16th Annual Congress of the International Association for Mass Communication Research, Barcelona, Spain].

Fortner, R. S. (1988b). Technological, political, and economic prospects for DBS-audio in international communication. *Journal of Broadcasting & Electronic Media, 32,* 183–195.

Fortner, R. S. (1989, September 10–14). Effectiveness of religious broadcasting into closed societies: Relevant trends to the year 2000 [Paper presented to the Consultation on the Christian Church under Persecution, Glen Eyrie, CO].

Fortner, R. S. (1990). Saving the world? American evangelicals and transnational broadcasting. In Q. J. Schultze (Ed.), *American Evangelicals and the Mass Media.* Grand Rapids, MI: Eerdmans, 307–328.

Fortner, R. S. (1991a). Analysis of VOA broadcasting. In *Analysis of Voice of America Broadcasts to the Middle East During the Persian Gulf Crisis.* Washington, DC: Center for Strategic and International Studies, 3–56.

Fortner, R. S. (1991b). Current controversies in technology transfer. In I. B. Singh & J. Hanson (Eds.), *Advances in Telematics, 1.* Norwood, NJ: Ablex, 149–173.

Fortner, R. S. (1991c, December 9). *Double Side-band, Single Side-band and Out-of-band Short-wave Broadcasting to International Audiences.* [Report to the British Broadcasting Corporation, IBAR].

Fortner, R. S. (forthcoming). *Public Diplomacy and International Politics: The Symbolic Constructs of Summitry and International Radio Communication.* New York: Praeger.

Fortner, R. S., & Durham, D. A. (1986). *A Worldwide Radio Receiver Population Analysis* (USIA Contract No. IA-22188-23). Washington, DC: Academy for Educational Development.

Fortner, R. S., & Durham, D. A. (1988). *The Future of Shortwave for International Broadcasting* [Briefing paper prepared for the Voice of America].

Forty years of wireless. (1936, June). *Radio Intelligence, 81,* 1, 3.

Foulkrod, M. (1947, July). Short wave of the future. *Current History, 13,* 12–16.

Fowler, G., & Crawford, B. (1987). *Border Radio: Quacks, Yodelers, Pitchmen, Psychics and Other Amazing Broadcasters of the American Airwaves.* Houston, TX: Pacesetter Press.

Fraenkel, P. (1986b). The BBC external services: Broadcasting to the USSR and Eastern Europe. In K. R. M. Short (Ed.), *Western Broadcasting over the Iron Curtain.* New York: St. Martin's Press, 139–157.

Frederick, H. H. (1986). *Cuban-American Radio Wars: Ideology in International Telecommunications.* Norwood, NJ: Ablex.

Freed, P. E. (1979). *Towers to Eternity.* Nashville, TN: Thomas Nelson.

Friedman, B. (1992, January 27). Soviet-American TV. Associated Press report.

Frost, M. A. (1938, October 19). [BBC internal circulating memo]. Caversham Park, England: BBC Written Archives Centre.

Ganley, G. D., & Ganley, O. H. (1987). *Global Political Fallout: The VCR's First Decade.* Norwood, NJ: Ablex.

Ganley, O. H. (1987). Information exchange as communications trade. In A. W. Branscomb (Ed.), *Toward a Law of Global Communications Networks.* New York: Longman, 55–62.

Garratt, G. R. M. (1958). Telegraphy. In C. Singer, E. J. Holmyard, A. R. Hall, & T. I. Williams (Eds.), *A History of Technology. Vol. 4: The Industrial Revolution, c. 1750–1850.* New York: Oxford University Press, 644–662.

General Post Office. (n.d., June 17). Relay exchanges: Control of programmes after outbreak of war (HO256. Piece 83). Public Records Office, London.

Gerbner, G. (1967). Mass media and human communication theory. In F. E. X. Dance (Ed.), *Human Communication Theory: Original Essays.* New York: Holt, Rinehart & Winston, 40–60.

Ghorpade, S. (1984). Foreign correspondents cover Washington for the world. *Journalism Quarterly, 61,* 667–671.

Gibbons, A. (1985). *Information, Ideology and Communication: The New Nations' Perspectives on an Intellectual Revolution.* Lanham, MD: University Press of America.

Giffard, C. A. (1984). Developed and developing nation news in U.S. wire service files to Asia. *Journalism Quarterly, 61,* 14–19.

Giffard, C. A. (1985). The inter press service: New information for a new order. *Journalism Quarterly, 62,* 17–23, 44.

Giffard, C. A. (1989). *Unesco and the Media.* New York: Longman.

Gifreu, J. (1986). *El Debate Internacional de la Comunicación.* Barcelona, Spain: Editorial Ariel.

Glenn, R. D. (1987). Legal issues affecting licensing of TV programs in the European Economic Community from the perspective of the U.S. exporter. In *Copyright Law Symposium* (No. 33). New York: Columbia University Press, 115–157.

Global television prices. (1989, January 18–24). *Variety.*

Godson, R. (1988). "AIDS: Made in the USA": Moscow's contagious campaign. In L. Bittman (Ed.), *The New Image-Makers: Soviet Propaganda & Disinformation Today.* Washington, DC: Pergamon-Brassey, 221–226.

Going Hollywood: Foreign companies look for part in U.S. studios. (1989, April 17). *Broadcasting, 116,* 40–41.

Goldey, M. J. (1986). International voice communication. In A. W. Branscomb (Ed.), *Toward a Law of Global Communications Networks.* New York: Longman, 63–76.

Golomstock, I. (1990). *Totalitarian Art in the Soviet Union, the Third Reich, Fascist Italy, and the People's Republic of China.* New York: Icon Editions.

Gorlin, J. (1987, July 30). Protecting intellectual property. *Wall Street Journal.*

Gorove, S. (1984). Major legal issues arising from the use of the geostationary orbit. In *Regulation of Transnational Communication.* In *Michigan Yearbook of International Legal Studies 1984.* New York: Clark Boardman, 3–12.

Goshko, J. M. (1985, June 3). Radio Marti broadcasts soft-sell propaganda. *Washington Post,* A20.

Goshko, J. M. (1987a, January 22). Soviets stop radio jamming, BBC says. *Washington Post.*

Goshko, J. M. (1987b, January 31). Wary VOA praised Iran in broadcast following administration request. *Washington Post.*

Goshko, J. M. (1991, August 20). U.S. stations try to fill in blanks for Soviet listeners. *Washington Post,* A20.

Goulet, D. (1977). *The Uncertain Promise: Value Conflicts in Technology Transfer.* New York: IDOC/North America.

Graff, R. D. (1983). *Communication for National Development: Lessons from Experience.* Cambridge, MA: Oelgeschlager, Gunn & Hein.

Graham, B. (1988, March 10). TV opens up remote villagers' world. *Washington Post,* A37, A38.

Graham, G. S. (1967). Imperial finance, trade, and communications, 1895–1914. In J. B. Benians & C. E. Carrington (Eds.), *The Cambridge History of the British Empire.* Cambridge: Cambridge University Press, 438–489.

Graham, J. (1983). *The Penguin Dictionary of Telecommunications.* London: Penguin.

Grandin, T. (1971). *The Political Use of Radio.* In *History of Broadcasting: Radio to Television* (1939). New York: Arno Press.

Granger, J. V. (1979). Technology and International Relations. San Francisco: Freeman.

Graves, C. (n.d.). *The Thin Red Lines.* London: Standard Art Book.

Great Britain. (1914). Royal Commission on the Natural Resources, Trade and Legislation of Certain Portions of His Majesty's Dominions [Second interim report]. In *Parliamentary Papers.*

The Great Soviet Encyclopedia (1970 ed., translated). (1973). New York: Macmillan.

Green, F. (1988). *American Propaganda Abroad.* New York: Hippocrene Books.

Greenberger, R. S. (1991, June 13). Angry critics say U.S. Arabic language service was not the Voice of America during Gulf War. *Wall Street Journal.*

Gregg, R. B. (1984). *Symbolic Inducement and Knowing: A Study in the Foundations of Rhetoric.* Columbia: University of South Carolina Press.

Grenier, R. (1987, December 7). In case you missed the show. *Washington Times.*

Griffith, W. E. (1980). Communist propaganda. In H. D. Lasswell, D. Lerner, & H. Speier (Eds.), *Propaganda and Communication in World History. Vol. 2: Emergence of Public Opinion in the West.* Honolulu: University Press of Hawaii, 239–258.

Group agrees to merge TAT-9A and TAT-X; rename TAT-G. (1991, November 11). *Fiber Optics News, 11,* 10.

Grun, B. (1979). *Timetables of History: A Horizontal Linkage of People and Events.* New York: Simon & Schuster.

Gryspeerdt, A. (1985). Active audiences in Europe: Public participation in the media. In E. M. Rogers & F. Balle (Eds.), *The Media Revolution in America and Western Europe.* Norwood, NJ: Ablex, 165–176.

GTE spacenet in Soviet venture. (1991, July 10). *Washington Post.*

Guback, T. (1969). *The International Film Industry.* Bloomington: Indiana University Press.

Guiding ITU in a brave new telecommunications world. (1989, December 4). *Broadcasting, 117,* 101.

Guttman, W. L. (1986, December). Telecommunications and sub-Saharan Africa: The continuing crisis. *Telecommunications Policy, 10.*

Hadamovsky, E. (1972). *Propaganda and National Power* (A. Mavrogordata & I. De Witt, Trans.). New York: Arno Press.

Hale, J. (1975). *Radio Power: Propaganda and International Broadcasting.* Philadelphia: Temple University Press.

Hall, P., & Preston, P. (1988). *The Carrier Wave: New Information Technology and the Geography of Innovation 1846–2003.* London: Unwin Hyman.

Hamelink, C. (1986). Dependency and cultural choice. In U. Kivikuru & T. Varis (Eds.), *Approaches to International Communication: Textbook for Journalism Education.* Helsinki, Finland: Finnish National Commission for UNESCO, 221–247.

Hamelink, C. (1990). Unesco and Alice in wonderland. *Media Development, 37*(3), 27–28.

Hancock, A. (1978). UNESCO. In J. A. Lent (Ed.), *Broadcasting in Asia and the Pacific: A Continental Survey of Radio and Television.* Philadelphia: Temple University Press, 368–374.

Hannan, E. (1988, Fall). Censorship during the Grenada invasion: The Pentagon, the press and the public. *International Communication Bulletin, 23,* 15–25.

Hanson, J., & Narula, U. (1990). *New Communication Technologies in Developing Countries.* Hillsdale, NJ: Lawrence Erlbaum.

Harbutt, F. J. (1986). *The Iron Curtain: Churchill, America, and the Origins of the Cold War.* New York: Oxford University Press.

Harden, B. (1991, October 21). Cultural pirates bring the world, and U.S. wrath, to Warsaw. *Washington Post,* A1, A14.

Hardman, T. H. (Compiler). (1909). *A Parliament of the Press: The First Imperial Press Conference.* London: Horace Marshall.

Harms, L. S., & Richstad, J. (Eds.). (1977). *Evolving Perspectives on the Right to Communicate.* Honolulu, HI: East-West Communication Institute.

Harms, L. S., Richstad, J., & Kie, K. (Eds.). (1977). *Right to Communicate: Collected Papers.* Honolulu, HI: Social Sciences and Linguistics Institute, University of Hawaii at Manoa.

Harriman, E. (1987). *Hack: Home Truths About Foreign News.* London: Zed.

Harrington, R. (1986, May 25). Battle of the bootlegs. *Washington Post,* G1, G4.

Harris, P. (1977). *News Dependence: The Case for a New World Information Order* [Final report to UNESCO]. Paris: UNESCO.

Haslach, R. D. (1983). *Netherlands World Broadcasting.* Media, PA: Lawrence Miller.

Hawker, P. (1985, March). DBS — progress and problems. *International Broadcast Engineer, 16,* 7–10.

Hay, J. (1987). *Popular Film Culture in Fascist Italy: The Passing of the Rex.* Bloomington: Indiana University Press.

Head, S. W. (1985). *World Broadcasting Systems: A Comparative Analysis.* Belmont, CA: Wadsworth.

Headrick, D. R. (1981). *The Tools of Empire: Technology and European Imperialism in the Nineteenth Century.* New York: Oxford University Press.

Headrick, D. R. (1988). *The Tentacles of Progress: Technology Transfer in the Age of Imperialism, 1850–1940.* New York: Oxford University Press.

Headrick, D. R. (1991). *The Invisible Weapon: Telecommunications and International Politics 1851–1945.* New York: Oxford University Press.

Heaton, J. H. (1890, June). A penny post for the Empire. *The Nineteenth Century,* 918.

Heil, A. (1992, February 18). Personal communication.

Heil, A., & Schiele, B. (1986). The voice past: The USSR and Communist Europe. In K. R. M. Short (Ed.), *Western Broadcasting over the Iron Curtain.* New York: St. Martin's Press, 98–112.

Henry, G. (1989, August 28). Murdoch sets the agenda. *The Guardian (London),* 21.

Hester, A. (1974). The news from Latin America via a world news agency. *Gazette, 17,* 82–91.

Hickman, T. (1991, November). Eastward and onward. *London Calling, 20,* 19.

Hift, F. (1991a, May 9). Can American TV stay on top of the market? *Christian Science Monitor.*

Hift, F. (1991b, August 8). Soviet video pirates run amok. *Christian Science Monitor,* 12.

Hift, F. (1991c, October 31). E. Europe's broadcasters see a harsh future. *Christian Science Monitor.*

Hind, J., & Mosco, S. (1985). *Rebel Radio: The Full Story of British Pirate Radio.* London: Pluto Press.

Hinsley, F. H. (1986). *Sovereignty* (2nd ed.). Cambridge: Cambridge University Press.

Hirsch, M. (1986). The doldrums of Europe's TV landscape: Coronet as catalyst. In D. A. Demac (Ed.), *Tracing New Orbits: Cooperation and Competition in Global Satellite Development.* New York: Columbia University Press, 114–129.

Hitler, A. (1939). *Mein Kampf.* New York: Reynal & Hitchcock.

Hoagland, J. (1989, May 19). Blanket television coverage gives demonstrators a media security blanket. *Washington Post.*

Hobday, M. (1985, January 25). *The Brazilian Telecommunication Industry: Accumulation of Microelectronic Technology in the Manufacturing and Service Sectors* (UNIDO Doc. UNIDO/IS.511).

Hoffman, D. (1991, August 23). Global communications network was pivotal in defeat of junta. *Washington Post,* A27.

Hoffman-Riem, W. (1987). National identity and cultural values: Broadcasting safeguards. *Journal of Broadcasting & Electronic Media, 31,* 57–72.

Hollis, J. S. (1984, March). Introduction to satellite communications. *CATJ,* 6–19.

Hollywood's biggest ever: Matsushita buys MCA. (1990, December 3). *Broadcasting, 119.*

Holmstrom, D. (1991, May 9). USA: Big seller everywhere. *Christian Science Monitor.*

Holt, R. T. (1958). *Radio Free Europe.* Minneapolis: University of Minnesota Press.

Hondius, F. W. (1984). Steps toward a European agreement on satellite broadcasting. In *Regulation of Transnational Communication.* In *Michigan Yearbook of International Legal Studies 1984.* New York: Clark Boardman, 103–124.

Horowitz, I. L. (1972). *Three Worlds of Development: The Theory and Practice of International Stratification.* New York: Oxford University Press.

Horton, P. C. (Ed.). (1978). *The Third World and Press Freedom.* New York: Praeger.

Hoskins, C., Mirus, R., & Rozeboom, W. (1989). U.S. television programs in the international market: Unfair pricing? *Journal of Communication, 39,* 55–75.

A hot new cold war at ICA. (1981, November 6). *Newsweek, 98,* 36–37.

House subcommittee votes to end TV Marti. (1991, June 3). *Broadcasting, 121,* 80.

Howell, W. J., Jr. (1986). *World Broadcasting in the Age of the Satellite.* Norwood, NJ: Ablex.

Howell, W. S. (1960). The North American service of Radio Moscow. *Quarterly Journal of Speech, 46.*

Hudson, H. E. (1985, March). Access to information resources: The developmental impact of the space WARC. *Telecommunications Policy, 9,* 23–30.

Hudson, H. E. (1990). *Communication Satellites: Their Development and Impact.* New York: Free Press.

Hughes, J. (1991, December 26). When words are better than weapons. *Christian Science Monitor,* 19.

Hungarian shoppers beat a path to West, buying in Vienna. (1989, April 10). *Washington Post.*

Hunter, A. (1935, September). Is foreign reception entertainment? *Wireless and Television Review, 2,* 136, 172.

Hutchins, R. (1947). Chairman, Commission on Freedom of the Press. *A Free and Responsible Press.* Chicago: University of Chicago Press.

Hutzler, C. (1991, August 29). "Radio Free China" plan discussed. *Christian Science Monitor,* 13.

IFPI (1991). *IFPI 1991 Review: The Challenge of the 1990s* (M. Kingston, Ed.). London: IFPI.

IFRB backs U.S. claim of Soviet jamming. (1986, September 22). *Broadcasting, 111.*

Imperial Wireless Telegraphy Committee. (1920). *Report.* London: HMSO.

Imperial Wireless Telegraphy Committee. (1923). *Imperial Wireless Scheme. Report* [Post 33, Minute 9544/1923]. Post Office Archives, London.

Imperial Wireless Telegraphy Committee. (1924). *Report.* London: HMSO.

Information Computer Communication Policy. Vol 8: An Exploration of Legal Issues in Information and Communication Technologies. (1983). Paris: OECD.

INMARSAT. (1987/88). *Annual Review.*

Innis, H. A. (1951). *The Bias of Communication.* Toronto: University of Toronto Press.

Innis, H. A. (1972). *Empire and Communications.* Toronto: University of Toronto Press.

Instituto Nacional de Investigacion y Capacitacion de Telecomunicaciones. (1985/86). Sector Transporte y Comunicaciones. *Memoria.*

Intelsat. (1988–90). *Annual Report.*

Intelsat. (1990–91). *Annual Report.*

Intelsat approves Orion plan. (1989, July 24). *Broadcasting, 117,* 85.

Intelsat approves system coordination. (1987, March 2). *Broadcasting, 112,* 76.

Intelsat board pases [sic] on coordination question. (1984, December 31). *Broadcasting, 107,* 112, 113.

Intelsat Upon. (1992, February 22). *The Economist, 322,* 65.

Intelsat VA. (1987, October). *Satellite Communications, 11,* 41.

International Broadcasting. (1930–1935a). In *File on the Netherlands.* London: BBC, IBAR.

International Broadcasting. (1930–1935b). In *File on the Soviet Union.* London: BBC, IBAR.

International Broadcasting Union. (1934, September). *Radio Intelligence, 60,* 7.

International Conference on Wireless Telegraphy. (1906). Observations on Draft Convention and Regulations by: Post Office

Conference in the Spring of 1905 [HO 257/22]. Public Records Office, London.

International conventions: Address by Mr. W. Platt to the Seaways Society. (1935, November). *Radio Intelligence, 74,* 4–7.

International HDTV progress. (1987, December 7). *Broadcasting, 113,* 97.

The international movie marketplace: Mother lode, or just fool's gold? (1989, February 22–28). *Variety,* 35, 47, 67.

International Telecommunication Union. (1965). *From Semaphor to Satellite.* Geneva, Switzerland: ITU.

International Telecom Statistics. (1989). Siemens.

Interview aftermath. (1989, June 19). *Broadcasting, 116,* 46, 47.

ITAA. (1991). The U.S. information technology industry. Reston, VA: ITAA.

Italia on the air! (1935, November). *Wireless and Television Review, 2,* 261–262.

ITU. (1988, August/October). *WARC on the Use of the Geostationary-Satellite Orbit and the Planning of Space Services Utilizing It.* In *Second Session, Geneva* [ORB-88]. Geneva, Switzerland: ITU.

ITU. (1989a, March 6). Minutes of the First Plenary Meeting [Corrigendum 1 to Document 47-E]. In *World Administrative Telegraph and Telephone Conference, Melbourne, November–December 1988.*

ITU. (1989b, May 30). Minutes of the Ninth Plenary Meeting. In *Plenipotentiary Conference, Nice.* Geneva, Switzerland: ITU.

ITU. (1989c, May 30). Minutes of the Ninth Plenary Meeting [Document 173-E]. In *Plenipotentiary Conference, Nice.* Geneva, Switzerland: ITU.

ITU. (1989d, June 22). United States of America. Statement Relevant to the Speech of the Representative of Cuba at the Ninth Plenary Meeting [Document 335-E]. In *Plenipotentiary Conference, Nice.* Geneva, Switzerland: ITU.

ITU. (1989e, June 28). Statement in Reply to Document 335 of the United States Delegation and Its Statement at the Twelfth Plenary Meeting [Document 496-E]. In *Plenipotentiary Conference, Nice.* Geneva, Switzerland: ITU.

ITU. (1989f, June 30). Declarations and Reservations made at the end of The Plenipotentiary Conference of the International Telecommunication Union. In *Plenipotentiary Conference, Nice.* Geneva, Switzerland: ITU.

ITU-COM explores problems ahead for international regulation. (1989, October 9). *Broadcasting, 117,* 63–65.

Izcaray, F., & McNelly, J. T. (1987). Selective media use by Venezuelans: The passing of the passive audience in a rapidly developing society. *Studies in Latin American Popular Culture, 6,* 27–41.

Jacobs, G. (1988, June). The renaissance of privately licensed short-wave broadcast stations in the United States. *IEEE Transactions in Broadcasting, 34,* 87–93.

Jakubowicz, K. (1985). Third world news cooperation schemes in building a new international communication order: Do they stand a chance? *Gazette, 36,* 81–93.

Jakubowicz, K. (1988, February 8–11). The media-political and economic dimensions of television programme exchange between Poland and Western Europe [Paper presented at the Conference: International Information Flows Between Eastern and Western Europe; Towards Confidence, Mutual Understanding and Cooperation, Arnoldshain, Germany].

Jakubowicz, K. (1990). NWICO is dead. Long live NEURICO? *Media Development, 37* (3), 33.

Jansky/Barmat Telecommunications. (1987). *What Has and Is About to Become of the Geostationary Orbit?* [Unpublished research paper].

Janus, N., & Roncagliolo, R. (1986). Advertising, mass media and dependency. In U. Kivikuru & T. Varis (Eds.), *Approaches to International Communication: Textbook for Journalism Education.* Helsinki, Finland: Finnish National Commission for UNESCO, 95–112.

Japan Electronics Almanac 1985. (1985). Tokyo: Dempa.

Japan Electronics Almanac. (1990). Tokyo: Dempa.

Japan's NHK details plans for global news network. (1991, June). *Broadcasting Abroad, 3,* 14.

Jenkins, R. (1987). *Transnational Corporations and Uneven Development: The Internationalization of Capital and the Third World.* New York: Methuen.

Jéquier, N. (1984). Telecommunications for development: Findings of the ITU-OECD project. *Telecommunications Policy, 8,* 83–88.

Jimmy Carter tells journalists not to be so "timid." (1989, May 15). *Broadcasting, 116,* 61.

Johnson, A. W. (1981). The cultural impact of technological change on broadcasting. In *Symposium 2 on Public Role and Systems of Broadcasting* [Summary report]. Tokyo: Hōsō-Bunka Foundation, 175–185.

Jones, C. (1991, May 30). Japan tries to organize Asia-wide network. *Christian Science Monitor.*

Jowett, G. S., & O'Donnell, V. (1986). *Propaganda and Persuasion.* Beverly Hills, CA: Sage.

Judd, F. C. (1987). *Radio Amateur's Guide: Radio Wave Propagation (HF Bands).* London: William Heinemann.

Jussawalla, M. (1982). International trade theory and communications. In M. Jussawalla & D. M. Lamberton (Eds.), *Communication Economics and Development.* New York: Pergamon Press, 82–99.

Jussawalla, M. (1985). Constraints on economic analysis of transborder data flows. *Media Culture and Society, 7,* 297–315.

Jussawalla, M., & Cheah, C. (1987). *The Calculus of International Communication: A Study in the Political Economy of Transborder Data Flows.* Littleton, CO: Libraries Unlimited.

Jussawalla, M., & Lamberton, D. M. (1982). Communication economics and development: An economics of information perspective. In M. Jussawalla & D. M. Lamberton (Eds.), *Communication Economics and Development.* New York: Pergamon Press, 1–15.

Kagan, D. (1989, April 24). Shortwave signals a new competitive era. *Insight,* 8–17.

Kahn, D. (1991). *Seizing Enigma: The Race to Break the German U-Boat Codes, 1939–1943.* Boston: Houghton Mifflin.

Kahn, F. J., (Ed.). (1973). *Documents of American Broadcasting.* Englewood Cliffs, NJ: Prentice-Hall.

Kalb, M. (1990). Foreword. In H. N. Tuch, *Communicating with the World: U.S. Public Diplomacy Overseas.* New York: St. Martin's Press, ix–xii.

Kang, J. G., & Morgan, M. (1988). Culture clash: Impact of U.S. television in Korea. *Journalism Quarterly, 65,* 431–438.

Kanocz, S. (1989). European Non-English-speaking influences on British and third world television — existing and potential. In C. W. Thomsen (Ed.), *Cultural Transfer or Electronic Colonialism? The Impact of American Television Programs on European Television.* Heidelberg, Germany: Carl Winter Universitätsverlag, 49–56.

Kariel, H. G., & Rosenvall, L. A. (1984). Factors influencing international news flow. *Journalism Quarterly, 61,* 509–516, 666.

Kashel, A. A. (1987). The use of satellites for television and sound broadcasting. *Radio and Television, 2,* 29–37.

Kaundinya, P. J. (1978). Recording and tape piracy a worldwide problem. *Interauteurs, 189,* 68–79.

Kavanaugh, A. (1986, June). Star WARCs and new systems: An analysis of US international satellite policy formation. *Telecommunications Policy, 10,* 93–105.

Kazansky, P. (1897). *The Universal Telegraph Union* (abridged translation from Russian). Odessa, Russia: no publisher.

Kellaway, L. (1990, April 19). A definite article of dissent. *Financial Times.*

Kenez, P. (1985). *The Birth of the Propaganda State: Soviet Methods of Mass Mobilization, 1917–1929.* Cambridge: Cambridge University Press.

Kennedy, R. (1979). The radio missionaries. In *World Radio TV Handbook.* New York: Billboard Publications, 71–77.

Kershaw, I. (1983). *Popular Opinion & Political Dissent in the Third Reich: Bavaria 1933–1945.* New York: Oxford University Press.

Kieve, J. (1973). *The Electric Telegraph: A Social and Economic History.* Devon, England: David & Charles.

Kilpatrick, J. J. (1987, August 19). No glasnost on the radio dial. *Washington Post.*

Kim, L., Lee, J., & Lee, J. (1987). Korea's entry into the computer industry and its acquisition of technological capability. *Technovation, 6,* 277–293.

Kincaid, S. K. (1986). The record carrier industry. In A. W. Branscomb (Ed.), *Toward a Law of Global Communications Networks.* New York: Longman, 77–88.

King, J. C. (1973). *A Survey and Analysis of the Major International Evangelical Short Wave Broadcasters: Trans World Radio, HCJB and the Far East Broadcasting Company* [Dissertation]. University of Michigan.

Kinner, J. (1988). Nigeria. In P. T. Rosen (Ed.), *International Handbook of Broadcasting Systems.* New York: Greenwood Press, 225–236.

Kirkpatrick, E. (1956). *Target: The World. Communist Propaganda Activities in 1955.* New York: Macmillan.

Kirsch, B. (1986). Deutsche Welle's Russian service, 1962–85. In K. R. M. Short (Ed.), *Western Broadcasting over the Iron Curtain.* New York: St. Martin's Press, 158–171.

Kissinger, H. (1985, November 17). An opportunity for a breakthrough. *Washington Post.*

Kitatani, K. (1988). Japan. In P. T. Rosen (Ed.), *International Handbook of Broadcasting Systems.* New York: Greenwood Press, 173–186.

Kleinwächter, W. (1986). Legal basis of a new information order. In U. Kivikuru & T. Varis (Eds.), *Approaches to International Communication: Textbook for Journalism Education.* Helsinki, Finland: Finnish National Commission for UNESCO, 205–216.

Knaplund, P. (1941). *The British Empire 1815–1939.* New York: Harper & Brothers.

Knight, P. (1990, April 19). The paper chase. *Financial Times.*

Knightley, P. (1975). *The First Casualty.* New York: Harcourt Brace Jovanovich.

Koehler, J. E. (1987, January). Satellite communications — international considerations. *IEEE Communications Magazine, 25,* 33–35.

Konstantinov, E. (1989). Direct broadcasting by satellite (DBS) between East and West: an international legal controversy? In J. Becker & T. Szecskö (Eds.), *Europe Speaks to Europe: International Information Flows Between Eastern and Western Europe.* New York: Pergamon Press, 406–420.

Konstantinova, R. (1991, April 16). Bulgaria-Radio. Associated Press report.

Kottak, C. (1990). *Prime-Time Society: An Anthropological Analysis of Television and Culture.* Belmont, CA: Wadsworth.

Kottak, C. P. (1991, Winter). Television's impact on values and social life. *Journal of Communication, 41,* 70–87.

Kretzmann, E. M. J. (1967, February). McCarthy and the Voice of America. *Foreign Service Journal.* 26–27, 44–46.

Kris, E., & Speier, H. (1944). *German Radio Propaganda: Report on Home Broadcasts During the War.* London: Oxford University Press.

Krutogorov, Y. (1991, July 21). Radio for Europe: Tiny "echo" is helping Russians find their voice. *Washington Post.*

Kumar, K. (1980). Social and cultural impact of transnational enterprises: An overview. In K. Kumar (Ed.), *Transnational Enterprises: Their Impact on Third World Societies and Cultures.* Boulder, CO: Westview Press, 1–43.

Kurian, G. T. (Compiler). (1984). *The New Book of World Rankings.* New York: Facts on File.

Kurtz, H. (1987, March 18). Reagan "interview" on Cuba had script. *Washington Post,* A4.

LaFranchi, H. (1991, May 30). Europeans want their own CNN. *Christian Science Monitor.*

Laïdi, Z. (1990). *The Superpowers and Africa: The Constraints of Rivalry 1960–1990.* Chicago: University of Chicago Press.

Lambert, P. (1992, January 13). Global satellite deregulation and separate systems: Off to a running start in 1992. *Broadcasting, 122,* 100.

Lansipuro, Y. (1987). Asiavision news exchange. *InterMedia, 15,* 22–27.

Lardner, G. (1991, November 22). Create "Radio Free China," Hill is urged. *Washington Post,* A23.

Larson, J. F. (1986). Television and U.S. foreign policy: The case of the Iran hostage crisis. *Journal of Communication, 36,* 108–130.

Lasker, B., & Roman, A. (1938). *Propaganda from China and Japan: A Case Study in Propaganda Analysis.* American Council, Institute of Pacific Relations.

Lasswell, H. D. (1927). *Propaganda Technique in the World War.* New York: Knopf.

Lasswell, H. D. (1960). The structure and function of communication in society. In W. Schramm (Ed.). *Mass Communications* (2nd ed.). Urbana: University of Illinois Press, 117–130.

Lasswell, H., & Blumenstock, D. (1970). *World Revolutionary Propaganda* (1939). Westport, CT: Greenwood Press.

The late night pirate show. (1981, October 17). *The Economist, 52.*

Latin American movie plan. (1990, January 22). *Broadcasting, 118,* 39.

Lavine, H., & Wechsler, J. (1940). *War Propaganda and the United States.* New Haven, CT: Yale University Press.

Lawrenson, J., & Barber, L. (1985). *The Price of Truth: The Story of the Reuters £££ Millions.* Edinburgh, Scotland: Mainstream.

Le Duc, D. R. (1981). East-West news flow "imbalance": Qualifying the quantifications. *Journal of Communication, 31,* 135–141.

Ledyard, G. H. (1963). *Sky Waves: The Incredible Far East Broadcasting Co. Story.* Chicago: Moody Press.

Lee, C. (1979). *Media Imperialism Reconsidered: The Homogenizing of Television Culture.* Beverly Hills, CA: Sage.

Lee, G. (1987a, January 2). Soviets broadcast Reagan's greeting. *Washington Post.*

Lee, G. (1987b, May 4). Soviets extent "glasnost" to airwaves. *Washington Post.*

Lee, G. (1987c, May 26). Soviets seem to halt VOA jamming. *Washington Post.*

Lee, J. (1968). *The Diplomatic Persuaders: New Role of the Mass Media in International Relations.* New York: Wiley.

LeFloch, B., Halbert-Lassalle, R., & Castelain, D. (1989). Digital sound broadcasting to mobile receivers. *IEEE Transactions in Consumer Electronics, 35.*

Legum, C., & Cornwell, J. (1978). Background paper. In *A Free and Balanced Flow.* Lexington, MA: Lexington Books, 15–72.

Leinwoll, S. (1988). The future of high frequency broadcasting. *IEEE Transactions in Broadcasting, 34,* 94–101.

Leive, D. M. (1984). Some conflicting trends in satellite communications. In *Regulation of Transnational Communications.* In *Michigan Yearbook of International Legal Studies 1984.* New York: Clark Boardman, 73–82.

Lendval, P. (1981). *The Bureaucracy of Truth: How Communist Governments Manage the News.* London: Burnett Books.

Lerner, D. (1958). *The Passing of Traditional Society.* Glencoe, IL: Free Press.

Lerner, D. (1960). Communication systems and social systems. In W. Schramm (Ed.), *Mass Communications* (2nd ed.). Urbana: University of Illinois Press, 131–140.

Letters to the hostages travel via VOA airmail. (1990, November 7). *Washington Post.*

Levin, H. (1971). *The Invisible Resource: Use and Regulation of the Radio Spectrum.* Baltimore, MD: Johns Hopkins University Press.

Lewis, C. A. ([1924]). *Broadcasting from Within.* London: George Newnes.

Lewis, T. (1991). *Empire of the Air: The Men Who Made Radio.* New York: Edward Burlingame Books.

Liebes, T., & Katz, E. (1990). *The Export of Meaning: Cross-Cultural Readings of Dallas.* New York: Oxford University Press.

Liebovich, L. (1988). *The Press and the Origins of the Cold War, 1944–1947.* New York: Praeger.

Lindahl, R. (1978). *Broadcasting Across Borders: A Study on the Role of Propaganda in External Broadcasts* [Göteborg Studies in Politics 8]. Lund, Sweden: C. W. K. Gleerup.

Linking lines in Europe. (1989, November 20). *The Times (London),* 38.

Lisann, M. (1975). *Broadcasting to the Soviet Union: International Politics and Radio.* New York: Praeger.

Liska, V. P. (1987, October). Astra: Closer to reality. *Satellite Communications, 11,* 45–46.

A listener. (1940). The political use of broadcasting. *The Political Quarterly, 11,* 234–248.

Lithuania applies to join Eutelsat TV and telephone network. (1991, October 15). Reuters report.

Ljunggren, D. (1991, October 9). BBC's world service signs deal on Russian radio. Reuters report.

Locksley, G. (1987, June). Direct broadcast satellites: The media-industrial complex in the UK and Europe. *Telecommunications Policy, 11,* 193–207.

Long, M. (1987). *World Satellite Almanac: The Complete Guide to Satellite Transmission & Technology* (2nd ed.). Indianapolis, IN: Howard W. Sams.

Lozoya, J. A., & Birgin, H. (Eds.). (1981). *Social and Cultural Issues of the New International Economic Order.* New York: Pergamon Press.

Lubis, M. (1986). Cultural integrity: Free and balanced information flow, mutually exclusive terms or parts of the same thing? *MediaAsia, 13,* 63–70.

Lukes, I. (1988). Radio Moscow's North American service: A study in radio propaganda. In L. Bittman (Ed.), *The New Image Makers: Soviet Propaganda and Disinformation Today.* Washington, DC: Pergamon-Brassey, 77–112.

Lumsden, J. (1984, July/August). The Greenville giant. *Broadcast Sound,* 12–13.

Lundgren, M. ([1983]). *Proclaiming Christ to His World: The Experience of Radio Voice of the Gospel, 1957–1977.* Geneva, Switzerland: Lutheran World Federation.

Luther, S. F. (1988). *The United States and the Direct Broadcast Satellite: The Politics of International Broadcasting in Space.* New York: Oxford University Press.

M.P. wants an answer to Haw-Haw. (1940, January 1). *News Chronicle.*

MacBride, S. (1980). Chairman, International Commission for the Study of Communication Problems (MacBride Commission). *Many Voices, One World* (abridged ed.). Paris: UNESCO.

MacKenzie, J. M. (1984). *Propaganda and Empire: The Manipulation of British Public Opinion 1880–1960.* Manchester: Manchester University Press.

MacKenzie, J. M. (1987). Propaganda and the BBC Empire Service, 1932–42. In J. Hawthorn (Ed.), *Propaganda, Persuasion and Polemic.* London: Edward Arnold, 37–54.

Madge, T. S. (1988). Great Britain. In P. T. Rosen (Ed.), *International Handbook of Broadcasting Systems.* New York: Greenwood Press.

Madrid Radio Telegraphic Conference. (1932, October). *Radio Intelligence, 37,* 7.

Maeda, Y. (1981). On the international role of broadcasting. In *Symposium 2 on Public Role and Systems of Broadcasting* [Summary report]. Tokyo: Hōsō-Bunka Foundation, 163–174.

Magoma, A. R. (1974). United Nations Radio. In S. W. Head (Ed.), *Broadcasting to Africa: A Continental Survey of Radio and Television.* Philadelphia: Temple University Press, 199–200.

"Make it known." (1991, August 20). *Washington Post,* A15.

Mainland, E., & Pomar, M. (1986). The voice present and future: VOA, the USSR and Communist Europe. In K. R. M. Short (Ed.), *Western Broadcasting over the Iron Curtain.* New York: St. Martin's Press, 113–138.

Maitland, D. (1984). Chairman, Independent Commission for World Wide Telecommunications Development (Maitland Commission). *The Missing Link*. Geneva, Switzerland: International Telecommunication Union.

Maletzke, G. (1986). Relations between communications, programs, and audiences in broadcasting. *The Third Channel, 2,* 436–447.

Malitza, M., & Sandi, M. (1981). The NIEO and the learning process of society. In J. A. Lozoya & H. Birgin (Eds.), *Social and Cultural Values of the New International Economic Order*. New York: Pergamon Books, 41–69.

Mañach, J. (1975). *Frontiers in the Americas: A Global Perspective* (P. H. Phenix, Trans.). New York: Teachers College Press.

Mankekar, D. A. (1986). Synthesis of third world viewpoints. In U. Kivikuru & T. Varis (Eds.), *Approaches to International Communication: Textbook for Journalism Education*. Helsinki, Finland: Finnish National Commission for UNESCO, 29–36.

Mankekar, D. R. (1981). *Whose Order? A Plea for a New International Information Order by the Third World*. Delhi, India: Clarion Books.

Mansell, G. (1982). *Let Truth Be Told: 50 Years of BBC External Broadcasting*. London: Weidenfeld & Nicolson.

Marhold, J. (1987). Our theme — social processes. *Radio and Television, 37*(5), 19–21.

Marinov, Z., Trichkov, V., & Todorov, T. (1989). Co-operation between Bulgaria and information systems in Western Europe. In J. Becker & T. Szecskö (Eds.), *Europe Speaks to Europe: International Information Flows Between Eastern and Western Europe*. New York: Pergamon Press, 250–258.

Markoff, J. (1991, January 16). News from the Mideast via the P.C. *New York Times,* C3.

Marshall, P. (1989, January). Global television by satellite: Choice for viewers, a threat to national broadcasters. *Space Communication and Broadcasting, 6,* 264–265.

Martin, E. (1985, December). DBS systems: Perspectives from a profit-seeking company. *Telecommunications Policy, 9,* 291–300.

Martin, J. L. (1984). Private leased telecommunications lines: Threats to continued international availability. In *Regulation of Transnational Communication*. In *Michigan Yearbook of International Legal Studies 1984*. New York: Clark Boardman, 219–239.

Martin, K. (1939). The ministry of information. *The Political Quarterly, 10,* 502–516.

Martin, L. J. (1958). *International Propaganda: Its Legal and Diplomatic Control*. Minneapolis: University of Minnesota Press.

Martin, L. J. (1980). The moving target: General trends in audience composition. In H. D. Lasswell, D. Lerner, & H. Speier (Eds.), *Propaganda and Communication in World History. Vol. 3: A Pluralizing World in Formation*. Honolulu: University Press of Hawaii, 249–294.

Martin, L. J. (1988). Kenya. In P. T. Rosen (Ed.), *International Handbook of Broadcasting Systems*. New York: Greenwood Press, 187–200.

Marvin, C. (1988). *When Old Technologies Were New: Thinking About Electric Communication in the Late Nineteenth Century*. New York: Oxford University Press.

Masani, M. (1976). *Broadcasting and the People*. New Delhi: National Book Trust, India.

Masmoudi, M. (1981). The new world information order. In J. Richstad & M. H. Anderson (Eds.), *Crisis in International News: Policies and Prospects*. New York: Columbia University Press, 77–96.

Mathews, J. (1985, October 10). TV station accused of propaganda. *Washington Post.*

Matta, F. R. (1980). The information bedazzlement of Latin America. In K. Kumar (Ed.), *Transnational Enterprises: Their Impact on Third World Societies and Cultures*. Boulder, CO: Westview Press, 187–206.

Mattelart, A. (1991). *Advertising International: The Privatisation of Public Space* (M. Chanan, Trans.). London: Comedia.

Mattelart, A., Delacourt, X., & Mattelart, M. (1984). *International Image Markets: In Search of an Alternative Perspective* (D. Buxton, Trans.). London: Comedia.

Mattelart, A., & Piemme, J. (1982). The internationalization of television in Belgium. In *Cultural Industries: A Challenge for the Future of Culture.* Paris: UNESCO, 102–111.

Mattelart, A., & Schmucler, H. (1985). *Communication and Information Technologies: Freedom of Choice for Latin America?* (D. Buxton, Trans.). Norwood, NJ: Ablex.

Mayo, O. N. (1980). *La Radio Sin Fronteras: Radiodifusión Exterior y Comunicación de Masas.* Pamplona, Spain: Ediciones Universidad de Navarra.

Mazrui, A. A. (1980). The impact of transnational corporations on educational processes and cultural change: An African perspective. In K. Kumar (Ed.), *Transnational Enterprises: Their Impact on Third World Societies and Cultures.* Boulder, CO: Westview Press, 207–229.

McAllister, B. (1987a, March 31). Fiscal laryngitis lowers "the voice." *Washington Post.*

McAllister, B. (1987b, September 1). Executives blamed for delays at VOA. *Washington Post.*

McAnany, E. G. (1987). Cultural policy and television: Chile as a case study. *Studies in Latin American Popular Culture, 6,* 55–67.

McCartney, N. (1990, April 19). The heavy cost of unregulated growth. *Financial Times.*

McKnight, L. (1987). The international standardization of telecommunications services and equipment. In E. Mestmächer (Ed.), *The Law and Economics of Transborder Communications: A Symposium.* Baden-Baden, Austria: Nomos Verlagsgesellschaft, 415–436.

McLuhan, M., & Fiore, Q. (1968). *War and Peace in the Global Village.* New York: Touchstone.

McPhail, T. L. (1987). *Electronic Colonialism: The Future of International Broadcasting and Communication.* In *Sage Library of Social Research* (Vol. 26). Beverly Hills, CA: Sage.

McQuail, D. (1983). *Mass Communication Theory: An Introduction.* Beverly Hills, CA: Sage.

McQuail, D. (1989). Commercial imperialism and cultural cost. In C. W. Thomsen (Ed.), *Cultural Transfer or Electronic Colonialism? The Impact of American Television Programs on European Television.* Heidelberg, Germany: Carl Winter Universitätsverlag, 207–218.

Medis, P. (1987, November). Sri Lanka — absorbing technology for survival. *InterMedia, 15*(6), 33–35.

Mehra, A. (1985). Freedom champions as freedom muzzlers: U.S. violations of free flow of information. *Gazette, 36,* 3–20.

Mehta, D. S. (1987). *Mass Media in the USSR.* Moscow: Progress.

Memoria Anual. (1986). Spain.

Mestmächer, E. (1987). *The Law and Economics of Transborder Telecommunications: A Symposium.* Baden-Baden, Austria: Nomos Verlagsgesellschaft.

Mestmächer, E. (1988, February). Toward a new international telecomm regime. *Transnational Data and Communications Report, 11,* 11–16.

Meyers, A. W. (1990, January) . . . And the walls come tumbling down — record breaking coverage of historic events. *INTELSAT News, 6,* 18.

Meyrowitz, J. (1985). *No Sense of Place: The Impact of Electronic Media on Social Behavior.* New York: Oxford University Press.

Mickelson, S. (1983). *America's Other Voice: The Story of Radio Free Europe and Radio Liberty.* New York: Praeger.

Mickiewicz, E. P. (1988). *Split Signals: Television and Politics in the Soviet Union.* New York: Oxford University Press.

Mill, J. S. (1947). *On Liberty* (A. Castell, Ed.). Northbrook, IL: AHM.

Millard, C. (1985). *Legal Protection of Computer Programs and Data.* London: Sweet & Maxwell.

Miller, J. E. (1987a). *Advanced Digital Technology for Satellite Sound Broadcasting in Band 9* [Study Group JWG 10-11S] (Doc. No. USSG 10-11S/2B). Geneva, Switzerland: CCIR.

Miller, J. E. (1987b). *Advanced Vehicular Receiving Antenna Technology* [Study Group JWG 10-11S] (Doc. No. USSG 10-11S/2A). Geneva, Switzerland: CCIR.

Miller, J. E. (1987c). *Satellite Transmitting Antenna Technology* [Study Group JWG 10-11S] (Doc. No. USSG 10-11S/2C). Geneva, Switzerland: CCIR.

Miller, J. E. (1987d). Technical possibilities of DBS radio at or near 1 gHz [Paper presented at the 15th International Television Symposium and Exhibition, Montreux, Switzerland].

Milner, R. (1983). *Reith: The B.B.C. Years.* Edinburgh: Mainstream.

Milton, J. (1951). *Aereopagitica and On Education* (G. H. Sabine, Ed.). Northbrook, IL: AHM.

Ministry of Posts and Telecommunications. (1988). *Communications in Japan.* Tokyo: Ministry of Posts and Telecommunications.

Minnesota close to red abyss as murder terrorizes voters. (1936, January 22). *Pelley's Weekly, 1.*

Mintz, J. (1992, January 15). AT&T, Ukraine agree on phone joint venture. *Washington Post,* F1, F2.

MIP-TV convenes in Cannes. (1988, April 25). *Broadcasting, 114,* 58.

Mirow, K. R., & Maurer, H. (1982). *Webs of Power: International Cartels and the World Economy.* Boston: Houghton Mifflin.

Modelski, T. (1986). *The Polish Contribution to the Ultimate Allied Victory in the Second World War.* Worthing, England: privately printed.

Mojkowski, J. (1987). The prospects of satellite television in Poland. *Radio and Television, 37*(5), 22–24.

"Monitor": Reaching around the world with radio. (1989, March 27). *Broadcasting, 116,* 54.

More freedom sought for world media. (1988, September 19). *Broadcasting, 115,* 49.

Morgan, W. L. (1988, October). C-band geostationary satellite locations. *Satellite Communications, 12.*

Moscow TV comparison of Gorbachev interview. (1987, December 3). [Foreign Broadcast Information Service (FBIS) Report]. In Soviet Union, 87-232.

Motion Picture Export Association of America. (1991, April 2). Press release.

Mowlana, H. (1984). The role of the media in the U.S.-Iranian conflict. In A. Arno & W. Dissanayake (Eds.), *The News Media in National and International Conflict.* Boulder, CO: Westview Press, 71–99.

Mowlana, H. (1985). *International Flow of Information: Global Report and Analysis.* Paris: UNESCO.

Mowlana, H. (1986). *Global Information and World Communication: New Frontiers in International Relations.* New York: Longman.

Mowlana, H. (1990). Old wine in new bottles. *Media Development, 37* (3), 25–26.

Mowlana, H., & Wilson, L. J. (1988). *Communication Technology and Development.* Paris: UNESCO.

MTV's "cultural colonialism." (1991, August 6). *Christian Science Monitor.*

MTV's reach around the world. (1991, August 6). *Christian Science Monitor,* 11.

Mufson, S. (1991, April 28). IMF shift to Eastern Europe stirs discontent in third world. *Washington Post.*

Murdoch takes big hit on Britain's Sky TV. (1990, February 26). *Broadcasting, 118.*

Mushi, S. S. (1966). The role of the ministry of culture in national development. In *East Africa's Cultural Heritage.* In *Contemporary African Monographs Series No. 4.* Nairobi, Kenya: East African Institute of Social and Cultural Affairs.

Mwaffisi, M. S. (1991). Direct broadcast satellites and national sovereignty: Can developing nations control their airwaves? *Africa Media Review, 5,* 87–95.

Mytton, G. (1983). *Mass Communication in Africa.* London: Edward Arnold.

Mytton, G. (1986, March). Audience research for international broadcasting. *InterMedia, 14,* 35–39.

Mytton, G. (1988, October 30). Developments in African broadcasting during the 1980s [Paper presented at the African Studies Association annual conference, Chicago.].

Mytton, G., & Forrester, C. (1988). Audiences for international radio broadcasts. *European Journal of Communication, 3,* 457–481.

N. Va. company to build satellite for Afrispace. (1990, November 19). *Washington Business Journal.*

Näslund, R. (1983). ITU conference in Nairobi: Confrontation or mutual understanding? *Telecommunications Policy, 7,* 100–110.

Naylor, R. (1991, September 5). AT&T—Soviets. Associated Press report.

NBC gets Gorbachev. (1987, November 30). *Broadcasting, 113,* 118.

NBC unveils new HDTV standard. (1988, October 17). *Broadcasting, 115,* 31.

Negroponte, N. P. (1991, September). Products and services for computer networks. *Scientific American, 265,* 76–83.

Neher, J. (1989, March 5). A revolution brews in European television. *Washington Post,* H2.

Nelson, W. D. (1991, August 21). Soviet coup—telephones. Associated Press report.

Netherlands East Indies Government. ([1942]). *Ten Years of Japanese Burrowing in the Netherlands East Indies: Official Report on Japanese Subversive Activities in the Archipelago During the Last Decade.* New York: The Netherlands Information Bureau.

Network news going international. (1987, January 26). *Broadcasting, 112,* 52.

Neumann, K. (1987). The international system of telecommunications tariffs. In E. Mestmächer (Ed.), *The Law and Economics of Transborder Communications: A Symposium.* Baden-Baden, Austria: Nomos Verlagsgesellschaft, 373–411.

Nevitt, B. (1982). *The Communication Ecology: Re-presentation Versus Replica.* Toronto: Butterworths.

New China book: VOA waging war on socialism. (1991, November 16). United Press Report.

A new approach to radio jamming abroad. (1986, October 19). *New York Times.*

Newcity, M. A. (1980). The Universal Copyright Convention as an agent of repression: The Soviet experiment. In *Copyright Law Symposium* (No. 24). New York: Columbia University Press, 1–50.

News drives global satellite traffic. (1991, October). *Broadcasting Abroad, 3,* 4.

New factors in bid to rule the (air) waves. (1990, October 21). *German Tribune,* 12.

New kids on the bloc: Commercial broadcasting struggling for toehold in Eastern Europe. (1990, January 8). *Broadcasting, 118,* 101.

Newton, A. P. (1940). *A Hundred Years of the British Empire.* London: Duckworth.

News agencies and the issues: Comments from the transnational news agencies. (1981). In J. Richstad & M. H. Anderson (Eds.), *Crisis in International News: Policies* and Prospects. New York: Columbia University Press, 268–282.

The New World Information Order, Issues in the World Administrative Radio Conference and Transborder Data Flow. (1979). New York: New York Law School.

The new world of international TV programming. (1989, October 23). *Broadcasting, 117.*

Nichols, J. S. (1984). When nobody listens: Assessing the political success of Radio Martí. *Communication Research, 11,* 281–304.

Nickelson, R. L. (1990, May). HDTV standards—understanding the issues. *Telecommunication Journal, 57,* 302–312.

Nigeria: Problems and opportunities. (1984, July). *IFPI Newsletter, 2,* 6.

Nillesen, A. B., & Stappers, J. G. (1987). The government as communicator: The Dutch dilemma. *European Journal of Communication, 2,* 491–512.

No connection. (1992, January 18). *The Economist, 322,* 76.

Nordenstreng, K. (1984). *The Mass Media Declaration of Unesco.* Norwood, NJ: Ablex.

Nordenstreng, K., Manet, E. G., & Kleinwächter, W. (Eds.). (1986). *New International Information and Communication Order Sourcebook.* Prague, Czechoslovakia: International Organization of Journalists.

Nordenstreng, K., & Schiller, H. I. (Eds.). (1979). *National Sovereignty and International Communication.* Norwood, NJ: Ablex.

Nordenstreng, K., & Varis, T. (1973). The non-homogeneity of the national state and the international flow of communication. In G. Gerbner, L. P. Gross, & W. H. Melody (Eds.), *Communications Technology and Social Policy: Understanding the New "Cultural Revolution."* New York: Wiley, 393–412.

Nordenstreng, K., & Varis, T. (1974). *Television Traffic—A One Way Street? A Survey*

and Analysis of the International Flow of Television Programme Material. Paris: UNESCO.

Norris, B. (1983, July/September). A thieves' bonanza of a billion pounds a year. *Inter-Media, 11,* 25–27.

Norwegian Telecommunications Administration (1982). *Statistics* [Summary of Norwegian Edition]. Oslo, Norway: Grondahl & Son Trykkeri.

Norwegian Telecommunications Administration. (1983). *Statistics* [Summary of Norwegian Edition]. Oslo, Norway: Grondahl & Son Trykkeri.

Norwegian Telecommunications Administration. (1984). *Statistics* [Summary of Norwegian Edition]. Oslo, Norway: Grondahl & Son Trykkeri.

Norwegian Telecommunications Administration. (1985). *Statistics* [Summary of Norwegian edition]. Oslo, Norway: Grondahl & Son Trykkeri.

O'Brien, R. C., Cooper, E., Perkes, B., & Lucas, H. (1977). *Communications Indicators and Indicators of Socio-Economic Development, 1960–1970.* Paris: UNESCO.

Ogan, C. L. (1985, March). Media diversity and communications policy: Impacts of VCRs and satellite TV. *Telecommunications Policy, 9,* 63–73.

Ogan, C. L. (1988). Developing policy for eliminating international video piracy. *Journal of Broadcasting & Electronic Media, 32,* 183–195.

Olenick, L. S. (1979). Transnational data flow: Data protection or economic protectionism? In *The New World Information Order, Issues in the World Administrative Radio Conference and Transborder Data Flow.* New York: Communications Media Center, New York Law School, 21–36.

Oliveira, O. S. (1988). Brazil. In P. T. Rosen (Ed.), *International Handbook of Broadcasting Systems.* New York: Greenwood Press, 35–46.

Ollivier, M. (Ed.). (1954). *The Colonial and Imperial Conferences from 1887 to 1937* [Imperial Conference of 1918, London]. London: Edmond Clotier.

Ong, W. J. (1982). *Orality and Literacy: The Technologizing of the Word.* London: Methuen.

The opening of the New York Radio Central. (1922, January). *The Radio Review, 3,* 3–13.

Organisation for Economic Co-operation and Development. (1989). *Competition Policy and Intellectual Property Rights.* Paris: OECD.

Ospina, S. (1986). Piracy of satellite-transmitted copyright material in the Americas: Bane or boon. In D. A. Demac (Ed.), *Tracing New Orbits: Cooperation and Competition in Global Satellite Development.* New York: Columbia University Press, 166–198.

Ottaway, D. B. (1988a, January 17). U.S. links Soviets to disinformation. *Washington Post.*

Ottaway, D. B. (1988b, December 1). After 35 years, Soviets stop jamming of U.S. broadcasts. *Washington Post.*

Overy, R. (1989). *The Road to War.* London: Macmillan.

Owens, R. C., Jr. (Ed.). (1986). *Piracy of U.S. Satellite Programming in the Western Hemisphere.* Washington, DC: International Law Institute.

Palmer, M. (1988, Winter). Deregulation and competition in European telecommunications. *Journal of Communication, 38,* 60–69.

Panel on International Telecommunications Policy of the American Society of International Law. (1971, June). *The International Telecommunication Union: Issues and Next Steps* [Occasional Paper No. 10]. New York: Carnegie Endowment for International Peace.

Panfilov, A. (1981). *Broadcasting Pirates, or Abuse of the Microphone.* Moscow: Progress.

Paper, L. J. (1987). *Empire: William S. Paley and the Making of CBS.* New York: St. Martin's Press.

The Paris Radio Central. (1921, March). *The Radio Review, 2,* 125–133.

Parry, R., & Kornbluh, P. (1988, September 4). Reagan's pro-Contra propaganda machine. *Washington Post.*

Partner, P. (1988). *Arab Voices: The BBC Arabic Service 1938–1988.* London: BBC External Services.

Patrick condemns international program piracy. (1987, March 16). *Broadcasting, 112,* 78, 79.

Pavlic, B., & Hamelink, C. J. (1985). *The New International Economic Order: Links Between Economics and Communications.* Paris: UNESCO.

Peel, G. (1905). The nerves of empire. In C. S. Golden (Ed.), *The Empire and the Century.* London: John Murray, 249–287.

Peers, F. W. (1969). *The Politics of Canadian Broadcasting 1920–1951.* Toronto: University of Toronto Press.

Pejman, P. (1986, September 7). Shah's son surprises TV viewers in Iran. *Washington Post,* A20.

Pelton, J. N. (1984). Intelsat, Communications development and world communications year. *Telematics and Informatics, 1,* 75–85.

Pelton, J. N. (1986a). The technological environment. In A. W. Branscomb (Ed.), *Toward a Law of Global Communications Networks.* New York: Longman, 37–48.

Pelton, J. N. (1986b). INTELSAT: Responding to new challenges. In D. A. Demac (Ed.), *Tracing New Orbits: Cooperation and Competition in Global Satellite Development.* New York: Columbia University Press, 58–74.

Pendakur, M. (1985). Dynamics of cultural policy making: The U.S. film industry in India. *Journal of Communication, 35,* 52–72.

Perry, S. (1991, December 19). EC countries agree on HDTV strategy in race with Japan. Reuters report.

Peterson, H. C. (1939). *Propaganda for War: The Campaign Against American Neutrality, 1914–1917.* Norman: University of Oklahoma Press.

Picard, R. G. (1991). Global communications controversies. In J. C. Merrill (Ed.), *Global Journalism: Survey of International Communication* (2nd ed.). New York: Longman.

Pichter, M. H. (1987). *Copyright Problems of Satellite and Cable Television in Europe.* London: Graham & Trotman.

Pincher, C. (1985). *The Secret Offensive, Active Measures: A Saga of Deception, Disinformation, Subversion, Terrorism, Sabotage and Assassination.* London: Sidgwick & Jackson.

Pirard, T. (1988, September). Astra gets Murdoch nod. *Satellite Communications, 12,* 25–26.

Pleydell-Bouverie, J. (1991, July). To what extent have telecommunications created the "global village"? *Geographical, 63,* 6–11.

Ploman, E. W. (1982). *International Law Governing Communications and Information: A Collection of Basic Documents.* Westport, CT: Greenwood Press.

Plomley, R. (1980). *Days Seemed Longer: Early Years of a Broadcaster.* London: Eyre Methuen.

Podmore, C., & Faguy, D. (1986, December). The challenge of optical fibres. *Telecommunications Policy, 10,* 341–351.

Poor man's burden: A survey of the third world. (1989, September 23). *The Economist, 312* [Special section following p. 86].

Possner, K. B. (1979). Legislative involvement in telecommunications policy: The 1979 World Administrative Radio Conference. In *The New World Information Order, Issues in the World Administrative Radio Conference and Transborder Data Flow.* New York: Communications Media Center, New York Law School, 17–20.

Powell, J. T. (1985). *International Broadcasting by Satellite: Issues of Regulation, Barriers to Communication.* Westport, CT: Quorum Books.

Prasad, B. S. (1986). Technology transfer: The approach of a Dutch multinational. *Technovation, 4,* 3–15.

Prentiss, S. (1985). *Television from Analog to Digital.* Blue Ridge Summit, PA: TAB Professional and Reference Books.

President extends free-market doctrine to space. (1984, December 3). *Broadcasting, 107,* 37, 38.

President's Task Force on U.S. Government International Broadcasting. (1991, December). *Report* (advance copy).

Price, R. B. (1984). Jamming and the law of international communications. In *Regulation of Transnational Communication.* In *Michigan Yearbook of International Legal Studies 1984.* New York: Clark Boardman, 391–403.

Prince of the global village. (1992, January 6). *Time, 139,* 20–23.

Pritchard, J. (1989). *Newnes Shortwave Listening Handbook.* Oxford: Heinemann Newnes.

Pye, L. (1963). Communication, development and power. In *Communications and Political Development.* Princeton, NJ: Princeton University Press.

Py, R., Sams, C., & Aluise, S. J. (1991a, November). AT&T offers 800 listing, MCI expands globally, Sprint has China connection. *The Long-Distance Letter, 9,* 7, 8.

Py, R., Sams, C., & Aluise, S. J. (1991b, November). Soviets place first call to United States over AT&T 5ESS switch. *The Long-Distance Letter, 9,* 9.

Quester, G. H. (1990). *The International Politics of Television.* Lexington, MA: Lexington Books.

Quimpo, M. G. (1990, August 14). AT&T in deal to expand China links. *Washington Post.*

R. M. (1923, January 27). [Memorandum. Post 33. Minute 9594/1923]. Post Office Archives, London.

Rachty, G., & Sabat, K. (n.d.). *Communication and Society. Vol 7: Importation of Films for Cinema and Television in Egypt.* Paris: UNESCO.

Radiat. (1934, December). Wireless in the Great War. *Wireless and Television Review, 1,* 13–14.

Radiat. (1935, February). Wireless in the Great War. *Wireless and Television Review, 1,* 121–122, 139.

Radio Free Afghanistan to air in Pashto. (1987, September 1). *Washington Post.*

Radio from foreign fields. (1934, June). *Radio Magazine, 1,* 23.

Radiosat International. (1991, February 13). Introducing: Radio without frontiers—by satellite [Unpublished paper].

Radio station identification guide. (1932, January). *Radio, 2,* 2.

Radiotelegraphy in the Dutch East Indies. (1921, November). *The Radio Review, 2,* 576.

The radio war. (1974, March 23). *The Economist,* 18.

Radio "Worldwide." (1966). *Ears That Hear: Some Thoughts on Missionary Radio.* London: Radio "Worldwide."

Rainger, P., Gregory, D., Harvey, R., & Jennings, A. (1985). *Satellite Broadcasting.* New York: Wiley.

Ramirez, A. (1991, September 10). A. T. & T. in link to Armenia. *New York Times,* C1, C4.

Randolph, E. (1989a, June 13). Clampdown on coverage seen in China. *Washington Post.*

Randolph, E. (1989b, October 7). Lack of viewers forces USIA's WorldNet off the air. *Washington Post.*

Rao, Y. V. L. (1981). Information imbalance: A closer look. In J. Richstad & M. H. Anderson (Eds.), *Crisis in International News: Policies and Prospects.* New York: Columbia University Press, 140–150.

Rathkolb, O. (1987). Voice of America's political propaganda for Austria 1945–1950. *Gazette, 39,* 31–45.

Ravault, R. (1981). Information flow: Which way is the wrong way? *Journal of Communication, 31,* 135–141.

Read, J. M. (1941). *Atrocity Propaganda 1914–1919.* New Haven, CT: Yale University Press.

Read, W. H. (1976). *America's Mass Media Merchants.* Baltimore, MD: Johns Hopkins University Press.

Read, W. H. (1986). International radio broadcasting: Sovereignty vs. free flow. In A. W. Branscomb (Ed.), *Toward a Law of Global Communications Networks.* New York: Longman, 89–94.

Rees, D. W. E. (1990). *Satellite Communications: The First Quarter Century of Service.* New York: Wiley.

Reiss, J. (1986). Deutschlandfunk: Broadcasting to East Germany and Eastern Europe. In K. R. M. Short (Ed.), *Western Broadcasting over the Iron Curtain.* New York: St. Martin's Press, 172–184.

Reith, J. (1928). Empire Broadcasting [Memorandum. E4/2. Empire Service Policy 1928–1929]. Caversham Park, England: BBC Written Archives Centre.

Reith, J. (1929, February 25). Empire Broadcasting. [Your report of 6th December. Memo to the Chief Engineer. E4/2. Empire Service Policy 1928–1929]. Caversham Park, England: BBC Written Archives Centre.

Reith, J. (1931, November 5). [Letter. E4/5. Empire Service Policy 1931]. Caversham

Park, England: BBC Written Archives Centre.

Religious broadcasters clean house, eye perestroika. (1990, February 5). *Broadcasting, 118,* 72.

Remington, T. F. (1988). *The Truth of Authority: Ideology and Communication in the Soviet Union.* Pittsburgh: University of Pittsburgh Press.

Remnick, D. (1989a, January 6). Refocusing the image of Soviet TV. *Washington Post.*

Remnick, D. (1989b, May 18). Moscow TV shutters glasnost in coverage of Beijing protests. *Washington Post.*

Remnick, D. (1991, August 21). Soviets getting all the news that fits. *Washington Post,* A29.

Remnick, D., & Diehl, J. (1988, March 18). Soviet sales seen for Western press. *Washington Post.*

Renaud, J. (1985). U.S. government assistance to AP's worldwide expansion. *Journalism Quarterly, 62,* 10–16.

Renaud, J. (1986). A conceptual framework for the examination of transborder data flows. *The Information Society, 4,* 145–185.

Renaud, J. (1987, June). The ITU and development assistance: North, south and the dynamics of the CCIs. *Telecommunications Policy, 11,* 179–192.

Renaud, J., & Litman, B. R. (1985, September). Changing dynamics of the overseas marketplace for TV programming: The rise of international co-production. *Telecommunications Policy, 9,* 245–261.

Renier, O., & Rubenstein, V. (1986). *Assigned to Listen: The Evesham Experience 1939–43.* London: BBC External Services.

Research and Analysis Reports. (1942a, March 19). *Design of Propaganda in German Foreign Newsreels.* In *Department of State General Records* [RG 59, No. 608]. National Archives, Washington, DC.

Research and Analysis Reports. (1942b, March 21). *The Radio Propaganda Atmo-sphere of the German Public.* In *Department of State General Records* [RG 59, No. 616]. National Archives, Washington, DC.

Research and Analysis Reports. (1942c, March 30). *Strategic Aims of Axis vs. American Broadcasts.* In *Department of State General Records* [RG 59, No. 615]. National Archives, Washington, DC.

Research and Analysis Reports. (1942d, November 1). *Attitudinal Atmosphere of the French People Provided by Radio Propaganda.* In *Department of State General Records* [RG 59, No. 200]. National Archives, Washington, DC.

Research and Analysis Reports. (1942e, December 7). *What the Axis Is Telling the Near East.* In *Department of State General Records* [RG 59, No. 436]. National Archives, Washington, DC.

Research and Analysis Reports. (1943a, November 26). *"Free Germany": An Experiment in Political Warfare.* In *Department of State General Records* [RG 59, No. 1593]. National Archives, Washington, DC.

Research and Analysis Reports. (1943b, December 24). *German Radio Propaganda to South Africa.* In *Department of State General Records* [RG 59, No. 1709]. National Archives, Washington, DC.

Research and Analysis Reports. (1944, March 30). *Japanese Films: A Phase of Psychological Warfare.* In *Department of State General Records* [RG 59, No. 1307]. National Archives, Washington, DC.

Reuters' Way. (1987, February). *Satellite Communications, 11,* 14–16.

Rich, N. (1970). *The Age of Nationalism and Reform, 1850–1890.* New York: Norton.

Richards, E. (1988, December 19). Pentagon aims to revive U.S. TV industry. *Washington Post,* A1, A4.

Richards, E. (1989, June 15). HDTV provides spark of hope for failing Silicon Valley firm — and U.S. electronics industry. *Washington Post.*

Righter, R. (1978). *Whose News? Politics, the Press and the Third World*. New York: Times Books.

RITA ousts TASS as new-look Russian news agency. (1992, January 22). Reuters report.

Roach, C. (1987). The U.S. position on the new world information and communication order. *Journal of Communication, 37*, 36–51.

Roach, C. (1990). Limitations and new possibilities. *Media Development, 37*(3), 28–30.

Roberts, R. (1990, August 14). CNN, on top of the world. *Washington Post.*

Roberts, R. (1991a, August 23). The BBC's coup. *Washington Post,* C1.

Roberts, R. (1991b, August 21). The librarian's chapter in history. *Washington Post,* B1, B9.

Robertson, E. H. (1974). Christian broadcasting in and to Africa. In S. W. Head (Ed.), *Broadcasting to Africa: A Continental Survey of Radio and Television*. Philadelphia: Temple University Press, 204–210.

Robins, K., Webster, F., & Pickering, M. (1987). Propaganda, information and social control. In J. Hawthorn (Ed.), *Propaganda, Persuasion and Polemic*. London: Edward Arnold, 1–18.

Robinson, P. (1985, December). Telecommunications, trade & TDF. *Telecommunications Policy, 9*, 310–318.

Rogers, E. M. (1969). *Modernization Among Peasants: The Impact of Communication*. New York: Holt, Rinehart & Winston.

Rogers, E. M. (1983). *Diffusion of Innovations* (3rd ed.). New York: Free Press.

Rogers, T. F. (1985). *Space-Based Broadcasting: The Future of Worldwide Audio Broadcasting*. Washington, DC: National Academy Press.

Rogers, T. F. (1988, September 1). Using satellite direct audio broadcasting to conduct public diplomacy [Paper prepared for the United States–Soviet Union Agenda Project of The Johns Hopkins University Foreign Policy Institute, Baltimore, MD].

Rolo, C. J. (1942). *Radio Goes to War: The "Fourth Front."* New York: Putnam.

Romania to Host East Europe's First Eutelsat Ground Station. (1991, December 17). Reuters report.

Rondolino, G. (1983). Italian propaganda films: 1940–1943. In K. R. M. Short (Ed.), *Film and Radio Propaganda in World War II*. London: Croom Helm, 230–244.

Roscher, R. (1921, February). Nauen and Togoland: A tragedy of radio-telegraph development. *The Radio Review, 2*, 68–75.

Rose, C. (1988). *The Soviet Propaganda Network*. London: Pinter.

Rosenfeld, S. (1985, April 5). Sandanista disinformation? *Washington Post,* A17.

Roser, C., & Brown, L. (1986). African newspaper editors and the new world information order. *Journalism Quarterly, 63*, 114–121.

Rostow, W. W. (1960). *The Stages of Economic Growth: A Non-Communist Manifesto*. Cambridge: Cambridge University Press.

Roxburgh, A. (1987). *Pravda: Inside the Soviet News Machine*. New York: George Braziller.

Royal Commission on the Natural Resources, Trade and Legislation of Certain Portions of His Majesty's Dominions. (1914). *Second Interim Report* [Parliamentary Paper, 1914, Cd. 7210].

Rubin, B. (1988). Worlds apart: Disinformation versus public interest. In L. Bittman (Ed.), *The New Image Makers: Soviet Propaganda and Disinformation Today*. Washington, DC: Pergamon-Brassey, 35–76.

Rundt, S. J. (1942, September 12). Short-wave artillery. *The Nation.*

Russell, N. (1981). The impact of facsimile transmission. *Journalism Quarterly, 58*, 406–410.

Russia's martial music. (1938, April 15). In *File on the Soviet Union*. London: BBC, IBAR.

Rutkowski, A. M. (1979). International data transfer, satellite communication and the 1979 World Administrative Radio Conference. In *The New World Information Order, Issues in the World Administrative Radio Conference and Transborder Data Flow.* New York: Communications Media Center, New York Law School, 3–16.

Rutkowski, A. M. (1981). *United States Policy Making for the Public International Forums on Communication.* New York: Communication Media Center, New York Law School.

Rutkowski, A. M. (1986). Integrated services digital network. In A. W. Branscomb (Ed.), *Toward a Law of Global Communications Networks.* New York: Longman, 121–140.

Ryan, P. (1989, November 10). Arabsat brings the region together. *Meed Special Report Telecommunications.*

Ryō, N. (1983). Japanese overseas broadcasting: A personal view. In K. R. M. Short (Ed.), *Film & Radio Propaganda in World War II.* London: Croom Helm.

Rydström, B. (1986, March). Videos, pirates and the underground. *Index on Censorship, 15,* 18–22.

Safety of life at sea. (1932, September). *Radio Intelligence, 36,* 3.

Safire, W. (1991, July 1). The raid of R. F. E. *New York Times,* A11.

Safire, W. (1992, February 10). Radio Free Asia. *New York Times,* A15.

Salerno, S. (1987, July). Spreading freedom's word. *American Legion Magazine,* 28–29, 46.

Sanders, M. L., & Taylor, P. M. (1982). *British Propaganda During the First World War, 1914–18.* London: Macmillan.

Sanger, D. E. (1991, December 9). NHK of Japan ends plan for global news service. *New York Times,* C8.

Sarnoff, D. (1931, November/December). Transatlantic wireless anniversary. *The Marconi Review,* 29–32.

Sarnoff, D. (1955, April 5). *Program for a Political Offensive Against World Communism.*

Satellite Communications: Developments, Applications and Future Prospects (1984). [Proceedings of the 1984 International Conference]. Pinner, England: Online.

Satellite digital TV coming into focus. (1991, October 28). *Broadcasting, 121,* 36–40.

Satellites serving the Pacific. (1988, February). *Satellite Communications, 12,* 20–21.

Satellite versus fibre — neither a clear winner. (1989, November). *Communications Systems Worldwide.*

Saunders, R. J., Warford, J. J., & Wellenius, B. (1983). *Telecommunications and Economic Development.* Baltimore, MD: Johns Hopkins University Press.

Sauvant, K. (1986a). Policies of transborder data flows. In U. Kivikuru & T. Varis (Eds.), *Approaches to International Communication: Textbook for Journalism Education.* Helsinki, Finland: Finnish National Commission for UNESCO, 53–62.

Sauvant, K. P. (1986b). Trade in data services: The international context. *Telecommunications Policy, 10,* 282–298.

Sauvant, K. P., & Mennis, B. (1980). Sociocultural investments and the international political economy of North-South relations: The role of transnational enterprises. In K. Kumar (Ed.), *Transnational Enterprises: Their Impact on Third World Societies and Cultures.* Boulder, CO: Westview Press, 275–296.

Savage, J. G. (1989). *The Politics of International Telecommunications Regulation.* Boulder, CO: Westview Press.

Sayre, N. (1982). *Running Time: Films of the Cold War.* New York: Dial Press.

Schaeffer, K. (1986). A television window on the Soviet Union. In D. A. Demac (Ed.), *Tracing New Orbits: Cooperation and Competition in Global Satellite Development.* New York: Columbia University Press, 305–311.

Schement, J. R., Gonzalez, I. N., Lum, P., & Valencia, R. (1984). The international flow of television programs. *Communication Research, 11,* 163–182.

Schiller, H. I. (1971). *Mass Communications and American Empire.* Boston: Beacon Press.

Schiller, H. I. (1976). *Communication and Cultural Domination.* White Plains, NY: International Arts and Sciences Press.

Schiller, H. I. (1989). Disney, Dallas and electronic data flows: The transnationalization of culture. In C. W. Thomsen (Ed.), *Cultural Transfer or Electronic Colonialism? The Impact of American Television Programs on European Television.* Heidelberg, Germany: Carl Winter Universitätsverlag, 33–44.

Schmitt, H. O. (1972). The national boundary in politics and economics. In R. L. Merritt (Ed.), *Communication in International Politics.* Urbana: University of Illinois Press, 405–422.

Schneider, I. (1989). American and British feature films broadcast by the ARD between 1954 and 1985: An outline of their development. In C. W. Thomsen (Ed.), *Cultural Transfer or Electronic Imperialism? The Impact of American Television Programs on European Television.* Heidelberg: Carl Winter Universitätsverlag, 71–76.

Schneiderman, R. (1988, August). HDTV: The resolution revolution. *Microwaves & RF,* 35–41.

Schrage, M. (1984, October 10). Intelsat future uncertain. *Washington Post,* C1, C4.

Schrage, M. (1985, May 7). Murdoch takes his boldest step yet. *Washington Post,* E1, E2.

Schramm, W. (1964). *Mass Media and National Development: The Role of Information in the Developing Countries.* Stanford, CA: Stanford University Press.

Schramm, W. (1980). The effects of mass media in an information era. In H. D. Lasswell, D. Lerner, & H. Speier (Eds.), *Propaganda and Communication in World History. Vol 3: A Pluralizing World in Formation.* Honolulu: University Press of Hawaii, 295–305.

Schultz, R. H., & Godson, R. (1984). *Dezinformatsia: Active Measures in Soviet Strategy.* Washington, DC: Pergamon-Brassey.

Schwartz, E. (1989, February 25). UNESCO chief vows major reforms. *Washington Post.*

Schwarzkopf, D. (1989). Dynasty, Dallas über alles? The American share in European TV-programmes: Origin, development, limits. In C. W. Thomsen (Ed.), *Cultural Transfer or Electronic Colonialism? The Impact of American Television Programs on European Television.* Heidelberg, Germany: Carl Winter Universitätsverlag, 21–32.

Schwoch, J. (1990). *The American Radio Industry and Its Latin American Activities, 1900–1939.* Urbana: University of Illinois Press.

Scott, G. (1973). *The Rise and Fall of the League of Nations.* New York: Macmillan.

Screen Digest. (1987, December). 275.

Screen Digest. (1988, February). 48.

Sedykh, I. (1992, February 21). All the news that's deemed fit. *Christian Science Monitor,* 19.

Senior, J. M. (1985). *Optical Fiber Communications: Principles and Practice.* London: Prentice-Hall.

Sepstrup, P. (1989). Transnationalization of television in Western Europe. In C. W. Thomsen (Ed.), *Cultural Transfer or Electronic Colonialism? The Impact of American Television Programs on European Television.* Heidelberg, Germany: Carl Winter Universitätsverlag, 99–136.

Servaes, J. (1986). Development theory and communication policy: Power to the people! *European Journal of Communication, 1,* 203–229.

Shakespeare, F. (1986). International broadcasting and US political realities. In K. R. M. Short (Ed.), *Western Broadcasting over the Iron Curtain.* New York: St. Martin's Press, 57–68.

Shanor, D. R. (1985). *Behind the Lines: The Private War Against Soviet Censorship.* New York: St. Martin's Press.

Sherman, C. E. (1974). International broadcasting unions. In S. W. Head (Ed.), *Broadcasting in Africa: A Continental Survey of Radio and Television.* Philadelphia: Temple University Press, 259–264.

Shirer, W. L. (1943, October). The American radio traitors. *Harper's, 187.*

Short, K. R. M. (1986). The real masters of the black heavens: Western broadcasters over the iron curtain. In K. R. M. Short (Ed.), *Western Broadcasting over the Iron Curtain.* New York: St. Martin's Press, 1–26.

Short future for shortwave? (1991, June 3). *Broadcasting, 121,* 57.

Shortwave radio tunes more Americans into international listening. (1987, October). *Wall Street Journal.*

Show business tries to balance books. (1991, October). *Broadcasting Abroad, 3,* 5.

Shulman, H. C. (1990). *The Voice of America: Propaganda and Democracy, 1941–1945.* Madison: University of Wisconsin Press.

Sibley, T. (1991, May 3). Congress seeks to establish shortwave service to Asia. *Christian Science Monitor,* 4.

Siebert, F. S., Peterson, T., & Schramm, W. (1956). *Four Theories of the Press.* Urbana: University of Illinois Press.

Siemens releases world telephone stats. (1990, January 1). *Telephone News, 11,* 5.

Signs of truce between Europe and U.S. (1989, April 25). *Broadcasting, 114,* 22.

Silburn, P. A. (1910). *The Governance of Empire.* Port Washington, NY: Kennikat Press (reprint).

Silvershirts instructed to prepare for nation's upset. (1936, May 20). *Pelley's Weekly, 2.*

Silvey, J. E. (1940). Internal BBC memorandum. In *Enemy Broadcasting Policy Record File 1939–1943* [E2/177]. Caversham Park, England: BBC Written Archives Centre.

Sinai, R. (1991, August 20). [No title]. Associated Press report.

Singh, S. N. (1991, April 30). The second revolution. *India Today.*

Sington, D., & Weidenfeld, A. (1943). *The Goebbels Experiment: A Study of the Nazi Propaganda Machine.* New Haven, CT: Yale University Press.

Sint, P. P. (1988, April). Role of Radio Austria in West-East data flow. *Transnational Data and Communications Report, 11,* 12–13.

Sint, P. P. (1989). The role of Radio Austria in West-East data flow. In J. Becker & T. Szecskö (Eds.), *Europe Speaks to Europe: International Information Flows Between Eastern and Western Europe.* New York: Pergamon Press, 216–232.

Sivowitch, E. N. (1975). A technological survey of broadcasting's prehistory, 1876–1920. In L. W. Lichty & M. C. Topping (Eds.), *American Broadcasting: A Source Book on the History of Radio and Television.* New York: Hastings House, 17–31.

Skoczylas, E. (1984). *Audiences and Frequency Use: VOA Broadcasting Options* [Unpublished report. Office of Research, USIA]. Washington, DC.

Skrzyski, C. (1991, August 22). FCC allows increased phone service to Soviet Union. United Press report.

The sky's the limit for broadcasters. (1986, February 8). *The Economist,* 25–26.

Smirnov, O. L. (1989). Experience in automated data exchange and prospects for improvement of international information flows between the USSR and Western Europe. In J. Becker & T. Szecskö (Eds.), *Europe Speaks to Europe: International Information Flows Between Eastern and Western Europe.* New York: Pergamon Press, 233–237.

Smith, A. (1979). *The Newspaper: An International History.* London: Thames & Hudson.

Smith, K. B. (1980). The impact of transnational book publishing on knowledge in less-developed countries. In K. Kumar (Ed.), *Transnational Enterprises: Their Impact on Third World Societies and Cultures.* Boulder, CO: Westview Press, 169–186.

Smith, R. J. (1991, December 7). Task force urges creation of radio for a free Asia. *Washington Post,* A10.

Smith, T. J. I. (Ed.). (1989). *Propaganda: A Pluralistic Perspective.* New York: Praeger.

Sneider, D. (1991, October 31). New Russian leaders threaten curbs on independent press. *Christian Science Monitor,* 3.

Snow, M. S. (1986). Competition by private carriers on international commercial satellite traffic: Conceptual and historical background. In D. A. Demac (Ed.), *Tracing New Orbits: Cooperation and Competition in Global Satellite Development.* New York: Columbia University Press, 33–57.

Software piracy costs firms billions. (1992, January 17). *Christian Science Monitor,* 8.

Soley, L. (1982, Winter). Radio: Clandestine broadcasting, 1948–1967. *Journal of Communication, 32,* 165–180.

Soley, L. C. (1989). *Radio Warfare: OSS and CIA Subversive Propaganda.* New York: Praeger.

Soley, L. C., & Nichols, J. S. (1987). *Clandestine Radio Broadcasting: A Study of Revolutionary and Counterrevolutionary Electronic Communication.* New York: Praeger.

Soley, L. C., & O'Brien, S. (1987, Spring). Clandestine broadcasting in the Southeast Asian peninsula. *International Communication Bulletin, 22,* 13–20.

Solomon, L. D. (1978). *Multinational Corporations and the Emerging World Order.* Port Washington, NY: Kennikat Press.

Somavia, J., & Reyes-Matta, F. (1981). Mass media in the third world and NIEO. In J. A. Lozoya & H. Birgin (Eds.), *Social and Cultural Values of the New International Economic Order.* New York: Pergamon, 70–89.

Soviet coup worries, then reassures U.S. partners. (1991, October). *Broadcasting Abroad, 3,* 3.

Sowers, M. W., Hand, G., & Rush, C. M. (1988). Jamming to the HF broadcasting service. *IEEE Transactions in Broadcasting, 34,* 109–114.

Space Applications Board. (1989). Commission on Engineering and Technical Systems, National Research Council. *NASA Space Communications R&D: Issues, Derived Benefits, and Future Directions.* Washington, DC: National Academy Press.

Speaking for America. (1991, June 21). [Editorial]. *New York Post.*

Special report: Toward liberalized, global communications. (1991, December 16). *Satellite News, 14,* 4, 5.

Spiegel, W. E. (1984). Prior consent and the United Nations human rights instruments. In *Regulation of Transnational Communication.* In *Michigan Yearbook of International Legal Studies 1984.* New York: Clark Boardman, 379–389.

Sreberny-Mohammadi, A., Nordenstreng, K., Stevenson, R., & Ugboajah, F. (Eds.). (1985). *Foreign News in the Media: International Reporting in 92 Countries.* Paris: UNESCO.

Staple, G. (1984, December 22). The assault on Intelsat. *The Nation.*

The Statesman's Year-Book. (1914). London: Macmillan.

Steele, R. W. (1985). News of the "good war": World War II news management. *Journalism Quarterly, 62,* 707–716.

Stephens, G. M. (1987, October). Intelsat's growing IBS. *Satellite Communications, 11,* 14–17.

Sterling, C. H., & Kittross, J. M. (1990). *Stay Tuned: A Concise History of American Broadcasting* (2nd ed.). Belmont, CA: Wadsworth.

Sterritt, D. (1991, May 9). Hollywood dominates style and substance of movies worldwide. *Christian Science Monitor.*

Stevenson, R. L. (1988). *Communication, Development, and the World: The Global Politics of Information.* New York: Longman.

Stott, J. H. (1985). *Satellite Sound Broadcasting to Fixed, Portable and Mobile Radio Receivers* [Unpublished report. BBC RD 1985/19]. London: BBC.

Stover, W. J. (1984). *Information Technology in the Third World: Can I.T. Lead to Humane National Development?* Boulder, CO: Westview Press.

Strabolgi, L. (1935, September). Broadcasting and the Indian Empire. *Wireless and Television Review, 2,* 139–140.

Stratigos, J. (1990, May). VSAT networking with OSI. *Via Satellite, 5,* 20–22, 24.

Straubhaar, J. D., & Viscasillas, G. M. (1991, Winter). Class, genre, and the regionalization of television programming in the Dominican Republic. *Journal of Communication, 41,* 53–69.

Strebel, E. (1983). Vichy cinema and propaganda. In K. R. M. Short (Ed.), *Film and Radio Propaganda in World War II.* London: Croom Helm, 271–289.

Stuart-Linton, C. E. T. (1912). *The Problem of Empire Governance.* London: Longmans, Green.

Sturmey, S. G. (1958). *The Economic Development of Radio.* London: Gerald Duckworth.

Sukow, R. (1991, June 27). Scrambling in wake of S-band selection. *Broadcasting, 121.*

Sullivan, T., & Miller, J. E. (1987). *Frequency Sharing Between Broadcasting-Satellite Service (Sound) in Band 9 and Terrestrial Services* [Study Group JWG 10-11S] (Document No. USSG 10-11S/2D (Rev. 1)). Geneva, Switzerland: CCIR.

Suplee, C. (1991, June 27). When communications system fails, civilization's lifeline seems to snap. *Washington Post.*

Sussman, L. R. (1977). *Mass News Media and the Third World Challenge.* Beverly Hills, CA: Sage.

Sutphin, S. E. (1986). *Understanding Satellite Television Reception.* Englewood Cliffs, NJ: Prentice-Hall.

Swahili by satellite. (1991, October 7). *Broadcasting, 121.*

Szesckö, T. (1987, March). The colours of change: Communication policies in Hungary. *InterMedia, 15*(2), 39–43.

Taishoff, M. N. (1987). *State Responsibility and the Direct Broadcast Satellite.* London: Francis Pinter.

Tallents, S. G. (1938, October 19). [Memorandum]. Caversham Park, England: BBC Written Archives Centre.

Tat, H. K. (1991, October 16). Asian broadcasters brace for spread of satellite TV. Reuters report.

Taubman, P. (1985, December 9). Oh comrade, can I borrow your Rambo cassette? *New York Times.*

Taylor, A. J. P. (1967). *English History 1914–1945.* London: Readers Union, Oxford University Press.

Taylor, P. M. (1983). Propaganda in international politics, 1919–1939. In K. R. M. Short (Ed.), *Film and Radio Propaganda in World War II.* London: Croom Helm, 17–47.

TBS sues Treasury over TV service to Cuba. (1991, October 21). *Broadcasting, 121.*

Technical Operations Study Committee for the Voice of America. (1986). Board on Telecommunications and Computer Applications, Commission on Engineering and Technical Systems, National Research Council. *Modern Audio Broadcasting Facilities for the Voice of America 1986–2001.* Washington, DC: National Academy Press.

Televerket (the Swedish Telecommunications Administration). (1985). *Annual Report* [July 1, 1984–June 30, 1985].

Television too. (1985, July 29). *Broadcasting, 109,* 52.

Thomas, I. (1935). Systems of broadcasting. *The Political Quarterly, 6,* 489–505.

Thomas, L. (1991, November 4). Synchronization of international networks. *Telephony, 221,* 29–35.

Thomsen, Christian W. (1989). Eurostrategists between cultural message and transnational commercialization: How to counter the North American media challenge. In *Cultural Transfer or Electronic Imperialism? The Impact of American Television Programs on European Television.* Heidelberg, Germany: Carl Winter Universitätsverlag, 9–20.

Thomson-CSF. (1982). *Etude Exploratoire des Performances de la Technologie Repeteur pour Satellite de Radiodiffusion Sonore* [Rapport Final] (Contract 4061/79/F/FC). Paris: Agence Spatiale Europeenne.

Thorson, L. (1991, June 21). Your local RFE. Associated Press report.

Thurber, D. (1991, November 23). Japan — HDTV. Associated Press report.

Till, D. (1983). *New Communication Order. Vol 10: A Study on the Feasibility of the Installation and Operation of Satellite Earth Stations for Broadcasting Organizations, News Agencies and Newspapers.* Paris: UNESCO.

Tomaru, H. (1991, December 9–15). BBC sets up 24-hour station to challenge CNN in Japan. *The Japan Times Weekly International Edition,* 18.

Transatlantic Wireless Anniversary. (1931, November/December). *The Marconi Review, 33,* 29–32.

Trescott, J. (1989, June 8). Signals of China's hope and turmoil. *Washington Post.*

Trevor-Roper, Hugh (Ed.). (1978). *The Goebbels Diaries: The Last Days* (R. Barry, Trans.). London: Book Club Associates.

Trezise, P. H. (1987). INTELSAT and competing private satellite systems. In E. Mestmächer (Ed.), *The Law and Economics of Transborder Communications: A Symposium.* Baden-Baden, Austria: Nomos Verlagsgesellschaft, 333–345.

Trotter, W. (1953). *Instincts of the Herd in Peace and War 1916–1919* (1919, 2nd ed.). London: Oxford University Press.

Truman, H. S. (1962). Fight false propaganda with truth. In U. G. Whitaker, Jr. (Ed.), *Propaganda and International Relations* [Speech to the American Society of Newspaper Editors, Washington, DC, April 20, 1950] (rev. and enlarged ed.). San Francisco: Chandler.

Trusov, V. A. (1987). Soviet television in the 70th year after the revolution. *Radio and Television, 37*(5), 3–10.

Truth is in the air. (1987, June 6). *The Economist,* 19–20, 22.

Tsui, L. S. (1991). The use of new communication technologies in third world countries: A comparison of perspectives. *Gazette, 48,* 69–93.

Tuch, H. N. (1990). *Communicating with the World: U.S. Public Diplomacy Overseas.* New York: St. Martin's Press.

Tunstall, J. (1977). *The Media Are American: Anglo-American Media in the World.* New York: Columbia University Press.

Tunstall, J. (1981). Worldwide news agencies: Private wholesalers of public information. In J. Richstad & M. H. Anderson (Eds.), *Crisis in International News: Policies and Prospects.* New York: Columbia University Press, 258–267.

Tunstall, J. (1983). *The Media in Britain.* New York: Columbia University Press.

Turner, L. (1973). *Multinational Companies and the Third World.* New York: Hill & Wang.

Tusa, A., & Tusa, J. (1988). *The Berlin Blockade.* London: Hoddler & Stoughton.

Tusa, J. (1990). *Conversations with the World.* London: BBC.

TV Martí bill approved by house. (1989, April 17). *Broadcasting, 11,* 33.

Twelve that would be HDTV. (1988, October 17). *Broadcasting, 115,* 38–39.

Twentieth Century Fund Task Force on the International Flow of News. (1978). *A Free and Balanced Flow.* Lexington, MA: Lexington Books.

Tydeman, J., & Kelm, E. J. (1986). *New Media in Europe: Satellites, Cable, VCRs and Videotex.* London: McGraw-Hill.

Tyrer, T. (1991, October 14). Sony buys new world TV assets. *Electronic Media, 10.*

Tyson, J. L. (1983). *U. S. International Broadcasting and National Security.* New York: Ramapo Press.

U.S. and USSR continue to find communications common ground. (1990, March 5). *Broadcasting, 118,* 60.

U.S. film industry is big winner in Europe's TV boom. (1989, March 5). *Washington Post.*

U.S. group has "jam" session in Cuba. (1990, January 1). *Broadcasting, 118,* 94.

U.S. says Moscow spread lies about baby-organ trafficking. (1988, October 21). *Washington Post,* A28.

U.S. shortwave station in Israel. (1990, March 19). *Broadcasting, 118,* 66.

U.S. takes over short waves to win air propaganda war. (1942, October 19). *Newsweek, 20.*

U.S. urged to increase spending on international broadcasting. (1991, June 17). *Broadcasting, 121,* 26.

U.S.A. (1986a). *Advanced Vehicular Antenna Technology for Satellite Sound Broadcasting in Band 9* [Contribution to Section 4.3 (System Characteristics) of JIWP 10-11/1 Report. Study Group 10-11] (Document No. US JIWP 10-11/1-2 (Rev. 3)). Geneva, Switzerland: CCIR.

U.S.A. (1986b). *The Use of Digital Technology for Satellite Sound Broadcasting in Band 9*

[Contribution to Section 4.3 (System Characteristics) of JIWP 10-11/1 Report. Study Group 10-11] (Document No. US JIWP 10-11/1-1 (Rev. 3)). Geneva, Switzerland: CCIR.

U.S.A. (1986c). *The Use of Digital Technology for Satellite Sound Broadcasting in Band 9* [Contribution to Section 4.3 (System Characteristics) of JIWP 10-11/1 Report. Study Group 10-10-11] (Document No. US JIWP 10-11/1-2 (Rev. 3)). Geneva, Switzerland: CCIR.

Ugboajah, F. O. (Ed.). (1985). *Mass Communication, Culture and Society in West Africa.* München, Germany: Hans Zell.

Ullswater Broadcasting Committee. (1935). [Paper No. 89. Overseas Broadcasting from Japan. Post 98. Number Papers]. Post Office Archives, London.

Ullswater Broadcasting Committee. (1935). [Paper No. 93. Report from the General Advisory Council of the British Broadcasting Corporation on Some of the Principles Involved in the Renewal of the Corporations Charter. 26 June 1935. Post 89. Numbered Papers]. Post Office Archives, London.

Ullswater Broadcasting Committee. (1935). [Paper No. 134. BBC Introductory Memorandum on Broadcasting and the Colonial Empire. 25 October 1935. Post 89. Numbered Papers.] Post Office Archives, London.

Ullswater Broadcasting Committee. (1936). *Report of the Broadcasting Committee 1935* [Cmd. 5091]. London: HMSO.

UNESCO. (1981a). *Cultural Co-operation: Studies and Experiences.* Paris: UNESCO.

UNESCO. (1981b). *Three weeks of television: An international comparative study.* Paris: UNESCO.

UNESCO. (1986). Division of Statistics on Culture and Communication. Office of Statistics. *International Flow of Selected Cultural Goods.* Paris: UNESCO.

UNESCO. (1987). Division of Statistics on Culture and Communication. Office of Statistics. *Latest Statistics on Radio and Television Broadcasting.* Paris: UNESCO.

UNESCO Executive Board, 129th Session. (1988). *Impact Evaluation (Type III Evaluation) of Unesco's Activities Related to the Endogenous Production of Programmes and Messages in Communication Since 1981* [Document 129 EX/INF.9]. Paris: UNESCO.

United Nations. (1983). Transnational Corporations and Transborder Data Flows. In R. C. O'Brien, (Ed.), *Information, Economics, and Power: The North-South Dimension* [UN Doc. E/C.10/87]. Boulder, CO: Westview Press.

United Nations General Assembly. (n.d.). Resolution 36/40.

United Nations General Assembly. (1982, March 23). *Report on the United Nations International Seminar on Remote Sensing Applications and Satellite Communications for Education and Development* [A/AC.105/PV.230].

United States. (1973). Presidential Study Commission on International Radio Broadcasting. *The Right to Know.* Washington, DC: U.S. Government Printing Office.

United States. (1982, September 30). Presidential Commission on Broadcasting to Cuba. *Final Report.* Washington, DC: U.S. Government Printing Office.

United States Advisory Commission on Public Diplomacy. (1986a). *Report.* Washington, DC: U.S. Government Printing Office.

United States Advisory Commission on Public Diplomacy. (1986b). *Soviet Advocacy and the U.S. Media.* Washington, DC: U.S. Government Printing Office.

United States Advisory Commission on Public Diplomacy. (1989). *Report.* Washington, DC: U.S. Government Printing Office.

United States Advisory Commission on Public Diplomacy. (1991a, November). Public diplomacy in the Soviet Union and the Republics. Washington, DC: no publisher.

United States Advisory Commission on Public Diplomacy. (1991b). *Report.* Washington, DC: U.S. Government Printing Office.

United States Congress. (1935). House Special Committee on Un-American Activities. *Investigation of Nazi and Other Propaganda* (Report No. 153) (74th Cong., 1st sess.). Washington, DC: U.S. Government Printing Office.

United States Congress. (1979). House Committee on Interstate and Foreign Commerce. *International Barriers to Data Flows: Background Report* (96th Cong., 1st sess.). Washington, DC: U.S. Government Printing Office.

United States Congress. (1983). Senate Committee on Commerce, Science, and Transportation. *Long-Range Goals in International Telecommunications and Information: An Outline for United States Policy* (98th Cong., 1st sess.). Washington, DC: U.S. Government Printing Office.

United States Congress. (1985). House Subcommittee on Courts, Civil Liberties, and the Administration of Justice of the Committee on the Judiciary. *Copyright and Technological Change* (99th Cong., 1st sess.). Washington, DC: U.S. Government Printing Office.

United States Congress. (1987). Senate Subcommittee on Patents, Copyrights and Trademarks of the Committee on the Judiciary. *U.S. Adherence to the Berne Convention* (99th Cong., 2nd sess.). Washington, DC: U.S. Government Printing Office.

United States Congress. (1988). Senate Subcommittee on Patents, Copyrights and Trademarks of the Committee on the Judiciary. *The Berne Convention* (100th Cong., 2nd sess.). Washington, DC: U.S. Government Printing Office.

Urivazo, R. I. (1987). 25 years of the Cuban Radio and Television Institute. *Radio and Television, 37*(6), 4–7.

Usabel, G. S. de. (1982). *The High Noon of American Films in Latin America.* Ann Arbor, MI: UMI Research Press.

USIA publishes guide to TV in Eastern Europe. (1990, March 5). *Broadcasting, 118,* 16, 17.

Valerdi, J. (1985, September). Regulatory issues in regional satellite communications: Towards a USA-Mexico bilateral agreement. *Telecommunications Policy, 9,* 191–202.

Varis, T. (1984, Winter). The international flow of television programs. *Journal of Communication, 34,* 143–152.

Varis, T. (1985). *International Flow of Television Programmes.* Paris: UNESCO.

Varis, T. (1986). Transnational flow of mass media materials. In U. Kivikuru & T. Varis (Eds.), *Approaches to International Communication: Textbook for Journalism Education.* Helsinki, Finland: Finnish National Commission for UNESCO. 117–129.

Varis, T., & Jokelin, R. (1976). *Television News in Europe: A Survey of News-film flow in Europe.* Tampere, Finland: University of Tampere.

Veale, N. (1991, July 5). Germany — phones. Associated Press report.

Vejjajiva, V. (1989, April 5). Intellectual property rights [Letter to the editor]. *Washington Post.*

Vernon, R. (1977). *Storm over the Multinationals: The Real Issues.* Cambridge, MA: Harvard University Press.

Videocassettes earned 50% more than cinemas in West Germany. (1988, June 8). *Variety,* 67.

Video compression: Multiplying satellite capacity from the ground in the '90s. (1991, July 29). *Broadcasting, 121.*

Viereck, G. S. (1930). *Spreading Germs of Hate.* New York: Horace Liveright.

Vines, Stephen. (1989, July 17). China sacks colony media chief. *The Guardian (London).*

Vinogradoff, I. (1945). *History of English Advertising Programmes Broadcast to the United Kingdom down to the Outbreak of War* [R34/961. Policy. Commercial Broadcasting History (Vinogradoff) 1945]. Caversham Park, England: BBC Written Archives Centre.

Vita, M. C. (1990, January 28). Radio riding wave of freedom. *Indianapolis Star.*

Vizas, C. J. II. (1986). The reality of change, satellite technology, economics, and institutional resistance. In D. A. Demac, (Ed.), *Tracing New Orbits: Cooperation and Competition in Global Satellite Development.* New York: Columbia University Press, 75–87.

VOA and the Soviet coup. (n.d.). Washington, DC: Voice of America.

VOA cuts services, lays off employees to meet budget. (1990, 5 February). *Broadcasting, 118,* 32.

VOA "does" journalism: It's the law. (1991, July 10). [Letter to the Editor by R. W. Carlson]. *Wall Street Journal.*

VOA, RFE/RL victorious after failed Soviet coup. (1991, September 2). *Broadcasting, 121,* 37–38.

VOA-2001 Committee. (1987). *VOA's Future in Shortwave Broadcasting* [Unpublished report].

Voice of America. (1992a). *Program Placement Catalog.* Washington, DC: Voice of America.

Voice of America. (1992b). Transmitter network.

Voice of America defends role in Gulf War. (1991, July 2). [Letters to the Editor by R. W. Carlson and H. F. Radday]. *New York Post.*

Voice of America 1988. (1988). Washington, DC: VOA.

Voice of America 1989. (1989). Washington, DC: VOA.

Volkogonov, D. (1986). *The Psychological War.* Moscow: Progress.

Vyvyan, R. N. (1974). *Marconi and Wireless.* Yorkshire, UK: EP.

Wallis, R., & Baran, S. J. (1990). *The Known World of Broadcast News: International News and the Electronic Media.* New York: Routledge.

War news by satellite. (1991, March). *BSI: Broadcast Systems International, 23,* 24.

The war of words. (1985, October 7). *U.S. News & World Report,* pp. 34–39.

Warr, M. (1991, October 28). SONET edging closer to global reality. *Telephony, 221,* S4.

Wasburn, P. C. (1988). Voice of America and Radio Moscow newscasts to the third world. *Journal of Broadcasting & Electronic Media, 32,* 197–218.

Washburn, P. S. (1985). FDR versus his own attorney general: The struggle over sedition. *Journalism Quarterly, 62,* 717–724.

Wassiczek, N., Waters, G. T., & Wood, D. (1990, May). European perspectives in the development of HDTV standards. *Telecommunication Journal, 57.*

Waterman, D. (1988, June). World television trade: The economic effects of privatization and new technology. *Telecommunications Policy, 12,* 141–151.

Weaver, C. (1988, November/December). When the Voice of America ignores its charter. *Columbia Journalism Review, 27,* 36–43.

Webster, D. (1990). New communications technology and the international political process. In S. Serfaty (Ed.), *The Media and Foreign Policy.* New York: St. Martin's Press, 219–227.

Weibul, L., Olsson, C., & Lundquist, L. (1971). *Nordick Nyhesformedling.* Statsvetenskapliga Institutionen: Goteborgs Universitet.

Weinraub, B. (1992, January 22). Ready for prime time in Moscow. *New York Times,* C1, C5.

Weinthal, L. (1923). The trans-African telegraph line. In L. Weinthal (Ed.), *The Story of the Cape to Cairo Railway and River Route from 1887 to 1922.* London: Pioneer, 211–218.

Weir, E. A. (1965). *The Struggle for National Broadcasting in Canada.* Toronto: McClelland & Stewart.

Welch, D. (1983). Nazi wartime newsreel propaganda. In K. R. M. Short (Ed.), *Film and Radio Propaganda in World War II.* London: Croom Helm, 201–219.

Welchman, G. (1982). *The Hut Six Story: Breaking the Enigma Codes.* London: Allen Lane.

Weldon, J. O. (1988). The early history of U.S. international broadcasting from the start of World War II. *IEEE Transactions in Broadcasting, 34,* 82–86.

Wells, A. (1972). *Picture-Tube Imperialism? The Impact of U.S. Television on Latin America.* New York: Orbis Books.

Wells, C. (1987). *The UN, UNESCO and the Politics of Knowledge.* London: Macmillan.

Wert, M. C., & Stevenson, R. L. (1988). Global television flow to Latin American countries. *Journalism Quarterly, 65,* 182–185.

West, N. (1986). *GCHQ: The Secret Wireless War 1900–86.* London: Weidenfeld & Nicolson.

West, N. (1988). *The SIGINT Secrets: The Signals Intelligence War 1900 to Today.* New York: William Morrow.

West, W. J. (1987). *Truth Betrayed.* London: Duckworth.

Whaley, B. (1980). Deception — its decline and revival in international conflict. In H. D. Lasswell, D. Lerner, & H. Speier (Eds.), *Propaganda and Communication in World History. Vol 2: Emergence of Public Opinion in the West.* Honolulu: University Press of Hawaii, 339–367.

Wheatley, L. J. (n.d.). Shortwave, anybody? Manila, The Philippines: Far East Broadcasting Company.

Wheatley, L. J. (1992, March 6). Personal communication.

Wheelon, A. D. (1983, October 28). Trends in satellite communications [Paper presented to the 4th World Telecommunications Forum, Geneva, Switzerland].

Whitaker, U. G., Jr. (1962). History and definition of propaganda. In U. G. Whitaker, Jr. (Ed.), *Propaganda and International Relations* (rev. and enlrg. ed.). San Francisco: Chandler.

White, A. B. (1939). *The New Propaganda.* London: Victor Gollancz.

White, J. B. (1955). *The Big Lie.* London: Evans Brothers.

White House sees no problem with new international satellite systems. (1985, 11 February). *Broadcasting, 108,* 59.

Whittle, J. (1992). Privatisation worldwide: Global trend is fundamentally reshaping the way business is done. *Global Communications, 14,* 31–36.

Whitton, J. B., & Larson, A. (1964). *Propaganda: Towards Disarmament in the War of Words.* Dobbs Ferry, NY: Oceana.

Wick, Worldnet and the war of ideas. (1986, November 3). *Broadcasting, 111,* 80.

Wick proposes Soviet-U.S. TV exchange. (1985, February 18). *Broadcasting, 108,* 72.

Wie phoenix aus der asche. (1986, April). *Nieue Medien,* 34–39.

Wiesner, L. (1984). *Telegraph and Data Transmission over Shortwave Radio Links: Fundamental Principles and Networks* (3rd ed.). München, Germany: Siemens-Aktiengesellschaft.

Wigand, R. T. (1988, Winter). Integrated services digital networks: Concepts, policies, and emerging issues. *Journal of Communication, 38,* 29–49.

Wigand, R. T., Shipley, C., & Shipley, D. (1984, Winter). Transborder data flow, informatics, and national policies. *Journal of Communication, 34,* 153–175.

Wildman, S. S., & Siwek, S. E. (1988). *International Trade in Films and Television Programs.* Cambridge, MA: Ballinger.

Wilhelm, D. (1990) *Global Communications and Political Power.* New Brunswick, NJ: Transaction.

Wilkinson, J. (1989). The American television influence in Britain and Africa: Its assets and its dangers. In C. W. Thomsen (Ed.), *Cultural Transfer or Electronic Colonialism? The Impact of American Television Programs on European Television.* Heidelberg, Germany: Carl Winter Universitätsverlag, 147–160.

Williams, A. (1907). *The Romance of Modern Invention.* London: Seeley.

Williams, G. (1987). "Remember the Llandovery Castle": Cases of atrocity propaganda in the First World War. In J. Hawthorn (Ed.), *Propaganda, Persuasion and Polemic.* London: Edward Arnold, 19–36.

Williamson, J. (1984, November 26). Satellite industry addresses new challenges. *Telephony, 207,* 34–35.

Wilson, C. H. (1939). Hitler, Goebbels, and the Ministry for Propaganda. *The Political Quarterly, 10,* 83–99.

Wilson, W. (1917, April 30). Executive Order No. 2605-A. (Woodrow Wilson Papers). National Archives.

Winkler, A. M. (1978). *The Politics of Propaganda: The Office of War Information 1942–1945.* New Haven, CT: Yale University Press.

Winseck, D., & Cuthbert, M. (1991). Space WARC: A new regulatory environment for communication satellites? *Gazette, 47,* 195–203.

Winter, D. (1971). *Seychelles Calling.* Woking, UK: Far East Broadcasting Association.

Winterbotham, F. W. (1974). *The Ultra Secret.* London: Weidenfeld & Nicolson.

Wireless Communications and Broadcasting. (1927, May 20). [Post 33. Minute 15959/1924]. Post Office Archives, London.

The wireless service for press messages from Geneva. (1921, October). *The Radio Review, 2,* 535–537.

Wise, D., & Ross, T. (1964). *The Invisible Government.* New York: Random House.

Withers, D. (1985). Freedom of access to the radio spectrum for satellite communications. *Telecommunications Policy, 9,* 109–120.

Witt, D. (1987). The impact of national deregulation policies on the structure and activities of the ITU. In E. Mestmächer (Ed.), *The Law and Economics of Transborder Communications: A Symposium.* Baden-Baden, Austria: Nomos Verlagsgesellschaft, 353–372.

Wood, J. (1987, August). Broadcasting the Voice of America. *International Broadcasting, 10,* 38–40, 42.

The world's debt to 12 million refugees. (1988, August 21). *New York Times.*

World Intellectual Property Organization. (1981, March 25–27). *WIPO Worldwide Forum on the Piracy of Sound and Audiovisual Recordings.* Geneva, Switzerland: WIPO.

World Intellectual Property Organization. (1983, March 16–18). *WIPO Worldwide Forum on the Piracy of Broadcasts and of the Printed Word.* Geneva, Switzerland: WIPO.

World Intellectual Property Organization. (1988). *Background Reading Material on Intellectual Property.* Geneva, Switzerland: WIPO.

Worldnet begins South, Central America service. (1986, July 7). *Broadcasting, 111,* 87.

Worldnet's funding dilemma. (1989, April). *Satellite Communications, 13,* 29–30.

World public switching expenditure. (1990, April 19). *Financial Times.*

World Radio Missionary Fellowship. (n.d.). *HCJB World Radio: The Challenge of Missions.* Oka Locka, FL: World Radio Missionary Fellowship.

World Radio TV Handbook 1988. New York: Billboard.

World Radio TV Handbook 1989. New York: Billboard.

World Radio TV Handbook 1990. (1990). New York: Billboard.

World Radio TV Handbook 1992. (1992). New York: Billboard.

World Television. (1991). *World Radio TV Handbook.* New York: Billboard, 353–354.

World transmission equipment expenditure. (1990, April 19). *Financial Times.*

Worldwide TV network planned: USSR's Gostelradio formed joint venture with Fla-based World One, Inc. to start global TV network. (1991, November 25). *Television Digest, 31,* 7.

Yen, M. (1987, August 28). N.Y. "radio pirates" defy prosecutors' ultimatum. *Washington Post.*

Youm, K. H. (1991). The Radio and TV Marti controversy: A Re-examination. *Gazette, 48,* 95–103.

Young, J. (1991, October 2). Sending signals under the sea. *Christian Science Monitor.*

Young, R. G. (1987). "Not this way please!" Regulating the press in Nazi Germany. *Journalism Quarterly, 64,* 787–792.

Zeman, Z. A. B. (1973). *Nazi Propaganda* (2nd ed.). London: Oxford University Press.

Zoglin, R. (1992, January 6). Inside the world of CNN. *Time, 139,* 28–32.

INDEX

International Communication Time Line 1935–1992

Intelsat launched

Edward R. Murrow

1948
Universal Declaration of Human Rights adopted by UN General Assembly; United States creates a permanent international information agency under the Smith-Mundt Act

1949
NATO created; Radio Free Europe created

1935
Italy begins broadcasting in Arabic to the Middle East

1950
Korean War breaks out

1962
Telstar launched

1939–1945
World War II

| 1935 | 1938 | 1941 | 1944 | 1947 | 1950 | 1953 | 1956 | 1959 | 1962 |

1938
BBC begins foreign language broadcasting; Austria jams German radio broadcasts

1942
Office of War Information and VOA created

1944
Agence-France Presse founded

1951
Radio Liberty created

1952
Universal Copyright Convention adopted

1953
United States Information Agency created

1956
CCITT created under the ITU; first submarine transatlantic telephone link established

1958
United Press International created from UP and the International News Service

1961
Eurovision and Intervision linked across the Gulf of Finland; International Convention for the Protection of Performers, Producers of Phonograms and Broadcasting Organizations (Rome Convention) adopted; Novosti Press Agency established

United Nations

1945
United Nations created